I0606379

Connections

Editorial Board

General Editors

JOEL B. GREEN (The United Methodist Church), Professor of New Testament Interpretation, Fuller Theological Seminary, Pasadena, CA

THOMAS G. LONG (Presbyterian Church (U.S.A.)), Bandy Professor Emeritus of Preaching at Candler School of Theology, Emory University, Atlanta, GA

LUKE A. POWERY (Progressive National Baptist Convention), Dean of Duke University Chapel and Associate Professor of Homiletics at Duke Divinity School, Durham, NC

CYNTHIA L. RIGBY (Presbyterian Church (U.S.A.)), W. C. Brown Professor of Theology, Austin Presbyterian Theological Seminary, Austin, TX

CAROLYN J. SHARP (The Episcopal Church), Professor of Homiletics, Yale Divinity School, New Haven, CT

Volume Editors

ERIC D. BARRETO (Cooperative Baptist Fellowship), Frederick and Margaret L. Weyerhaeuser Associate Professor of New Testament, Princeton Theological Seminary, Princeton, NJ

GREGORY CUÉLLAR (Baptist), Associate Professor of Old Testament, Austin Presbyterian Theological Seminary, Austin, TX

WILLIAM GREENWAY (Presbyterian Church (U.S.A.)), Professor of Philosophical Theology, Austin Presbyterian Theological Seminary, Austin, TX

CAROLYN B. HELSEL (Presbyterian Church (U.S.A.)), Assistant Professor of Homiletics, Austin Presbyterian Theological Seminary, Austin, TX

JENNIFER L. LORD (Presbyterian Church (U.S.A.)), Dorothy B. Vickery Professor of Homiletics and Liturgical Studies, Austin Presbyterian Theological Seminary, Austin, TX

SONG-MI SUZIE PARK (The United Methodist Church), Associate Professor of Old Testament, Austin Presbyterian Theological Seminary, Austin, TX

ZAIDA MALDONADO PÉREZ (The United Church of Christ), Retired Professor of Church History and Theology, Asbury Theological Seminary, Orlando, FL

EMERSON B. POWERY (The Episcopal Church), Professor of Biblical Studies, Messiah College, Mechanicsburg, PA

WYNDY CORBIN REUSCHLING (The United Methodist Church), Professor of Ethics and Theology, Ashland Theological Seminary, Ashland, OH

DAVID J. SCHLAFER (The Episcopal Church), Independent Consultant in Preaching and Assisting Priest, Episcopal Church of the Redeemer, Bethesda, MD

ANGELA SIMS (National Baptist Convention), President, Colgate Rochester Crozer Divinity School, Rochester, NY

DAVID F. WHITE (The United Methodist Church), C. Ellis and Nancy Gribble Nelson Professor of Christian Education, Professor in Methodist Studies, Austin Presbyterian Theological Seminary, Austin, TX

Psalms Editor

KIMBERLY BRACKEN LONG (Presbyterian Church (U.S.A.)), Editor, *Call to Worship: Liturgy, Music, Preaching, and the Arts,* Louisville, KY

Sidebar Editor

RICHARD MANLY ADAMS JR. (Presbyterian Church (U.S.A.)), Director of Pitts Theology Library and Margaret A. Pitts Assistant Professor in the Practice of Theological Bibliography, Candler School of Theology, Emory University, Atlanta, GA

Project Manager

JOAN MURCHISON, Austin Presbyterian Theological Seminary, Austin, TX

Project Compiler

PAMELA J. JARVIS, Austin Presbyterian Theological Seminary, Austin, TX

Year A, Volume 2

Lent through Pentecost

Joel B. Green
Thomas G. Long
Luke A. Powery
Cynthia L. Rigby
Carolyn J. Sharp
General Editors

WJK Westminster John Knox Press
Louisville • Kentucky

© 2019 Westminster John Knox Press

First edition
Published by Westminster John Knox Press
Louisville, Kentucky

19 20 21 22 23 24 25 26 27 28—10 9 8 7 6 5 4 3 2 1

All rights reserved. No part of this book may be reproduced or transmitted in any form or by any means, electronic or mechanical, including photocopying, recording, or by any information storage or retrieval system, without permission in writing from the publisher. For information, address Westminster John Knox Press, 100 Witherspoon Street, Louisville, KY 40202-1396, or contact us online at www.wjkbooks.com.

Unless otherwise indicated, Scripture quotations are from the New Revised Standard Version of the Bible, copyright © 1989 by the Division of Christian Education of the National Council of the Churches of Christ in the U.S.A., and are used by permission. Scripture quotations marked NJPS are from *The TANAKH: The New JPS Translation according to the Traditional Hebrew Text.* Copyright 1985 by the Jewish Publication Society. Used by permission. Scripture quotations marked NIV are from *The Holy Bible, New International Version.* Copyright © 1973, 1978, 1984, 2011 by Biblica, Inc.® Used by permission. All rights reserved worldwide.

Excerpts from "You, Lord, Are Both Lamb and Shepherd" by Sylvia G. Dunstan, © 1991 GIA Publications, Inc. All rights reserved. Used by permission. Excerpts from "Crucifixion" in *New Poems,* translation © 2015 Len Krisak. Reprinted by permission of Cambden House. All rights reserved. Excerpt from "The Third Day," by Amos N. Wilder, from *Grace Confounding,* copyright © 1972 Amos Wilder. Used by permission. Excerpt from "Stay," by Jan Richardson, from *Circle of Grace: A Book of Blessings for the Seasons,* copyright © 2015 Jan Richardson. All rights reserved. Used by permission.

Book and cover design by Allison Taylor

The Library of Congress has cataloged an earlier volume as follows:
Names: Long, Thomas G., 1946- editor.
Title: Connections : a lectionary commentary for preaching and worship / Joel B. Green, Thomas G. Long, Luke A. Powery, Cynthia L. Rigby, Carolyn J. Sharp, general editors.
Description: Louisville, Kentucky : Westminster John Knox Press, 2018- | Includes index. |
Identifiers: LCCN 2018006372 (print) | LCCN 2018012579 (ebook) | ISBN 9781611648874 (ebk.) | ISBN 9780664262433 (volume 1 : hbk. : alk. paper)
Subjects: LCSH: Lectionary preaching. | Bible—Meditations. | Common lectionary (1992) | Lectionaries.
Classification: LCC BV4235.L43 (ebook) | LCC BV4235.L43 C66 2018 (print) | DDC 251/.6—dc23
LC record available at https://lccn.loc.gov/2018006372

Connections: Year A, Volume 2
ISBN: 9780664262389 (hardback)
ISBN: 9780664264802 (paperback)
ISBN: 9781611649727 (ebook)

PRINTED IN THE UNITED STATES OF AMERICA

♾ The paper used in this publication meets the minimum requirements of the American National Standard for Information Sciences—Permanence of Paper for Printed Library Materials, ANSI Z39.48-1992.

Most Westminster John Knox Press books are available at special quantity discounts when purchased in bulk by corporations, organizations, and special-interest groups. For more information, please e-mail SpecialSales@wjkbooks.com.

Contents

Sidebars

Publisher's Note

"The preaching of the Word of God is the Word of God," says the Second Helvetic Confession. While that might sound like an exalted estimation of the homiletical task, it comes with an implicit warning: "A lot is riding on this business of preaching. Get it right!"

Believing that much does indeed depend on the church's proclamation, we offer Connections: A Lectionary Commentary for Preaching and Worship. Connections embodies two complementary convictions about the study of Scripture in preparation for preaching and worship. First, to best understand an individual passage of Scripture, we should put it in conversation with the rest of the Bible. Second, since all truth is God's truth, we should bring as many "lenses" as possible to the study of Scripture, drawn from as many sources as we can find. Our prayer is that this unique combination of approaches will illumine your study and preparation, facilitating the weekly task of bringing the Word of God to the people of God.

We at Westminster John Knox Press want to thank the superb editorial team that came together to make Connections possible. At the heart of that team are our general editors: Joel B. Green, Thomas G. Long, Luke A. Powery, Cynthia L. Rigby, and Carolyn J. Sharp. These gifted scholars and preachers have poured countless hours into brainstorming, planning, reading, editing, and supporting the project. Their passion for authentic preaching and transformative worship shows up on every page. They pushed the writers and their fellow editors, they pushed us at the press, and most especially they pushed themselves to focus always on what you, the users of this resource, genuinely need. We are grateful to Kimberly Bracken Long for her innovative vision of what commentary on the Psalms could accomplish, and for recruiting a talented group of liturgists and preachers to implement that vision. Bo Adams has shown creativity and insight in exploring an array of sources to provide the sidebars that accompany each worship day's commentaries. At the forefront of the work have been the members of our editorial board, who helped us identify writers, assign passages, and carefully edit each commentary. They have cheerfully allowed the project to intrude on their schedules in order to make possible this contribution to the life of the church. Most especially we thank our writers, drawn from a broad diversity of backgrounds, vocations, and perspectives. The distinctive character of our commentaries required much from our writers. Their passion for the preaching ministry of the church proved them worthy of the challenge.

A project of this size does not come together without the work of excellent support staff. Above all we are indebted to project manager Joan Murchison. Joan's fingerprints are all over the book you hold in your hands; her gentle, yet unconquerable, persistence always kept it moving forward in good shape and on time. Pam Jarvis skillfully compiled the volume, arranging the hundreds of separate commentaries and Scriptures into a cohesive whole.

Finally, our sincere thanks to the administration, faculty, and staff of Austin Presbyterian Theological Seminary, our institutional partner in producing Connections. President Theodore J. Wardlaw and Dean David H. Jensen have been steadfast friends of the project, enthusiastically agreeing to our partnership, carefully overseeing their faculty and staff's work on it, graciously hosting our meetings, and enthusiastically using their platform to promote Connections among their students, alumni, and friends.

It is with much joy that we commend Connections to you, our readers. May God use this resource to deepen and enrich your ministry of preaching and worship.

WESTMINSTER JOHN KNOX PRESS

Introducing Connections

Connections is a resource designed to help preachers generate sermons that are theologically deeper, liturgically richer, and culturally more pertinent. Based on the Revised Common Lectionary (RCL), which has wide ecumenical use, the hundreds of essays on the full array of biblical passages in the three-year cycle can be used effectively by preachers who follow the RCL, by those who follow other lectionaries, and by non-lectionary preachers alike.

The essential idea of Connections is that biblical texts display their power most fully when they are allowed to interact with a number of contexts, that is, when many connections are made between a biblical text and realities outside that text. Like the two poles of a battery, when the pole of the biblical text is connected to a different pole (another aspect of Scripture or a dimension of life outside Scripture), creative sparks fly and energy surges from pole to pole.

Two major interpretive essays, called Commentary 1 and Commentary 2, address every scriptural reading in the RCL. Commentary 1 explores preaching connections between a lectionary reading and other texts and themes within Scripture, and Commentary 2 makes preaching connections between the lectionary texts and themes in the larger culture outside of Scripture. These essays have been written by pastors, biblical scholars, theologians, and others, all of whom have a commitment to lively biblical preaching.

The writers of Commentary 1 surveyed five possible connections for their texts: the immediate literary context (the passages right around the text), the larger literary context (for example, the cycle of David stories or the Passion Narrative), the thematic context (such as other feeding stories, other parables, or other passages on the theme of hope), the lectionary context (the other readings for the day in the RCL), and the canonical context (other places in the whole of the Bible that display harmony, or perhaps tension, with the text at hand).

The writers of Commentary 2 surveyed six possible connections for their texts: the liturgical context (such as Advent or Easter), the ecclesial context (the life and mission of the church), the social and ethical context (justice and social responsibility), the cultural context (such as art, music, and literature), the larger expanse of human knowledge (such as science, history, and psychology), and the personal context (the life and faith of individuals).

In each essay, the writers selected from this array of possible connections, emphasizing those connections they saw as most promising for preaching. It is important to note that, even though Commentary 1 makes connections inside the Bible and Commentary 2 makes connections outside the Bible, this does not represent a division between "what the text *meant* in biblical times versus what the text *means* now." *Every* connection made with the text, whether that connection is made within the Bible or out in the larger culture, is seen as generative for preaching, and each author provokes the imagination of the preacher to see in these connections preaching possibilities for today. Connections is not a substitute for traditional scriptural commentaries, concordances, Bible dictionaries, and other interpretive tools. Rather, Connections begins with solid biblical scholarship, then goes on to focus on the act of preaching and on the ultimate goal of allowing the biblical text to come alive in the sermon.

Connections addresses every biblical text in the RCL, and it takes seriously the architecture of the RCL. During the seasons of the Christian year (Advent through Epiphany and Lent through Pentecost), the RCL provides three readings and a psalm for each Sunday and feast day: (1) a first reading, usually from the Old Testament; (2) a psalm, chosen to respond to the first reading; (3) a second reading, usually from one of the New Testament epistles; and (4) a Gospel reading. The first and second readings are chosen as complements to the Gospel reading for the day.

During the time between Pentecost and Advent, however, the RCL includes an additional first reading for every Sunday. There is the usual complementary reading, chosen in relation to the Gospel reading, but there is also a "semicontinuous" reading. These semicontinuous first readings move through the books of the Old Testament more or less continuously in narrative sequence, offering the stories of the patriarchs (Year A), the kings of Israel (Year B), and the prophets (Year C). Connections covers both the complementary and the semicontinuous readings.

The architects of the RCL understand the psalms and canticles to be prayers, and they selected the psalms for each Sunday and feast as prayerful responses to the first reading for the day. Thus, the Connections essays on the psalms are different from the other essays, and they have two goals, one homiletical and the other liturgical. First, they comment on ways the psalm might offer insight into preaching the first reading. Second, they describe how the tone and content of the psalm or canticle might inform the day's worship, suggesting ways the psalm or canticle may be read, sung, or prayed.

Preachers will find in Connections many ideas and approaches to sustain lively and provocative preaching for years to come. Beyond the deep reservoir of preaching connections found in these pages, preachers will also find here a habit of mind, a way of thinking about biblical preaching. Being guided by the essays in Connections to see many points of contact between biblical texts and their various contexts, preachers will be stimulated to make other connections for themselves. Connections is an abundant collection of creative preaching ideas, and it is also a spur to continued creativity.

JOEL B. GREEN
THOMAS G. LONG
LUKE A. POWERY
CYNTHIA L. RIGBY
CAROLYN J. SHARP
General Editors

Introducing the Revised Common Lectionary

To derive the greatest benefit from Connections, it will help to understand the structure and purpose of the Revised Common Lectionary (RCL), around which this resource is built. The RCL is a three-year guide to Scripture readings for the Christian Sunday gathering for worship. "Lectionary" simply means a selection of texts for reading and preaching. The RCL is an adaptation of the Roman Lectionary (of 1969, slightly revised in 1981), which itself was a reworking of the medieval Western-church one-year cycle of readings. The RCL resulted from six years of consultations that included representatives from nineteen churches or denominational agencies. Every preacher uses a lectionary—whether it comes from a specific denomination or is the preacher's own choice—but the RCL is unique in that it positions the preacher's homiletical work within a web of specific, ongoing connections.

The RCL has its roots in Jewish lectionary systems and early Christian ways of reading texts to illumine the biblical meaning of a feast day or time in the church calendar. Among our earliest lectionaries are the lists of readings for Holy Week and Easter in fourth-century Jerusalem.

One of the RCL's central connections is intertextuality; multiple texts are listed for each day. This lectionary's way of reading Scripture is based on Scripture's own pattern: texts interpreting texts. In the RCL, every Sunday of the year and each special or festival day is assigned a group of texts, normally three readings and a psalm. For most of the year, the first reading is an Old Testament text, followed by a psalm, a reading from one of the epistles, and a reading from one of the Gospel accounts.

The RCL's three-year cycle centers Year A in Matthew, Year B in Mark, and Year C in Luke. It is less clear how the Gospel according to John fits in, but when preachers learn about the RCL's arrangement of the Gospels, it makes sense. John gets a place of privilege because John's Gospel account, with its high Christology, is assigned for the great feasts. Texts from John's account are also assigned for Lent, the Sundays of Easter, and summer Sundays. The second-century bishop Irenaeus's insistence on four Gospels is evident in this lectionary system: John and the Synoptics are in conversation with each other. However, because the RCL pattern contains variations, an extended introduction to the RCL can help the preacher learn the reasons for texts being set next to other texts.

The Gospel reading governs each day's selections. Even though the ancient order of reading texts in the Sunday gathering positions the Gospel reading last, the preacher should know that the RCL receives the Gospel reading as the hermeneutical key.

At certain times in the calendar year, the connections among the texts are less obvious. The RCL offers two tracks for readings in the time after Pentecost (Ordinary Time/standard Sundays): the complementary and the semicontinuous. Complementary texts relate to the church year and its seasons; semicontinuous emphasis is on preaching through a biblical book. Both approaches are historic ways of choosing texts for Sunday. This commentary series includes both the complementary and the semicontinuous readings.

In the complementary track, the Old Testament reading provides an intentional tension, a deeper understanding, or a background reference for another text of the day. The Psalm is the congregation's response to the first reading, following its themes. The Epistle functions as the horizon of the church: we learn about the faith and struggles of early Christian communities. The Gospel tells us where we are in the church's time and is enlivened, as are all the texts, by these intertextual interactions. Because the semicontinuous track prioritizes the narratives of specific books, the intertextual connections are not as apparent. Connections still exist, however. Year A pairs Matthew's account with Old Testament readings from the first five books; Year B pairs Mark's account with stories of anointed kings; Year C pairs Luke's account with the prophetic books.

Historically, lectionaries came into being because they were the church's beloved texts, like the scriptural canon. Choices had to be made regarding readings in the assembly, given the limit of fifty-two Sundays and a handful of festival days. The RCL presupposes that everyone (preachers and congregants) can read these texts—even along with the daily RCL readings that are paired with the Sunday readings.

Another central connection found in the RCL is the connection between texts and church seasons or the church's year. The complementary texts make these connections most clear. The intention of the RCL is that the texts of each Sunday or feast day bring biblical meaning to where we are in time. The texts at Christmas announce the incarnation. Texts in Lent renew us to follow Christ, and texts for the fifty days of Easter proclaim God's power over death and sin and our new life in Christ. The entire church's year is a hermeneutical key for using the RCL.

Let it be clear that the connection to the church year is a connection for present-tense proclamation. We read, not to recall history, but to know how those events are true for us today. Now is the time of the Spirit of the risen Christ; now we beseech God in the face of sin and death; now we live baptized into Jesus' life and ministry. To read texts in time does not mean we remind ourselves of Jesus' biography for half of the year and then the mission of the church for the other half. Rather, we follow each Gospel's narrative order to be brought again to the meaning of Jesus' death and resurrection and his risen presence in our midst. The RCL positions the texts as our lens on our life and the life of the world in our time: who we are in Christ now, for the sake of the world.

The RCL intends to be a way of reading texts to bring us again to faith, for these texts to be how we see our lives and our gospel witness in the world. Through these connections, the preacher can find faithful, relevant ways to preach year after year.

JENNIFER L. LORD
Connections Editorial Board Member

Connections

Ash Wednesday

Isaiah 58:1–12
Psalm 51:1–17
2 Corinthians 5:20b–6:10
Matthew 6:1–6, 16–21
Joel 2:1–2, 12–17

Isaiah 58:1–12

1Shout out, do not hold back!
Lift up your voice like a trumpet!
Announce to my people their rebellion,
to the house of Jacob their sins.
2Yet day after day they seek me
and delight to know my ways,
as if they were a nation that practiced righteousness
and did not forsake the ordinance of their God;
they ask of me righteous judgments,
they delight to draw near to God.
3"Why do we fast, but you do not see?
Why humble ourselves, but you do not notice?"
Look, you serve your own interest on your fast day,
and oppress all your workers.
4Look, you fast only to quarrel and to fight
and to strike with a wicked fist.
Such fasting as you do today
will not make your voice heard on high.
5Is such the fast that I choose,
a day to humble oneself?
Is it to bow down the head like a bulrush,
and to lie in sackcloth and ashes?
Will you call this a fast,
a day acceptable to the LORD?

6Is not this the fast that I choose:
to loose the bonds of injustice,
to undo the thongs of the yoke,
to let the oppressed go free,
and to break every yoke?
7Is it not to share your bread with the hungry,
and bring the homeless poor into your house;
when you see the naked, to cover them,
and not to hide yourself from your own kin?
8Then your light shall break forth like the dawn,
and your healing shall spring up quickly;
your vindicator shall go before you,
the glory of the LORD shall be your rear guard.
9Then you shall call, and the LORD will answer;
you shall cry for help, and he will say, Here I am.

If you remove the yoke from among you,
  the pointing of the finger, the speaking of evil,
10if you offer your food to the hungry
  and satisfy the needs of the afflicted,
then your light shall rise in the darkness
  and your gloom be like the noonday.
11The LORD will guide you continually,
  and satisfy your needs in parched places,
  and make your bones strong;
and you shall be like a watered garden,
  like a spring of water,
  whose waters never fail.
12Your ancient ruins shall be rebuilt;
  you shall raise up the foundations of many generations;
you shall be called the repairer of the breach,
  the restorer of streets to live in.

Commentary 1: Connecting the Reading with Scripture

Isaiah 58:1–12 resides in the section of the book to which scholars typically refer as Third Isaiah (chaps. 56–66). The events of the entire book of Isaiah span three centuries. In Third Isaiah, the tone and style of poetry shifts from the longer poetic reflections on restoration in Second Isaiah to shorter oracles of judgment that are loosely tied together. The oracles in Third Isaiah reflect a time after the exile but before a full realization of the restoration Second Isaiah (chaps. 40–55) promised. Isaiah 58 seems to fit this time period well, especially with its reference in verse 12 to the rebuilding of ancient ruins, streets, and walls. Perhaps this text reflects the tumultuous time of reconstruction, between 536 BCE and 520 BCE in the Persian period, when certain projects such as the temple rebuilding had commenced, but faltered. It probably predated rebuilding projects such as those by Nehemiah. There are, however, no precise historical markers in this passage to suggest a specific date during the reign of a particular Persian emperor or Judean official.

In 58:1–12, the prophet suggests that the current state of economic and national malaise is due to the people's disregard for the poorest in society. The prophet utters an oracle against public displays of piety that ignore the plight of those suffering economic injustice, though the prophet seems to suggest that the people are earnestly seeking to know God's ways and have a personal encounter with their God. Verse 3 suggests that God's apparent absence befuddles them. God refuses to bless them in their current circumstances despite their intention of piety.

The prophet directly answers this inquiry with an indictment. Even though the people have performed a ritual fast (and made a show of it), they still go about daily business practices that take advantage of the working poor. Verse 4 suggests that the pursuit of piety is a competitive one: "Look, you fast only to quarrel and to fight and to strike with a wicked fist." The following verse suggests a scene in which those participating in the fast are comparing their misery almost as if they are asking whose belly is growling the loudest or whose demeanor is the most sullen. God, however, disregards such pompous piety.

The prophet does not simply call out the wickedness of false piety, but outlines actionable items the community can perform in order to rectify the communal order, thereby repairing their relationship with God. God does not call the people to fast, but to feed. Instead of taking a few days intentionally to make themselves hungry, the prophet instructs the people to feed those who are legitimately and perpetually hungry.

Give Pleasure to Your Lord

Above everything else, choose for yourself humility. Set an example and foundation by means of all your good words. Bend down as you worship, let your speech be lowly, so that you may be loved by both God and other men and women.

Allow the Spirit of God to dwell within you; then in his love he will come and make a habitation with you; he will reside in you and live in you. If your heart is pure you will see him and he will sow in you the good seed of reflection upon his actions and wonder at his majesty. This will happen if you take the trouble to weed out from your soul the undergrowth of desires, along with the thorns and tares of bad habits.

Have a love for penitence, then; put your neck under its yoke. Give pleasure to your Lord by changing from bad actions to good. Be reconciled readily, while there is still time, while you still have authority over your soul.

Evagrius, "Admonition on Prayer," in Sebastian Brock, ed. and trans., *The Syriac Fathers on Prayer and the Spiritual Life* (Kalamazoo, MI: Cistercian Publications, 1987), 68–69.

Instead of calling the people to bind themselves with cords of self-ablation, the prophet calls them to loose the cords of the oppressed, setting them free. Instead of bowing themselves low under the yoke of a self-imposed sense of depravity, the prophet suggests that they break the yoke of the heavily burdened labor class.

As if anticipating the challenge that such lofty goals are impossible to realize in the face of systemic injustice, the prophet gives even more direct and specific instructions in verse 7: share bread with the hungry, shelter the homeless, clothe the naked, and pay attention to everyone in the community. The practices that create a socially and economically just society are the fast that God desires. These actions will garner the positive attention of God once more, and the inclusion of the poor in restored Israel's social vision will hasten the rebuilding process for the entire community (Isa. 58:12).

Isaiah 58 itself may seem to stand in tension with the other lectionary texts from the Hebrew Bible on Ash Wednesday: Joel 2:1–2, 12–17 and Psalm 51:1–17. Joel 2:12 calls the people to fast in response to the terrible coming of the Day of YHWH. Joel 2:14 suggests that such a fast, coupled with weeping and lament (Joel 2:12), might persuade God to relent and restore. Isaiah 58, however, reminds the people that the inward piety of Joel 2:12 ("return to me with all your heart") must also manifest itself in outward expression. It is almost as if the people asking why their fast did not work in Isaiah 58:3 recalled a sentiment similar to Joel 2:12–17. God, through the prophet, condemns their self-interested piety.

The literary context of the superscription of Psalm 51 attributes the psalm to David after Nathan confronted him regarding his adultery and murder. One might imagine those who fast in Isaiah 58 reciting this psalm during their pretense of self-deprecation. We might ask, Does the prophet in Isaiah 58 agree with the psalmist on what an acceptable sacrifice is (in Ps. 51:17, a broken or contrite spirit)? Would a broken and contrite spirit inherently lead one toward breaking the bonds of injustice?

The understanding that true piety must always include economic justice stands in continuity with the greater Isaiah tradition and previous prophets, particularly Amos and Micah, who also decry the practice of false piety divorced from an ethic that maintains justice for the poor. Amos, for example, indicts the Jerusalem elites for oppressing the poor and flaunting said oppression in the context of worship as they recline on garments taken in pledge and drink wine bought with fines they imposed on the poor in God's house (Amos 2:8; cf. Exod. 22:26–27).

The familiar passage in Micah 6 asks what type of sacrifice would appease God. Instead of burnt offerings, thousands of rams, or even human sacrifice, God demands justice, kindness, and modesty (Mic. 6:7–8). None of these texts suggest that there is anything inherently wrong or otherwise displeasing about fasting or sacrifice. Rather, these texts, particularly Micah, demand an inward attitude of humility, coupled with the outward practices of economic justice and opportunity for all within the community.

The New Testament lectionary passages also reflect Isaiah 58's concern that social ethics must accompany religious ritual. Second Corinthians 5:20 reflects the goal of the fasts in Isaiah 58 and Joel 2 with its emphasis on reconciliation with God. The passage calls on the community to be ambassadors of God's righteousness (2 Cor. 5:20–21), while warning them not to accept God's grace in vain (6:1). The claim in 6:10 that "as poor, yet making many rich; as having nothing, and yet possessing everything" also connects to the prophet's admonishment to attend to the social needs of the oppressed (Isa. 58:6–7).

Of course, Jesus' condemnation of brash public piety in Matthew 6:1–6, 16–21 has strong connections to Isaiah 58's understanding of fasting. Both texts suggest that empty piety displeases God. Matthew 6 assumes economic assistance to the poor is a standard practice (Matt. 6:3–4), reflecting the prophet's concern to feed, shelter, and clothe the needy (Isa. 58:7). Matthew's condemnation of storing wealth can also be an expression of Isaiah 58's admonitions to use wealth to help those whom society leaves behind, a sentiment that is also pivotal in one of Jesus' most famous teachings (Matt. 25:31–40) to feed the hungry, give water to the thirsty, welcome the stranger, clothe the naked, care for the sick, and visit the incarcerated. As Ash Wednesday ushers in some of the most prominent rituals of the Christian tradition, Isaiah 58 reminds us that true piety involves loving all our neighbors publicly by creating a just and equitable society.

DAVID G. GARBER JR.

Commentary 2: Connecting the Reading with the World

Ash Wednesday. It has always struck me as peculiar that on Ash Wednesday the lectionary suggests a text in which God seems to spurn the wearing of ashes (Isa. 58:5). The very practices of penitence that characterize the season of Lent appear at first glance to be rejected. Should we not impose ashes to mark the beginning of Lent? Is the prophet calling to the twenty-first-century-CE church from his sixth-century-BCE vantage point to tell it to be less liturgical? No. This prophecy is concerned not about correcting worship practices but, rather, about fostering a holistic spiritual life, wherein social justice is itself a spiritual practice, a means of encountering God.

The people long to encounter God—the text does not question their sincerity on this point—and so formally abstain from certain physical needs in order to draw God's attention. Like Christian observances of Ash Wednesday, where the imposition of ashes and exhortation to "remember you are dust" remind worshipers of their own inevitable deaths, fasting in postexilic Israel also evoked mortality. Sackcloth and ashes (v. 5) suggested the burial shroud and earthen grave.[1] By contrast, the prophet describes the elements of God's desired fast with images that portray the everyday corporeal needs of life: food, shelter, clothing, and human companionship (v. 7). Even the word translated in the NRSV as "kin" is *basar*, most literally "flesh," emphasizing the physical body: "not to hide yourself from your *flesh*." While the addressees of Isaiah 58 humble themselves in ways that mimic death, they neglect to lift up the needy toward a flourishing life. God remains distant.

My grandfather, a United Methodist pastor, used to remind me that "death is a part of life." Read in the liturgical context of Ash Wednesday, Isaiah 58:1–12 emphasizes a similar sense of the ways in which life and death are intertwined. Moreover, the prophet tells us "life" itself is not divided into compartments; God desires no separation between our physical, spiritual, and moral lives. One's behavior in the workplace is as relevant to worship as one's behavior in the sanctuary.

Preachers might catalog the rituals that define many of our daily activities—banter with the

1. Joseph Blenkinsopp, *Isaiah 56–66*, Anchor Bible 19B (New York: Doubleday, 2003), 183.

barista who sells our morning coffee, shared exasperation with a coworker about the weather, bedtime routines with children—in order to show how even the most banal parts of our lives have a liturgical flavor. In every encounter with our neighbors, we encounter God; our neglect of the neighbor impedes the encounter with God.

Spirituality and Wealth. Relationship with the neighbor has a specifically economic resonance in Isaiah 58. The petitioners addressed in the text seem to be people of some wealth; they have power over laborers (v. 3), and they have houses, bread, and clothes to share (v. 7). Isaiah 58:6 is thick with the vocabulary of "fetters" and "yokes," painting a clear picture of their fellow human beings in slavery—physical entrapment and forced labor. Ending this captivity is the "fast" God chooses, and implied throughout the poem is the fact that the Israelites being addressed have some power to do that.

The passage begins with a strident tone: God calls for the people to be condemned loudly, exposing their piety as hypocrisy.[2] This brash beginning crescendoes through the series of rhetorical questions in verses 5–7. Then, at verses 8–12, the tone begins to level off, revealing that the passage is not built on sheer condemnation but, rather, also finds its roots in God's pastoral care for the powerful Israelites whom the prophet is addressing. God is ready to answer their calls of distress (v. 9), offer them strength (v. 11), and provide restoration in the midst of devastation (v. 12).

In congregations where worshipers possess significant socioeconomic advantages, this text, like much of the prophetic corpus, calls for individuals with power to act with justice. Be they business owners or policymakers, CEOs or middle managers, people who have authority over employees and who hold significant wealth can be found in the pews of Christian churches across the world. Pastors who minister to power brokers have a sacred obligation to keep God's desire for economic justice at the forefront of their consciousness. At the same time, those pastors also know that feelings of loss, divine abandonment, and spiritual longing can be acute for any person, regardless of social status. Isaiah 58 addresses this dynamic well.

Far from portraying a strict dichotomy between the privileged and the oppressed, the Isaiah text acknowledges that *all* people long for God, even as the ways in which they seek access to God may differ. The poem draws attention to the petitioners' need for God's healing and vindication (v. 8) as they experience "parched places" (v. 11) and "ruins" (v. 12). Their worldly economic power does not eliminate their need for a restorative power beyond themselves, both as individuals and as a people. At the same time, the prophet does not claim that sincere spiritual need replaces the obligation to pursue social justice; instead, enacting social justice is itself a salve for the weary power broker's soul and a manifestation of a deep spiritual connection with the Divine.

The text's direct address to the economically advantaged does not preclude its proclamation to other communities. For individuals more likely to identify with the oppressed workers than the wealthy managers, this passage is a reminder that God values their physical and economic flourishing as much as their spiritual well-being. Moreover, the text can also draw attention to questions of systemic injustice: the ways that all people participate in the oppression of others, often unwittingly and unwillingly. Do we wear clothes sewn in dangerous, ultralow-wage factories? Do we use mobile phones containing "conflict minerals," mined in ways that perpetuate war and exploit civilians? Do we acquire consumer goods whose production erodes the environment, affecting the poor first?

These kinds of systemic ills have no easy solutions, and we cannot always extricate ourselves from our culpability in them. Nevertheless, Isaiah 58 calls us all to identify where we may have some agency to "loose the bonds of injustice" (v. 6) and "satisfy the needs of the afflicted" (v. 10), and to

2. Literature and film provide a bounty of examples of hypocritical characters, including ones with public religious or political personas subverted by criminality or immorality. Think of the titular character in Sinclair Lewis's novel *Elmer Gantry*, Robert Duvall's character Sonny in the 1997 film *The Apostle*, the warden in *The Shawshank Redemption*, or Frank Underwood in the Netflix television series *House of Cards*. While some of these characters only feign piety, Isaiah's addressees seem sincerely to desire a relationship with God.

understand that justice work is an integral part of our religious lives or, rather, simply part of our *lives* overall, whole and unsegmented.

Finally, this text can be a call to faith communities to examine whether their corporate lives balance care for worship practices with a robust sense of external mission. Measured by the prophetic words of Isaiah 58, a congregation's spiritual vitality does not lie solely, or even predominantly, in its liturgies, its pipe organs and praise bands, or the particulars of its Ash Wednesday service. A church encounters God when it pairs its worship with an active, justice-seeking love for the neighbor. Isaiah 58 ultimately reminds us—in ways that both convict and assure—that God cares about the totality of our lives. Pursuing freedom and justice for the oppressed amplifies our prayers before the God we seek.

CAMERON B. R. HOWARD

Psalm 51:1–17

1Have mercy on me, O God,
according to your steadfast love;
according to your abundant mercy
blot out my transgressions.
2Wash me thoroughly from my iniquity,
and cleanse me from my sin.

3For I know my transgressions,
and my sin is ever before me.
4Against you, you alone, have I sinned,
and done what is evil in your sight,
so that you are justified in your sentence
and blameless when you pass judgment.
5Indeed, I was born guilty,
a sinner when my mother conceived me.

6You desire truth in the inward being;
therefore teach me wisdom in my secret heart.
7Purge me with hyssop, and I shall be clean;
wash me, and I shall be whiter than snow.
8Let me hear joy and gladness;
let the bones that you have crushed rejoice.
9Hide your face from my sins,
and blot out all my iniquities.

10Create in me a clean heart, O God,
and put a new and right spirit within me.
11Do not cast me away from your presence,
and do not take your holy spirit from me.
12Restore to me the joy of your salvation,
and sustain in me a willing spirit.

13Then I will teach transgressors your ways,
and sinners will return to you.
14Deliver me from bloodshed, O God,
O God of my salvation,
and my tongue will sing aloud of your deliverance.

15O Lord, open my lips,
and my mouth will declare your praise.
16For you have no delight in sacrifice;
if I were to give a burnt offering, you would not be pleased.
17The sacrifice acceptable to God is a broken spirit;
a broken and contrite heart, O God, you will not despise.

Connecting the Psalm with Scripture and Worship

Psalm 51 represents the very soul of Lent. While the other lections for the day reflect concepts related to Lent, the psalm eloquently crystalizes the meaning and the feeling, the purpose and the path, of Ash Wednesday and the season it initiates. As such, it may present an opportunity to build the day's proclamation, or even the entire service, around the psalm.

One possibility is to remind the congregation that psalms are prayers and then share a congregational reading of the entire seventeen-verse text (this will be easier if it is printed in easily readable type in the bulletin or projected onto a screen). With everyone now familiarized with the text, pray it again as a body, proceeding through it in sections, each section followed by a brief meditation.

We may divide the text in various ways, while still remaining sensitive to its overall flow. One example: treat verses 1–6 as a unit of prayer, then verses 7–11 as a unit, and then verses 12–17 as a unit. Begin each of these short readings with, "Let us pray," and follow each unit with a reflection on that particular segment of the psalmist's prayer. Such an immersive exploration of Psalm 51 will produce a distinctive homily that is a Scripture-drenched experience of Lenten prayer. Such a prayerful experience is ideal preparation for ashes on the forehead and the Lenten journey ahead.

If, however, your context does not permit so adventuresome an approach, the psalm is still a helpful companion. This is the quintessential psalm of penitence, which means that it relates directly to both of today's other Hebrew Bible texts, each of which urges repentance.

Today's reading from Joel describes a catastrophic plague of insects, which the writer interprets as divine punishment and judgment: "the day of the LORD" (Joel 2:1). After quoting YHWH as inviting the people to repent and return (v. 12), the author adds an endorsement of God's merciful and loving nature, and suggests that it may not be too late for the people's salvation (vv. 13–14). He goes on to describe an extensive communal act of repentance that must be orchestrated among all the faithful, from infants to elders, newlyweds to priests (vv. 15–17).

A sermon might juxtapose this public expression of penitence with Psalm 51's private, personal expression. In its mood, the Joel passage feels almost frantic with noise and activity, while the psalm is intense, intimate, and inwardly focused. In its theology, the Joel passage enumerates human actions aimed at changing God's mind, while the psalm is all about God's actions to transform the penitent. Exploring that theological difference would be fruitful for an Ash Wednesday sermon. Although Joel clings to a hope that God might relent (v. 14), the psalmist begins by claiming God's grace (Ps. 51:1), which is the foundation upon which our faith is built. A sermon might also examine shared vocabulary, notably "steadfast love" (Joel 2:13; Ps. 51:1) and "return" (Joel 2:12, 13; Ps. 51:13), or shared concepts, including "mercy" (Joel 2:13; Ps. 51:1) and "heart" (Joel 2:12, 13; Ps. 51:6, 10).

Today's lection from the book of Isaiah is another glimpse into the reality of communal guilt and how that can—and must—be amended. A sermon about the hypocrisy condemned by this passage (Isa. 58:1–5) would be a potent way to launch Lenten disciplines. And the focus in Psalm 51 on fervent reliance on God's grace and transformative power offers a strong remedy that you can invite your congregation to ponder as the means by which they can be made people whose "light shall break forth like the dawn" (v. 8), people who are continually guided by the Lord (v. 11), people who "shall be called the repairer of the breach" (v. 12).

Psalm 51 is unmatched as a prayer of confession. The Hebrew Bible's full array of terminology for sin is present, translated as "transgression(s)/transgressor(s)," "iniquity(ies)," "sin(s)/sinner(s)," "evil," and "guilty" (vv. 1, 2, 3, 4, 5, 9, 13). If the entire reading seems too long for your service, consider omitting verses 5–8, or build a responsive confession in which one reader names specific sins to which the congregation repeatedly responds by praying the psalm's first verse.

For millennia, Psalm 51's beauty and power has been a liturgical resource. It is, therefore, easy to find it set to music. In addition to those direct settings of the text, hymns that complement this psalm include "Amazing Grace," "There's a Wideness in God's Mercy," "God of Compassion, in Mercy Befriend Us," and, with its deeply faithful yearning for God's transformative companionship, "I Want Jesus to Walk with Me."

Ash Wednesday is the door that leads into Lent. Psalm 51 is not only the key to that door; it is also a map of the journey we will walk with Jesus from here to the cross and onward to the empty tomb.

LEIGH CAMPBELL-TAYLOR

2 Corinthians 5:20b–6:10

> 5:20b We entreat you on behalf of Christ, be reconciled to God. 21 For our sake he made him to be sin who knew no sin, so that in him we might become the righteousness of God.
>
> 6:1 As we work together with him, we urge you also not to accept the grace of God in vain. 2 For he says,
>
> > "At an acceptable time I have listened to you,
> > and on a day of salvation I have helped you."
>
> See, now is the acceptable time; see, now is the day of salvation! 3 We are putting no obstacle in anyone's way, so that no fault may be found with our ministry, 4 but as servants of God we have commended ourselves in every way: through great endurance, in afflictions, hardships, calamities, 5 beatings, imprisonments, riots, labors, sleepless nights, hunger; 6 by purity, knowledge, patience, kindness, holiness of spirit, genuine love, 7 truthful speech, and the power of God; with the weapons of righteousness for the right hand and for the left; 8 in honor and dishonor, in ill repute and good repute. We are treated as impostors, and yet are true; 9 as unknown, and yet are well known; as dying, and see—we are alive; as punished, and yet not killed; 10 as sorrowful, yet always rejoicing; as poor, yet making many rich; as having nothing, and yet possessing everything.

Commentary 1: Connecting the Reading with Scripture

On Ash Wednesday, we stand at a characteristic tension of the Christian life. As we receive ashes as visible, tangible reminders of our mortality, we also confess the hope of the resurrection. We will die, yes, but Jesus has already lifted us up from the clutches of death. One day, yes, our breath will still, but Jesus walks before us through that death and into everlasting life. Yes, we are divided now, but God has promised the gift of reconciliation.

Our passage helps cast a vision of the shape of reconciliation, but also of the paths upon which such reconciliation is experienced and tested. The verses immediately preceding our text help contextualize our passage. Second Corinthians 5 explores the tension of earthly lives infused with the resurrection power of Jesus and the "eternal" (2 Cor. 5:1), heavenly existence that awaits us. That tension, however, ought not to hamper our confidence in God's deliverance of our communities, according to Paul. Such confidence inspires his continued ministry in the midst of many challenges and travails, "for the love of Christ urges us on, because we are convinced that one has died for all; therefore all have died. And he died for all, so that those who live might live no longer for themselves, but for him who died and was raised for them" (vv. 14–15). This storytelling echoes the Adam and Christ typology Paul evokes in Romans 5:12–21. That is, Paul's confidence is rooted not in his own power, but in what God has already done for all of us. Here Paul is telling a story not just about himself but about the whole of humanity. After all, "all have died," and "one died for all" (2 Cor. 5:14–15). Jesus' death and our death along with him means a radical shift in our perspective. We see Christ in a new light, for he indeed has made us a "new creation" (vv. 16–17). This is how "reconciliation" has been effected. This is how God has drawn us to God's embrace and toward one another.

Thus our passage begins with the admonition to "be reconciled to God" (v. 20). This is not so much exhortation as recognition, not a command to be as much as a call to see and experience whom God has made us to be. Live as if you have already been reconciled to God by God! It is in this way that we "become the righteousness of God" (v. 21). Note here that the term translated "righteousness" (Gk. *dikaiosynē*) could also be translated as "justice."[1]

What would it mean for us to imagine ourselves as the "justice of God," as embodiments of God's setting right of the world? Righteousness might suggest to some a religious correctness that does not encompass such justice for all. Such justice, however, is at the center of God's reconciling activity with, through, and among us. After all, what shape would reconciliation take if not for the presence and power of God's justice? As Lois Malcolm notes, "Being reconciled to God is not an escape to some transcendent sphere (an easy ticket to heaven) but a call to serve in God's reconciling work (2 Corinthians 5:18)."[2] Reconciliation comes at a heavy cost, as Paul will outline soon.

The next chapter starts with stirring admonition. God's promises to listen, to intervene, to save are trustworthy; for this reason, "we urge you also not to accept the grace of God in vain" (6:1). God's grace is trustworthy and true. It is also timely. As Paul seems to cry out, "See, now is the acceptable time; see, now is the day of salvation" (v. 2). This prophetic promise is fulfilled before us, experienced right here and right now. Before we assume that such salvation is an easy path, Paul reminds the Corinthian followers of Jesus of the vibrant tensions he has experienced in his ministry. In a litany of marked contrasts, Paul notes that the day of salvation has included all kinds of turmoil for him (v. 5). In the midst of such travails, Paul names the values that keep his eyes on God's righteousness and grace (vv. 6–7), including a reference to weapons that I find particularly provocative in a US context so frequently interlaced with gun violence.

Paul wields "the weapons of righteousness for the right hand and for the left" (v. 7; Eph. 6:10–17). Once again, the tensions of faithfulness emerge. These metaphorical "weapons" have nothing to do with retribution or bitterness or fear of neighbor or violence against the other. These weapons do not kill; they proclaim God's abundant life. These weapons do not pave a path to grief and loss; they reconcile erstwhile enemies. These weapons do not tear apart communities; they draw them back together.

Yet, even as Paul subverts the power of weaponry by turning this image upside down, does he not also create the possibility that some might understand that these are not "weapons" in any significant sense? Worse yet, might not the appeal to the language and imagery of weapons already limit our ability to proclaim the gospel because we are participating under the terms such metaphors have set for us? Can we ever escape the use and purpose of weapons, even as we draw upon this image metaphorically and subversively? Perhaps even metaphorical "weapons" cannot be stripped of their intended use and purpose. Isaiah's call to "beat . . . swords into plowshares" (Isa. 2:4) may apply to our words and metaphors as much as it does to metallic arms.

Paul closes with particularly striking contradictions. An impostor yet true. A stranger yet known by all. Dead yet alive. Afflicted but breathing. Grieving yet joyful. Poor yet having it all. These tensions are characteristic of Paul's ministry. Resolving them would oversimplify the gospel. Choosing one or another of a binary pair would leave us poorer still.

A sermon might invite a community to name the living tensions that characterize them, to claim the ways they are living here and in between, and to embrace an interstitial reality. For instance, we might name how our hopes for racial reconciliation are both a sure promise God has made and also a distant reality in so many of our communities; even as we hope for freedom from racism, we remain embedded within cultures and systems that continue to feed us the lie of white supremacy.

Just as important may be to return to the very notion of reconciliation, a notion running

1. Cf. Elsa Tamez, *The Amnesty of Grace: Justification by Faith from a Latin American Perspective*, trans. Sharon H. Ringe (Eugene, OR: Wipf & Stock, 1991).
2. Lois Malcolm, "Commentary on 2 Corinthians 5:20b–6:10," n.p. https://www.workingpreacher.org/preaching.aspx?commentary_id=3571.

through our text. For many, reconciliation is a compelling theological idea pointing to a resetting of relationships among human and God. Reconciliation shimmers with the hope that those things that divide us may one day fade, but in other communities, reconciliation may sound a bit hollow. In communities that have expressed historic oppressions, the "re" in reconciliation makes us wonder when we were all conciliated in the first place!

Reconciliation is not a return to a unified past, after all, but a transformation of relationships in the future. Such transformation cannot come about without repair, without the setting right of injustice.[3] Reconciliation is not just mutual forgiveness but a mutual commitment to God's justice. Reconciliation does not erase a dark history; true reconciliation wonders how such a history can be told well, reconstructed honestly, and its effects repaired justly.

ERIC D. BARRETO

Commentary 2: Connecting the Reading with the World

One of the first rules a researcher working with data learns is the crucial distinction between correlation and causation. The fact that two patterns seem to have something to do with each other does not mean that one causes the other. Many a mistaken finding has resulted from a researcher claiming causation when that which was binding two patterns was more complicated than what first met the eye.

At the beginning of the season of Lent, as faithful people commit to aligning their lives more attentively with God's will, the distinctions between correlation and causation become important to the believer's relationship with God. We do not give up for Lent that which is repelling us from God because we think we can get God to love us more; we do not embrace new spiritual disciplines to cause God to approve of us over our less-observant neighbor. Yet giving up that which is not life-giving does cause us to feel closer to God, and taking up new faith practices can be deeply satisfying. What does the apostle Paul have to say about the connections—or lack thereof—between the *actions* of the faithful and God's *unconditional* love?

Second Corinthians 5:20b–6:10 opens with a stark contrast, and then the paradoxes just keep on coming. The passage, appointed for Ash Wednesday, opens with the sinlessness of Jesus and the sinfulness of humanity. Jesus takes on our sin in order to bury it, and then to rise again. Paul next moves into what sounds like a locker-room pep talk at halftime for a team that is losing, enumerating the adversities the church has overcome. This series of what New Testament scholar Wayne A. Meeks calls "antithetic clauses,"[4] followed by paradoxes regarding the suffering and success of the church, speaks volumes about Paul's understanding of God's grace. That understanding surely had as much to do with Paul's life experiences and culture as it did with his faith.

Paul's second letter to the church in Corinth is known among Pauline scholars as the one most impervious to interpretation. Gathered together from a set of fragments, the boastful and confident tone suggests that Paul was seeking to distinguish himself among competing Christian missionaries. We do not know who the rivals were, but the passion in Paul's tone might suggest that tensions were running high due to fear of losing the battle. Perhaps Paul was concerned that the church was losing faith in his leadership.

Grace is the gift of God's love. It can be neither earned nor lost based on human behavior. Why is it, then, that Paul goes to such great lengths to describe the good that has come from the hard work and suffering of the church? Why does he suggest that those in Christ not "accept the grace of God in vain" (2 Cor. 6:1b)? One possible explanation is that Paul and his

3. See Jennifer Harvey, *Dear White Christians: For Those Still Longing for Racial Reconciliation* (Grand Rapids: Eerdmans, 2014).
4. Wayne A. Meeks, ed., *HarperCollins Study Bible*, New Revised Standard Version ed. (London: HarperCollins, 1993), 2172.

listeners were speaking to those shaped in a culture of highly choreographed gift giving.

In his article entitled "The Expectation of Grace: Paul on Benefaction and the Corinthians' Ingratitude," B. J. Oropeza suggests that it would have been inconceivable for recipients of a gift in Paul's time to accept that gift without a strong sense of obligation toward reciprocity.[5] Believers in Corinth would surely understand concepts of giving and receiving gifts much more readily than they would grasp the idea of unconditional love. Oropeza suggests that the culture of reciprocity, with its attendant taboo against failing to respond to one gift with another, played a shaping role in Paul's theology of grace. Paul seizes on the church's impulses to give back, teaching them that the appropriate response to God's grace is a deeper faith and a stronger church. Today, social graces call upon us to be good hosts and good guests, and to say "please" and "thank you." Because these conventions are still widely held, helping a community to understand the passage within the context of reciprocity is both possible and useful.

Preaching about the potential benefits of Christian self-sacrifice presents nettlesome liturgical and ecclesiastical challenges. From an ecclesiastical perspective, many in our pews are suffering already for reasons that have nothing to do with Lent. Telling them that they need to suffer even more can be alienating in the extreme. Yet the connection—correlative, not causative—between self-sacrificial suffering and a deepening of a person's faith is unmistakable.

The social and ethical dimensions of this text provide fertile soil for preachers who appreciate paradox. I once had a colleague teach me a valuable lesson about ministering to youth and young adults: *adversity builds community*. I have chanted those words to myself like a mantra during many a difficult ministry moment—not to mention family reunions, and marriage and parenting in general. Adversity calls upon us to trust God more deeply and to get over our illusions of control. Yet it is hard to imagine a God who loves us wanting us to present our suffering as an offering. God's grace understood as anything other than a gift that cannot be reciprocated in kind is simply not grace.

In my education of seminary students, I have worked closely with clergy mentors. One of the lessons I teach regarding appropriate professional boundaries is this: amid unequal power relationships we can find mutuality, even when we cannot find reciprocity. The mentor might find great satisfaction in her work with a student. The student might find tremendous learning in the mentoring relationship. When the giver and the receiver do not stand on equal footing, reciprocity is not expected or appropriate; but mutuality, where both receive something good, is what makes a relationship worthwhile.

When preaching on this appointed text on Ash Wednesday, we must avoid the temptation to point to the suffering of the early church as a way in which those churches were somehow inherently better than ours. We must also defuse any interpretation suggesting that human suffering, in the form of grief or pain or depression, is somehow pleasing to God. We can, however, name the fact that, from the very beginning, Christians saw a connection between their striving for what is good and the depth of their faith. Sometimes that striving came at a high cost, but it was worth it.

The human knowledge and personal resources this text provides come in the form of encouragement to live abundantly, even amid adversity, in response to God's gift of love. The sacrifices we make during Lent indeed can bring us closer to God, but they should be understood as a response to God's grace, not as what earns it. Reciprocity is not the name of the game, as we do not have God's power to give without counting the cost. However, mutuality is possible; in fact, a response of striving to be more and more faithful might be exactly the appropriate gift we can give to God. Suffering for Christ and depth of faith: yes, there is a correlation. No, there is no simple causation. At least not one we can, through this mirror dimly, understand.

SARAH BIRMINGHAM DRUMMOND

5. B. J. Oropeza, "The Expectation of Grace: Paul on Benefaction and the Corinthians' Ingratitude (2 Corinthians 6:1), " *Bulletin for Biblical Research* 24, no. 2 (2014): 207-226.

Ash Wednesday

Matthew 6:1–6, 16–21

1“Beware of practicing your piety before others in order to be seen by them; for
then you have no reward from your Father in heaven.
2“So whenever you give alms, do not sound a trumpet before you, as the hypocrites do in the synagogues and in the streets, so that they may be praised by
others. Truly I tell you, they have received their reward. 3But when you give alms,
do not let your left hand know what your right hand is doing, 4so that your alms
may be done in secret; and your Father who sees in secret will reward you.
5“And whenever you pray, do not be like the hypocrites; for they love to stand
and pray in the synagogues and at the street corners, so that they may be seen
by others. Truly I tell you, they have received their reward. 6But whenever you
pray, go into your room and shut the door and pray to your Father who is in
secret; and your Father who sees in secret will reward you. . . .
16“And whenever you fast, do not look dismal, like the hypocrites, for they dis-
figure their faces so as to show others that they are fasting. Truly I tell you, they
have received their reward. 17But when you fast, put oil on your head and wash
your face, 18so that your fasting may be seen not by others but by your Father
who is in secret; and your Father who sees in secret will reward you.
19“Do not store up for yourselves treasures on earth, where moth and rust
consume and where thieves break in and steal; 20but store up for yourselves treasures in heaven, where neither moth nor rust consumes and where thieves do
not break in and steal. 21For where your treasure is, there your heart will be also.”

Commentary 1: Connecting the Reading with Scripture

Today is Ash Wednesday, the beginning of Lent, the beginning of Eastertide. Today, we begin to prepare for the Great Feast. We fast. We receive ashes. We are reminded that we will, all of us, sooner rather than later, die: “From ashes, you were made; to ashes, you will return.” We are marked as walking dead. We are marked as dust of stars. We set our face as flint toward Jerusalem. We commit ourselves to confront empire. We follow Jesus on the way of sorrows. All this on this one day in the annual journey that helps us, all of us, little by little, year by year, decade by decade, to walk nearer and nearer to the path Jesus walked.

Then, just then, we read: “But when you fast, put oil on your head and wash your face, so that your fasting may be seen not by others” (Matt. 6:17–18a). If this is a day—and a season—of imitating Christ, of getting back on track, it seems rather odd, does it not, that we do not actually listen to what Jesus, rather plainly, is saying.[1] In the midst of this collection of teachings that the author of the Gospel we call “Matthew” has gathered into a rather disjointed sermon, Jesus counsels the crowd about religious practices: “Give alms, but do so in secret. Pray, but do not make a show of it. Fast, but do not look pained as you do. Wash your face!” The preacher should not run away from this clash of lectionary, festival, and contemporary circumstance. Often the homiletical key emerges in the struggle to hold such tensions. What might we say at the intersection of Jesus’ words and our imposing ashes and our sending of the people out as witnesses?

1. For historical roots of this disjuncture, see Thomas J. Talley, *Worship: Reforming Tradition* (Washington, DC: Pastoral Press, 1990), 61–64. For a constructive critique of Lenten lectionary selections, see J. Frank Henderson, “The Lectionary for Ash Wednesday and the Sundays of Lent: Critique and Alternative Vision,” at www.jfrankhenderson.com/pdf/lentstudy.pdf.

Our reading falls at the midpoint of Jesus' rather choppy Sermon on the Mount, his first extended teaching in this Gospel. In chapters 1 to 4 (and we read from chap. 4 in the upcoming Sunday, Lent 1), Jesus' identity is established and his mission defined. The commencement of his public ministry is preceded by his own forty-day fast, out in the wilderness; he asks no more of us than he asks of himself (4:2). As chapter 4 ends, Jesus has called the first four disciples and begun to teach, to announce the coming new kingdom, and to heal. He is getting famous. He is drawing larger and larger crowds. He climbs a hill and sits down and begins to teach.

First come the Beatitudes, which Matthew (as opposed to Luke) tends to spiritualize: blessed are the poor in spirit (not just those who are actually poor) and those who hunger after righteousness (rather than those who simply do not have adequate food). Perhaps here is a clue: Does our fasting retune our hungers? Despite his weakened state and his power to transform stones into bread, Jesus stays hungry as he debates the tempter. Might our fasting help us retain our saltiness, our leaven, our light? Here, Jesus suggests, just a chapter earlier, that we remove the covering over ourselves so that others "may see [our] good works" and give God glory (5:16). In fact, despite his contentions with Pharisees and other interpreters of the law, here Jesus is quite explicit that he has not come to abolish the Torah but to fulfill every jot and tittle of the Torah. Further, if one does not keep every commandment and avoid leading others astray, if one does not in fact exceed the righteousness of scribes and Pharisees, one cannot enter the kingdom that he has come to announce (5:20).

As the sermon goes on, Jesus continues to "amp up" the commandments. From "do not commit adultery" to "do not lust"; from the concession for men to declare divorce to no divorce at all; to no oath-taking; to turning the second cheek; to giving one's cloak as well as one's coat; to loving enemies. His talk about almsgiving and fasting (and his instruction to pray oh-so-simply, 6:7–15, which we skip over today) is situated within this larger discussion about exceeding the law, about being more righteous . . . even . . . about being perfect!

In our chapter, chapter 6, Jesus speaks in terms of contrasting models: do not be like *A*; be *B*. In verses 7–15 and 22–34, those in the *A* category are Gentiles. Gentiles apparently heap up empty phrases as they pray. Instead, pray simply and directly; God already knows what you need anyway. Gentiles also strive for material comforts, for food and fashion and finery. Again, God knows what you need; do not worry. God will provide.

In our verses, Jesus castigates the "hypocrites." Whether in synagogue or on the street corner, these fellow Jews call attention to themselves. The almsgiving is appropriate, so too the praying—but not the style. While these are those whose righteousness we are to exceed, we are not to imitate them. It is not others whom we need to impress. It is only God who is to confirm our fulfillment of the commandments—unto excess, unto perfection. Jesus seems to want it both ways: "Fast, but wash your face, show no discomfort," and God will reward you; but also, "Do your good works openly so that others may bear witness and give God glory." Just here we must study our own intentions and attitudes, the why and the how of our Lenten disciplines.

So too our other lections build bridges between Jesus' teaching and our practices. "Create in me a clean heart, O God," we sing with the psalmist. Perhaps this and similar passages motivated Jesus' teaching: what God desires is not public sacrifice but a broken and contrite heart—so that we are enabled to move from acknowledgment of sin to an acceptance of guilt and so to repentance and on to joy and praise. For Joel, the call to fast, to weep over our failings, and to gather to plea for mercy responds to an existential threat. If God does not relent, the people truly will be no more. The relatively secure may contemplate the efficacy of acts of contrition; those at risk assemble and cry out for the blessing, for the divine help that will sustain them.

Isaiah presses us beyond reflection on personal failings to critique of the social structures that foster inequity and exploitation. The prophet, like Jesus in Matthew 25, challenges us to concrete acts of compassion and justice on behalf of the poor, the homeless, the naked, those in prison. Here the consequence concerns not our final resting place but our present situation. If we change our ways, light will dawn upon us now, our ruins will be restored now, our streets will be tranquil, the nation and the world will be at peace . . . now!

Similarly, in his letter to the community in Corinth, Paul—while tooting his own horn a bit—counsels us not just to receive grace, but to do something with it. God, in Christ, has banished sin and established us as righteous. So let our ministries commend themselves to all as witness to God's grace. Let the fast we choose—like the hardships we may endure—issue in the declaration of good news, the building up of the body, the invitation to all to the feast.

W. SCOTT HALDEMAN

Commentary 2: Connecting the Reading with the World

On Ash Wednesday, congregants around the world will hear in their native tongues the words "Remember that you are dust, and to dust you shall return" (see Gen. 3:19). We are reminded of our solidarity with every human being with whom we share mortality and finitude. In modern American culture, the rituals of death and burial have mostly been scrubbed clean of earlier Christian practices in which the living saints care for and accompany the body of the deceased believer to his/her final resting place "in sure and certain hope of the resurrection to eternal life though our Lord Jesus Christ."[2] In place of this liturgical drama that recalls the life, death, and resurrection of Christ, we find memorial services under the direction of professional funeral directors (whose role has displaced the minister in much the same way that the wedding planner has usurped the role of the minister in Christian marriage ceremonies). In contrast, Ash Wednesday calls for deep and slow theological reflection on mortality and death.

It is in this Lenten context that the preacher leads the congregation in meditating on Matthew 6. Jesus explores three expressions of authentic Jewish piety: almsgiving, prayer, and fasting. This triad of Jewish practices was widely recognized in antiquity, and these practices continue, in varying degrees, to remain part of the church's mission and purpose. Prayer is central to the life of faith, yet its practice both in the life of individual believers and the communal life of congregations is sometimes thin. Fasting has diminished in its importance as a Christian practice, though it is still observed, especially during Lent.

Christian believers, during the Lenten season, might learn from the Ramadan experience and practice of Muslim neighbors. Ramadan is the ninth month in the Islamic calendar and is a holy time devoted to fasting and spiritual devotion. Making time for the required prayers five times a day, daily readings from the Qu'ran, fasting between sunrise and sunset, and attending evening mosque services can be challenging for any busy Muslim with family and work responsibilities, especially in a non-Muslim country.

Dilshad Ali, a Muslim journalist and social-media blogger from Richmond, Virginia, has written in "Ramadan: It's Not Just a Food Fast" of the challenges and rewards from her religious experiences with prayer during Ramadan over the past twenty years. Her advice is helpful not only to the Muslim observing Ramadan, but also the Christian participating in Lent:

> Ramadan [is] a whole-body awareness of God and a humble thankfulness for whatever blessings He has granted. . . . Do dhikr (reciting short du'as, or supplications) silently while you're driving, waiting in line somewhere, or doing endless household tasks. . . . Not Muslim? Spending whatever downtime you have to remember God or peacefully meditate is a great idea for everyone. Thousands of hours go by every year in our work commutes, in chauffeuring our kids around, in keeping the house going. Why not try to use that time to quiet our minds, remind ourselves of a higher being, and appreciate what we've been given?[3]

2. "The Committal," *The Book of Common Prayer* (New York: Oxford University Press, 2007), 485
3. Dilshad Ali, "Ramadan: It's Not Just a Food Fast"; http://www.beliefnet.com/faiths/islam/2009/08/ramadan-its-not-just-a-food-fast.aspx.

Almsgiving in the form of charitable giving is a regular congregational activity (though the average percentage of charitable giving per person has decreased in modern society). What is often missing in the modern appropriation of these practices is the understanding of their redemptive nature, particularly of almsgiving. The book of Tobit observes, "Prayer with fasting is good, but better than both is almsgiving with righteousness. A little with righteousness is better than wealth with wrongdoing. It is better to give alms than to lay up gold. For almsgiving saves from death and purges away every sin. Those who give alms will enjoy a full life" (Tob. 12:8–9). In some quarters of the early church almsgiving was elevated to the level of a commandment (1 Tim. 6:14; *Didache* 1:5; Polycarp, *Phil.* 3.3–5.1).

The impact of prayer and fasting on individual spiritual life is at least acknowledged (if only, at times, in lip service), but making charitable contributions or almsgiving is generally viewed as an altruistic act, whose only beneficiary is the recipient(s) of the charitable deed. Atoning almsgiving in the early church, however, was believed to hold the power to cleanse the sins of those who practiced this mercy, a point Jesus makes later in this text when he says, "Store up for yourselves treasures in heaven" (Matt. 6:20; Jas. 5:2 details the consequences of ignoring the almsgiving command). This view and practice stood in sharp contrast to docetic Christianity, which had disregard for the bodies of the poor and for the harm such disregard had on the social body. The benefits of almsgiving to both giver and receiver could be explored in a Lenten meditation.

The preacher might also explore the social and ethical implications of the Matthean text. Up to this point in the Sermon (chap. 6), the implied audience, it seems, is male: the would-be murderer's anger is directed toward a brother (5:21–22); the adulterer lusts after a woman (v. 28); the husband initiates divorces with his wife (vv. 31–32); the one who has been sued is commanded to give not only his overcoat but his inner tunic as well (v. 40), an impossibility for a female auditor. Generally speaking, contemporary preachers are encouraged to put the male-dominated language of ancient patriarchal society into more inclusive idiom.

The preacher might explore the implications of these instructions for Matthew's male auditors from a gender-specific point of view. With a presumed male audience, these instructions from Jesus to pray, fast, and give alms "in secret" are countercultural. They represent a shift from the male-dominated public space of the house of worship or the street corner to the home, and the "male listener, lover of public recognition of his worth, is expected to forgo that reward."[4] The shift from public to domesticated space removes the honor that accrues to the *man* publicly engaged in these practices and turns the focus to interior benefits of intimate encounter with God, our guest. Once that point is made, the preacher can then draw out its "inclusive" implications!

Finally, a brief glimpse of the history of interpretation of the *place* of prayer (6:6) might also reward the proclaimer. We typically imagine Jesus instructing believers to withdraw to their "prayer closet" in solitude, but the call to pray "in secret" is not necessarily a call to do so in solitude. In the ancient urban setting in which Matthew's Gospel would have first been heard, the "room" (*tameion*) was often a storeroom or room for sleeping. Jerome later translates the word as *cubiculum*, a term connoting a small bedroom (from which we also get the word "cubicle"), but without the connotation of a storeroom. These rooms were not very private and were often in plain view. The *cubiculum* was the site of activities intended to be done in secret, concealed from the public at large, but still not in private, as least not in the sense in which that word functions in the modern West. Sometimes they functioned as a reception area for guests of similar social standing or intimate friends. It is no wonder that the cubiculum became a metaphor for the human heart that receives God as its guest during prayer.

MIKEAL C. PARSONS

4. Carolyn Osiek, "'When You Pray, Go into Your *TAMEION*' (Matthew 6:6): But Why?" *Catholic Biblical Quarterly* 71 (2009): 723–40 (737).

Joel 2:1–2, 12–17

1Blow the trumpet in Zion;
sound the alarm on my holy mountain!
Let all the inhabitants of the land tremble,
for the day of the LORD is coming, it is near—
2a day of darkness and gloom,
a day of clouds and thick darkness!
Like blackness spread upon the mountains
a great and powerful army comes;
their like has never been from of old,
nor will be again after them
in ages to come.
. . . .
12Yet even now, says the LORD,
return to me with all your heart,
with fasting, with weeping, and with mourning;
13rend your hearts and not your clothing.
Return to the LORD, your God,
for he is gracious and merciful,
slow to anger, and abounding in steadfast love,
and relents from punishing.
14Who knows whether he will not turn and relent,
and leave a blessing behind him,
a grain offering and a drink offering
for the LORD, your God?

15Blow the trumpet in Zion;
sanctify a fast;
call a solemn assembly;
16gather the people.
Sanctify the congregation;
assemble the aged;
gather the children,
even infants at the breast.
Let the bridegroom leave his room,
and the bride her canopy.

17Between the vestibule and the altar
let the priests, the ministers of the LORD, weep.
Let them say, "Spare your people, O LORD,
and do not make your heritage a mockery,
a byword among the nations.
Why should it be said among the peoples,
'Where is their God?'"

Commentary 1: Connecting the Reading with Scripture

Repent: the Day of the Lord is near. The fourth-century-BCE prophet Joel provides a classic "repent now before disaster strikes the nation" warning. Repentance or change of life direction will avert God's punitive action.

I suspect that many folks in contemporary congregations do not find threats of divine punishment helpful. Only some would admit to seeing forecast catastrophes—whether economic, weather, contagions, political or international conflicts—as instruments of divine punishment. Such forecasts do not usually prompt repentance as prevention. We do not think much about repentance anyway, do we?

More likely, I suspect, disasters and crises overtake us—whether "natural" (weather, earthquakes, floods, and so on), health, family, financial, work, relationships, damage from alcohol/drug dependency, violent verbal and/or physical attacks, and so on. We respond, lamenting, "Why me/us? What did I/we do to deserve this?" We might, perhaps, see it as a wake-up call and change our eating habits, start exercising, undergo therapy or medical treatment, abandon or repair a relationship, go to church, or . . . and we would not call any of this repentance. Life happens.

Perhaps this passage will prompt us to think about what comprises repentance, if repentance is required, what it signifies, what place it might have for lives lived faithfully in relationship to God. Is repentance reserved, or even appropriate, for all crises? Might it take its place in the rhythm of faithful living—along with confession, worship, thanksgiving, learning, service, fellowship, faithful endurance—when it is not automatically linked with crises?

Joel 2 anticipates the approaching Day of the Lord, first mentioned in 1:15. This proverbial day of destruction denotes the action of the powerful God, "the Almighty." This is not a "day" in which God saves and blesses the people. Like previous prophets (Amos 5:18–20; Zeph. 1:14–18), Joel warns that it is a day of judgment, a day of "darkness and gloom" (cf. Amos 5:18, 20), to be met with trembling, not eager expectation.

This day "is coming, it is near," he declares (Joel 2:1–2). The trumpet blast and the alarm should alert residents of Jerusalem to danger from an approaching enemy army (cf. Hos. 5:8). This army approaches "like blackness spread upon the mountains." It is "great and powerful" (Joel 2:2b), incomparable in size. According to verse 11, this is God's army; God is the commander-in-chief "at the head of his army; how vast is his host! Numberless . . . . Truly the day of the Lord is great; terrible indeed—who can endure it?" This army seems to be metaphorical (note the comparative "like" in vv. 4–5). It is an unparalleled "apocalyptic" army bringing judgment. Joel sees it. Can his listeners? He warns them: the enemy is on its way, and the enemy is God. God is attacking God's people in judgment.

Some congregants know the experience of God the enemy, of being overrun by "God's army" of disease, family crisis, financial ruin, the daily news, professional sabotage. They know the experience of feeling judged, punished, condemned—whether it is merited or not. Others?

The passage constructs the people under the curses of the covenant. It assumes disobedience; judgment is punishment. In the covenant curses, the many punitive options comprise "disaster, panic, and frustration . . . defeat before your enemies" (Deut. 28:20–25).

Yet the curses are not the final word. A change of ways will mean blessing instead of curse (30:1–10).

Do crises and disasters always portend punishment? What about those circumstances *people perceive to be judgment* but about which they/we can do nothing, concerning which we have no agency? The passage does not consider them; the preacher must break the nexus that "disaster equals (avoidable) punishment."

Assuming agency, verses 3–11 (omitted from the lectionary reading) continue to describe the approaching army of God.

Verses 12–14 issue the call to repent. "Even now," says the Lord, there is an opportunity to "return to me." God initiates this invitation to reorient whole lives and society toward God's ways. God the enemy becomes God the gracious inviter. To embrace this invitation will change the course of history. The call is very general, not specifying particular sins or injustices.

The call evokes the covenant summons to repent by using the covenant phrase "with all your heart" (Deut. 30:2, 10). This interior reorientation, this change of heart and mind, is manifested in external practices of fasting, weeping, and mourning. Genuine repentance is rooted in the heart: "rend your hearts and not your clothing" (Joel 2:13). The contrast does not disparage the latter rite of lament, but it insists on joining the interior and exterior (so Matt. 6:16–18).

Verse 13 continues to evoke the covenant to encourage repentance. God is described as merciful and gracious. On Sinai, God reveals Godself to Moses as merciful, gracious, slow to anger, abounding in steadfast love (Exod. 34:6). In Numbers 14, the people complain against the Lord, who threatens to punish them. Moses intercedes for the people, reminding the Lord of precisely these qualities of mercy and grace so as to "forgive their iniquity" (Num. 14:18–19). So here God reminds the people that God "abounds in steadfast love and relents from punishing." The terrible, punitive Day of the Lord offers the possibility of blessing prevailing over curse, mercy over punishment, new life over destruction (so Ps. 51), God the gracious over God the enemy.

God can repent.

Verse 14a reasserts the possibility of this divine turning or "relenting" from punishing sin. To relent means that God abandons curse for blessing. God restores the blessings of productivity annihilated by the plague of locusts described in chapter 1, which preceded this imminent Day of the Lord. Several verses note the devastation of food supplies in that plague (Joel 1:7, 10–12, 17, 19) including the loss of grain supplies (1:11, 17). Verse 9 specifically mentions that "the grain offering and the drink offering are cut off from the house of the LORD"; the priests cannot offer them.

The situation of curse and punishment can be reversed with human *and* divine turning. Not only will the created order be realigned with the divine purposes of fertility; but so also will the covenant relationship and worship in the sanctuary.

Verses 15–17 summon the people again to gather and express repentance. The command to gather the people repeats 1:14. The trumpet blast echoes the warning about the approaching army of verse 1, but foregrounds the call to repent. That is, fear of God's enmity and punitive army should motivate a return to God the gracious and merciful. Again, fasting is mentioned as an appropriate act (1:14; 2:12, 15). It involves serving God, forgoing food, work, and sex in mourning sin, reorienting life to the Lord.

Verse 16 depicts the gathered congregation very deliberately. The elders or the aged were addressed in 1:2, suggesting those with some communal power and leadership. Then follow the children and infants, the next generation that will not exist unless the terrible army is turned back with human and divine repentance. Then follow the bridegroom and bride, the source of future generations. The future of the people and its well-being are incentives for repentance.

The priests lead the assembly with weeping and prayer. The priestly prayer adds a further reason for divine action. Whereas verses 13–14 appeal to God's character, verse 17's prayer appeals to God's honor and reputation among the nations. If God wipes out the people, the nations will respond with mockery (compare Num. 14:13–16).

The passage foregrounds a nexus of disobedience, crisis, and judgment, but also the possibility of divine and human turning. It does not consider scenarios of crisis not linked to disobedience and not requiring repentance. Preachers must engage them.

WARREN CARTER

Commentary 2: Connecting the Reading with the World

Ash Wednesday services take place with death and disaster in the wings. In the church year, Jesus has turned his face toward Jerusalem. In every year, fear lurks that, as W. B. Yeats writes in "The Second Coming," "the centre cannot hold," and that some "rough beast" is slouching toward birth, even in our sacred places. It has always been so on Ash Wednesday, from the trembling potential martyrs of the early church, to the grieving woman with ashes on her forehead at the Parkland, Florida, high school mass-murder scene in 2018.

Life's fragility encircles Ash Wednesday liturgies. From a global vantage point, the earth is sick with chills and fever from climate change; nuclear weaponry increases along with war talk; and pandemic disease stalks an ever-increasing world population. In smaller frames, images arise of children gassed, of refugees drowning in hopelessness, of schools converted to charnel houses. Science and technology offer us a clearer view of the big picture, and a closer view of its consequences than ever before; but suffering and death continue unabated. The task for the Ash Wednesday liturgy is, first, to confess this personal, communal, and global reality—and then to respond to it in faith.

Joel issues trumpet calls to awaken and to respond to this reality. The first trumpet (Joel 2:1) calls complacent mortals to see their vulnerability in the face of an annihilating plague of locusts, and links this vulnerability to the unendurable last judgment facing unrepentant humanity. Following Joel's description of the only path from death to life—an appeal to God for deliverance (vv. 12–14)—the second trumpet (v. 15) calls God's repentant people to their proper faithful response: a worship service (vv. 16–17).

Joel's call to gather in solemn assembly gives Ash Wednesday worship its proper template. In the prophet's summoned assembly and in Ash Wednesday services, confession of oneness with a creation in which death and dissolution are natural and inevitable opens the possibility of hope through oneness with the God of that creation. This Creator God, infinitely merciful, may yet offer deliverance to those with repentant hearts.

Ash Wednesday, in parallel with Joel 2, calls first for confession of our inability to save ourselves; then it points a way forward: "Remember, you are dust and to dust you will return. Repent and believe in the gospel." Like steps one and two of the Alcoholics Anonymous twelve-step program, recovery begins with admitting we are powerless to manage our lives, and that only a higher power can restore us. Many contemporary media portray a distorted intuition of this human condition. The global or even universal disaster genre (whether of natural, human, or alien origin) is a cinema staple of the last fifty years. Its resolution usually comes through violent resistance (*Star Wars: The Last Jedi*, 2017), modern technology (*Armageddon*, 1998), or submission to inevitable death (*Melancholia*, 2011). In most of these films, modern media sound Joel's cry to awaken to death's approach; but Joel's second call to dependence upon God as the sole sane response is missing.

Ash Wednesday offers an alternative to futile violent resistance and to nihilistic resignation in the face of approaching apocalypse: communal repentance before God. Acceptance of ashes on the forehead confesses mortality. This is more a humble (from the Indo-European root for ground) admission of earthy reality than a confession of wrongdoing, more an acknowledgment that we are creatures than a confession that we are evil. The ashes in cross shape link our gifts of earthy life and death to those same gifts in Jesus, who created new life through them. To "repent and believe the gospel," is to accept death itself as a servant of life in oneness with a merciful God who leaves a grain offering in a loaf of bread and a drink offering in a cup of wine. Symbols of a broken and bloody body become the doorway to new life rather than to life's end.

Ash Wednesday's communal confession of mortality and heartrending return to God's good news is not a deterrent against sorrow, loss, or death. It is, however, a stand against ultimate entropy, the inevitable gradual decline of all things into disorder. Christians weep, but our tears plead our hope (v. 17). Iwan Russell-Jones contrasts T. S. Eliot's poems *The Waste Land* and *Ash Wednesday* to show how art can reveal this truth.[1] In the former, the pre-Christian Eliot portrays modern life as fragmentary, disconnected, and meaningless. In the latter, after his conversion, the same realities become charged with meaning through seeing

1. Iwan Russell-Jones, "Shall These Bones Live? The Ash Wednesday Promise of Art," *CRUX* 50, no. 1 (Spring 2014): 13–20.

human life and death in light of Christ's habitation in the flesh. Russell-Jones quotes literary critic Northrup Frye's summary of Eliot's *Ash Wednesday*, "a desert, a garden, and a stairway between them." In the Ash Wednesday service, we stand on the stairway, we orient ourselves to our dusty home via ashes and locusts, and we turn, repent, believing the gospel life will lead to a garden door.

Ash Wednesday, like Joel's solemn assembly, requires a communal act of worship. It takes the whole *ecclesia* to shift reality. Joel calls everyone: the aged, the children, unweaned infants, brides and bridegrooms, as well as priests (vv. 16–17). All lament how things are, and hope for how things may become, God willing.

Can a liturgical service change the world's condition? For many, worship has a poor reputation in our day. Many Christians prefer action over liturgy, but in Joel liturgy *is* action. Some current scholarship supports this. The idea that gathered communities with focused hearts and minds change community consciousness, thereby changing lived reality, is growing in acceptance. David Nicol writes of "subtle activism," the use of meditation and prayer to support collective transformation.[2] Drawing on the thought of such writers as Teilhard de Chardin and Wendell Thomas, as well as various mystical religious traditions, Nicol explores the hidden spiritual connections within large social changes. Social activism of the traditional sort necessarily continues, but in a new reality created by communal spiritual practices. What worshipers once saw from a human point of view, they now see differently. The facts remain, but worship changes the communal vision, like one of those "magic eye" pictures for the soul. Through worship, a greater power, deep in reality, offers active alignment with a new communal future enabled by a new consciousness of belief in good news.

The individual's task in the Ash Wednesday liturgy is to prepare for a holy death, one that opens the door to life rather than closing it. The ashes symbolize oneness with personal mortality as part and parcel of an impermanent creation in which all passes away. Realizing this dusty state frees mortals to look beyond themselves, perhaps to glimpse the loving One who first breathed life into that dust, and might again. Julian of Norwich's visions enabled her to see an undying Love at the heart of all creation, and to know that it is knotted up with every human soul, which she called oneing with God.[3] The incarnate Christ is the clearest evidence of this merciful Love knot. The Love at work in creation during the darkest times, as Joel intuited, is merciful (v. 13). Those under the mark of ashes and the cross have reason to believe God may remain in and with us when dissolution, decline, and death have done their worst. All manner of things shall be well.

WM. LOYD ALLEN

2. David Nicol, *Subtle Activism* (Albany, NY: SUNY Press, 2015).
3. See Julian of Norwich, *Revelations of Divine Love* (New York: Paulist, 1978), chap. 53, 284.

First Sunday in Lent

Genesis 2:15–17; 3:1–7
Psalm 32
Romans 5:12–19
Matthew 4:1–11

Genesis 2:15–17; 3:1–7

[2:15]The LORD God took the man and put him in the garden of Eden to till it and
keep it. [16]And the LORD God commanded the man, "You may freely eat of every
tree of the garden; [17]but of the tree of the knowledge of good and evil you shall
not eat, for in the day that you eat of it you shall die." . . .

[3:1]Now the serpent was more crafty than any other wild animal that the LORD
God had made. He said to the woman, "Did God say, 'You shall not eat from any
tree in the garden'?" [2]The woman said to the serpent, "We may eat of the fruit of
the trees in the garden; [3]but God said, 'You shall not eat of the fruit of the tree that
is in the middle of the garden, nor shall you touch it, or you shall die.'" [4]But the
serpent said to the woman, "You will not die; [5]for God knows that when you eat of
it your eyes will be opened, and you will be like God, knowing good and evil." [6]So
when the woman saw that the tree was good for food, and that it was a delight
to the eyes, and that the tree was to be desired to make one wise, she took of its
fruit and ate; and she also gave some to her husband, who was with her, and he
ate. [7]Then the eyes of both were opened, and they knew that they were naked;
and they sewed fig leaves together and made loincloths for themselves.

Commentary 1: Connecting the Reading with Scripture

It comes as no surprise on the First Sunday in Lent to find lectionary readings pondering temptation. The Genesis reading focuses on God's first prohibition. Despite this text's rich history of interpretation, many questions remain. Why does God place the tree of knowledge in the garden in the first place? What is the nature of the knowledge it bestows? Why does God not want the first humans to have this knowledge, a knowledge that would also grant them moral agency? Why do the first humans not die on the day in which they eat the fruit as God has threatened? Our obsession with such questions, however, testifies to our resistance to learning the lessons the text itself wants to teach, lessons about the consequences of human decisions.

Genesis 3:1 describes the serpent as the craftiest (*'arum*) of all the wild animals. In Genesis 2:25, we learn that the man and woman were naked (*'arummim*), yet unabashed. The use of *'arum*, the Hebrew term that describes the serpent as "crafty" or "clever" in 3:1, links this verse to the previous chapter and introduces a pun that envelops 3:1–7 when the first humans realize their nakedness (*'arummim*) and experience shame. Elsewhere in Scripture, the term *'arum* designates the crafty language of iniquity: "For your iniquity teaches your mouth, and you choose the tongue of the crafty [*'arum*]" (Job 15:5). The serpent displays its craftiness, anticipating the first woman's own "why" questions by offering a plausible interpretation of God's words in 2:17: God does not want the humans to partake of the fruit because they will become like gods themselves, knowing both good and evil. While the narrative does not reveal the serpent's inner motivation, paradise begins to crumble as the serpent introduces suspicion into the relational dynamic between God and humankind. While some might characterize the serpent in this case as deceptive, Genesis 3:22

confirms God's fear that the humans would become like God.

As Phyllis Trible has argued, the first theological conversation in the Bible occurs between the woman, still unnamed, and the serpent.[1] Eve becomes the first interpreter when she adds to the prohibition "nor shall you touch it," reckoning that in order to eat the fruit, she must first touch it (Gen. 3:3). The woman ponders three categories of delight as she contemplates the fruit of knowledge. First, she sees the fruit as good for food. Second, she sees it as pleasing to the eyes. Third, and perhaps most importantly, she considers the wisdom the fruit offers. Throughout the text, the man remains silent, but the suggestion that the man is "with her" in verse 6 implies that he has overheard the conversation, thereby making him complicit in the disobedience.

The fate of the first humans' forbidden feast is death, but death from a certain point of view. While we know that the first humans did not die immediately, they did suffer many allegorical deaths. First was a death of the bliss that stems from ignorance. Their realization of nakedness is not necessarily shame over their sexual nature, but with their newfound knowledge, they now realize the potential for abuse. As two autonomous moral agents, they can now recognize the potential in the other for both good and evil, a potential that can also awaken mutual suspicion in the same way the serpent aroused the woman's suspicion of God.

As we see in the verses following the lectionary reading, this suspicion leads to accusation. When God interrogates the man, the man points a finger first at the woman and by proxy at God, blaming his decision to take the fruit on "the woman whom *you* gave to be with me" (3:12, emphasis added). The first man's refusal to accept responsibility for his own actions constitutes the original sin of patriarchy, which haunts the Western tradition to this day. Likewise, the woman blames the trickster serpent (v. 13). The humans' disobedience leads to alienation from each other, from the created order (represented by the serpent and the work needed to yield a crop), and from God (vv. 14–19). Finally, they experience the death of exile, as God casts them out of the garden, lest they eat also of the tree of life that grants immortality. At the beginning of Lent, the text invites us to contemplate these "deaths" that result from our decisions.

Trible's reading suggests that God's original intent for humanity involved a more egalitarian relationship between man and woman, suggesting that patriarchy was the result of the post-Eden curse in 3:16.[2] Others, however, have pointed out that the history of interpretation too often shapes our understanding more than the original text. Gale Yee, for instance, cites the deuterocanonical book of Sirach: "From a woman sin had its beginning, and because of her we all die" (Sir. 25:24). Similarly, 1 Timothy 2 justifies the silencing of women by using this sentiment and shifting the blame from Adam to Eve: "and Adam was not deceived, but the woman was deceived and became a transgressor" (1 Tim. 2:14), a clear misreading if we take into account God's punishment of all parties—man, woman, and serpent—in Genesis 3:14–19.[3] While the history of interpretation might consistently blame the fall of humankind on the woman, the epistolary reading offers a countertext to this idea, reminding the reader that death entered into the world through the sin of one man (not Eve) and has perpetually haunted humankind (Rom. 5:12–14).

The remaining lectionary readings support a traditional theological understanding of Genesis 3 representing the fall of humankind. Psalm 32 suggests that acknowledgment of and repentance from sin lead to redemption (Ps. 32:5). An intertextual reading with this psalm might suggest that the main point of the Genesis narrative is not the original sin of partaking the fruit or even of disobedience. Disobedience is part of the human condition that the Genesis narrative describes. What may matter more is the reaction of the first humans, once they realize their nakedness. Additionally, the Gospel reading, Matthew 4:1–11, illustrates Jesus' capacity to

1. Phyllis Trible, *God and the Rhetoric of Sexuality* (Philadelphia: Fortress, 1978), 109–10.
2. Trible, *God and the Rhetoric of Sexuality*, 128.
3. Gale A. Yee, *Poor Banished Children of Eve: Woman as Evil in the Hebrew Bible* (Minneapolis: Fortress, 2003), 59.

resist sin. When taken in tandem, these three lectionary texts provide hope through God's willingness to accept those who repent (Ps. 32), to God's plan for redeeming the world from the consequences of sin (Rom. 5:12–19), and to Jesus' perfect example as one who resists temptation (Matt. 4:1–11).

When we read beyond the confines of the lectionary text in Genesis 3, we also see the grace of God from the beginning. In addition to God providing clothes to the first humans, Eve gains a name: the mother of all living. Ultimately, this lectionary reading is not a text about the doctrine of sin, about the fall of humankind, or about the "why" questions behind God's motivations. The text, however, does describe the little deaths that occur as the result of our knowledge of good and evil. We are dead to the ignorance of sin and corruption. We are dead to an anxiety-free existence in paradise. We continually experience the death of alienation from one another, from creation, and from God, but the text also introduces the possibility for reconciliation between Eve and Adam, who perpetuate life through their children, as well as between humanity and a gracious God, who remains in relationship with humans despite our disobedience.

DAVID G. GARBER JR.

Commentary 2: Connecting the Reading with the World

Reading this text within the liturgical season of Lent inevitably draws attention to the theme of sin. Yet the story also invites consideration of the relationship between work and the human condition. The opening line of this lection asserts that God put the first human in the garden "to till it and keep it" (Gen. 2:15). Life in Eden was never one of pure leisure, but instead involves work from the start. Only after the humans' disobedience does the ground become cursed and the work become painful (3:17–19). That very first work was stewardship of the rest of God's creation: keeping—as in both guarding from harm and tending with care—the vegetation in the garden, along with the waters and soil that make the garden thrive. In the Eden story, work, understood as the daily, God-given, life-giving activity with which humans occupy themselves, is stewardship; humanity's first job is to care for creation.

So often today our work is at odds with an Edenic vision of stewardship. We produce goods in ways that exploit the earth rather than care for it. We value the things produced more than the people who produce them. We have been offered the earth's abundance, and yet we keep reaching for more and more beyond our own need, while others go without. We tend to value the *pain* of work rather than the primordial joy of the work itself. We "humble-brag" about how busy we are, how tired we are, what time we sent that e-mail, forgetting all the while that we human beings are part of God's creation, and thus in stewarding creation, we must also take care of ourselves.

Reading Genesis 2–3 through the lens of work has ecclesial implications as well. Rather than reserving talk of stewardship for the church's fund-raising season, broaching the topic in Lent helps to cultivate a year-round consciousness of how a congregation and its members spend their time and money. Moreover, sustained, honest talk about work and finances with congregants can also help to establish healthy parameters for salary, work hours, and expectations for pastors in their service. Given the Ash Wednesday reading from Isaiah 58:1–12, which names injustice in the workplace as an impediment to encountering God, and the vocational overtones of the call of Abraham passage (Gen. 12:1–4a) appointed for the Second Sunday in Lent, the Year A Old Testament readings open space for sustained Lenten reflection on work as both a blessing from God and a context for sin.

References to the story of Adam and Eve in art, literature, music, and popular culture are legion. Among the most enduring retellings of Genesis 2–3 is John Milton's seventeenth-century masterpiece *Paradise Lost*. While the lengthy epic poem offers innumerable points of connection with the biblical account, I find its emphasis on human companionship to be among its most compelling angles. Watching Adam and Eve in love in the garden, a jealous Satan describes them as "Imparadised in one another's arms, / The happier Eden" (*Paradise Lost* 4.504–5). The first couple's relationship, which includes both desire and fulfillment, is acknowledged as its own form of paradise.

The last four lines of the poem, which describe the couple's journey out of the garden, strike a surprisingly optimistic note, reminding the reader that despite their expulsion, they face their new life together, and under God's watchful care:

> The world was all before them, where to choose
> Their place of rest, and Providence their guide:
> They, hand in hand, with wandering steps and slow,
> Through Eden took their solitary way.
> *Paradise Lost* 12.646–49

Milton's juxtaposition of "their solitary way" with the image of Adam and Eve walking "hand in hand" emphasizes that, despite the losses the two have suffered and the distinct struggles each one now faces, they have not lost each other. Although sin and disobedience have driven them from paradise, Adam and Eve still retain "the happier Eden" of their love.

While Milton highlights Adam and Eve's conjugal joys, the notion of human companionship in Genesis 2–3 need not be limited to romantic pairings. The ending of *The Fellowship of the Ring*, the first film in Peter Jackson's adaptation of J. R. R. Tolkien's *Lord of the Rings* trilogy, provides a different example with overlapping themes. Frodo Baggins, the hobbit protagonist, is on an epic quest only he can fulfill: to destroy the one ring of power by throwing it into the fires of Mordor. When it becomes clear that his journey is endangering his friends, he tries to run off for Mordor by himself, only to be tracked down by his dearest friend and caretaker Samwise Gamgee. Frodo waves him off, shouting, "I'm going to Mordor alone, Sam!" Undeterred, Sam yells back, "Of course you are! And I'm coming with you!" Like Milton's Adam and Eve, Frodo and Sam have their own daunting quests to fulfill, their own vocations to inhabit, and yet their solitary journeys are made possible by the companionship they provide for each other. For us, as for Frodo and Sam, friendship mitigates hardship; relationships mitigate the fractures wrought by human sin.

The lectionary's particular choice of verses from Genesis 2–3 draws attention to the apparent discrepancy between what God says (2:16–17), what the woman says that God said (3:2–3), and what the serpent says (3:1, 4–5). Emily Dickinson's poem "Tell All the Truth but Tell It Slant—" can provoke reflection on which of these characters is telling the whole truth. When juxtaposed with the biblical text, Dickinson's assertion that "Success in Circuit lies" invites readers to reflect on which of the story's character(s) has rightly characterized the conditions in the garden, and which character(s) has achieved some success through subterfuge.[4] Dickinson's poetry also contains many more direct references to "Eden," especially to convey the idea of "paradise."[5]

Finally, Genesis 2–3 functions as an etiology: an origin story for all of humanity. Most comic-book superheroes have origin stories that describe how those heroes come to be who they are and do what they do. Many involve some sort of childhood trauma, such as the death of a parent. In the Black Panther series, T'Challa's mother dies in childbirth, and his father is later murdered. In the Batman comics, Bruce Wayne witnesses his parents' murder. Superman is sent away from his home planet just before it explodes.

The Eden account in the book of Genesis likewise provides an explanatory backstory, not to describe an individual, but to provide a narrative backdrop against which to understand human nature as a whole. Adam and Eve's disobedience does lead to a superpower of sorts: knowing good and evil, described as becoming like gods (3:5,

4. For more on truth-telling in this lection, see Cameron B. R. Howard, "Commentary on Genesis 2:15–17; 3:1–7," http://www.workingpreacher.org/preaching.aspx?commentary_id=3183. The language of "alternative facts" or "fake news" that has entered media discourse may also illuminate some of the ambiguities in the story.

5. See, for example, "Wild nights—Wild nights!" and "Eden is that old-fashioned House."

22). That newfound knowledge opens the possibility of immortality, resulting in the trauma of being expelled from the garden (3:22–24). Read next to the classic comic-book genre, Genesis 2–3 resounds with both tragedy and promise in ways that once again recall the end of *Paradise Lost*: humanity, flawed yet still cherished by God, leaves home to venture into the rest of God's creation, where new adventures await.

CAMERON B. R. HOWARD

Psalm 32

[1]Happy are those whose transgression is forgiven,
whose sin is covered.
[2]Happy are those to whom the LORD imputes no iniquity,
and in whose spirit there is no deceit.

[3]While I kept silence, my body wasted away
through my groaning all day long.
[4]For day and night your hand was heavy upon me;
my strength was dried up as by the heat of summer.

[5]Then I acknowledged my sin to you,
and I did not hide my iniquity;
I said, "I will confess my transgressions to the LORD,"
and you forgave the guilt of my sin.

[6]Therefore let all who are faithful
offer prayer to you;
at a time of distress, the rush of mighty waters
shall not reach them.
[7]You are a hiding place for me;
you preserve me from trouble;
you surround me with glad cries of deliverance.

[8]I will instruct you and teach you the way you should go;
I will counsel you with my eye upon you.
[9]Do not be like a horse or a mule, without understanding,
whose temper must be curbed with bit and bridle,
else it will not stay near you.

[10]Many are the torments of the wicked,
but steadfast love surrounds those who trust in the LORD.
[11]Be glad in the LORD and rejoice, O righteous,
and shout for joy, all you upright in heart.

Connecting the Psalm with Scripture and Worship

Given that Lent is our traditional time of repentance, it is hardly surprising that the season's first Sunday would feature this collection of lections: the Genesis text that recounts sin's origin story; a passage from Romans that considers that ancient story along with the God-given antidote to sin, namely, Jesus Christ; the Gospel of Matthew's demonstration of Jesus' perfect resistance to temptation and sin; and Psalm 32, which needs only eleven verses to move from the blessedness of forgiveness (Ps. 32:1–2) to the wretchedness of guilt (vv. 3–4) to the relief of confession (vv. 5–9) and, finally, to the joy of righteousness (vv. 10–11). The psalm, thus, is an overview of the human experience of sin and, therefore, this poetic prayer relates to each of today's other texts.

Losing the Holy Image of God

Let us never set up our own will against the holy will of God. There was not only liberty allowed to man, in taking the fruits of paradise, but everlasting life made sure to him upon his obedience. There was a trial appointed of his obedience. By transgression he would forfeit his Maker's favour, and deserve his displeasure, with all its awful effects; so that he would become liable to pain, disease, and death. Worse than that, he would lose the holy image of God, and all the comfort of his favour; and feel the torment of sinful passions, and the terror of his Maker's vengeance, which must endure for ever with his never dying soul. The forbidding to eat of the fruit of a particular tree was wisely suited to the state of our first parents. In their state of innocence, and separated from any others, what opportunity or what temptation had they to break any of the ten commandments? The event proves that the whole human race were concerned in the trial and fall of our first parents. To argue against these things is to strive against stubborn facts, as well as Divine revelation; for man is sinful, and shows by his first actions, and his conduct ever afterwards, that he is ready to do evil. He is under the Divine displeasure, exposed to sufferings and death. The Scriptures always speak of man as of this sinful character, and in this miserable state; and these things are true of men in all ages, and of all nations.

Matthew Henry, *Matthew Henry's Concise Commentary on the Bible*, Monograph, Christian Classics Ethereal Library, https://www.ccel.org/ccel/henry/mhcc.ii.ii.html.

Psalm 32 may be especially helpful as a counterbalance to today's Genesis lection. Seasoned worshipers will be aware that following today's lesson, the Genesis text goes on to recount the expulsion of the first man and the first woman from God's garden, a fate that follows the awful moment when God lays curses upon each of the two. Mindful that those ominous developments are in the wings, we may welcome Psalm 32 as something of a balm for that accursed banishment: while the Genesis text makes clear that God will not abide human efforts to make ourselves godlike, the psalm makes clear that God is also ready to forgive us (vv. 1, 5), to preserve us (v. 7), and to surround us with "steadfast love" (v. 10).

This image of God "surrounding" (vv. 7b, 10b) us "with glad cries of deliverance" (v. 7b) as well as with "steadfast love" (v. 10) is an especially potent and poignant contrast to the idea of God exiling people from God's presence. Even in the wasteland of sin, we are never beyond God's gracious reclamation.

Psalm 32's initial two verses are parallel lines of poetry, each with the classic beatitude opening: "Happy [or blessed] are those . . ." (vv. 1–2). While these verses are similar in form, the subtle difference in their content could be useful in preaching on the accompanying lections.

In the psalm's first verse, the reality of sinfulness—and our resulting need for forgiveness—is acknowledged: we are happy when our sins are forgiven. In the second verse, by contrast, although the initial phrase continues the preceding verse's focus, the second phrase modulates to a slightly different idea: we are happy when "in [our] spirit there is no deceit" (v. 2b).

This could provide a helpful angle for preaching today's Genesis lection, in which we uneasily witness the moment in which deceit is born. Note that the woman has not practiced deceit simply by talking with the serpent, nor are she and the man being deceitful even when they eat the forbidden fruit (that action is a sin because it contradicts God's instructions, but it is not "deceit"). Only when they eat the fruit and thereby become "wise" (3:6) do these people choose to practice deceit by hiding from God, as related in the verse that immediately follows this story.

Sin is sometimes defined as that which separates us from God, and these chapters in Genesis are telling a tale of exactly that sort of deliberate human participation in what we know is in opposition to God's will. Psalm 32 also includes such a story; it begins, "While I kept silence, my body wasted away" (Ps. 32:3a). The psalmist quickly resolves the story: "Then I acknowledged my sin to you, and I did not hide my iniquity . . . and you forgave the guilt of my sin" (v. 5).

This sequence of events is ideal material for constructing a confession sequence. In calling the people to confession, one might say, "The psalmist speaks to God, saying: 'While I kept silence, my body wasted away through my groaning all day long. Then I acknowledged my sin to you, I did not hide my iniquity, and you forgave the guilt of my sin.' Confident that we too may rely on God's steadfast love and forgiveness, let us now confess our sin." The final verse of the psalm might serve as the basis for a declaration of forgiveness: "Be glad in the Lord and rejoice, O righteous, and shout for joy, all you upright in heart. Know that you are forgiven and be at peace."

To know that we are forgiven and, therefore, able to be truly at peace is to follow the outline of Christian salvation history, moving from the despair of leaving Eden behind to the glory of leaving the tomb behind. Every Lent is a miniaturized version of that transformative arc: through the journey of Lenten penitence, we leave behind the solemnity of Ash Wednesday and move toward celebrating the joy of Easter Sunday. Psalm 32 offers welcome signposts.

The psalm also serves well as a call to worship, for example using verses 1 and 6:

Reader 1: Happy are those whose transgression is forgiven, whose sin is covered.
Reader 2: Therefore let all who are faithful offer prayer to God.

In addition to musical settings of Psalm 32 are some well-known hymns that complement the day's texts: "Come, Ye Sinners, Poor and Needy," "Forgive Our Sins as We Forgive," "Jesus, Lover of My Soul," "O Love That Wilt Not Let Me Go," "O Worship the King, All Glorious Above," and "Rock of Ages, Cleft for Me."

In Lent, when we are called to recognize our sin in order to repent of it, Psalm 32 is like a kindly companion who tells us the truth. With its happy opening verses and its glad closing verse, the psalm sets our Lenten penitence within the surrounding embrace of God's gracious Easter promise.

LEIGH CAMPBELL-TAYLOR

Romans 5:12–19

[12]Therefore, just as sin came into the world through one man, and death came
through sin, and so death spread to all because all have sinned— [13]sin was
indeed in the world before the law, but sin is not reckoned when there is no law.
[14]Yet death exercised dominion from Adam to Moses, even over those whose
sins were not like the transgression of Adam, who is a type of the one who was
to come.
[15]But the free gift is not like the trespass. For if the many died through the one
man's trespass, much more surely have the grace of God and the free gift in the
grace of the one man, Jesus Christ, abounded for the many. [16]And the free gift
is not like the effect of the one man's sin. For the judgment following one trespass brought condemnation, but the free gift following many trespasses brings
justification. [17]If, because of the one man's trespass, death exercised dominion
through that one, much more surely will those who receive the abundance of
grace and the free gift of righteousness exercise dominion in life through the one
man, Jesus Christ.
[18]Therefore just as one man's trespass led to condemnation for all, so one
man's act of righteousness leads to justification and life for all. [19]For just as by
the one man's disobedience the many were made sinners, so by the one man's
obedience the many will be made righteous.

Commentary 1: Connecting the Reading with Scripture

Romans is bursting at the seams with stories. What if more of our preaching of Romans took on this narrative dimension? This lection provides an ideal text, but also an ideal point in the liturgical calendar to recount the cosmic story Paul tells. In brief, the story is this: Through one person, Adam, sin entered and wrecked the world God created. Through one person, Jesus, sin and death are not just held at bay but utterly defeated. If these are the basic contours, the details and the theological imagination evoked here take a bit more work to unpack.

First, we ought to remember where we stand in Paul's argument. Romans 4 recounted Abraham's faithfulness as proof that God's grace comes by faith, for Abraham's trust in God preceded the law and circumcision alike. In that way, Abraham becomes an ancestor to both Jews and Greeks. Thus, chapter 5 begins by summarizing, "since we are justified by faith, we have peace with God through our Lord Jesus Christ" (Rom. 5:1). Thus we can boast in the gift of "our hope of sharing the glory of God" (v. 2), but also boast in the travails we face because "God's love," the guarantor of our salvation and wholeness in the midst of joy and suffering alike, "has been poured into our hearts" (v. 5). That is, God is faithful, through and through. So faithful is God that Jesus dies for us while we were still mere sinners, enemies of God.

In this way, Paul brings us to a narrative contrast between Adam and Christ. These two are types or symbols. They represent two distinct trajectories in the story of God's intervention to deliver the world. So also, death and sin perhaps ought to be read as Death and Sin. That is, death and sin are not mere nouns or things, one pointing to the moment our lives end, and the other to the many ways we break relationship with God and one another. No. Death and Sin need to be capitalized, for they represent personified forces.[1] They are the names of those

1. See Katherine Grieb, *The Story of Romans: A Narrative Defense of God's Righteousness* (Louisville, KY: Westminster John Knox, 2002), 56–84.

who afflict us but whom Jesus defeats. They are leading actors in the narrative Paul is recounting, not just bit characters.

Thinking of Death and Sin as personified forces helps bring additional exegetical clarity to verses 12–14. Sin is an invading force, an impostor smuggling itself into a law meant to bring life and grace. Sin's interference has distorted the law from within, and Sin draws Death in its wake. Death here certainly includes when we draw our last breath; but also every instance of harm, oppression, injustice. Death breaks God's good world; but the power of Sin and Death, while widespread, even universal, is not absolute. Death *has had* dominion, but something has changed. Paul weaves a story about these forces, Death and Sin, between a story about Adam and Jesus.

Notice that Paul never names Adam explicitly, though the reference to this figure of the Hebrew Scriptures is unquestionable (cf. the first reading, Gen. 2:15–17; 3:1–7). Why not name Adam if Paul names Christ explicitly? Perhaps because of the caution of verse 15: "But the free gift is not like the trespass." We are misled if we assume that Jesus is a mere counterweight to Adam's disobedience and fall in the garden. The scales in Paul's narrative are not equal.

Indeed, many have died on account of "one man's trespass" (v. 15), but God's grace and Jesus' "free gift . . . abounded for the many" (v. 15). The trade is not fair. The terms of the negotiation are not equitable. Why? Because God's grace, love, and free gift are in no way comparable to the story of death one man inaugurated. After all, "the free gift is not like the effect of the one man's sin" (v. 16). Indeed, Paul's argument will reach a crescendo at the end of chapter 8 when he declares that nothing whatsoever "will be able to separate us from the love of God in Christ Jesus our Lord" (8:39).

What is parallel is the scope of the effect of these two men, Adam and Jesus. One imprisoned us all; the other frees us all. Jesus' obedience is key. His faithfulness to proclaim the good news, to heal and exorcise, to die an unjust death, and to rise makes all the difference. His obedience is not the inverse of Adam's disobedience; Jesus' faithfulness obviates Adam's fall. Jesus' resurrection is a resounding rejection of the twin forces of Sin and Death, and his overcoming of them is immediate. We are living in the aftermath of the defeat of Sin and Death, not just in anticipation of this eventual conclusion.

Psalm 32 evokes many of the themes we have named above. The deep need for sin to be forgiven, for our broken relationships to God and one another to be healed echo in the voice of the psalmist yearning for confession, deliverance, and forgiveness. Perhaps Romans and the psalm together can help us voice our own deep yearning for deliverance from our iniquities. A preacher might note the personal dimensions of such sin, the weight of guilt we carry about things done and left undone.

To that personal dimension, a preacher might draw us to see the relational, communal, systemic aspects of such yearnings. We yearn for deliverance also from the plagues of racism, sexism, homophobia, gun violence, environmental degradation. Both the psalm and Romans echo in response that God's love and grace abound, since God has already forgiven and restored us. The question that lingers is how we will live into God's embrace. How will we embrace forgiveness? How will we live as if we really truly believed that Death and Sin have been defeated, even as they surround us?

Romans is full of stories. What are the defining stories in your community? Are they stories about loss or progress, resentment or joy? A combination of both? How can those local stories be woven into this cosmic story of fall and deliverance; defiance and obedience; death, injustice, and scarcity over against abundant resurrection life? The first step in drawing these stories together may be to preach this text less as a list of theological assertions and more like the persuasive, compelling story it was for Paul and the Roman churches.

This homiletical challenge reminds me of the story within the story told in the last installment of the *Harry Potter* films. Hermione, one of Harry's best friends and constant companions in danger and adventure, reads a child's story about three magical items called "The Deathly Hallows." The details of the story are not as important for us as the mode of storytelling. The live-action movie shifts to an animated mode for the first time in eight films, the look of this part of the movie jarring in its symbolic representation and artistic rendering. That is, the director could have had Hermione simply read the story while capturing the reactions of the other characters. Instead, a shift in visual cues alerts the audience that something pivotal is happening. Stories are made memorable not just in what they narrate but how they are told. Perhaps then our understanding of the genre of the sermon might itself come into question in light of this text from Romans. We are accustomed to mining Paul's letter for theological insight, less so to hearing—and even living—the story he weaves.

ERIC D. BARRETO

Commentary 2: Connecting the Reading with Scripture

In the cosmic battle between life and death, life now wins—every time—but it has not always been that way. These words would be a fitting "once upon a time" preamble to the campfire story that Christians gathered around the fire hear from Paul in the fifth chapter of his Letter to the Romans.

Paul's Letter to the Romans includes significant attention to the way of the world before Jesus. In the passage appointed for the First Sunday in Lent, Paul's letter draws attention to Adam and Adam's sin. Paul argues that all of humanity suffered for Adam's sin, paying the price for it as though the sin were their own, until Jesus redeemed humanity through his death and resurrection. The Letter to the Romans argues that the law, as received by Moses on Mount Sinai, interrupted but did not upend that history of all humanity suffering for Adam's misconduct. If anything, the law might have made matters more complicated, misleading people into thinking that they knew all they needed to know about what God wanted from them. Only Jesus' free gift of love was enough to reverse the fortunes of a humanity that had inherited sin from its earliest ancestor. Jesus' forgiving, redeeming love is mightier than Adam's sin. Where Adam's sin held onto us, Jesus' gift of love releases humanity from bondage, once and for all.

Paul expresses this view of human history through a series of binary contrasts: Adam versus Christ, death versus life, sin versus righteousness, transgression versus free gift, condemnation versus justification.[2] Peter Leithart, president of the Theopolis Institute in Birmingham, Alabama, writes of two dimensions in this passage from Romans that are significant for Christians today. First, he says, this text deals with the heart of Christian Scripture: "The fundamental problem the Gospel addresses is the reign of Death."[3] Second, he points out that Augustine's doctrine of original sin uses language from this particular passage, helping us to understand how Augustine came to the conclusion that we are born in sin and must convert through accepting Christ's free gift.

The liturgical significance of this text, perhaps due to Augustine's interpretation of it, points directly to the practice of Christian baptism, for all practices of baptism but particularly for those groups that practice infant baptism. Why would a baby need to have sin washed away if not for the fact that the baby has inherited sin as though it were a genetic condition? Furthermore, and perhaps more relevantly to the position of this text in the liturgical year, Lent descends upon us every year, whether or not we have experienced a particularly vice-filled year. Every year during Lent, we have something on which we must work, something for which to atone. Our fallenness is our natural state, and the free gift is all that will relieve us; we cannot do anything rightly enough to redeem ourselves the way Jesus redeems us at Easter. In Lent we reenact this history in order to connect with human beings from every time, even before humanity received the gift of God's love.

2. Peter J. Leithart, "Adam, Moses, and Jesus: A Reading of Romans 5:12–14," *Calvin Theological Journal* 43, no. 2 (2008): 263.
3. Leithart, "Adam, Moses, and Jesus," 273.

These practices of infant baptism and Lenten disciplines of self-sacrifice do raise questions about how free the free gift of Jesus' love actually is. It would be unbecoming for Christians saved by Jesus to cheer, "I can do whatever I wish!" as a response to Jesus' crucifixion. We hear in this text that Jesus' free gift of love is so very much stronger than Adam's sinfulness. The ethical and cultural significance of the practice today of infant baptism (babies born sinful, already in need of turning around) and Lenten self-sacrifice therefore must be framed as a response to God's love, not an act meant to earn God's love. Our goodness and our humility in the face of sin is our thank-you gesture, not our penance. When a parent presents an infant for baptism, the parent is saying, "I know I am not enough for this child." When a good person takes on a Lenten discipline, the person says, "I know God loves me the way I am, and I also know that I have work to do."

Personal implications of this text, and the passage's connection to larger human knowledge, can be found in the arc of human history Paul presents. Paul describes human history as fallen from the start (Adam), relying on laws as a temporary stopgap measure (the law) en route to true redemption (Jesus). We experience a similar arc in our human lives. First, we are born in a literal mess, crying and bloody and unable to take care of ourselves. Those who care for us, or those who control us, give us rules to live by. We need those rules to be safe, at first, and then later we need rules to relate appropriately with each other. As we mature, we shed those rules as snakes shed skin. Our characters and our morals develop over time, gradually replacing a rule-bound approach to living together with a deeper set of commitments to goodness and righteousness. The ultimate accomplishment takes place when we transfer our dependence upon rules to rootedness in love, where our conduct might look the same, but wells up from the depth of our souls.

The Picasso Museum in Madrid, Spain, displays Pablo Picasso's paintings in chronological order, over the course of his life. The visitor can see that as a boy Picasso did not just follow the rules; he mastered them. His early work evidences classical training and studied determination to capture outward reality. Over time, Picasso's work changes. One can almost sense the moment when the source of his genius transitioned from the rules he had learned to a creative vision originating from within him. The arresting beauty of his later work is, of course, less concrete; and in its abstract nature, it is difficult to describe. Yet its capacity to connect with its viewer makes one mindful that the rules get us only so far. As Paul expresses in this and other letters, the greatest gift and guide is love.

My husband teaches high school English. In the beginning of the year, he requires his students to write twelve-sentence paragraphs, with each sentence serving a particular function. Midway through the year he loosens that requirement. Unfailingly, a student or two asks, "Mr. Drummond, is it okay if I keep writing twelve-sentence paragraphs?" The discipline is something of which they are not ready to let go, and of course he says yes. Until the law is fulfilled, it remains a needed guide. When that law is fulfilled in a new ethic of love, the law remains respected and appreciated, but it no longer has nor needs to have the last word. To say the law has been fulfilled does not mean it has been replaced, but rather that it has found the destination toward which it was pointed all along.

During the season of Lent, we build structure around the conduct we think a fitting response to God's love for us. We impose rules on ourselves. The best goal to which we can strive during Lent is that our motivations gradually transition from a desire to follow self-imposed rules to a deep need to respond to God's love. That love, unlike our rules, never runs dry and can carry us into Eastertide changed, renewed, and redeemed.

SARAH BIRMINGHAM DRUMMOND

Matthew 4:1–11

1 Then Jesus was led up by the Spirit into the wilderness to be tempted by the
devil. 2 He fasted forty days and forty nights, and afterwards he was famished.
3 The tempter came and said to him, "If you are the Son of God, command these
stones to become loaves of bread." 4 But he answered, "It is written,

'One does not live by bread alone,
but by every word that comes from the mouth of God.'"

5 Then the devil took him to the holy city and placed him on the pinnacle of the
temple, 6 saying to him, "If you are the Son of God, throw yourself down; for it is
written,

'He will command his angels concerning you,'
and 'On their hands they will bear you up,
so that you will not dash your foot against a stone.'"

7 Jesus said to him, "Again it is written, 'Do not put the Lord your God to the
test.'"
8 Again, the devil took him to a very high mountain and showed him all the
kingdoms of the world and their splendor; 9 and he said to him, "All these I will
give you, if you will fall down and worship me." 10 Jesus said to him, "Away with
you, Satan! for it is written,

'Worship the Lord your God,
and serve only him.'"

11 Then the devil left him, and suddenly angels came and waited on him.

Commentary 1: Connecting the Reading with Scripture

In the construction of the lectionary, especially in the great seasons of Resurrection and Incarnation, the choice of the Gospel text governs the choice of the other readings, especially the second text from the New Testament. However, this week, the Romans texts seems to challenge the pattern. Whatever one may make of Paul's description of the typological economy of salvation—that through one man's trespass came condemnation and, just so, through one man's act of righteousness comes grace sufficient to wipe away both sin and death—it demands the preacher's attention. What is our Gospel text about but the exploration of this righteous one, Jesus the Christ, who—as Paul will tell us a few chapters later—not only refuses to condemn us but actively intercedes for us, claiming us with a love from which nothing can separate us?

The question of who this Jesus might be is also highlighted by our move backward in Matthew's carefully constructed chronology. On Ash Wednesday, we read from chapter 6; on this First Sunday in Lent, we now read from chapter 4. What is chapter 4 but the culmination of Matthew's construction of our introduction to this one man, Jesus the Messiah, Jesus the Christ?

Matthew establishes Jesus' place in the ongoing history of Israel, but over and over again, with little twists. In the first half of chapter 1, Matthew demonstrates Jesus' royal, even foundational, lineage. He is son of Abraham, son of David, son of the exiles, son of those who return—fourteen generations and fourteen generations and fourteen generations of continuity. He is also son of: a prostitute spy, a survivor of rape, an adulterer and murderer, captives, rebuilders, the occupied, a carpenter. Of course, all this is actually his "stepfather's" lineage—Jesus' only by adoption.

In the second half of chapter 1, we are introduced briefly to his mother. Fulfilling a prophecy, she bears Emmanuel without intimate relations with Joseph. This child is special—so Joseph is assured; accept him, name him, make him yours, an angel in a dream counsels. The child's distinctiveness is again emphasized in the first half of chapter 2, as we meet foreign astrologers who know of him, who seek him. They follow a star. They offer gifts. They are changed and take a different route home. In the second half of chapter 2, this Jesus is under threat, flees to exile, lives as a refugee until the death of the king who fears him. He returns. His father being first assured and then cautioned in two subsequent dreams, the family moves not back to Bethlehem but to Nazareth in the Galilee. Having grown up, in chapter 3 this Jesus approaches John the Baptist, asking to be baptized. John protests but acquiesces. Immersed in the waters of the Jordan River, this one is claimed as Beloved by a voice from the heavens as the Spirit alights. A royal if tainted bloodline. A complex—even scandalous—nuclear family. The fulfillment of prophecy. Subject of devotion of foreign dignitaries. Threat to a vassal king. Crosser of borders. Successor to the Baptizer. Beloved. Emmanuel, God-with-us. Here is Matthew's Jesus, the Messiah, the Christ.

There is one more step to take before beginning his public ministry—and so the story in our passage, the first half of chapter 4: Jesus, like Moses, like Elijah, must fast. The excursion into the wilderness is Spirit-led. Forty days, like Noah, like Moses, like the years of wandering, speaks of fullness. Enough! He is famished. Emmanuel is weak with hunger. Right on time, the tempter arrives. It is better to remain hungry than to take the bait. He knows he is Beloved; there is no need to call upon angels to prevent his crash into the temple courtyard. He has no need of worldly kingdoms and their splendors; he knows who holds the future. Scripture twisted. Scripture claimed. Away with you, Satan. Now the angels can come. They minister, not in dreams as to his adopted father, but directly, to this one man. It is time for him to begin. Matthew has made clear to us who this Jesus is.

To return to Paul's letter, this is the one man whose "act of righteousness leads to justification and life for all" (Rom. 5:18), the one who has grace abundant enough to bestow righteousness as a free gift upon all. Paul's Jesus Christ is a type. Matthew's Jesus is a man—a branch on a twisted family tree, a vulnerable child, a refugee who dares to return despite ongoing imperial rule, one who submits to baptism, one who becomes famished, one who faces the tempter. Perhaps the power of the type is precisely in the particularity of the life of the man; Paul needs Matthew to make the identity of this righteous one stick.

I must note at this point that I have not written the word "man" this many times when thinking homiletically and theologically since encountering Phyllis Trible at Union Theological Seminary more than thirty years ago.[1] Paul led me this way, but Matthew too suffers from phallocentric logic. Yes, women appear in his genealogy—and are crucial to it—but he traces Joseph's line. His birth narrative is about Joseph; Mary barely appears and neither speaks nor is spoken to. To the contrary, as Sojourner Truth reminded opponents of woman's suffrage more than a century ago: "That little man in black there, he says women can't have as much rights as men 'cause Christ wasn't a woman! Where did your Christ come from? Where did your Christ come from? From God and a woman! Man had nothing to do with Him."[2]

Further, this tale of fasting is shaped as a hero's journey—a man overcoming obstacles to prove his worth. Today's text from Genesis provides an important counternarrative. Eve is the central figure. She too faces a tempter. She carefully

1. See Phyllis Trible, *God and the Rhetoric of Sexuality* (Philadelphia: Fortress, 1978).
2. Sojourner Truth, "Ain't I a Woman?" (1851 speech), in Miriam Schneir, *Feminism: The Essential Historical Writings* (New York: Vintage Books, 1994), 94–95.

considers the tempter's words, God's words, the quality of the fruit, and the likely benefits; she may not exactly have counted the costs. Having engaged in reasonable if incomplete theological reflection, she takes and eats. She hands what was probably a pomegranate to the man. He does not hesitate. He does not think. He does not weigh costs and benefits. He eats. For Paul, this Adam is the one man through whom sin entered the good, the very good, creation—and so death too. Eve disappears.

A third and final counternarrative comes in our psalm: the sinner who does not hide iniquity, who acknowledges sin, receives simple, uncomplicated forgiveness—and shelter, instruction, and guidance. The body wastes and strength dissipates, not from fasting, but because faults are hidden in silence. Confess and know grace. Turn and you will be delivered, you will be glad and rejoice.

Our story of temptation is the final episode in Matthew's "introductory chapter." We now know who Jesus is. As a character, Jesus also now knows who he is. The public ministry is begun. As a Lenten Gospel text, the story invites us to follow Jesus in fasting. We too should prepare ourselves to confront those who twist Scripture. We too should not take the bait, keeping our eyes on the prize. Here is one last twist. The one who refuses to turn stones into bread is the same one who feeds more than five thousand with only five loaves and who offers himself as bread, as body, to satisfy all hunger . . . all!

W. SCOTT HALDEMAN

Commentary 2: Connecting the Reading with the World

Drawing on a vast amount of data, including some 500,000 interviews, Robert Putnam, in *Bowling Alone*, demonstrated how increasingly isolated we are from family, neighbors, and friends.[3] According to Putnam, we visit with family and friends less frequently, know our neighbors less well, belong to fewer social organizations, and even, as the title suggests, bowl alone rather than participate in bowling leagues. The reasons for this ironic increasing person-to-person isolationism in the midst of our high connectivity to the "virtual community" are complex, but one result is clear. "Alone" has become a frightening word. Being alone can mean having no friends and no community. It can mean feeling excluded and left out. Being alone, though, can also mean inhabiting a stretch of time all alone with nothing. No distractions, no books, no TV, no magazines, no video games. We tend to avoid that kind of aloneness as well. Most of us do everything possible not to go there.

The wisest people among us have always chosen times of aloneness. They have chosen aloneness in order to open themselves to prayer, to letting go, to making choices. Anthony the Great was among the first of the so-called desert fathers who ventured alone into the wilderness in the third century to confront temptations and his struggle to obey God. The life of faithfulness was not easy, but it was not impossible. This time of solitude enabled Anthony to pursue the virtuous life with more clarity.

Jesus too pursued solitude before he started his ministry. Before he was healer, teacher, and liberator, he chose aloneness. In the desert, Jesus considered unworthy alternatives and overcame them. Empty and vulnerable by choice, Jesus was brought face-to-face with the dark options of another path. In those moments, he remembered who he was, who God declared him to be at the river just days before: "My Son." "My Beloved." When the seducer came, Jesus could speak from the deep wellspring of knowing who he was—God's Beloved Son—and say, "No." However vast the difference between Jesus' relationship with God and ours, we too are daughters and sons of God. We too are God's Beloved—and we do the work of aloneness to confirm, clarify, and sustain that identity.

We do not do all the work of aloneness by ourselves. There is a kind of being alone that we

3. Robert D. Putnam, *Bowling Alone: The Collapse and Revival of American Community* (New York: Simon & Schuster, 2000).

share communally. Part of the purpose and mission of the church is to remind believers through life together that they have been made sons and daughters of God. We come to worship to enrich and clarify that identity. We form our identity as God's children through the study of the living Word and celebration of the Table. We strengthen that identity in community together.

When assaulted by the adversary, Jesus did not have to make up a response on the fly, but he could speak it from the overflow of instruction from family and synagogue. This then is the church's mission too. The work of sustaining and clarifying our identity as God's Beloved never ceases, because in this world of clamoring idolatries, it is easy to forget what the beloved daughters and sons of God must affirm and what they must deny. This work of faith is done best in communal aloneness.

Other monastics knew this truth. Pachomius (292–348) emphasized cenobiticism, communal monastic life. In his community, Pachomius sought a balance of the solitary life, in which the monks lived in individual cells, with communal life in which the believers worked together for the common good. In his novel *Jayber Crow*, through his fictional protagonist Wendell Berry has captured this vision of the church as gathered community working, sometimes imperfectly, for the common good and each other:

> My vision of the gathered church that had come to me. . . had been replaced by a vision of the gathered community. . . . My vision gathered the community as it never has been and never will be gathered in this world of time, for the community must always be marred by members who are indifferent to it or against it, who are nonetheless its members and maybe nonetheless essential to it. And yet I saw them all as somehow perfected, beyond time, by one another's love, compassion, and forgiveness, as it is said we may be perfected by grace.[4]

The liturgical season of Lent, in which this text is read, provides believers the same opportunity to enter together as a community a period of aloneness, of self-emptying, of ego-denial, in order to remember who they are. Lent, of course, points toward its culmination in Holy Week. Jesus spoke to the theme of remembrance on that last night at the table with his friends: "Do this in remembrance of me." Jesus said it twice. Over broken bread, he said, "Remember." Over the cup, he said, "Remember" (1 Cor. 11:23–25). So we look to Jesus, and we recall all that he refused, and all that he embraced, and all that he gave for the sake of us all. We can live in the great remembrance of who we are: God's Beloved daughters and sons.

The preacher might also attend to the order of the temptations in Matthew. Unlike Luke's version (which has the last temptation occurring at the temple), the third temptation in Matthew occurs on a very "high mountain." Rhetoricians and preachers alike know that the last (or first) item in a story usually holds special significance. Settings can provide points of continuity for a story. In Nathaniel Hawthorne's 1850 novel *The Scarlet Letter*, there are three scaffold scenes, which serve as pivotal moments in plot development and character identity. In the first scaffold scene, at the beginning of the book (chaps. 1–3), Hester Prynne, holding her infant daughter, is publicly humiliated and condemned for adultery. Her lover, the Rev. Arthur Dimmesdale, conceals his own guilt and participates in the judgment of Hester. In the second scene, in the book's middle (chap. 12), seven years after the first scene, Dimmesdale surreptitiously scales the scaffold in the middle of the night to confront his demons. Hester and her daughter, Pearl, hear his cry, and join him on the scaffold, and he reveals to Hester what she already knows. In the last scaffold scene (chap. 23), a dying Dimmesdale publicly confesses his role in Pearl's birth. With his death, Pearl is freed to live her life more fully and compassionately. The scaffold scene serves both to advance and resolve deep conflicts in the novel's plot and to reveal the characters' development.

So it is with Matthew's Gospel, in which mountains provide the setting for important moments of disclosure of Jesus' identity. Here in Matthew 4, Jesus is revealed as the "obedient

4. Wendell Berry, *Jayber Crow: A Novel* (Washington, DC: Counterpoint, 2000), 205.

Messiah." Other mountain scenes also reveal important aspects of Jesus' identity and vocation: the teaching Messiah (5:1); the praying Messiah (14:23); the healing Messiah (15:29); the glorified Messiah (17:1–2); and the apocalyptic Messiah (24:3).

Finally, Matthew ends with the resurrected Jesus, the universal Messiah, taking his disciples to a "high mountain" and commissioning them to go to "all nations" (28:16–20). From beginning to end, mountains function as the revelatory locus of Jesus' identity and vocation. Connecting the purpose of the last temptation of Jesus with similar settings in a modern novel such as *The Scarlet Letter* provides a compelling resource for fresh theological reflection on this Scripture text.

MIKEAL C. PARSONS

Second Sunday in Lent

Genesis 12:1–4a
Psalm 121
Romans 4:1–5, 13–17
John 3:1–17
Matthew 17:1–9

Genesis 12:1–4a

> [1]Now the LORD said to Abram, "Go from your country and your kindred and your father's house to the land that I will show you. [2]I will make of you a great nation, and I will bless you, and make your name great, so that you will be a blessing. [3]I will bless those who bless you, and the one who curses you I will curse; and in you all the families of the earth shall be blessed."
> [4]So Abram went, as the LORD had told him; and Lot went with him.

Commentary 1: Connecting the Reading with Scripture

On the Second Sunday in Lent, the Old Testament passage from Genesis 12:1–4a reminds us of the God who makes promises and who wishes to bless humanity. This same God, however, makes difficult demands of Abram, asking him to break with his past—his homeland—and travel to a new land of promise. This faithful immigrant, in turn, will become the agent of blessing for all nations. The promise here includes three elements: the land, the promise of great progeny, and the promise of blessings. In this simple introduction to Abram's story, we do not hear from Abram himself. All the narrative tells us is that Abram followed God's call and embarked on the journey at seventy-five years of age.

While one might consider the beginning of Abram's story in Genesis 12 to mark a change between the literature of the primeval history in Genesis 1–11 and the stories of the matriarchs and patriarchs in the rest of Genesis, this passage also offers some connective tissue. The story that began with the first family in Genesis 2–3 and begins anew with Noah's family in Genesis 8 has become the story of a larger human community in Genesis 11. The world in which Abram finds himself is a cosmopolitan world of many nations that now have various languages and cultures (Gen. 11:9). The genealogy in Genesis 11:10–31 connects Abram, through his father, Terah, back ten generations to Noah's son Shem. In the narrative, the wide-angle perspective on all of humanity in chapter 11 once again zooms in to focus on one family, the family of Terah and his son. Abram is actually continuing the journey Terah himself began, though the biblical text does not give us a window into Terah's own motivations (11:31).

The connections between Abram's story and the primeval history are more than just genealogical. Michael Fishbane points out a thematic connection to the creation narratives. He suggests that the ten generations between Abram and Noah are comparable to the span between Adam and Noah, reinforcing the idea of another new beginning with Abram's story. Moreover, Fishbane posits a typological connection between God's promises of land, progeny, and blessing, suggesting these are a reversal of the curses in Genesis 3 "against the earth, human generativity, and human labour."[1] Abram's blessing carries the promise of a new creation in which his family will bless all other people groups.

As a transition passage in the grand narrative of Genesis, this promise looks backward,

1. Michael Fishbane, *Biblical Interpretation in Ancient Israel* (Oxford: Oxford University Press, 1985), 372–73.

at the connections between Abram's family and Noah's and Adam's families, while launching Abram's particular story forward. It is the thesis statement of the life story of Abram (later known as Abraham) and is reiterated and expanded at critical junctures in his life. The promise to become a great nation comes under threat later in Genesis 12, when Abram lies to Pharaoh about Sarai's identity. In that context, because of Sarai's beauty, Pharaoh might have taken her into his harem, ending Abram's hope of having an heir in this marriage. God's protection in this episode manifests itself in plagues on Pharaoh's house that spur Pharoah to release Abram and Sarai.

The promise narratively recurs and gains a liturgical context in the covenant scene and circumcision ceremony of Genesis 17. In this text, God reiterates that Abram will father not only one son, but two, and that many nations will trace their lineage to him. God changes Abram's name to Abraham as a marker that he will become the father of many nations (17:5). God then reaffirms the promise of the land and adds some scope by defining the land of Canaan as the perpetual homeland of Abraham's offspring (v. 8).

God also promises that the son by Sarai, now renamed Sarah, will be the son who carries forward the covenant (v. 19). Abraham exhibits his own ability to be a blessing to the nations by interceding on Ishmael's behalf (v. 18). Though Isaac will bear the covenant, Ishmael will also inherit God's blessings and become a great nation (v. 20). Abraham ratifies Ishmael's inclusion in these promises through the circumcision ritual (v. 23). As in any good narrative, the threat to the promise does not end in this scene, and the tension continues, as Sarah does not give birth until chapter 21. In the meantime, Abraham again demonstrates his ability to bless the nations by interceding for the people of Sodom in Genesis 18. God's decision to reveal the plan for Sodom's destruction to Abraham centers on Abraham's role as the patriarch of a great nation that will bless all others (18:17–18). After the sordid tale of Sodom and Lot, Abraham once again passes Sarah off as his sister, this time to the king of Gerar, in a tale that echoes the initial threat to the promise by Pharaoh (Gen. 20).

One might assume that the promise finally comes to fruition in Genesis 21 with the birth of Isaac. The birth, however, leads to further tension between Sarah and Hagar, Ishmael's mother, resulting in the expulsion of Hagar and Ishmael. The promise once again faces the threat of God's own challenge to Abraham to sacrifice his only son. Only after Abraham complies with the request does God stop him and reiterate the promise once more, saying that Abraham's descendants will be more numerous than the sands on the seashore and that all the nations of the world will find blessing through them (22:16–18). This blessing will weave its way through the successive generations of Abraham's family, first to Isaac (26:1–5) and then to Jacob (28:13–15).

Later literature recalls this promise in efforts to reassure the people of Judah and Israel. Referring to the exiles in Isaiah 44 as Jacob, the prophet of comfort offers language very similar to the Abrahamic promise: "For I will pour water on the thirsty land, and streams on the dry ground; I will pour my spirit upon your descendants, and my blessing on your offspring" (Isa. 44:3). The reassurance is particularly poignant in Isaiah 51:1–2, written to encourage a colonized people in an exilic context: "Listen to me, you that pursue righteousness, you that seek the LORD. Look to the rock from which you were hewn, and to the quarry from which you were dug. Look to Abraham your father and to Sarah who bore you; for he was but one when I called him, but I blessed him and made him many." The prophet continues to base God's coming restoration on these ancient promises throughout the passage (51:4–5). Likewise, the prophet Zechariah renews the promise to a generation that has experienced the curses of exile and colonization, suggesting that God will reverse the people's fortune, and they will once again become a blessing (Zech. 8:13).

This text is the basis for the three great Abrahamic faiths: Judaism, Islam, and Christianity. Judaism traces its lineage through Isaac and Islam through Ishmael. In the Christian context, the lectionary text in Romans 4:1–5, 13–17 democratizes the Abrahamic promise, suggesting that Christians are coinheritors of the promise because "he is the father of all of us" (Rom. 4:16). Perhaps the text can remind those of us in an increasingly shrinking and cosmopolitan world of the interrelatedness of all humanity and the church's responsibility to become a blessing to all nations.

DAVID G. GARBER JR.

Commentary 2: Connecting the Reading with the World

Scholarship on biblical narrative often draws attention to the efficiency of biblical prose. Old Testament narrative rarely provides elaborate, descriptive detail about scenery, nor does it give much access to the inner thoughts of its characters. Instead, biblical prose prioritizes dialogue and action.[2] We hear what characters say, and we observe what they do, but we do not always receive much insight from the narrator into *why* they do what they do, or what feelings may lurk, hidden, behind their speech. Readers are left to fill in these "gaps" in the narrative; in fact, much biblical interpretation, particularly of the homiletical variety, happens in these gaps.[3]

As the story of the call of Abram, Genesis 12:1–4a invites reflection on vocation, that sense of divine call that pulls our lives toward particular choices or roles. Nonetheless, to connect these three and a half quick verses to the lives of Christians in today's pews will require as much reading in the gaps as it will attending to the words on the page. True to the efficiency of biblical narrative, the lectionary passage consists almost entirely of speech by God ("Now the Lord said to Abram, 'Go . . .'"), followed by Abram's response, an action: "So Abram went, as the Lord had told him."

The text describes from where Abram should depart (familiar, familial territory), where Abram should go (unfamiliar, unspecified territory), and what God promises to do with and for him. The text does *not* describe a multitude of other things, including why Abram is the one chosen; why God requires or desires Abram's departure in order to realize these promises; whether or how Abram knows God is really talking to him; whether Abram has any questions or concerns about the process; whether any time has lapsed between the call and Abram's response; and whether Abram has consulted with, or even informed, the rest of his household, including his wife Sarai.

Abram's willingness to do as God had told him playfully recalls Dr. Seuss's children's book *Marvin K. Mooney, Will You Please Go Now!* (New York: Random House, 1972)—a connection I am sure many preachers have made in their sermons or children's messages. In the Seuss book, a voice represented only by a giant hand with a pointing finger commands Marvin K. Mooney to "go," suggesting such modes of transportation as a broomstick or a camel. The only rationale offered for Marvin's imminent departure is that "the time has come." In the final pages of the book, the voice shouts with frustration, "I said GO, and GO I meant!" In a conclusion that closely, if probably unintentionally, echoes Genesis 12:4a, the narrator remarks, "The time had come, so Marvin went."

God's speech—God's *call*—turns Abram's focus away from his past concerns and toward God's agency in his life. The familiar location from which Abram must depart is marked by second-person possessive pronouns: "*your* country and *your* kindred and *your* father's house" (Gen. 12:1). Six first-person-singular verbs follow, all with God as the subject and Abram as the object of God's action: "I will show you," "I will make of you," and so forth. Perhaps, then, to answer a call from God is to be willing to submit to God's agency: to be reoriented from subject to object, or from the familiar to the unknown. Even so, a glaring gap remains: How does Abram—and how do any of us—know when we are responding to *God's* voice, rather than social pressure, our own whims, or some other force?

2. See Robert Alter, *The Art of Biblical Narrative* (New York: Basic Books, 1981).

3. The ancient Jewish rabbinic practice of midrash—deeply imaginative and deeply faithful—was the original exercise in biblical gap filling. For more on midrash and its intersections with modern Christian biblical interpretation, see Wilda C. Gafney, *Womanist Midrash: A Reintroduction to the Women of the Torah and the Throne* (Louisville, KY: Westminster John Knox, 2017).

One reading of this passage acknowledges the speed with which Abram obeys, in order to encourage a great leap of vocational faith. When God calls, go! Trust God's voice, relinquish control, "let go and let God." Yet most pastoral leaders giving counsel to parishioners about whether to move, change jobs, or make other major life decisions would encourage them to embark upon a period of discernment: to talk it over with their families, to weigh the pros and cons, to make a budget, and certainly to "pray on it." According to the details provided in the narrative, Abram does none of these things. Must we therefore assume Abram simply heard these words from God and got up to go without hesitation, and that we in turn should emulate him? It is all well and good for the great patriarch of three world religions to have followed the voice of God into the unknown, but what about the rest of us?

Somewhere in the gap between verses 3 and 4 is Abram's own process of discernment. This is a space in which the preacher's homiletical imagination around vocation can take flight. What did God's voice sound like, and where did Abram hear it, that he knew it to be genuine? Was Abram already on speaking terms with this God? Did he think this journey would be easier or harder than his current situation? What did Sarai say when Abram asked her to pack up the tents?

Perhaps contrary to our expectations, the brevity of this passage—it would fit in two tweets, with characters to spare!—expands, rather than limits, its homiletical potential. Preachers can name its unanswered questions, acknowledge them, and multiply them to find the connections that will speak to the unique contexts of their congregations. Discernment, in this passage as in everyday life, bridges the distance between call and response. Even though Abram's discernment process, whatever it may have looked like, is not detailed in the text, the gaps in the narrative help us to host better questions.

The same kinds of vocational connections that this text inspires for individuals can also provide guidance for Christian communities today. As churches face a narrative of decline spurred by aging and shrinking congregations, they must discern where God is calling them in this new era. No longer a dominant cultural voice, many churches face a journey into unfamiliar, unspecified territory, reimagining their ministries for a changing context. The call of Abram can offer hope and guidance in this process, pulling faith communities away from "we've always done it this way" and reorienting them toward God's agency, which leads to newness and blessing. Pausing in the "gap" between God's call and Abram's response can remind congregations to undertake deliberate processes of discernment, rather than jumping—as a consequence of excitement or panic—to the next new idea.

At the same time, some communities may need the push to action that Abram's ostensibly quick response can provide. In any case, the text also provides a word of hope in the promise of blessing that lies ahead. God's blessing of Abram is radically expansive, pushing beyond self, family, or tribe to all families of the earth. We know from the rest of Abram's story that his confidence in God's promises falters time and again, and yet God's faithfulness to the promise persists. Genesis 12:1–4a reminds us that God can draw out infinite blessings from the life of one person, or one community, simply trying to respond faithfully to God's call.

CAMERON B. R. HOWARD

Psalm 121

[1]I lift up my eyes to the hills—
from where will my help come?
[2]My help comes from the LORD,
who made heaven and earth.

[3]He will not let your foot be moved;
he who keeps you will not slumber.
[4]He who keeps Israel
will neither slumber nor sleep.

[5]The LORD is your keeper;
the LORD is your shade at your right hand.
[6]The sun shall not strike you by day,
nor the moon by night.

[7]The LORD will keep you from all evil;
he will keep your life.
[8]The LORD will keep
your going out and your coming in
from this time on and forevermore.

Connecting the Psalm with Scripture and Worship

If God called you to leave behind all that you know—homeland, family, inheritance—what would you do? Today's Genesis passage tells us what Abram did. When he heard such a call—"Go from your country and your kindred and your father's house" (Gen. 12:1)—Abram just went. This first of Abram's famous displays of faith, which, combined with famous lapses of faith, create one of the Hebrew Bible's epic sagas, is astonishing. How might we act with such astonishing faith, such confident trust in God? One way could be to internalize Psalm 121.

Known as a Song of Ascent—songs that may have been sung by pilgrims journeying up to Jerusalem—Psalm 121 is recognized as a psalm of trust. From start to finish, it exudes a serenely rooted trust in God's power and in God's loving care.

The psalm begins with one of the most basic actions a person can take: "I lift up my eyes" (Ps. 121:1a). It then asks one of the most basic questions a person can ask: "from where will my help come?" (v. 1b). In response to this human-centric question, comes the God-centric answer: "My help comes from the LORD" (v. 2a). Immediately acknowledging the human need for help and the divine capacity to give that help creates a sense of relationship: the trustworthiness of God enables us to live in trusting reliance on God. Perhaps that is how Abram was able to leave behind all he knew.

The vocabulary of those opening two verses is personal, with both including the phrase "my help." Then, in verses 3–8, the pronouns shift from first-person singular to second-person singular, and the key terminology shifts from "help" to "keep," versions of which appear six times in those six verses. This is "keep" in the sense of "guard," "protect," "watch over," "care for." How appropriate, as the psalm proceeds to focus on God's comprehensive (e.g., v. 6's "day . . . night," and v. 8's "going out . . . coming in") caregiving.

Like the Genesis passage, which simply presents God's sweeping promise of blessing to and through Abram, Psalm 121 is uncomplicated by details of specific difficulties that might necessitate help. Instead, it emphasizes the value of God's help by exploring the nature of the One who provides it.

The psalmist leads with God's surpassing strength: God "made heaven and earth" (v. 2b). Yet this almighty Creator is also as near as your next footfall (v. 3a). This marvelous juxtaposition of God's transcendence and God's immanence describes the perfect traveling Companion!

Three repetitions underscore God's faithful wakefulness (vv. 3b–4). As Abram traveled to "the land" that God would show him (Gen. 12:1), how vital it must have been to know that God was keeping watch, even after each evening's fire burned low.

In the center of the psalm, the psalmist carefully arranges the word order to emphasize that it is "*the Lord* [who] is your keeper" (Ps. 121:5a). We can reasonably imagine that Abram's ability to leave everything behind grew from his confidence that it is none other than the Lord with whom he would journey.

The psalm continues to explore the totality of this trust-based relationship, delineating the 24/7 nature of God's care (v. 6) and declaring that it provides protection against nothing short of "all evil" (v. 7a). Furthermore, the subject of this all-encompassing care is our *nephesh* (v. 7b). Frequently translated "life" or "soul," the *nephesh* is our very being; God's embracing care is for our essential essence.

The final verse includes the psalm's most overtly journey-related language: "your going out and your coming in," which will be guarded by God forever (v. 8b). Whether the journey in question is Abram's journey to an unknown land, or a pilgrim's journey to Jerusalem, or a congregation's journey through Lent, what better reassurance can there be than that our eternal God cares for us eternally?

Lent helps us hear God's call to leave behind the sin that we know and to travel toward new life in God. Psalm 121 accompanies worshipers on today's leg of that trip. A call to worship could be fashioned from any verses (for nongendered language, substitute "God" for "he"). As a call to confession, one might say: "The psalmist reminds us that the Lord is our keeper, who will keep us from evil, who will keep our very lives. Confident that we are so cared for by the almighty and all-merciful God, let us confess our sins." Responsive intercessory prayers might include a congregational refrain after each petition: "Help comes from the Lord, who made heaven and earth" (v. 2). Verse 8 of the psalm offers a ready benediction: "The Lord will keep your going out and your coming in from this time on and forevermore."

To help worship continue beyond the benediction, encourage your congregation to engage this Scripture directly. Ask children to hand out slips of paper printed with a phrase drawn from the psalm (e.g., "My help comes from the Lord, who made heaven and earth" (v. 1), "God who keeps me will not slumber" (v. 3b), "The Lord is my keeper" (v. 5a), "The Lord will keep me from all evil" (v. 7a), "God will keep my life" (v. 7b), "The Lord will keep my going out and my coming in from this time on and forevermore" (v. 8)), or invite parishioners to choose a phrase that especially speaks to them of God's care and to write it on paper they will carry with them for the rest of Lent.

For hymns, "Sing Praise to God Who Reigns Above" is a solid choice, and "Go, My Children, with My Blessing" could highlight the relationship described in the psalm. That trust-based relationship was crucial for Abram and is crucial for us, because, when God calls us to leave behind all the priorities we know and journey with the sent-to-be-crucified Jesus, we struggle. So let us lift our eyes to God, from whom our help comes.

LEIGH CAMPBELL-TAYLOR

Romans 4:1–5, 13–17

[1]What then are we to say was gained by Abraham, our ancestor according to the
flesh? [2]For if Abraham was justified by works, he has something to boast about,
but not before God. [3]For what does the scripture say? "Abraham believed God,
and it was reckoned to him as righteousness." [4]Now to one who works, wages
are not reckoned as a gift but as something due. [5]But to one who without works
trusts him who justifies the ungodly, such faith is reckoned as righteousness. . . .

[13]For the promise that he would inherit the world did not come to Abraham or
to his descendants through the law but through the righteousness of faith. [14]If it
is the adherents of the law who are to be the heirs, faith is null and the promise
is void. [15]For the law brings wrath; but where there is no law, neither is there
violation.

[16]For this reason it depends on faith, in order that the promise may rest on
grace and be guaranteed to all his descendants, not only to the adherents of
the law but also to those who share the faith of Abraham (for he is the father of
all of us, [17]as it is written, "I have made you the father of many nations")—in the
presence of the God in whom he believed, who gives life to the dead and calls
into existence the things that do not exist.

Commentary 1: Connecting the Reading with Scripture

Preaching from Romans requires us to look in several directions at once. Any particular lection will emerge and flow from arguments Paul has been building. That same lection will also anticipate arguments that follow. That is, preaching a particular Pauline text means looking back and forward at the same time, even as we keep the assigned text before us. Not only that! Paul's imagination is also shaped by his reading of texts from the Hebrew Bible. So we must also draw connections to these ancient stories and the traditions that had accrued around them.[1] When Paul refers to "Abraham" in 4:1, the name evokes to Paul and his audience a litany of stories and traditions. "Abraham" evokes a particular person; even more, the name evokes a fully formed character and story.

Romans 4, therefore, starts with a pregnant question: "What then are we to say was gained by Abraham, our ancestor according to the flesh?" First, we have to remind ourselves why Paul asks this question. The previous chapter similarly begins with a vivid question (Rom. 3:1): What advantage is there to be a Jew, a member of a people chosen by God? What advantage is there if Paul is right that all of us are caught up in the web of sin and death so vividly described in chapters 1 and 2?

Paul suggests there are many advantages to being called by God to be a Jew. After all, God's faithfulness is absolute. The promises God has made God will keep. What is also true for Paul is that "the power of sin" (3:9) has imprisoned "both Jews and Greeks," a reality confirmed by the Hebrew Scriptures (see 3:10–18). Jesus, however, subverts this deadly reality, for "he will justify the circumcised on the ground of faith and the uncircumcised through that same faith" (3:30). That is, the diagnosis and prescription are identical for all people. As chapter 3 closes, Paul seems to realize a potential implication of this teaching. What role does the law, the Torah, play if we are all caught in the same web of sin and delivered by the same righteous Jesus?

1. For such traditions, see James L. Kugel, *The Bible As It Was* (Cambridge, MA: Belknap, 1997).

Be Still and Wait God's Pleasure

1 If you but trust in God to guide you
and place your confidence in him,
you'll find him always there beside you
to give you hope and strength within;
for those who trust God's changeless love
build on the rock that will not move.

2 Only be still and wait his pleasure
in cheerful hope with heart content.
He fills your needs to fullest measure
with what discerning love has sent;
doubt not our inmost wants are known
to him who chose us for his own.

3 Sing, pray, and keep his ways unswerving,
offer your service faithfully,
and trust his word; though undeserving,
you'll find his promise true to be.
God never will forsake in need
the soul that trusts in him indeed.

Georg Neumark, "If Thou But Suffer God to Guide Thee," trans. Catherine Winkworth, in *The United Methodist Hymnal: Book of United Methodist Worship* (Nashville: United Methodist Pub. House, 1989), #142.

Notice that Paul says he confirms the law by teaching this (3:31)!

So we arrive at our passage. If we start in the same place and are saved by the same Jesus, what do we make of Abraham? What did Abraham "gain"? Abraham, Paul suggests, did not merit righteousness as a laborer earns a paycheck; instead, Abraham's righteousness was a gift, through and through. Because it was a gracious, divine gift, righteousness remains a gift available to all of Abraham's descendants.

Here is where Paul's argumentation becomes particularly bold, and perhaps where our preaching might match Paul's boldness too. Gentiles get *grafted* into Abraham's lineage (cf. 11:17–21), not by standing in place of Israelites or Abraham's descendants according to the flesh but beside, or even better, behind them, as Paul suggested in 1:16 ("to the Jew first and also to the Greek"). It is God's faithfulness to Israel that opens up the possibility that Gentiles too might be counted as heirs of Abraham, for God's grace and righteousness are rooted in God's faithfulness, a faithfulness that is expansive and embraces "many nations" (4:17). Moreover, God is a God "who gives life to the dead and calls into existence the things that do not exist" (v. 17b). Such is God's grace that a people who were not called are now called after Israel.

In this way, Paul suggests, Abraham becomes an exemplar of faith, not so much because Abraham was bold but because he trusted God's faithfulness. Abraham trusted God's faithfulness when he left his country because he believed God's promise that Abraham would father a "great nation" (Gen. 12:2). Abraham trusted, and Isaac was born (21:1–7). Abraham believed even as he lifted a knife above the same boy (22:1–19). Yet behind these memories of Abraham's trusting of God is a query that rings throughout the letter to the churches in Rome: What do we make of God? Are God's promises to Abraham mutable, changeable, revocable? Is the God of Abraham a God who has been proven worthy of trust? Is God a God of justice and righteousness? Answering these questions in the affirmative is not just a matter of confession. Answering in the affirmative requires a different way of life than we have known before.

These were pressing questions for Paul, so pressing that they anchor the long, complex argumentation of Romans. Is this still a question that haunts people of faith today in quite the same way? Do we worry that God may prove to be faithless in the end?

I think these questions are still with us, though they take various and diverse shapes in our communities. Here, the preacher must practice a careful listening of the community to which she is called, in order to discern the reverberations of this ancient question today. For one, we might turn to the incredible amount of mistrust we find in many Western communities and political contexts. Surveys suggest that our mistrust of our neighbors has grown as we know them less and less.[2] In addition, we might consider the ways in which our political discourse has devolved into isolated silos of (mis)information; in such silos, our political opponents are taken to be not just misguided but deluded, partners in evil, or barely even human. Such mistrust of our neighbors must overflow into our theologies. If we cannot trust those who bear the image of God, then how can we trust the God who gifted them with God's own image? A sermon may explore how a rising tide of cynicism and mistrust creates a God who looks less like the God of Abraham and more like a God of vengeance or wrath or resentment.

A sermon might also draw us to the verses that follow our text, especially verses 18–19, as Paul retells the story of Isaac's conception and birth as a long-delayed promise. "Hoping against hope" is a resonant way to consider the shape of faithfulness in a world of uncertainty. Does Abraham's faithfulness preclude doubt, exclude questioning and wondering if God's promises would be kept? Of course not (see Gen. 15:1–6!), though Paul seems to be a bit more certain in Romans 4:20 than we might be. Belief is not absolute certainty. Faith is not unswerving assurance.

Instead, Abraham's life included not just a visit from angels to assure him of the promise, not just the long-awaited birth of Isaac. His life included Hagar and Ishmael as well as the story of Isaac's near-sacrifice. When Paul evokes "Abraham," he brings to mind not just the heights of Abraham's life but its darkest moments too. Faith can be found in both.

So a sermon might invite us to remember that faith is not linear, growing more and more day by day. Faith rides on the waves of life, rising and falling. Faith is not just a matter of individual belief, of *my* certainty in times of trouble. Faith is nurtured and held by our neighbors, our siblings in faith. "Hoping against hope" may mean that sometimes I need someone else to hold my trust in God for me when my trust is slipping. After all, we follow a Jesus who preached the good news *and* prayed in grief in a garden, who rose from the dead *and* who cried out when he felt deserted by God.

ERIC D. BARRETO

Commentary 2: Connecting the Reading with the World

Sequence matters. Trust God. Grace is guaranteed.

These three themes emerge from the section of Paul's Letter to the Romans appointed for the Second Sunday in Lent. They *emerge*, rather than being stated outright, from a series of twists and turns that could cause the reader to wonder if Paul's cryptic expository style is purposeful. Does Paul seek to provide an object lesson for the complex and intertwined relationship between faith and works? A Christian who takes Lent seriously might turn to this passage, two weeks into Lent, and start to flag in zeal; they might find that where they hoped all their questions would be answered, all of their answers are questioned.

Sequence Matters. Ask any elementary school teacher, merger negotiator, or entrepreneur: the way in which we sequence what we do is just as important as the doing, and sometimes it is more important. Paul writes to the Romans that the sequence that led to Abraham becoming the spiritual parent of Christians was important to the faith journeys of all of us, Abraham's spiritual children. Abraham was asked by God to do something difficult and costly. Abraham believed in God and followed God's instruction. Good things then happened.

Of course, we could easily understand the good things that happened to Abraham to be wages earned, writes Paul. To do so would get the sequence wrong. Abraham did not follow God's instruction to cause God to love him, but to respond to God's love for him. Anything one could find in God's call to Abraham that we

2. George Gao, "Americans Divided on How Much They Trust Their Neighbors," Pew Research Center (April 13, 2016), http://www.pewresearch.org/fact-tank/2016/04/13/americans-divided-on-how-much-they-trust-their-neighbors/.

could now view as a transaction, Paul's analysis in Romans throws into question. God's love is a free gift, and Abraham's faith is a free response to that gift. Who loved and honored whom first, and who responded how and when, matter, because God does not invite us to play manipulative games in the interest of garnering favor.

We live in a culture where tried and true societal rules about sequence are collapsing, in large part due to the way in which new technologies make it possible to do so many different things at once. In intimate partnerships, couples become sexually involved before they connect emotionally. They begin to share a life before they have created a covenant with one another. Bridal salons now offer maternity collections. One does not have to have puritanical morals regarding sexuality to say that this type of sequence presents challenges for the building of lasting relationships. No judgment, truly, but in intimate relationships we as a human community have quite recently disregarded the societal norm suggesting that sequence matters.

Similarly, and far less sexily, curricula in theological seminaries have had to let go of the idea that sequence matters. Seminary educators face resistance to sequencing, and in a student-driven educational marketplace, such resistance is on one hand understandable, and on the other hand, armed and dangerous. Some start out in ministry before they have gone to seminary, and then bring to seminary different needs and questions than the seminary was built to address. Students chafe against having to take courses that interest them less, and they ignore prerequisites expected for upper-level courses. This lack of concern for ordered learning does not necessarily stem from arrogance; rather, students generally lack respect for the notion that sequence matters. They want it all; they want it now.

Trust God. This passage from Romans makes clear that the best thing Abraham ever did was trusting God. Christians, Jews, and Muslims share a common understanding that Abraham was the first human being to talk to the God we all now worship in our different ways. Abraham therefore had no frame of reference for who God was and what God would call him to do. God tells him to change his name, and he changes it. God tells him he will start a great nation, and Abraham gets down to the business of doing so.

He was righteous by trusting God, not trusted by God for being righteous. Therefore, Paul makes a strong argument in this passage that trusting God is in itself good, and it is the beginning of good things that can happen to those who trust God.

Grace Is Guaranteed. Grace is not earned like wages and cannot be lost like squandered wages. Abraham did not receive God's grace for being a good man, or even for trusting God. He received God's grace because God is God. God's economy does not resemble a market economy, where earnings and expenditures come as a result of effort. Grace, God's currency distributed with abundance, does not follow predictable human rules, which means it cannot be fully understood. Only in cases where human beings become overconfident of their self-perceived understanding of how to earn God's favor are they in real trouble. All their answers are questioned.

All three of these premises call on us to examine our assumptions about how Christians are supposed to observe Lent. Many give up bad habits during Lent, with the hope that God will help them work on their character and improve as human beings. Others take on new spiritual practices, including a generalized seriousness and restraint that make them less fun to be around. Whereas these observances surely provide opportunities for reflection and spiritual growth, it is a mistake to understand them in any transactional way. We do not give things up, or take things on, during Lent in an effort to bring God closer to us. Our efforts at faithfulness have no earning power.

They are, rather, evidence of the work God has already done in us. One particularly helpful definition of the distinction between faith and works favored among Luther adherents is that faith is the apple tree planted by God, faith itself being a gift (2 Pet. 1:1); and works are the apples. Good apple trees, healthy and strong and reaching up toward the sunlight, grow good apples. In terms of personal piety and larger human knowledge, this distinction is important, as it reminds the pious that they are not earning anything by their actions; their actions are fruits of the grace God has already given everyone.

Liturgically, and in an ecclesial context, this passage reminds us that piety is not a contest. Those who are most faithful are not racking up points for entry into heaven, and they should not be allowed to conduct themselves as if they were. Language used in worship during Lent should carefully describe Lenten faith practices not as a ploy to get on God's good side, but as a response to God's ultimately self-giving love. That love places in us gratitude beyond what we can express in any way other than by striving to be the very best versions of ourselves we can be. Culturally and ethically, Paul's depiction of Abraham's relationship with God upends conventional stereotypes about how Christians ought to be good. The notion that Christians attempt to collect good works like chits to trade in for prizes misses the mark completely.

Perhaps Robert Wadsworth Lowry's hymn best captures the nature of sequence, trust in God, and grace: our good works are our song. Christians do good, and are good, because as the hymn goes, "How can I keep from singing?"

> What though my joys and comforts die?
> I know my Savior liveth.
> What though the darkness gather round?
> Songs in the night he giveth.
>
> The peace of Christ makes fresh my heart,
> a fountain ever springing!
> All things are mine since I am his!
> How can I keep from singing?[3]

SARAH BIRMINGHAM DRUMMOND

3. Robert Lowry, "My Life Flows On (How Can I Keep from Singing?)," in *Glory to God* (Louisville, KY: Westminster John Knox Press, 2013), 821.

John 3:1–17

1Now there was a Pharisee named Nicodemus, a leader of the Jews. 2He came
to Jesus by night and said to him, "Rabbi, we know that you are a teacher who
has come from God; for no one can do these signs that you do apart from the
presence of God." 3Jesus answered him, "Very truly, I tell you, no one can see the
kingdom of God without being born from above." 4Nicodemus said to him, "How
can anyone be born after having grown old? Can one enter a second time into
the mother's womb and be born?" 5Jesus answered, "Very truly, I tell you, no one
can enter the kingdom of God without being born of water and Spirit. 6What is
born of the flesh is flesh, and what is born of the Spirit is spirit. 7Do not be astonished that I said to you, 'You must be born from above.' 8The wind blows where
it chooses, and you hear the sound of it, but you do not know where it comes
from or where it goes. So it is with everyone who is born of the Spirit." 9Nicode-
mus said to him, "How can these things be?" 10Jesus answered him, "Are you a
teacher of Israel, and yet you do not understand these things?

11"Very truly, I tell you, we speak of what we know and testify to what we have
seen; yet you do not receive our testimony. 12If I have told you about earthly
things and you do not believe, how can you believe if I tell you about heavenly
things? 13No one has ascended into heaven except the one who descended from
heaven, the Son of Man. 14And just as Moses lifted up the serpent in the wilderness, so must the Son of Man be lifted up, 15that whoever believes in him may
have eternal life.

16"For God so loved the world that he gave his only Son, so that everyone who
believes in him may not perish but may have eternal life.

17"Indeed, God did not send the Son into the world to condemn the world, but
in order that the world might be saved through him."

Commentary 1: Connecting the Reading with Scripture

Dear Nicodemus is trying. He has seen the signs and wonders. He is Pharisee without being antagonist. He would follow this teacher. Jesus is not taking it easy on him. He deals in puzzles: "You must be born from above!"

"How can one who is old be born again?" Nicodemus sputters in reply. How indeed?

Jesus pivots: "Do not be astonished. The Spirit blows where it will." Jesus seems to point to a salvation of surrender. The Son has been sent. The Son will be lifted up. The Spirit moves like a rushing wind, and one is (voila!) reborn. The Spirit rushes on.

The crux here seems to be belief—but belief in what? That one can be born again? That one can ascend to heaven? That those born of water *and* Spirit will enter the kingdom? That the Son was sent? That eternal life is a gift? The negative case seems clearer but no less troubling. One who does not believe Jesus' take on earthly matters cannot hope to understand what he says about heavenly things. One who does not believe will perish. One who does not believe may not have eternal life.

How does this square with the conclusion, that the Son was sent not to condemn but to save? Even this most well-known and cherished verse, "For God so loved the world . . . ," may now feel less reassuring than anxiety producing. Perhaps it has always been so. How can we ever know for sure whether we are among those who belong to the "everyone who believes in him"?

Of course, we are reading from what we name the Gospel of John. We break from the overall pattern of the year and from our primary focus on Matthew. The shift provides opportunity to show contrasts between the Gospel portrayals. For instance, John's Jesus functions primarily in the realm of rhetoric; Matthew's prefers concrete action. John's Jesus declares, "I am . . . !" regularly: I am Bread of Life (John 6:35, 41, 48, 51); I am Light of World (8:12; 9:5); I am Good Shepherd (10:11, 14); I am Resurrection and Life (11:25); I am Way–Truth–Life (14:6); I am Vine (15:1, 5); and so on. Matthew's Jesus clarifies that those who do unto the least of these—clothe them, feed them, visit them—do such acts of charity and love and justice unto Jesus himself, and that it is these who will be welcomed into the new age, to the banquet, to the feast (Matt. 25:31–46). John's Jesus wants us to assent, to believe his claims about himself. Matthew's wants us to go and do likewise.

The portraits are not oppositional but cumulative. We have four Gospels for precisely this reason: to tell a life, especially a messianic one, one needs multiple versions. That John appears in Lent 2 helps round out our preparations: to examine ourselves and to consider what we believe, even as we continue to fast, refraining from certain indulgences; and to give alms, pursuing new or deepened acts of charity and justice making.

As for Nicodemus, he may leave the scene of our text perplexed, but he is not a quitter. He appears again in chapter 7 at verse 50, still asking questions—this time to his colleagues, pleading with them to accord Jesus due process. He also shows up after Jesus has died (John 19:39). He supplies ointments necessary for a proper burial. He is steadfast both in contemplating Jesus' teachings, even as they confound him; and in generous compassion, as he attends to the body of this crucified rabbi. Was he eventually "born from above," touched by the Spirit, numbered among those gifted with eternal life? We will answer this question differently; the real question is, What does our answer to this mean for our preaching, for our ministries, for us?

In our epistle, Paul presses the question of faith and works. Using Abraham as an illustration, he seems to construct a different economy of salvation than John's Jesus during this first conversation with Nicodemus. A brief excerpt of Abraham's story (when he is still called Abram) constitutes our first reading. God says, "Go, and I will bless you, and you will be a blessing to everyone else." Abram goes—simple as that, no questions asked, no protest, no apparent anxiety. This, Paul concludes, is faith, the kind of faith that is rewarded by astonishing grace. Paul likens works to employment—if you earn your wages, they are no gift. God is in the gift business. When God promised him blessings, Abram believed—and so was reckoned righteous. Just so, both those who adhere to the Law and those who claim freedom from the Law, if they believe, if they share Abraham's faith; they too partake of the promise, they too receive grace, they too receive life though they die.

Adherence to Law, in fact, seems wrongheaded; given human frailty, it leads justly to wrath. Faith alone is the dependable way to salvation. All of Paul's talk of works and laws seems in tension with a "spirit that blows where it will" to realize a rebirth from above. Perhaps, however, they are not so different after all?

Where Paul wants to deliver us from the trap of legality into an economy of freedom and gift, John's Jesus seems to toss all reason into the air. They may get us to the same end point but by different routes. Jesus speaks nonsense and yet tells us not to be astonished. We have little enough to do with being born the first time. To be born again is an impossibility. There is nothing any of us can do. It is completely up to the whimsy of Spirit—this Spirit that is as unpredictable as wind.

Ah—but, what of wind? Perhaps there is a clue here. Gusting winds bear away debris but also branches, roofs, sometimes even cars and boats. What if those who are being borne by Spirit are actually being carried away—perhaps to "come 'round right," as the old Shaker hymn puts it. Now free of "the way things are" we can see, we can enter this "kingdom of God," this alternative reality where justice reigns and mercy abounds, where all are fed and satisfied, where every tear is wiped away and death is no more. This is Jesus' perplexing invitation to Nicodemus . . . and to us.

Our psalmist seems to understand this. There is trouble in the valley. There is need for aid. Do the crests of the hills promise rescue or demise? No matter. God is near. God is the only sure help. God keeps us safe . . . despite attack. Keeps us sheltered. Keeps evil at bay. With nothing to fear, we can . . . simply live!

Finally, wind seems often to appear near water. Hovering over the deep "in the beginning," that life-giving Spirit must have blown fiercely to stir life, and then, gently, to be first breath of all creatures. Parting seas. Alighting over a baptism in the Jordan. Touching down on every font. In chapter 7, Jesus promises a permanent end to thirst to any who would come to him. Another puzzle. The narrator must explain—as John's narrator loves to do—that, by this, Jesus meant not actual water but the Spirit. More puzzles. More promises. More grace. More life. Such are the gifts of John's Jesus for us this Lent.

W. SCOTT HALDEMAN

Commentary 2: Connecting the Reading with the World

"John Cougar, John Deere, John 3:16." So go the lyrics to country and western singer Keith Urban's tribute to rural living. John 3:16 is arguably one of the best-known Bible verses, if not *the* best-known. Tim Tebow famously called attention to the verse with his eye black for the January 8, 2009, NCAA championship football game. Three years later, on January 8, 2012, Tebow led the Denver Broncos to a 29–23 playoff win over the Pittsburgh Steelers. He passed for 316 yards and averaged 31.6 yards per completion. Once the coincidences were noticed, Google searches for John 3:16 exploded, and *Time* magazine dubbed the game the "John 3:16 game." Perhaps no one in modern American culture has contributed more to the popularity of the verse, especially among evangelical Christians, than the Rev. Billy Graham, who once called John 3:16 his favorite verse, labeling it "the gospel in miniature."

However ubiquitous the verse is in popular culture, it is apparently still not a universally recognized icon. Legend has it that former baseball player and broadcaster Tim McCarver was calling a New York Mets game and noticed a person holding a sign behind home plate that read simply, "John 3:16." "Look," McCarver quipped, "Tommy John has lowered his E.R.A. [earned run average] again!" The preacher could explore these and other examples of the impact of the verse on popular culture and imagination in an effort to get beyond its "sound bite" or "bumper sticker" status.

One might begin exploring the theological depths of this familiar verse by engaging the homiletical work of William Hull, who places John 3:16 in "conversation" with a text from Ephesians: "I pray that you may have the power to comprehend, with all the saints, what is the breadth and length and height and depth, and to know the love of Christ that surpasses knowledge, so that you may be filled with all the fullness of God" (Eph. 3:18–19). In a series of published sermons, Hull argues that the dimensions of divine love described in Ephesians—love's breadth, length, height, and depth—are given substance by John 3:16:

> When following Ephesians 3:18, we ask, "How *broad* is the love of God? John 3:16 replies, "For God so loved the *world*. . . ." When we ask, "To what *length* did God go to love a world like ours?" John 3:16 replies, "He gave up his *only* Son." When we ask, "To what *depth* did that Son descend on our behalf?" John 3:16 replies, "He went where people were *perishing*." And, finally, when we ask, "To what *height* did he lift those who were perishing in the depths?" John 3:16 replies, "He provided them with *eternal life*."[1]

It is difficult, if not impossible, for us to fathom the *breadth* of God's love. Loving the world can seem a trite truism, yet it is what separates human from divine love. Dietrich

1. William E. Hull, *Love in Four Dimensions* (Nashville: Broadman, 1982), 23–24.

Bonhoeffer has written penetratingly about the limits of human love: "We are separated from one another by an unbridgeable gulf of otherness and strangeness which resists all attempts to overcome it by means of natural association or emotional or spiritual union. There is no way from one person to another. . . . Christ stands between us, and we can only get in touch with our neighbors through him."[2]

God's love knows no favorites. Too often we give in to our base inclinations to build walls, real and metaphorical, between ourselves and others, focusing on differences of culture, language, customs, creed, and ethnicities. Even in our best moments, we struggle to honor those differences that distinguish us as individuals and peoples, while affirming at the same time the deep connections that bind us together as human beings. God's love transgresses all human barriers placed in the way, embracing and enveloping persons for who they are—God's children formed in God's image. "There's a Wideness in God's Mercy," as the old hymn declares.

The *lengths* to which God has gone to express concern and affection for the world are remarkable. Into the formlessness and void that humans have created, by "reverse engineering" through careless and cruel treatment of themselves, their neighbor, and the environment, God spoke the Word once again, reclaiming humanity once again through the gift of that Word. God continues to speak that Word in every act of compassion and kindness we do in God's name to enable our neighbors to flourish and fulfill their God-given vocations.

The Lenten season, the liturgical context for our text, reminds us of our mortality; we are flesh and blood, subject to death and decay; we are constantly perishing. We are also capable of unthinkable atrocities toward our fellow humans. God stands with us in the *depths* of this decay, in our perishing. An explorer investigating uncharted oceans, whose instruments could not register the impenetrable depths of the sea, simply recorded in his log, "Deeper still." When we contemplate the depths of God's reach, we finally must confess with breathless wonder, "Deeper still."

Elie Wiesel has provided an unforgettable description of the depths of God's loving presence. As he watched a youth, hanged by the Nazi SS, struggle for breath and life, he heard a man call out: "'For God's sake, where is God?' And from within me, I heard a voice answer, 'Where is he? This is where—hanging there on the gallows.'"[3]

The *height* of God's love is eternal life. In Johannine idiom, however, eternal life has both present and eschatological qualities. For the Johannine Jesus, eternal life is not some disembodied escapism into a remote space known as "heaven." N. T. Wright has attempted to capture the intended sense with this translation: "everyone who believes in him may share in *the life of God's new age*."[4] For Wright, life after life after death is the joining together heaven and earth in seamless fashion, a day-to-day divine reality in which we participate and flourish.

Several other themes can be profitably pursued by the proclaimer. For example, John 3:8, "The wind blows where it chooses, and you hear the sound of it, but you do not know where it comes from or where it goes. So it is with everyone who is born of the Spirit," bears witness to the mystery of the Spirit, which, like the wind, comes and goes "where it chooses." The Spirit cannot be tamed; it cannot be domesticated. Putting John 3:8 in dialogue with Native American understandings of the Spirit world could be instructive for a congregation. In *The Wind Is My Mother*, Marcellus "Bear Heart" Williams, a traditionally trained shaman of the Muskogee Nation–Creek tribe and an ordained American Baptist minister, observed: "Someone once said to me, 'I wish I had the same amount of spirit that you have.' I turned to him and said, 'We were all given the same amount of spirit. None more, none less. The difference between individuals is allowing the Spirit to have more of you.' So that's where the difference is, yielding to that spirit more."[5]

MIKEAL C. PARSONS

2. Dietrich Bonhoeffer, *The Cost of Discipleship* (New York: Macmillan, 1959), 87–88.

3. Elie Wiesel, *Night* (New York: Farrar, Straus and Giroux, 2006), 64–65.

4. N. T. Wright, *The Kingdom New Testament: A Contemporary Translation* (New York: HarperCollins, 2011), 176, emphasis added.

5. Bear Heart with Molly Larkin, *The Wind Is My Mother: The Life and Teachings of a Native American Shaman* (New York: Berkley Books, 1996), 246.

Matthew 17:1–9

[1]Six days later, Jesus took with him Peter and James and his brother John and led
them up a high mountain, by themselves. [2]And he was transfigured before them,
and his face shone like the sun, and his clothes became dazzling white. [3]Sud-
denly there appeared to them Moses and Elijah, talking with him. [4]Then Peter
said to Jesus, "Lord, it is good for us to be here; if you wish, I will make three
dwellings here, one for you, one for Moses, and one for Elijah." [5]While he was
still speaking, suddenly a bright cloud overshadowed them, and from the cloud
a voice said, "This is my Son, the Beloved; with him I am well pleased; listen
to him!" [6]When the disciples heard this, they fell to the ground and were overcome by fear. [7]But Jesus came and touched them, saying, "Get up and do not be
afraid." [8]And when they looked up, they saw no one except Jesus himself alone.
[9]As they were coming down the mountain, Jesus ordered them, "Tell no one
about the vision until after the Son of Man has been raised from the dead."

Commentary 1: Connecting the Reading with Scripture

Most Protestant communions celebrate the Transfiguration of the Lord on the Last Sunday after Epiphany, just before Ash Wednesday; and the Transfiguration is commemorated on August 6 in the cycle of holy days. Roman Catholic tradition, however, has long included an account of the transfiguration as the Gospel lection for the Second Sunday in Lent. The Revised Common Lectionary honors this tradition by offering Matthew 17:1–9 as an alternate reading for John 3:1–17. Preaching from the story of the Transfiguration in the context of Lent invites a different interpretation than a preacher might explore in Ordinary Time.

Our familiarity with this story should not keep us from recognizing how odd it is among the Gospel traditions. The presence of Moses and Elijah, the overshadowing cloud, the dialogue between Jesus and the disciples, and the heavenly voice all point to very complex intertextual connections for this story. We will note only two that are especially important for preaching during Lent: Moses on Sinai and Elijah on Horeb.

In the Bible, mountains symbolically designate places of divine revelation (Ps. 74:2). The story of the exodus and of the ensuing wilderness wandering is especially full of mountain experiences. Both Moses (e.g., Exod. 3 and 24) and Elijah (1 Kgs. 19) have epiphanic experiences on mountains. One of Moses' experiences includes coming down with his face shining (Exod. 34). Matthew draws on this background, using mountains at critical places in his narrative; a key example is the appearance of the risen Christ in 28:16–20. Throughout Matthew, Jesus is presented in the typology of Moses, and John the Baptist is said to be Elijah. So Elijah, representing the prophets, is a forerunner of the Messiah; and Moses, representing the Law, is the messianic prototype. Indeed, both Moses and Elijah were claimed not to have died. Elijah in 2 Kings 2:11 ascends in a whirlwind into the heavens. While Deuteronomy 34 reports Moses' death on a mountaintop overlooking the promised land, later midrashic tradition retells this story in terms of a cloud surrounding Moses, followed by his sudden disappearance.

The importance of these interconnections becomes clear in the conclusion to the transfiguration story. As Jesus leads the disciples down the mountain after the epiphany, he orders them to tell no one about the "vision" they have seen until after the resurrection (Matt. 17:9). Therefore, this story foreshadows Jesus' resurrection. As the transfigured Jesus appears on a mountain, the risen Christ appears on a mountain.

Elijah and Moses do not die, and Jesus is raised from the dead. In preaching this text on the Second Sunday in Lent, then, preachers should help congregations lean toward Easter without yet getting there. (After all, the scene in Matthew follows on the heels of Jesus' first passion prediction, 16:21.)

Preachers must keep a healthy tension in place: We do not skip over Holy Week to get to the empty tomb, but we also do not become morose in meditating on the cross as if we did not know that Christ arose from the dead. Indeed, is this not the way we always experience resurrection? It is an eschatological experience, an already/not yet experience. To bring the theme of resurrection into a Lenten sermon is to remind the congregation that although we proclaim Jesus was raised two thousand years ago, we experience resurrection as only partly in our grasp, and not yet fully manifested in our lives and in the world.

At the same time in which the context of Lent calls us to squint ahead toward resurrection, and to worship (even in Lent) one who is risen; reading this passage on the Second Sunday in Lent gestures backward to the previous Sunday. When Matthew's story of Jesus' transfiguration is preached on the last Sunday of Epiphany, it is liturgically placed so as to recall the story of Jesus' baptism. In other words, The Baptism of the Lord and Transfiguration Sunday serve as bookends for the Sundays after Epiphany, with each containing the heavenly voice declaring Jesus to be God's Son. In Lent, however, the connection between this story and that of Jesus' temptation (Matt. 4:1–11, always read on the first Sunday in Lent) cannot be missed.

In the temptation story, which follows on the heels of Jesus' baptism, the devil sets up the first two trials by saying, "*If* you are the Son of God . . ." (emphasis added). Jesus is being tempted to deny the very identity just proclaimed to the crowd in his baptism. In the transfiguration, long after the temptation, it is clear that Jesus' identity remains intact.

Moreover, in the temptation story, the devil takes Jesus up to "a very high mountain," offering him all the kingdoms of the world if he will only worship the devil. In Luke's version of the temptation (Luke 4:1–13), this is the second of the three trials, but Matthew makes it the final, climactic test. In a sense, on Lent 1 we see Jesus being victorious, claiming the mountain as a symbol of his approach to God's kingdom over Satan's; on Lent 2 we see that eschatological victory confirmed by God's own voice.

Therefore, to preach the Transfiguration in Lent is to preach a middle mountain, if you will. The mount of transfiguration stands between the mountain of temptation and the mountain of resurrection.

Preachers are often attracted to the idea of asking congregations to identify with Peter. Like Peter, we strive to hold onto mountaintop religious experiences and resist having to return down the mountain to the everyday humdrum of regular life. There is nothing wrong with this identification, but it is an easy homiletical grab that does not go to the center of the text. The mountaintop setting, the physical transfiguration of Jesus, the appearance of Elijah and Moses, and the declaration of the heavenly voice all show that this story depicts a scene that is thoroughly christological. Asking a congregation to identify with Jesus in order to better understand who Jesus is as the Son of God is a more fruitful homiletical approach.

A common misunderstanding people have of this story is that transfiguration means transformation. True, the dictionary definition of "transfigure" is "to transform into something better." Theologically and narratively speaking, Jesus was not changed at the Transfiguration. His true nature, his fuller nature, was revealed.

We, like Peter, often domesticate Jesus so he can be easy to understand, easy to access, easy to keep in a tent. However, there is no boxing in the One who bests the devil in an apocalyptic battle of wits, whose face shines like the sun, whose clothes are dazzling white, who converses with Elijah and Moses, whom God publicly claims as God's own, and who commissions his followers to make disciples of all nations, now that he has risen from the dead and has been given all authority in heaven and earth.

The story of the Transfiguration presents Jesus as more than just a moral exemplar, prophet, political martyr, or "what a friend we have in Jesus." This is a high Christology. The story, of course, does not dictate what kind of

Christology preachers or congregations must hold. It does, however, demand serious homiletical consideration and interpretation. Preachers grounded in a specific historical religious tradition and shaped by various contemporary theologies should use this text as an opportunity to help their congregations explore what they consider to be a credible Christology and, perhaps, be challenged by the "vision" of the transfiguration. In a day when preaching is dominated by hortatory and experientially oriented sermons, a doctrinal sermon can be a surprising gift for the community of faith.

O. WESLEY ALLEN JR.

Commentary 2: Connecting the Reading with the World

The essence of Jesus' transfiguration is encapsulated in one word: glory. It may be helpful for preachers to describe ordinary understandings of glory as distinguished from transfiguration glory. There is "intrinsic glory," pertaining to a majestic beauty associated with an object of admiration. The grandeur of a beautiful sunset is a manifestation of glory that exists whether acknowledged or not. There is also "attributed glory," the honor and public acclaim piled onto a recipient as a means of exceptional recognition. The world gives glory to people for a grand achievement or distinctive accomplishment.

Jesus' glory, however, is qualitatively different from and immeasurably superior to any glory imaginable on earth. So the event of the Transfiguration is a theophany. The blinding brightness of Jesus' appearance puts his transcendent glory on full display before Peter, James, and John. The voice from heaven further commands that Jesus, the beloved Son of God, Servant, and Messiah be recognized and obeyed. Although the totality of Jesus' divine glory is beyond human comprehension in substance and gravitas, God still chooses to reveal it to these three disciples. Despite their cowering fear and limited ability fully to grasp Jesus' glory, even a glimpse of it is sufficient to engender faith, command obedience, and cultivate hope for the rewarding but treacherous journey of discipleship.

Faith needs a context, hence the significance of the presence of Moses and Elijah standing next to Jesus in their glorified states. For the disciples, Moses and Elijah not only remind them of God's saving acts in Israel's history; their discussion with Jesus about his impending departure (i.e., death) also links what God did for Israel through them with what God has been doing and is about to do through Jesus. Even though Moses, Elijah, and Jesus appear at different points along Israel's historical timeline, they are key figures in the same mission of salvation orchestrated by the same God.

Jesus, however, towers over his predecessors Moses and Elijah by virtue of his divine identity. As Messiah and Son of God, Jesus is God's eschatological Servant who is about to bring God's plan to a climax when he arrives in Jerusalem, offering salvation not only to Israel but through Israel to the nations as well. Because of their obedience to the task entrusted to them, Moses, Elijah, and Jesus set an example for Peter, James, and John, that they remain faithful to the One whom they call Lord and Master. When the disciples follow diligently and faithfully, their obedience is an acknowledgment of and participation in Jesus' glory.

The followers of Jesus in subsequent generations and various contexts continue to face the same challenge and promise. Living in between the "already" of Jesus' first coming and the "not yet" of his future return, Christians must, in matters of faith, decide repeatedly whether to obey the voice of the exalted Lord or the voice of the unbelieving world.

Obedience and faith are especially difficult—yet all the more necessary—when opposition and persecution rear their ugly heads. In the Gospel of Matthew, the account of the transfiguration is both preceded and followed by a prediction of Jesus' passion (Matt. 16:21; 17:22–23; cf. 17:12). By sandwiching the divine identity and glory of the Messiah in between twin assurances of his suffering and death, the author creates a jarring juxtaposition. This seeming dissonance is precisely the crux of the matter, that in God's wisdom and divine economy, Jesus' suffering and glory are two sides of the same coin, so that one cannot be embraced without the other. If this is the case even for the Messiah, why should it be any different for Peter, James, John, and for all other followers of Jesus who come after them?

Suffering and glory, in this particular order, will soon be demonstrated for Peter, James, and John in the death, burial, resurrection, and exaltation of Jesus. Seen from this perspective, it is fitting for later Christians to ponder the meaning of this passage at this juncture of the liturgical calendar on the Second Sunday in Lent. The revelation of Jesus' divine glory continues to offer hope and confidence as Christians meditate upon Jesus' suffering on their behalf in the upcoming readings and services of Holy Week. Things will get worse before they get better; evil will appear to triumph before it is soundly and unequivocally defeated. During Lent, if the focus lies solely on the shame and injustice of Jesus' death, there will only be anger and discouragement, especially when believers continue to be persecuted and reviled for their Christian witness and convictions.

In today's world, people taunt the almighty God with impunity and seem to get away with destroying human lives, the moral fabric of society, and even creation itself with little consequence. Gun violence is rampant, the threat of global warming is unheeded, and migrant children are torn from their parents in the name of national security. It is easy for Christians to complain that God is not doing enough to right the wrongs of the world. It is easy to lose hope and become cynical because nothing seems to change for the better.

However, just as lasting glory can only be eschatological glory, true hope can only be eschatological hope, grounded in God's redemptive promise. Human aspirations for harmonious society, equal treatment of persons, and world peace are admirable, but they are unrealizable except by the power of the Holy Spirit. Therefore, if the Transfiguration is meant to point to the distant future, then the kind of hope it generates must carry believers beyond the victory of the first Easter, over the hurdles of evils in every generation, to the heavenly denouement when God will set all things right. Faith, in the meantime, is, on the one hand, believing that the final outcome has already been determined and, on the other hand, living in hope within the tension of suffering and glory.

Of the paintings of the transfiguration depicted by famous artists from Titian and Giovanni Bellini to Fra Angelico and Tissot, Raphael's *The Transfiguration* stands out in its portrayal of the twin themes of glory and suffering. In the upper part of this painting, Jesus, Moses, and Elijah are suspended in midair, and the three disciples, still atop the mountain, look up in fear after having fallen to the ground. Below them, the lower half of the canvas depicts what is happening meanwhile at the foot of the mountain. The remaining disciples are struggling to cast a demon out of an epileptic boy (17:14–18). Using these twin images, Raphael sends an important theological message often missing from other paintings of the Transfiguration that spotlight only the mountaintop experience: While faithlessness and evil forces, causing fear and confusion, may seek to derail Jesus' disciples, in the end they are no match for Jesus, whose divine glory and power guarantee victory over all, for himself and for those who do his bidding.

Therefore, consider the cruciform discipleship and countercultural mission to which the worldwide church throughout the ages has been called. While the account of the Transfiguration, read during Lent, serves to foreshadow Jesus' exaltation beyond death, it is also a text for all times and seasons. The church universal constantly needs to envision Jesus' glory in front of it, even as it brings light into darkness and speaks healing into brokenness in a world that responds with suspicion, vengeance, and ingratitude. It is this hope of future glory that beckons the church and encourages Christians, especially the ones in the direst of circumstances, to take the long view, to remain faithful, and not to give up.

DIANE G. CHEN

Third Sunday in Lent

Exodus 17:1–7
Psalm 95
Romans 5:1–11
John 4:5–42

Exodus 17:1–7

> 1From the wilderness of Sin the whole congregation of the Israelites journeyed
> by stages, as the LORD commanded. They camped at Rephidim, but there was
> no water for the people to drink. 2The people quarreled with Moses, and said,
> "Give us water to drink." Moses said to them, "Why do you quarrel with me? Why
> do you test the LORD?" 3But the people thirsted there for water; and the people
> complained against Moses and said, "Why did you bring us out of Egypt, to kill
> us and our children and livestock with thirst?" 4So Moses cried out to the LORD,
> "What shall I do with this people? They are almost ready to stone me." 5The LORD
> said to Moses, "Go on ahead of the people, and take some of the elders of Israel
> with you; take in your hand the staff with which you struck the Nile, and go. 6I will
> be standing there in front of you on the rock at Horeb. Strike the rock, and water
> will come out of it, so that the people may drink." Moses did so, in the sight of the
> elders of Israel. 7He called the place Massah and Meribah, because the Israelites
> quarreled and tested the LORD, saying, "Is the LORD among us or not?"

Commentary 1: Connecting the Reading with Scripture

It is easy to grumble about the grumbling Israelites. Already God has fixed their water supply (Exod. 15:23–25a), given them quail to eat (16:13), and provided manna (16:14). Now they are whining again. On the one hand, this seems a more legitimate complaint than some of their others later on, when they tire of the manna and want "the fish that we used to eat free in Egypt, the cucumbers, the melons, the leeks, the onions, and the garlic" (Num. 11:5 NJPS). Water is necessary for life; it is far from a luxury. On the other hand, they *have* just experienced God's care for them after their wild escape from Egypt. God *has* provided water, quail, and manna already. Why do they assume that God cannot or will not supply them with water once again?

Their complaint is also directed at their leader, Moses, probably because he is physically present in a way they can confront directly. "Why did you bring us out of Egypt, to kill us and our children and our livestock with thirst?" (Exod. 17:3b). Moses seems truly frightened as he reports to God, "Before long they will be stoning me!" (NJPS). As on the previous occasions, God gives instructions to Moses that, when carried out, lead to the solving of the problem.

God's instructions have some interesting details. Moses is to pass in front of the people. Is he supposed to show that he is not afraid of them or that he is not running away? Is the point to make clear that all is being done above board and in public? Moses is also to take some of the elders of the people along with him as he goes to the particular rock from which will come their water supply. Is this so that the leaders will see that Moses is powerful, and then later act to help keep the rest of the people in line? Are the elders supposed to be learning from Moses what to do in case another crisis arises in the future? Are they a sort of band of bodyguards, to protect Moses from the thirsty mob reaching for stones to hurl in his direction?

Moses is also told to take the rod with which he struck the Nile some two months before, causing it to part in front of them and making a way for Israel to escape the Egyptian army.

Perhaps the rod is to be a visual reminder to the people that the same God who has saved them before can save them again. (Surely they are not supposed to look on the rod itself as the source of the power working on their behalf?) Maybe even if one rod looks pretty much like another to the crowd, the specific rod is to be a reminder to Moses himself of God's previous salvific power.

Then God declares that when Moses strikes the rock at Horeb ("the" rock? Is not the whole area a jumble of crags and rocks and boulders and stones?), God will be standing on the rock. God often gives assurances of being with people; rarely is the assurance in such a physically specific manner. Perhaps the divine presence on the rock is to be transferred metaphorically to that rock, for the tradition knows of calling God "my rock and my redeemer" (cf. Pss. 19:14; 78:35) and "rock of my salvation" (cf. 2 Sam. 22:47; Pss. 62:2; 89:26). There is also a tradition, known in both Jewish and Christian sources, that the rock followed Israel miraculously throughout their generation of desert wandering (*Targum Jonathan* to Num. 21:19 and 1 Cor. 10:4).

Our text then reports that Moses does as he had been told and strikes the rock with his rod "in the sight of the elders of Israel." Surprisingly, the text does not report that water comes out or that the people's thirst is quenched. Of course the water did, or the story would have said the people kept complaining, or something along that line. What is reported after Moses' striking the rock is the naming of the place with the double name Massah (strife, trial) and Meribah (quarrelling, contention). The point is not that the naming is more important than the supply of water, but that once God has said there will be water, there will be water. One knows that without further words.

What one cannot know without being told is the name given to the place. The double naming memorializes not what God did for the people, but how the people fussed at Moses and at God. There is an honesty about these names that is at the same time both touching and brutal. One wonders what would happen if churches were named in a similar manner. Instead of Grace and Holy Trinity and St. Mary's or even the more mundane First and Community, would one see Bickering United Methodist and Tightfisted Episcopal, Gossiping Lutheran, and Lazy Baptist? (Please, dear readers, do not exegete the names as they are attached to the denominations. I have nothing specific in mind by these pairings.)

The people have the last word in today's reading, and it is a telling one: "Is the LORD present among us or not?" (NJPS). The Lord's presence seems to them to be primarily as a dispenser of good things. If they do not have what they want at a particular moment, then they question whether the Lord is actually present with them. Presumably if they had all they thought they needed or wanted, they would not ask this question. In that case they would not necessarily be celebrating the Lord's presence. The idea has arisen—and lives on mightily to this day in some quarters—that the presence of the Lord is supposed to guarantee freedom from all wants and to assure freedom from all difficulties. This notion is another perversion of the equation on the individual level that one who is experiencing severe hardships is being punished thereby by God for major sins and that one who is faithful to God will be materially blessed as a reward.

The people's need for water is genuine. The issue is whether or not they are willing to trust that God both knows that need and can meet it. They have seen as recently as Exodus 15:22–25a that God does know how to provide potable water. They have seen as recently as the previous chapter that God does know how to provide enough food for them. Not only is God capable of providing for them; God wants to and will provide for them. What they lack at Massah and Meribah is any sense of trust in God's faithfulness. They act like spoiled children, whining, "What have you done for me lately?"

Even after Moses follows God's instructions and we may reasonably assume that they have drunk their fill, the people ask, "Is the LORD present among us or not?" If this question had come at the beginning of the account, it would not be so serious. That they are still asking it, even after having their needs met, is troubling. It may be at this point that the preacher will find ties to the contemporary world. We seem to be a generation—perhaps not all that different from all other generations—looking for signs, for proofs not so much for God's presence as for God's beneficent and bountiful favor to be showered upon *us* at our every whim.

REBECCA ABTS WRIGHT

Commentary 2: Connecting the Reading with the World

Rocks and sand, scrubby bushes, occasional wildflowers, but not much water. A stark and startling, dramatic landscape and the setting of our story, where Moses leads the people of Israel out of the wilderness of Sin to camp at Rephidim—where there is *no* water! Adult human bodies are composed of at least 60 percent water. Baby bodies are 75 percent. Human beings are made of water and cannot live long without it.

No wonder the people are fearful, desperate, and grieving their lost life. They are also forgetful. Not long ago, in the wilderness of Sin God heard their complaints of starvation and supplied them with manna and quail. Fear drowns out memory and reason. People complain when they are afraid, when they fear they will lose everything or die. Even leaders forget at times. How often do we try to figure out a crisis by ourselves? Meet everyone's needs? Answer every complaint? Hard times confront us all with our propensity for functional atheism: voicing belief in God but not trusting in God.

Leading a congregation as pastor and preacher through a discipleship journey in Lent, or any other time, can be metaphorically like Moses leading the people through the wilderness. It is a journey that some parishioners do not want to endure. Complaints abound. "Confession of sins, spiritual disciplines, stories of sacrifice? Is life not hard enough? Do we not give enough to the church, volunteer enough in the church? Why are you picking on us, challenging us to dig deeper, study harder, pray more, have more faith, take more risks in mission? You are asking us to change?"

Life is a journey that seeks stability in the midst of constant change. Change is more apparent than ever in the breaking-news, social-media world in which we live. Change brings fear. Change brings grief that comes from letting go of the way things were. Were things not better in the "good old days"? Better back in Egypt? The pastor/preacher, like Moses, feels as if she is between a rock and a hard place, the proverbial Scylla and Charybdis, in leading the people. Congregational lay leaders often join the pastor in this bind. As leaders, both lay and clergy, do we run about saving each individual who complains from Scylla, the six-headed monster of change, while the whole of the congregation is being sucked into Charybdis, the whirlpool of anxiety?[1] At such times we cannot foster the functional atheism of the people or ourselves. The tough love and discipline of learning to trust God *is* comfort in the midst of change, fear, and grief in the wilderness.

How can we nurture faith in authentic ways in the midst of complaint and bitterness? Moses is at his wit's end in this story. Pastors, lay leaders, fearful parishioners often feel at their wits' ends in the midst of change. What does Moses do? He cries out to God in desperation and frustration, possibly some anger. In that cry he *relinquishes* the people's complaints to God, lets them go. Moses does not try to fix the situation on his own power. Whether out of pure faith or the weariness of despair, Moses throws up his hands, trusts, and stops to listen. Trusting God when we feel despairingly helpless means admitting we are not in control. That is a hard and a liberating choice. How do we lead in the tough times? By admitting that the abundant Spirit of God is ultimately in control. Like Moses, our actions as pastors, lay leaders, and congregation are to stop, trust, and listen.

How does God respond? With criticism or ridicule or impatience? God, who has already saved these forgetful people time and again, responds calmly. God is not stressed with the

1. Homer, *The Odyssey,* trans. Robert Fitzgerald (New York: Vintage Classics, 1990), 217–18.

people's continued complaints. God responds with seemingly simple instructions. Go to the place I will show you. I will be there. Strike a rock. There will be water.

These are not logical instructions, researched through congregational study and tested leadership skills. They are not based on a geologic survey. There is not even a dowsing rod! Following these instructions requires acting on faith rather than fact. However, the fact is that faith can be acted on, because Moses will use the rod that struck the Nile as the people were liberated from Egypt. The rod is a sign of God's presence that Moses carries with him. It is tried and true. Following on faith when it seems there are but scanty facts is the discipleship of trust. Moses follows. The people follow. There is water.

Let us imagine that when the water comes pouring out from the rock like a fountain, a spring in the desert, it flows so abundantly that it creates a pool in a cleft in the rocky hillside. As the people drink they can see themselves reflected in the pool. Perhaps, they see the streaks of tears down their sandy cheeks. Tears from their thirsty anguish turned to tears of relief. Do they see God in their reflection in this pool of water? In their tears? In their joy-filled faces? The water is a mirror of who God really is. God is love, abundance, forgiveness, providence.

"How we see God is a direct reflection of how we see ourselves. If God brings to mind mostly fear and blame, it means there is too much fear and blame welled inside us. If we see God as full of love and compassion, so are we."[2] This is the first rule of love, according to Shams of Tabriz, the spiritual mentor of the great thirteenth-century Sufi poet, Rumi. How we mirror God is also how we see God.

The Hebrew people in the desert saw God through the lens of fear and blame. They assumed that God was out to get them. Yet God, in steadfast love and faithfulness, responds to their complaints and doubts in the midst of their fear with water to keep them alive. God mirrors back redemption instead of condemnation. What a miracle! How do we mirror God in our world? How do we lead people to see God in steadfast love and faithfulness, instead of in their own image of stress, worry, judgment, and complaint?

Out of the bitterness and complaint can come sustenance. When we take the risk to learn the discipline of trust, we free ourselves from functional atheism. Relationship with God deepens. In Ellen Bass's poem "The Thing Is," the process of trust is illuminated. Bass challenges us to love life, in the midst of unimaginable grief, grief that weighs us down physically. To love life in the midst of grief that physically sickens us. When we are so sick of life that we think we can stand it no longer, Bass encourages us to think of life as a plain, sad face held between our hands and to say to it, "I will take you, I will love you, again."[3]

In our story, Moses is leading people so tired of change that they are sick of life. He relinquishes his anguish, his doubts, to God in trust. The people follow his lead. God responds with compassion. Water gushes from the rock with renewing life. The journey in the wilderness of change continues with new hope.

JANE ANNE FERGUSON

2. Elif Shafak, *The Forty Rules of Love* (New York: Penguin Random House, 2010), 30.
3. Ellen Bass, "The Thing Is," in *Mules of Love* (Rochester, NY: BOA Editions, 2002), Kindle edition location 865.

Psalm 95

1O come, let us sing to the LORD;
let us make a joyful noise to the rock of our salvation!
2Let us come into his presence with thanksgiving;
let us make a joyful noise to him with songs of praise!
3For the LORD is a great God,
and a great King above all gods.
4In his hand are the depths of the earth;
the heights of the mountains are his also.
5The sea is his, for he made it,
and the dry land, which his hands have formed.

6O come, let us worship and bow down,
let us kneel before the LORD, our Maker!
7For he is our God,
and we are the people of his pasture,
and the sheep of his hand.

O that today you would listen to his voice!
8Do not harden your hearts, as at Meribah,
as on the day at Massah in the wilderness,
9when your ancestors tested me,
and put me to the proof, though they had seen my work.
10For forty years I loathed that generation
and said, "They are a people whose hearts go astray,
and they do not regard my ways."
11Therefore in my anger I swore,
"They shall not enter my rest."

Connecting the Psalm with Scripture and Worship

For many people, the ancient scenario referenced in both of today's OT passages is baffling. In fact, pastors may very well stand with their parishioners in thinking that the Israelites' request for water (Exod. 17:1–3) was hardly unreasonable (and do not get me started on the fact that, in the Num. 20:12 telling of this episode, Moses' action on behalf of his parched people is named as the reason he is prohibited from entering the promised land!). As you strive for a sermon that will connect your congregation with this challenging Exodus text, Psalm 95 can be of assistance.

Psalm 95 is an "enthronement psalm," composed to celebrate God's sovereignty. This somewhat bookish designation may be helpful in understanding the transgression that so greatly displeases God: one way to interpret the conflict in today's texts is to view the Israelites' demand for water as their doubting God's fitness to be sovereign. Here in the midst of Lent, when the novelty of the season has worn off, it can be instructive to ponder a sin that we may pay little attention to but which God, evidently, takes very seriously.

Psalm 95 consists of two dramatically different sections: the hymnic opening (Ps. 95:1–7a), and the concluding admonition (vv. 8–11). In the first section, the psalmist highlights God's credentials as sovereign; in its second section, the psalmist imagines God's side of the story from that thirsty day at Rephidim (Exod. 17:1). Connecting the contrasting voices and purposes of these two segments is the psalmist's heartfelt exclamation: "O that today you would listen to his voice!" (Ps. 95:7b).

Look at Psalm 95's opening section as a step-by-step depiction of the proper relationship between God and God's people. First, we are to approach God with joyful, thankful praise (vv. 1–2). Why? Because God created all that is, and no other god is worthy of consideration (vv. 3–5). Next, we are humbly to worship God (v. 6). Why? Because God is our God, and we are God's own (v. 7a). It is then, while we are reverently focused on the rightly sovereign God, that the psalmist exhorts us to listen to God's voice (v. 7b). Such worshipful attentiveness to God is the correct attitude for faithful people. If you can help your congregation hold onto that image—joyful people obediently gathered to glorify God and attend to God's word—then they will be better able to consider what went wrong at Massah and Meribah when the Israelites failed to live in such a posture of grateful praise and humble veneration.

By doubting that God would provide water in the wilderness, the Israelites were questioning God's willingness and/or ability to care for God's people. To doubt God's sure provision is to doubt God's love and/or power. The Israelites—like contemporary disciples—could doubt those constants only by forgetting God's character and ignoring God's history of gracious sovereignty. God became angry at being put to the test by the Israelites because "they had seen [God's] work" (v. 9b) and yet questioned God's fitness as sovereign.

The second section of Psalm 95 is presented in the voice of God and is a condemnation of the Israelites in the wilderness (vv. 9–11), introduced by a plea (v. 8) that the audience of "today" (v. 7b) not commit the same sin. This is how the psalm calls us to avoid the sin that the Exodus passage cites.

For liturgy, each section of the psalm is useful. The opening segment is intended literally to call the faithful to worship, so open your service with any or all of this (from vv. 1–7):

Reader 1:	O come, let us sing to the LORD!
Reader 2:	Let us make a joyful noise to the rock of our salvation!
Reader 1:	Let us come into God's presence with thanksgiving.
Reader 2:	Let us make a joyful noise to God with songs of praise!
Reader 1:	For the LORD is a great God!
Reader 2:	In God's hand are the depths of the earth; the heights of the mountains are God's also.
Reader 2:	The sea is God's, for God made it, and the dry land, which God's hands have formed.
Reader 1:	O come, let us worship and bow down, let us kneel before the LORD, our Maker.
Reader 2:	For this is our God, and we are the people of God's pasture, and the sheep of God's hand.

The psalm's second section is helpful in a confession; these phrases are drawn from verses 7–11:

> Forgetting that you are our God and we are your people,
> we have hardened our hearts and refused to listen to your voice.
> Our hearts go astray and we do not regard your ways, even though we have seen your works.
> Though you would be justified in loathing us, do not be angry, O God.
> Forgive us and let us enter your rest today and forevermore. Amen.

Given the psalm's central exhortation for us to listen to God, Psalm 95 also provides inspiration for a prayer for illumination. Concepts and vocabulary from verses 6–8 yield a prayer such as this: "Come, Holy Spirit. As the Scriptures are read and proclaimed, help us listen to your voice. Open our hearts to receive your word so that we may follow your ways. Amen."

Hymnals likely include some version of this psalm. These familiar hymns might also be helpful: "Glorious Things of Thee Are Spoken," "Guide Me, O Thou Great Jehovah," "He Is

King of Kings," "I Sing the Mighty Power of God," and "Rejoice, the Lord Is King!"

When we—like the wilderness generation long ago—ask, "Is the Lord among us or not?" (Exod. 17:7), Psalm 95 flips the question to demand, "Are we properly attentive to the Lord among us or not?" In the wilderness of our Lenten journey, we are cared for by the sovereign God who creates, redeems, and sustains us. It is this God's voice to which we are to listen today.

LEIGH CAMPBELL-TAYLOR

Romans 5:1–11

[1]Therefore, since we are justified by faith, we have peace with God through our
Lord Jesus Christ, [2]through whom we have obtained access to this grace in
which we stand; and we boast in our hope of sharing the glory of God. [3]And not
only that, but we also boast in our sufferings, knowing that suffering produces
endurance, [4]and endurance produces character, and character produces hope,
[5]and hope does not disappoint us, because God's love has been poured into our
hearts through the Holy Spirit that has been given to us.

[6]For while we were still weak, at the right time Christ died for the ungodly.
[7]Indeed, rarely will anyone die for a righteous person—though perhaps for a
good person someone might actually dare to die. [8]But God proves his love for
us in that while we still were sinners Christ died for us. [9]Much more surely then,
now that we have been justified by his blood, will we be saved through him from
the wrath of God. [10]For if while we were enemies, we were reconciled to God
through the death of his Son, much more surely, having been reconciled, will we
be saved by his life. [11]But more than that, we even boast in God through our Lord
Jesus Christ, through whom we have now received reconciliation.

Commentary 1: Connecting the Reading with Scripture

Romans 5:1–11 argues that since we are made right with God ("justified") by means of faith (Rom. 5:1, 9), we are reconciled to God and now at peace with God (vv. 1, 10, 11). For Paul this marks the pivotal shift in humanity's relationship with the creator. Once under God's wrath (v. 9), living as enemies with God (v. 10), we live now in a state of peace and reconciliation made possible by the death of Christ (vv. 6–9).

The immediate context in Romans is crucial for understanding what Paul means by "we are justified by faith" (v. 1). "Justified" essentially means "declared right." Being "right" does not mean right from a legal point of view. Paul makes clear in Romans 4:9–18 that no one is right in this sense (see 4:9). The word refers to being in right relationship, which is typically the meaning of this language in the Old Testament.

The word translated "justified" in verse 1 comes from the same root word as the word translated "righteousness" in Romans 4:22 (*dikaiosynē*). In that verse Paul quotes Genesis 15:6, which says Abraham's faith "was reckoned to him as righteousness." Throughout Romans 4 Paul rehearses the Abraham story, asking, How was it that Abraham was justified before God (4:1)? Was it because he submitted to circumcision (4:10)? For the descendants of Abraham, is the promise of justification because of obedience to the law, or through some other means (4:13–15)?

Paul's main point is that Abraham was declared right with God because he trusted God, not because Abraham adhered to a law. Although Abraham was obedient to God's command to circumcise male members of his household (Gen. 17:23–27), he "believed God and it was reckoned to him as righteousness" prior to circumcision (Gen. 15:6; Rom. 4:22). For Paul, the order of events was crucial. God declared Abraham righteous; *then* Abraham was circumcised, and then he circumcised the men in his house as a sign of the covenant. Abraham's obedience was his faithful response to God's grace, not a prerequisite for God's blessing.

So, Paul says, the declaration that Abraham's faith was reckoned as righteousness was "not written for his sake alone, but for ours also," so that "it will be reckoned to us" who believe in God "who raised Jesus our Lord from the dead"

(4:23–25). In other words, Paul argues that those who believe in Jesus are the true heirs to the promises of God to Abraham.

The relationship of Romans 5:1–11 to the larger argument of Romans is also a key to Paul's statement that we were once enemies of God and under God's wrath. It is possible to conclude that this language assumes God requires blood sacrifice for sinners to be made right with God (5:9). In this way of thinking, God is inherently angry, and humans must appease that anger through sacrifice in order to escape punishment. Paul does use the language of sacrificial atonement in Romans 3:21–26. Throughout this argument, however, and in Romans 5:1–11, Paul's point is that the peace we have with God is because of God's own initiative, a sign of God's love.

What then do we make of references to God's wrath? When the word "wrath" appears first in Romans 1:18, Paul does not use it to speak of God's anger and intention to punish. Rather, God's wrath is the natural outcome of the creation's turning away from the creator. Instead of punishing the creatures directly, God simply lets them go their own way. Wrath is being left in a state of sinfulness that leads to self-destruction. Paul then says the law was a human-centered solution that was no solution at all to the problem of being separated from God (Rom. 3). The only real solution to the human problem was God's action.

Paul speaks of this coming through Christ's death "for us" (5:8). Since this is a sign of God's love "for us," it is better to understand Christ's death as martyrdom and not as the satisfying of a legal requirement.[1] Regardless of how we read the sacrificial language, the notion that God in Romans 5:1–11 must be appeased so as to vent divine wrath is off base. Such ideas rely in part on a separation of the work of God and the work of Christ. Romans 5:8, however, clearly holds the two together. God proves love for us by the death of Christ. Moreover, if Christ's death reconciled us to God, his life is the vehicle by which we are saved (v. 10). Paul concludes his argument by saying we can "boast in God"; that is, we tout the work of God that we experience in Jesus Christ as the reason for our salvation. Far from being full of wrath that must be appeased, God actively sought a way for us to be reconciled.

The theme of human righteousness as something given to believers by means of God's righteousness appears throughout Scripture. For example, the psalmist recognizes that salvation comes through the abundance of God's steadfast love (Ps. 5:7) and prays, "Lead me, O Lord, in *your* righteousness" (v. 8). The notion that salvation depends solely on God's faithfulness and initiative was true even for God's people who received the law at Sinai. There was never a sense that they could *be* righteous by adhering to a set of legal requirements. Rather, the law Moses delivered was intended as their response to God's deliverance.

This is apparent in the structure of the Ten Commandments. It begins with a prologue that recalls God's salvation (Exod. 20:1–3). The Commandments provide opportunity for Israel to respond to what God did for them. As Deuteronomy 7:7–11 also says, God did not choose the Israelites because of their power, ability, or faithfulness. It was because the "Lord loved you" (Deut. 7:8). Passages like these imply what Romans 5:11 says directly, that God's people can boast only of God's love, faithfulness, and saving action on their behalf.

Romans 5:1–11 connects to the other lectionary readings through its focus on trust in God. Exodus 17:1–7 tells how the Israelites complained in the wilderness about having no water. Psalm 95 recalls this event and concludes that the wilderness generation's lack of trust was the reason those people would not enter God's "rest" (Ps. 95:11). Romans affirms trust that grows out of the experience of God's work in Christ. Thus Romans 5:1–11 presents a life of faith the wilderness generation seemed unable to embrace. Moreover, Romans 5:3–5 comes alive when read against the backdrop of Israel's wilderness experience. If a person trusts in God, then he or she can endure suffering and hardship with certainty that God has a better future in store. Again, the Israelites in the wilderness lacked faith and so also did not have the resources to endure suffering. John 4:5–42 shares with Romans an interest in

1. Joseph A. Fitzmyer, *Romans: A New Translation with Introduction and Commentary*, Anchor Bible 33 (New York: Doubleday, 1993), 401.

justification by faith that is open to Gentiles, they being rightful heirs to the promises of Abraham (Gen. 12:1–3).

Romans 5:1–11 has an important place in the Christian canon. Paul's argument about being justified before God draws a direct connection between Abraham's faith and the faith of those who trust in Jesus Christ. This connection appears prominently also in other Pauline letters, especially Galatians 3–4, as well as in other New Testament letters. As Ephesians 2:8 says, "For by grace you have been saved through faith, and this is not your own doing; it is the gift of God."

JEROME F. D. CREACH

Commentary 2: Connecting the Reading with the World

In the progressive Christian context in which many of us live, the sacrificial, salvific death of Christ is seldom if ever mentioned. There are both theological and ontological reasons for rejecting or at least ignoring "the atonement." (I am using the term as a shorthand for the story of God sacrificing Jesus for the sins of humanity irrespective of various doctrinal interpretations.) The theological objections have to do with what God's redemptive sacrifice of Jesus says about God. If God would stay the hand of Abraham as he was about to sacrifice Isaac, if the horror of a father killing his son on God's orders is redeemed by the last-minute reprieve, what kind of God would kill His *own* son for any reason? The connection between atonement claims and the nature of God was stated forcefully in 1980s and 1990s feminist theological writings. A Google search uncovers more contemporary writings with the same theme. In these analyses, God is depicted as male—an abusive father. Various theological and psychological strategies are offered to move past, heal, transform this image of God.

It is useful to highlight the fact that only God's actions can atone for the sin of humanity and to contrast atonement and making amends. Persons sometimes can and do make amends for the harm they have caused in the world. However, as powerfully depicted in Ian McEwan's novel *Atonement*,[2] atonement itself includes the power to change the narrative of human life, to control history, something no human has the power to do except in fictional form. Paul's claim in Romans 5:1–11 is that God changed the narrative with the sacrificial death of Jesus so that humans, once enemies of God, are now reconciled to God. In Paul and in Christian theology, the atonement is a story about God and God's actions.

Contemporary objections to the way that story depicts the nature of God have led progressive Christianity away from embracing the atonement as part of its lived theology and toward strategies of healing from what was, for Paul, the healing center of God's love. Paul marveled that Christ would die for sinners, when most would not die even for a righteous person. The wonder of this, which Paul expresses here, is lost in the haze of abuse that hovers over this story in many contemporary hearts and minds. The powerful scenes of Christ on the cross throughout the history of Christian art are treated as historical artifacts, portrayals belonging to the passions of another time. Even in contemporary Christian circles where at least the eucharistic words of institution include the body and blood of Christ, atonement is not often featured outside of discussions of Christian doctrine. It is seen as confusing, if not dangerous, and thus not engaged by preachers or parishioners.

Progressive Christianity's ontological objections to the atonement accompany a shift from understanding humanity as ineluctably flawed by sin, to the claim that humans are basically good. This shift was articulated clearly and influentially in 1983 by Matthew Fox in his classic *Original Blessing: A Primer in Creation Spirituality Presented in Four Paths, Twenty-Six Themes, and Two Questions*.[3] If humanity is not sinking

2. Ian McEwan, *Atonement* (New York: Random House, 2001).
3. Matthew Fox, *Original Blessing: A Primer in Creation Spirituality Presented in Four Paths, Twenty-Six Themes, and Two Questions* (Santa Fe: Bear & Co., 1983).

under the weight of original sin against which it has no effective guards or defenses, then it does not need salvation in the historically interruptive, narrative-altering way that the atonement provides. The reconciliation claimed by Paul to be the result of God's sacrifice of Jesus is, in fact, a human birthright; it is ours through the magnificent grace of our creator God, there to claim and enact throughout our lives. Endurance becomes transformation. Baptism is not a seal against eternal damnation but a public communal acknowledgment that we are all beloved children of God to be embraced by the love of Christian community. The "peace with God through our Lord Jesus Christ" of which Paul writes (Rom. 5:1) is ours now and forever merely because we are human.

Let us now leave behind progressive Christianity's thoughtful, if sometimes sanitized, objections to the atonement. Let us enter a state prison in Georgia, a death-penalty state. Let us walk through the sally ports, through the metal detectors, past guards who look both bored and threatening. We enter a small room with large glass windows outside of which sit one or more of those guards, and we listen to a person on death row.

Theological and ontological claims adhere once again. The death-row inmate has done something truly terrible, sinful by any definition. Whatever action resulted in her conviction to death was not her first offense, her first experience of herself as a sinful person, so that her sense of her sinfulness is not dependent upon or confined to one or more specific acts. Certainly anyone on death row is subject to being labeled "sinful," even by themselves. When the person is first convicted and confined to death row, there are often protests of innocence, rages against an unfair system, an unfair life, incompetent lawyers, ill treatment of all kinds. If that inmate is lucky enough to be exposed to and even slightly open to messages of forgiveness from chaplains, visiting pastors, or other inmates, then over time the person will shift from looking outward for relief, and begin to look inward at the realities of their past and present.

What I observed in my sixteen years of being a pastor to someone on death row is that an emerging sense of being forgiven preceded acknowledgment of sin. In a long, slow process, drip by tiny drip, through study of Scripture and assurances of God's pardon from many sources, the person on death row began to believe she was forgiven, accepted, loved by God. The sense of sinfulness never went away. It is not that she experienced the shift from original sin to original blessing that Matthew Fox's work articulated. There was no ontological transformation. Instead, there was her profound experience of grace. "But God proves God's love for us in that while we were still sinners, Christ died for us" (Rom. 5:8).

The power of that biblical verse and others like it was almost tangible, certainly observable. She did not have somehow to convince herself that she was a good person. She did not have to enter profound and soul-crushing denial. The deeper the message of God's love could penetrate her heart and soul, the more she was able to acknowledge the horror of what she had done, and the more she was able to acknowledge that horror, the more she could embrace God's love and acceptance. God's wrath was an ever-present possibility, and God's grace was a miracle moment by moment. Like Romans 5:8, Romans 5:9 was a lived reality: "Much more surely then, now that we have been justified by his blood, will we be saved through him from the wrath of God." Only the blood of Christ, and God's love expressed in the blood of Christ, was powerful enough to overcome her sin—and overcome it, it did. As she was being executed, she sang "Amazing Grace."

As it has through the centuries, Romans 5:1–11 raises many questions, both theoretical and existential. Does God's sacrifice of Jesus on the cross signify an abusive father-God or a God whose love is so profound that no human sin can diminish it? Are humans fundamentally good so that Christian exhortations to renounce sin distort fundamental humanity, or is sin our condition, expressed in myriad awful ways? Given Christian theology's embrace of paradox, might both be true?

SALLY B. PURVIS

Third Sunday in Lent

John 4:5–42

5So he came to a Samaritan city called Sychar, near the plot of ground that Jacob had given to his son Joseph. 6Jacob's well was there, and Jesus, tired out by his journey, was sitting by the well. It was about noon.

7A Samaritan woman came to draw water, and Jesus said to her, "Give me a drink." 8(His disciples had gone to the city to buy food.) 9The Samaritan woman said to him, "How is it that you, a Jew, ask a drink of me, a woman of Samaria?" (Jews do not share things in common with Samaritans.) 10Jesus answered her, "If you knew the gift of God, and who it is that is saying to you, 'Give me a drink,' you would have asked him, and he would have given you living water." 11The woman said to him, "Sir, you have no bucket, and the well is deep. Where do you get that living water? 12Are you greater than our ancestor Jacob, who gave us the well, and with his sons and his flocks drank from it?" 13Jesus said to her, "Everyone who drinks of this water will be thirsty again, 14but those who drink of the water that I will give them will never be thirsty. The water that I will give will become in them a spring of water gushing up to eternal life." 15The woman said to him, "Sir, give me this water, so that I may never be thirsty or have to keep coming here to draw water."

16Jesus said to her, "Go, call your husband, and come back." 17The woman answered him, "I have no husband." Jesus said to her, "You are right in saying, 'I have no husband'; 18for you have had five husbands, and the one you have now is not your husband. What you have said is true!" 19The woman said to him, "Sir, I see that you are a prophet. 20Our ancestors worshiped on this mountain, but you say that the place where people must worship is in Jerusalem." 21Jesus said to her, "Woman, believe me, the hour is coming when you will worship the Father neither on this mountain nor in Jerusalem. 22You worship what you do not know; we worship what we know, for salvation is from the Jews. 23But the hour is coming, and is now here, when the true worshipers will worship the Father in spirit and truth, for the Father seeks such as these to worship him. 24God is spirit, and those who worship him must worship in spirit and truth." 25The woman said to him, "I know that Messiah is coming" (who is called Christ). "When he comes, he will proclaim all things to us." 26Jesus said to her, "I am he, the one who is speaking to you."

27Just then his disciples came. They were astonished that he was speaking with a woman, but no one said, "What do you want?" or, "Why are you speaking with her?" 28Then the woman left her water jar and went back to the city. She said to the people, 29"Come and see a man who told me everything I have ever done! He cannot be the Messiah, can he?" 30They left the city and were on their way to him.

31Meanwhile the disciples were urging him, "Rabbi, eat something." 32But he said to them, "I have food to eat that you do not know about." 33So the disciples said to one another, "Surely no one has brought him something to eat?" 34Jesus said to them, "My food is to do the will of him who sent me and to complete his work. 35Do you not say, 'Four months more, then comes the harvest'? But I tell you, look around you, and see how the fields are ripe for harvesting. 36The reaper is already receiving wages and is gathering fruit for eternal life, so that sower and reaper may rejoice together. 37For here the saying holds true, 'One sows and another reaps.' 38I sent you to reap that for which you did not labor. Others have labored, and you have entered into their labor."

[39]Many Samaritans from that city believed in him because of the woman's testimony, "He told me everything I have ever done." [40]So when the Samaritans came to him, they asked him to stay with them; and he stayed there two days. [41]And many more believed because of his word. [42]They said to the woman, "It is no longer because of what you said that we believe, for we have heard for ourselves, and we know that this is truly the Savior of the world."

Commentary 1: Connecting the Reading with Scripture

On his way from Judea to Galilee, Jesus chooses to go through Samaria, a land that is at once rich with stories of Israel's past and fraught with Samaritan-Jewish hostility. When Jesus arrives in the Samaritan city of Sychar and rests by Jacob's well, we are reminded of the importance of this place. An apparent reference to Shechem or its vicinity, Sychar is steeped in Israel's history. This setting is closely associated with God's promise to Abram (Gen. 12:6–7), with Jacob's land (Gen. 33:18–19), and with Joseph's burial (Josh. 24:32).

However, by the time Jesus arrives at Sychar, animosity between Samaritans and Jews is an ancient, open secret (2 Kgs. 17:24–41). Jesus and the disciples would not expect Samaritan hospitality in Sychar, any more than Samaritans would expect a warm welcome in Emmaus.

This long-simmering tension between Jews and Samaritans is referenced immediately in the conversation between Jesus and the Samaritan woman at the well. She asks Jesus, "How is it that you, a Jew, ask a drink of me, a woman of Samaria?" (John 4:9). Her surprise and the cultural explanation that follows (v. 10) find an echo in other NT passages. In John's Gospel, Jewish authorities insult Jesus by calling him a Samaritan (8:48), and in Luke's Gospel, people in a Samaritan village turn away Jesus and his disciples (Luke 9:51–56).

The Jewish-Samaritan tension in our text is accompanied by issues related to gender. A scene such as this, in which a Jewish man speaks with a woman in a public place, comes as a surprise; it runs counter to social mores of Jesus' day. Thus, when the disciples return from an errand, their astonishment springs not from Jesus conversing with a Samaritan but from his conversing with a woman (John 4:27).

Furthermore, historic male-female encounters at wells (Gen. 24:10–27; 29:1–11; Exod. 2:15–22; 1 Sam. 9:3–12) provide a backdrop for this scene at Jacob's well. Unlike these betrothal scenes in Hebrew Scripture, our text does not hold the hues of courtship, but one could be forgiven for looking twice at the sight of a Galilean man conversing with a woman.

Nevertheless, Jesus neither flinches nor flees from the Samaritan woman at the well. In contrast to the relatively brief exchange between Jesus and Nicodemus in the middle of the night (3:1–21), Jesus and the Samaritan woman carry on conversation at some length at midday.

This lengthy conversation is composed of three waves. First, Jesus reveals himself as a source that satisfies the kind of spiritual thirst expressed by the psalmist: "As a deer longs for flowing streams, so my soul longs for you, O God. My soul thirsts for God, for the living God" (Ps. 42:1–2). The "living water," like the "rivers of living water" (John 7:37–38), is not explicitly defined, but it suggests a holy provision of basic human needs and an endless connection to God in Christ. The Samaritan woman may not understand how a request for well water has turned into something far deeper, but her appetite for spiritual nourishment is awakened.

Second, Jesus reveals to the Samaritan woman a deep understanding of her marital history. The number of times she has been married raises questions, if not eyebrows, as does her current relationship outside of marriage. However, the underlying message here does not seem to be Jesus' gracious welcome of a prodigal wife. Rather, the emphasis is on Jesus' knowledge of her past and present. This theme of Jesus' omniscience is established in the earlier stories of Peter and Nathanael (1:42–51), in which Jesus knows

These Countless Benefits

If He reconciled us when we were in open war with Him, it is reasonable that we should abide in a state of reconciliation, and give unto Him this reward for that He may not seem to have reconciled untoward and unfeeling creatures to the Father. . . If then He hath brought us near to Himself, when we were far off, much more will He keep us now that we are near. . . . For He died for us, and farther reconcile us, and brought us to Himself, and gave us grace unspeakable. But we brought faith only as our contribution. And so he says, "by faith, unto this grace." What grace is this? Tell me. It is the being counted worthy of the knowledge of God, the being forced from error, the coming to a knowledge of the Truth, the obtaining of all the blessings that come through Baptism. For the end of His bringing us near was that we might receive these gifts. For it was not only that we might have simple remission of sins, that we were reconciled; but that we might receive also these countless benefits. Nor did He even pause at these, but promised others, namely, those unutterable blessings that pass understanding alike and language. And this is why he has set them both down also. For by mentioning grace he clearly points at what we have at present received, but by saying, "And we rejoice in hope of the glory of God," he unveils the whole of things to come. And he had well said, "wherein also we stand." For this is the nature of God's grace. It hath no end, it knows no bound, but evermore is on the advance to greater things, which in human things is not the case. . . And so if thou feel in doubt about those to come; from those now present, and from what thou hast already received, believe in the other also. . . For it is not only for what hath been given, but for what is to be given, that we ought to be filled with confidingness, as though it were already given.

John Chrysostom, "Commentaries on the Epistle to the Romans," in *Nicene and Post Nicene Fathers* Series 1, Vol. 11 (Peabody, MA: Hendrickson, 2004), 396.

Peter's name before any formal introduction, then demonstrates knowledge of Nathanael, the skeptical "Israelite." Indeed, Nathanael's pale-faced question, "Where did you get to know me?" (1:48), may cross the mind of the Samaritan woman. While Nathanael's meteoric response, "Rabbi, you are Son of God! You are the King of Israel!" (1:49), sails above the Samaritan woman's reply, "Sir, I see that you are a prophet" (4:19), she is far from finished with this conversation.

Third, Jesus reveals to the Samaritan woman his divine identity. In the wake of her statement, "'I know that Messiah is coming'" (v. 25), Jesus says, "'I am he, the one who is speaking to you'" (v. 26)—or, literally, "'*I* AM, the one who is speaking to you.'" We may be familiar with the metaphorical "I AM" sayings in John's Gospel (6:35, 48, 51; 8:12; 9:5; 10:7, 9; 10:11, 14; 11:25; 14:6; 15:1). This rendering of "it is I" appears in three other passages: when Jesus walks on the sea, "'it is I; do not be afraid'" (6:20); when he teaches in the treasury of the temple (8:24, 28, 58); and when he identifies himself to the police on the night of his arrest (18:5). When Jesus identifies himself in divine terms to the Samaritan woman, she leaves her jar at the well, returns to town, and invites her Samaritan kin to "come and see."

"Come and see" is a key refrain in the opening chapters of John's Gospel. When two disciples of John the Baptist ask Jesus, "Rabbi, where are you staying?" Jesus replies, "come and see" (1:38–39). Seven verses later, Nathanael's question concerning Jesus, "Can anything good come out of Nazareth?" is met with Philip's invitation, "come and see" (1:46). In a series of unlikely turns, the Samaritan woman becomes the only other character on this Gospel's stage to offer such an invitation. "Come and see" bids would-be Jewish disciples and Samaritans alike to respond to the claim that Jesus is I AM. Throughout the Fourth Gospel, there is a question—sometimes explicit, sometimes implicit—that asks each of us: "Do you see? Do you see God in Christ?"

When the disciples return to the well with food for Jesus, Christ declines their offer in order to reveal his appetite for God's "work" and the "harvest" that is underway. Just as Jesus is at once thirsty for well water and eager to offer a "spring of water gushing up to eternal life" (4:14), whatever physical hunger he may feel in Sychar is far surpassed by his hunger to do God's will and work (see 6:27–29).

The work to which Jesus refers is a symbolic harvest of people. The chapter of Luke's Gospel that contains the parable of the Good Samaritan begins with similar language; Jesus sends seventy followers into the field, saying, "The harvest is plentiful, but the laborers are few" (Luke 10:2). Christ's purpose, like the aim of his laborers, is to bring people to God and God to people, and this mission clearly includes Samaritans.

This radical inclusion of a historically dreaded "other" speaks volumes about Jesus. A *Samaritan* apostle? A Samaritan *woman* apostle? This passage responds to these questions with a resounding *Yes*. To place the unnamed Samaritan woman in the saintly company of Peter, Philip, and Nathanael is to watch long-standing barriers of race and gender fall and the reconciling message of Christ rise.

We might, upon our first reading of this text, wonder why Jesus decides to go through Samaria. There *are* alternative routes between Judea and Galilee. When we allow ourselves to sink into this story, and to let our eyes adjust to its place within the Gospel and the canon of Scripture, we can understand that Jesus is not merely trying to make good time to Galilee. He is much more intent on revealing his divine nature and helping us see that something good can come out of Samaria.

ANDREW NAGY-BENSON

Commentary 2: Connecting the Reading with the World

The twelve chapters of John's Gospel between the prologue and chapter 13 are often called the Book of Signs. The story of Jesus' encounter with the Samaritan woman at the well assigned for this Third Sunday in Lent is not counted as one of the seven signs, though the Gospel lections for the next two Lenten Sundays are. Read back to back in the days before Easter, these passages from the Book of Signs function liturgically much as John meant them to function theologically. The Book of Signs points readers toward the consummate disclosure of who Jesus is, which truth is revealed in the Book of Glory's presentation of Jesus' deeply ironic glorification in his crucifixion and resurrection. Placed in Lent, these readings point the congregation toward Easter, much as a road sign with a directional arrow tells a driver that the road ahead is going to curve in a certain way.

Lent, like Advent, is a season of liturgical imagination for Christians. In Advent, we imagine what it would be like if the darkness were never to be conquered by the light, or what it would be like if God were eternally distant and utterly inconceivable. In Lent, we imagine what it would be like if hatred and death, rather than love and life, were to have the last word. John's Book of Signs, not just the seven he identifies, but the whole sweep of its twelve chapters, points us toward the deep truth about God and God's way in the world that is to be revealed in crucifixion and resurrection. The Book of Signs is to the Book of Glory as Lent is to Good Friday and Easter.

The long story of Jesus' encounter with the woman at Jacob's well points us toward the truth about him in at least two ways. The first is disclosed in the image of water. John's well-wrought story contrasts both who is giving water to whom, and the emblematic nature of the water offered. The water the woman would draw from Jacob's well to give Jesus quenches thirst for but a moment. The "living water" he offers her gushes "up to eternal life."

If choosing to follow the water metaphor in the passage, the preacher should be careful to avoid hints of supersessionism, implications that Christianity supersedes or replaces either orthodox Judaism or the woman's heterodox Judaism. Indeed, Jesus says in verse 22 that "salvation is from the Jews." The contrast is more properly between any hollow religiosity and a fulsome faith in the God who is worshiped "in spirit and truth."

Another way in which the story points us toward the truth about Jesus comes in remembering how culturally improper—indeed radical—it would have been in his time and place for a Jewish man to take water from a Samaritan woman, much less hold an extended conversation with her, especially one that takes her seriously as a person and potential follower. It is important to remember that most modern Christians associate the word "Samaritan" with the more famous "good" Samaritan of Luke 10, and might conceivably hear the word as a marker of virtue, rather than as an indicator of suspect and impure otherness, which it would have invoked for Jesus' Jewish contemporaries and John's later readers.

Indeed, Jesus' world, as much as or more than ours, was one of sharp racial, ethnic, class, and gender distinctions: Jew and Gentile, Jew and Samaritan, free and slave, male and female. Both the woman herself and Jesus' disciples are astonished that he touches a cup she has touched and then—even more incredibly—actually speaks to her. John notes in an aside, perhaps for the sake of Gentile readers, that "Jews do not share things in common with Samaritans." Jesus' defiance of racial, ethnic, and gender boundaries in this story is shot through all four Gospels. It is a theme echoed by Paul's repeated declarations, as in Galatians 3:28, that in Christ "there is no longer Jew or Greek, . . . slave or free, . . . male and female."

One might picture the story by playing with the juxtaposed images of centrifugal and centripetal social forces at work in Jesus' world and ours. Picture, for instance, spinning a ball on a string over your head. The motion pulls the ball outward; the string holds it in place. Imagine a group of children holding hands in a circle, running as fast as they can. The centrifugal force of their circular motion would pull them apart. The centripetal force of their grasp of each other's hands holds them together.

So it is with social forces in Jesus' world and in ours. Distinctions of race, language, immigration status, nationality, and gender function as centrifugal social forces that pull us outward, apart, away from each other. To the right end of the present political spectrum, a resurgent populism and white identity politics would name race, national origin, and immigration status as defining identities that trump our common humanity as children of God. At the left end of the current cultural scene, another form of identity politics elevates certain racial, class, and gender groups to a victimization status that effectively separates and even alienates them from others.

Jesus, in this story and throughout the Gospels, defies such centrifugal social and cultural forces, powers that worked to spin his world apart. Likewise, Christian faith at its most faithful has defied such centrifugal forces. Unhappily, both history and the present moment are replete with examples of individual Christians and the church working in exactly the opposite way, to pull humanity apart. When they have been most faithful, Christians and the church have worked as a powerful centripetal force, pulling humanity to the center, together like a circle of children spinning while tightly grasping each other's hands.

Some years ago, I met Elias Chacour in northern Israel, in a little town in Galilee called Ibillin, not far from Nazareth. Chacour is an incarnation of multiple centripetal identities. He is an Israeli citizen, an Arab, and a Christian. Later an archbishop in the Melkite Church, Father Chacour then ran a remarkable school and college in Ibillin, one of the few educational institutions in Israel where Christian, Jewish, Muslim, and Druze students are invited to study side by side.

Father Chacour was clear about why his school had to be this way. It had to be this way, he said, because the God he worships has no regard for human divisions. The God he worships loves Christians. The God he worships loves Muslims. The God he worships loves Jews. The God he worships loves Druze. The God he worships loves agnostics, loves atheists, loves Arabs and Israelis.

One evening we were talking on his rooftop overlooking the hills of the Galilee, the very hills Jesus had once walked. He told us that when people in that part of the world first meet, they often ask each other a routine question, "What were you born?" It is a big question, and you are supposed to answer, "I was born a Melkite Christian," or "I was born a Shia . . . or an Israeli . . . or a Lebanese." Chacour told us that when people ask him this question, he always answers the same way. He always says, "I was born a baby." He said it on the rooftop that night: "I was born a baby," and then he laughed and laughed, laughed till tears came. His obvious point was that there is no "us" and "them" in the love of God.

MICHAEL L. LINDVALL

Fourth Sunday in Lent

1 Samuel 16:1–13
Psalm 23

Ephesians 5:8–14
John 9:1–41

1 Samuel 16:1–13

[1]The LORD said to Samuel, "How long will you grieve over Saul? I have rejected him from being king over Israel. Fill your horn with oil and set out; I will send you to Jesse the Bethlehemite, for I have provided for myself a king among his sons." [2]Samuel said, "How can I go? If Saul hears of it, he will kill me." And the LORD said, "Take a heifer with you, and say, 'I have come to sacrifice to the LORD.' [3]Invite Jesse to the sacrifice, and I will show you what you shall do; and you shall anoint for me the one whom I name to you." [4]Samuel did what the LORD commanded, and came to Bethlehem. The elders of the city came to meet him trembling, and said, "Do you come peaceably?" [5]He said, "Peaceably; I have come to sacrifice to the LORD; sanctify yourselves and come with me to the sacrifice." And he sanctified Jesse and his sons and invited them to the sacrifice.

[6]When they came, he looked on Eliab and thought, "Surely the LORD's anointed is now before the LORD." [7]But the LORD said to Samuel, "Do not look on his appearance or on the height of his stature, because I have rejected him; for the LORD does not see as mortals see; they look on the outward appearance, but the LORD looks on the heart." [8]Then Jesse called Abinadab, and made him pass before Samuel. He said, "Neither has the LORD chosen this one." [9]Then Jesse made Shammah pass by. And he said, "Neither has the LORD chosen this one." [10]Jesse made seven of his sons pass before Samuel, and Samuel said to Jesse, "The LORD has not chosen any of these." [11]Samuel said to Jesse, "Are all your sons here?" And he said, "There remains yet the youngest, but he is keeping the sheep." And Samuel said to Jesse, "Send and bring him; for we will not sit down until he comes here." [12]He sent and brought him in. Now he was ruddy, and had beautiful eyes, and was handsome. The LORD said, "Rise and anoint him; for this is the one." [13]Then Samuel took the horn of oil, and anointed him in the presence of his brothers; and the spirit of the LORD came mightily upon David from that day forward. Samuel then set out and went to Ramah.

Commentary 1: Connecting the Reading with Scripture

Although this text recounts David's anointing by Samuel to be king over Israel, the narrative is more about Samuel than David. Since his first speech in 1 Samuel 3, Samuel has been an enigmatic figure. He did not recognize God's voice when called in that earlier chapter, but because he was young, and since both the word of the LORD and visions were rare in those days (1 Sam. 3:1), we can overlook this seeming dullness.

Now it is a different matter. God chides him more than once in today's reading. First there is the matter of his "grieving" over Saul. Samuel had not wanted Saul—or anyone else, for that matter—to be king over Israel. Why is he now grieving Saul's rejection? Perhaps it is inertia. Perhaps as the old saying has it, "Better the devil you know than the devil you don't."

Samuel responds fearfully to God's instruction to go to Bethlehem and anoint Saul's replacement: "If Saul finds out, he will kill me" (NJPS). "No," says the LORD, "go to Bethlehem for a sacrificial feast, and anoint the son I tell you to anoint."

As soon as Samuel sees Eliab, the eldest of Jesse's sons, he is sure this is to be the new king. God says he is not the chosen one, despite his height (a reminder, perhaps, of Saul's commanding height above other Israelites? [1 Sam. 10:23]). Then comes a sentence often quoted but rarely translated adequately. The NRSV renders it "for the LORD does not see as mortals see; they look on the outward appearance, but the LORD looks on the heart" (16:7b). This is certainly true, as far as it goes. Taken by itself, in the words of Peter Miscall, the statement "is a platitude with little determinable relevance to the context."[1]

Isaiah 55:8–9 reminds us that the LORD's ways and our ways are vastly different from each other. Miscall goes on to say that "God's ways are not human ways, and neither Samuel nor we are to know why the Lord has rejected Eliab or why he has chosen David."[2] Divine choice, selection, election remain matters of mystery.

It is also good to remember that the rejection of Eliab is mentioned only in terms of his not being chosen to be king. That is, there is no indication that Eliab is not otherwise a perfectly good person, a fine son and brother, and a faithful member of the community. Eliab is not a failed human being. He simply is not the one God has chosen for Saul to anoint as king.

None of the people whom God chooses in the Bible from Abram/Abraham onward is said to be chosen because of a set of sterling inner qualities that only God can see. Undoubtedly God does know a person's "true inner self," but we are never told that it is on such basis that any person is selected for any task. No call narrative—whether Moses' long conversation with God at the burning bush (Exod. 3–4), the shorter calls of Gideon (Judg. 6:11–17), Jeremiah (Jer. 1:4–19), or any of the others for whom we have such an account—specifies any qualities of the individual as leading to the choice. Neither God nor the narrator ever gives a rationale for any selection. Neither outward nor inward qualities are cited as motivating God's decision. Apparently God chooses whomever God chooses.

This need not be taken as meaning God's decisions are random, and even less that human decision makers such as Saul can be satisfied with choosing for superficial reasons or with no thought at all. This, I think, is the point of verse 7b. What would be the use of reminding Samuel that he and God are not on the same plane, unless there is also an admonition? A more literal translation of the phrase is "humans see with the eyes and the LORD sees with the heart." What does "seeing with the heart" mean? If "heart" is what we usually assume in English with such phrases as "wearing one's heart on one's sleeve," then it seems hardly as good as seeing with the eyes, let alone any sort of improvement. If we remember, however, that in the ancient Hebrew figurative division of the body, the "heart" stands for the locus of thinking and decision making, the difficulty can be resolved.

Samuel is not to rely on outward appearance in making the choice for Saul's successor, but to think carefully about the choice. Actually, in this case, the Lord has already said that Samuel is to rely on God's pointing out the chosen son, and not to make a hasty decision on his own. As a more general maxim, the saying would seem to commend thought, pondering, consultation with God, in place of quick conclusions at first sight. (Pairing this lection with the Gospel appointed from John 9 is another indication that sight/insight is a major theme of the day.)

For each of the seven sons of Jesse, Samuel receives the same message from God: "Not this one." He asks Jesse if there is not another boy somewhere. Upon being told that there is one more, out with the flocks, Samuel says, "Send someone to bring him, for we will not sit down to eat until he comes here" (1 Sam. 16:11 NJPS). This detail may be intended to remind us of the clandestine anointing of Saul by Samuel, after a delayed feast (chap. 9).

When the youngest son appears, the message from the Lord is finally, "Rise and anoint him, for this is the one." Having been told that the handsome and tall Eliab is not the chosen, some might assume God's choice will be the ugliest and shortest. Lest we think that, the narrator

1. Peter D. Miscall, *1 Samuel: A Literary Reading* (Bloomington: Indiana University Press, 1986), 117.
2. Miscall, *1 Samuel*, 117.

tells us that David is "ruddy-cheeked, bright-eyed, and handsome" (16:12 NJPS). So the meaning of verse 7b becomes clearer: it really is *not* by assessing the outward appearance, either positively or negatively, that the proper decisions can be made. Searching for the apparently least likely candidate is no more relying on God's guidance than assuming the most likely looking one is to be chosen.

Samuel anoints David in front of his brothers. Just as Samuel had predicted to Saul (10:6) and just as it had happened to Saul (10:10), the spirit of the Lord grips David from that time on (16:13). The spirit had come upon Saul, he had defeated the Ammonites, and he had been acclaimed king by the people.

Is something similar, something new and decisive, to happen with David? Will he soon be king? Are defeat and destruction of the Philistines (as when the spirit came upon Samson [Judges 14–16]) to occur? What is the significance of "from that day forward"? Is it a sign of permanence, a sign that David's possession by the spirit is to be qualitatively different from that of Samson and Samuel?[3]

The narrator's choice of details paralleling the account of Saul certainly seems to steer us to comparisons of the two stories.

In the final sentence, Samuel returns to Ramah. Although not apparent at the time, this is almost the last we hear of him. He will not leave Ramah again. Saul will come to him there (chap. 19), and there he will die (chap. 25). On the eve of his own death, the desperate Saul will have the woman of Endor bring up the ghost of Samuel (chap. 28). However, once he anoints David, Samuel's active role in the story is over.

REBECCA ABTS WRIGHT

Commentary 2: Connecting the Reading with the World

With an anointing of oil and the blessing of God's Spirit, the saga of David, iconic shepherd king of Israel, begins. Behind the intrigue and suspense of this well-told tale, the text poses questions about leadership and answering God's call. The old prophet, Samuel, has been called by God to choose a *new* king for Israel. King Saul's leadership is over in God's eyes, because Saul has disobeyed God's instructions. Samuel is fearful of Saul's anger and the anger of the people when they discover God has chosen a new king. These fears are not important to God. God is on the move, choosing to act on what matters, rather than what is practical. God's ways are persistent, perhaps a bit subversive, in leading Samuel to the newly chosen king. God effectively says to the prophet, "Have faith! The answer to 'how?' is 'yes!'"[4] Bring a sacrifice to Bethlehem. Invite Jesse and his sons. Conduct worship. The new king will be revealed.

Worship is always an occasion for forming and reforming community. In this story worship is the place where God's moves lead the community forward. They *discover* God's vision for the people in worship. What can we learn from this auspicious, spontaneous, and community-changing worship in Bethlehem? Leadership consultant Peter Bloch writes, "Choosing to act on 'what matters' is the choice to live a passionate existence, which is anything but controlled and predictable."[5] Sounds a bit like the life David led. Sounds a bit like the life Jesus led. As God's church seeking new ways in changing times, will we encourage the boldness of "yes!" as we recognize and anoint new leaders for the future? Will we commit, time and again, to worship that facilitates the opportunities for God's Spirit to come mightily upon our leaders, old and new, as well as upon all of God's people?

Carol Newsom gives us insight into where we might find new leaders as she writes of the folkloristic element of this anointing story, "the motif of the overlooked or neglected child who becomes a king or queen . . . is, in short, the Cinderella story."[6] In folk literature around the world, the

3. Miscall, *1 Samuel*, 117.
4. Peter Bloch, *The Answer to How Is Yes: Acting on What Matters* (San Francisco: Berrett-Koehler, 2003).
5. Bloch, *The Answer*, 7.
6. Carol A. Newsom, "Exegetical Essay," in *Feasting on the Word: Year A, Lent Through Eastertide* (Louisville, KY: Westminster John Knox, 2010), 101.

Cinderella motif is ubiquitous. Human beings love the story of the outlier, the deserving hero or heroine, the surprise leader, found on the margins of society. Do we all secretly harbor images of ourselves as worthy outliers?

These Cinderella leaders bring with them an empathy and intuition that is often not found in mainstream leaders. They can be experienced first as "ugly," coarse, or odd in appearance, not worthy of a second look. They are often in the role of servant. They have a greater connection to animals and the earth, to the sustenance and welfare of all the people, not only of the elite. When their inner beauty and wisdom attract the attention of a good person in power, their outer beauty is revealed. Eventually they are awarded their rightful place as leaders of the people.

David is the Cinderella leader coming from the margins of the tribe rather than the main stream. He is the outlier, the brother who is not remembered until last, because he is so far down on the inheritance list. He is young, maybe naive, not as acquainted with the ways of society, because he has been in the fields with his harp and the sheep for company. Music and nature are good teachers of the soul. Sheep teach good leadership skills, because they desperately need good leadership. They are easily spooked and separated into factions that take wrong paths, finding themselves in quicksand or at the edge of a cliff. David has learned to provide direction and protection for his sheep, to lead them to green pasture and still water. He knows the value of solitude, singing, and prayer. God recognizes in David a heart that will look to God for direction, protection, and abundance—and the ability to lead God's people to these things as well.

Young people in literature and real life bring us many examples of Cinderella leaders. Meg Murray, the teenage protagonist in Madeleine L'Engle's young adult science fiction/fantasy classic *A Wrinkle in Time,* and Harry Potter, the beloved boy wizard of J. K. Rowling's seven-book fantasy series, are two who stand out.

Meg is an awkward young teen, a math prodigy struggling to fit in at school and often in trouble for her outspoken defense of the underdog. Yet she is chosen by a celestial being to be a leader, an anointed one in a monumental act of change. She must rescue her scientist father and her younger brother from the control of evil on a planet lacking love as it is gripped by a fascist-like entity who disguises rigid social conformity as safety and security. Her actions for family shift the balance of universal power toward the light.

Harry is orphaned as a babe in the cradle when he unwittingly defends his parents against the power of an evil wizard. He is left with a lightning-bolt scar on his forehead, a constant reminder that he is different. Branded as strange by his adopted family, he discovers his true family at Hogwarts School of Witchcraft and Wizardry, and grows into his anointed leadership when the struggle between good and evil reaches epic proportions in the wizarding community. Both of these young people confront inner personal battles as they create change by following their anointed calls.

In the news we learn of young people around the world taking up the mantles of David, Meg, and Harry as unexpected leaders. Deemed outliers by society because of age or gender, they are saying "yes!" rather than "how?" to change. Students leaders such as Cameron Kasky, Emma Gonzalez, Alex Wind, Jaclyn Corin, and David Hogg, from Marjory Stoneman Douglas High School in Parkland, Florida, have emerged as national spokespeople in the call for gun control in the United States after their school was assaulted by a lone gunman who killed fourteen of their peers and three staff members. At the age of fifteen, Malala Yousafzai was shot in the head by a member of the Taliban in Pakistan for her efforts to support education for girls. She survived to become a world-renowned activist for children's education, and in 2014 she became the youngest recipient of the Nobel Peace Prize. Xiuhtezcatl Martinez, a young adult indigenous environmental activist in Boulder, Colorado, has been speaking out for the environment since the age of six, particularly on the issue of fracking.

All these young people teach us to be bold in saying "yes!" to God's Spirit in the call to change that can shift the balance of the universe from greed-loving power to justice-loving power. In Lent, the story of David's anointing points toward his descendant, Jesus of Nazareth. Jesus, an outlier, a Cinderella leader, called and anointed by God, to shift the balance of the universe from the evil of oppression, scarcity, and hatred to freedom, abundance, peace, and love. Jesus who calls to other outliers, such as the blind man in John, offering healing and recognizing their potential to lead. In turn, they witness mightily, and the ripples spread. Who is waiting to be anointed in the midst of your community? Who is waiting to say, "yes!"?

JANE ANNE FERGUSON

Mingled with Sounds of Joy

David has left no sweeter psalm than the short twenty-third. It is but a moment's opening of his soul; but, as when one, walking the winter street, sees the door opened for some one to enter, and the red light streams a moment forth, and the forms of gay children are running to greet the comer, and genial music sounds, though the door shuts and leaves the night black, yet it cannot shut back again all that the eye, the ear, the heart, and the imagination have seen—so in this psalm, though it is but a moment's opening of the soul, are emitted truths of peace and consolation that will never be absent from the world.

The twenty-third psalm is the nightingale of the psalms. It is small, of a homely feather, singing shyly out of obscurity; but oh! It has filled the air of the whole world with melodious joy, greater than the heart can conceive. Blessed be the day on which that psalm was born!

What would you say of a pilgrim commissioned of God to travel up and down the earth singing a strange melody, which, when one heard, caused him to forget whatever sorrow he had? And so the singing angel goes on his way through all lands, singing in the language of every nation, driving away trouble by the pulses of the air which his tongue moves with divine power. Behold just such an one! This pilgrim God has sent to speak in every language on the globe. It has charmed more griefs to rest than all the philosophy of the world. It has remanded to their dungeon more felon thoughts, more black doubts, more thieving sorrows, than there are sands on the sea shore. It has comforted the noble host of the poor. It has sung courage to the army of the disappointed. It has poured balm and consolation into the heart of the sick, of captives in dungeons, of widows in their pinching griefs, of orphans in their loneliness. . . . It has made the dying Christian slave freer than his master, and consoled those whom, dying, he left behind mourning, not so much that he was gone, as because they were left behind and could not go too. Nor is its work done. It will go singing to your children and my children, and to their children, through all the generations of time; nor will it fold its wings till the last pilgrim is safe, and time ended; and then it shall fly back to the bosom of God, whence it issued, and sound on, mingled with all those sounds of celestial joy which make heaven musical for ever.

Edna Dean Proctor, ed., *Life Thoughts Gathered from the Extemporaneous Discourses of Henry Ward Beecher* (Edinburgh: A. Strahan, 1858), 6-7.

Psalm 23

[1]The LORD is my shepherd, I shall not want.
  [2]He makes me lie down in green pastures;
he leads me beside still waters;
  [3]he restores my soul.
He leads me in right paths
  for his name's sake.

[4]Even though I walk through the darkest valley,
  I fear no evil;
for you are with me;
  your rod and your staff—
  they comfort me.

[5]You prepare a table before me
  in the presence of my enemies;
you anoint my head with oil;
  my cup overflows.
[6]Surely goodness and mercy shall follow me
  all the days of my life,
and I shall dwell in the house of the LORD
  my whole life long.

Connecting the Psalm with Scripture and Worship

Beloved and familiar, Psalm 23 affirms the shepherding activity of God with a series of short phrases in which God is the subject and the psalmist is the object of God's care. God is the one who "makes me lie down in green pastures," who "leads me beside still waters," who "restores my soul," and who "leads me in right paths" (Ps. 23:2–3). As the psalm continues, the relationship between the subject (God) and the object (psalmist) deepens, as indicated by the more intimate second-person point of view. "You are with me; your rod and your staff—they comfort me. You prepare a table before me in the presence of my enemies; you anoint my head with oil" (vv. 4–5). God is active and involved, gracious and compassionate, tender and loving. The psalmist marvels at the abundance of grace: "my cup overflows" (v. 5). The psalm concludes with the assurance that God will remain the faithful shepherd who seeks out and gathers in, and that the psalmist will continue as the object of God's care: "Surely goodness and mercy shall follow me all the days of my life" (v. 6). No wonder generations of believers have kept this psalm close!

There is no obvious reason for what the psalmist receives. The psalmist lists no accomplishments or credits. God's favor has come apart from whatever the psalmist has done or left undone. It is pure grace, a gift the giver wants to give without regard for or interest in the worthiness of the recipient. God's motivations are generous and mysterious, beyond expectation and calculation.

Divine inscrutability is on display in the lesson from 1 Samuel. God has decided to move the monarchy in a new direction, away from Saul and toward one of Jesse's sons. Samuel is enlisted in this task. He fills his horn with oil, heads to Bethlehem, and prepares to anoint the one God has selected. As the sons of Jesse gather around, drawn by the sacrifice of a heifer, Samuel anticipates what is to come, presuming to know already that God has chosen Eliab (1 Sam. 13:6). It must be so, Samuel assumes. Eliab looks the part; he has the right stature and appearance. Eliab's outward characteristics resemble those of Saul (9:2), the last king Samuel anointed and the king God subsequently rejected.

Samuel has it wrong. God is taking a fresh approach with the new king. The categories for consideration are different now. External features are no longer necessary credentials. "The LORD does not see as mortals see; they look on the outward appearance, but the LORD looks on the heart" (16:7). What is God looking for on the heart of the new king? It is not clear to Samuel or to Jesse (or to the reader). It is known only to God. Seven sons of Jesse parade before Samuel, but none of them has been selected. It takes a further inquiry of Jesse by Samuel before the youngest son, David, is called from the field where he has been keeping the sheep—perhaps even making them to lie down in green pastures.

Mysteriously, beyond expectation and calculation, God has chosen David. The object of God's search, the target for God's grace, David offers no list of accomplishments. He is simply the one whose heart God has seen, the one whom God has favored. Samuel anoints David's head with oil. God's spirit comes mightily upon him (v. 13). His cup overflows. Over the days and the pages that follow, David's life journey is filled with twists and turns, peaks and valleys; yet he remains the object of God's care; goodness and mercy continually pursue him. That is how it is with grace.

The Gospel lesson for this day, John 9:1–41, offers another example of the unpredictable and abundant flow of grace. The passage begins with Jesus seeing the man blind from birth. Jesus is the subject, and the blind man is the object of his gaze and then the object of his healing mercy. In this opening scene, the blind man does not clamor for Jesus' attention, deliver a statement of faith, or present a case for his healing. Instead, he is simply one whom Jesus has seen, one on whom the light of the world has shined. The story moves through several scenes of accusation, testimony, and recrimination, until eventually the man is driven out of the community. Hearing what has happened, Jesus seeks out the healed man, for he is still the object of Jesus' care. When Jesus finds him (John 9:35), he engages the man in conversation, through which the man comes to state his belief (v. 38). The grace he has received, the transformation of his life, moves him to faith and worship. His cup overflows.

Lent is a time when many take on various disciplines to nourish the soul and revitalize the spirit. There is much to commend an increased attention to the practices of study, worship, and service over these forty days. However, the texts for today gently remind us that Lent is not just about what *we* are doing; instead, it is an opportunity to regain an awareness of what *God* is doing. How is God active in our lives? Where is God leading us? How is God tending us? How have we experienced the mysterious contours of God's grace? How has God sought us out? As we consider what God is doing within us and among us, these texts can help shape our faithful responses, pointing us to belief and worship, affirmation and assurance.

JOHN W. WURSTER

Fourth Sunday in Lent

Ephesians 5:8–14

[8]For once you were darkness, but now in the Lord you are light. Live as children
of light— [9]for the fruit of the light is found in all that is good and right and true.
[10]Try to find out what is pleasing to the Lord. [11]Take no part in the unfruitful works
of darkness, but instead expose them. [12]For it is shameful even to mention what
such people do secretly; [13]but everything exposed by the light becomes visible,
[14]for everything that becomes visible is light. Therefore it says,

"Sleeper, awake!
  Rise from the dead,
and Christ will shine on you."

Commentary 1: Connecting the Reading with Scripture

Ephesians 5:8–14 gives instructions for how Christians should live as those God has transformed through Jesus Christ. The reading comes in the middle of a larger set of instructions on this subject (Eph. 4:17–6:20). Although the original purpose of Ephesians is uncertain, the focus in the letter on the nature of life after conversion is striking. This feature of the writing has led many Christians to read it as a baptismal liturgy.[1] The traditional practice of preparation for baptism in the Lenten season and the Lenten focus on new life in Christ make Ephesians 5:8–14 particularly appropriate for this time in the church year.

This reading opens with a causative particle "for" (Gk. *gar*) that indicates the passage is part of an argument already in progress. The first verse has a declaration followed by an imperative: "For once you were darkness, but now in the Lord you are light. Live as children of light" (v. 8). "For once you were darkness" refers to the change from the "old self" before Christ (4:22) to the "new self" "in the likeness of God" (4:24) that the preceding section of the letter emphasizes.

The section immediately preceding the reading gives two sets of examples of "darkness" Christians should eschew in favor of new-life actions (4:25–5:7). First, Ephesians 4:25–32 lays out rules for new life in Christ, including put away falsehood (4:25); do not let anger lead to evil acts (4:26–27); do honest work (4:28); be kind and forgiving (4:31–32). Ephesians 5:1–2 sums up this list with the injunctions "be imitators of God" (5:1) and "live in love, as Christ loved us" (5:2). Then Ephesians 5:3–5 gives a second list, of dark action to reject in favor of light: do not mention fornication or greed (5:3); avoid obscene and vulgar acts; and embrace thanksgiving (5:4). Verse 5 sums up by saying no one who engages in the dark behaviors listed will have a share in God's kingdom.

Ephesians 5:6–7 implores the reader to dissociate from the disobedient. Verses 8–9 tell why. "You are light," and the "fruit of the light" is found in good actions, not in the dark actions listed in 4:25–5:5. Verses 10–14 take this reasoning further. They hint that acts done in secret are by nature acts contrary to God. Therefore, the believer must bring all things into the light. Verses 13–14 suggest that anything visible, that can stand being exposed to the light and done openly, is by nature of God. Verse 14 ends with a three-line poem that was perhaps part of an early Christian hymn. It enhances the messages of verses 13–14 by saying that Christ "will shine" only on "children of light" (v. 8).

1. Ernst Best, *Ephesians: A Shorter Commentary* (London: T. & T. Clark, 2003), xxxi.

Following our lection the author gives more specific instructions as to actions and attitudes to avoid (5:15–20), and principles for relating to members of one's household (5:21–6:9). With each example the writer fills out what a life "in the light" looks like. The household code may seem to contradict contemporary understandings of the Christlike life, since it reinforces hierarchical relationships between husbands and wives (5:22–33), and supports slavery (6:5–9). The principle that runs throughout this section, however, which applies to every person, is to love "as Christ loved us" (5:2). The household code, anachronistic as it may be, envisions radical self-giving that is "fruit of the light" (5:9). This portion of the letter ends with an emblem of how to stand against the "powers of this present darkness" (6:12): "put on the whole armor of God" (6:11–17).

Ephesians 5:8–14 has significant connections with at least two dominant themes in Scripture. First, the theme of living separate from the surrounding culture is common. The Old Testament has many expressions of this idea, but perhaps the most direct is Leviticus 11:44, "Be holy, for I am holy." "Holy" seems to mean separate from those things that are ritually unclean, morally impure, and socially unjust. The OT legal tradition includes commands concerning each of these dimensions of holiness. In each case, however, the call to holiness arises from awareness that God has transformed the people from slave to free (Lev. 11:45, "For I am the Lord who brought you up from the land of Egypt, to be your God"). So also Ephesians 5:8–14 commands Christians to have a pure life because God has transformed them. Once they were subject to the "ruler of the power of the air" (Eph. 2:2), but now they are free and live in the love of the God of mercy (2:4–5). Other NT letters also take up this same injunction to "be separate" (2 Cor. 6:17; 1 Peter 1:16). The letters typically have a section on ethical behavior that gives concrete examples of actions Christians should engage in or avoid because of their new life in Christ (Rom. 12–14; Col. 3–4; 1 Thess. 4:1–12). Ephesians is dominated by this kind of instruction.

The second major theme is darkness and light. From the very first chapter in the Bible, light and darkness have signaled the difference between order and chaos, purpose and randomness, good and evil (Gen. 1:2, 3). When Pharaoh refused to comply with God's command to release the Israelites, God's last-ditch effort was to plunge the Egyptian king and his people into darkness in hopes of bringing them to God's way (Exod. 10:21–29). The psalmist speaks of God as "my light and my salvation" (Ps. 27:1). John's Gospel uses light as a primary symbol for the incarnation. Jesus was "the true light, which enlightens everyone" (John 1:9). This light "shines in the darkness, and the darkness did not overcome it" (1:5). Light reflects the purposeful work of the Creator to bring good; darkness represents the forces of this world. As 1 John 1:5 says, "God is light and in him there is no darkness at all." Ephesians 5:8–14 makes a unique contribution to this theme by saying, "You are light." In other passages God is light and Christians are "in the light" (1 John 2:9), but Ephesians 5:8 uses a bold metaphor when it says that "you are light." Perhaps the closest parallel is Jesus' statement that "you are the light of the world" (Matt. 5:14).

Ephesians 5:8–14 relates most closely to John 9:1–41 among the other lections. The Gospel lesson is a narrative about Jesus healing a man born blind. Jesus' teaching immediately after the miracle makes clear that the point of the story is spiritual blindness (John 9:35–41). In the previous chapter Jesus declared, "I am the light of the world. Whoever follows me will never walk in darkness" (8:12). Thus, Jesus' healing of the blind man contributes to the Fourth Gospel's use of light and darkness as symbols of the spiritual life (3:2; 13:30).

The most obvious connection of the Ephesians passage to Psalm 23 is in the psalm's reference to "the darkest valley" (Ps. 23:4). The psalmist is sure that God leads through such a dark place, just as the writer of Ephesians is sure God shines on believers (Eph. 5:14) and protects them from the powers of darkness (Eph. 6:12). If Psalm 23's "darkest valley" refers to death, then Ephesians 5:14's promise of resurrection is an even closer connection.

At first reading 1 Samuel 16:1–13 may seem to have no connection to the Ephesians lection.

A close reading, however, reveals an important thematic link. God tells Samuel not to judge Jesse's sons by "outward appearance" because God "looks on the heart" (1 Sam. 16:7). This reflects the same bifurcation of perspectives that appears in the light/darkness of Ephesians 5:8–14.

JEROME F. D. CREACH

Commentary 2: Connecting the Reading with the World

This short passage in Ephesians invites reflection on some very complex issues: the nature and process of conversion, the relationship between Christian communities and the world around them, and the apocalyptic context of Paul's teachings.

Conversion is complete: once in darkness, now in light. Conversion is a process: now that you are in the light, live as children of light. Ephesians 5:8 is a succinct statement of the dynamics of conversion: the change has happened, now live out the change. The instructional tone of the verse's context reminds new converts that though they can claim the new life God offers them in the gospel of Jesus Christ, they can do so only if they live it out.

Conversion is from God: they are in light in the Lord. Conversion is a partnership with God, as in verse 10 they are reminded that living in the light requires discernment to find out what pleases God. While the behavioral outcomes of conversion are relatively fixed, this passage reminds us that the internal process required to reach those behavioral outcomes can be complex and difficult in particular situations. I am reminded here of the complexity of such processes as overcoming addiction, mastering Bach's Goldberg Variations, or climbing a steep mountain. The end, the goal, is clear, even simple. The process is anything but.

Put yet another way, conversion shows as a moral face in the world. At least for Paul and those writing in his name, there is no possibility of an internal, private conversion that does not enact goodness. In fact, there is no *complete* conversion that does not demand constant embodiment in the form of what Paul called "the fruits of the Spirit." The lists of those fruits, behavior that exhibits the love of God in the world, in concrete ways and in concrete communities, vary from passage to passage, but they all signal that the reality of conversion is found in behavior. Our souls are visible in our actions.

The phrase "children of light" in verse 8 calls to mind the Qumran community, where that designation functioned as a kind of title for those who chose to live by the community's rules. Their writings made clear that the moral purity of their community included separation from the world around them. They treated exposure to other persons and groups as though it were exposure to a contagious disease, and isolation was their strategy for maintaining their version of communal health.

The picture is more complicated in our passage. Verses 6 and 7 immediately preceding might suggest that the Ephesians (and other communities who might have been the recipients of this letter) should have no contact with those who speak "empty words." However, verses 11, 12, and 13 suggest a more active role for members of Christian communities in exposing secretive, immoral behavior on the part of those for whom conversion has not taken place. Children of light expose by the light the "unfruitful works of darkness."

This somewhat ambiguous passage raises two issues that still confront Christian communities today. First, Ephesians is clear that if the acts of darkness take place among members of the community, those acts should be exposed. In the past, in the Puritan communities, for example, persons were brought before the community to account for and repent of certain behaviors. This is a rare to nonexistent occurrence in liberal Protestantism today. Taking the place of exposure in the churches with which I am familiar is at least the attempt to create an atmosphere of acceptance and forgiveness such that a person who has indulged in immoral behavior could face his or her problem(s) in the context of the community.

The second and more complicated issue is the role of Christian communities with regard to the moral or immoral behavior of those outside of the community. What are *the* Christian values and moral standards? Who defines or identifies them? Why and how are they to be ascendant among other candidates for moral standards? These questions have been addressed in our North American context largely by the doctrine of the separation of church and state enshrined in the US Constitution. Common moral standards are inscribed in our laws that apply to all persons and groups, and religious bodies have influence outside their communities (ideally) through the power of persuasion. That separation is currently under challenge with new legislation that will allow religious communities to be active political groups, but as of now the church/state separation is largely intact.

This passage also raises the specter of the Christian person or community bringing condemnation on those that are different and/or have different values or simply do not acknowledge that authority of Christian teachings. As church membership has declined in North America—and studies proliferate searching for the reasons—there has arisen a chorus of complaints that Christian communities are judgmental. This passage in Ephesians almost demands that we be judgmental when we see and know of "unfruitful works of darkness."

As we penetrate more deeply into the theological and moral commitments of this passage from Ephesians, it seems to recede further and further from our current reality. In liberal Protestant circles, we do not, by and large, think of ourselves as more enlightened than those from other religions or no religion, at least not in the moral realm. We may hold the conviction that Jesus showed us a relationship to God and a way of life that is beautiful and true, and while it calls us and leads us, it also constantly reminds us how far we fall short of the way. To summon another Pauline term, our Christian convictions offer us no cause for boasting, for we are constantly falling short.

When we read these epistles, it is easy to forget their eschatological and apocalyptic setting. I think it is crucial that we remember it. Paul and his students were not offering long-term, universal strategies for dealing with a multicultural, global environment but, rather, a prescription for living out the end of days in the light of a new relationship to God. The experience of conversion and of a new identity in a close-knit group with similar values has been repeated countless times in the history of Western Christianity. Outside Christianity, cults have arisen from a similar dynamic, and for the most part they end badly. In a wider, more socially integrated context, however, an ecstatic experience like that alluded to in the hymn fragment in verse 14 is very hard to sustain. Apocalyptic scenarios include a sense of urgency, of ultimacy, that simply dissipates in the course of mundane daily life, although crises, personal or communal, may awaken an apocalyptic-like sensibility.

What might we take away from this passage for the long-term, multicultural, global complexity of our context? First, Ephesians offers a clear and convincing picture of the challenge of living out even our most deeply held convictions and the value and power of those convictions to call us back to the person we are striving to be. Second, our relationship to God is always expressed in how we treat others; there is no gap between theology and morality.

Finally, perhaps the urgency and ultimacy of the eschatological setting of this epistle can encourage some yearning in us for a more enlivened faith and call us to look again at conversion even in our world.

SALLY B. PURVIS

Fourth Sunday in Lent

John 9:1–41

1As he walked along, he saw a man blind from birth. 2His disciples asked him, "Rabbi, who sinned, this man or his parents, that he was born blind?" 3Jesus answered, "Neither this man nor his parents sinned; he was born blind so that God's works might be revealed in him. 4We must work the works of him who sent me while it is day; night is coming when no one can work. 5As long as I am in the world, I am the light of the world." 6When he had said this, he spat on the ground and made mud with the saliva and spread the mud on the man's eyes, 7saying to him, "Go, wash in the pool of Siloam" (which means Sent). Then he went and washed and came back able to see. 8The neighbors and those who had seen him before as a beggar began to ask, "Is this not the man who used to sit and beg?" 9Some were saying, "It is he." Others were saying, "No, but it is someone like him." He kept saying, "I am the man." 10But they kept asking him, "Then how were your eyes opened?" 11He answered, "The man called Jesus made mud, spread it on my eyes, and said to me, 'Go to Siloam and wash.' Then I went and washed and received my sight." 12They said to him, "Where is he?" He said, "I do not know."

13They brought to the Pharisees the man who had formerly been blind. 14Now it was a sabbath day when Jesus made the mud and opened his eyes. 15Then the Pharisees also began to ask him how he had received his sight. He said to them, "He put mud on my eyes. Then I washed, and now I see." 16Some of the Pharisees said, "This man is not from God, for he does not observe the sabbath." But others said, "How can a man who is a sinner perform such signs?" And they were divided. 17So they said again to the blind man, "What do you say about him? It was your eyes he opened." He said, "He is a prophet."

18The Jews did not believe that he had been blind and had received his sight until they called the parents of the man who had received his sight 19and asked them, "Is this your son, who you say was born blind? How then does he now see?" 20His parents answered, "We know that this is our son, and that he was born blind; 21but we do not know how it is that now he sees, nor do we know who opened his eyes. Ask him; he is of age. He will speak for himself." 22His parents said this because they were afraid of the Jews; for the Jews had already agreed that anyone who confessed Jesus to be the Messiah would be put out of the synagogue. 23Therefore his parents said, "He is of age; ask him."

24So for the second time they called the man who had been blind, and they said to him, "Give glory to God! We know that this man is a sinner." 25He answered, "I do not know whether he is a sinner. One thing I do know, that though I was blind, now I see." 26They said to him, "What did he do to you? How did he open your eyes?" 27He answered them, "I have told you already, and you would not listen. Why do you want to hear it again? Do you also want to become his disciples?" 28Then they reviled him, saying, "You are his disciple, but we are disciples of Moses. 29We know that God has spoken to Moses, but as for this man, we do not know where he comes from." 30The man answered, "Here is an astonishing thing! You do not know where he comes from, and yet he opened my eyes. 31We know that God does not listen to sinners, but he does listen to one who worships him and obeys his will. 32Never since the world began has it been heard that anyone opened the eyes of a person born blind. 33If this man were not from God, he could do nothing." 34They answered him, "You were born entirely in sins, and are you trying to teach us?" And they drove him out.

35Jesus heard that they had driven him out, and when he found him, he said,
"Do you believe in the Son of Man?" 36He answered, "And who is he, sir? Tell me,
so that I may believe in him." 37Jesus said to him, "You have seen him, and the
one speaking with you is he." 38He said, "Lord, I believe." And he worshiped him.
39Jesus said, "I came into this world for judgment so that those who do not see
may see, and those who do see may become blind." 40Some of the Pharisees
near him heard this and said to him, "Surely we are not blind, are we?" 41Jesus
said to them, "If you were blind, you would not have sin. But now that you say,
'We see,' your sin remains."

Commentary 1: Connecting the Reading with Scripture

Blindness and *sight* are prominent themes in this well-crafted text. The words appear in more than half of the chapter's verses, and, characteristic of the Fourth Gospel, they hold multiple meanings.

On the surface, this is a story about a blind man miraculously healed by Jesus. Jesus puts mud on the eyes of the blind man, and the man can see. It is the only instance of Jesus giving sight to the blind in the Fourth Gospel, but this story runs alongside six similar accounts in the Synoptic Gospels (Matt. 9:27–31; 12:22–23; 20:29–34; Mark 8:22–26; 10:46–52; Luke 18:35–43). Like our text, each of these stories ends with a man, once blind, who now can see, but John's telling is much longer and more developed than these companion stories.

Also, unlike the others, John's story does not begin with a blind man crying to Jesus for mercy, or with people bringing a blind man to Jesus. In our text, the blind man does not speak until after the healing, and is not led by friends to Jesus. Rather, this story begins with a question. When Jesus sees a man "blind from birth," the disciples ask, "Rabbi, who sinned, this man or his parents, that he was born blind?" (John 9:2).

The disciples' question is rooted in an ancient, if contested, understanding that the sins of parents are visited on their children. The Ten Commandments' admonition against "bowing down to idols" includes this warning: "for I the Lord your God am a jealous God, punishing children for the iniquity of parents, to the third and fourth generation of those who reject me" (Exod. 20:5). Traces of this belief resurface throughout Hebrew Scripture (Num. 14:18; Ps. 109:13–14; Jer. 32:18). Other OT passages, most notably Ezekiel 18, challenge the belief that God punishes children for the transgressions of their parents (see also Jer. 31:29–30).

"Rabbi, who sinned, this man or his parents, that he was born blind?" In a sense, Jesus answers the disciples' question twice—first in word, then in action. As he does in Luke 13:1–5, Jesus rejects the idea that sin has anything to do with the man's suffering. Then he demonstrates what it means to do the "works of God" by relieving the misery of the blind beggar (John 9:3–5).

More questions surface in the wake of the healing act. Did this really happen? If so, how did this happen? Who but God has the power to give sight to the blind? These questions not only carry the narrative forward; they invite the formerly blind man to bear witness to his experience of healing and to express his developing sense of Jesus' divinity.

Some of the "neighbors" who have seen the blind beggar in the streets are not convinced that this sighted man is the same fellow who formerly could not see (v. 9). Similarly, some of the Jewish leaders "[do] not believe that he had been blind and had received his sight" (v. 18), so they call in the man's parents for questioning. In both instances, it is made clear that this is not a case of mistaken identity (vv. 9, 20).

According to the blind man and his parents, this healing did happen—but how? "How" is not a fleeting concern here; the word appears six times in this story. The newly sighted man twice tells the story of how the healing happened

(vv. 11, 15), first to his neighbors, then to the Pharisees.

Despite his clear testimony, the man's explanation of what happened does not quell the disquiet among Jewish leaders. Beyond the mechanics of putting mud on the eyes and washing them clean, the Pharisees wrestle with a bigger "how?"

Because Jesus performed this healing on the Sabbath (v. 14), some of the Pharisees consider Jesus a sinner, and they reject the possibility that a sinner could do such wonders (vv. 16, 24). This controversy around healing on the Sabbath appears earlier in John's Gospel (5:1–18) and is numbered among similar stories in the other Gospels (Mark 3:1–6; Luke 13:10–17; 14:1–6).

Other Pharisees are less convinced of Jesus' sinfulness. In their words, "How can a man who is a sinner perform such signs?" (John 9:16). This sentiment is echoed in the following chapter, when "the Jews" say, "These are not the words of the one who has a demon. Can a demon open the eyes of the blind?" (10:21).

The healed man is brought into the fray of the Pharisees' disparate views on Jesus. They ask him "how?" in three separate scenes. In each instance, the newly sighted man's eyes adjust and glimpse more clearly the holy source of his healing.

While this story's focal point is God's works made manifest in Christ, our text has much to say about one's experience of seeing God in Christ and saying so. The blind man's recognition of his healer's identity is not instantaneous. It comes in stages. It comes by telling his truth in confrontational exchanges with the Pharisees. Interestingly, it comes in the absence of Jesus. Jesus is absent from this story for far longer than in any other episode in the Gospels, from verse 8 through verse 34! In a sense, the blind man becomes a disciple as he gradually "sees" who Jesus is and testifies through a progression of professions: from "the man called Jesus" (9:11) to "a prophet" (v. 17) to a man "from God" (v. 33).

The author of the Fourth Gospel portrays the healed man's response to Jesus in stark contrast to that of the Pharisees. Reflective of the Jewish-Christian tensions in the Johannine community, our text underscores the risk of confessing faith in Jesus (v. 22). If the healed man is a symbolic representative of the Johannine community, then he stands for those who have professed faith in Jesus Christ and have been rejected by the Jewish religious community.

The Johannine Christians' belief that Jesus is the light of the world is shared by early Christians in the second half of the first century. In the epistle text for this Fourth Sunday in Lent, Paul urges the Christian community in Ephesus to *be* the light (Eph. 5:8–9). Perhaps the healed man's brave truth-telling in our text reflects the spirit of the apostle's words.

At the end of our story, the blind man sees and understands. Not only do his eyes open, but his heart opens to the truth about the one who gave him sight. Ultimately, the man declares, "Lord, I believe," and he worships Jesus (v. 38). Conversely, the Pharisees' question, "Surely we are not blind, are we?" (v. 40), seems to provide its own answer. The learned ones who find offense in the suggestion that a healed blind man would have something to teach them about God do not see that the Lord has opened "the eyes of the blind" (Ps. 146:7).

As the preacher alights this text's paths toward the pulpit, she will do well to provide context for the strained ties between "the Jews" and Jesus' first-century followers. She will walk mindfully, of course, around the suggestions that "dark" is bad and "light" is good, and that "the Jews" are blind and Christ's disciples can see. Surely, such binaries have caused much pain in interracial and interfaith relations.

ANDREW NAGY-BENSON

Commentary 2: Connecting the Reading with the World

The Gospel lections for the final two Sundays in Lent are the last two of the seven signs in the section of John's Gospel called the Book of Signs. Each involves what we would name a miracle, but for John his signs are even more than that. Each of them, like a road sign offering a driver critical information about the road that lies ahead, points the reader toward the full disclosure of the truth about Jesus that will be revealed in his crucifixion and resurrection, narrated in the next section of the Gospel, the Book of Glory. Thus these "signs," read and proclaimed at the end of Lent, point the preacher and congregation toward Good Friday and Easter.

The forty-one verses of John's story of the healing of the man born blind, the man's conversion, and the conflict with authorities that ensues, form one of the longest readings the Common Lectionary offers. A worship planner will need to determine whether to read it in its entirety or only one or more portions. There are several natural breaks in the narrative, after verses 12, 17, and 34, for instance, but any editing will affect the focus of the sermon to follow. This lengthy reading is beautifully constructed, a gem with multiple facets offering a wide range of preaching trajectories.

One sermon direction might respond to the question that will rise in the minds of most modern listeners as they hear the first three verses of the reading, namely, the assumption that Jesus' disciples casually make that illness and ill fortune are occasioned by sin: "Rabbi, who sinned, this man or his parents, that he was born blind?" A sermon might remember that this is much the same question unpacked in the book of Job. Jesus' one-sentence response echoes that suggested by the forty-two chapters of Job: "Neither this man nor his parents sinned; he was born blind so that God's works might be revealed in him" (John 9:2).

A sermon might explore the reality that even though moderns generally reject the idea that illness and misfortune are simply the wages of sin, there is something in all of us that is nevertheless attracted to the notion. Part of us longs for a clear causal connection between what I do and what happens to me, simply because it implies that I can closely control my fortune with my behavior. If bad things generally happen to "bad" people, I can avoid them by being "good." I recall a church committee meeting I attended years ago. A member of the committee arrived late with a grim look on his face and explained that a common acquaintance had just been diagnosed with lung cancer. There was silence, followed by someone hesitantly asking the question that was on all our minds, "Did he smoke?" When the answer was yes, a palpable sense of relief rose around the table. His behavior, we could believe, had obviously led to his illness, and if I do not do what he did, I will be OK. It is not so simple, of course, but we are tempted to want it to be truer than it is.

Jesus denies the causal connection, but he does affirm that the man's blindness and healing can still have meaning and purpose: "so that God's works might be revealed in him." In my work as a pastor, I have often counseled people facing loss or tragedy to try to avoid asking the "why?" question and, rather, to struggle to ask the "how?" question. Asking *why* a death has come too early or *why* suffering has suddenly enveloped a good life are questions that usually lead nowhere. Asking *how*—*how* one might find a way through the pain to a strong and vibrant life in spite of it all—is a question with answers. A preacher might remember the familiar but jolting statement attributed to Helen Keller: "I thank God for my handicaps. For through them I have found myself, my work, and my God."

The central portion of the lection focuses on the tension that arises after the healing with persons first identified as "the Pharisees" and then as "the Jews." John's use of the term "the Jews" throughout his Gospel to name Jesus' adversaries has contributed to centuries of Christian anti-Semitism. Indeed, I once heard a Jewish friend refer to John as "that anti-Semitic Gospel." When passages from the Fourth Gospel that speak negatively of "the Jews" are read in worship, a preacher might remind the congregation of several things. First, all the characters in the story are Jews. Jesus was a Jew; Jesus' followers were Jews; and John himself was most surely a Jew. Secondly, John uses the term as a signal word to identify Jesus' opponents in a historical context that did not yet know what would later become anti-Semitism.

John knows that all the players in the story are Jews and uses the term to identify certain members of the Jewish community, principally the power structure in Jerusalem that will later be complicit in Jesus' execution. Finally, the Greek word traditionally translated as "Jews" can just as well be translated as "Judeans." One could faithfully read this and other John lections substituting "the Judeans" for "the Jews."

A sermon might note that the objections that the Pharisees and "the Judeans" raise to Jesus' healing of the man born blind arise initially because he did so on the Sabbath. A sermon might build on a contrast between modern forms of pious but small-minded literalism that lose themselves in "jots and tittles," and faith that gives sight to the blind, even if rules are violated in the process, all the while being careful to vilify neither "the Jews" or "the Pharisees." A wise homiletical mantra declares that whenever Pharisees find their way into a sermon, they must be "us" not "them."

That John understands the contrast between blindness and sight to be metaphorical becomes entirely clear in the last six verses of the lection. The formerly blind man has, gradually, come to "see" who Jesus is. He first names him "the man called Jesus," then "a prophet," next "from God," and finally with the messianic title "the Son of Man." Like most conversions, his is more gradual than precipitous.

"Amazing Grace" has become what is arguably the most popular hymn in the English-speaking world. Its familiar first verse includes the line "I once was blind, but now I see," an obvious echo of verse 25 of the lection. The hymn's author, John Newton, once a slave trader, later came to Christian faith and leadership in the movement to abolish the slave trade. Blindness and sight were for Newton both metaphorical and autobiographical.

At the conclusion of the passage, Jesus suggests that it is the Pharisees who are blind. Another faithful sermon trajectory might explore those things which, metaphorically speaking, make us "blind" today. One might reference the political and cultural "echo chambers" that have become all too common in our time. Politically skewed news outlets, especially on cable television, internet websites that link us only to like-minded blogs, edited social media circles, and our temptation to choose friends, indeed communities, where our perspectives will not be challenged can all work to blind us to the complexity of the issues that face our nation and world. Blindness is not just not seeing; it is also not seeing everything, the whole of truth, all the nuances of reality that can be seen only from perspectives outside the familiarity of our comfort zones.

MICHAEL L. LINDVALL

Fifth Sunday in Lent

Ezekiel 37:1–14
Psalm 130
Romans 8:6–11
John 11:1–45

Ezekiel 37:1–14

1The hand of the LORD came upon me, and he brought me out by the spirit of the
LORD and set me down in the middle of a valley; it was full of bones. 2He led me
all around them; there were very many lying in the valley, and they were very dry.
3He said to me, "Mortal, can these bones live?" I answered, "O Lord GOD, you
know." 4Then he said to me, "Prophesy to these bones, and say to them: O dry
bones, hear the word of the LORD. 5Thus says the Lord GOD to these bones: I will
cause breath to enter you, and you shall live. 6I will lay sinews on you, and will
cause flesh to come upon you, and cover you with skin, and put breath in you,
and you shall live; and you shall know that I am the LORD."
7So I prophesied as I had been commanded; and as I prophesied, suddenly
there was a noise, a rattling, and the bones came together, bone to its bone. 8I
looked, and there were sinews on them, and flesh had come upon them, and
skin had covered them; but there was no breath in them. 9Then he said to me,
"Prophesy to the breath, prophesy, mortal, and say to the breath: Thus says the
Lord GOD: Come from the four winds, O breath, and breathe upon these slain,
that they may live." 10I prophesied as he commanded me, and the breath came
into them, and they lived, and stood on their feet, a vast multitude.
11Then he said to me, "Mortal, these bones are the whole house of Israel. They
say, 'Our bones are dried up, and our hope is lost; we are cut off completely.'
12Therefore prophesy, and say to them, Thus says the Lord GOD: I am going to
open your graves, and bring you up from your graves, O my people; and I will
bring you back to the land of Israel. 13And you shall know that I am the LORD,
when I open your graves, and bring you up from your graves, O my people. 14I will
put my spirit within you, and you shall live, and I will place you on your own soil;
then you shall know that I, the LORD, have spoken and will act, says the LORD."

Commentary 1: Connecting the Reading with Scripture

The exile was not a short event in the life of Israel, lasting longer than the wilderness wanderings after the exodus from Egypt. Perhaps at first it was not hard for the people to keep up their hopes that God would rescue them from Babylon; but as years piled up into decades and they continued to languish in captivity, despair began to replace hope. Finally it had been too long; they considered themselves as good as dead. This is the setting for Ezekiel's chapter 37 vision.

In contrast to the vision in chapter 1, with its opaque and grotesque symbolism, this vision seems fairly transparent. Israel is in exile. The people have nearly given up hope. Their expectation for a better future is as alive as a valley full of dry, disconnected bones. Not only do the bones symbolize death; they stand for ritual uncleanness as well.

When God asks Ezekiel whether or not the bones can live, the prophet gives a careful reply: "O Lord GOD, you know."

If only we could hear the prophet's tone of voice! Perhaps Ezekiel said this with robust confidence. "O God, you know that you can do all things. If you want these bones to live, then of course they will." Ezekiel may not have been able to rouse more than a tired whisper: "O God, I don't know anything anymore. Everything seems bleak. Do you not see how bad off we are? But if anyone knows, you do."

God instructs Ezekiel to prophesy to the bones. Why does God make such a request? Could the Lord not have revived those bones without Ezekiel's help? Well, yes and no. Here we are at a major message of this lection. First, God desires an interactive, cooperative relationship with human beings. This relational nature seems to be so much a part of the definition of the biblical God that an aloof or absolutely separated "God" would be as impossible for the prophets to conceive as a notion of dry rain or frigid fire. Of course the sovereign God could act alone, but God chooses instead to act in concert with human beings. (See also the interaction between God and Job, in chaps. 38–42, esp. 40:3–7, where Job decides to give up the argument, but God urges him to continue.)

Second, the instruction God gives Ezekiel is not random, although it does not seem to be particularly practical. God does not tell Ezekiel to start gathering up the bones or sorting them into skeletons. Rather, the command fits who Ezekiel is as an individual. If Ezekiel had been a singer, God would have said, "Sing to the bones." Had he been a baker, the order would have been, "Bake for the bones." God tells him to prophesy to the bones, because Ezekiel is a prophet. That is, God is not asking him to do something that is outside his nature or something that he is incapable of doing. Notice too that the Lord helps Ezekiel by giving him the message to proclaim. The point can be stated positively as well. It is not just that the divine command is neither impossible nor contrary to Ezekiel's nature. The task God sets for Ezekiel is simply and profoundly to *do* what he *is*.

Ezekiel does not argue or object. He prophesies, and the bones begin to connect to each other. The restoration does not end with bare skeletons; sinews and flesh and skin are added; bodies are formed. They look like people, but they are not alive because "there was no breath in them" (Ezek. 37:8). They are, perhaps, in the state of the first protohuman being of Genesis 2:7 before being enlivened by the breath of God. God gives further orders that Ezekiel prophesy to the breath to enter them. The bodies then come alive and stand up on their feet.

There is a wordplay here that is not possible to capture in a simple English translation. The Hebrew word for "breath" also means "wind," "spirit," and "Spirit." In verses 8, 9, 10, and 14 the same word is translated these different ways. One meaning that can be conveyed in this polyvalent manner is that merely having "breath" does not make one alive. It is the "spirit"/"Spirit" which gives true life. The breath is necessary, of course, but not sufficient. (The parallel obtains also in the Greek of the NT, most familiarly, perhaps, in the conversation between Nicodemus and Jesus in John 3. Cf. John 3:5, 6, 8.)

God then explains the meaning of the vision Ezekiel has just witnessed and participated in. The exiles are saying, "We might as well be dead because we have no future. There is no hope for us." God proclaims that they do indeed have a future because God will revive them and even return them to their homeland. God's spirit will be in them, and they will know the Lord. The culmination of the promise is not only that they will be able to return home, but also that they will know "that I, the Lord, have spoken and will act" (37:14). The source of their hope is not in their own abilities. It is not even in their prophet. The source of their hope is in the God who has not abandoned them, who continues to be with them even in their exile. God does not require the people to do anything here except to be the recipients of the proffered grace, to receive the Spirit of God within them.

Genesis 1:26–27 says humans are created in the image of God, not in the image of each other. Paul uses the metaphor of the body of Christ, with the reminder that bodies are made of different parts, each having its own particular function (1 Cor. 12:12–31). Is this not similar to what can be seen functionally in 1 Samuel 17:31–51? When David approaches King Saul and offers to fight Goliath, Saul gives David his own armor to use. David tries it on, but it does not seem right to him, so he removes and returns it. Rather than using the royal armor and weaponry, David approaches battle "in the name of the Lord" (1 Sam. 17:45–46) *and* with the particular shepherd's skills with the sling that he has spent years honing. Both sides are important: the king is willing to offer and share his equipment. David is willing to try something new. After the trial, however, Saul is willing for David to use what is best for David. The Spirit that we are told came on him at his anointing (1 Sam. 16:13), goes with him to his victory over Goliath. To follow Ezekiel's pattern in this text is to do three simple-sounding things—remembering that simple is not the same as simplistic. First, Ezekiel saw the circumstances of the people as they really were. He did not look at that valley of bones in his vision and say, "Oh, it's not really so bad. Everyone will feel better tomorrow." Second, he was willing to listen for God and listen to God. Finally, whether or not Ezekiel thought it would make any difference in the reality of his world, he did what he heard God ask. What God required of him was none other than to be his own true self and to use what was his own true gift. By being faithful both to his own identity and to the call of God, Ezekiel is the catalyst for the reviving of those bones.

REBECCA ABTS WRIGHT

Commentary 2: Connecting the Reading with the World

The young woman had spoken her mind, acted her truth, and gained the disapproval of the tribe. The elders sentenced her to death. "Throw her off the cliff into the sea!" Now she is a skeleton woman at the bottom of the ocean. Bones picked bare by the fish and bleached by the salt. All alone she waits. For what? To be saved? For new life? Can a disgraced skeleton dare to hope for such things?

So begins the Inuit story of "Skeleton Woman," a profound folktale of death and rebirth.[1] In the story the skeleton is hooked by a fisherman who is lonely and despairing with hunger. When he brings her up from the depths, thinking she is a huge fish, he is so frightened by her staring face full of barnacles and sea worms coming out the eye holes that he forgets to release his hook from her breast bone. He rows furiously back to shore, terrified because, still hooked on his line, she continues following him the whole way. On shore he runs for home, heedless that his line is tangled in his clothing. She rattles close behind. Oblivious in his fear, he brings her all the way into his hut, barring the door behind him, only to turn and discover her leering presence.

Finally he stops. Catching his breath, he sees her in her tangled mess on his floor. The man is moved to a strange pity. Vowing to bury her the next day, he makes a fire. In the light he straightens out her bones into their proper order and covers her with a blanket. Then he falls into his own lonely bed to escape his great hunger in sleep. In the night a small tear escapes his eye. A tear of despair, of longing? A simple, single tear of profound feeling.

Curious, the Skeleton Woman moves close to the man. An enormous thirst rises up in her. A thirst for sustenance, for connection? A thirst for life. She drinks the single tear. It is a deeply satisfying drink. Just enough to give her the courage to reach inside the man's chest and bring out his beating heart. Using it as a drum, the Skeleton Woman sings the flesh back onto her bones until she is a whole woman once again. She returns the man's heart to his chest and climbs beneath his furs into his bed. All night long they give each other comfort and love as two lonely hearts can do when they find one another. In the morning they are no longer despairing. They emerge from the man's hut hand in hand. They never go hungry again. The Skeleton Woman's time in the ocean gives her a special gift for calling fish to the fisherman's hook. With love, they feed the people as well as one another.

Ezekiel, the prophet, tells us his vision of dry, bleached bones covering the desert. A frightening sight. Imagine the jolt to body and soul of being carried away by the Spirit of God, then

1. Christina Pinkola Estes, *Women Who Run with the Wolves; Myths and Stories of the Wild Woman Archetype* (New York: Ballantine Books, 1992), 132–34. "Skeleton Woman" can also be found online. The telling in this essay is original to me.

finding yourself in a valley full of bones as far as the eye can see. The sun beats down upon your head and shines blindingly in your eyes. You cannot step without encountering a bone. They are so dry they are almost crumbling. Imagined eyes stare out empty sockets. Then the Spirit says the most preposterous thing: "Can these bones live?" "O God," you think, "I don't know." Then you realize who has asked. "O God," you reply, "you know."

Ezekiel's vision is familiar, vivid, and much beloved. Hearing it in on a Sunday when Easter is fast approaching, we are tempted to move to the "good" part—the part where the bones do live again! Spirit moves the bones to connect one with another so that they may rise in full bodies and take flesh. Spirit breathes into them the breath of life. "The toe bone connects to the foot bone, the foot bone connects to the ankle bone . . . ," sings the old song joyfully! No more dead bones staring us in the face with their message of despair and failure and defeat. It is best to get past the bones and to the life of the story.

Or is it? In her essay on this story of Spirit's power, Katherine Amos asks a powerful Lenten question. "What can your spiritual dry bones teach you?"[2] What are the dry bones in the life of your spirit? Would you *like* for them to live again? Faced with the foreboding specter of a valley of dead bones, I wonder if one of the prophet's first responses to Spirit's question, "Can these bones live?" is, instinctively, "I certainly hope not!" Who would these bones become? Friend or foe? In his fear, the Inuit fisherman could have put Skeleton Woman out in the snow for the bears and wolves to consume rather than straighten her out by the fire and cover her tenderly with a blanket. Before we ask for new life, perhaps we too can simply sit with our bones. Get to know them. Grieve with them. Let Spirit teach us. Are we ready for the challenge of new life?

What about the spiritual dry bones of your congregation? Who, what, and where are they? What is your prophetic role as pastor and preacher in opening the eyes of your church to see its dry spiritual bones? How will you sit with the people and their bones? What fears and grief could arise? How will you lead the people to pray over and learn from the bones? Where will the compassion for these bones come from in your community? How will you lead the people in surrendering to the power of the Spirit, in discovering where Spirit needs to hover in your community with the breath of life? We can ask the same questions of our denominational associations, jurisdictions, and national organizations. What can our spiritual dry bones teach us as the gathered church in our wider settings?

In the contemporary folktale "The Rabbi's Best Gift," Spirit's movement among the dry spiritual bones of a monastic community comes from an unexpected source, from one outside the community.[3] A rabbi gives an abbot a secret to share among despairing monks: "The Messiah is among you!" Though they never speak the secret, Spirit weaves its gift through the dry bones of their life together, bringing recognition, repentance, and forgiveness. New life comes in abundance.

Living with the rabbi's secret reveals the wounds, the dryness of our spiritual bones. Then Spirit can enliven them as in Ezekiel's vision. Then Spirit as the force of compassion can bring new life as it did to Skeleton Woman through the tears of the Inuit fisherman. Then Spirit as inner wisdom can empower abundance as in the monastery. It all starts with a prophet, a lover, a teacher willing to see the bones.

JANE ANNE FERGUSON

2. Katherine A. Amos, "Pastoral Perspective, Ezekiel 37:1–14," in *Feasting on the Word; Preaching the Revised Common Lectionary, Year A, Volume 2,* ed. David L. Bartlett and Barbara Brown Taylor (Louisville, KY: Westminster John Knox, 2010), 124.

3. William R. White, "The Rabbi's Gift," in *Stories for the Journey: A Sourcebook for Christian Storytellers* (Minneapolis: Augsburg Publishing House, 1988), 108–110.

Psalm 130

[1]Out of the depths I cry to you, O LORD.
  [2]Lord, hear my voice!
Let your ears be attentive
  to the voice of my supplications!

[3]If you, O LORD, should mark iniquities,
  Lord, who could stand?
[4]But there is forgiveness with you,
  so that you may be revered.

[5]I wait for the LORD, my soul waits,
  and in his word I hope;
[6]my soul waits for the Lord
  more than those who watch for the morning,
  more than those who watch for the morning.

[7]O Israel, hope in the LORD!
  For with the LORD there is steadfast love,
  and with him is great power to redeem.
[8]It is he who will redeem Israel
  from all its iniquities.

Connecting the Psalm with Scripture and Worship

A plaintive cry for deliverance opens Psalm 130, giving voice to profound anguish. The psalmist has descended to a point where there is no one to help but God. Described as "the depths" (Ps. 130:1), it is a dark and bleak place in which resources have been exhausted. The way forward is unclear. Fear is close; despair looms. Mustering faith, the psalmist cries to God, begging to be heard. In a reflective way that seems to boost confidence, the psalmist remembers God's persistent mercy (vv. 3–4). Memories of God's past faithfulness build hope for the present. Though still in the depths, the psalmist adopts a posture of anticipation of how God will respond to the cries of help. "I wait for the LORD, my soul waits, and in his word I hope" (v. 5). It is an eager expectation, a waiting even more intense than that of those watching for the dawn of a new day in a dark night (v. 6).

A psalm that begins with lament transitions to hope in just a few lines. By the end of the psalm, the individual experience of the psalmist becomes an encouraging lesson for many, an emphatic plea for Israel to "hope in the LORD" (v. 7). What begins in the depths becomes a resounding affirmation of faith.

The vision of Ezekiel in the day's first lesson begins in a bleak place, a valley of dry bones. Again, we are in the depths. The signs of decay are numerous and stark. The lament is represented in a physical way: the bones are "very many" and "very dry" (Ezek. 37:2). The situation is dire; the possibilities seem grim. Is there a way forward, a way that leads to life? Is there any hope?

The prophet is asked about the future of these dry bones. Ezekiel responds by correctly and humbly acknowledging that the future

Christ the True Door and Anchor

When we know and consider that Christ came down from heaven and loved sinners in obedience to the Father, then there springs up in us a bold approach to and firm hope in Christ. We learn that Christ is the real epistle, the golden book, in which we read and learn how he always kept before him the will of the Father. . . . Now we see that there is no shorter way to the Father except that we love Christ, hope and trust in him, boldly look to him for everything good, learn to know and praise him. For then it will be impossible that we should have a miserable, frightened, dejected conscience; in Christ it will be heartened and refreshed. . . . For when the conscience does not hope and trust in God it cowers and trembles before the purity and righteousness of God. It can have no sweet assurance; it flees and still has nowhere to go unless it finds and catches hold of Christ, the true door and anchor. . . . So God has nothing but the best and he offers it to us, weeds us, sustains us, and cares for us through his Son. That's the way our hearts are changed to follow Christ.

Martin Luther, "Sermon on the Raising of Lazarus," in *Luther's Works, Volume 51: Sermons,* trans. John W. Doberstein, general ed. Helmut T. Lehmann (Philadelphia: Fortress, 1959), 45–47.

belongs to God alone. "O Lord God, you know" (v. 3). Only God is able to reach into a valley so deep; only God can transform bones so dry. It is God's work, but Ezekiel has a part to play, voicing what God seeks to do in animating sinew, tissue, skin, and breath.

Bit by bit, it happens as God directs. Life comes again to the valley. Where dry bones once lay, a vast multitude now stands—breathing, alive, transformed (v. 10). The scene is hope enfleshed, a sign of encouragement to a nation in exile, an inspiration to a people convinced that they would never return from the depths of their despair. The promise of this vision is that God will not leave them in the valley, but rather God will raise them to new life. God's dynamic word transforms the text from a description of death to a promise of life. "I am going to open your graves and bring you up from your graves, O my people; . . . then you shall know that I, the Lord, have spoken and will act" (vv. 12, 14). There is no depth beyond God's reach.

The transformation theme of the Ezekiel 37/Psalm 130 pairing is furthered in the Gospel lesson from John 11. It is another desperate scene. Lazarus is in the tomb dead. The cry of lament comes to Jesus from the depths of the grieving Martha. She knows her brother is dead. She knows the situation is dire. Still, she musters a bit of hope, perhaps drawing on her past experiences of Jesus' mercy for encouragement: "I know that God will give you whatever you ask" (John 11:22). There is a sense of anticipation as Martha speaks, an eagerness resembling that of those who spend a grim night watching for the morning.

The transforming work is for Jesus alone to do, but others have a part in it. The stone is rolled away from the tomb as Jesus directs. He then calls into the deep darkness, "Lazarus, come out!" (v. 43). The dynamic word of Jesus calls forth life from death, and Lazarus stumbles out of the tomb. A story that begins bleakly concludes with a demonstration of love stronger than death. There is no depth beyond God's reach.

As Easter draws near, this Sunday in Lent offers a powerful foretaste of the promise and power of resurrection. These texts provide opportunities for acknowledgment and exploration of the various forms of the deep valley. That bleak place goes by many names: grief, anxiety, illness, despair, loss, fear, doubt, sorrow, and more. It is a place in which we all find ourselves from time to time, a low place where resources seem exhausted and hope feels thin, a dry place starkly filled with signs of decay. Even in that place, the psalm urges us to voice our prayer to God and to cry for deliverance. For as lonely as that valley may feel, God is still present in it. As high as the dry bones are stacked, God insists on life. As tightly as the tomb is sealed, God refuses to let death have the last word.

A sermon taking note of the drear and darkness of the depths where we inevitably have to travel will also want to point to signs of hope relentlessly, even impossibly, pushing through the barrenness. What are the signs of a breaking new day? Where is the surprising and fresh connection of sinew, tissue, and skin? Where have we sensed the animating breath that revitalizes? Where have we seen one stumbling out of the grave, who, though still in need of unbinding, is resolutely reaching for God's future?

JOHN W. WURSTER

Romans 8:6–11

[6]To set the mind on the flesh is death, but to set the mind on the Spirit is life and peace. [7]For this reason the mind that is set on the flesh is hostile to God; it does not submit to God's law—indeed it cannot, [8]and those who are in the flesh cannot please God.

[9]But you are not in the flesh; you are in the Spirit, since the Spirit of God dwells in you. Anyone who does not have the Spirit of Christ does not belong to him. [10]But if Christ is in you, though the body is dead because of sin, the Spirit is life because of righteousness. [11]If the Spirit of him who raised Jesus from the dead dwells in you, he who raised Christ from the dead will give life to your mortal bodies also through his Spirit that dwells in you.

Commentary 1: Connecting the Reading with Scripture

The lectionary reading from Romans is part of a larger unit (Rom. 8:1–11) in which Paul celebrates Christian freedom from the "condemnation" of the law (v. 1). In the previous chapter Paul argues that the ultimate effect of the Mosaic law is to make humans aware of their own sinfulness (7:7–13). He is careful not to say that the law is the source of sin (7:7), but that the law has no power to free a person from it. It can only point out what is sinful. When a person knows the law, that knowledge generates a heightened awareness of disobedience. Paul uses the example of the Tenth Commandment, "You shall not covet" (Exod. 20:17; Deut. 5:21). He says that just knowing the command made him more aware of how much he coveted! Then in Romans 7:14–25 Paul laments the state of humans who are left to wallow in their own guilt because they cannot obey the law. In verse 24 Paul sums up the frustration over his disobedience when he exclaims "Wretched man that I am! Who will rescue me from the body of death?" The answer is Jesus Christ (Rom. 7:25). Jesus did what the law could not do. By taking on flesh in Jesus Christ, God overcame the sin humans experience in the flesh (8:3). Paul now contrasts the life of faith in Jesus Christ, which he calls life in the Sprit, with the attempt to obey the law, which he refers to as life in the flesh (8:5).

Romans 8:6–11 presents a distinct message within this section of Romans. The passage has two parts. Verses 6–8 expound a principle based on the argument in previous verses. Verse 6 expresses it in sum: "To set the mind on the flesh is death, but to set the mind on the Spirit is life and peace." In verses 7–8 Paul goes further to say that the mind "set on the flesh" directly opposes God and cannot please God.

The second part of the passage (vv. 9–11) begins with a declaration and expounds on it: "But you are not in the flesh; you are in the Spirit" (v. 9). Here Paul argues that the Spirit of God who raised Jesus from the dead dwells within those who have accepted the saving power of Christ's death. The result is that those who were once "dead" because of sin now have life because of God's righteousness (v. 10). This is the culmination of what Paul celebrates in Romans 8:1–11: believers now have life, because the Spirit of God lives within them.

Paul's argument rests on his understanding of several key terms: "body," "flesh," and "Spirit." For Paul there is no human life without a body. A body is necessary for existence in the present life and in the life to come. So, when Paul speaks of the believer's transformation in the age to come, he talks in terms of getting a new body that is imperishable (1 Cor. 15:42–44). Thus the word "body" refers to our existence as humans and as the possibility of relating to others.[1]

In this way of thinking, the body is not good or bad; it is simply the reality of human existence. Since the world is dominated by forces that oppose God's purpose, Paul recognizes that our bodily existence can be dominated by the tendency to rebel against God. So Paul sometimes speaks of the "body of death" (Rom. 7:24). The body is "dead" because of sin (8:10). Here "death" refers to a state of being out of touch with the intentions and work of the Creator. When Paul speaks of death in Romans 8:6–11, he refers to an orientation toward the world dominated by sin. As he says in Romans 7:13, "It was sin, working death in me."

The main word Paul uses for this death-orientation is "flesh." "Flesh" can refer to the physical body, but Paul mainly uses it figuratively. The physical body represents a human-generated effort to direct one's life. Paul insists in Romans 7:14–25 that such efforts lead only to failure, for the human is not capable of obedience. Thus he says the law is "weakened by the flesh" (8:3). It is a human effort to please God, and therefore it is ultimately futile. The opposite of flesh is Spirit. "Spirit" connotes that orientation to the world through God's work on our behalf, that is, through Christ's death and resurrection.

In Romans 8:12–17 Paul further clarifies the difference between flesh and Spirit with a concrete image. Living "according to the flesh" is like being a slave (vv. 12, 15). Most slaves in Paul's world were debt slaves. They worked to pay what they owed the master. All the work they did, therefore, grew out of obligation. Paul says living "by the Spirit" is like being adopted into a family (vv. 15–17). As members of God's family, our relationship with God has changed completely. We no longer work to pay off a debt, for there is none. In fact, we are heirs to the riches of God's household (v. 17). Therefore, our work for God is not obligation, but a sign of gratitude.

As Paul makes his argument about being "in the Spirit," he seems to draw ideas from the prophet Ezekiel, who declared that God would give Israel "a new spirit" that would allow them to obey the law (Ezek. 11:19; 36:27). Ezekiel was addressing the same reality as Paul: God's people were not capable of obeying God's commands. The only hope was for God to transform them, which is what Ezekiel says God would do. Ezekiel describes the transformation in terms of God replacing Israel's "heart of stone" with a "heart of flesh" (11:19; 36:26). The people would become obedient because God would give them God's spirit (36:27, "I will put my spirit within you").

Romans 8:6–11 connects with the other lections for the Fifth Sunday in Lent in its promise that God gives new life to believers and redeems them from sin (the main connection to Ps. 130). Ezekiel 37:1–14 and John 11:1–45 are classic resurrection texts. Paul's promise that God will "give life to your mortal bodies" speaks in concert with them (Rom. 8:11). Pairing Romans 8:6–11 with Ezekiel 37:1–14 gives opportunity to acknowledge that the New Testament belief in resurrection is rooted in the Old Testament. Ezekiel's vision of dry bones expresses the conviction that God is a God of life, and God's spirit is at work to bring the dead to life (Ezek. 37:1, 5, 6, 9, 10).[2]

Romans 8:6–11 fits within the larger Christian canon also through this notion that God is the God of life, and the primary work of God's Spirit is to bring and sustain life. This appears first in Genesis 1:2. The world was "a formless void" and thus not able to sustain life; but the Spirit of God was hovering over the chaotic waters. The Spirit of God is the animating force in the world. Thus, the Hebrew word *ruach* may be translated also "wind" or "breath." The NIV prefers "Spirit" in most cases. This connects with Paul's comments about the life-giving Spirit in Romans 8:6–11. The theme appears in many OT texts, particularly psalms that affirm that God rescues the faithful from the grave (Ps. 16:10–11).

JEROME F. D. CREACH

1. Paul J. Achtemeier, *Romans*, Interpretation (Atlanta: John Knox, 1988), 132–33.
2. Jon D. Levenson, *Resurrection and the Restoration of Israel: The Ultimate Victory of the God of Life* (New Haven, CT: Yale University Press, 2008).

Commentary 2: Connecting the Reading with the World

These six verses in Romans 8 are densely packed, less like something organic whose parts work together and more like random items crowded together in an attic. Instead of forcing connections that Paul apparently did not make, let us examine these verses on their own terms.

Paul's unfortunate flesh/spirit dualism, where flesh equals death and spirit equals life, has wreaked havoc of all kinds throughout Christian history. Late-twentieth-century Christian feminist critiques were perhaps the most pointed, noting that flesh became associated with females and spirit with males, reinforcing a gendered hierarchy in church institutions, and well beyond. Alongside and sometimes entwined with the feminist critique is the damage done by Christianity's denigration of the body, its pleasures, its sensual connection to its natural context, human sexuality—the list goes on. Guilt and shame became the cloaks in which the Christian body was adorned. While Paul is not solely responsible for this trajectory, he is surely one of its prominent contributors.

Christian spiritual practice, then, often involved denial of physical pleasure. In fact, physical pleasure was seen as antithetical to Christian spirituality; and thanks to Augustine, we have a graphic memoir of the conflict. The desert fathers and mothers engaged in a range of ascetic practices. "Mortification of the flesh" is a phrase that belongs in the history, and perhaps the present, of Christian spiritual life. Flesh = death, and spirit = life.

The negativity and warnings of verses 6–8 give way to the main thrust of our passage, which is harmony with God and communion with Christ. Paul's claim that those who are "of the Spirit" have Christ in them (Rom. 8:10) is a claim about intimacy. Likewise, the statement that God's Spirit dwells in those who live in the Spirit (v. 11) is remarkable, if unremarkably Pauline. It is as though there is a new spiritual energy available in the world, one not dependent upon any specific set of behavioral requirements, but only on a relationship, an intimate relationship at that, with God as revealed in Christ.

Let us pause here and ask ourselves what it might mean to "have the Spirit of Christ," or to have "Christ in you," or to have God's Spirit indwelling Christian believers. Paul is pointing us to a mystery here, but what mystery? I think he is evoking a kind of attraction, like a love affair, one that is profound and undeniable. In fact, I read this as Paul's suggestions of a mystical connection between believers and God, a sense of being overtaken, of being filled with the Spirit of Christ such that there can be no other passion. It is as though intimacy with Christ, with God, leaves no room, no spiritual space, for that which is not of God.

A fun exercise in a classroom or just about any other setting is to ask folks to tell the group why they love someone whom they love, to convince the rest of us that this person is lovable. It is, of course, an impossible task, since verbal descriptions can reach only observable qualities and actions; and love is way beyond those, much deeper and more inchoate than we can articulate. I know Paul does not here use the word "love," but when I read this passage, I am reminded of that pedagogical exercise. Just as in the classroom setting, persons end up just speaking more loudly and then finally giving up trying to articulate love, so in Romans, Paul's often convoluted arguments are attempts to articulate a mystery, albeit a common mystery, an available mystery, of intimacy with God. Even Paul can only point to, but not articulate, the ineffable.

We need to recall that in many cases, extreme Christian asceticism was in service of mystical connection with God. Denial of "the flesh" was not usually for its own sake. Though there are surely examples of pathological behavior, to label all extreme Christian ascetic practices as pathological would be a shallow reading of the history of Christian spiritual practices. On the other hand, it is important to note that in Romans 8:6–11, intimacy with God is not something that human activity brings about. No set of precepts, behavioral guidelines, even laws can create it; only hearing the gospel and giving oneself over to it will result in being "in the Spirit." Elsewhere in Romans and in his other writings, Paul speaks about the "fruits of the Spirit" being a varying list of good behaviors. There is no doubt that living "in the Spirit" has an ethical dimension. However, this passage makes it clear that intimacy with the Divine is the core of Christian life.

Verse 11 announces the third item in this dense set, a startling if somewhat understated consequence of life in the Spirit: bodily resurrection. It is a startling claim in at least two ways. First of all, it highlights a disconnect between Paul's use of the term "flesh" to denote sinful life and his belief in, and claim of, bodily resurrection. Surely if human flesh were as negative as Paul depicts it, resurrection would be only spiritual in nature, with the spirit leaving the body behind and enjoying freedom for eternity. Jesus' bodily resurrection with its universe-altering consequences does not allow Paul to take that path. Yet the verses themselves convey no sense of tension between "flesh" and "bodily resurrection." Somehow, they stand comfortably side by side in Paul's teachings.

Second, bodily resurrection for all believers, eternal life with God, is an enormous promise; but here it is mentioned almost as an aside. It certainly is not offered up as an incentive for accepting the life in the Spirit, as I would think it could. Rather, it is mentioned as a quiet outcome of the more important, distinctive life in the Spirit before death.

Here the historical/cultural distance between the communities in which I participate and the community in Rome to which Paul wrote is pronounced. In my liberal Christian context, any discussion of bodily resurrection will catch folks' attention. By and large we do not mention it. When we do, it is with caveats about the difference between something being literal and something being true; or we note that belief in a bodily resurrection is not a requirement for participation in our community (contra Paul!), and so on. Paul's casual mention of bodily resurrection here is most simply explained, I think, by the assumption that it was taken for granted as a part of the Christian gospel. Like the negativity of the flesh, bodily resurrection was a common Christian truth in the Roman community.

What of the intimacy with God, with Christ, that this passage lifts up? Must we leave it behind, with our questions about bodily resurrection? I think not. Like a love affair, that intimacy begins with longing; and longing for God has not vanished from our world. There are many Christian—and for that matter non-Christian—people today helping to lead people closer to God. Christian meditation has seen a resurgence. New forms of worship are being created, even as the old forms seem to have lost some of their power. In fact, we may be in the midst of a spiritual revolution that will open new pathways to intimate, even mystical connections.

With all its complexity, negative impact on Christians' views of the body, and perhaps inconsistency, this passage reminds us that the gospel offers intimacy with God, for anyone in any context. That is good news indeed.

SALLY B. PURVIS

Fifth Sunday in Lent

John 11:1–45

1Now a certain man was ill, Lazarus of Bethany, the village of Mary and her sister
Martha. 2Mary was the one who anointed the Lord with perfume and wiped his
feet with her hair; her brother Lazarus was ill. 3So the sisters sent a message to
Jesus, "Lord, he whom you love is ill." 4But when Jesus heard it, he said, "This
illness does not lead to death; rather it is for God's glory, so that the Son of God
may be glorified through it." 5Accordingly, though Jesus loved Martha and her
sister and Lazarus, 6after having heard that Lazarus was ill, he stayed two days
longer in the place where he was.

7Then after this he said to the disciples, "Let us go to Judea again." 8The disciples said to him, "Rabbi, the Jews were just now trying to stone you, and are you
going there again?" 9Jesus answered, "Are there not twelve hours of daylight?
Those who walk during the day do not stumble, because they see the light of this
world. 10But those who walk at night stumble, because the light is not in them."
11After saying this, he told them, "Our friend Lazarus has fallen asleep, but I am
going there to awaken him." 12The disciples said to him, "Lord, if he has fallen
asleep, he will be all right." 13Jesus, however, had been speaking about his death,
but they thought that he was referring merely to sleep. 14Then Jesus told them
plainly, "Lazarus is dead. 15For your sake I am glad I was not there, so that you
may believe. But let us go to him." 16Thomas, who was called the Twin, said to his
fellow disciples, "Let us also go, that we may die with him."

17When Jesus arrived, he found that Lazarus had already been in the tomb
four days. 18Now Bethany was near Jerusalem, some two miles away, 19and many
of the Jews had come to Martha and Mary to console them about their brother.
20When Martha heard that Jesus was coming, she went and met him, while Mary
stayed at home. 21Martha said to Jesus, "Lord, if you had been here, my brother
would not have died. 22But even now I know that God will give you whatever
you ask of him." 23Jesus said to her, "Your brother will rise again." 24Martha said
to him, "I know that he will rise again in the resurrection on the last day." 25Jesus
said to her, "I am the resurrection and the life. Those who believe in me, even
though they die, will live, 26and everyone who lives and believes in me will never
die. Do you believe this?" 27She said to him, "Yes, Lord, I believe that you are the
Messiah, the Son of God, the one coming into the world."

28When she had said this, she went back and called her sister Mary, and told
her privately, "The Teacher is here and is calling for you." 29And when she heard
it, she got up quickly and went to him. 30Now Jesus had not yet come to the village, but was still at the place where Martha had met him. 31The Jews who were
with her in the house, consoling her, saw Mary get up quickly and go out. They
followed her because they thought that she was going to the tomb to weep
there. 32When Mary came where Jesus was and saw him, she knelt at his feet
and said to him, "Lord, if you had been here, my brother would not have died."
33When Jesus saw her weeping, and the Jews who came with her also weeping,
he was greatly disturbed in spirit and deeply moved. 34He said, "Where have you
laid him?" They said to him, "Lord, come and see." 35Jesus began to weep. 36So
the Jews said, "See how he loved him!" 37But some of them said, "Could not he
who opened the eyes of the blind man have kept this man from dying?"

38Then Jesus, again greatly disturbed, came to the tomb. It was a cave, and a
stone was lying against it. 39Jesus said, "Take away the stone." Martha, the sister

of the dead man, said to him, "Lord, already there is a stench because he has
been dead four days." 40Jesus said to her, "Did I not tell you that if you believed,
you would see the glory of God?" 41So they took away the stone. And Jesus
looked upward and said, "Father, I thank you for having heard me. 42I knew that
you always hear me, but I have said this for the sake of the crowd standing here,
so that they may believe that you sent me." 43When he had said this, he cried with
a loud voice, "Lazarus, come out!" 44The dead man came out, his hands and feet
bound with strips of cloth, and his face wrapped in a cloth. Jesus said to them,
"Unbind him, and let him go."
45Many of the Jews therefore, who had come with Mary and had seen what
Jesus did, believed in him.

Commentary 1: Connecting the Reading with Scripture

Throughout the Gospel of John, Jesus demonstrates power to give life. From the opening verses of the prologue, Jesus (the Word) is the source of all creation (John 1:3). He also brings into the world "eternal life"—a life-force stronger than death and the wellspring of abundant living. For John, eternal life is given, here and now, to those who believe "that Jesus is the Messiah, the Son of God" (John 20:31). At the heart of our Gospel passage lies the miracle of life given. At the heart of the miracle lies an invitation to believe that Jesus is sent from God.

The opening verses of our text signal a belief in Jesus. Martha and Mary send word to Jesus that their brother Lazarus is ill. The nature of his illness is unnamed, but the reality of Lazarus's condition is clear; the words "ill" or "illness" appear in each of the first five verses of our text. The sisters' initial message to Jesus suggests considerable confidence in Jesus' power to heal their brother.

Martha and Mary's confidence in Christ is made explicit when they see him in Bethany. Martha meets Jesus and the disciples on the outskirts of town and says to him, "'Lord, if you had been here, my brother would not have died'" (11:21). Later, Mary greets Jesus the same way (v. 32). Furthermore, "the Jews" who accompany Mary ask a rhetorical question among themselves: "Could not he who opened the eyes of the blind man have kept this man from dying?'" (v. 37). There seems to be no question that Jesus *could have* healed Lazarus, which helps to explain the sisters' accusatory tone.

We need not soften the hard edges of Mary and Martha's complaint or the Jews' question. The spirit of their words belongs to an ancient tradition of crying out to God. The book of Psalms, in particular, provides ample context for the complaints brought to Jesus (Pss. 13; 77:7–10; 88; 142:1–2).

Martha and Mary would have reason to hope that Jesus could make Lazarus well. Jesus has demonstrated great power to heal the infirm and the blind prior to this scene in Bethany (4:43–54; 5:1–19; 9:1–41). The healing of the royal official's dying son seems particularly noteworthy, as it portrays Jesus' ability to heal a dying boy from a distance (4:43–54). With this story in mind, one could wonder why Jesus does not extend healing from afar to Lazarus, and similarly, why Jesus delays his trip to Bethany by two days.

These curiosities lead us closer to the central message of this text. By his own admission, Jesus has something other than healing in mind. When the sisters' message reaches Jesus, he frames Lazarus's grave illness in terms of the Son of God's power to bring about life—even in places where death's shadow is dark (2:11; 9:3; 11:40; 13:31–32; 14:13; 17:1). Mary and Martha's faith that Jesus could heal their brother is not misplaced; there is simply more to the message that Jesus needs to deliver, a message expressed in Paul's Letter to the Romans (Rom. 8:38–39).

The disciples may labor to read Jesus' mind and to understand what Lazarus' illness has to do with "God's glory" (John 11:4). Nevertheless, when Jesus states his intentions to go to Bethany, the disciples understand very well the risks involved. Their concern is warranted. Earlier in the Fourth Gospel, after a contentious exchange with Jewish leaders in which Jesus reveals his divine identity (8:24; 58), Jesus' opponents "picked up stones to throw at him" (8:59). Later, Jesus and "the Jews" verbally spar again; when Jesus says, "the Father and I are one" (10:30), the crowd "took up stones again to stone him" (10:31).

The disciples' caution also serves to remind us of Jesus' teaching in the previous chapter. Jesus' willingness to go to Bethany, at great risk to himself, underscores the meaning of "I am the good shepherd. The good shepherd lays down his life for the sheep'" (10:11). In a similar vein, the disciples' concern serves to foreshadow the Jewish leaders' response to the raising of Lazarus. Immediately after our Gospel lesson, news that Lazarus has been raised reaches the Pharisees and chief priests, and after much handwringing "they planned to put [Jesus] to death" (11:53).

When the Good Shepherd arrives in Bethany, we learn (with Jesus and the disciples) that Lazarus died four days earlier (v. 17). What follows is an important, two-part exchange between Jesus and Martha. First, Jesus tells his friend that her brother will "rise again" (v. 23). Martha believes this. She has given her heart to the Jewish concept of a final resurrection in the messianic age, an idea stunningly conveyed by Ezekiel's vision of the valley of dry bones and expressed, albeit in less dramatic ways, in the New Testament (Mark 12:18–27; Acts 23:6–8; 24:15, 21).

Second, Jesus conveys his own stunning truths to Martha. In essence, Jesus brings the promise of future resurrection into the present; death has no power, today or tomorrow, over those who believe in him (John 5:28–29; 6:39–40, 44, 54). He also brings eternal life into the here and now; abundant life is given to those who believe in him (3:16, 36; 5:24; 6:47; 10:28; 17:2). With this, Jesus asks Martha if she believes, and she replies with one of the most astounding confessions in the Fourth Gospel: "'Yes, Lord, I believe that you are the Messiah, the Son of God, the one coming into the world'" (11:27).

Martha then exits the Gospel stage, and Mary enters. The mood changes. Few words are exchanged between Jesus and Mary, but the emotional intensity climbs. Mary kneels at Jesus' feet, as she will in chapter 12 when she anoints Christ's feet with costly perfume (12:1–8). Mary is weeping in grief. Jesus himself is "greatly disturbed" and "deeply moved," and he weeps as well.

Even in his emotional state, Jesus drives the narrative to its conclusion. At the tomb, Jesus orders the stone to be removed. Jesus asks for the stone to be moved and for the crowd to withstand the stench of death, "so that" (11:42) they will see the glory of God and may believe that Jesus is sent by God. With three startling words—"Lazarus, come out!"—comes a most startling sight: "the dead man came out, his hands and feet bound with strips of cloth, and his face wrapped in a cloth" (vv. 43–44). With six more startling words, Lazarus is unbound and freed.

John's account of the raising of Lazarus can be celebrated for its elaborate telling and its theological heights. If the Gospel of John were a range of high peaks, chapter 11 would be among its most majestic. However, this story of Lazarus is not the only one of its kind in Scripture. There are several other stories that tell of a dead person being brought to life (1 Kgs. 17:17–24; 2 Kgs. 4:18–37; Luke 7:11–15; 8:49–55; Acts 9:36–41.)

Each of these stories, like our Gospel text, is well beyond logical explanation. Yet explaining how these miracles occur is not the point. The central issue, especially for John, is the response of those who witness the inexplicable revelation of God. As our Gospel text ends, "Many of the Jews . . . who had seen what Jesus did, believed in him" (John 11:45). Believed in him. This is what the Fourth Gospel's Jesus wants to know: how will you respond to the life-giving power of God *in me*?

ANDREW NAGY-BENSON

Commentary 2: Connecting the Reading with the World

On this Last Sunday in Lent, the lectionary offers the last of Jesus' seven signs in John's Book of Signs. Like the others, this sign points toward the full disclosure of who Jesus is and the nature of God's way in the world, truths that are to be revealed in the drama of crucifixion and resurrection of the Book of Glory. This last sign is the boldest of them all: Jesus gives life to the dead. John offers the raising of Lazarus from the grave as a dramatic harbinger of Jesus' own resurrection, but remember that Lazarus is merely resuscitated; he lives to die another day. Jesus' resurrection is of a different kind. It is resurrection and no mere resuscitation, the hinge point in human history, the definitive triumph over death that offers eternal life to all. John, unlike the Synoptic Gospels, understands the raising of Lazarus to be the critical act that leads directly to the conspiracy to crucify Jesus. So, ironically, in John's Gospel Jesus' giving of life to another leads to his own death. (Do note that this connection is made only in the last verses of chapter 11, which lie outside the assigned lection for the day.) The obvious challenge facing the preacher is to proclaim this passage about triumphant life in a way that does not become too much like an Easter sermon on this Last Sunday in Lent.

Embedded in this long narrative is a series of verses affirming the vulnerability, compassion, and love of Jesus. Verse 3 has Lazarus's sisters communicate to Jesus, "He whom you love is ill." Verse 5 tells us that "Jesus loved Martha and her sister and Lazarus." When Jesus sees the sisters weeping, verse 33 tells us that "he was greatly disturbed in spirit." In verse 35, as he is about to be shown the tomb of his friend, John tells us that "Jesus began weeping." In verse 36, fellow Jews who have come to comfort the sisters see Jesus in tears and comment, "See how he loved him." Finally, in verse 38, as he approaches the tomb, Jesus is "again greatly disturbed."

Christians, steeped in a faith that assumes divine compassion, love, and even vulnerability, often forget how radically peculiar it is to ascribe such attributes to God, as seen here through Jesus. In the long and diverse history of theism, God has more often been imagined as distant and impassive, if not angry and punitive. The love, compassion, indeed vulnerability (this last to be made brutally clear in the crucifixion) of God that are so transparent in this lection are central to the Christian understanding of the Divine. In a culture more comfortable with a vague divine transcendence than an insistent divine immanence, such a reminder of our understanding of God would be particularly fitting in Lent. Further reading on this theme might include William Placher's classic 1994 book *Narratives of a Vulnerable God.*[1]

The core theme of the lection—even more than Jesus' love, compassion, and vulnerability—is the defiance of death. Jesus does not just raise Lazarus from the grave; he mocks the grave in his almost blasé attitude toward the last enemy. He says, "This illness does not lead to death," and then waits two days before setting out for Bethany, refusing to let death set his agenda. Later, but before he goes to Lazarus's tomb, he declares to Martha, "I am the resurrection and the life. Those who believe in me, even though they die, will live" (11:25).

Such a ringing affirmation of life, both physical and spiritual, is a word that aches to be spoken in a world grown inured to its own cultures of death. The distant Syrian and Afghan wars plod on, taking thousands of lives with no conclusion in sight. Fallen from the news cycle, the death they rain on innocents evokes little outrage. An unprecedented opioid addiction crisis ravages our nation, so deadly that it has actually led to a decline in average life expectancy, yet our political leadership makes but the feeblest of responses. Mass shootings, often in schools, have become so regular that we have become numb to their abject horror, but a nation locked in culture war and a bottomless debate about guns does next to nothing. All summed up, such cultural indifference to death stands in starkest contrast to Jesus' defiance of death and insistence on life, the theme most central to this story.

The twin facts that Jesus knew and loved Lazarus, and that Lazarus is given his life back, have naturally led to speculation about Lazarus's life before and after that day in Bethany. Fictional works such as Richard Zimler's 2016 novel *The Gospel according to Lazarus*[2] imagine Jesus and Lazarus to have been childhood friends. Eastern Christian tradition suggests that Lazarus lived another thirty years and was appointed by Paul and Barnabas to be the first bishop of Kition, modern Larnaka, in Cyprus.

1. William C. Placher, *Narratives of a Vulnerable God: Christ, Theology, and Scripture* (Louisville, KY: Westminster John Knox, 1994).
2. Richard Zimler, *The Gospel according to Lazarus* (London: Peter Owen Publishers, 2016).

Western church tradition made him bishop of Marseilles in France.

Such speculation, however questionable, might provide a door into a sermon reflecting on the truth that when each of us awakens each morning, we are like Lazarus, given the gift of yet more life. Such a parallel should invite us to remember that our waking is a gift, a grace for which we are rightly thankful. It invites the very question that led to traditions about Lazarus's later life, namely, just how are we to spend the precious "Lazarus life" we are given upon waking? Indeed, the lection itself references this obvious metaphor: sleep and waking lying parallel to death and life. In a culture too often characterized by an overwrought sense of entitlement, a sermon on the story of the raising of Lazarus might offer a strong affirmation of the raw giftedness of this life, precious and undeserved as it is, and the claim it makes upon us to use the gift well.

A pastor once was privileged to read a portion of the diary of a young man who had put thoughts to paper one late night in a hospital room while sitting beside his critically ill wife. He waited and worried, wondered and wrote through the night. Toward morning the young man wrote that, in spite of the possibility of his wife's death, he could not feel that life had dealt him an injustice. The time during which his wife had been in his life came to him as gift, one that he had neither brought about nor deserved. Although he had himself not lived what most would consider a full measure of years, were his own life to end that day he would count himself more fortunate than so many whose lives had ended sooner, and who had received less happiness than he had. At the end, the young husband thanked God for the miracle of his life and that of his beloved, and the gift, at least for that moment, of being together.

MICHAEL L. LINDVALL

Liturgy of the Palms

Psalm 118:1–2, 19–29 Matthew 21:1–11

Psalm 118:1–2, 19–29

1O give thanks to the LORD, for he is good;
his steadfast love endures forever!

2Let Israel say,
"His steadfast love endures forever."

. . . .

19Open to me the gates of righteousness,
that I may enter through them
and give thanks to the LORD.

20This is the gate of the LORD;
the righteous shall enter through it.

21I thank you that you have answered me
and have become my salvation.
22The stone that the builders rejected
has become the chief cornerstone.
23This is the LORD's doing;
it is marvelous in our eyes.
24This is the day that the LORD has made;
let us rejoice and be glad in it.
25Save us, we beseech you, O LORD!
O LORD, we beseech you, give us success!

26Blessed is the one who comes in the name of the LORD.
We bless you from the house of the LORD.
27The LORD is God,
and he has given us light.
Bind the festal procession with branches,
up to the horns of the altar.

28You are my God, and I will give thanks to you;
you are my God, I will extol you.

29O give thanks to the LORD, for he is good,
for his steadfast love endures forever.

Connecting the Psalm with Scripture and Worship

Psalm 118 begins by laying a foundation emphasizing God's faithfulness. Each of the first four verses affirms that God's "steadfast love endures forever." The verses omitted in the lection (Ps. 118:3–18) describe the psalmist's experience of deliverance through God's merciful acts. Having been saved by God's hand, the psalmist arrives at the gates of the temple in verse 19, and the appointed passage resumes. The grateful psalmist seeks to enter the gates to offer thanksgiving to God. Here is the classic cycle of grace and gratitude: the experience of God's steadfast love evokes thanksgiving. "I thank you that you have answered me and have become my salvation" (v. 21).

As the psalm continues, a chorus of voices joins the psalmist, amplifying the praise of God's gracious activity. God's deeds are acknowledged and celebrated: "This is the LORD's doing; it is marvelous in our eyes. This is the day that the LORD has made; let us rejoice and be glad in it" (vv. 23–24). God's persistent grace flows forth day by day. Each day is to be received with gratitude and joy. The choir moves in verse 26 to bestow a blessing upon the one entering the gates, the "one who comes in the name of the LORD." This solo voice returns in verse 28 to continue the psalmist's act of gratitude. As it concludes, the psalm expands from this single scene of thanksgiving to return to the general affirmation with which it began: "O give thanks to the LORD, for [God] is good, for [God's] steadfast love endures forever" (v. 29).

God's faithful love through the ages takes a particular shape as a congregation gathers on Palm Sunday. Psalm 118 almost functions as a script as Matthew describes Jesus' triumphal entry into Jerusalem in this day's Gospel lesson. The love of God expressed through the generations is present and vital as Jesus enters the city. God's deliverance is at hand again. *Let us give thanks for what God is doing this day. Let us give thanks for God is good this day.* Jesus enfleshes God's goodness, and the crowds respond to Jesus with shouts of praise. He is the one who comes in the name of the Lord (Matt. 21:9). The cries of "Hosanna" that come from the people's lips rehearse the song of the choir in Psalm 118:25: "Save us" (*hoshiana*). The spreading of leafy branches on the road as Jesus rides along correlates with the instruction in Psalm 118:27b: "Bind the festal procession with branches." The promise of the psalm is being enacted in a dramatic way, and the enthusiasm of the parade places the "whole city" in "turmoil" (Matt. 21:10).

While not in his Palm Sunday account, Psalm 118:22 holds significance for Matthew. The writer retains this verse ("the stone that the builders rejected has become the chief cornerstone") for a bit later in chapter 21, where it is quoted by Jesus as part of a stinging attack on the religious authorities (21:42). This stunning reversal, whereby that which has been rejected in turn becomes central, is puzzling in the context of the psalm, where it seems out of place, disrupting the experience of deliverance and the song of praise and thanksgiving.

Matthew, however, seizes upon this verse as crucially reflective of God's amazing work, which is inherently disruptive. The humble Jesus receives a triumphant reception. The crucified Jesus is raised from the dead. His teaching lifts up the lowly. His deeds bring healing to the sick. The gospel is outside of the usual categories and the customary expectations. Stones that seem worthless to many are in fact crucial. This reappraisal is the Lord's doing. It is marvelous and amazing.

Several verses of Psalm 118 have long been a part of the liturgical manual for the church. Who does not have at the ready for use as a call to worship verse 24, "This is the day the LORD has made; let us rejoice and be glad in it"? At the Lord's Table the *Sanctus*, sung or spoken, regularly keeps before us verse 26, "Blessed is the one who comes in the name of the LORD." Another liturgically useful phrase is the one that occurs most frequently in the psalm, "O give thanks to the LORD, for [God] is good; [God's] steadfast love endures forever." This verse could function as a refrain in a litany of a thanksgiving, chronicling experiences of grace, past and present, and offering affirmations of God's enduring love.

More particularly, at the beginning of Holy Week, a litany could be crafted highlighting key moments of Jesus' passion, starting with his procession into Jerusalem and then on to his praying in the garden, his betrayal, his arrest, his denial, his trial, his beating, and his crucifixion. After each of these moments is invoked, the congregation would affirm that God's steadfast love endures forever, even in the midst of such sorrow and agony, especially in the midst of such sorrow and agony. It is boundless love, love for which to be ever thankful.

JOHN W. WURSTER

Matthew 21:1–11

[1]When they had come near Jerusalem and had reached Bethphage, at the Mount of Olives, Jesus sent two disciples, [2]saying to them, "Go into the village ahead of you, and immediately you will find a donkey tied, and a colt with her; untie them and bring them to me. [3]If anyone says anything to you, just say this, 'The Lord needs them.' And he will send them immediately." [4]This took place to fulfill what had been spoken through the prophet, saying,

> [5]"Tell the daughter of Zion,
> Look, your king is coming to you,
> humble, and mounted on a donkey,
> and on a colt, the foal of a donkey."

[6]The disciples went and did as Jesus had directed them; [7]they brought the donkey and the colt, and put their cloaks on them, and he sat on them. [8]A very large crowd spread their cloaks on the road, and others cut branches from the trees and spread them on the road. [9]The crowds that went ahead of him and that followed were shouting,

> "Hosanna to the Son of David!
> Blessed is the one who comes in the name of the Lord!
> Hosanna in the highest heaven!"

[10]When he entered Jerusalem, the whole city was in turmoil, asking, "Who is this?" [11]The crowds were saying, "This is the prophet Jesus from Nazareth in Galilee."

Commentary 1: Connecting the Reading with Scripture

Palm/Passion Sunday opens with shouting, waving palms, and a triumphal entry into Jerusalem. It ends with darkness, death, and the pronouncement over a dead body, "Truly this man was God's Son." With Matthew 26:14–27:66 (or the shorter reading, 27:11–54) serving as the climactic lesson for the day, many a preacher will need to use Matthew 21:1–11 only in the introduction of a sermon focusing more emphatically on the Passion Narrative. In such a situation, it will call our attention to the contrast between the opening and closing of Holy Week, between the crowd first shouting hosannas and later shouting, "Crucify him!"

While such an approach would be homiletically reasonable, it is a shame when the story of the triumphal entry does not receive its due. This story offers a moment of incisive christological insight in the Synoptic Gospels. If a congregation attends well to Holy Thursday and Friday, preachers could do more than simply use this text as an introduction to the sermon and show, instead, the significance of the triumphal entry alongside the day's passion account.

Matthew's version of the triumphal entry is well-known for its unique approach to linking this story to the Hebrew Bible text on which it is based. Mark bases this scene on Zechariah 9:9, and Matthew makes that relationship explicit. As is Matthew's custom, he uses a fulfillment notice: "This was done to fulfill what was spoken by the prophet . . ."

Two things stand out about this particular quotation. First, Matthew 21:4–5 represents the first time Matthew has used a fulfillment notice since 13:35, and the first prophetic citation since 15:7, where Jesus indicts the Pharisees and scribes for hypocrisy. The recurrence of a prophetic citation after a lag of six chapters would have been striking to the original readers and should be flagged as theologically significant to contemporary congregations.

Second, in Matthew's desire to present Jesus as the ultimate fulfillment of Scripture, he presents Jesus as doing something of a circus act in riding into Jerusalem. Zechariah 9:9 uses poetic parallelism, a poetic device constitutive of ancient Hebraic poetry, just as schemes of rhyming and meter are constitutive of some forms of modern poetry in English. In synonymous parallelism, the poet repeats something with an artful variation. In this case the repetition on which Matthew focuses is,

> humble, and mounted on a donkey,
> and on a colt, the foal of a donkey.

Zechariah is referring to a single animal, as is Mark (11:7); but Matthew, in his zeal to present Jesus as the fulfillment of the passage, presents Jesus as riding two animals at the same time (Matt. 21:6–7).

Matthew's decision to present Jesus in this way should not be the central focus of a Palm Sunday sermon, but neither should it be neglected. This is one of those places in Scripture that provides preachers with the opportunity to teach a little about the authority of Scripture, hermeneutics, and exegesis. Matthew used Mark as a source, so he knew the tradition of Jesus riding a single animal. He certainly knew how poetic parallelism worked. So Matthew is not making a literal assertion. His point is theological. Helping a congregation see this can free them from thinking they have to interpret Scripture literally or that textual discrepancies fatally undermine the authority of Scripture. In this case, if they can see that Matthew was not concerned with presenting a journalistic, historical picture of the triumphal entry, they may be able to open themselves to Matthew's theological claim.

This theological claim is also a political claim. In this scene, Matthew echoes the infancy narrative (which is the section of the Gospel narrative most densely populated with citation formulas: 1:22; 2:6, 15, 16, 23) to highlight Jesus' kingship. Let us see the different ways this text lifts up that Christology before we consider the theme homiletically.

First, we return to Matthew's explicit use of Zechariah 9:9. Interpreters are always on thin ice when trying to decipher how fully New Testament authors considered the historical-literary context of Hebrew Bible passages they quote. The case is no different here, but that context is instructive. Zechariah 9–11 presents YHWH as a divine warrior-king who processes to Jerusalem to take the throne and restore peace and unity to Israel in the face of conquering foreign powers. There is irony in the presentation of YHWH entering Jerusalem humbly but also victoriously. This irony is also evident in Matthew's application of the text to Jesus. He is named as entering Jerusalem humbly, but he does so with a parade!

Matthew emphasizes Jesus' kingship in other ways as well. The large crowds roll out a royal "red carpet" for him (Matt. 21:8), surround him with praise (v. 9), and tell "the whole city" of Jerusalem who he is (vv. 10–11). In the praise they offer during the parade, the crowds call Jesus the "Son of David" and "the one who comes in the name of the Lord," explicit messianic terminology.

In the infancy narrative, it is clear that Jesus is born a king, and indeed must be taken to Egypt to be kept from being killed by Herod. It is at this point in the narrative, when Jesus choreographs the entry into Jerusalem, that Matthew presents Jesus as claiming that kingship for himself. This is the beginning of a coronation ceremony that will end with Jesus ironically proclaimed messiah and king (26:63–64, 68; 27:11, 17, 22, 29, 37); crowned (with thorns) and robed (27:28–29), and finally enthroned (on the cross, 27:35–37).

In contemporary theological and liturgical language, it is a good practice to avoid using terms such as "king" and "kingdom" because of their patriarchal and militaristic implications, but in preaching on this passage, set in its ancient context, the terms are useful. So often, preachers lift up Jesus as Messiah in relation to Israel without taking seriously enough the political language as it stands over against the Roman Empire. Too often we emphasize that the Jews expected a different kind of messiah, so as to evacuate Jesus' identity and mission of political implications.

The coronation parade into Jerusalem, however, is an unmistakable challenge to Caesar. Jesus enters Jerusalem, which was the former capital of Israel and Judah and the current regional capital from which Caesar's representative, the prefect Pontius Pilate, governs. Jesus enters the city as if he is claiming it as his own, as the capital of the near-at-hand reign of God!

The Passion Narratives we read during Holy Week, be it the story from Matthew read as part of the liturgy this day or John's version read on Good Friday, have far-reaching theological, ecclesiological, and devotional implications; but the Liturgy of the Palms makes clear at the beginning of the week that these stories and this season also have political implications. Preachers should help their congregations claim this political aspect of the gospel as part of the church's identity and mission in the world. Christ is king in the sense of one who leads the church to march victoriously, nonviolently, and even foolishly (riding two donkeys!) into the center of politics, offering a different vision of God's will for the world from what any Caesar, ancient or contemporary, has ever offered. Seen this way, waving those palms in worship is not just something the children do as amused adults watch; it is a political act claiming the church's allegiance to God's vision for the world.

O. WESLEY ALLEN JR.

Palms before My Feet

When fishes flew and forests walked
And figs grew upon thorn,
Some moment when the moon was blood
Then surely I was born.

With monstrous head and sickening cry
And ears like errant wings,
The devil's walking parody
On all four-footed things.
The tattered outlaw of the earth,
Of ancient crooked will;
Starve, scourge, deride me: I am dumb,
I keep my secret still.

Fools! For I also had my hour;
One far fierce hour and sweet:
There was a shout about my ears,
And palms before my feet.

G. K. Chesterton, "The Donkey," in *The Wild Knight*, 4th ed. (London: J. M. Dent and Sons, 1914), 16–17.

Commentary 2: Connecting the Reading with the World

Palm Sunday marks the start of Holy Week in the liturgical calendar. The church winds down its observance of Lent and enters into a sobering but grateful remembrance of the Last Supper on Maundy Thursday and the crucifixion of Jesus on Good Friday. In the span of a few chapters, Matthew's readers experience a rapid swing from the jubilatory tone of Jesus' entry into Jerusalem to the deep anguish of Gethsemane and Golgotha. This precipitous emotional dive is followed by the astonishing reversal on Easter Sunday, when exhilaration and triumph return with the risen Jesus.

Even though most English Bibles assign the title "Triumphal Entry" to this story, the descriptor needs qualification. First, there was nothing particularly triumphant about the event by first-century standards. This was not a kingly parade to celebrate an actual victory, whether that of the Jews against the Romans or the Romans against another nation. Even from the Christian point of view, the triumph was a proleptic one, anticipated but not yet accomplished at this juncture of the narrative. Jesus would suffer and die before being raised on the third day. This triumph was still to come, understandable in retrospect from the spiritual, postresurrection, and eschatological point of view.

Two millennia later, Christians continue to commemorate Palm Sunday with a sense of "qualified triumphalism" that looks back at Jesus' work on the cross and looks ahead toward God's final triumph over all evil to usher in the age to come. Between the "already" of Jesus' victory over death and the "not yet" of the final consummation of God's reign, two reminders for today's church are in view from this text. First, there is dissonance between worldly standard and divine standard when it comes to humility and meekness, the modus operandi of Jesus the king and his followers. Second, beware of the fickleness of the human heart.

What is the world's standard and expectation of a royal figure or, for that matter, a president, premier, or prime minister? These days, what qualifies a person to occupy the top seat of power in a regime? Strength, power, wealth, and influence are the usual qualifiers. A self-serving agenda is especially prevalent in today's political and social climate, from the individual to the national level, from insisting on bearing arms to protecting one's Second Amendment rights to a new era of arms race and trade wars for military and economic hegemony. The same standards and attitudes filter down from the political sphere to business corporations, educational institutions, and—sad to say—the church. Humility and meekness are seen as weakness, and weakness a sure route to failure.

In the famous 1970 musical *Jesus Christ Superstar*, by Andrew Lloyd Webber and Tim Rice, Jesus enters into Jerusalem with the crowd hailing: "Hosanna!" "Hey JC, JC, won't you fight for me?"[1] Stemming from its Hebrew root words, "hosanna" means "we beseech you to save [us]." The crowd expects Jesus to be the warrior king on a stallion, poised to annihilate the armies of their Roman overlords. The strong leader must fight for the underdogs by subduing force with greater force. Is this picture congruent with Jesus' definition of messiahship, or with the actions and attitudes of Jesus in his ministry among his followers?

Closer to the spirit of the text, Christian tradition offers an alternate vision to that of Webber and Rice. The words from the hymn "Ride On! Ride On in Majesty," penned by Henry Milman in 1827, hold in tension the kingly esteem of Jesus and a God-infused humility: "In lowly pomp ride on to die."[2] "Lowly pomp" is an oxymoron in the world's calculation. Jesus' triumph emerged from shame and suffering. Jesus' vision and interpretation of his entry into Jerusalem, a place both of death and of exaltation, must be embraced through eyes of faith and hearts of hope. At present, earthly triumphalism will always dismiss humility and meekness, though this does not have to be the case. Effective Christian witness can interrupt the existing state of affairs. Preachers could include examples of leaders whose humility creates an environment of trust and respect that can achieve much more than the sheer use of force or charisma.

In 2015, Pope Francis visited Philadelphia for the World Meeting of Families. Much to the curiosity and delight of the public, the Holy Father chose to ride in a tiny Fiat for a pope-mobile, rather than a fancy limousine or large protected vehicle worthy of an honored dignitary. Like Jesus on his borrowed colt, the pope demonstrated that humility and simplicity best suited his style of leadership and, more profoundly, the mission of his calling. Riding in the Fiat, he frequently stepped out to talk to people or bless a child. The pope was seen, but he also saw; the pope was honored, but he also extended honor. Indeed, a ruler on a beast of burden and a pope in a compact car challenged the status quo and invited self-reflection on one's definition of greatness. It is in the relinquishing of the world's trappings of greatness that true greatness is embodied (Matt. 20:26).

Oblivious to Jesus' hint that God's Messiah was a humble king on a donkey (Zech. 9:9), the

1. Tim Rice, "Jesus Christ Superstar Soundtrack—Hosanna Lyrics," http://www.songlyrics.com/jesus-christ-superstar-soundtrack/hosanna-lyrics/.
2. Henry Hart Milman, "Ride On! Ride On in Majesty," in *The Presbyterian Hymnal* (Louisville, KY: Westminster/John Knox, 1990), 90.

crowd nevertheless gave him a royal reception of sorts, carpeting the way with clothing and branches while bestowing upon him the messianic title "Son of David." Matthew notes that "the whole city was in turmoil" (21:10). Some celebrants knew Jesus as the prophet from Nazareth, while others doubtless had no idea who he was. Some were caught up by the jubilant hysteria, like a modern-day flash mob, and joined in the praise without understanding what it was about. Soon enough, some in this crowd would end up in another crowd, shouting repeatedly to Pilate, "Let him be crucified!" (27:22–23).

People in a crowd tend to feed off collective energy. That said, a crowd disperses as easily as it gathers. In the unexpected defeat of the New England Patriots by the Philadelphia Eagles in Super Bowl LII, strangers became fast friends for a short while, swept up in the euphoria of victory. People all over Philadelphia and its vicinity sang, "Fly, Eagles, fly," and wore Eagles gear. Even those who cared little about football became fans by proximity or osmosis, but that newfound enthusiasm was short-lived. Not long after the parade, only the most dedicated fans remained for the next season. The true fans set themselves apart from the crowd.

Preachers can help congregations on this Palm/Passion Sunday learn again that commitment is for the long haul, not for a sudden burst of excitement that changes from cheer to jeer as the winds of circumstance shift. The crowd in Jerusalem was fickle. When people thought Jesus had potential to be their warrior king, they rallied behind him. When they saw Jesus dragged before Pilate, they sided with the temple leaders. The way of the world is shortsighted. People support the party, the leader, and the program as long as they perceive the possibility of personal gain.

Jesus holds his disciples and the church to a higher standard and a tougher hope. The bleaker the world looks, the greater the temptation to give up hope that in God's time justice will be served and all will be made whole. Praise be to God that every Easter this hope is renewed, so that the church may celebrate the triumph of this special day in confidence, faithfulness, and patience. Come, Lord Jesus!

DIANE G. CHEN

Liturgy of the Passion

Isaiah 50:4–9a
Psalm 31:9–16
Philippians 2:5–11
Matthew 27:11–54
Matthew 26:14–27:66

Isaiah 50:4–9a

4The Lord GOD has given me
   the tongue of a teacher,
that I may know how to sustain
   the weary with a word.
Morning by morning he wakens—
   wakens my ear
   to listen as those who are taught.
5The Lord GOD has opened my ear,
   and I was not rebellious,
   I did not turn backward.
6I gave my back to those who struck me,
   and my cheeks to those who pulled out the beard;
I did not hide my face
   from insult and spitting.

7The Lord GOD helps me;
   therefore I have not been disgraced;
therefore I have set my face like flint,
   and I know that I shall not be put to shame;
   8he who vindicates me is near.
Who will contend with me?
   Let us stand up together.
Who are my adversaries?
   Let them confront me.
9It is the Lord GOD who helps me;
   who will declare me guilty?

Commentary 1: Connecting the Reading with Scripture

The Old Testament passage for this Sunday of the Passion is the third of four so-called Servant Songs in Isaiah 40–55. The other Servant Songs are 42:1–4; 49:1–6; and 52:13–53:12. Though the word "servant" does not appear in this particular passage, the verse immediately following the passage refers back to the speaker of the song as YHWH's Servant (Isa. 50:10).

Much has been written about the Servant Songs, in particular about the identity of the Servant. The Servant has been identified over the centuries in various ways: as a royal figure, as a prophet (whether Isaiah himself or another prophet), as Israel, and in Christian tradition, as Christ. Rather than dwelling on the issue of the Servant's identity, this essay will explore the connections between this passage and the wider context of Isaiah, the other Servant Songs, and the other texts appointed for the day. This exploration will focus on three themes: teaching, suffering, and servanthood.

First, some background. Chapters 40–55 of Isaiah, commonly referred to by scholars as Second Isaiah, are addressed to the Judean exiles in Babylon. The prophet promises a return from exile and a restoration of Judah, through the power and faithfulness of YHWH. In the tradition of the eighth-century prophet Isaiah, the unnamed prophet of the exile reminds the people of the faithfulness of God in the exodus and promises a new exodus (43:14–21; cf. 11:15–16).

Teaching. The passage, as translated in the NRSV, begins with the phrase, "The Lord God has given me the tongue of a teacher," but the Hebrew actually says, "the tongue of those who are taught" (50:4). "Those who are taught" are disciples. The same word is used of the disciples of the eighth-century prophet Isaiah, among whom his teaching will be preserved (8:16). Perhaps the exilic prophet is claiming here a lineage with the earlier prophet; he is one of "those who are taught," and he continues the legacy of Isaiah. The word appears again in a later passage in Second Isaiah, where God promises that all of Zion's children will "be taught" by YHWH, and that their prosperity/peace (*shalom*) shall be great (54:13). The latter passage asserts that not only the Servant but all of Zion's children will be disciples of YHWH.

Given these connections, the statement of the Servant—that God has given him the tongue of a disciple in order "to sustain the weary with a word"—becomes both a fulfillment of earlier prophecy and a promise of future *shalom* for the returning exiles. Preachers might emphasize that the word the Servant speaks comes from YHWH, not from himself: "Morning by morning he wakens—wakens my ear to listen as those who are taught" (50:4). YHWH is the one who teaches; the disciple listens and only then speaks.

Suffering. The announcement in Second Isaiah of the restoration of Judah is met with resistance, resistance that entails suffering for YHWH's Servant. The Servant, identified as Israel in 49:3, is in our passage apparently an individual in Israel, one who experiences physical violence for the sake of the teaching that he brings: "I gave my back to those who struck me, and my cheeks to those who pulled out the beard; I did not hide my face from insult and spitting" (50:6).

The suffering of the Servant in this passage foreshadows the even more severe suffering of the Servant in the fourth Servant Song, Isaiah 52:13–53:12. That more familiar passage develops the theme of suffering found in chapter 50, but it differs from it in two significant ways. First, the fourth Servant Song is spoken by the community, not by the Servant himself. The community comments on the suffering of the Servant. Secondly, the fourth Servant Song bears witness to the realization that the Servant suffers not just *at the hands of* the community, but *for the sake of* the community: "He was wounded for our transgressions, crushed for our iniquities; upon him was the punishment that made us whole, and by his bruises we are healed" (53:5).

The idea of the vicarious suffering of the Servant for the sake of the community is not as explicit in our passage. Certainly, the Servant suffers as a result of his obedient discipleship, but whether the suffering is redemptive for the community or not is a matter of interpretation. What is clear from the last two Servant Songs is the assertion that the Servant will be vindicated by YHWH, in spite of or even through his suffering: "The Lord God helps me; therefore I have not been disgraced; therefore I have set my face like flint, and I know that I shall not be put to shame; he who vindicates me is near" (50:7–8; see 53:12).

The rhetorical questions at the end of the passage offer particularly rich possibilities for preaching. Through these questions, even in the midst of suffering the Servant proclaims faith in the God who will defend and uphold him against his enemies: "Who will contend with me? Let us stand up together. Who are my adversaries? Let them confront me. It is the Lord God who helps me; who will declare me guilty?" (50:8–9). The preacher can help hearers connect this with Romans: "If God is for us, who is against us? . . . Who will bring any charge against God's elect? It is God who justifies. Who is to condemn?" (Rom. 8:31, 33–34). Both the Servant in Isaiah and the apostle Paul faced harsh opposition. Both, however, also proclaimed faith in the God whose grace enabled them to follow where God's call led them.

Servanthood. The Servant of YHWH in our passage, like the Servant in Isaiah 52–53, suffers because of the call of God. This is always the case, biblically speaking, for God's servants. To be called "my servant" by YHWH is no small thing. The people so designated in the Hebrew Bible are the elect—either the Israelites as a whole or faithful individuals from within Israel—but the choosing is always a mixed blessing. With the designation "my servant" comes a relationship with the God of Israel, but with it comes also hardship and persecution.

This is true not just in Isaiah's Servant Songs, but also in the other texts for this Sunday, as the preacher might note. The writer of Psalm 31 is surrounded by enemies and calls on God to save him: "Let your face shine upon *your servant*; save me in your steadfast love" (Ps. 31:16). Paul invokes Christ as the example of faithful obedience: "Let the same mind be in you that was in Christ Jesus, who, though he was in the form of God, did not regard equality with God as something to be exploited, but emptied himself, taking the form of a slave" (Phil. 2:5–7). Of course, the Gospel lesson for this Passion Sunday speaks in great detail of the suffering that Christ endured as a slave/servant.

The Servant in Isaiah 50 is an obedient disciple, one who speaks the word of God and suffers for it, but one who also proclaims faith in the God who will not let him go. This figure plays a role that foreshadows the vocation of faithful servants of God through the centuries, a fact we remember especially this day as we hear again the story of the one who, though he was in the form of God, took the form of a servant/slave and humbled himself to the point of death, even death on a cross.

KATHRYN SCHIFFERDECKER

Commentary 2: Connecting the Reading with the World

The Liturgy of the Passion occurs after the Liturgy of the Palms. Whereas the Liturgy of the Palms famously tells of Jesus' triumphal entry, the texts for the Liturgy of the Passion comprise a dark counterpoint: they are the somber reminder of how fast things can, and will, turn grim for Jesus. The readings that accompany Isaiah 50:4–9a, especially Psalm 31:9–13 and Philippians 2:6–8, drive the point home . . . with nails.

Ever since Bernard Duhm's 1892 commentary on Isaiah, biblical scholars have identified Isaiah 50:4–9a as belonging to the Servant Songs in this portion of Isaiah (chaps. 40–55, typically dated to the exilic period). There is considerable debate about these Servant Songs—their demarcation, meaning, and so forth. The present lection belongs to the third in a sequence of at least four (42:1–9; 49:1–6; 50:4–11; 52:13–53:12). One important question facing the interpretation of these songs is the identity of this unnamed Servant. Christians have long seen in the fourth song, if not also the others, an anticipation of the vicarious suffering of Jesus.

In this light, in the Liturgy of the Passion, Isaiah 50:4–9a can also be profitably considered with reference to Jesus, his suffering, and his death. "Who is the Servant?" can be answered—at least in liturgical time—straightforwardly: he is Jesus of Nazareth, the Christ, even if other answers were also at work for the original context and audience of Isaiah.

What, then, do we learn about the Servant who is Christ when Isaiah 50:4–9a is read at the start of Holy Week? First, we learn that the Servant is a teacher (see Matt. 7:28–29) who sustains "the weary with a word" (Isa. 50:4aβ; see 42:3; Matt. 11:28–30). This ability, we are told, is the gift of the Lord God (v. 4aα), who is the Servant's own teacher (v. 4b; see John 5:19; 15:15). Next, we learn of the Servant's obedience, even his submission to violence (vv. 5–6; see 53:7; Phil. 2:8). The language of verse 6 is worth dwelling on. The Servant claims to have bared his back to his attackers and to have given his cheeks to those who would abuse him (v. 6a); it is not hard to see here an adumbration of Matthew 5:39.

Perhaps Jesus, in the Sermon on the Mount, had Isaiah 50 in mind. Maybe the same is true when Jesus stood before Caiaphas (see Matt. 26:67). The Servant also claims to have not hidden his face from insult and spitting (Isa. 50:6b), something with which Jesus too was familiar (Matt. 26:67; 27:30; Luke 18:32). The hiding of God's face is often a trope for judgment in the Old Testament (Deut. 31:17–18; 32:20; Jer. 33:5), but here the face of God's Son is *not* hidden—a sign of mercy perhaps, if not hope? No. Here the revealing of the face facilitates the *abuse* of the one who took the very form of a servant (Phil. 2:7).

According to some scholars, this is something new in Israel's history. In Claus Westermann's opinion, "Some radical change has come about . . . a new factor entered into God's dealings . . . the lament of the mediator who is attacked and defamed because of his task here develops, for the first time, into assent to and acceptance of this suffering."[1] Brevard Childs puts things somewhat differently, characterizing the Servant's words here as a "confession of unswerving trust." He states that the Servant "is now led along a new path of suffering and deepest humiliation" with a transfer taking place "from Israel, the servant nation, to Israel, the suffering individual who now embodies the nation's true mission."[2] It is not surprising, then, to find commentators speaking of this text as a kind of autobiography and noting connections between it and the laments of various psalmists (see Pss. 5, 7, 17, 26, 27, 69), Jeremiah, or Moses.[3]

Or Jesus.

What would that mean? What would be the significance of that? It is not unusual to associate Jesus' life and ministry with suffering, especially during Holy Week—even suffering that is on behalf of others, suffering that is perhaps willingly chosen. However, such notions are in bad repute today, hard to imagine. Nowadays, the majority of human energy goes to minimize suffering as much as possible. Medicine and technology are only two of the most powerful ways we do that. The impression, if not explicit message, of those attempts is that suffering is altogether bad, an evil to avoid at all costs. As for suffering intentionally for someone else? Simply unbelievable (cf. Rom. 5:7–8). Then again, there is Isaiah 50:4–9a, and there is Jesus in Holy Week. Preachers must somehow reckon with such theological realities—no easy task.

Jesus' suffering has long been a central trope in Christian art; in some periods, in fact, it was the primary artistic image produced and seen. Before the internet and screens of every kind, what must have been the effect of seeing so many images of Christ's suffering?

One possibility is that this ubiquitous image suggested—not unlike Isaiah 50:4–9a itself—that suffering was to be expected (see Heb. 2:18; 4:15), that it was a kind of practice, perhaps even a way to obey God, and that therefore suffering, as horrible as it can and might be, is not beyond redemption. Once again, such sentiments are almost unimaginable, now, in our day with its screens, medicine, and technology, but such sentiments are not wrong, according to Isaiah 50 and Jesus Christ. Preachers must somehow reckon with such theological realities, not to mention their ethical outcomes—again, no easy task.

There is another, perhaps correlative, possibility of this art: that dwelling on images of Jesus' suffering trains a viewer to see all that as decidedly *his* suffering, not one's own. So, despite the fact that suffering might be expected, it could be a practice and way to obey God, one not entirely beyond redemption. Despite that, not all suffering *should* be expected, not all suffering *is* a practice or way of obedience, and some suffering may *not* be redemptive. These latter types are *not* Christ's suffering and therefore *not* Christ-*like*.

That is a very important distinction between two very different kinds of suffering. It is only those who know *Christ's* kind of suffering—whether borne solely by him or somehow also now, belatedly, in one's own body (see Gal. 6:17; Phil. 1:20; Col. 1:24)—who are able to face suffering, like the Servant in Isaiah, like Jesus himself, like Paul and so many others (cf.

1. Claus Westermann, *Isaiah 40–66*, Old Testament Library (Philadelphia: Westminster, 1969), 230.
2. Brevard S. Childs, *Isaiah*, Old Testament Library (Louisville, KY: Westminster John Knox, 2001), 395.
3. See Klaus Baltzer, *Deutero-Isaiah*, Hermeneia (Minneapolis: Fortress, 2001), 19–22, 339–40.

1 Pet. 2:11–4:11), and who know the deepest truths about suffering, its significance, and, finally, its impermanence (Isa. 50:7–9a; Rom. 8:31). These are those who can pray, using the more recent phrasing from the Morning Prayer collect for Fridays in the 1979 Episcopal *Book of Common Prayer*: "Almighty God, whose most dear Son went not up to joy but first he suffered pain, and entered not into glory before he was crucified: Mercifully grant that we, walking in the way of the cross, may find it none other than the way of life and peace; through Jesus Christ your Son our Lord. *Amen*."

BRENT A. STRAWN

Psalm 31:9–16

9 Be gracious to me, O LORD, for I am in distress;
  my eye wastes away from grief,
  my soul and body also.
10 For my life is spent with sorrow,
  and my years with sighing;
my strength fails because of my misery,
  and my bones waste away.

11 I am the scorn of all my adversaries,
  a horror to my neighbors,
an object of dread to my acquaintances;
  those who see me in the street flee from me.
12 I have passed out of mind like one who is dead;
  I have become like a broken vessel.
13 For I hear the whispering of many—
  terror all around!—
as they scheme together against me,
  as they plot to take my life.

14 But I trust in you, O LORD;
  I say, "You are my God."
15 My times are in your hand;
  deliver me from the hand of my enemies and persecutors.
16 Let your face shine upon your servant;
  save me in your steadfast love.

Connecting the Psalm with Scripture and Worship

Crying for deliverance, the psalmist is in a desperate place. The situation is bleak: soul and body waste away, life is marked by sorrow and sighing, strength fails (Ps. 31:9–10). The psalmist's condition is an object of scorn, horror, and dread in the community. "Those who see me in the street flee from me" (v. 11). Meanwhile, others are plotting the psalmist's demise, whispering and scheming to end the psalmist's life (v. 13). In desperation, the psalmist cries to God for help. There is no one else available. There are no other resources.

The lection concludes with the psalmist declaring faith in God. In spite of all that has happened, in spite of what life has become, the psalmist will still trust in God. "My times are in your hand" (v. 15). God's steadfast love and enduring faithfulness give the psalmist encouragement, even amid difficult and agonizing circumstances. The pain of the present situation does not negate God's persistent goodness. Beyond the appointed reading, the remainder of Psalm 31 deepens this affirmation of God's merciful deliverance, especially verses 19–24. While the situation is dire, the psalmist maintains confidence in God.

The day's lesson from Isaiah is the third Servant Song. Read through the lens of Psalm 31, the passage evidences a similar confidence. Though treated badly by some, the speaker persists with the assigned task of bringing words of hope and comfort to "sustain the weary" (Isa.

50:4). Obediently responding to what God has given and taught, the speaker finds strength to continue to walk a challenging path, bearing up against attacks and insults (v. 6). God is perceived as close and supportive, enabling the completion of a difficult task. "The Lord God helps me; therefore I have not been disgraced. . . . Who are my adversaries? Let them confront me. It is the Lord God who helps me" (vv. 7a, 8b). God's faithfulness overcomes the experiences of rejection. With God's endorsement, the speaker will prevail.

The New Testament lessons for Passion Sunday exhibit similar themes of obedience to God's call and confidence in God's presence, even amid otherwise desperate circumstances. The majestic Christ hymn in Philippians 2:5–11 portrays Jesus as setting aside divine glory to enter human life. Emptying himself, his humanity takes a particular form of lowliness, the form of a slave. From this position of humility, Jesus pursues the mission given to him, speaking words to the weary and persistently extending mercy and love, even when opposed by others. Jesus is obedient even as his journey takes him to death. He humbly continues to point to God's forgiving love even as he himself is attacked, beaten, and crucified. Through Christ's obedience and perseverance, God's saving work is revealed. In raising Jesus from the dead and giving him "the name that is above every name" (Phil. 2:9), God vindicates the way of suffering and endorses the gospel message Jesus' opponents thought they had buried.

Matthew's account of the passion describes the depth of anxiety in Jesus' final days, as some plot and scheme to end his life, as his own body is wracked by sorrow and pain. Through it all, Jesus maintains his focus on what he has been called to do. He knows what is to come. "One of you will betray me" (Matt. 26:21), he tells the Twelve at the Passover table. They cannot believe it, but Jesus remains resolute. He shares the bread and the cup with them and then predicts that they will all desert him and that Peter will deny even knowing him (vv. 26–35). Again they protest, but Jesus is continuing his journey.

He acknowledges his grief as he prays in the garden, turning to God for deliverance because there is no one else to help. The prayer is balanced with acceptance and confidence as Jesus faces the future set before him, trusting God is with him. After his arrest, he endures trials, humiliations, and beatings, even as his disciples abandon him. His opponents appear to have the upper hand; still Jesus presses on. His demeanor amazes Pontius Pilate (27:14), and his self-assured silence builds the drama of what is to come. There are more mocking and physical beatings. The torment resembles the psalmist's plight in Psalm 31. At the moment of his death, Jesus is acclaimed God's Son by the Roman centurion, as if Jesus' true identity is revealed in his willingness to suffer.

However, Matthew does not conclude the story with Jesus' death. The passage continues by giving careful attention to the disposition of his body. Matthew notes the "great stone" that seals the tomb and the posting of guards to make it secure, underscoring the human efforts to muffle the gospel (vv. 60–66). The progression of Holy Week chronicles the attempts of Jesus' adversaries to eliminate him and destroy his message. Their success seems to grow with each passing day. By Friday, Jesus is broken and dead. As the guards seal his tomb, it seems the adversaries have done all they could possibly do. Their victory appears complete; yet the presence of the women in verse 61 suggests that there is more to come. Not even death can thwart God's goodness.

The Liturgy of the Passion is an invitation for the preacher to help the congregation voice the words of Psalm 31:9, "Be gracious to me, O Lord, for I am in distress." Here is an occasion for the preacher to name the sorrow and the pain of the world, as well as the anguish that frequently marks human life. Between Palm Sunday "hosannas" and Easter "alleluias" there is the deep valley of rejection, humiliation, and apparent defeat. It is a valley we all travel at different times and at many times. It is a valley where the preacher is called to speak a word to the weary, while also pointing to the faithful presence of the God who refuses to leave us alone. For in Jesus, God knows about deep valleys, great sorrows, and tombs that appear irreversibly sealed. God knows about these things, and God has also prevailed against them.

JOHN W. WURSTER

Philippians 2:5–11

5Let the same mind be in you that was in Christ Jesus,
6who, though he was in the form of God,
did not regard equality with God
as something to be exploited,
7but emptied himself,
taking the form of a slave,
being born in human likeness.
And being found in human form,
8he humbled himself
and became obedient to the point of death—
even death on a cross.

9Therefore God also highly exalted him
and gave him the name
that is above every name,
10so that at the name of Jesus
every knee should bend,
in heaven and on earth and under the earth,
11and every tongue should confess
that Jesus Christ is Lord,
to the glory of God the Father.

Commentary 1: Connecting the Reading with Scripture

The larger literary and historical connections are key to interpreting this passage. The social world to which Paul wrote Philippians 2:5–11 had much in common with the world today. Then, as now, many people acted according to self-interest. The social structure of the Roman age was hierarchical, with people in the upper echelons in positions of status, controlling material resources, benefiting from keeping others in lower places in the social pyramid, and enforcing their will through violence. The preacher can show such connections.

Paul, an apocalyptic theologian, sees God ending the present broken age and, through Jesus Christ, the church beginning to manifest qualities of the future realm of God, with the expectation that the second coming will bring the final and full realm. The church is to be a community whose life in the present alerts the wider world to these great transitions, embodies the qualities of the realm of God, and offers people the opportunity to be part of it.

However, the Philippian congregation faced both external and internal conflict. Paul was imprisoned by the external force of the Roman Empire (Phil. 1:12–18). The Philippians faced similar harassment (1:27–30). Internally, the community was beset by false teachers (3:2–4, 17–19) and by differences of perspective regarding how to make Christian witness (4:1–2).

Paul's exhortations to the congregation to be of the same mind (1:27; 2:2, 5; 3:15; 4:2, 8) and admonitions to unity (1:27; 2:2) indicate that the community had become fragmented in its response to these threats. Some community members acted from "selfish ambition or conceit," focusing on their own interests instead of seeking to support the mission of the community (2:2, 4; see 2:21).

The preacher can help us identify how the Philippian congregation was similar to many congregations today, in that the core values and practices of the eschatological community conflict with those of the surrounding culture. At the same time, many congregations struggle to consider which voices to regard as authentic Christian teaching and how to make Christian witness.

Paul's call to unity is not for its own sake, but is to strengthen the congregation for witness so they will stand firm in the trauma of the present and will become citizens of the new world after the apocalypse (3:20–4:1; see 1:5–6, 10–11).

In its immediate literary context, Paul's admonition to "have the same mind" (2:2, 4) is to share a common commitment to living together in community in ways that provide vital support for one another and that witness to the coming new world (3:17–19; see 1:28; 2:14–15). Paul uses Philippians 2:5–11 as the decisive picture of the pathway to forming such a community.

Preachers may recall that Philippians 2:5–11 interprets the event of Christ in three phrases. In the first phrase (2:6), Christ preexisted, that is, Christ was with God in heaven before being incarnated in human form. Yet Christ did not regard that exalted stature as something "to be exploited," that is, as something to use for his own benefit in the manner of the Roman social world. Congregations in every age need to learn from Christ's example, for our faith communities have their own ways of exploiting power. A preacher might point out how the congregation's life and witness are part and parcel of current "Roman"-like social order. The church—and ministers—often benefit from keeping things the way things are.

In the second phase (2:7–8), Christ emptied himself, that is, gave up the security and honor he had in heaven. Instead, he acted on behalf of the interest of others by witnessing to God's purpose to replace the present broken world with a transformed one. Jesus took the form of a slave who died on a cross, an especially painful and humiliating death. The reference to slavery is a double entendre. At one level, slaves were at the bottom of the social pyramid. The slave was obedient to the master. At another level, most people in the ancient world believed that everyone served a deity (or deities). Jesus was obedient to God, which meant being obedient to the divine purpose of effecting the transition from the old age to the new.

As Paul wanted the Philippians to be obedient to the purpose to which Jesus was obedient, namely, manifesting the realm of God, so the preacher might encourage today's community, on Palm/Passion Sunday, in a similar direction. The preacher might further offer the congregation the same pastoral advisory that Paul offered the Philippians. As the Romans put Jesus to death in order to end what they perceived as a threat to their control, so the church can expect conflict with self-interested forces today.

In the third phase (2:9–11), God vindicated the coming of God's realm through Jesus by exalting Jesus as ruler of the cosmos. This exaltation demonstrates the trustworthiness of Paul's claim that the turning of the ages is underway through Jesus. The theological claim in this ancient text is consistent with the canon's broader notion that God often uses the unlikely or the seemingly powerless to expose the falsehood of those who deem themselves powerful; through unexpected agents, Scripture regularly reveals the way to authentic life and community.

For examples, we might consider Moses confronting Pharaoh, the prophets preaching against monarchs, or Mary giving birth to the Savior. This motif comes to expression in another lectionary reading for today: Isaiah 50:4–9a, one of the Servant Songs, wherein the Servant has remained faithful even in the face of threat. Jesus, similarly, remained faithful in witness to God's realm, even when the Romans executed him. God used the crucifixion to show that God's renewing purposes, represented through Christ, are at work even in the most desperate situation.

Philippians 2:5–11 functions in two ways in the Philippian community and can function similarly for congregations today. First, it shows the Philippians how the congregation can become an eschatological community: by having the same mind that was in Christ Jesus, setting aside self-interest in the interest of the well-being of others. A preacher might help listeners begin to imagine practical steps they can take in the life of the congregation and in broader witness in this direction.

Second, the story of Jesus in Philippians 2:5–11 bespeaks the source of power out of which the church can take the dramatic step of self-emptying, of giving up status and control according to Roman social expectation, for the sake of eschatological witness. God is present to work with the Philippians as they seek a community that embodies the mind that was in Christ Jesus.

Moreover, a life self-emptying for the sake of others that is begun in the present will come to completion at the day of Jesus Christ, the second coming (Phil. 1:6; see 1:10–11; 3:10–11, 20–21). The sermon might call attention to ways in which the congregation can feel the force of God's presence and working in their midst. For example, the congregation can become aware of this presence through studying the Bible, through partaking of the loaf and the cup, and by participating with others in a public demonstration for justice.

Scholars generally agree that Paul cited Philippians 2:5–11 from preexisting tradition, perhaps a hymn. However, scholars differ greatly on interpreting the details of the hymn. For Passion Sunday, it is enough to note how Paul uses the broad lines of the text: the self-emptying of Christ for the sake of the eschatological transformation of the world is both model for the Philippians to develop the same mind and the source of power for them to do so.

RONALD J. ALLEN

Commentary 2: Connecting the Reading with the World

It sounds like a pipe dream, this grand vision of unity where believers are of the same mind. For some, these words may conjure up hazy memories of a bygone era, for others a lofty goal for which to aim. For others, they strike the ear as just a pipe dream.

In any given gym or sports bar there will be television screens set to various stations. CNN and Fox may be reporting the same story at the same moment, but given the vastly differing details and analyses, they might as well be reporting on different events. In our highly polarized world, chances are good that if two people cannot be of the same mind politically or theologically, they cannot be friends. Perhaps they cannot even have a civil conversation. For all of their benefits, social-media platforms have made personal attacks much easier. Charges of "fake news" can leave those in our pews wondering which sources to trust and what can possibly provide a foundation for unity.

Talk of "having the same mind" can be troubling in an era when facts are what anyone declares them to be, where truth is whatever an individual or group or political party defines it to be. Ideology that does not tolerate dissent can be dangerous. When journalism is labeled "the enemy," anxieties rise over the prospect of the loss of free thought and free speech. Leaders in Nazi Germany were of the same mind. Jim Jones's cult members were of the same mind. How is this being of one mind a good thing?

Given such concerns, what can Paul's fervent words hold for us today? "Mind" is used three times in the first five verses of this chapter in Philippians. "Mind," as Paul asserts here, connotes aligning one's life, orienting one's self in a particular way, the way of Jesus. This is not groupthink or moving in lockstep. Paul is addressing the crucial power of a unified mind-set, of the disciplined, generative efforts of the faithful. Countless issues, needs, deadlines, and opportunities cry out for our attention; choosing that to which we give our attention, our mindfulness, can be a powerful spiritual practice.

Use of the terms "slave," "obedient," and "humbled" should also give us pause. Framing these verses in a way that is scripturally accurate and at the same time culturally and pastorally sensitive can be challenging. A good starting place is to consider how these words might sound to a person of color, an immigrant or refugee, the survivor of an abusive relationship. There are congregants who bear the scars of being part of a church or family, or both, where they were told in a variety of ways to obey authority, to submit even when doing so caused them great harm.

Wrestling with how we speak of and embody the way of humility and obedience so as not to cause further harm is a challenge to which Jesus calls us in the present moment. In our time, as in Paul's, the need for both genuine community and bold commitment to the way of Christ is apparent, and makes such wrestling worth every ounce of effort. Jesus had been quite clear that status seeking and manipulative power had no place in his movement. Jesus chose the way of humility, of self-emptying in the benefit of a greater good.

In Paul's world there were those who sought status and honor in ways that had the potential to erode the community of faith. Paul was less interested in self-abasement than he was in avoiding the cultural practices that could destroy the church and dilute its message and witness. Paul's respect for the community in Philippi moved him to call forth the best from them.

Healthy unity requires some level of humility. How we speak of and practice that humility can be the difference between effective and ineffective witness.

Tourists visiting the Church of the Holy Sepulchre in Jerusalem have likely experienced the cacophony of voices chanting, singing, and preaching in the sanctuary and adjacent chapels. Multiple Christian groups compete for air space, with the sounds bouncing off the ancient walls in an ironic and sometimes overwhelming assertion of theological wills. Churches in our own culture often compete not for air space but for members, for recognition. Church marketing efforts can reveal subtle (and sometimes not so subtle) implications of a bigger program, a larger building, or a better-funded music program. What if churches intentionally practiced humility, shedding the fear of the future, fear of the unknown, fear of the other, the striving for status or superiority, the competitive attitudes?

What does it look like when a congregation acknowledges its privilege and uses that privilege in the service of others? One predominantly white congregation studies its history, learns that the building was constructed by slaves, and invites descendants of those slaves who are members of a nearby African American congregation to break bread together with them, and humbly asks forgiveness. Another congregation invites the impoverished families who now inhabit the neighborhood to come to share their stories and their hopes. Yet another congregation welcomes an undocumented immigrant family into sanctuary to give them time and space as their legal case is adjudicated, and over time is humbled by the realization that everyone, immigrant and church member alike, needs sanctuary. Across town, Jewish, Muslim, and Christian congregations pool resources and volunteers in an anti-hunger project. Such efforts involve the hard work of emptying of self (Phil. 2:7) for a greater good, releasing what was in order to make space for what might be. Institutional humility may not pack the pews, but it may prove a more faithful, fruitful, and spiritually enriching mind-set for the believers gathered at that altar.

Communities across the country are seeing a rise in grassroots, people-centered efforts such as totally free markets, community sings, pop-up dinners, and tiny houses. These are collaborative efforts aimed not at self-aggrandizement or profit but at building up community, fostering a sense of belonging among residents. They are humble efforts. While they pale in comparison to Jesus' emptying himself in obedience, they do reflect a type of downward mobility, an eschewing of ladder climbing in favor of real community. Congregations might learn from such efforts.

Sooner or later life will empty us: the phone call in the middle of the night, the serious look on the surgeon's face, the note left on the kitchen counter. Emptying can consist of the long, slow diminishing of joy and purpose, or it can crash upon us in an instant. Faith communities also experience seasons of great loss and grief. Acknowledging Jesus' own emptying can be a welcome reminder that we are never alone in such times.

This passage also offers an invitation to preachers in this busy time of Holy Week and Easter. Philippians calls to us to let go, to take the time to be in the presence of the Holy, emptying ourselves of those expectations and workaholic tendencies, giving ourselves over to simple moments of praise.

Paul's lyrical words invite us to pause, to breathe, to take stock, and once again to allow the full depth of Jesus' mind-set, his attitude, and his actions to settle into the marrow of our bones. Praise and passion are both reflected in these powerful words for Passion-Palm Sunday. Making space for both the hosannas of Palm Sunday and the desolation of Good Friday is a challenge for preachers, not just on this Sunday, but on most Sundays. Paul offers us an opportunity to clarify whom it is we are praising, and how we can best follow in faith. Paul calls us to praise the God who is with us always.

JULIE PEEPLES

And Then He Broke

Long practiced prodding up the hill the mob
clambering Golgotha's bare-gallows skull,
the heavy henchmen lay there in a lull,
with only now and then some beefy gob
turned up to gaze at three so all-consumed.
But still their killing—rushed beyond all
measure;
sloppy, yet finished and perfected—loomed
above the free men lolling at their leisure . . .

Till one as splattered as a butcher "Sir"ed
his captain: "One of these three just cried
out!"
The mounted captain turned (he thought
he'd heard
it, too), with "Which one?" *Had* there been
some shout

or groan—a calling on Elijah? All
of them now burned to see with one desire.
And so, to stay Him from His final fall,
the greedy offered vinegar to gall
the dwindling cough with which He would
expire.

For they still hoped for some dramatic
stroke—
perhaps Elijah might materialize?
But then the distance echoed Mary's cries,
as He himself roared out. And then He broke.

Rainer Maria Rilke, "Crucifixion," in *New Poems,* trans. Len Krisak (Rochester, NY: Camden House, 2015), 229–30.

Matthew 27:11–54

11Now Jesus stood before the governor; and the governor asked him, "Are you
the King of the Jews?" Jesus said, "You say so." 12But when he was accused by
the chief priests and elders, he did not answer. 13Then Pilate said to him, "Do you
not hear how many accusations they make against you?" 14But he gave him no
answer, not even to a single charge, so that the governor was greatly amazed.
15Now at the festival the governor was accustomed to release a prisoner for
the crowd, anyone whom they wanted. 16At that time they had a notorious prisoner, called Jesus Barabbas. 17So after they had gathered, Pilate said to them,
"Whom do you want me to release for you, Jesus Barabbas or Jesus who is
called the Messiah?" 18For he realized that it was out of jealousy that they had
handed him over. 19While he was sitting on the judgment seat, his wife sent word
to him, "Have nothing to do with that innocent man, for today I have suffered
a great deal because of a dream about him." 20Now the chief priests and the
elders persuaded the crowds to ask for Barabbas and to have Jesus killed. 21The
governor again said to them, "Which of the two do you want me to release for
you?" And they said, "Barabbas." 22Pilate said to them, "Then what should I do
with Jesus who is called the Messiah?" All of them said, "Let him be crucified!"
23Then he asked, "Why, what evil has he done?" But they shouted all the more,
"Let him be crucified!"

24So when Pilate saw that he could do nothing, but rather that a riot was beginning, he took some water and washed his hands before the crowd, saying, "I am
innocent of this man's blood; see to it yourselves." 25Then the people as a whole
answered, "His blood be on us and on our children!" 26So he released Barabbas
for them; and after flogging Jesus, he handed him over to be crucified.

27Then the soldiers of the governor took Jesus into the governor's headquarters, and they gathered the whole cohort around him. 28They stripped him and
put a scarlet robe on him, 29and after twisting some thorns into a crown, they put
it on his head. They put a reed in his right hand and knelt before him and mocked
him, saying, "Hail, King of the Jews!" 30They spat on him, and took the reed and
struck him on the head. 31After mocking him, they stripped him of the robe and
put his own clothes on him. Then they led him away to crucify him.

32As they went out, they came upon a man from Cyrene named Simon; they
compelled this man to carry his cross. 33And when they came to a place called
Golgotha (which means Place of a Skull), 34they offered him wine to drink, mixed
with gall; but when he tasted it, he would not drink it. 35And when they had crucified him, they divided his clothes among themselves by casting lots; 36then they
sat down there and kept watch over him. 37Over his head they put the charge
against him, which read, "This is Jesus, the King of the Jews."

38Then two bandits were crucified with him, one on his right and one on his
left. 39Those who passed by derided him, shaking their heads 40and saying, "You
who would destroy the temple and build it in three days, save yourself! If you are
the Son of God, come down from the cross." 41In the same way the chief priests
also, along with the scribes and elders, were mocking him, saying, 42"He saved
others; he cannot save himself. He is the King of Israel; let him come down from
the cross now, and we will believe in him. 43He trusts in God; let God deliver him
now, if he wants to; for he said, 'I am God's Son.'" 44The bandits who were crucified with him also taunted him in the same way.

45From noon on, darkness came over the whole land until three in the afternoon. 46And about three o'clock Jesus cried with a loud voice, "Eli, Eli, lema
sabachthani?" that is, "My God, my God, why have you forsaken me?" 47When
some of the bystanders heard it, they said, "This man is calling for Elijah." 48At
once one of them ran and got a sponge, filled it with sour wine, put it on a stick,
and gave it to him to drink. 49But the others said, "Wait, let us see whether Elijah
will come to save him." 50Then Jesus cried again with a loud voice and breathed
his last. 51At that moment the curtain of the temple was torn in two, from top to bottom. The earth shook, and the rocks were split. 52The tombs also were opened,
and many bodies of the saints who had fallen asleep were raised. 53After his
resurrection they came out of the tombs and entered the holy city and appeared
to many. 54Now when the centurion and those with him, who were keeping watch
over Jesus, saw the earthquake and what took place, they were terrified and
said, "Truly this man was God's Son!"

Commentary 1: Connecting the Reading with Scripture

Because of the expansive nature of the day, Palm/Passion Sunday is a difficult occasion on which to preach. The movement from a focus on Jesus' triumphal entry into Jerusalem at the beginning of the service to the cross at the end serves as an important correction for congregants who do not participate in Holy Week services between this Sunday and Easter. Focusing on Jesus' passion on this Sunday reminds people of the stark reality of a world that would execute the Christ, in order to prepare them for the radical reversal of our situations that occurs with the resurrection.

That said, this is quite a long text from which to preach (and it is the shorter of the alternatives; see the essay on Matthew 26:14–27:66 for commentary on the longer option for the passion lection). To try to treat the whole within the context of a single sermon will lead to a superficial interpretation at best. Preachers will do well to focus on a single passage while using the rest as context or look for some overarching theme or element of the whole upon which to focus. This essay will focus on the first of these two options (see the essay on Matt. 26:14–27:66 for an exploration of the latter option).

One of the benefits of preaching from the Revised Common Lectionary is that it invites the preacher to compare and contrast readings from across the canon. Most commonly this occurs with the four readings (or some subset) assigned to each Sunday. The lectionary also invites comparison and contrast between the different Gospels. Many congregations tend to harmonize the Gospels, as if they presented a unified historical picture. Instead, the four Gospels (and especially the Synoptics) function like a theological conversation where there are some points of agreement and other points of divergence in their understanding of Jesus as the Christ and the salvation he brings.

Preachers who have been working with Matthew since the First Sunday of Advent have already had the opportunity to point out some of the First Gospel's unique literary techniques and theological claims, such as Matthew's use of formula citations in the infancy narrative, Matthew's presentation of the magi, the unique dialogue between John and Jesus at the Jordan, and Matthew's collection of Jesus' teachings into discourses, especially the Sermon on the Mount. Year A departs from Matthew during most of Lent, but on Palm/Passion Sunday it returns to Matthew, inviting the congregation to remember that Matthew has a unique view of Jesus' death as well.

While some congregants are likely quite familiar with the broad strokes of Matthew's passion story (especially those details shared with the other Gospels), they may have never attended to 27:51b–53 closely. At the moment of Jesus' death there is an earthquake that opens tombs of the saints, and they are raised from the dead! What an odd little notice Matthew inserts into his revision of Mark's passion story between the ripping of the temple curtain and the centurion proclaiming Jesus to be God's Son!

The significance of this element of the scene can be viewed from several angles. First, the earthquake itself. In the ancient Mediterranean world generally, earthquakes were often seen as accompanying the arrival of a god or an action of a god. This is true in the Hebrew Bible (see Judg. 5:4–5; 2 Sam. 22:8; 1 Kgs. 19:11–12; Job 9:6; Pss. 18:7; 68:7–8; Isa. 29:6; Joel 2:10; 3:16; Nah. 1:5; Hag. 2:6, 21). Perhaps the most significant reference to earthquakes in the background of Matthew's use here is his earlier use in 24:7. This is part of the eschatological discourse. The disciples have asked Jesus about signs of his coming and the end of the age. Along with false messiahs, wars, and famines, earthquakes will arise. Jesus says, "All this is but the beginning of the birth pangs." Matthew's use of the trope, then, signifies that Jesus' death was more than a tragic death caused by the political powers of the day. God was/is at work through this death. What God is doing (or at least part of what God is doing) through the crucifixion is seen in the results of the earthquake.

Tombs are opened and the bodies of saints are raised from the dead (v. 52). The raising of these saints clearly foreshadows the resurrection of Jesus himself. Matthew, after all, is the only evangelist to include an earthquake in the story of the empty tomb (28:2). Preachers should note this connection without washing away the stench of the cross to move to the glory of Easter. Reference to Jesus' resurrection in a Passion Sunday sermon should follow Matthew's example in speaking only in a proleptic manner. Instead, it is better to focus primarily on how the notice functions *within* this passage.

Before we do that, however, it might be helpful to warn about avoiding distractions. Congregants may well want to ask about the identity of the saints and about what happened to them after they were raised, as if Matthew were making a historical assertion. Matthew instead is making a theological claim, using evocative literary and mythological imagery. Likely, he means "saints" in the generic sense of righteous ones (since righteousness is a pervasive theme throughout Matthew). He simply does not care about the question of whether the saints are resuscitated (like Lazarus) and die again or are raised to ascend with Jesus or such. Their appearance at this juncture in Matthew's narrative should focus our attention on Jesus and not on them.

Now, what theological and homiletical claims are to be made about this odd little notice in the midst of the crucifixion scene, then? There are two complementary emphases to consider.

First, the contrast between Jesus' crucifixion and the raising of the saints (mentioned in almost the same breath) could not be more striking: this death brings about life! The religious and political authorities thought they were putting an end to Jesus and his movement, but the power of humans to kill is proclaimed to be powerless in the face of God, even at the very moment death arrives. For Matthew, clearly then, the crucifixion is not defeat, with the resurrection being a delayed victory. While the crucifixion is tragic in that it reveals humanity's predilection for evil and violence and its rejection of Jesus, it is life-giving. Resurrection, for us, begins with the cross. This is why we Christians use the ironic label for the liturgical day, commemorating Jesus' death as *Good* Friday.

Second, the earthquake and the raising of the saints show that much contemporary talk of the cross is too small. We often preach the cross only in terms of forgiveness of sins. Clearly, this sort of understanding is an element of Matthew's theology. He presents Jesus as describing his death as a ransom for many (20:28), and the cup of the Last Supper as his "blood of the covenant, which is poured out for many for the forgiveness of sins" (26:28). The mention of the earthquake and raising of the saints shows, however, that for Matthew that element is part of a wider eschatological understanding of the cross. Jesus' death marks the beginning of the birth pangs, so that we the church now and forevermore live in the last days; we live in the "already" of experiencing God's salvation in Christ and the "not yet" of seeing that salvation manifested throughout the whole of the earth.

O. WESLEY ALLEN JR.

Commentary 2: Connecting the Reading with the World

This text, from Jesus' trial before Pilate to his death, is the shorter of two Gospel reading options for the Liturgy of the Passion in Year A, the other spanning the events from Jesus' betrayal by Judas to his burial by Joseph of Arimathea. Either one of these Gospel readings is, in this lectionary, set alongside the Gospel reading for the Liturgy of the Palms, earlier in the worship service. The purpose of having both liturgies (Palms and Passion) on the same Sunday to lead off Holy Week is to highlight the contrast between the exuberant welcome of the Messiah and, a few days later, the cruel rejection of the same Messiah. This tension invites the congregation into meditation of the unfathomable wisdom and grace of God in offering forgiveness and salvation through the death of his own Son, thereby preparing believers for heightened joy and gratitude on Easter Sunday.

This segment of the Passion Narrative is a stark reminder of the paradoxical nature of God's salvation, imparting life through the death of the Messiah. The Son of God, innocent and undeserving of all the torture and mockery inflicted on him by his detractors, goes to the cross in absolute obedience to the divine will with neither protest nor self-justification. Jesus' only words in this reading come in a cry of dereliction: "My God, my God, why have you forsaken me?" (Matt. 27:46). He identifies not only with the anguish of the righteous sufferer in the opening verse of Psalm 22, but also, implicitly, with that sufferer's trust in God's vindication toward the end of the psalm (Ps. 22:19–31).

On the surface, the gospel message of Jesus Christ appears to be a tough sell. Even Paul admits that the message of the crucified Messiah was "a stumbling block to Jews and foolishness to Gentiles" (1 Cor. 1:23). It is still the case today: people look to a strong leader to take charge in the political arena, the business world, and even the church. Surely a savior worthy of that title could do better than ending his life humiliated by his enemies and abandoned by his closest friends. Yet here lies the point of misunderstanding by those who do not believe. Death is not the end of the promise of eternal life, but its beginning.

This order, from death to life, and from suffering to vindication, is essential for the salvation of individual Christians as well as for the proclamation and mission of the church. The resurrection was God's vindication of Jesus' messiahship. Christians follow this Messiah, and relinquishing their lives to the lordship of Jesus is a form of dying. Through faith in Jesus, death to one's self yields a transformed life on this earth and an indestructible life in eternity. Preachers might remind the congregation that, in Christ, death is not to be feared, but is all within the process of God's redemption and regeneration, bringing Christ's own to maturity in faith, both now and for eternity.

If Jesus' path was cruciform, why would his followers expect theirs to be any different? Whether it is a tough sell or not, the Christian message and mission must not deviate from this core historical and theological sequence—from death to life, from suffering to vindication—just to make it more palatable to a skeptical and rebellious world. Jesus trusts God to the point of death in total surrender. Is the church today bold enough to do the same? Given that most people in the pews do not face the threat of martyrdom on account of their faith, preachers might challenge the congregation to reflect on surrendering their time, resources, and relationships to the lordship of Christ.

Related to the issue of suffering is the more specific focus in this reading on injustice, especially in the proceedings of Jesus' trial, sentencing, and death. Although Jesus does not defend himself against the false charges lodged against him before Pilate, the text explicitly states that both the governor and his wife are cognizant of Jesus' innocence. After the death of Jesus, the centurion's acknowledgment of Jesus' sonship affirms not only his innocence, but also his messianic identity.

Injustice, whether individual or systemic, still pervades the world in spite of two millennia of technological and societal advancement. From genocide, discrimination of all stripes, and racial profiling to corruption in law enforcement, human trafficking, and inhumane exploitation of the poor, the propensity of human beings to oppress those who are weak has not diminished. In Jesus' case, the Jewish leaders are motivated by jealousy, and Pilate by expediency. The mob, poised to start a riot unless the governor releases Barabbas for them, is probably fueled by nationalistic fervor, spurred by the religious elite. Each has a self-focused agenda, which is carried out at another's expense. These motivations still thrive in the twenty-first century, as injustice and violence often remain rampant and unchecked.

When Jesus stands before Pilate, nobody speaks up for him. That hardly excuses the church today from staying silent and not speaking up against blatant injustice. To address this, the work of a contemporary artist may offer some food for thought.

Jesus' crucifixion is among the most oft-painted scenes within the Passion Narrative in Western religious art. Consider, for example, *Christ Crucified between Two Thieves: The Three Crosses*, a 1653 drypoint print by Rembrandt. The composition of this print is typical, drawing upon the biblical narratives directly. At the center, Jesus hangs on the cross between two criminals. There are women at the foot of the cross and soldiers looking on nearby. The dark gray tones deliver an ominous signal of the power of darkness.

He Qi, a Chinese Christian artist, provides instead a thought-provoking interpretation that takes liberties with a strictly historical reconstruction. In his 1999 work of colored ink on paper, *The Crucifixion*, Jesus is positioned at the center of the painting. The Holy Spirit, in the form of a dove, replaces the titulus above his head. The other two crosses, while still there, are but tiny strokes in the background. The painting highlights the characters around Jesus—a man behind bars, a nude woman, a woman holding a baby, a man on the ground with his eyes closed, and another man with a cane, who is propped up, half-standing, by a hatted man behind him. These figures wear a range of skin tones, from light to yellow to brown and dark. It is this motley crew, not Jesus' own disciples, who hold vigil under the cross. All of them carry the shame of low status in Jesus' day. They represent sinners, tax collectors, the blind, the lame, women, children, and Gentiles. Jesus was nailed to the cross because of his politically radical mission to restore these nameless and powerless people to physical, spiritual, and communal wholeness. Ironically, in embodying God's justice, Jesus suffered the epitome of injustice from those who were fully intentional about brutally torturing and executing thousands of people.

For Christians today, He Qi's message is urgent and relevant. Every day there are numerous opportunities to do justice and embody the saving grace of Jesus. Preachers might encourage the hearers to identify specific individuals God has placed in their paths for whom they are called to advocate. An act of generosity, a gift of time, or a touch of welcome—nothing goes unnoticed by God. For Jesus himself said, "Just as you did it to one of the least of these . . . you did it to me" (Matt. 25:40).

DIANE G. CHEN

Matthew 26:14–27:66

26:14Then one of the twelve, who was called Judas Iscariot, went to the chief
priests 15and said, "What will you give me if I betray him to you?" They paid him
thirty pieces of silver. 16And from that moment he began to look for an opportunity
to betray him.
17On the first day of Unleavened Bread the disciples came to Jesus, saying,
"Where do you want us to make the preparations for you to eat the Passover?"
18He said, "Go into the city to a certain man, and say to him, 'The Teacher says, My
time is near; I will keep the Passover at your house with my disciples.'" 19So the
disciples did as Jesus had directed them, and they prepared the Passover meal.
20When it was evening, he took his place with the twelve; 21and while they
were eating, he said, "Truly I tell you, one of you will betray me." 22And they
became greatly distressed and began to say to him one after another, "Surely not
I, Lord?" 23He answered, "The one who has dipped his hand into the bowl with
me will betray me. 24The Son of Man goes as it is written of him, but woe to that
one by whom the Son of Man is betrayed! It would have been better for that one
not to have been born." 25Judas, who betrayed him, said, "Surely not I, Rabbi?"
He replied, "You have said so."
26While they were eating, Jesus took a loaf of bread, and after blessing it he
broke it, gave it to the disciples, and said, "Take, eat; this is my body." 27Then he
took a cup, and after giving thanks he gave it to them, saying, "Drink from it, all of
you; 28for this is my blood of the covenant, which is poured out for many for the
forgiveness of sins. 29I tell you, I will never again drink of this fruit of the vine until
that day when I drink it new with you in my Father's kingdom."
30When they had sung the hymn, they went out to the Mount of Olives.
31Then Jesus said to them, "You will all become deserters because of me this
night; for it is written,

'I will strike the shepherd,
and the sheep of the flock will be scattered.'

32But after I am raised up, I will go ahead of you to Galilee." 33Peter said to him,
"Though all become deserters because of you, I will never desert you." 34Jesus
said to him, "Truly I tell you, this very night, before the cock crows, you will deny
me three times." 35Peter said to him, "Even though I must die with you, I will not
deny you." And so said all the disciples.
36Then Jesus went with them to a place called Gethsemane; and he said to his
disciples, "Sit here while I go over there and pray." 37He took with him Peter and
the two sons of Zebedee, and began to be grieved and agitated. 38Then he said
to them, "I am deeply grieved, even to death; remain here, and stay awake with
me." 39And going a little farther, he threw himself on the ground and prayed, "My
Father, if it is possible, let this cup pass from me; yet not what I want but what you
want." 40Then he came to the disciples and found them sleeping; and he said to
Peter, "So, could you not stay awake with me one hour? 41Stay awake and pray
that you may not come into the time of trial; the spirit indeed is willing, but the
flesh is weak." 42Again he went away for the second time and prayed, "My Father,
if this cannot pass unless I drink it, your will be done." 43Again he came and found
them sleeping, for their eyes were heavy. 44So leaving them again, he went away
and prayed for the third time, saying the same words. 45Then he came to the

disciples and said to them, "Are you still sleeping and taking your rest? See, the
hour is at hand, and the Son of Man is betrayed into the hands of sinners. 46Get
up, let us be going. See, my betrayer is at hand."

47While he was still speaking, Judas, one of the twelve, arrived; with him was
a large crowd with swords and clubs, from the chief priests and the elders of the
people. 48Now the betrayer had given them a sign, saying, "The one I will kiss is
the man; arrest him." 49At once he came up to Jesus and said, "Greetings, Rabbi!"
and kissed him. 50Jesus said to him, "Friend, do what you are here to do." Then
they came and laid hands on Jesus and arrested him. 51Suddenly, one of those with
Jesus put his hand on his sword, drew it, and struck the slave of the high priest, cut-
ting off his ear. 52Then Jesus said to him, "Put your sword back into its place; for all
who take the sword will perish by the sword. 53Do you think that I cannot appeal to
my Father, and he will at once send me more than twelve legions of angels? 54But
how then would the scriptures be fulfilled, which say it must happen in this way?"
55At that hour Jesus said to the crowds, "Have you come out with swords and clubs
to arrest me as though I were a bandit? Day after day I sat in the temple teaching,
and you did not arrest me. 56But all this has taken place, so that the scriptures of the
prophets may be fulfilled." Then all the disciples deserted him and fled.

57Those who had arrested Jesus took him to Caiaphas the high priest, in
whose house the scribes and the elders had gathered. 58But Peter was following
him at a distance, as far as the courtyard of the high priest; and going inside, he
sat with the guards in order to see how this would end. 59Now the chief priests
and the whole council were looking for false testimony against Jesus so that
they might put him to death, 60but they found none, though many false witnesses
came forward. At last two came forward 61and said, "This fellow said, 'I am able to
destroy the temple of God and to build it in three days.'" 62The high priest stood
up and said, "Have you no answer? What is it that they testify against you?" 63But
Jesus was silent. Then the high priest said to him, "I put you under oath before
the living God, tell us if you are the Messiah, the Son of God." 64Jesus said to him,
"You have said so. But I tell you,

From now on you will see the Son of Man
   seated at the right hand of Power
   and coming on the clouds of heaven."

65Then the high priest tore his clothes and said, "He has blasphemed! Why do we
still need witnesses? You have now heard his blasphemy. 66What is your verdict?"
They answered, "He deserves death." 67Then they spat in his face and struck him;
and some slapped him, 68saying, "Prophesy to us, you Messiah! Who is it that
struck you?"

69Now Peter was sitting outside in the courtyard. A servant-girl came to him
and said, "You also were with Jesus the Galilean." 70But he denied it before all
of them, saying, "I do not know what you are talking about." 71When he went out
to the porch, another servant-girl saw him, and she said to the bystanders, "This
man was with Jesus of Nazareth." 72Again he denied it with an oath, "I do not
know the man." 73After a little while the bystanders came up and said to Peter,
"Certainly you are also one of them, for your accent betrays you." 74Then he
began to curse, and he swore an oath, "I do not know the man!" At that moment
the cock crowed. 75Then Peter remembered what Jesus had said: "Before the
cock crows, you will deny me three times." And he went out and wept bitterly.

27:1When morning came, all the chief priests and the elders of the people conferred together against Jesus in order to bring about his death. 2They bound him,
led him away, and handed him over to Pilate the governor.

3When Judas, his betrayer, saw that Jesus was condemned, he repented and brought back the thirty pieces of silver to the chief priests and the elders. 4He said, "I have sinned by betraying innocent blood." But they said, "What is that to us? See to it yourself." 5Throwing down the pieces of silver in the temple, he departed; and he went and hanged himself. 6But the chief priests, taking the pieces of silver, said, "It is not lawful to put them into the treasury, since they are blood money." 7After conferring together, they used them to buy the potter's field as a place to bury foreigners. 8For this reason that field has been called the Field of Blood to this day. 9Then was fulfilled what had been spoken through the prophet Jeremiah, "And they took the thirty pieces of silver, the price of the one on whom a price had been set, on whom some of the people of Israel had set a price, 10and they gave them for the potter's field, as the Lord commanded me."

11Now Jesus stood before the governor; and the governor asked him, "Are you the King of the Jews?" Jesus said, "You say so." 12But when he was accused by the chief priests and elders, he did not answer. 13Then Pilate said to him, "Do you not hear how many accusations they make against you?" 14But he gave him no answer, not even to a single charge, so that the governor was greatly amazed.

15Now at the festival the governor was accustomed to release a prisoner for the crowd, anyone whom they wanted. 16At that time they had a notorious prisoner, called Jesus Barabbas. 17So after they had gathered, Pilate said to them, "Whom do you want me to release for you, Jesus Barabbas or Jesus who is called the Messiah?" 18For he realized that it was out of jealousy that they had handed him over. 19While he was sitting on the judgment seat, his wife sent word to him, "Have nothing to do with that innocent man, for today I have suffered a great deal because of a dream about him." 20Now the chief priests and the elders persuaded the crowds to ask for Barabbas and to have Jesus killed. 21The governor again said to them, "Which of the two do you want me to release for you?" And they said, "Barabbas." 22Pilate said to them, "Then what should I do with Jesus who is called the Messiah?" All of them said, "Let him be crucified!" 23Then he asked, "Why, what evil has he done?" But they shouted all the more, "Let him be crucified!"

24So when Pilate saw that he could do nothing, but rather that a riot was beginning, he took some water and washed his hands before the crowd, saying, "I am innocent of this man's blood; see to it yourselves." 25Then the people as a whole answered, "His blood be on us and on our children!" 26So he released Barabbas for them; and after flogging Jesus, he handed him over to be crucified.

27Then the soldiers of the governor took Jesus into the governor's headquarters, and they gathered the whole cohort around him. 28They stripped him and put a scarlet robe on him, 29and after twisting some thorns into a crown, they put it on his head. They put a reed in his right hand and knelt before him and mocked him, saying, "Hail, King of the Jews!" 30They spat on him, and took the reed and struck him on the head. 31After mocking him, they stripped him of the robe and put his own clothes on him. Then they led him away to crucify him.

32As they went out, they came upon a man from Cyrene named Simon; they compelled this man to carry his cross. 33And when they came to a place called Golgotha (which means Place of a Skull), 34they offered him wine to drink, mixed with gall; but when he tasted it, he would not drink it. 35And when they had crucified him, they divided his clothes among themselves by casting lots; 36then they sat down there and kept watch over him. 37Over his head they put the charge against him, which read, "This is Jesus, the King of the Jews."

38Then two bandits were crucified with him, one on his right and one on his left. 39Those who passed by derided him, shaking their heads 40and saying, "You who would destroy the temple and build it in three days, save yourself! If you are the Son of God, come down from the cross." 41In the same way the chief priests also, along with the scribes and elders, were mocking him, saying, 42"He saved others; he cannot save himself. He is the King of Israel; let him come down from the cross now, and we will believe in him. 43He trusts in God; let God deliver him now, if he wants to; for he said, 'I am God's Son.'" 44The bandits who were crucified with him also taunted him in the same way.

45From noon on, darkness came over the whole land until three in the afternoon. 46And about three o'clock Jesus cried with a loud voice, "Eli, Eli, lema sabachthani?" that is, "My God, my God, why have you forsaken me?" 47When some of the bystanders heard it, they said, "This man is calling for Elijah." 48At once one of them ran and got a sponge, filled it with sour wine, put it on a stick, and gave it to him to drink. 49But the others said, "Wait, let us see whether Elijah will come to save him." 50Then Jesus cried again with a loud voice and breathed his last. 51At that moment the curtain of the temple was torn in two, from top to bottom. The earth shook, and the rocks were split. 52The tombs also were opened, and many bodies of the saints who had fallen asleep were raised. 53After his resurrection they came out of the tombs and entered the holy city and appeared to many. 54Now when the centurion and those with him, who were keeping watch over Jesus, saw the earthquake and what took place, they were terrified and said, "Truly this man was God's Son!"

55Many women were also there, looking on from a distance; they had followed Jesus from Galilee and had provided for him. 56Among them were Mary Magdalene, and Mary the mother of James and Joseph, and the mother of the sons of Zebedee.

57When it was evening, there came a rich man from Arimathea, named Joseph, who was also a disciple of Jesus. 58He went to Pilate and asked for the body of Jesus; then Pilate ordered it to be given to him. 59So Joseph took the body and wrapped it in a clean linen cloth 60and laid it in his own new tomb, which he had hewn in the rock. He then rolled a great stone to the door of the tomb and went away. 61Mary Magdalene and the other Mary were there, sitting opposite the tomb.

62The next day, that is, after the day of Preparation, the chief priests and the Pharisees gathered before Pilate 63and said, "Sir, we remember what that impostor said while he was still alive, 'After three days I will rise again.' 64Therefore command the tomb to be made secure until the third day; otherwise his disciples may go and steal him away, and tell the people, 'He has been raised from the dead,' and the last deception would be worse than the first." 65Pilate said to them, "You have a guard of soldiers; go, make it as secure as you can." 66So they went with the guard and made the tomb secure by sealing the stone.

Commentary 1: Connecting the Reading with Scripture

Palm/Passion Sunday combines palm and passion themes into a single Sunday as an important resource for congregations with little observance of Holy Week days between this Sunday and Easter. A community should not sing hosannas one Sunday and alleluias the next without pausing at the cross. A sermon about Jesus' passion on this Sunday, then, may be the only chance for many congregants to stand in the shadow of the cross before rejoicing at the empty tomb.

This is an extremely long text from which to preach. Indeed, given its length, sometimes congregations may be satisfied simply to read the story dramatically, letting it stand on its own without a sermon. While there can be great significance in this approach, it would be a shame if year after year, preachers failed to offer their congregations interpretations of the Passion Narrative, as if its meaning were self-evident. Believers need help making sense of the crucifixion theologically.

A preacher can no more do justice to the whole of this lection than can this brief commentary. A preacher would do well to focus on a single scene (perhaps that of the cross) while using the rest of the narrative as context; for an example of this option, see the commentary on the shorter alternative reading, Matthew 27:11–54. Alternatively, the preacher might look for some overarching theme or element of the whole upon which to focus. This essay will address the latter of these two options. One way to do this would be for the preacher to interject commentary at key junctures in the story instead of reading the entire lengthy text and then offering a short homily. Focusing on the pathos evoked as the story unfolds will tie these comments together.

Before we explore a homiletical approach to this pathos, it will be helpful to offer a caveat. A long homiletical tradition in the church is to focus on Jesus' suffering, even to the point of the preacher pounding the pulpit along with the description of nails piercing Jesus' wrists and explicitly describing the blood dripping down Jesus' body. While the scene of Jesus' suffering and death is certainly filled with narrative pathos, it is not of the sort that is usually preached these days. One should note that the actual act of crucifying Jesus is told in very little detail. There is no depiction of nailing or bleeding. These sorts of elements come more from the Hebrew Bible readings (Isa. 50:4–9a, one of the Suffering Servant passages) and the Psalter reading (Ps. 31:9–16, an individual lament) than from the Gospel. Matthew names the act of crucifixion in a subordinate clause, almost in passing: "And when they had crucified him . . ." (Matt. 27:35). Humanity's obsession with the morbid and grotesque should not be entertained in a sermon on the cross. It is *the fact* that Jesus was crucified and died that is important to the Gospel writers, not the horrific details of that death.

The pathos to which preachers should attend, then, is the progressive emotional experience the narrative creates for the readers. This experience is not of the sort one would experience when hearing the story for the first time. Matthew was written for people who already knew of Jesus' death and were dedicated members of the church, a situation analogous to preaching in a congregational setting on Palm/Passion Sunday. Preachers should not pretend that the story is new to hearers and that they do not know of the resurrection to follow the crucifixion. The pathos is that of followers of Jesus reliving the tragic and eschatological death of their leader, a death that changed us and is still changing the world.

The best way preachers can help hearers experience this pathos is to invite them to identify with the disciples in the story (just as Matthew's original hearers would have done). In the earlier material of the narrative, Matthew often redeems Mark's presentation of the disciples, making them appear more faithful and having better theological understanding. In this lection, however, we see the disciples at their worst.

Gospel texts rarely describe the emotional state of characters in the story, though this does not stop preachers from psychologizing biblical characters in their sermons. In the Jerusalem narrative, however, we have a number of references to emotions upon which preachers could comment as they progress through the story.

First, just prior to the beginning of the lection, the disciples become inappropriately angry (*aganakteō*) when a woman anoints Jesus in preparation for his death (Matt. 26:6–13).

Second, during the Passover meal the disciples are greatly saddened (*lypeō*) when Jesus announces that one of them will betray him (26:22).

Third, the narrator explicitly names Jesus' emotions in the scene in Gethsemane when Jesus withdraws with his inner circle of disciples (26:36–46). At the transfiguration (17:1–8), they saw his true glory. Now they see his deepest angst. Matthew describes Jesus as starting to become distressed (*lypeisthai*) and troubled or "agitated" (*adēmonein*) in 26:37. Jesus names himself similarly in the next verse when he tells the inner group of disciples how he is feeling. Translated woodenly, his words are, "My life is grieved to death" (*perilypos estin hē psychē mou heōs thanatou*). Jesus then throws himself on the ground in isolation (vv. 38–39). Strikingly, however, the disciples show neither emotion nor any signs of empathy. They are simply sleepy. Even when they abandon Jesus at his arrest and flee, the narrator assigns them no explicit emotion (v. 56). The contrast is painful for those of us identifying with the disciples. Matthew seems to be indicting *our* apathy in response to Jesus' suffering.

Fourth, while the narrator withholds comment on Peter's emotional state as he denies knowing Jesus (vv. 69–75), the scene ends with the emotional display of Peter weeping bitterly. With the exception of Judas repenting and hanging himself (27:1–10), the disciples disappear from the story of the passion following Peter's denial.

Working through the long Jerusalem narrative, the preacher could trace the disciples' emotions at the beginning of the story, and then through the trials and crucifixion repeatedly ask something like, "I wonder what they would have been feeling if they had still been by Jesus' side at this point."

The final emotions evoked by the sermon, however, should not be in the realm of melancholy or guilt. Having portrayed the disciples' failure of nerve and unfaithfulness, a preacher would do well after narrating Jesus' death to offer a flashback to Jesus' promise of enduring presence. Earlier, even while he was understandably preoccupied with his coming death, Jesus was also concerned for the fate of the disciples. After his Last Supper he tells them that they will desert and deny him, but he also promises that after the resurrection he will meet them in Galilee (26:31–32). So, we too will meet Christ again on Easter.

One way that preachers might have the hearers experience the passion story while simultaneously foreshadowing hope is to look to the other lections of the day. The preacher could draw in the epistle reading as a way of connecting passion and proleptic hope. Philippians 2:5–11 is fitting for the day because it portrays Christ's passion in terms of his self-emptying. There is pathos in this language as well, but the Christ hymn ends with language of eschatological exaltation. Reading (or rereading) this Pauline text at the end of a sermon on Matthew would be like ending the sermon with an ellipsis indicating more to come.

O. WESLEY ALLEN JR.

Commentary 2: Connecting the Reading with the World

The Revised Common Lectionary appoints one of the Synoptic Gospels' passion accounts for Palm/Passion Sunday, in addition to the reading at the Liturgy of the Palms. Compared to the other suggested Gospel reading for Year A for the Liturgy of the Passion (the complementary reading), this one (the standard reading) is almost thrice as long. Time constraints may be a factor as to which reading is chosen. If many in the congregation do not attend other services during Holy Week, then the longer Gospel reading is an opportunity for them to reflect on the entire story of Jesus' suffering, beginning with the betrayal of Judas, through his arrest and trials, to his death and burial. Listening to these events, one after another, can be highly instructive in this day and age to many churchgoers for whom biblical literacy can no longer be assumed.

Two connections are offered in relation to this reading. The first has to do with how Jesus' suffering emboldens, rather than stifles, the mission of the church. The word "rejection" encapsulates the type of suffering that the Messiah endured in these two chapters. Judas betrayed him. Peter denied knowing him. All the other disciples deserted him. The Jewish leaders and their cronies piled false accusations on him, abused him verbally and physically, and incited the crowd to call for his death. The Roman soldiers flogged and mocked him, and out of expediency, Pilate turned a blind eye to justice and ordered his crucifixion.

Any one of these forms of rejection would be hard enough, let alone having all of them hurled continuously at Jesus until his final breath. A crucified Messiah would have been a contradiction in terms for the Jews, but a Messiah who had endured such abandonment and hostility would actually provide the best encouragement to his followers, who sooner or later would find themselves on a path of discipleship that is likewise riddled with rejection.

The rejection of God's salvation and its messengers has not let up in the last two millennia. Many believers have suffered, and others have died. In China, North Korea, Afghanistan, Somalia, and Sudan, the persecution of Christians is a present threat. Even in places where there is supposed to be freedom of religion, believers can find themselves facing misunderstanding, apathy, or ridicule. In fact, if followers of Jesus cause no ripple, face no resistance, and make no impact in the secular world, something is amiss.

Not that Christians should actively seek martyrdom or glorify suffering as proof of their commitment to Jesus, but if they are blissfully at ease with society and its values, one wonders whether the salt has lost its saltiness (Matt. 5:13; Mark 9:50; Luke 14:34). Preachers might challenge their congregation to engage in some honest self-reflection: Have they become too inward-looking without realizing it? As a church, are they offering their neighbors an authentic gospel or a comfortable self-help gathering? Are they prepared to risk opposition for the sake of Christ? These are hard but necessary questions.

Note that Jesus' cry of dereliction, "My God, my God, why have you forsaken me?" (Matt. 27:46), is not included in the types of rejections mentioned above. At first glance, Jesus' words from Psalm 22:1 may easily be interpreted as an anguished cry of abandonment of a dying man. On further reflection, it makes better theological sense to consider not only the first verse but the entire psalm of lament, so that the righteous sufferer's trust in God's faithfulness and deliverance is not lost to the reader (Ps. 22:19–31).

Lest this tidal wave of Jesus' rejection leave his readers swamped by fear and hopelessness, the evangelist extends the trajectory implied in Psalm 22 by offering a glimmer of hope near the end of this reading. Several supernatural occurrences immediately after Jesus' death—the tearing of the temple veil, the earthquake, the raising of many from death to life—anticipate God's vindication of Jesus in the final chapter of Matthew's narrative. Even here, the truth is articulated, ironically, on the lips of the centurion and those who were with him: "Truly this man was God's Son!" (27:54).

Preachers must encourage their hearers, individually and together as a church, to press forward in bold and compelling witness, for they already know how all this will end according to God's sovereign and salvific purposes. By trusting in God's promises and relying on the power of the Holy Spirit, believers will receive grace to face whatever hardship comes their way on account of their faithfulness.

Another connection may be drawn from the contemporary culture through the use of film that brings the story of Jesus to a wider audience. In the last sixty years, many movies have been made on the life of Jesus. While most of them portray Jesus' teaching and healing ministry in Galilee before his final week in Jerusalem, only one, *The Passion of the Christ* (2004), written, directed, and produced by Mel Gibson, is entirely devoted to the twelve hours culminating in Jesus' death—from Gethsemane to Golgotha, with a quick nod to the resurrection at the very end.

The materials in this movie are drawn from all four Gospels. Events particular to Matthew include the regret and suicide of Judas, Pilate washing his hands, the rending of the temple veil, the earthquake, and the emergence of the dead from the tombs. There are ample embellishments to heighten the dramatic effect of various scenes, such as an appearance of Satan at Gethsemane and Jesus crushing a serpent's head with his heels. Historical facts are thus intertwined with fiction and theatrical imagination. Only viewers familiar with the biblical accounts can tell what is actually in the Gospels, and what is drawn from later Christian tradition or other sources.

Reviews were mixed; concerns about anti-Semitism were debated. Viewers were united in underscoring the shock effect created by the film's unrelenting violence. Blood is everywhere, accompanied by blood-curdling screams and the most brutal of assaults to the human body and psyche in gory detail. Gibson has succeeded in giving viewers a visceral sense of the torture

Jesus endured, eliciting a range of responses from deep sympathy and righteous indignation to horror and revulsion.

For some people, the graphic nature of the film heightens their appreciation of how much Jesus suffered and died for them. For others, the sensory overload is so overwhelming that it becomes a hindrance to reflection on the significance of Jesus' death. It becomes difficult to look past the violence. Because the movie covers only the last twelve hours of Jesus' life, it lacks the broader context found in all four Gospels. Despite its limited focus and selective departure from the scriptural narrative, this movie can still serve as an accessible starting point for a more robust conversation about God's salvation through Jesus the Messiah. A nonbeliever may never pick up a Bible but may be curious enough to see a box-office hit. Used properly, this movie, its flaws notwithstanding, may be cautiously employed to serve an evangelistic end. In no way, though, should a movie be deemed an adequate substitute for the biblical account.

Lasting faith cannot be sustained merely by an emotional impact, however strong and impressionable it might be. What makes Jesus' unimaginably grisly death meaningful is precisely its theological underpinning. The death of God's own Son sealed with blood the covenant between God and God's people for the forgiveness of sins, in order that Scripture be fulfilled (26:26–28). No human rejection can change this fact of history, that God's redemption of humankind is embodied in Jesus' passion—in the suffering love of a Savior.

DIANE G. CHEN

Holy Thursday

Exodus 12:1–4 (5–10), 11–14
Psalm 116:1–2, 12–19

1 Corinthians 11:23–26
John 13:1–17, 31b–35

Exodus 12:1–4 (5–10), 11–14

[1]The LORD said to Moses and Aaron in the land of Egypt: [2]This month shall mark for you the beginning of months; it shall be the first month of the year for you. [3]Tell the whole congregation of Israel that on the tenth of this month they are to take a lamb for each family, a lamb for each household. [4]If a household is too small for a whole lamb, it shall join its closest neighbor in obtaining one; the lamb shall be divided in proportion to the number of people who eat of it. [5]Your lamb shall be without blemish, a year-old male; you may take it from the sheep or from the goats. [6]You shall keep it until the fourteenth day of this month; then the whole assembled congregation of Israel shall slaughter it at twilight. [7]They shall take some of the blood and put it on the two doorposts and the lintel of the houses in which they eat it. [8]They shall eat the lamb that same night; they shall eat it roasted over the fire with unleavened bread and bitter herbs. [9]Do not eat any of it raw or boiled in water, but roasted over the fire, with its head, legs, and inner organs. [10]You shall let none of it remain until the morning; anything that remains until the morning you shall burn. [11]This is how you shall eat it: your loins girded, your sandals on your feet, and your staff in your hand; and you shall eat it hurriedly. It is the passover of the LORD. [12]For I will pass through the land of Egypt that night, and I will strike down every firstborn in the land of Egypt, both human beings and animals; on all the gods of Egypt I will execute judgments: I am the LORD. [13]The blood shall be a sign for you on the houses where you live: when I see the blood, I will pass over you, and no plague shall destroy you when I strike the land of Egypt.

[14]This day shall be a day of remembrance for you. You shall celebrate it as a festival to the LORD; throughout your generations you shall observe it as a perpetual ordinance.

Commentary 1: Connecting the Reading with Scripture

The instructions for the first Passover meal in Exodus 12 provide the background for the events of Holy Thursday as described in the Gospels, as well as for the recitation of those events in Paul's letter to the church at Corinth. One might picture the different texts as points along a time line, a time line that stretches back to the time of the exodus and forward to the "marriage supper of the Lamb" (Rev. 19:9).

At the beginning, of course, is the story in Exodus 12. In its immediate context, the chapter serves as the culmination of the story of the conflict between Pharaoh and Moses over the fate of the Hebrew slaves. Moses, acting as the messenger of God, tells Pharaoh over and over again, "Let my people go." Pharaoh's heart is hardened again and again, and the plagues mount up to the point that even Pharaoh's counselors beg him to let the Hebrew people go: "Do you not yet understand that Egypt is ruined?" (Exod. 10:7).

Pharaoh's pride and greed indeed lead him to ruin Egypt instead of giving in to the demands of Israel's God. In this single-minded, destructive obsession, Pharaoh is the prototype for countless despots who have done the same over the centuries, grasping power desperately even as their nations disintegrate around them and their people suffer. The preacher has many examples from which to draw. Like these despots, Pharaoh refuses to obey God, even though his people suffer because of his stubbornness and sin.

The culmination of the story, then, is the last and most terrible plague of all: the death of the Egyptian firstborn. Though a difficult story, this narrative repays the preacher's close attention. The death of the firstborn must be understood in the context of the whole book of Exodus. The book begins with a failed attempt at genocide. Pharaoh, afraid of the burgeoning population of Israelites, orders his people to kill every Hebrew baby boy (1:22). Pharaoh defies God's will for life. He works against God's commandment to humanity at creation, to "be fruitful and multiply" (Gen. 1:28), a commandment that has begun to be lived out by the Israelites, who "were fruitful and prolific; they multiplied and grew exceedingly strong" (Exod. 1:7).

Pharaoh's actions are, as Terence Fretheim has shown, "anticreational." So the plagues are a natural response to and an outgrowth of those antilife measures. The plagues can be understood as "the effect of Pharaoh's anticreational sins upon the cosmic order writ large."[1] In the plagues, the order established by God at creation is broken. Pests like frogs and locusts overrun the boundaries set for them at creation. Primordial darkness—the same darkness (*hoshek*) that covered the deep before creation—engulfs the land of Egypt so that the world, or that corner of it, returns again to primeval chaos (Gen. 1:2; Exod. 10:21–23).

The last plague, then, is the culmination of the anticreational forces that Pharaoh himself has brought upon his land. In particular, the death of the Egyptian firstborn is the result of the antilife measures that Pharaoh and all the Egyptian people perpetrated against God's firstborn son, Israel, in the first chapter of Exodus. That connection is made even before Moses first appears before Pharaoh: "Thus says the Lord: Israel is my firstborn son. I said to you, 'Let my son go that he may worship me.' But you refused to let him go; now I will kill your firstborn son" (4:22–23). Later, God's special claim on Israel's own firstborn is asserted. This claim results not in death, however, but redemption (Exod. 13:11–16).

In contrast to the dismay modern hearers may feel about the death of the Egyptian firstborn, the Exodus 12 text does not dwell on that death. Instead, it celebrates the deliverance of God's people from slavery and teaches subsequent generations how to commemorate that event. In particular, God gives instructions before the Passover about how the Israelites are to prepare. At the center of the preparations is the Passover lamb, whose blood—painted on the door frame of each family's house—will save the inhabitants of that house from death, and whose body will serve as the food for the Passover meal.

This focus on the Passover lamb, of course, makes for a natural connection homiletically with the Gospel text for Holy Thursday. Unlike the other Gospels, John does not speak of the dinner that Jesus eats with his disciples as a Passover meal; it occurs "before the festival of the Passover" (John 13:1). Instead, Jesus is crucified on the day of preparation for the Passover (19:14); in other words, on the day that the Passover lambs are slaughtered. The body and blood of this Passover lamb will save God's people from the forces of oppression and death, just as in the first Passover, though this time the victory is cosmic in scope. Not just Pharaoh, but death itself is defeated.

The Exodus 12 text places a strong emphasis on remembrance. The Passover meal, even in its first enactment, is not understood merely as a onetime event. God instructs Israel to remember and to reenact that meal: "This day shall be a day of remembrance for you. You shall celebrate it as a festival to the Lord; throughout your generations you shall observe it as a perpetual ordinance" (Exod. 12:14). Even after entering the promised land, the Israelites are to remember and reenact the deliverance of their ancestors, as if it had happened to them. "You shall tell your child on that day, 'It is because of what the Lord did for me when I came out of Egypt'" (13:8).

1. Terence E. Fretheim, *Exodus* (Louisville, KY: John Knox, 1991), 107.

The act of remembrance guards against nostalgia. The bitter herbs and unleavened bread eaten with the Passover lamb remind future generations of Israelites that their lot was bitter in Egypt and that their deliverance was sudden, so sudden that their bread had no time to rise (12:8–11). When they are tempted to return to Egypt, to oppression and slavery, the Passover reminds them what life in Egypt was like and what kind of God they serve—a God of deliverance.

This theme of remembrance resonates strongly with the Gospel accounts of the Last Supper (which is a Passover meal in the Synoptic Gospels), and with the epistle lesson for today. Paul describes Jesus' last meal with his disciples as a feast of remembrance, "'This is my body that is for you. Do this in remembrance of me. . . . This cup is the new covenant in my blood. Do this, as often as you drink it, in remembrance of me'" (1 Cor. 11:24–25). The preacher might remind the congregation that the Lord's Supper, like the first Passover meal, is not a onetime event. It is a meal that is to be remembered and reenacted throughout subsequent generations, proclaiming to each new generation the wonder of God's deliverance: "For as often as you eat this bread and drink the cup, you proclaim the Lord's death until he comes" (1 Cor. 11:26).

Passover, the Last Supper, and the continuing reenactment of both meals through the centuries as feasts of liberation and life, and as "foretaste[s] of the feast to come"[2]—these texts hold rich possibilities for preaching. The focus on this Holy Thursday will undoubtedly be on the Gospel account, but the story of Passover provides the necessary background for understanding the events of that night, as Jesus himself becomes the Passover lamb given for the sake of the world.

KATHRYN SCHIFFERDECKER

Commentary 2: Connecting the Reading with the World

To read the story of Passover on Holy Thursday is to invite and invoke—celebrate, even—the many connections between the story of the exodus, the story of Jesus' last meal with the disciples, and the Eucharist that memorializes Jesus' death. There are, of course, possible historical connections at work here. While the Gospel chronologies differ, Luke is quite clear that this is a Passover meal (Luke 22:1, 7, 8, 11, 13, 15). Things are less certain according to John. Regardless, what cannot be gainsaid are the strong echoes and allusions found in the timing of the Last Supper (according to the Synoptics) and the content of the Passion Narratives, which together seem to connect Jesus' last meal with his disciples to the meal first legislated in Exodus.

Whatever the possible *historical* connections or *literary* relationships, there are also *liturgical* considerations: so, again, to read this story on Holy Thursday before Good Friday is to entertain the deeply comparable, even parallel, nature of God's redemptive activity in Israel and in Christ, the exodus and the cross. Preachers should help congregants see such deep connections between the testaments, to help prevent ever-present Marcionite tendencies to see otherwise.

Exodus 12 begins with a chronological notice: the culminating, climactic tenth sign (see Exod. 11:1–10) is, first and foremost, *calendarized.* The importance of the event about to transpire—both in terms of what God does to Egypt and what God does *not* do to Israel—is of such magnitude that the reckoning of the year must be thoroughly reconsidered. This significance of the event means that the month in which it happens (Abib, see Exod. 13:4; April–May in contemporary calendars) must now be considered the first month in the year. The year is not to be reckoned by lunar or solar considerations, nor by agriculture cycles, but by God's redemptive action. This is not unlike how the Western church's calendar begins in Advent, not in January, though if Exodus 12 were the

2. "Holy Communion, Setting One," *Lutheran Book of Worship* (Philadelphia: Augsburg Fortress, 1978), 66.

model, the Christian year would begin not at Advent, but at Eastertime.

The event in Exodus 12 is not only calendarized; it is *liturgized*. Still further, "liturgy *precedes* the liberative event," according to this text.[3] The death of the firstborn will lead directly to Israel's release from Egypt (11:1; 12:31–32), but before the exodus and before the last plague, there is liturgical commemoration *in advance*. So, also, with the Eucharist: God's work in Christ's death on the cross is now past and accomplished, but in the meal we proclaim Christ's death "until he comes again" (1 Cor. 11:26). The liturgical enactment of the Lord's Supper, like the Passover meal, hearkens back to the past but also points to the future. In a very real sense, in both cases the still-to-be-realized future is the ultimate moment of redemption: freedom from Egypt, the hope of glory.

Both Israel and the church thus commemorate and celebrate God's ultimate victory *before* experiencing it. Therefore, the futuristic or eschatological aspects of the meal are just as important as the past, memorializing ones, if not more important. Liturgy is indeed a way the past is made present, but it is also a way to make the future present. One might go so far to say that liturgy is *timeless*, somehow outside of or above time—hence the mystery of faith: "Christ *has* died, Christ *is* risen, Christ *will* come again"—even as liturgy *shapes time*, including the rather mundane reckoning of days, months, years, calendars. How could this be true for local Christian communions?

Oddly, the lectionary commends the reading of verses 3–4 and 11, which concern the lamb for the meal and the manner of its consumption, but leaves as optional verses 5–10, which contain important details about the lamb and the symbol of its blood on the door frames of Israelite homes. Verse 4 is worth dwelling on, as it is additional evidence for the flexibility of Old Testament law and its concern for those households, whether smaller or poorer or both, that may not otherwise be able to meet the standard requirements (Lev. 12:8; Luke 2:24).

The meal is familial and communal, and everyone is to have enough—just enough, or so it would seem. Hoarding and gluttony, at any rate, are not envisioned (see 1 Cor. 11:17–26); also not envisioned is leisurely supping until one is pleasantly satisfied, since the meal is to be eaten in haste, as if the diners are ready to leave at a moment's notice (Exod. 12:11; see Matt. 24:42; Mark 13:33, 35). There is no time for leftovers, therefore; anything that is not consumed must be destroyed (12:10). This anticipates the manna account (Exod. 16), which likely underlies Jesus' prayer for "daily bread" (Matt. 6:11; Luke 11:3). Once again, from two testaments grow one Scripture (John Donne).

The blood of the lamb is obviously a pregnant symbol in Exodus 12 and beyond. The blood is explicitly said to be a sign "for you" (Exod. 12:13)—not, that is, for God. True, God will see the blood and pass over Israelite houses during the last plague, but the sign is for Israel. It is thus a sign of "divine promise: *God commits himself* to pass over the blood-marked houses."[4] The external or public nature of this sign—as opposed to an internal reminder to God—is also present in the Eucharist, which is to be "proclaimed" (NRSV) or "broadcasted" (CEB) until the Lord's return.

Lamb imagery is frequently found in the New Testament with reference to Christ (John 1:29, 36; Rev. 5:6; and so on), with the blood of the lamb that is Christ explicitly mentioned three times (1 Pet. 1:19; Rev. 7:14; 12:11). In these texts, no less than in Exodus 12, the blood represents great cost, the very sacrifice of life, even as it protects those who are now marked by it. This too is a mystery: "*God uses creation to achieve redemption*."[5]

One last comparison between Passover and Eucharist might be drawn. Despite the clear instructions for roasting, not boiling, the lamb in Exodus 12:8–9, other texts offer different, even contradictory, instructions: Deuteronomy 16:7 allows for boiling after all; and 2 Chronicles 35:13 seems to harmonize the options. Such

3. Terence E. Fretheim, *Exodus* (Louisville, KY: John Knox, 1991), 137.
4. Fretheim, *Exodus*, 138 (emphasis original).
5. Fretheim, *Exodus*, 138 (emphasis original).

discrepancies often cause problems of logic for preachers and laity alike. Are the accounts of the Eucharist any different? There is comparable, if not much wider, disagreement on the practice and meaning of the Lord's Supper, as regards notions of transubstantiation of elements, the real presence of Christ in the sacrament, or the meal as a memorial. Perhaps variation in the Passover meal permits, even authorizes, variation in Christian attitudes toward the Lord's Supper, paving the way for generosity toward those who view or celebrate in different ways without mandating strict uniformity.

As a further example, we might return to the Lord's Prayer. According to Luke's account, when one prays, one is to "say" (*legete*, Luke 11:2) the prayer Jesus offers. The prayer is thus a *script* to be recited verbatim. In Matthew, however, one is to pray "in this way" or "thusly" (*houtōs*; Matt. 6:9). Here the prayer is not a script but a *model*. Perhaps the Lord's Supper, no less than the Lord's Prayer and the Passover meal, can be similarly understood. Good preaching can help overcome faux distinctions between the testaments and can help unite Christians despite distinctive beliefs and practices.

BRENT A. STRAWN

Psalm 116:1–2, 12–19

1I love the LORD, because he has heard
my voice and my supplications.
2Because he inclined his ear to me,
therefore I will call on him as long as I live.
. . . .
12What shall I return to the LORD
for all his bounty to me?
13I will lift up the cup of salvation
and call on the name of the LORD,
14I will pay my vows to the LORD
in the presence of all his people.
15Precious in the sight of the LORD
is the death of his faithful ones.
16O LORD, I am your servant;
I am your servant, the child of your serving girl.
You have loosed my bonds.
17I will offer to you a thanksgiving sacrifice
and call on the name of the LORD.
18I will pay my vows to the LORD
in the presence of all his people,
19in the courts of the house of the LORD,
in your midst, O Jerusalem.
Praise the LORD!

Connecting the Psalm with Scripture and Worship

Maundy Thursday takes its name from the Latin word for commandment, *mandatum*. On this day we remember God's commandment to keep the Passover (Exod. 12:14), we celebrate the feast that Jesus commanded us to share in his name (1 Cor. 11:23), and we proclaim Christ's new commandment: to love one another as he has loved us (John 13:34). How does Psalm 116 help us respond to this triple commandment, both in the liturgy and in our daily life?

"I love the LORD" (Ps. 116:1), declares the psalmist, setting the tone for this ballad of trauma and triumph. Biblical scholars classify Psalm 116 as an individual song of thanksgiving. True to its literary form, this psalm has a simple, three-part structure—opening with an exclamation of gratitude to God (vv. 1–2), recounting an experience of distress and deliverance (vv. 3–9), and concluding with the promise of public thanks and praise (vv. 10–19). The theme of love unites these disparate parts: the saving love of God and the adoration of the one whom God has saved.

Along the way, Psalm 116 contributes a remarkable array of vivid imagery to the vocabulary of prayer: "The snares of death encompassed me" (v. 3); "You have delivered my soul from death, my eyes from tears, my feet from stumbling" (v. 8); and "I walk before the LORD in the land of the living" (v. 9). Particularly relevant to the commandments of Maundy Thursday is this couplet: "What shall I return to the LORD for all [God's] bounty to me? I will lift up the cup of salvation and call on the name of the LORD" (vv. 12–13).

As Old Testament scholar Bernhard Anderson points out, the lifting of a cup as a votive offering to a deity was a familiar ritual act in the ancient Near East. Anderson wonders if the reference to the cup in Psalm 116:13 might be metaphorical; nevertheless, it is consistent with descriptions of daily drink offerings in Exodus 29:40 and Numbers 28:7. Indeed, Anderson notes that the elevation of the chalice as an act of thanksgiving remains a common gesture in Jewish and Christian worship; accordingly, his discussion of Psalm 116 is offered under the heading "Eucharistic Praise."[1] For contemporary Jews, Psalm 116 is at the heart of the group of Hallel Psalms (Pss. 113–118) recited at Pesach, or Passover. In Jewish tradition, the first half of the psalm (vv. 1–11) is sometimes omitted; similarly, the RCL omits verses 3–11 on Maundy Thursday, but highlights the cup by picking back up at verse 12.

In the context of the Maundy Thursday service, Psalm 116 functions in three ways. First, it responds to the call of Exodus to celebrate the mighty acts of the Lord, as the psalmist exclaims: "I love the LORD, . . . [who] has heard my voice and my supplications" (v. 1). Second, it anticipates Christ's instructions over the bread and cup, "Do this in remembrance of me" (1 Cor. 11:24), as the psalmist promises: "I will lift up the cup of salvation and call on the name of the LORD" (v. 13). Third, it reflects and embodies Jesus' posture of faithful love and humble service in washing the disciples' feet, as the psalmist prays: "O LORD, . . . I am your servant, the child of your serving girl. You have loosed my bonds" (v. 16).

These three functions of Psalm 116 in the Maundy Thursday liturgy point to three applications in our daily service of God, and three potential avenues for proclamation. First, there is the theme of liberation. How might we share in God's work of delivering the oppressed and setting captives free? Second, there is the theme of self-offering. How might we fulfill Jesus' call to "do this" in remembrance of him, devoting ourselves to others? Third, there is the theme of humble service and love in Christian community. How might we demonstrate to the world that we are Christ's disciples? The thread that runs through all of this is thanksgiving. All of these may be understood as expressions of gratitude for God's amazing grace.

Three very different musical works help to convey the enduring strength of this psalm and its breadth of application in human life. The sixteenth-century Lutheran hymn CHRIST LAG IN TODESBANDEN ("Christ Jesus Lay in Death's Strong Bands") seems to have drawn inspiration from the "snares of death" in Psalm 116:3. While its concluding hallelujahs give it a place among the Easter hymns, the text also has clear allusions to Exodus 12. The eighteenth-century Isaac Watts paraphrase of Psalm 116, "I Love the Lord, Who Heard My Cry," particularly as it is set to Richard Smallwood's arrangement of an African American spiritual, evokes the psalmist's confidence, resilience, and determination. The twentieth-century praise song "You Are My Strength When I Am Weak" may not have been directly inspired by Psalm 116, but its references to the cup and Lamb of God offer connections to Maundy Thursday.[2]

Psalm 116 helps us understand that God's gracious acts and our grateful response are both deeply rooted in love. Following God's command is not a heavy burden or a dull obligation, but an act of joyful devotion, a true labor of love. Christ's "new commandment" (John 13:34) thus encapsulates the "greatest and first commandment" and the "second [that] is like it" (Matt. 22:38–39; see also Deut. 6:5 and Lev. 19:18). We love God—and love one another—because God first loved us (1 John 4:7, 19). All of Christian faith, life, and worship can be summarized in these opening words of Psalm 116: "I love the LORD."

DAVID GAMBRELL

1. Bernhard W. Anderson, *Out of the Depths: The Psalms Speak for Us Today*, 3rd ed., with Steven Bishop, rev. and expanded (Louisville, KY: Westminster John Knox, 2000), 107–13.
2. *Glory to God: The Presbyterian Hymnal* (Louisville, KY: Westminster John Knox, 2013), 237, 799, and 519.

1 Corinthians 11:23–26

> [23]For I received from the Lord what I also handed on to you, that the Lord Jesus on the night when he was betrayed took a loaf of bread, [24]and when he had given thanks, he broke it and said, "This is my body that is for you. Do this in remembrance of me." [25]In the same way he took the cup also, after supper, saying, "This cup is the new covenant in my blood. Do this, as often as you drink it, in remembrance of me." [26]For as often as you eat this bread and drink the cup, you proclaim the Lord's death until he comes.

Commentary 1: Connecting the Reading with Scripture

A lectionary connection with this text can spark preaching for Holy Thursday.[1] Some churches both wash feet (John 13:1–17) and partake of the loaf and the cup (1 Cor. 11:23–26). To help the congregation recognize the different nuances in Scripture, the preacher could call attention to the distinctive role each rite plays in the worldview of its theological family: foot washing in John and the sacred meal in Paul. Indeed, the preacher might replace the one longer sermon with two minisermons, each focused on one rite, showing how the two rites can work together on the eve of Jesus' trial, crucifixion, and resurrection.

The larger and immediate literary connections in 1 Corinthians frame the interpretation of Paul's account of the institution of the bread and the cup in 11:23–26. For Paul, Christ is God's apocalyptic agent in ending the present evil age and replacing it—after the second coming—with the eschatological realm of God (e.g., 1 Cor. 15:24). The church is the body of Christ in the world; its mission is to continue the witness of Christ to the coming transformation and to embody the future qualities of the realm of God, which includes being a genuine community of mutual support in the service of witness to God's purposes in Christ.

The preacher can remind listeners that, by contrast with the realm of God, Roman society was a social pyramid in which the upper classes lived above the other classes in every way, especially with respect to wealth, power, social recognition, and material resources. The Romans designed this exclusive pyramid to allow the privileged class to control and exploit people below. In this regard, the world of today is not so different from the world of antiquity. The preacher can point to an abundance of examples.

The ancient churches, including the Corinthian congregation, were unusual social groups for the first century CE, in that the churches often included people from up and down the social pyramid. The church was called to be an inclusive, mutually supportive community that anticipated the eschatological world. However, Paul wrote 1 Corinthians in response to the breakdown of such community in that congregation. The congregation had divided into competing, hostile groups (e.g., 1 Cor. 1:10–17), thereby simply reproducing in the church the brokenness of the social pyramid characteristic of Roman society. Theological disagreements had resulted from outside teachers introducing doctrines that differed from Paul's views; and the congregation was conflicted regarding whom and what to believe.

The preacher can help us see that these conditions are hauntingly familiar to the church today as our ecclesial landscape is a minefield of theological and ethical disagreements. Indeed, the composition of many congregations in the

1. Holy Thursday is often known as Maundy Thursday, from the Latin *mandatum novum*, the "new commandment" Jesus gives the disciples to love one another (John 13:31b–35).

United States reflects the social divisions of wider early-twenty-first-century society, and the social order within many congregations today is, in certain respects, almost as hierarchical as that of the Roman period. We are not the first ones in history to negotiate these challenges in church.

When we turn to the text itself, positive themes surface. Many apocalyptic writers believed that after the apocalypse, God would celebrate the beginning of the new world with a great banquet, sometimes called the eschatological or messianic banquet. Furthermore, the Jewish people believed that the power of past and future events can operate in the present. For instance, the Passover—mentioned in the reading from Exodus for today—not only recalled the events of the exodus but released the liberating power of that event for the later generations partaking of the meal. The community gathered at the Passover table today says, "When *we* were slaves in Egypt . . ." Preachers can make these past-tense and future-tense connections, bringing the liberating power of the past events and the eschatological promises of the future to speak to present-day struggles.

In 1 Corinthians 11:23–26, Paul turns to an ancient tradition of the sacred meal as the starting point for reflecting theologically on the congregation's situation. The church has struggled with what happens to the bread and the cup when the church pronounces the words of institution. "This [bread] is my body. . . . This cup is the new covenant." Transubstantiation? Consubstantiation? Real presence? Commemoration? Something else? For the first-century congregation, gathering around the loaf and the cup was supposed to be a protoeschatological banquet. As the community ate and drank, they had a momentary realization of the coming eschatological world.

First Corinthians 10:16 refers to drinking the cup as sharing in the blood of Christ, that is, of receiving the eschatological benefit of Jesus' death. The same passage refers to eating the bread as sharing the life of the risen One. The resurrection is the first fruit of the new world. In 1 Corinthians 10:16–18, Paul employs the word "share" (*koinōnia*) to indicate that by eating the meal, the congregation becomes partners with Christ in the coming new world. Paul makes this meaning explicit in 1 Corinthians 11:26: "For as often as you eat . . . and drink . . . you proclaim the Lord's death *until he comes.*"

Paul believed that the experience of mutual support through eating together should be an experience that embodied eschatological community. It was intended to strengthen the church's witness to egalitarian eschatological community in the face of the rigid, self-serving, and exploitative social pyramid of the old Roman social world.

The immediate literary context (1 Cor. 11:17–22, 27–34) reveals that the social divisions of the old world had undermined the eschatological quality of the sacred meal. It appears that members in the upper reaches of the Roman social pyramid were eating their fill prior to the arrival of "those who have nothing." Indeed, some elites became drunk. The problem with drunkenness at the sacred meal may be that inebriated persons are not fully available for mutual, eschatological solidarity; their overindulgence shows disregard for the needs of others, and they may be completely self-absorbed.

Paul counsels the congregation to "examine" themselves so that they will not eat or drink unworthily and so that they will "discern" the "body" (vv. 28–29). Christians often take these directives to push individuals to examine their personal worthiness to partake. However, Paul has the congregational situation in view. The apostle wants the congregation to examine the degree to which the people gathering at the table do so as truly eschatological community. The apostle prescribes a corrective action: "When you come together to eat, wait for one another" (v. 33). This behavior is more than being polite. This behavior enacts the values and practices of the realm of God.

On Holy Thursday, this passage has three important functions for today's community. First, it affirms that the congregation is partnered with Jesus in bringing the realm of God in the things that lie ahead—not only the crucifixion and resurrection of Jesus, but also their own confrontation with modern-day "Romans" who would extinguish the community pointing to the possibility of the realm of God. Second, it assures the congregation that the power of the eschaton is working through them as they struggle to witness to the eschatological world. Third, the passage is a norm for evaluating the degree to which the congregation's meeting around chalice and paten reflects the inclusivity and mutual solidarity of eschatological community. If not, the preacher could help the congregation ask, "How might we wait for one another today?"

RONALD J. ALLEN

Commentary 2: Connecting the Reading with the World

"For I received from the Lord what I also handed on to you" (1 Cor. 11:23). There are things we hand on to our children and grandchildren without their having any say in it: physical features, place of birth, birth order, relatives. There are things we hand on without intending to: the way we do or do not deal with conflict, a sense of humor or lack thereof, a certain outlook on life. There are things we hand on quite intentionally: our values, work ethic, family history. What do we intentionally hand on of our faith?

In church we hand all sorts of things on to each other: casseroles, committee assignments, resources, prayer concerns. How do we hand on the living bread, especially with our own children and with the children of those in our congregations? We make sure they know the overarching story of Scripture, or the ancient creeds, or a particular catechism—but do we hand on what we have received from Jesus? Even beyond what is taught in classes, what do we hand on by our example, our attention, our faith, hope, and love?

Speaking to the church in Corinth, Paul has much to say about community. Things are to be done so as to build up the body. The church is to be the antithesis of the everyone-for-themselves mentality. In the verses preceding and following this passage, Paul makes clear that there are respectful and disrespectful ways to partake in the Lord's Supper, and they have nothing to do with intinction versus a common cup, or wine versus grape juice. They have to do with the community itself, and leaving no one behind. "One goes hungry and another becomes drunk" (1 Cor. 11:21), Paul admonishes. Partaking in communion with no regard for the needs of others around you violates the spirit of the Table. Who is missing? Who is going hungry, whether for food, housing, companionship, or spiritual nurture?

For the church in Corinth, to partake in the meal, to remember, came with a challenge. Paul urged them to put aside the culturally accepted practices of class divisions and social status, and to be one as they shared the bread and cup. Followers of Jesus Christ had no business marring the meal with social distinctions.

Are there subtle fault lines still present in our churches, our traditions? Are there divisions that, while perhaps less obvious than those in the Corinthian church, are still understood and even taken for granted? Who might not feel particularly welcome in our pews? How are our congregations cultivating community, encouraging all to develop meaningful and healthy relationships beyond social media and the ever-present electronic screens?

There is an intimacy about sharing in Communion; clergy and deacons often remark how moving it is to offer this simple meal of bread and cup to friends and strangers alike. A brand-new deacon stood beside the communion table, eager to serve the cup for the first time. As an elderly member of the congregation approached the cup, the deacon burst into a grin and said lovingly, "Hey, sweetie." Their mutual affection more than made up for the lack of any proper liturgical words.

How do we remember Jesus' death as we reenact the meal? Each communion becomes a reminder of both death and life. Walking up the aisle comes one recently widowed whose husband of sixty-five years died suddenly. Here come a middle-aged mother whose marriage just dissolved and a young man fresh out of rehab. All who partake on any given Sunday are part of a community experiencing more than its share of violence, and part of a global community where destruction is an everyday occurrence. Death is all around, and death is swallowed up in Christ's death and resurrection.

The pain is real; so is the tender balm of a community where folks look out for one another, where they hold faith for those whose faith may be at an ebb.

We remember Christ's death and together, we trust that death does not have the final word. At least for a moment, we are one indeed. Artificial lines of saint and sinner, worthy and unworthy, are erased. People and relationships and all manner of situations get broken and poured out. So did Jesus. He feeds us and is healing our brokenness, our emptiness, and he has promised that he is coming again.

Communion can happen in all sorts of places; no white linens are required. Anxious family members and strangers crowding in a small hospital waiting room pass around the cookies someone brought; a thermos or two of coffee appears. A place of stressful waiting becomes sacred space. A table is set up under a city bridge where men and women dealing with homelessness often camp out. Sandwiches and lemonade take the place of white bread and grape juice as volunteers and guests break bread together.

Years ago, while traveling with my six-year-old daughter in Guatemala for a nonprofit organization, we gathered at a local restaurant with a half dozen other staffers. Toward the end of our meal, a young boy about my daughter's age appeared by her side and asked in Spanish if he could have her leftovers. We boxed up all that we could, and watched as he took the food outside, sat on a curb, and broke the uneaten sandwich into three portions, sharing with two other children. I have never witnessed a more powerful, more holy communion, and my daughter has never forgotten the experience.

The services for Maundy Thursday often recall the upper room, with Jesus washing the feet of the disciples, giving them the new commandment, that they love one another as he has loved them. Many of us love the drama of Maundy Thursday, and faith communities find different ways to retell the story. A mime troupe came to church one year, and with Samuel Barber's "Adagio for Strings" playing throughout, the performers told the story of the Last Supper, the passion and death of Christ. This gripping story became even more powerful without words.

On Maundy Thursday, we will once again remember the upper room, the betrayal, the garden, the denials, the cross. Jesus' hands, which shared the bread and cup only hours before, will soon be wounded, hurting, his actual body broken. If we eat this bread and drink this cup in remembrance of Jesus, we need to remember that story. If we do this in remembrance of Jesus, we need to connect that story to our own and that of our congregation, just as Paul connected it with the community in Corinth. If we do this in remembrance of Jesus, then we do it also in remembrance of those Jesus loves, who are facing their own imprisonment, their own suffering and death. Where is Jesus being crucified today? We remember the individuals and families facing the possibility of death by deportation. We remember those forgotten in our prisons and those imprisoned by fear, by bigotry and hatred. We remember victims of senseless violence. We bring them all with us to the Table, acknowledging our great need for healing, our hunger for the bread of life.

With each Maundy Thursday, with each communion in whatever form, we are fed, strengthened for the road ahead, where we will have the opportunity to be food for a hungry world. Not long after the meal in the upper room, the risen Christ would send his disciples out into the world to follow in his way, healing the sick, feeding the hungry, proclaiming the good news. We offer ourselves as they did, to a world hungry to be fed.

JULIE PEEPLES

John 13:1–17, 31b–35

[1]Now before the festival of the Passover, Jesus knew that his hour had come to
depart from this world and go to the Father. Having loved his own who were in
the world, he loved them to the end. [2]The devil had already put it into the heart
of Judas son of Simon Iscariot to betray him. And during supper [3]Jesus, knowing
that the Father had given all things into his hands, and that he had come from
God and was going to God, [4]got up from the table, took off his outer robe, and
tied a towel around himself. [5]Then he poured water into a basin and began to
wash the disciples' feet and to wipe them with the towel that was tied around
him. [6]He came to Simon Peter, who said to him, "Lord, are you going to wash my
feet?" [7]Jesus answered, "You do not know now what I am doing, but later you will
understand." [8]Peter said to him, "You will never wash my feet." Jesus answered,
"Unless I wash you, you have no share with me." [9]Simon Peter said to him, "Lord,
not my feet only but also my hands and my head!" [10]Jesus said to him, "One who
has bathed does not need to wash, except for the feet, but is entirely clean. And
you are clean, though not all of you." [11]For he knew who was to betray him; for this
reason he said, "Not all of you are clean."

[12]After he had washed their feet, had put on his robe, and had returned to
the table, he said to them, "Do you know what I have done to you? [13]You call me
Teacher and Lord—and you are right, for that is what I am. [14]So if I, your Lord and
Teacher, have washed your feet, you also ought to wash one another's feet. [15]For
I have set you an example, that you also should do as I have done to you. [16]Very
truly, I tell you, servants are not greater than their master, nor are messengers
greater than the one who sent them. [17]If you know these things, you are blessed
if you do them. . . .

[31b]Jesus said, "Now the Son of Man has been glorified, and God has been glorified in him. [32]If God has been glorified in him, God will also glorify him in himself
and will glorify him at once. [33]Little children, I am with you only a little longer. You
will look for me; and as I said to the Jews so now I say to you, 'Where I am going,
you cannot come.' [34]I give you a new commandment, that you love one another.
Just as I have loved you, you also should love one another. [35]By this everyone will
know that you are my disciples, if you have love for one another."

Commentary 1: Connecting the Reading with Scripture

This Gospel reading for Holy (or Maundy) Thursday appears every year in the lectionary, an obvious selection, since it includes the only report of Jesus' new commandment: "that you love one another" (John 13:34), the theme of the day. However, several other dimensions of this text can command the attention of the preacher, in particular *time, movement,* and *event.*

Time. The first time reference is that these events happened "before the festival of the Passover." For John, this naming of Passover is not merely a reference to the liturgical calendar but a nod to his theological conviction that the death and resurrection of Jesus constituted a fulfillment of the Passover, the festival in which the faithful commemorated Israel's freedom from slavery, redemption, formation as a people, and feeding in the wilderness. John keeps saying that "Passover's coming!" The Passover "was near," John says, right before the story of Jesus cleansing the temple and promising to raise up a new temple "in three days" (2:13–22). Again, John says the Passover "was near" right before Jesus fed the five thousand (6:4–14). Once more, John tells his readers that the Passover "was near" right before Jesus was anointed by Mary as a sign of his burial, an event that occurred "six days before the Passover" (11:55–12:8).

At one level, these references point to different Passovers, but at another level they all point to the great Passover that culminates the story of Jesus. Now, as Jesus gathers with his disciples on this Thursday night, that Passover, the Passover approaching with urgency throughout the entire Gospel, has finally come. This is a cosmic event. The whole world has come to this Passover—Jews (12:9) and Greeks (12:20)—and even the Pharisees have to admit about Jesus, "Look, the world [*kosmos*] has gone after him" (12:19).

The preacher may describe how this story shows that God is always a "Passover God," a God of redemption. God redeems the people of Israel by bringing them through the waters of the sea, and in this story, Jesus gives his disciples a "share" of his life, by filling a basin with water and washing their feet (13:5–8). In the wilderness, God fed the people with manna, and in this story, Jesus gathers at table and feeds his disciples. At Sinai, God gave the people the law, the commandments that set them apart as a holy people and led them in the paths of life. Here, Jesus gives his disciples "a new commandment" of love that will set them apart as "my disciples" (13:34–35).

Another key reference to time in this passage is Jesus' "hour" (13:1). In John, Jesus' ministry moves inexorably toward his "hour," that is, his death, resurrection, and ascension. Jesus comes from God; he is the eternal Word become flesh and living among us. His mission is to gather his sheep and then to return to God (his "hour"), making a "way" ("I am the way, the truth, and the life," 14:6) for his sheep to join him in his glory. The ministry of Jesus creates a deep communion between Jesus, God, and the believer: "On that day you will know that I am in my Father, and you in me, and I in you" (14:20).

At Cana, Jesus at first resists performing the sign of changing water into wine, because it is too early, "My hour has not yet come" (2:4). Later, Jesus taught bold and controversial truths in the very treasury of the temple, but no one harmed him because it was too early, "his hour had not yet come" (8:20). Now, the hour has come. A preaching connection here is the opportunity to describe how the death of Jesus was no accident. In John's Gospel, Jesus did not get crucified because he suddenly ran out of luck and ran out of time. He gave his life as a gift (10:18), and his "hour" had come to fulfillment. He had accomplished that which he was sent to do, and "having loved his own who were in the world, he loved them to the end" (13:1b). Here the word "end" almost surely has a double meaning—until the last and to the full extent[1]—in other words, Jesus loved them both until his hour had come and until his love was filled to the brim.

Movement. Once more John's Gospel communicates irony by speaking on two levels at once. Jesus is on the move here, but where is he going? On the level of ordinary time and history, Jesus is in a downward spiral, moving from the table to betrayal to being accused to the humiliation of the cross. He goes from the room where he shares the supper with his disciples, across the Kidron Valley to a garden where he is arrested (18:1–12), and then on to his trial, and finally to Golgotha, where he is crucified (19:16–18). On the higher theological level, though, Jesus is moving upward toward God: "Jesus knew that his hour had come to depart from this world and go to the Father" (13:1). The world believes that it is finishing Jesus off, putting him to death, but Jesus himself knows the truth, that "he had come from God and was going to God" (v. 3). These movements trace the two basic paths, the two roads that diverge and beckon all humanity, the way of darkness and evil and the way of light and glory. Despite what the world thinks is happening to Jesus, he is traveling the way to glory, and the implication of this movement is shown in the contrasting movements of the disciples (which unfortunately are edited out of the lectionary reading). After receiving the bread from Jesus,

1. Gail R. O'Day, "The Gospel of John," in Leander E. Keck et al., eds., *The New Interpreter's Bible* (Nashville: Abingdon, 1995), 9:491–875 (721).

The Solicitude of Our Love

Think not then, my brethren, that when the Lord says, "A new commandment I give unto you, that ye love one another," there is any overlooking of that greater commandment, which requires us to love the Lord our God with all our heart, and with all our soul, and with all our mind; for along with this seeming oversight, the words "that ye love one another" appear also as if they had no reference to that second commandment, which says, "Thou shalt love thy neighbor as thyself." For "on these two commandments," He says, "hang all the law and the prophets." But both commandments may be found in each of these by those who have good understanding. For, on the one hand, he that loveth God cannot despise His commandment to love his neighbor; and on the other, he who in a holy and spiritual way loveth his neighbor, what doth he love in him but God? That is the love, distinguished from all mundane love, which the Lord specially characterized, when He added, "as I have loved you." For what was it but God that He loved in us? Not because we had Him, but in order that we might have Him; and that He may lead us on, as I said a little ago, where God is all in all. It is in this way, also, that the physician is properly said to love the sick; and what is it he loves in them but their health, which at all events he desires to recall; not their sickness, which he comes to remove? Let us, then, also so love one another, that, as far as possible, we may by the solicitude of our love be winning one another to have God within us. And this love is bestowed on us by Him who said, "As I have loved you, that ye also love one another." For this very end, therefore, did He love us, that we also should love one another; bestowing this on us by His own love to us, that we should be bound to one another in mutual love, and, united together as members by so pleasant a bond, should be the body of so mighty a Head.

"By this," He adds, "Shall all men know that ye are my disciples, if ye have love one to another:" as if He said, Other gifts of mine are possessed in common with you by those who are not mine,—not only nature, life, perception, reason, and that safety which is equally the privilege of men and beasts; but also languages, sacraments, prophecy, knowledge, faith, the bestowing of their goods upon the poor, and the giving of their body to the flames: but because destitute of charity, they only tinkle like cymbals; they are nothing, and by nothing are they profited. It is not, then, by such gifts of mine, however good, which may be alike possessed by those who are not my disciples, but "by this it is that all men shall know that ye are my disciples, that ye have love one to another."

Augustine, "Tractate 65," in Saint Augustine, *Homilies on the Gospel of John; Homilies on the First Epistle of John; Soliloquies*, trans. John Gibb, Nicene and Post Nicene Fathers of the Christian Church 7, ed. Philip Schaff (Edinburgh: T. & T. Clark, 1888), 318–19.

Judas "immediately" goes out and takes the downward path, into the night, into the darkness (v. 30). The other disciples are anxious about where Jesus is going and where they are going. Peter asks, "Lord, where are you going?" Jesus reassures him and the others that, while they cannot follow him in this moment, they will ultimately follow him into the light, into the dwelling place of God (13:36–14:7).

Event. There are three primary events in this passage—the meal, the foot washing, and the giving of the new commandment—and they are interconnected theologically. The meal starts first, but it is soon interrupted by the foot washing, and this interruption is the key to understanding everything that happens. The description of the foot washing is complex (for example, the language about bathing in vv. 8–11 may have a baptismal referent), but the main thrust is clear: the foot washing is an invitation to enjoy the life of glory made possible by Jesus. It does not seem like glory, with Jesus acting as a servant and washing the disciples' feet, but that is the point. Glory, as revealed by Jesus, is hospitality, service, and mutual love, and Jesus tells Peter that unless he allows Jesus to express this hospitality and love toward him, he will not be a part of Jesus' life (13:8–9). When Jesus and the disciples return to the table (v. 12), the lesson of the foot washing is reverberating in the air. The host at this meal is "Teacher and Lord" (v. 13), but those roles of authority have been radically redefined. True teaching and true lordship are now seen as loving service—something new, worthy of a "new commandment," that "you also should love one another" (v. 34).

THOMAS G. LONG

Commentary 2: Connecting the Reading with the World

We have all heard that God is love (1 John 4:8). Fewer of us have interrogated the full meaning of this claim. John 13 provides us with an instructive example. This Scripture lesson says much about how God chooses to reveal Godself in the world. Here we witness Jesus insisting on washing the feet of his disciples. To love is to serve. Love demands that we stretch beyond the boundaries of comfort to attend to the needs of others. Jesus thus models the mores of God's kingdom by performing an act otherwise reserved for servants or the enslaved. Possibly this is why Peter protests, "You will never wash my feet" (John 13:8). Yet Jesus makes clear that participating in God's kingdom demands such gracious care. Though power and rank define our worldly kingdom, humility and generosity represent God's kingdom. Jesus' orientation toward his followers typifies the Christian life of service and sacrifice.

Jesus' example provides both moral challenge and inspiration. We live in a society that all too often encourages us to acquire social status, "move up" the professional ladder, and gain enough clout to ignore tasks that we consider menial. Think of most public settings. Undesirable activities tend to roll down the proverbial hill. The invisible labor that makes our lives possible—serving food, sweeping floors, cleaning streets, and emptying trash—is most often the responsibility of those compensated most poorly. We tend to look down on occupations in the public and service sectors.

It is this vertical understanding of power that Jesus seeks to invert. The kingdom of God exalts those who are willing to lower themselves to aid others. This is a challenge that many of us in pulpit leadership would do well to assume. Too many of us in professional ministry forget the time-tested truism: hands that serve are as valuable as lips that pray. More importantly, Jesus' example ought to remind us that "to whom much has been given, much will be required; and from the one to whom much has been entrusted, even more will be demanded" (Luke 12:48). We must remember that God's kingdom upends the power and rank of our earthly kingdoms. We follow a God who serves.

Beyond the moral challenge, Jesus' actions can inspire us to look beyond ourselves. In what ways might we get involved in our community to "wash the feet" of others? Volunteering time at a homeless shelter, serving at a community food bank, providing homework assistance at an underresourced school: these are acts of love consistent with Jesus' example. If our churches are concerned only with the souls of individuals, while ignoring their material needs, we will soon be a church that is so heavenly minded that we are no earthly good. Jesus' life should inspire us to pursue those whose feet we might wash, just as it calls us to interrogate why the feet of some are more entrenched in the muck and mire of social misery than others. This is the Christian life. People will recognize us by how we love one another (John 13:35).

This theme of love and service is also a valuable lesson for the church during Holy Week. Now is when we focus on Christ's atoning work on the cross. Ransom and satisfaction theories tend to predominate: many preachers will focus on Jesus' death as a payment to liberate sinful humanity. Jesus' crucifixion will thus satisfy our debt to Satan. John 13 provides a complementary point. Rather than concentrate exclusively on Jesus' crucifixion, the moral exemplar theory of atonement affirms Jesus' life, teachings, and ethical example. Consider how this lesson begins and ends. The first verse speaks to Jesus showing the "full extent of his love" (v. 1 NIV), and the lesson concludes with Jesus encouraging his disciples to distinguish themselves by their love for one another. Between these verses rests the example of Jesus washing his disciples' feet. Jesus' exemplary behavior serves as the crux of positive moral change and hence redemption for the church and society.

The moral exemplar theory of atonement does not diminish the role of the crucifixion. To the contrary, even a cursory reading of the Gospels reveals that Jesus' care and compassion were the source of his ultimate trouble with both temple and Roman authorities. Inspired by the Hebrew prophets, Jesus showed concern for the most vulnerable in a way that attracted crowds throughout Galilee and Judea and subsequently threatened the status quo. His example of compassion and pleas for justice revived the teachings of the Law and the Prophets, thus challenging religious officials who sought to maintain a semblance of power under the crushing weight of Roman imperialism. Jesus' teachings about an inverted kingdom, where the "first shall be last" (Matt. 20:16), surely provoked the ire of an empire that deemed Caesar the savior of the world.

This is why we cannot focus on Jesus' death without equal attention to his life. Jesus' crucifixion was not inevitable, but a result of his moral courage and magnanimous example. He offered a different vision of life and a contrasting example of power. Jesus provides examples of power defined by neither high status nor military might. Instead, we witness power in the form of amity and affection, service and humble sacrifice.

Unfortunately, anyone willing to confront power and oppression with love and justice should be prepared to suffer persecution and the possibility of death. The tragic history of the United States bears witness to this fact. In the early nineteenth century, Presbyterian minister Elijah Parish Lovejoy dared to use his newspaper the *Observer* to challenge the peculiar institution of slavery in the United States. In 1837, a rabid pro-slavery mob in Alton, Illinois, destroyed his printing press and murdered Lovejoy at the scene.[2]

Similar was the case for Juliette Hampton Morgan. Though from a privileged white family in Montgomery, Alabama, she raised her voice regularly in the *Montgomery Advertiser* to condemn Jim Crow. She also participated in interracial prayer groups in the city as a way of publicly washing the feet of black women. Segregationists attacked her home and burned crosses in her yard. Eventually, the constant threats and persecution led to Morgan taking her own life.[3] Today, however, we revere both Lovejoy and Morgan for their moral courage. They, like so many other martyrs of the faith, are moral exemplars of love and service to the point of death.

John 13 provides us with a clarion call and ethical example. The Christian life encourages us to reimagine prominence and revise our definitions of power. Dr. Martin Luther King Jr. stated this claim eloquently in his famous address "The Drum Major Instinct": "Everybody can be great, because everybody can serve. You don't have to have a college degree to serve. You don't have to make your subject and verb agree to serve. . . . You only need a heart full of grace, a soul generated by love."[4] By answering this call to serve during Holy Week, we can reflect the redemptive power of Jesus' sacrifice.

JONATHAN L. WALTON

2. Paul Simon, *Freedom's Champion: Elijah Lovejoy* (Carbondale: Southern Illinois University Press, 1994).

3. Mary Stanton, *Journey toward Justice: Juliette Hampton Morgan and the Montgomery Bus Boycott* (Athens: University of Georgia Press, 2006).

4. Martin Luther King Jr., "The Drum Major Instinct (4 February 1968)," in *A Testament of Hope: The Essential Writings and Speeches of Martin Luther King, Jr.*, ed. James M. Washington (San Francisco: HarperSanFrancisco, 1991), 265–66.

Good Friday

Isaiah 52:13–53:12
Psalm 22
Hebrews 4:14–16; 5:7–9
John 18:1–19:42
Hebrews 10:16–25

Isaiah 52:13–53:12

52:13See, my servant shall prosper;
he shall be exalted and lifted up,
and shall be very high.
14Just as there were many who were astonished at him
—so marred was his appearance, beyond human semblance,
and his form beyond that of mortals—
15so he shall startle many nations;
kings shall shut their mouths because of him;
for that which had not been told them they shall see,
and that which they had not heard they shall contemplate.
53:1Who has believed what we have heard?
And to whom has the arm of the LORD been revealed?
2For he grew up before him like a young plant,
and like a root out of dry ground;
he had no form or majesty that we should look at him,
nothing in his appearance that we should desire him.
3He was despised and rejected by others;
a man of suffering and acquainted with infirmity;
and as one from whom others hide their faces
he was despised, and we held him of no account.

4Surely he has borne our infirmities
and carried our diseases;
yet we accounted him stricken,
struck down by God, and afflicted.
5But he was wounded for our transgressions,
crushed for our iniquities;
upon him was the punishment that made us whole,
and by his bruises we are healed.
6All we like sheep have gone astray;
we have all turned to our own way,
and the LORD has laid on him
the iniquity of us all.

7He was oppressed, and he was afflicted,
yet he did not open his mouth;
like a lamb that is led to the slaughter,
and like a sheep that before its shearers is silent,
so he did not open his mouth.
8By a perversion of justice he was taken away.
Who could have imagined his future?
For he was cut off from the land of the living,
stricken for the transgression of my people.

[9]They made his grave with the wicked
and his tomb with the rich,
although he had done no violence,
and there was no deceit in his mouth.

[10]Yet it was the will of the LORD to crush him with pain.
When you make his life an offering for sin,
he shall see his offspring, and shall prolong his days;
through him the will of the LORD shall prosper.
[11]Out of his anguish he shall see light;
he shall find satisfaction through his knowledge.
The righteous one, my servant, shall make many righteous,
and he shall bear their iniquities.
[12]Therefore I will allot him a portion with the great,
and he shall divide the spoil with the strong;
because he poured out himself to death,
and was numbered with the transgressors;
yet he bore the sin of many,
and made intercession for the transgressors.

Commentary 1: Connecting the Reading with Scripture

Walter Brueggemann is right: "It is one of the great oddities of Old Testament studies that the very text that is taken to be *abundantly rich and theologically suggestive* is at the same time undeniably *inaccessible and without clear meaning*."[1] Yet we need not be too troubled by the complexity, mystery, and sheer potential of such a passage. In the way a docent in a museum directs attention to a marvelous painting, pointing out a few items but primarily inviting awe, the preacher might be wise to linger slowly over the words, and not overexplain. Let this text be heard in the shadows of the sanctuary; it can do its own work.

Readers of biblical Hebrew enjoy an advantage: they can relish the assonance and rhythm, noted well in James Muilenburg's 1956 *Interpreter's Bible* commentary. Even in English, the unexplained text moves us. The poetic artistry suggests the author was trying to capture something beyond simple words. The historical context matters: Israel, long in exile, had suffered enough, suspicious of Cyrus the Persian commandeering their fate and a bit baffled by the boundless hope voiced by the prophet we have dubbed Second Isaiah, the nameless prophet who took up Isaiah's preaching from the eighth century and reenvisioned it for the exiles in the sixth century. More baffling were the four Servant Songs (42:1–6; 49:1–7; 50:4–9; 52:13–53:12) depicting a puzzling figure—puzzling to us, but not to the Lord, who speaks first and last in our passage. This is "my" Servant, Yahweh almost boasts (Isa. 52:13). God certainly is intimately united with this unnamed soul who achieves God's will for the people and the world.

We are in uncharted territory as the opening line declares, "my servant *despite* his suffering" shall be exalted (52:13–15) while the closing line concludes, "my servant *because of* his suffering" shall be exalted (53:11–12). The "despite" we get, but "because of"? We look to the verses in-between to understand the shift. Most likely an admiring student of this Servant wrote these verses that are sandwiched between God's proud declarations. We read, not only was this Servant unattractive; there was something repulsive about him—yet people were drawn to him. He suffered in silence, in a world where piling up words of defense and right answers is

1. Walter Brueggemann, *Isaiah 40–66*, Westminster Bible Companion (Louisville, KY: Westminster John Knox, 1998), 141; emphasis original.

expected. In a survival-of-the-fittest world that has always looked for superheroes, this Servant was mocked, weak and timid, the victim rather than the perpetrator of violence. Preachers can invite listeners to reflect on ways that we still, in the twenty-first century, value strength in a way that does not allow for the ways of this Servant.

It sounds like a sorry story, but the overall impact, despite all the agony, is triumph. Suffering and exaltation are welded together. How could this be? The turn seems to come in "he was wounded for our transgressions." It turns out that the "our" refers to the Israelites who had hurt him! Was it really his physical ugliness that repulsed? Was it, rather, what he had done, and the consequences he suffered—but then that is the glory? What is going on here?

The underlying narrative is perceived well by John Goldingay: in exile, Israel was incapable of fulfilling its vocation to be the good news for all the nations. One Servant stepped forward to be Israel when Israel could not. No wonder he was abused, first by their captors and then by fearful Israelites themselves: "The message about Yahweh's intention to bring down the Babylonian empire would not endear him to Babylonians or to Judahites who identified with their rulers, while his critique of the Judahites would give them further reason for resentment."[2]

The surprise, shocking yet terribly hopeful? He stayed the course; he did not fight back. He loved. He suffered with them, but then some perceived he was actually suffering for them, paying the price for being in ministry to them. They had nothing to offer God, but he did: he gave himself. He was not a martyr; God's suffering is not simply weathering hard times or overcoming obstacles. His suffering itself was redemptive. Joseph Blenkinsopp wisely explains that at first the exiles, like Job's friends, concluded he was being punished by God. "But then it dawned on him" (the first disciple of the Servant) "that for some mysterious reason Yahweh had diverted the ills that should have fallen on the community onto this one individual."[3] This "dawning" led to the writing of our text. What can we call this dawning, this revolutionary understanding of redemptive suffering? Nothing but "inspired."

Preachers can remind listeners that we have seen redemptive suffering elsewhere in Scripture: Joseph's brothers treated him and their father cruelly, and Joseph suffered much. Then, when they met up years later, Joseph exhibited profoundly what is in the heart of God: "Even though you intended to do harm to me, God intended it for good, in order to preserve a numerous people" (Gen. 50:20–21). Astonishing. Joseph did not just forgive them, or give them another chance. God, while assuredly not causing them to sin, used their dastardly behavior for good. The Joseph story and our Isaiah text reveal a God whose redemptive purpose is powerful, and so very hopeful.

No wonder Christians found these words a focusing lens through which to ponder Jesus. Isaiah 52:13–53:12 does not predict or describe in advance Jesus' suffering. Christian readers need to let the text stand on its own as a Jewish text, not co-opting it as if it is purely Christian in intent. Yet the text does say this is God's way, and always has been. God, as we see clearly in Jesus, fulfills God's historic vocation, suffers silently for it, and yet that suffering is redemptive.

It is worth noting that, profound and evocative as our text is for pondering Good Friday, direct citations of it in the New Testament are rare. First Peter 2:18–25 expounds our text; in Luke 22:37, Jesus alludes to it. Most New Testament scholars understand that Jesus understood himself in this light, fully intending to fulfill Israel's calling and bear their sufferings himself. He did not quote Isaiah while standing before Caiaphas or Pilate, but instead articulated it through his actions, courageously engaging the dark powers, fulfilling his vocation to suffer and thereby redeem Israel from its long exile.

This servant labor, in Isaiah and also for Jesus, was not just for Israel or believers, but all the nations. "Kings shall shut their mouths" (Isa. 52:15a) seems unlikely—until we think eschatologically, as did Philippians 2 ("every knee shall bow . . ."). The few exiles who heard and were moved by the Servant no doubt hoped

2. John Goldingay, *The Theology of the Book of Isaiah* (Downers Grove, IL: IVP Academic, 2014), 70.
3. Joseph Blenkinsopp, *Isaiah 40–55*, Anchor Bible 19A (New York: Doubleday, 2002), 351.

against hope that this redemption of the nations would transpire sooner than later.

Preachers should take care not to preach this text as "Go thou and do likewise." The text is not about us, except as the beneficiaries of God's extraordinary mercy and curious power, which bring redemption through another's suffering. There is no takeaway except awe. This is why the text has lived so dynamically as Scripture: we get our best glimpse into the heart of the Creator, whose ongoing determination is to bring a broken, sinful humanity, and even creation itself, to God's good end, to the glory into which we are incorporated by such a surprising but wonderful method. A person. A Servant. Wounded with us and for us. Glorified for and with us and everything.

JAMES C. HOWELL

Commentary 2: Connecting the Reading with the World

On Good Friday, Christians gather to meditate on the sufferings of Christ, to contemplate the cost of our redemption, and to listen for an honest and unflinching word from the pulpit. The remembrance of Jesus' death is marked in Christian tradition by penitential prayer, fasting, veneration of the cross, and special liturgical forms such as litanies imploring God's mercy and antiphonal "reproaches" said or sung in the voice of Christ and answered by the people with the ancient hymn known as the Trisagion: "Holy God, Holy and Mighty, Holy Immortal One, have mercy upon us." Good Friday draws us toward a terrible paradox at the heart of incarnational theology: to be fully united with the world that God so loves (John 3:16), Christ must become vulnerable to the violence that has fractured creation ever since Cain killed Abel. Much is required of believers who keep watch during Christ's agony. At the foot of the cross, we confront the cruelty of worldly empires, admit our complicity in systemic evil, and hear a wrenching cry of dereliction met by the thunderous silence of God (Ps. 22:1; Matt. 27:46). Believers need a preacher who acknowledges trauma in history and lived experience while speaking a compelling word of grace. Here, Isaiah 52:13–53:12, the last of four Servant Songs in Isaiah, can be an extraordinary resource for Christian homiletics.

The Servant Songs offer glimpses into prophetic witness in the context of the Babylonian exile or its aftermath in the sixth century BCE. Nebuchadnezzar's army had besieged Jerusalem, causing enormous suffering (see Lam. 1–5). In 587 BCE, the wall of Jerusalem had been breached and the Jerusalem temple plundered. Many Judeans were slain; survivors were taken into captivity along with their shamed political and religious leaders. The first Song (Isa. 42:1–4) gives us God's Servant as one divinely appointed to teach and enact justice. The second Song (49:1–6) reflects on the Servant's mission in terms reminiscent of the call of Jeremiah (Jer. 1:4); his prophetic words will illumine even those outside the covenant community (Isa. 46:6). The third Song (50:4–11) shows us a Servant, identified as Israel, teaching and sustaining the community while enduring mockery and violence. In these three Songs, the Servant remains resilient in the face of fierce opposition; his prophetic work will have redemptive consequences for the whole earth. The fourth Song (52:13–53:12), then, takes up these themes in an artful poem in which the humiliation and unjust execution of the Servant constitute a source of theological resistance for those who remain faithful to the purposes of God.

More elaborate than the other Servant Songs and more elusive in its meanings, the fourth Song is built on elliptical clauses and obscure locutions that have spurred Jewish and Christian interpreters to explore many possibilities for historical referents. Is the Servant an unspecified messianic figure or a prophet, whether Isaiah, Jeremiah, or another? Are the Servant Songs instead about a political ruler, whether the reformer Josiah, the liberator Cyrus of Persia, or the exiled Jehoiachin? Might the Servant be a trope for the beleaguered covenant people Israel, whose communal vocation as Servant is proclaimed over and over in Isaiah

(41:8–9; 42:18–22; 43:8–10; 44:1–2, 21; 45:4; 48:20; 49:3)?

The complex figure of the Servant is painted in a rich variety of hues and textures. It may well have held several meanings even for those who originally composed the polyphonic Isaiah traditions. Within reception history, a focal understanding for Christians emerged while the New Testament writings were being shaped (see Acts 8:32–35; Rom. 4:24–25; 1 Pet. 2:21–25): these Songs may fruitfully be read as pointing to the ministry, suffering, death, and resurrection of Jesus.

For the Good Friday preacher, the fourth Servant Song offers much for homiletical reflection. Satisfaction and substitution theories of atonement find purchase in the claim (Isa. 53:4–6, 11) that the healing of the community's transgressions required that the Servant be afflicted. The preacher might mull how vast must be the compassion of God the Shepherd (Ps. 23) to have subjected the Beloved (Eph. 1:6) to such a torturous death for the sake of God's persecuted "sheep" (Ps. 44:9–22; Ezek. 34; Rom. 8:31–39). Stirring indeed is God's promise that in the future exaltation of the Servant, the world will witness a reversal that transforms the injustice of present hierarchies (52:13–15); here the prophet sings with matriarch Hannah (1 Sam. 2:1–10) a subversive melody that will be taken up by Mary in her Magnificat (Luke 1:46–55). The preacher could expound on the grievous harms wrought by sin, catalyzing in hearers gratitude for God's grace and a yearning for righteousness.

The traditional christological focus may be amplified by a catechetical move toward *imitatio Christi*: lifting up other faithful servants who have borne witness to the purposes of God. Given that anti-Semitism, white supremacy, and gender bias still find a firm footing in many Christian communities, radical witness might be explored in terms of God's servants Dietrich Bonhoeffer (1906–45), Martin Luther King Jr. (1929–68), and Pauli Murray (1910–85), modern prophets who strove mightily against prevailing prejudices in their own time. Modeling courageous Christian dissent in his resistance to Nazism, Bonhoeffer famously articulated the notion that costly grace lies at the foundation of discipleship: "the cross means sharing the suffering of Christ to the last and to the fullest. . . . The cross is laid on every Christian."[4] Martin Luther King Jr. worked tirelessly for racial equity in an era when the vicious subjugation of African Americans regularly went unpunished. King saw white and black Christian leaders as "caught in an inescapable network of mutuality," arguing that racist politics and extrajudicial violence should be seen as injurious to the body of Christ as a whole.[5] Pauli Murray pitched fierce battles for the civil rights of African Americans and women, seeing racism and misogyny as pernicious distortions of our common life. Many effects destructive to families and communities have been traced subsequently, from the drastically disproportionate representation of women in extreme poverty across the globe to the epidemic rates of incarceration of black men in the United States.[6]

Those obedient to the purposes of God, including believers originally from outside of Israel, will be honored as God's "servants" (Isa. 54:17; 56:6; 63:17; 65:8–16; 66:14) in the redeemed community envisioned in the latter chapters of Isaiah. In continuity with that theological trajectory, Isaiah 52:13–53:12 can help us proclaim Christ's death as a holy mystery through which all will be drawn into unity with God (John 12:32; Col. 1:19–20).

CAROLYN J. SHARP

4. Dietrich Bonhoeffer, *The Cost of Discipleship*, trans. R. H. Fuller (New York: Simon & Schuster, 1995), 89. For more on Bonhoeffer as pastor and preacher, see Michael Pasquarello III, *Dietrich Bonhoeffer and the Theology of a Preaching Life* (Waco, TX: Baylor University Press, 2017).

5. Martin Luther King Jr., "Letter from a Birmingham Jail," written on April 16, 1963, and published in several venues, including an August 1963 issue of the *Atlantic Monthly* and King's 1964 book, *Why We Can't Wait* (New York: Signet Classics, 2000). For more on King as preacher, see his sermons in *Strength to Love* (Minneapolis: Fortress, 2010) and Richard Lischer, *The Preacher King: Martin Luther King Jr. and the Word That Moved America*, rev. ed. (Oxford: Oxford University Press, 1997).

6. See Pauli Murray, *Song in a Weary Throat: An American Pilgrimage* (New York: Harper & Row, 1987). On the high rate of incarceration of black and brown persons in the United States, see Michelle Alexander, *The New Jim Crow: Mass Incarceration in the Age of Colorblindness* (New York: New Press, 2012); Bryan Stevenson, *Just Mercy: A Story of Justice and Redemption* (New York: Spiegel & Grau, 2015).

Psalm 22

1My God, my God, why have you forsaken me?
Why are you so far from helping me, from the words of my groaning?
2O my God, I cry by day, but you do not answer;
and by night, but find no rest.

3Yet you are holy,
enthroned on the praises of Israel.
4In you our ancestors trusted;
they trusted, and you delivered them.
5To you they cried, and were saved;
in you they trusted, and were not put to shame.

6But I am a worm, and not human;
scorned by others, and despised by the people.
7All who see me mock at me;
they make mouths at me, they shake their heads;
8"Commit your cause to the LORD; let him deliver—
let him rescue the one in whom he delights!"

9Yet it was you who took me from the womb;
you kept me safe on my mother's breast.
10On you I was cast from my birth,
and since my mother bore me you have been my God.
11Do not be far from me,
for trouble is near
and there is no one to help.

12Many bulls encircle me,
strong bulls of Bashan surround me;
13they open wide their mouths at me,
like a ravening and roaring lion.

14I am poured out like water,
and all my bones are out of joint;
my heart is like wax;
it is melted within my breast;
15my mouth is dried up like a potsherd,
and my tongue sticks to my jaws;
you lay me in the dust of death.

16For dogs are all around me;
a company of evildoers encircles me.
My hands and feet have shriveled;
17I can count all my bones.
They stare and gloat over me;
18they divide my clothes among themselves,
and for my clothing they cast lots.

[19]But you, O LORD, do not be far away!
O my help, come quickly to my aid!
[20]Deliver my soul from the sword,
my life from the power of the dog!
[21]Save me from the mouth of the lion!

From the horns of the wild oxen you have rescued me.
[22]I will tell of your name to my brothers and sisters;
in the midst of the congregation I will praise you:
[23]You who fear the LORD, praise him!
All you offspring of Jacob, glorify him;
stand in awe of him, all you offspring of Israel!
[24]For he did not despise or abhor
the affliction of the afflicted;
he did not hide his face from me,
but heard when I cried to him.

[25]From you comes my praise in the great congregation;
my vows I will pay before those who fear him.
[26]The poor shall eat and be satisfied;
those who seek him shall praise the LORD.
May your hearts live forever!

[27]All the ends of the earth shall remember
and turn to the LORD;
and all the families of the nations
shall worship before him.
[28]For dominion belongs to the LORD,
and he rules over the nations.

[29]To him, indeed, shall all who sleep in the earth bow down;
before him shall bow all who go down to the dust,
and I shall live for him.
[30]Posterity will serve him;
future generations will be told about the Lord,
[31]and proclaim his deliverance to a people yet unborn,
saying that he has done it.

Connecting the Psalm with Scripture and Worship

Why do we call this Friday "good"? The answer to this liturgical riddle may be found in the ancient song of the cross, Psalm 22.

Psalm 22 is an individual lament—in fact, a paradigmatic example of the genre.[1] It begins with a bitter complaint: "My God, my God, why have you forsaken me? . . . I cry by day, but you do not answer; and by night, but find no rest" (Ps. 22:1–2). It continues with a dire description of the psalmist's present situation (vv. 6–8, 11–18), seasoned with affirmations of God's faithfulness in better days (vv. 3–5, 9–10). The psalmist makes bold petitions for God's saving presence and power: "But you, O

1. Patrick D. Miller, *Interpreting the Psalms* (Philadelphia: Fortress, 1986), 100–111.

Lord, do not be far away! . . . Save me from the mouth of the lion!" (vv. 19–21).

Then a threshold is crossed; there is a sudden shift in the tone of the psalm from crisis to confidence, from jeopardy to joy. Some scholars attribute this rapid mood swing to a priestly oracle of salvation (something like a contemporary declaration of forgiveness); others insist we can only point to the mysterious mercy of God. In any case, the final section of the psalm (vv. 22–31) reflects a dramatic turn of events. Now delivered from the dust of death, the psalmist's praise resounds throughout the great congregation (vv. 22–26), to all the nations of the earth (vv. 27–28), and even to past and future generations (vv. 29–31).

Like other biblical laments, Psalm 22 makes evocative use of metaphorical imagery. The three typical subjects of the lament—God, self, and others—are described in language that is expansive enough to account for a variety of experiences, yet vivid and specific enough to elicit pangs of empathy. Consider these examples: God is a monarch (v. 3) and a midwife (v. 9); the psalmist is a worm (v. 6), an empty vessel (v. 14), a melted candle (v. 14), and a broken pot (v. 15); the psalmist's enemies are strong bulls (v. 12), roaring lions (v. 13), wild dogs (v. 16), and marauding bandits (v. 16). Certain images from this psalm had an especially strong resonance with the memory of Jesus' crucifixion: mocking crowds (v. 7), wounded hands and feet (v. 16), and the division of garments (v. 18). Two of the evangelists even recall Jesus speaking the opening words of this psalm from the cross (Matt. 27:46; Mark 15:34).

Interestingly enough, Matthew and Mark are not included among the readings for Good Friday in the RCL. (As we will see, there is a reason for this, related to the riddle of Good Friday.) In the RCL, Psalm 22 is offered as a response to Isaiah's fourth Servant Song (Isa. 52:13–53:12). With its first-person voice, the psalm becomes the Suffering Servant's prayer, using common images of derision (Isa. 53:3; Ps. 22:6), posterity (Isa. 53:10; Ps. 22:30), and self-emptying (Isa. 53:12; Ps. 22:14). Similarly, with respect to the two options for the epistle reading on Good Friday (Heb. 10:16–25 and Heb. 4:14–16; 5:7–9), the psalm reflects the description of Jesus as a great high priest (Heb. 10:21; Ps. 22:25) and gives voice to his loud cries and tears (Heb. 5:7; Ps. 22:1–2).

The lengthy Gospel reading for Good Friday (John 18:1–19:42) deserves a closer look, since it provides the primary focus for this liturgical event. Again, the parallels are striking. The evangelist recounts how Jesus was taunted as "King of the Jews" and slapped in the face (John 19:3); the psalmist is scorned, despised, and mocked (Ps. 22:6–7). The evangelist records the shouts of "Crucify him!" (John 19:6); the psalmist cries out, "a company of evildoers encircles me" (Ps. 22:16). The evangelist remembers soldiers gambling for Jesus' garments (John 19:23–24); the psalmist complains, "for my clothing they cast lots" (Ps. 22:18). The evangelist tells us that Jesus' penultimate words were, "I am thirsty" (John 19:28); the psalmist laments, "my mouth is dried up" (Ps. 22:15).

On this Friday we call "good," however, we must give special consideration to Jesus' *final* words from the cross, as recorded by John, and to their deep consonance with the concluding words of Psalm 22. Old Testament scholar Robert Davidson suggests the intriguing possibility that "the last words John's Gospel attributes to Jesus, 'It is finished' (John 19:30) echo the closing words of the psalm, 'he has done it.'"[2] It is finished: God has accomplished it. Could it be that, while Matthew and Mark recognized Jesus' voice in the desperate cry at the opening of Psalm 22, John heard the Word of the Lord in its confident conclusion? This would be consistent with the image of Jesus throughout the Fourth Gospel: clear in purpose, authoritative, and in control—even as he died on the cross.

With all of these strong reverberations among the texts, Good Friday is a day when it is best to allow the Scriptures to speak for themselves. It is hard to imagine what words the preacher might have to add to Isaiah's beloved Servant Song, the poignant poetry of the psalm, the high priestly Christology of Hebrews, and John's compelling Passion Narrative. Those responsible for proclaiming the Word would do well by simply

2. Robert Davidson, *The Vitality of Worship: A Commentary on the Book of Psalms* (Grand Rapids: Eerdmans, 1998), 82.

To Think of Ourselves as the Least of All

Jesus has always many who love His heavenly kingdom, but few who bear His cross. He has many who desire consolation, but few who care for trial. He finds many to share His table, but few to take part in His fasting. All desire to be happy with Him; few wish to suffer anything for Him. Many follow Him to the breaking of bread, but few to the drinking of the chalice of His passion. Many revere His miracles; few approach the shame of the Cross. Many love Him as long as they encounter no hardship; many praise and bless Him as long as they receive some comfort from Him. But if Jesus hides Himself and leaves them for a while, they fall either into complaints or into deep dejection. Those, on the contrary, who love Him for His own sake and not for any comfort of their own, bless Him in all trial and anguish of heart as well as in the bliss of consolation. Even if He should never give them consolation, yet they would continue to praise Him and wish always to give Him thanks. What power there is in pure love for Jesus—love that is free from all self-interest and self-love!

Do not those who always seek consolation deserve to be called mercenaries? Do not those who always think of their own profit and gain prove that they love themselves rather than Christ? Where can a man be found who desires to serve God for nothing? Rarely indeed is a man so spiritual as to strip himself of all things. And who shall find a man so truly poor in spirit as to be free from every creature? His value is like that of things brought from the most distant lands.

If a man give all his wealth, it is nothing; if he do great penance, it is little; if he gain all knowledge, he is still far afield; if he have great virtue and much ardent devotion, he still lacks a great deal, and especially, the one thing that is most necessary to him. What is this one thing? That leaving all, he forsake himself, completely renounce himself, and give up all private affections. Then, when he has done all that he knows ought to be done, let him consider it as nothing, let him make little of what may be considered great; let him in all honesty call himself an unprofitable servant. For truth itself has said: "When you shall have done all these things that are commanded you, say: 'we are unprofitable servants'" [Luke 17:10].

Then he will be truly poor and stripped in spirit, and with the prophet may say: "I am alone and poor." No one, however, is more wealthy than such a man; no one is more powerful, no one freer than he who knows how to leave all things and think of himself as the least of all.

Thomas à Kempis, *Imitation of Christ*; trans. Aloysius Croft and Harold Bolton (Milwaukee: Bruce, 1940), 75–76.

gesturing to God's Word made flesh. Indeed, Good Friday can be a wordy service—particularly with the church's traditional omission of the Eucharist on this day. Those responsible for planning worship should make generous use of contemplative silence, stirring music, ritual action, and embodied prayer.

Why do we call this Friday "good"? The psalmist seems to know. The good news of Good Friday is that God meets us in the dust of death, the depth of despair—and then takes us to the height of hallelujah, the pinnacle of praise. To borrow the words of a neighboring psalm, God leads us through the darkest valley to the very house of the Lord, where goodness and mercy follow us all the days of our lives (Ps. 23:4, 6). So it is that, even on this bleak day at the center of the Triduum and the heart of Holy Week, we may rejoice with the psalmist and evangelist: "It is finished; God has done it!"

DAVID GAMBRELL

Hebrews 4:14–16; 5:7–9

4:14Since, then, we have a great high priest who has passed through the heavens, Jesus, the Son of God, let us hold fast to our confession. 15For we do not have a high priest who is unable to sympathize with our weaknesses, but we have one who in every respect has been tested as we are, yet without sin. 16Let us therefore approach the throne of grace with boldness, so that we may receive mercy and find grace to help in time of need. . . .

5:7In the days of his flesh, Jesus offered up prayers and supplications, with loud cries and tears, to the one who was able to save him from death, and he was heard because of his reverent submission. 8Although he was a Son, he learned obedience through what he suffered; 9and having been made perfect, he became the source of eternal salvation for all who obey him.

Commentary 1: Connecting the Reading with Scripture

Hebrews 4:14–5:9 concerns not only Holy Week, but the Easter and Ascension triumph that follows. It begins with the victorious portrait of the One who has passed into the highest heavens on our behalf. Here, we find a summary of the astonishing Christology of the message to the Hebrews, where Jesus is both the Creator and the One who suffers and "learns obedience" (Heb. 5:8). We are in the realm of mystery.

The appointed passages, Hebrews 4:14–16 and 5:7–9, concentrate upon the archetypical sufferer on this holy day. Yet, in the immediate context, Hebrews links and contrasts Jesus with the Old Testament priest, and the strange figure of Melchizedek. Like the Aaronic priest, Jesus is vulnerable and so can understand the priestly risk involved in standing in the liminal space between God and humanity; yet he has no need to offer sacrifice for his own sins. The earthly priest was appointed and had neither the need nor the grounds for elevating himself to his office; Jesus *could* have claimed such rights (cf. Phil. 2:5–11), but instead relies upon God to exalt him. High priest forever, he has entered into the holiest place, and not simply into an earthly temple.

We are given Melchizedek as an Old Testament example of mysterious authority, but Jesus is even more awe-inspiring, and *eternal*! Melchizedek was honored in one of the Dead Sea Scrolls and in later rabbinic tradition, but within the pages of the Christian canon, his importance is eclipsed by that of Jesus, who is "the same yesterday and today and forever" (Heb. 13:8). Melchizedek, who bursts into the story in Genesis 14 with no pedigree, symbolizes one without father or mother; but Jesus has always been one with the heavenly Father. Preachers may warn against treating any penultimate authority with the loyalty that we should offer Jesus alone. Even the wisest and strongest among us cannot bear the burden meant only for our Lord; we build on sand if we think otherwise.

Very early in the book Jesus is commended to us as God. He is higher than the angels, greater than Moses, more honorable than Melchizedek—and we must worship! God the Father addresses the Son with the divine title "O God" (1:8; the author of Hebrews is reading Ps. 45:6 christologically). Similarly, the promise that he gives is higher than that which the Hebrews received. When we arrive, then, at chapters 4 and 5, we know about the glory of this One who yet can "sympathize with our weaknesses" (4:15). Now we explore the amazing humility of the One who suffered beyond all measure and meditate upon it for "Good" Friday. We stress one pole of the great paradox about our Lord's identity: he was (and remains) utterly human, and in the "days of his flesh" he suffered (5:7). Even though he was "Son"—the unique Messiah, and the only eternal Son of God—he prayed, and he learned obedience. This is particularly surprising in the light of Hebrews' introduction, about this One who is the "very stamp" of God's nature, who preserves the cosmos, and who has taken on the name above all names (1:1–4).

This paradox of Jesus' full humanity and divinity helps us through some questions of translation. In 5:8, we can be sure we are talking not about "a son" only. He is "Son"—and this is why we are startled. Although "Son" of God, this happens to him! Why does God allow such things—why not just teach us gently? The book of Hebrews responds: Jesus himself supplicated, cried out, humbled himself before the Father, learned, and was made perfect through suffering. Clearly, suffering and humility are not simply casualties of our existence, but are being used by God to bring about incalculable good. As a beloved Easter hymn of the Eastern Orthodox Church reminds us, "He trampled down death by death!"

Preachers can help us to see, though, that it would be masochistic and diabolical to seek out suffering, or to downplay the suffering of others. We cannot explain or minimize suffering, evil, and death: but God has and will use even these dark places to bring about light and life! Here preachers must tread carefully, never implying that God afflicts us *in order to* bring about the divine purposes. Still, in proclaiming the gospel, preachers can truthfully speak, with awe, of the comfort of *Good* Friday. Like a master artist, God takes the blot that we have put on the page and makes it the centerpiece of a great tableau.

The themes of the passage are wide-ranging, and found elsewhere in the New Testament. Here we find encouragement to pour out petition and intercession, for Christ did so—to the point of sweat and tears. We may not understand the mystery of prayer, but because we are members of God's beloved family with his Son, we are qualified to bring our concerns before God (2:11, 14). Preachers can help us to see that this theme is a very difficult one in our age of individualism. Without it, however, we cannot understand either how the gospel is good news or how we are meant to enjoy God. God cares for each one of us personally, but God gives us a place within his large family as we "go on to maturity" (6:1, RSV). It is not just deliverance from death and rescue from punishment for which we hope, but actual glory (John 17:10; 2 Cor. 5:21; Rom. 5:2; Rev. 21–22). This is a promise for each of us, and for all of us together!

We read this passage along with Isaiah 53 and John 18. There, Jesus is shown to be the ultimate fulfillment of the Servant who will suffer for others. The glorious One is the one who suffers and dies for us! Here, we relearn what Jesus taught Peter before the transfiguration (Mark 8:27–38): it is not enough to acknowledge his messiahship, nor even his divinity, but to press through to the outpouring of God's love on the cross, for us. Our Gospel reading for this day underscores the heartbreaking mystery: Jesus cries out both "I AM" (John 18:6) and "I thirst" (19:28). He holds the name of Lord, the I AM who made heavens and earth and sea; yet he thirsts for our sake. Though the other Gospels have him quote from the first verse of Psalm 22 ("Why have you forsaken me?"), the Gospel of John declares his final word to be "It is finished" ("God has done it!"; cf. Ps. 22:31b).

God has done it, provided us a way through, that we may see suffering as now full of meaning; in Christ we will be cleansed of our sins and raised from death, and finally we will ascend in glory. On this day opposites collide, bringing an unexpected conclusion. Hebrews 10:23–24, also appointed for today, encourages us to "consider how to stir up one another to love and good works" (RSV), and to hold on to this revolutionary story that has changed the entire world. The preacher may emphasize the wonder of the God-human, the continuity of Good Friday with Easter and Ascension, our solidarity in Christ, the invitation of God to pray, our call to humility and hope. Each of these challenges thinking that is individualistic, pessimistic, or prosaic. The story of the tender God-human who is made perfect can break through even our skepticism, and turn our eyes upwards.

EDITH M. HUMPHREY

Commentary 2: Connecting the Reading with the World

Worship spaces draped in black, somber music, mournful prayers, and heavy hearts: these are what we expect to encounter in a Good Friday worship service. On this holy day, we gather with the realization that we can neither turn back time nor stop time. The best we can do is move through the hours of Jesus' suffering and death together. Together we can find ways to confess, to reflect, and to survive the earth's darkest hours.

Congregations gather to honor Jesus' last hours in a variety of ways, from Tenebrae services, with the extinguishing of the light, to compilation readings of the seven last words of Christ, to a choir's presentation of a classic requiem. Preaching on Good Friday provides an opportunity to explore the pain of this world, while also offering the promise that death does not claim the final word. While we cannot rush the hours of Jesus' betrayal, suffering, and death, we can hold out the reminder of life renewed. The darkness of Good Friday can and should be balanced with a reminder that Easter will come. Death will be swallowed up by life.

It is a fine line, living in the silence and darkness of Good Friday while keeping the Easter miracle within reach. Christian educators remind those who work with children that it is vital that we never leave children in Good Friday's grip. Easter will come, we tell them. Children are not the only ones who need this reassurance.

This passage from Hebrews allows the preacher to bring that word of expectation to a grieving community. Here we read how we may embrace hope: trust in our empathic Savior, continue to profess the faith with conviction, and always acknowledge our crucified God. Preaching this particular text on Good Friday will set a more hopeful tone than other texts one might typically hear. If your congregation has entered Lent or Holy Week with heavier hearts than usual, this is their text. Has the congregation been going through its own time of trial and testing, or an unusually painful season of grief? Preach this passage as a word of hope for all God's children.

On Easter of 2018, NBC aired a live television broadcast of *Jesus Christ Superstar*. Those familiar with this 1970 rock opera by Andrew Lloyd Webber and Tim Rice will remember that the original stage play, as well as the 1973 film version directed by Norman Jewison, ends with Jesus on the cross. There is no resurrection, no redemption, no restoration. The 2018 version, however, rewrites the ending with an interpretive resurrection scene: Jesus' body fades away, but is replaced with blinding streams of light. If your church has the technology to project film clips, how might you use the crucifixion and resurrection scenes in conjunction with the Hebrews text? How might these beams of light be experienced as God's mercy? How might they be representative of the "throne of grace," and how might you invite congregants to approach that throne, understanding it as the source of reconciliation and restoration?

These are complex concepts, and this text could be a launching pad for exploring an affirmation of faith. "Let us hold fast to our confession" (Heb. 4:14b) is an invitation to help congregants unpack an affirmation of faith. For churches that recite an affirmation each week, the words may become rote. For them the Easter season could be an opportunity to incorporate a new affirmation, one that is introduced on Good Friday. In faith traditions that do not incorporate creeds, there are various scriptural confessions of faith that could be explored (e.g., Col. 1:15–20; Phil. 2:5–11). There is also the possibility of engaging others in writing a confession of faith inspired by the Hebrews passage for use in the Good Friday service. This could be done prior to worship and woven into the sermon, or created as a corporate act of worship.

Affirmations of faith feed our intellectual yearning for understanding, but our hearts also long for connection. For all who have suffered persecution, abuse, rejection, discrimination, here is a word of promise: Jesus identifies with our pain. Jesus our "high priest" has "passed through the heavens" in order to walk this world with humanity. The author of Hebrews offers a unique focus for this painful day. Instead of highlighting the cross and the cruelty it represents, the author invites the reader to turn around and face the "throne of grace," where Christ's healing may be found.

Preaching this truth may touch tender places, and it would be wise to offer opportunities for congregants to receive prayers of healing during or after the service. How might the congregation experience Good Friday if it were set in the context of a service for healing and wholeness? Instead of a day burdened by guilt, Good Friday could be an immersion in God's empathic mercy and grace.

Good Friday worship often touches people on a very personal level, but there are many vivid communal aspects of this day. Jesus was convicted by a community. A crowd screamed for his execution. This aspect of the story challenges us to look beyond our own walls. Churches seeking a way to carry Jesus' identification with human suffering into their local communities may draw inspiration from the work of pastors such as Nadia Bolz-Weber. In *Accidental Saints: Finding God in All the Wrong People*, Bolz-Weber writes of extending the message of Good Friday into the neighboring community. At the conclusion of their Good Friday service, participants collect the cross and purple tulips from their worship space and regather at the site of a recent tragedy.[1] Where violence has occurred, they bring the message that Jesus was himself the victim of violence.

This simple gift of presence, of seeing and naming a tragedy within the community, is transformative for those who participate in it and the neighbors who witness it. Where violent deaths are too quickly forgotten, especially within neglected communities, simply standing as witness is an offering of compassion. Within and beyond the church walls, how might this message of Jesus' sacrificial love bring people together in solidarity and hope?

Responding to the violence around us begs the question of how justice is carried out in our communities. Those who wait in death-row cell blocks are in need of the message of Jesus' compassion and salvation. Even as we are confronted with the reality that Jesus was unjustly executed, we live in one of the few societies that still embraces capital punishment. Our nation must acknowledge that we have executed innocent individuals, that our execution methods are potentially forms of torture, and that the system itself is rife with racial prejudice. We must ask ourselves if, in taking a life, we have eliminated any hope of reconciliation or redemption. Many family members of victims of violent crime have raised their voices in support of a moratorium on the death penalty. What if their stories could be heard on Good Friday? Our Scripture speaks to the truth of our brokenness and God's desire to meet us in our brokenness. In Jesus' death we witness God forgiving what we often deem unforgivable.[2]

Whether you have given more Good Friday sermons than you can remember, or never preached on this holy day, engaging in this text from Hebrews offers fresh insights, renewed hope, and the incredible assurance of Jesus' identification with the suffering of all creation. God has not and will never abandon God's children. Instead, God welcomes all to the throne of grace.

CATHY CALDWELL HOOP

1. Nadia Bolz-Weber, *Accidental Saints: Finding God in All the Wrong People* (New York: Convergent Books, 2016), 137.
2. Visit https://deathpenaltyinfo.org.

Good Friday

John 18:1–19:42

18:1After Jesus had spoken these words, he went out with his disciples across
the Kidron valley to a place where there was a garden, which he and his disciples entered. 2Now Judas, who betrayed him, also knew the place, because
Jesus often met there with his disciples. 3So Judas brought a detachment of
soldiers together with police from the chief priests and the Pharisees, and they
came there with lanterns and torches and weapons. 4Then Jesus, knowing all
that was to happen to him, came forward and asked them, “Whom are you looking for?” 5They answered, “Jesus of Nazareth.” Jesus replied, “I am he.” Judas,
who betrayed him, was standing with them. 6When Jesus said to them, “I am he,”
they stepped back and fell to the ground. 7Again he asked them, “Whom are you
looking for?” And they said, “Jesus of Nazareth.” 8Jesus answered, “I told you
that I am he. So if you are looking for me, let these men go.” 9This was to fulfill the
word that he had spoken, “I did not lose a single one of those whom you gave
me.” 10Then Simon Peter, who had a sword, drew it, struck the high priest’s slave,
and cut off his right ear. The slave’s name was Malchus. 11Jesus said to Peter,
“Put your sword back into its sheath. Am I not to drink the cup that the Father
has given me?”

12So the soldiers, their officer, and the Jewish police arrested Jesus and bound
him. 13First they took him to Annas, who was the father-in-law of Caiaphas, the
high priest that year. 14Caiaphas was the one who had advised the Jews that it
was better to have one person die for the people.

15Simon Peter and another disciple followed Jesus. Since that disciple was
known to the high priest, he went with Jesus into the courtyard of the high priest,
16but Peter was standing outside at the gate. So the other disciple, who was
known to the high priest, went out, spoke to the woman who guarded the gate,
and brought Peter in. 17The woman said to Peter, “You are not also one of this
man’s disciples, are you?” He said, “I am not.” 18Now the slaves and the police had
made a charcoal fire because it was cold, and they were standing around it and
warming themselves. Peter also was standing with them and warming himself.

19Then the high priest questioned Jesus about his disciples and about his
teaching. 20Jesus answered, “I have spoken openly to the world; I have always
taught in synagogues and in the temple, where all the Jews come together. I
have said nothing in secret. 21Why do you ask me? Ask those who heard what I
said to them; they know what I said.” 22When he had said this, one of the police
standing nearby struck Jesus on the face, saying, “Is that how you answer the
high priest?” 23Jesus answered, “If I have spoken wrongly, testify to the wrong.
But if I have spoken rightly, why do you strike me?” 24Then Annas sent him bound
to Caiaphas the high priest.

25Now Simon Peter was standing and warming himself. They asked him, “You
are not also one of his disciples, are you?” He denied it and said, “I am not.” 26One
of the slaves of the high priest, a relative of the man whose ear Peter had cut off,
asked, “Did I not see you in the garden with him?” 27Again Peter denied it, and at
that moment the cock crowed.

28Then they took Jesus from Caiaphas to Pilate’s headquarters It was early
in the morning. They themselves did not enter the headquarters, so as to avoid
ritual defilement and to be able to eat the Passover. 29So Pilate went out to them
and said, “What accusation do you bring against this man?” 30They answered, “If

this man were not a criminal, we would not have handed him over to you." [31]Pilate
said to them, "Take him yourselves and judge him according to your law." The
Jews replied, "We are not permitted to put anyone to death." [32](This was to fulfill
what Jesus had said when he indicated the kind of death he was to die.)

[33]Then Pilate entered the headquarters again, summoned Jesus, and asked
him, "Are you the King of the Jews?" [34]Jesus answered, "Do you ask this on your
own, or did others tell you about me?" [35]Pilate replied, "I am not a Jew, am I? Your
own nation and the chief priests have handed you over to me. What have you
done?" [36]Jesus answered, "My kingdom is not from this world. If my kingdom
were from this world, my followers would be fighting to keep me from being
handed over to the Jews. But as it is, my kingdom is not from here." [37]Pilate asked
him, "So you are a king?" Jesus answered, "You say that I am a king. For this I
was born, and for this I came into the world, to testify to the truth. Everyone who
belongs to the truth listens to my voice." [38]Pilate asked him, "What is truth?"

After he had said this, he went out to the Jews again and told them, "I find
no case against him. [39]But you have a custom that I release someone for you at
the Passover. Do you want me to release for you the King of the Jews?" [40]They
shouted in reply, "Not this man, but Barabbas!" Now Barabbas was a bandit.

[19:1]Then Pilate took Jesus and had him flogged. [2]And the soldiers wove a
crown of thorns and put it on his head, and they dressed him in a purple robe.
[3]They kept coming up to him, saying, "Hail, King of the Jews!" and striking him on
the face. [4]Pilate went out again and said to them, "Look, I am bringing him out to
you to let you know that I find no case against him." [5]So Jesus came out, wearing
the crown of thorns and the purple robe. Pilate said to them, "Here is the man!"
[6]When the chief priests and the police saw him, they shouted, "Crucify him! Crucify him!" Pilate said to them, "Take him yourselves and crucify him; I find no case
against him." [7]The Jews answered him, "We have a law, and according to that law
he ought to die because he has claimed to be the Son of God."

[8]Now when Pilate heard this, he was more afraid than ever. [9]He entered his
headquarters again and asked Jesus, "Where are you from?" But Jesus gave him
no answer. [10]Pilate therefore said to him, "Do you refuse to speak to me? Do you
not know that I have power to release you, and power to crucify you?" [11]Jesus
answered him, "You would have no power over me unless it had been given you
from above; therefore the one who handed me over to you is guilty of a greater
sin." [12]From then on Pilate tried to release him, but the Jews cried out, "If you
release this man, you are no friend of the emperor. Everyone who claims to be a
king sets himself against the emperor."

[13]When Pilate heard these words, he brought Jesus outside and sat on the
judge's bench at a place called The Stone Pavement, or in Hebrew Gabbatha.
[14]Now it was the day of Preparation for the Passover; and it was about noon. He
said to the Jews, "Here is your King!" [15]They cried out, "Away with him! Away with
him! Crucify him!" Pilate asked them, "Shall I crucify your King?" The chief priests
answered, "We have no king but the emperor." [16]Then he handed him over to
them to be crucified.

So they took Jesus; [17]and carrying the cross by himself, he went out to what
is called The Place of the Skull, which in Hebrew is called Golgotha. [18]There they
crucified him, and with him two others, one on either side, with Jesus between
them. [19]Pilate also had an inscription written and put on the cross. It read, "Jesus
of Nazareth, the King of the Jews." [20]Many of the Jews read this inscription,
because the place where Jesus was crucified was near the city; and it was written in Hebrew, in Latin, and in Greek. [21]Then the chief priests of the Jews said
to Pilate, "Do not write, 'The King of the Jews,' but, 'This man said, I am King of

the Jews.'" [22]Pilate answered, "What I have written I have written." [23]When the soldiers had crucified Jesus, they took his clothes and divided them into four parts, one for each soldier. They also took his tunic; now the tunic was seamless, woven in one piece from the top. [24]So they said to one another, "Let us not tear it, but cast lots for it to see who will get it." This was to fulfill what the scripture says,

"They divided my clothes among themselves,
  and for my clothing they cast lots."

[25]And that is what the soldiers did.

Meanwhile, standing near the cross of Jesus were his mother, and his mother's sister, Mary the wife of Clopas, and Mary Magdalene. [26]When Jesus saw his mother and the disciple whom he loved standing beside her, he said to his mother, "Woman, here is your son." [27]Then he said to the disciple, "Here is your mother." And from that hour the disciple took her into his own home.

[28]After this, when Jesus knew that all was now finished, he said (in order to fulfill the scripture), "I am thirsty." [29]A jar full of sour wine was standing there. So they put a sponge full of the wine on a branch of hyssop and held it to his mouth. [30]When Jesus had received the wine, he said, "It is finished." Then he bowed his head and gave up his spirit.

[31]Since it was the day of Preparation, the Jews did not want the bodies left on the cross during the sabbath, especially because that sabbath was a day of great solemnity. So they asked Pilate to have the legs of the crucified men broken and the bodies removed. [32]Then the soldiers came and broke the legs of the first and of the other who had been crucified with him. [33]But when they came to Jesus and saw that he was already dead, they did not break his legs. [34]Instead, one of the soldiers pierced his side with a spear, and at once blood and water came out. [35](He who saw this has testified so that you also may believe. His testimony is true, and he knows that he tells the truth.) [36]These things occurred so that the scripture might be fulfilled, "None of his bones shall be broken." [37]And again another passage of scripture says, "They will look on the one whom they have pierced."

[38]After these things, Joseph of Arimathea, who was a disciple of Jesus, though a secret one because of his fear of the Jews, asked Pilate to let him take away the body of Jesus. Pilate gave him permission; so he came and removed his body. [39]Nicodemus, who had at first come to Jesus by night, also came, bringing a mixture of myrrh and aloes, weighing about a hundred pounds. [40]They took the body of Jesus and wrapped it with the spices in linen cloths, according to the burial custom of the Jews. [41]Now there was a garden in the place where he was crucified, and in the garden there was a new tomb in which no one had ever been laid. [42]And so, because it was the Jewish day of Preparation, and the tomb was nearby, they laid Jesus there.

Commentary 1: Connecting the Reading with Scripture

This sweeping Passion Narrative moves from the arrest of Jesus, through the interrogation and trial, to his crucifixion and burial. Throughout it is deeply ironic, told on two levels simultaneously. On one level, Jesus is taunted, scourged, and ridiculed as a mocked and impotent king—a story of a ministry destroyed. On a higher level, however, the Jesus who said, "And I, when I am lifted up from the earth, will draw all people to myself" (John 12:32), is now, indeed, lifted up and revealed as the true king (and great priest; see Heb. 10:16–25, the second reading for Good Friday)—the story of a ministry fulfilled.

The passage opens with the nighttime arrest of Jesus, where Judas acts out his betrayal, and it ends with the burial of Jesus, where Nicodemus "acts out his love and reverence for Jesus"[1] by tenderly caring for his body at burial. The preacher might explore how Jesus in John's Gospel provokes a crisis that calls for a decision between light and darkness, contrasting Judas, who was called in the light and became an agent of the darkness, with Nicodemus, who came to Jesus by night (3:1–2) and then became allied with the light.

There is a second example of irony in the arrest scene. At one level Jesus is overpowered here, surrounded by a detachment of soldiers ("cohort," that is, as many as six hundred troops) who arrest and bind him. At another level, however, Jesus remains in charge. When the soldiers announce that they are looking for Jesus of Nazareth, he responds, "I am he" (in Greek it is simply *egō eimi,* "I am"), which connects to the great I AM divine revelation to Moses at the burning bush (Exod. 3:13–14), and the soldiers fall to the ground. In verse 8, it is Jesus who gives the orders. Earlier, Jesus taught that no one was going to take his life from him: "but I lay it down of my own accord" (John 10:18). So, what appears from one perspective to be the cornering of a criminal is revealed, from another point of view, to be Jesus calmly receiving the gift of the cup from the Father (18:11) and then giving his life for the sake of the world.

Jesus asks the soldiers, "Whom are you looking for?" That question appears three times in John's Gospel, and the preacher may want to explore them as a set. Jesus asks a similar question to two of John the Baptist's followers (1:38), who appear to be seeking Jesus out of curiosity. He asks it here of the soldiers, who are seeking him out of malice, and he asks it again of Mary Magdalene in the cemetery (20:15), who is seeking Jesus out of grief. Regardless of the motive, in each case the quest leads to Jesus, the light of the world.

The passage contains two accounts of Jesus being interrogated by the authorities, one in a Jewish setting before Annas of the high-priestly family, and the other in a Roman setting before Pontius Pilate. In the Annas scene, Jesus is bold and firm, even to the point that he is slapped by a police officer for seeming insubordination (18:22). The preacher may want to explore the stark contrast between Jesus' courage and the failure of nerve happening outside in the courtyard, where Peter "the Rock" is himself crumbling and denies Jesus three times (18:17, 25, 27).

The second interrogation, before Pilate, is a complex drama arranged in seven scenes (18:28–32; 18:33–38a; 18:38b–40; 19:1–3; 19:4–8; 19:9–11; 19:12–16a) in which a frantic Pilate scurries back and forth between outside his house, where he waffles in front of Jesus' accusers, and inside, where Pilate berates and flogs Jesus. Once again, the account is ripe with irony. It is the weak and panicky governor Pilate who is the official authority, but it is Jesus who exhibits calm control. It is Pilate who stands in judgment, but it is Jesus who is the true Judge.

The irony is at its deepest when it becomes clear that when Pilate, the vacillating politician, is outside addressing the accusers, he ironically becomes an evangelist. "This man is innocent. I find no case against him. Here is your king!" (18:38). When he is inside the house, he ironically acts as one leading the Johannine community in call-and-response worship (vv. 33–38). "What have you done?" ("The works of God who sent him," the congregation would reply.) "Are you a king?" ("Yes, he is.") "What is truth?" ("He is the way, and the truth, and the life.") "Where are you from?" ("From the Father who sent him.")

The last scene of the trial sequence is controversial. The accusers threaten Pilate with a charge of treason: "If you release this man, you are no friend of the emperor" (19:12). What Pilate does next is a matter of debate. Does Pilate bring Jesus outside and then sit on the judge's bench himself, or does Pilate bring Jesus out and put *Jesus* on the judge's seat? The underlying Greek can be translated either way, but dramatically and theologically, the latter reading is more compelling. Pilate responds to the crowd's bullying by bringing Jesus out, placing him on the seat of judgment. Then, taunting the accusers, he points toward Jesus: "Here is

1. Gail R. O'Day, "The Gospel of John," in Leander E. Keck et al., eds., *The New Interpreter's Bible* (Nashville: Abingdon, 1995), 9:491–875 (835).

your King. . . . Shall I crucify your King?" (vv. 14–15).

So the trial ends with the accused, Jesus, on the judge's bench and the supposed judge, Pilate, on the witness stand giving testimony. As pathetic and cynical as he is, Pilate is the unsuspecting player in a cosmic courtroom drama not of his own making. Despite himself, Pilate proclaims the truth: Jesus is the true Judge and King of the whole cosmos. The wheels of politics continue to spin, but human politics itself is finally gathered up into the great drama of God's redemption of the world.

As the crucifixion scene proceeds, Jesus' mother and "the disciple whom he loved" are among those standing near the cross. Jesus speaks to them from the cross ("here is your son. . . . here is your mother" (19:26–27), creating a new familial relationship. This is perhaps an indication that the death of Jesus makes possible what the narrator of John's Gospel saw from the beginning: a family of God's children who have relationships "not of blood or of the will of the flesh . . . but of God" (1:13).

Jesus also calls his mother "woman" (19:26), which is what he called her at the wedding at Cana (2:1–12, esp. v. 4). Mary's appearance at the "first sign" and now at the end serves to tie together the full span of Jesus' ministry. It also highlights the motif of water in John's Gospel. At Cana, Jesus requested water, and the result was an overflow of fine wine. He asked the Samaritan woman for water, only to promise that he would give "living water" that will become a spring "gushing up to eternal life" (4:7, 14). At the Festival of Booths, Jesus invited all who were thirsty to come to him because "out of his [Jesus'] belly will flow streams of living water" (7:38; my literal trans.). Now at the crucifixion, Jesus invokes our memory of Cana, saying, "I am thirsty." He is given wine as he dies. Then a soldier pierces his side, and water and blood gush out. From the cross flows the promised stream of living water, flowing to eternal life.

THOMAS G. LONG

Commentary 2: Connecting the Reading with the World

The term "Good Friday" seems counterintuitive when considered against the reality of what we gather to commemorate. The narrative of John 18:1–19:42 captures the terrifying details and the range of visceral responses to Jesus' final hours. Fear, dread, violence, pain, suffering, and death are a few of the terms that depict Jesus' crucifixion. Soldiers arrest Jesus, his disciples flee, Roman officials condemn him, his followers deny him, and Jesus dies a painful death while nailed to a cross. Nothing about this series of events is "good." Yet one archaic definition of good was "holy." This might help to explain why faith communities once referred to Holy Wednesday before Easter as "Good Wednesday." Thus it is important for preachers to prevent contemporary connotations of the term "good" from obscuring the sheer horror detailed in the account. Good Friday provides an opportunity for the church to recount and reflect on personal and communal suffering born of injustice.

Consider Peter's denial. It is easy to demonize this disciple as a lily-livered coward who turned on his friend and teacher. So often we depict Peter in our sermons as one who lost faith. This sort of interpretation misses the sociopolitical significance and intent of crucifixion. Roman officials reserved the act of crucifixion for those considered a threat to Roman imperial power. Crucifixion was state-sanctioned violence that targeted those persons deemed subversive. For instance, when given a choice between releasing Jesus and Barabbas, the crowd called for Barabbas, whom the Bible describes as a bandit (John 18:40). The Gospel of Mark states also that Pilate crucified Jesus alongside two bandits (Mark 15:27). In our context, the term "bandit" evokes images of thievery and criminality. Roman officials used the term in the first century to describe any Jew in Palestine whom they labeled insurrectionist. So-called bandits challenged the imperial power and divinity of the emperor. Crucifixion, then, was an act of terror with a dual aim: to punish political dissidents and to instill fear in all who might consider any strategy of resistance.

Theologian James Cone likens crucifixion to the practice of racist lynching in the United States. Cone argues in his book *The Cross and the Lynching Tree* that toward cultivating fear, crucifixions were accompanied by beatings, dismemberment, and prolonged suffocation (see John 19:31–34).[2] Jews were nailed to crosses, and their bodies were hung in the open air to terrify anyone with the slightest thought of dissent. In *The War of the Jews*, his first-century treatment of the period, Josephus described Rome's response to uprisings that precipitated the Jewish war in Jerusalem around 66 CE. It was the hope of the Roman military commander and future emperor Titus, according to Josephus,

> that the Jews might perhaps yield at that sight [of the crucifixions], out of fear lest they might themselves afterwards be liable to the same cruel treatment. So the soldiers out of the wrath and hatred they bore the Jews, nailed those they caught, one after one way, and another after another, to the crosses, by way of jest; when their multitude was so great, that room was wanting for the crosses, and crosses wanting for the bodies.[3]

To depict Peter's denial as either a lapse of faith or betrayal of Jesus diminishes the larger theater of terror that the empire produced. To paraphrase the haunting lyrics of Billie Holiday to describe the phenomenon of lynching in the American South, "Roman trees bore strange fruit."

Good Friday provides us an opportunity to acknowledge the legitimacy of fear. Too many of us have been conditioned to believe that fear is an antonym to faith. We equate anxiety with inadequacy and fear with failure. The horror of crucifixion Friday ought to disabuse us of this sort of simplistic thinking. There are times in life when our fears are founded, and a sense of dread and angst is appropriate. It is OK to be afraid and even have doubts. Fear and uncertainty are not the opposite of faith. To the contrary, doubt is a precondition of faith. According to the writer of Hebrews, "faith is the substance of things hoped for, the conviction of things not seen" (Heb. 11:1). Thus, the opposite of faith is not fear and doubt. The opposite of faith is our optimistic or pessimistic certainty. In the words of Søren Kierkegaard, "he who always hopes for the best becomes old, deceived by life, and he who always prepares for the worst becomes old prematurely; but he who has faith, retains eternal youth."[4]

Therefore, we can use Good Friday to acknowledge the legitimacy of fear. Every moment of transformation and positive change begins here. This is true for those who receive a negative diagnosis from a physician, experience the loss of a loved one, or face an impending divorce. Pastoral care ought to begin with a period of recognition. Certainly, we want to encourage parishioners to keep the faith and have hope in the future, but we also want to affirm their fears about the future. Momentous life events can be frightening, and people need to have their feelings corroborated.

The same is true in times of positive social change. Consider the #MeToo movement. Women at all levels of society have had much to fear. For generations, men in power have conditioned women to believe that they are of lesser value and expendable in the workplace and society at large, mere sexual cogs in the machines of masculinist pleasure. To raise a voice of protest is to risk retaliation: being overlooked for professional opportunities, losing income, and even being disparaged publicly. If this is true for women in Hollywood and on Wall Street, imagine the fear that poor and working-class women must face when trying to combat gender discrimination and sexual abuse. We can appreciate the courage of women who say, "Enough is enough," only after we acknowledge the fear they face as they take risks to stand against such devaluation. These are but some causes for our individual and shared fears.

Despite the reality of fear, Good Friday should also remind us that God is present. Suffering does not separate us from the love of God (Rom.

2. James H. Cone, *The Cross and the Lynching Tree* (Maryknoll, NY: Orbis, 2013), 31.
3. Flavius Josephus, *The War of the Jews* 5.11, in *The Complete Works of Josephus: New Updated Edition*, trans. William Whiston (Peabody, MA: Hendrickson, 1987), 720.
4. Søren Kierkegaard, *Fear and Trembling*, trans. Alastair Hannay (London: Penguin Classics, 1986), 52.

8:38–39). God is with us in the midst of our pain. There are so many examples throughout Scripture: Joseph imprisoned in Egypt (Gen. 39:21); Moses standing before Pharaoh (Exod. 8:20); the children of Israel wandering through the wilderness for forty years (Deut. 2:7); Ruth embracing the God of the Israelites as her own to follow her mother-in-law Naomi (Ruth 1:16–17); Esther intervening on behalf of her people with the Persian ruler, despite the fear of execution (Esth. 5 and 7); Shadrach, Meshach, and Abednego in a fiery furnace (Dan. 3); Daniel in the den of lions (Dan. 6); Jesus alone in the Garden of Gethsemane (Mark 14:36); Paul and Silas imprisoned in Philippi (Acts 16:25–31). The list goes on. Good Friday provides the preacher an opportunity to walk parishioners back and forth through Scripture to recall the one to whom Isaiah refers as Emmanuel, "God with us" (Isa. 7:14).

JONATHAN L. WALTON

Hebrews 10:16–25

16 “This is the covenant that I will make with them
after those days, says the Lord:
I will put my laws in their hearts,
I will write them on their minds,”

17 he also adds,

“I will remember their sins and their lawless deeds no more.”

18 Where there is forgiveness of these, there is no longer any offering for sin.
19 Therefore, my friends, since we have confidence to enter the sanctuary by
the blood of Jesus, 20 by the new and living way that he opened for us through
the curtain (that is, through his flesh), 21 and since we have a great priest over the
house of God, 22 let us approach with a true heart in full assurance of faith, with our
hearts sprinkled clean from an evil conscience and our bodies washed with pure
water. 23 Let us hold fast to the confession of our hope without wavering, for he
who has promised is faithful. 24 And let us consider how to provoke one another to
love and good deeds, 25 not neglecting to meet together, as is the habit of some,
but encouraging one another, and all the more as you see the Day approaching.

Commentary 1: Connecting the Reading with Scripture

This Hebrews lection is a complicated assignment for Good Friday. Of the other appointed readings for this day, John 18–19 narrates the passion, Psalm 22 laments divine abandonment before finding divine blessing (while it is usually read christologically, its reach is much greater), and Isaiah 52–53 tells of the Suffering Servant (also usually read christologically).

Throughout Hebrews, numerous passages reflect on Jesus' death, including the preceding section, 9:1–10:18. Today's passage, which concludes this section, refers to Jesus' death and the relationship with God that it accomplishes (Heb. 10:16–22). Alongside this focus it exhorts the recipients to live a communal and faithful way of life (10:23–25). This combination of doctrine and praxis makes a crucial statement. Jesus' death is not just to be affirmed doctrinally or its benefits enjoyed individually or passively, but it is to shape a way of life marked by actions of love that benefit others.

This combination of theological exposition and ethical exhortation pervades Hebrews. The whole document can be described as a homily or sermon that elaborates theological understandings along with pastoral implications. It alternates and combines exposition and exhortation from the outset. The christological argument of chapter 1 declaring that Jesus is superior to the angels leads to an appeal to pay attention (2:1–4). The instruction about Jesus as a human and faithful Son of God (2:5–3:6) gives way to a warning to avoid unbelief (3:7–19). This alternating yet connecting pattern continues into chapters 9 and 10. The preacher's sermon can reflect the genre of Hebrews in combining theological exposition with practical exhortation.

To whom are these expositions and elaborations addressed? Hebrews has remained somewhat elusive in yielding details about the situations it addresses. There are, however, some clues that help to account for the document's exhortations. The readers are constructed as Jesus-believers and seem to have been so for some time. They have been, according to the author, well instructed previously about basic doctrines (6:1–3). They also seem familiar with the Scriptures, since various Hebrew Bible texts are basic to the document's arguments. The writing is pastoral, not evangelistic. The preacher can follow the lead of Hebrews and do in the sermon what the text itself does: create pastoral connections between text and hearers.

In the time they have been believers, they have experienced hostility at the hands of others: "you endured a hard struggle with sufferings, sometimes being publicly exposed to abuse and persecution, and sometimes being partners with those so treated. For you had compassion for those who were in prison, and you cheerfully accepted the plundering of your possessions" (10:32–34). Their sufferings have included public abuse (what sort? by whom?), some seem to have been imprisoned (why? by whom?), and they have had possessions plundered (how? why?). Subsequent references mention unspecified hostility (12:3) and trials (12:7–11), which are to be endured as God's discipline.

While idealistically affirming their cheerfulness, the author perhaps senses discouragement among the folks. He writes a "word of exhortation" (13:22) to them: "Therefore lift your drooping hands and strengthen your weak knees" (12:12). Today's passage (10:16–25) addresses this discouragement by assuring them of their relationship with God and of their responsibilities to sustain one another with practical love. The preacher might remind the congregation that as much as these Good Friday events exhibit God's love for us, that love is often experienced in the supportive and practical ways we care for one another.

Additional aspects of the book influence how we understand today's text. Chapters 9–10 present Jesus, first as the high priest and then as the sacrifice that takes away sin. This analogical argument moves between the earthly and the heavenly arenas. The earthly site includes the wilderness tent shrine (Exod. 25–26) and the annual Day of Atonement ritual in which the high priest offers blood to cleanse himself and then the people (Heb. 9:1–10). In the heavenly tent, Christ the high priest offers his own blood. This thought is developed as chapter 10 presents Christ as the one who "offered for all time a single sacrifice for sins" (10:12). Our passage builds on several connections with these chapters.

Verse 16 takes up the concern with covenant. The argument moves by analogy, but the two parts of the analogy are not created equal. Consistent with the rest of Hebrews, the old covenant is constructed as inferior to the new covenant. For example, the old covenant is mediated by angels to Moses, confirmed with animal blood, enacted by the Levitical priesthood, temporary, with an earthly tabernacle, and yearly atonement. The new covenant is mediated by Jesus the Son, confirmed by his blood or death, enacted by the priesthood of Melchizedek, eternal, with a heavenly tabernacle, and once-for-all-time atonement. Here, verses 16–18 emphasize forgiveness as a key feature of the new covenant. Three times in verses 17–18 God's forgiveness is declared. God remembers their sins no more. God remembers lawless deeds no more. There is forgiveness and hence no need for any further offering for sin.

This argument presents a big challenge for preaching from Hebrews. Preachers have to be very careful with its analogies of old and new. The trap of supersessionism is everywhere: it is easy to reinforce prejudices of Jewish inferiority and Christian supremacy, pretend forgiveness is a Christian creation, and disparage Jews and Jewish sacred practices. Such attitudes and actions are deeply rooted in Christian identities marked by superiority and hate; the cycle must be broken with care-full and clear proclamation.

Preachers might address the issue directly, alerting hearers to the issue of hateful readings and their tragic consequences. They might show how the writer of Hebrews rereads Jeremiah 31:31–34 through Jesus-glasses in verses 16–17. A passage that addressed the end of Babylonian exile and a new start in the land is now used to interpret Jesus' death. That is, preachers' attention to the contexts might counter the textual contrasts of old and new, Jewish/Hebrew Bible and Christian Bible. Preachers might show that forgiveness was a well-established experience in the tradition—Psalm 51 is a good example—and here is linked with Jesus' death.

Verses 19–22 rehearse emphases from previous chapters. These verses interpret the death of

Jesus as facilitating the experience of the presence of God and encounter with God. Verse 20 uses a metaphor of moving through a curtain into the house of God in which Jesus is the high priest. It exhorts doing so in the assurance of faith, cleansed from sin, and washed in baptism (10:22). This encounter with God accompanies further practices that identify this household (10:23–25). First is a bold confession. A second involves being inspired by other confessors to practices of love and good deeds (10:24). This verse is often translated as "provoking" others to perform these deeds, but the Greek urges that they be inspired by other believers to live faithfully. Third, they are to be vigilant in meeting together, to support and encourage one another. All of this is framed by the expectation that the day of Christ's return and establishment of God's purposes approaches. The preacher might highlight these practices of confession, love, good deeds, and gathering together as expressions of and invitations to a Good Friday-shaped church praxis.

The passage celebrates God's action through Christ's death in establishing not only a new covenant but also a community charged with embodying the love displayed in Christ's act. Attention to both emphases allows the preacher to expand a common Good Friday piety of "Jesus and me" into a praxis of Jesus, congregants, and the world.

WARREN CARTER

Commentary 2: Connecting the Reading with the World

This Good Friday text addresses Jesus' crucifixion through the lens of the ancient Israelite Day of Atonement liturgy (Lev. 16:1–34). The nature of the atonement has consequences for gospel proclamation and life. The saying "You will always live out what you believe to be true about God" is particularly relevant on Good Friday. The character of God is acutely at issue in Good Friday proclamation.

Though numerous atonement theories exist, for most Western Christians some form of substitutionary atonement theory dominates. A particular difficulty of the substitutionary approach is reconciling the loving, forgiving God that Jesus proclaimed with the image of a wrathful God who required that Jesus be nailed to a cross, lest there be hell to pay. The idea that God incarnate endured torture and death rather than let humanity's debt go unpunished is little better. Bloodthirsty gods have bloodthirsty disciples. The shadow of the angry, vengeful god of ancient human sacrifice falls at least partially over even the most orthodox atonement theories.

Anthropologist René Girard's seminal work on the scapegoat mechanism as applied to the atonement by theologians such as James Alison has opened a fresh approach to Hebrews 10 and Good Friday.[1] Girard (1923–2015) roots human violence in unconscious, mimetic (imitative) desires that spread through cultures like a silent, subliminal contagion. Ensuing efforts to obtain what others have, which put self above others at everyone's expense, result in violence and alienation. For example, if a mimetic desire for money infects a culture, the society may assume that the one who dies with the most toys wins. The preacher can help listeners connect to these dynamics of scapegoating and ask how we see that mimetic desire infecting us, our community, our nation, and our world now.

This mimetic desire is almost an unconscious force among us. As violence builds in intensity, societies sense danger, but do not see their own unconscious desires as the cause. When we are caught in this cycle, we cannot answer why we "spend [our] money for that which is not bread and [our] labor for that which does not satisfy"

1. Girard's work is complex. See "Girard's Theory and Atonement," http://girardianlectionary.net/res/atonement_webpage.htm, an annotated catalogue of sources related to Girard and the atonement. For Alison, see James Alison, "An Atonement Update," *Australian eJournal of Theology*, no. 8 (October 2006), http://aejt.com.au/__data/assets/pdf_file/0008/378656/aejt_8.1_alison_atonement.pdf.

(Isa. 55:2). Such cultures feed the false self's imitative desires and starve the true self, all the while wondering why our citizens war against each other in the midst of terrible spiritual famine. Preachers could help listeners see how this cultural diagnosis applies to their local and the national cultural context—for instance, as we are shaped by forces of consumerism, competition, and captivation with disposable goods.

All of this may be easily recognizable when we look at societal forces, but it gets worse. For here enters Girard's scapegoat mechanism. A society senses and fears the destructive disorder building up, but cannot see that it arises from its own disordered values. Who, then, is to blame for the disorder? Is it those within the society, or those on its boundaries who least share the culture's contagion who are to be blamed? Girard helps us see that societies institutionalize scapegoating.

Preachers could use this scapegoat framework to diagnose the social and ethical issues generated by the United States' prison-industrial complex. This for-profit system has created in the United States the largest prison population per capita in the world, scapegoating a significant segment of our population by imprisoning African Americans at five times the rate of whites. As hate speech and fear-mongering flourish, the accused are victimized, often with shocking savagery. These systemic outbursts of violence may serve temporarily as release valves for pent-up fear and anxiety in the culture. Some may experience a sense of joyous victory over evil from this bloodletting, a misguided catharsis that reinforces the enduring attraction of the scapegoat mechanism.

We see this scapegoating functioning in the smile of the little white girl posed in 1935 before the lynched body of African American Rubin Stacy, as well as in the grinning American soldiers giving the "thumbs up" as they pose with tortured prisoners at Abu Ghraib in Iraq. Deep cultural fears and disorders have been projected onto those lynched and tortured. Religious scapegoating involves the mostly unconscious transfer of evil to innocent victims ("innocent" meaning punished due to prejudice) by religious people who fail to confront directly the evil within themselves and their cultural systems.

The Day of Atonement in Leviticus 16 is ancient Israel's scapegoat liturgy, and it lies behind Hebrews 10:16–25. The sins of the people are named by the priest, his hands placed on the head of a goat. The goat is then released into the wilderness, taking their sins with it. No human blood was shed—God forbade it. God did not require even the goat's blood for satisfaction. This enlightened transference of guilt created a cathartic calm, and the newly cleansed people may have recommitted themselves with joy to faithful observance of the Torah. The scapegoating mechanism remained—until Good Friday.

According to Hebrews, Good Friday's scapegoat, Jesus, has unveiled a "new and living way" (10:20) that renders scapegoating obsolete once and for all. A scapegoat revealed as scapegoat disarms the transfer ritual. As simultaneously the divine high priest and the innocent victim, exonerated by resurrection (Heb. 10:19, 21), Jesus reframes the ancient belief that the blood sacrifice appeases God. In fact, Jesus turns that idea on its head. The victims are not guilty; the accusers are. Bloodthirstiness is not in God; it is in us. Wrong and dangerous are Christian interpretations that claim the bloody execution of an innocent man made God forget sin. They are a sign that we, not God, have forgotten our sin. The blame game leaves no one justified. This error has led to tragic evil as some Christians scapegoated Jews for the Roman execution of Jesus.

The good news is this: God seeks no retribution whatsoever against the guilty. The divine priest's offering is a divine victim who absorbs violence and returns only forgiveness. God calls sinners to forgive and release the victimized in our midst, as God has forgiven and released us. The myth of divine violence ended once and forever when Jesus bodily endured accusers' abuse ("through his flesh," v. 20), but refused to respond in kind. Forgiveness, not vengeance, is God's offering. Rejoice, scapegoaters, for Jesus said, "Father, forgive them, for they know not what they do" (Luke 23:34 KJV).

Preachers can help listeners realize that atonement is more than just theory on Good Friday. First, we see that the sin problem is in us, no matter how hard we try to transfer it elsewhere. Second, as Jesus pulled back the curtain, we find we stand amazed in the presence of God, simultaneously sinners and forgiven (Heb. 10:19–20). God in Christ on Good Friday reverses scapegoat atonement from external ritual to internal reality (v. 16). Through the curtain of our sin—the lacerated flesh of Christ (v. 20)—we see undying forgiveness, which was always there.

This atonement makes believers bold (v. 19) to desire to imitate Christ, including his redemptive suffering. This new mimetic desire encourages believers to provoke one another to love and good deeds (v. 24) and not fail to meet together (v. 25), so that this contagion may spread among us deeper, faster, further. Atonement is seeing who we and God have been all along, and acting on that new understanding.

WM. LOYD ALLEN

Easter Day/Resurrection of the Lord

Jeremiah 31:1–6	John 20:1–18
Psalm 118:1–2, 14–24	Acts 10:34–43
Colossians 3:1–4	Matthew 28:1–10

Jeremiah 31:1–6

1At that time, says the LORD, I will be the God of all the families of Israel, and they shall be my people.

2Thus says the LORD:

The people who survived the sword
  found grace in the wilderness;
when Israel sought for rest,
  3the LORD appeared to him from far away.
I have loved you with an everlasting love;
  therefore I have continued my faithfulness to you.
4Again I will build you, and you shall be built,
  O virgin Israel!
Again you shall take your tambourines,
  and go forth in the dance of the merrymakers.
5Again you shall plant vineyards
  on the mountains of Samaria;
the planters shall plant,
  and shall enjoy the fruit.
6For there shall be a day when sentinels will call
  in the hill country of Ephraim:
"Come, let us go up to Zion,
  to the LORD our God."

Commentary 1: Connecting the Reading with Scripture

Not many preachers will lean into Jeremiah 31 on Easter, but perhaps Easter is the quintessential day to be attentive to the very Scriptures that Jesus, his mother, and his disciples treasured. The grave danger on Easter is that we might forget the larger drama of the Bible and reduce things to the individual's promise of eternal life. N. T. Wright has reminded us that God's historic labor to bring redemption to all of creation through Israel finds its culmination in Good Friday and Easter Sunday.[1] Jesus' mission was to bring scattered Israel home from exile.

Jeremiah 31:1–6 is nestled among a cluster of texts that pulsate with hope. Scholars believe chapters 30–33 were a distinct scroll at some point and they refer to the ways it comforts, consoles, and restores. Readers, be careful here; these words that speak so buoyantly of restoration are set in the larger context of Jeremiah's entire preaching career during Israel's most pathetic, catastrophic years. It is not mere comfort, which might imply nothing is lost or sacrificed, but restoration. We cannot fathom Jeremiah 31 without recalling that his calling was to "pluck up and destroy" before he was

1. See N. T. Wright, *Surprised by Hope: Rethinking Heaven, the Resurrection, and the Mission of the Church* (New York: HarperOne, 2008).

"to build and to plant" (Jer. 1:10); his scathing warnings and sentences of judgment are not erased by a few chapters of hope. Even on Easter Sunday, we cannot just lop off the Bible's appeals to repent and the inevitability of judgment. Easter, after all, did happen in a cemetery.

A prophet knows what time it is. When the people were cocky, complacent, self-indulgent, and secure, Jeremiah knew it was time for repentance and frank warnings that doom was looming. We cannot be sure when chapter 31 came to be. Some believe he was speaking to the fallen northern kingdom during the reign of Josiah; more scholars place these words after the annihilation of Jerusalem, capital of the southern kingdom, and deportation of the people. This ambiguity may be hopeful for us: his words can fit any and all situations of hopelessness. Jeremiah knew when it was time to bolster people's hopes. Preaching today requires a keen sense of timing: when to pluck up, when to build up.

A broad-minded canonical reading of Jeremiah 31 ties hope not only to judgment but also to love: "I have loved you with an everlasting love" (v. 3). Sarah Howell-Miller explored this connection: "If we continue to think about love in the context of the resurrection, there is an important question that needs to be asked. In order for resurrection to happen, first death must occur. So, the question is—what needs to die in order for love to rise? . . . We cannot be rebuilt in love until the rotten boards are torn out and thrown away."[2]

The linkage of love and Easter also teaches us what resurrection is—and is not. Eternal life is not a reward for a life well lived or faith properly declared. Rather, God forges a relationship of love with us that is so strong even death cannot cancel it out. Notice the way "again" recurs three times in verse 4. God's is a determined love. Walter Brueggemann spoke of "the relentlessness of Yahweh in the history of the Jews, relentlessness for newness which the world can neither evoke nor preclude."[3] It is both: biblical hope knows God's purpose cannot be forced or prevented. The preacher can help us see that it may be in politics or in church strategizing: we try to force God's hand, but God will do God's thing in good time.

The Hebrew of verse 3 is happily ambiguous. "The LORD appeared from far away." Interestingly, the Hebrew, *mērāḥôq*, may also mean "from long ago." The sense is both. The Lord's appearing was far away—from exile, geographically and psychically, but also long ago, in the days of Abraham, or at creation itself. If we consider this hopeful love in light of God's ancient promises, we begin to grasp that Israel is loved, not despite their disobedience, but because they have been, are, and will be God's covenant people, made in God's image, the recipients of outlandish promises. God loves despite our mess, but also precisely because of our inviolable identity. The world presses various identities upon us; but the preacher can help us know again that God's image was first, will be last, and trumps all others even now.

Our passage is replete with feminine images. Instead of typical military and political imagery, Jeremiah envisions a virgin people (miraculous indeed, as he had mocked their lustful infidelity in previous sermons!), "families" instead of "tribes," and female drummers and dancers instead of warriors and grandees. To press the feminine image, the exile must have felt like a time of barrenness, but God was already beginning a new, hidden work; Israel, clueless, was already bearing new, hidden life. The long years of exile were not a waste, or sheer evil, but a kind of pregnancy, a preparation for the new life, unseen but sure.

Three other items bear mention. Salvation here is not heaven or some idyllic state. Jeremiah envisions Israel living in the land, not lounging about, but working hard—and enjoying the fruits of their labors. For too long, Assyrian or Babylonian overlords, or even the kinds of corrupt Israelite kings God had warned of through Samuel (1 Sam. 8) had seized the people's produce and taxed them sorely. In God's new creation, people labor diligently, but then have enough; this is what the Bible means when it speaks of being blessed, having plenty or rich fare.

2. Sarah Howell-Miller, https://sarahshowell.wordpress.com/2017/08/18/do-you-love-me-more-than-these/.
3. Walter Brueggemann, *A Commentary on Jeremiah* (Grand Rapids: Eerdmans, 1998), 269.

The tambourines and dancing clearly evoke memories of Israel's epic deliverance from Egypt. Miriam, Moses' sister, led the twirling, percussion, singing, and dancing that day (Exod. 15:20). In Jeremiah's day, the people faced their own wilderness journey, through that wretched stretch of land between Babylon and Jerusalem. Israel's geography of salvation is paradoxical: in the place of judgment and loss comes the renewal; in the place of death, in the barren wilderness that seems God-forsaken, God never forsakes but shows up in mercy and strength. Grace is found in the wilderness.

Finally, Jeremiah 31 offers the picturesque image of a sentinel standing on top of a high tower, crying to Ephraim, "Come, let us go up to Zion." We hear echoes of those lovely psalms used during the long pilgrimage treks to the great festivals at the temple (Pss. 84, 122). More interestingly, the way Jeremiah speaks of Samaria and Ephraim (whether we date chapter 31 to the days of Josiah, or during the exile) reveals his robust hope in a more radical, downright miraculous restoration—and reconciliation. Ephraim, up in Samaria, had been crushed by the Assyrians generations earlier; and before that, for two centuries, the Judeans listening to Jeremiah had been at odds with the northern tribes of Ephraim.

The God of Jeremiah 31 will not settle for the redemption of Judah alone. This God will also regather the lost tribes; none will be lost. It will not simply be that they too get rescued; there will be a healing of the lingering strife. God's labor of restoration will involve reconciliation among those who have been divided. Christians dive forward to Paul's declaration that "in Christ God was reconciling the world to himself," and therefore God has entrusted "the ministry of reconciliation" to us (2 Cor. 5:18–19).

JAMES C. HOWELL

Commentary 2: Connecting the Reading with the World

Jeremiah 31:1–6 contains at least four prominent topics that any celebration of Easter exhibits. The first of these is surprise. From the darkness of the tomb of death and pain arises the surprise of new and unexpected life. As that is exemplified in the risen Christ, so does it appear in the promised return from exile by the people of Judah. Surprise and accompanying joy are welcome additions to human experience. Are we not surprised when we hear a child utter truths that we never imagined they could know? My granddaughter, aged three, recently grabbed a pen with which to draw and asked, "Doc [that's me], is this pen kid-proof?" Who knew that she knew to be worried about such things? A lovely surprise!

Jeremiah was called by God to a ministry of confrontation with evil and a promise of God's rebuilding of the ruined cities and the replanting of the sacred land (Jer. 1:10). Much of Jeremiah 1–29 contains oracles and narratives of God's anger with the people's continual acts of sin, but in the Book of Consolation (Jer. 30–31), the prophet enumerates God's unbroken covenant promises to the people, rooted deeply in God's vast love for them. The exile of the people, beginning in 597 BCE, was the result, says Jeremiah, of the chosen people's refusal to follow the ways of their God. When Judah and Jerusalem were swallowed up by the most powerful empire in the ancient Near East at that time, many thought the end of God's people had come—but God's great surprise was still to occur.

The oracle begins with the proclamation of that surprise. "At that time, says YHWH, I will be God for all the families of Israel, and they shall be my people" (31:1, my trans.). Like a thunderclap YHWH announces that exile is not the last word of Israel's history. Though the Assyrians destroyed the northern kingdom late in the eighth century BCE, YHWH now trumpets the news that the entire nation will once again unite, and God will be the God of all the families of the land. There can be no Israel, says YHWH, without all of Israel.

This call for unity among God's people, our second theme, strikes a crucial theological chord at a time when churches and society in general seem starved for unity. An Ethiopian proverb says, "When spiders unite, they can tie down a lion." So many congregations and denominations fracture over the issue of same-sex relationships; their search for unity seems too often divorced from the search for justice. The doing of justice (Mic. 6:8), the search for equality and inclusiveness, is one of the hallmarks of Micah's summary of what the Lord requires; a humble walk with God is based on that search for unity. Alexander Hamilton is often credited with having said, "I think the first duty of society is justice." Only in God's justice can we hope for lasting unity.

The third topic of this passage is God's unexpected forgiveness that will occur among the newly united ones. The Babylonian exiles had not dared hope that their God would forgive them for their sins, but "again, I will build you, and you shall be built," says God (Jer. 31:4a). Unlike the anti-God builders of the tower of Babel in Genesis 11, God will be the builder of a new Israel. Despite the destruction of the temple and palace at the hands of the Babylonians, God will rebuild the ruined city: "Again you shall adorn yourself, and with tambourines shall go forth in the dance of the merrymakers!" (v. 4b, my trans.). The days of sackcloth and ashes will end, and all Israel will dance again and play music: "Again you shall plant vineyards on the mountains of Samaria; the planters shall plant, and shall enjoy the fruit" (v. 5)! In direct rejection of Deuteronomy 28:30, where the disobedience of Israel leads to a lack of enjoyment of the planter's fruit, now enjoyment will reign as all the newly forgiven rejoice at the harvest on the mountains of Samaria, where vineyards have not existed for over two centuries.

Note too that God refers to Israel as "virgin" at verse 4. This image is in sharp contrast to the earlier image of the wanton woman who clothes herself to attract her lovers and as a result becomes pregnant, crying out "as one bringing forth a child" (4:30–31). God has expunged all that previously notorious activity and has made Israel virginal again, ready to receive God's good grace once more.

It is always difficult to receive forgiveness for a past error. When Jesus forgave the woman accused of adultery, bidding her, "Go, and sin no more" (John 8:11 KJV), he offered a living example of what it means to forgive fully. When we are forgiven and told that what we have done is no longer counted against us, the joy and freedom we feel are nothing less than astounding. When I spent far too much time traveling early in our marriage, my wife was left with sole care of our small children. Yet she was ultimately forgiving, enabling me to adjust my schedule and to focus more attention on our relationship. As of this writing we are coming up on our fiftieth wedding anniversary.

The fourth topic is without doubt the most important one, on which the others rest. The surprising promise of God is based squarely on God's amazing love for the people, no matter what they have done, no matter how hopeless they sense their futures to be. The announcement of this love is established by a brief history of God's relationship with Israel in 31:2: "Thus says YHWH, 'The people who survived the sword found grace in the wilderness . . . when YHWH appeared to them long ago'" (my trans.). This is a reference to the escape from slavery in Egypt, the wandering in the wilderness, and God's presence with them through the entire episode. Why? "I have loved you with an everlasting love; that is why I have continued my *hesed* to you" (v. 3, my trans.).

That wonderful Hebrew word is nearly untranslatable. NRSV reads "faithfulness," which is surely not wrong, but the word contains a world of power in it. Its basic meaning, when used as an attribute of God, is "unbreakable connection." It announces that there is finally nothing we can do that can separate us from this love of God. Paul's magnificent paean to the love of God in Romans 8:31–39 is precisely what this term means in the Hebrew Bible—which for Paul is modeled in the figure of the Christ.

God's *hesed* is the foundation of our relationship with God. When Moses asks after the glory of God on Mount Sinai, the answer involves *hesed*: "YHWH, YHWH, a God merciful and gracious, slow to anger, filled with *hesed* and faithfulness, keeping *hesed* to thousands of generations" (Exod. 34:6–7, my trans.). It is on this love of God that Israel depends for the surprising end to their exile, and for God's promise of forgiveness. It is precisely here, in the love of God, that Israel and we may find the rest we seek, just as Israel sought for rest in the land of promise so long ago. This portion of Jeremiah's Book of Consolation is well named, for in its words Israel and we moderns find a surprising and joyful consolation for our struggles, and forgiveness for our past errors. On Easter Sunday, the surprising joy of the love of our God is made manifest in the risen One. We welcome Christ with unbounded gladness and join the dance of the merrymakers once again!

JOHN C. HOLBERT

Psalm 118:1–2, 14–24

1O give thanks to the LORD, for he is good;
his steadfast love endures forever!
2Let Israel say,
"His steadfast love endures forever."
. . . .
14The LORD is my strength and my might;
he has become my salvation.

15There are glad songs of victory in the tents of the righteous:
"The right hand of the LORD does valiantly;
16the right hand of the LORD is exalted;
the right hand of the LORD does valiantly."
17I shall not die, but I shall live,
and recount the deeds of the LORD.
18The LORD has punished me severely,
but he did not give me over to death.

19Open to me the gates of righteousness,
that I may enter through them
and give thanks to the LORD.

20This is the gate of the LORD;
the righteous shall enter through it.

21I thank you that you have answered me
and have become my salvation.
22The stone that the builders rejected
has become the chief cornerstone.
23This is the LORD's doing;
it is marvelous in our eyes.
24This is the day that the LORD has made;
let us rejoice and be glad in it.

Connecting the Psalm with Scripture and Worship

"This is the day that the LORD has made; let us rejoice and be glad in it" (Ps. 118:24). The last words of this selection from Psalm 118 are often used as the first words in the Service for the Lord's Day. Indeed, they make a fitting "prelude and postlude" for this First Sunday of the season of Easter.

Psalm 118 is something of a medley in terms of its literary form: an individual song of thanksgiving (vv. 5–18), followed by a processional liturgy (vv. 19–28), all bookended with a classic hymn of praise (vv. 1–4, 29). It begins and ends with one of the great refrains of the Psalter: "O give thanks to the LORD, [who] is good; [whose]

steadfast love endures forever!" (vv. 1, 29).[1] The first section of the psalm (vv. 5–18) describes how the psalmist was delivered from the doorstep of death by the hand of the Lord. The second section of the psalm (vv. 19–28) finds the psalmist knocking at the gates of the temple to make an offering of thanks and praise.

Psalm 118 does double duty among the RCL texts for the Resurrection of the Lord, serving as the response to one of two potential first readings: Acts 10:34–43 and Jeremiah 31:1–6. In relation to the Acts reading, these verses from Psalm 118 become the altar call that follows Peter's sermon on the expansive implications of Christ's death and resurrection: "I truly understand that God shows no partiality" (Acts 10:34). Now the psalmist boldly sings, "Open to me the gates of righteousness" (Ps. 118:19). As a reflection on the alternate reading from Jeremiah, Psalm 118 is the homecoming hymn of a people returning from exile: "There are glad songs of victory in the tents of the righteous" (v. 15).

With its multiple references to the right hand of the Lord (vv. 15–16), Psalm 118 seems to anticipate the epistle for this day: "So if you have been raised with Christ, seek the things that are above, where Christ is, seated at the right hand of God" (Col. 3:1). At a deeper level, its astonished affirmation—"I shall not die, but I shall live" (Ps. 118:17)—proclaims the great mystery of faith in Christ's death, resurrection, and promised return (cf. v. 26).

As for the Gospel reading, whether John 20:1–18 or Matthew 28:1–10, Psalm 118 resonates with the witness of the evangelists (all four, in fact) that Jesus rose from the dead on the first day of the week. This is no minor plot point; it is essential to understanding the whole arc of salvation, from the first day of creation (Gen. 1:5) to the revelation of God's coming realm (Rev. 1:10). The day of Christ's rising stands at the center of the story. Accordingly, we should think of this feast of Resurrection as the center of the Christian year and the "Sunday of Sundays"—an archetype of the church's weekly worship. Once every seven days we gather to proclaim the good news of Christ's resurrection on the first day of the week; and for seven weeks (roughly a seventh of the year), we are called to "rejoice and be glad" in the season of Easter. This "day that the LORD has made" (Ps. 118:24) reveals God's purpose and promise for the whole creation.

Psalm 118 offers several valuable insights for preaching on the Resurrection of the Lord. First, the gift of new life is no garden-variety miracle, no springtime bud or chrysalis; Psalm 118 depicts resurrection as a hard-fought battle with the powers of evil and death (v. 5–18). Second, the work of resurrection is not something we can accomplish through our own best efforts and intentions; it is always the Lord's doing, and it is "marvelous in our eyes" (v. 23). Third, while Jesus' resurrection is a singular event in human history, it is nevertheless consistent with the gracious action of the God of all generations, the one whose "steadfast love endures forever" (v. 1). Fourth, resurrection involves a dramatic and scandalous reversal of fortune—a new creation established on the cornerstone the builders rejected (v. 22). Finally, our primary response to the gift of life redeemed and restored is that of gratitude: "O give thanks to the LORD" (v. 1); everything else in Psalm 118—and in Christian life—begins with this.

Psalm 118 is the last of the group of Hallel Psalms (Pss. 113–118), associated with the Passover, or Pesach, in Jewish tradition. Appropriately, the RCL makes prominent use of these Hallel Psalms throughout Holy Week: on Palm/Passion Sunday (Ps. 118), Maundy Thursday (Ps. 116), the Easter Vigil (Ps. 114), the Resurrection of the Lord (Ps. 118), and Easter Evening (Ps. 114). It is also worth noting that although these verses fall just outside the bounds of our present lection, Psalm 118 is the source for the well-known words of Palm/Passion Sunday and the Great Thanksgiving: "Hosanna! [Save us!] Blessed is the one who comes in the name of the LORD" (Ps. 118:25a, 26). Thus, a single psalm stands at the thresholds of Holy Week.

Given the psalms' heightened significance in this season, as well as their prominent place in helping centuries of Christians to interpret the death and resurrection of Jesus, worship

1. James Luther Mays, *Psalms*, Interpretation (Louisville, KY: John Knox, 1994), 373–81.

planners would be well advised to make careful and creative use of the psalms in Holy Week. This is not a time to skip the psalm! If anything, consider using the psalms in multiple ways—spoken and sung, in a variety of styles and settings, as a resource for proclamation, prayer, and praise.

From hosanna to hallelujah, Psalm 118 encompasses the mystery of our faith. On the first Sunday of Easter, this psalm helps us to proclaim that the risen Lord is the Alpha and the Omega, and that death will never have the last word.

DAVID GAMBRELL

Colossians 3:1–4

[1]So if you have been raised with Christ, seek the things that are above, where Christ is, seated at the right hand of God. [2]Set your minds on things that are above, not on things that are on earth, [3]for you have died, and your life is hidden with Christ in God. [4]When Christ who is your life is revealed, then you also will be revealed with him in glory.

Commentary 1: Connecting the Reading with Scripture

The reading reminds us of our interconnection with Christ, and how his death, resurrection, ascension, life in the Spirit, and future hope are linked. In conjoining these, we align ourselves with Eastern Christians, who, in the Divine Liturgy, picture even the second coming as something already accomplished: "Remembering . . . all that *has been done* for our sake: the Cross, the tomb, the Resurrection on the third day, the Ascension into heaven, the enthronement at the right hand, *and the second and glorious coming again.*"[1] In worship, we are connected with heavenly things and with the new creation.

Setting the passage in context helps us to avoid mistaking the apostle's meaning when he tells us to set our minds "not on things that are on earth" (Col. 3:2). The previous chapter had spoken about Torah's regulations, specifically concerning things that could not be handled or touched. Though these rules held sway for a time, their purpose was to point forward to the great triumph of Jesus, who would fulfill the Torah. Evidently, some Colossian Christians were tempted by a cult-like group that emphasized the ascetical life and strictly maintained the holy days prescribed by the Torah. The apostle (whether Paul or an associate) assures them that, now that Christ has reconciled things on earth and in heaven, God's mystery has been revealed. This mystery is *Christ himself* (2:2). The letter instructs them, and us, not to fixate upon "earthly things" of limited time or value. Rather, we should understand that earthly activities and physical things may indeed bear fruit so long as we relate them to Christ and do not see them as ends in themselves.

The letter is not world-denying, but world-transforming. Preachers can urge their congregations not to reject social and cultural realities summarily, since Jesus' incarnate participation among us has imbued such things with meaning. Music, housecleaning, art, intellectual pursuits, carpentry, gardening, or any other human endeavor may bring glory to our human-loving Lord.

The letter to Colossae is difficult because of controversy concerning its authorship and because we do not have enough information to understand fully whom the apostle was opposing. Recent scholars have been less reticent than the past generation to consider Paul as the author.[2] Following their cue, Reformed preachers need not reject the book's themes of mystery and ecclesial concerns, or think that these matters obscure the doctrine of justification, which an earlier generation thought summed up Paul's gospel. Instead, they may show how our life together in Christ may be embraced as an integral part of his mysterious gospel concerning Christ. Colossians includes dramatic hymns of praise (1:15–20) and practical advice for Christians in various situations (3:12–4:5),

1. *Liturgy of St. John Chrysostom*, https://www.goarch.org/-/the-divine-liturgy-of-saint-john-chrysostom, emphasis added.

2. N. T. Wright, *Colossians and Philemon*, Tyndale New Testament Commentaries (Grand Rapids: Eerdmans, 1986), 31–34; Peter T. O'Brien, *Colossians–Philemon*, Word Biblical Commentary 44 (Grand Rapids: Zondervan, 2000), xli–xlviii; John M. G. Barclay, *Colossians and Ephesians* (New York: T. & T. Clark, 2004), 18–36.

God Is in the Beginning and Will Be in the End

The God of the creation and of the real beginning is, at the same time, the God of the resurrection. From the beginning the world is placed in the sign of the resurrection of Christ from the dead. Indeed it is because we know of the resurrection that we know of God's creation in the beginning, of God's creation out of nothing. The dead Jesus Christ of Good Friday—and the resurrection κύριος (Lord) of Easter Sunday; that is creation out of nothing, creation from the beginning. The fact that Christ was dead did not mean the possibility of the resurrection, but its impossibility; it was the void itself, it was the *nihil negativum*. There is absolutely no transition or continuity between the dead and the resurrected Christ except the freedom of God which, in the beginning, created his work out of nothing. If it were possible to intensify the *nihil negativum* we would have to say here of the resurrection that with the death of Christ on the Cross the *nihil negativum* was taken into God himself. "O great affliction, God himself is dead"—but he who is the beginning lived, destroyed the void and created the new creation in his resurrection. By his resurrection we know of the creation—for if he were not resurrected the Creator would be lifeless and would not bear witness to himself. But by his creation we know once more of the power of his resurrection, because he remains the Lord.

In the beginning, out of freedom, out of nothing, God created the heavens and the earth. That is the comfort with which the Bible addresses us who are in the middle, who are anxious before the false void, the beginning without a beginning and the end without an end. It is the gospel, it is the resurrected Christ of whom one is speaking here. God is in the beginning and he will be in the end. He is free regarding the world. The fact that he lets us know this is mercy, grace, forgiveness and comfort.

Dietrich Bonhoeffer, *Creation and Fall: A Theological Exposition of Genesis 1–3*, trans. John C. Fletcher (London: SCM, 1959), 16.

reminding us that to "put on" the "new human being" (3:10) is both to live like the angels who see God's face and to serve on earth, for Christ was "pleased to dwell" among us. In preaching, we can encourage a well-balanced life that has its feet on the ground that Christ hallowed and eyes upon the glory of the heavens, which he fills.

The themes of the passage include our remembrance that we have died with Christ, our present resurrected status, our steady gaze upon the exalted Christ, and our anticipation of mysterious glory to come. We are encouraged to see ourselves as joined with the Lord in every way and in every movement of salvation history.

With the Lord we have died, and so we must continue to "put to death" those things that are merely earthly and have no continuing value: these will not survive God's judgment (3:5–11). Christ died in our place, indeed; but the preacher can help us understand that we *also* are called to die with him, and to continue dying daily to whatever separates us from him. Belief in Jesus' substitutionary death should not shield us from the command to "take up our cross": this will mean holding less tightly to comforts and even abstaining from what is "ours" to help those poor whom the Lord also loves.

With the Lord we *have been* raised. This emphasis is unusual in Paul, who speaks elsewhere about resurrection as a future hope (e.g., 1 Cor. 15). However, if we understand the enormity of chapter 1's message (we are in solidarity with Christ, the "firstborn"), we can truly speak of the resurrection as already accomplished. Similarly, the ascension, in which Christ took the human body with him as an offering to God, is also *our* triumph. We do not yet see what we shall be, but our hidden life looks for God's power that "is able to do far more abundantly than all that we ask or think" (Eph. 3:20 RSV). Christians are in a position to glimpse eternity even in humble circumstances, without yielding to an unreal triumphalism; a kind of "sober joy" becomes our birthright.

This same joy emerges in one of the Gospel readings for Easter morning, Matthew 28:1–10. There the dramatic pyrotechnics of the resurrection come upon the women who seek Jesus' body. The word of the angel, "Do not be afraid," coupled with instructions to tell the disciples that they will see Jesus, leads the women away from the place of the dead with both fear and joy. Even while they are on their way, Jesus himself affirms the angel's word and receives their worship. The women (whose witness would not be accepted by the conventions of their day) are used by Jesus to display the wonder of the resurrection, for they have set their mind on things above and have believed. The message that they pass on includes within it the great theme of Colossians, that we are now in solidarity with the *risen* Christ rather than with our *dying* first parents. Looking up, where he has taken our human natures, we are assured of what he has in store for us: to inherit the very glory of God.

We frequently speak about salvation as though it were simply a matter of being forgiven and avoiding the wrath of God. However, this connection made between our death and our glory reminds us that God the Son did not take on human flesh only to die, but to assume everything that we are, so that we could become what he is. The mystery we breathe as we read Colossians 3 reminds us of God's grand plan: to make us like Christ! As part of his body, we will inherit his splendor.

Yet, this solidarity is not automatic. We are called to act, to set our minds on Christ. All of Paul's letters, including Colossians, move from teaching the gospel to encouraging us to act in its light: this is who you are, so live like it! We set our minds on Christ; yet we should not be so "heavenly minded" that we are of "no earthly use."

These few verses are replete with preaching themes: what can distract us from Christ, solidarity with Christ, what it means to die and rise with him, why the ascension is an important finale to the Christian story, how mystery is interconnected with nitty-gritty matters, and how our perspective affects our fruitfulness. Whichever theme is accentuated, the preacher must always put Jesus Christ in the foreground, as this letter does.

EDITH M. HUMPHREY

Commentary 2: Connecting the Reading with the World

We have picked up this letter to the church at Colossae approximately halfway through its message. We have skipped over the greeting and the possible hymn text (Col. 1:15–20); we have moved past the admonitions about how to practice the faith. We find ourselves at the opening of chapter 3, receiving additional advice and listening to theological musings about things above and things below, death and life, things hidden and things revealed. Though brief, these four verses contain a multitude of theological puzzles one might ponder in an Easter sermon.

Hymn writer Sylvia Dunstan, author of the Ascension hymn "You, Lord, Are Both Lamb and Shepherd," originally titled the tune "Christus Paradox." Here are the lines of the concluding stanza:

> Worthy is our earthly Jesus! Worthy is our
> cosmic Christ!
> Worthy your defeat and victory; worthy still
> your peace and strife.
> You, the everlasting instant; you, who are our
> death and life.[3]

Dunstan echoes the theological contrasts expressed by the letter writer. Interweaving the stanzas of this hymn through a sermon could offer an interesting pairing. Have the congregation or choir sing a stanza, and then explore the lyrics in the light of the Scripture. While the third stanza specifically references the Colossians passage, "you sit in power at God's side" (3:1), each line of this hymn's intricate text offers insights through which we might see Jesus anew. Who is this Christ with whom we are hidden in God? Who is this Christ who is our life? He is much more than a man who was murdered on a cross. He is Lamb *and* Shepherd, prince *and* slave. He is the earthly Jesus

3. Sylvia G. Dunstan, "You, Lord, Are Both Lamb and Shepherd," in *Glory to God* (Louisville, KY: Westminster John Knox, 2013), 274.

and the cosmic Christ. If Jesus is our very life, then should not our desire be to get to know his multifaceted nature? Sometimes we need to be shaken from our preferred ways of seeing Jesus, so that we do not create him in our image.

Other Easter hymns would also pair well with this text. Open your hymnal and consider how you might place song and Scripture in conversation with one another. "Now the Green Blade Rises" offers imagery of the hiddenness of seeds and the breaking forth of new life. "Day of Arising" speaks of Jesus as our companion. Awaken sleepy worshipers by stepping outside the box and choosing a secular song that addresses the concepts of resurrection described in the text.

Just as music is essential to our worship, so are our sacraments. The actions described in these verses (dying, rising, hiding, revealing) are the movements of the baptismal liturgy. This sacrament has been linked with Easter celebrations since the days of the early Christian community. If your congregation is celebrating a baptism during the Easter season, take advantage of the opportunity to delve into your denomination's theology of the sacrament. What are the promises made at baptism, and how are they lived out in the congregation? What are the core concepts you want the congregation to understand about this sacred symbolic action?

Alternately, you might want to share the story of how the early Christians would prepare the catechumens to be welcomed into the body in the early hours of Easter morning. After an intensive period of study and preparation, those seeking to be baptized would fast during what we know as Good Friday and Holy Saturday. A candidate would undress, be anointed with oils of thanksgiving and exorcism (men by men and women by women), and then enter the baptismal waters. While in the water, the candidate would respond to the baptismal questions using the words we profess as the Apostles' Creed.

Unclothed adults professing their faith is a far cry from our contemporary practice of infants in heirloom baptismal gowns or even youth and adults in baptismal robes! Walk the congregants through the symbolism of the ancient sacrament, with its tangible expression of rebirth.[4] Do we get that same sense of dying and rising with Christ in our own worship experience? If not, how might we reclaim it?

Reflect on the anointing with the "oil of exorcism" as a possible sermon theme. In renouncing the power of evil in our lives and in our world, we are claiming God's dominion. The Colossians passage speaks of focusing on the things that are above, rather than the things that are on earth. This is not to say that the earth is evil; we know the earth is filled with God's good gifts. (Indeed, an evil to renounce is abuse of the earth itself.) Still, we know that God's intangible gifts of mercy, compassion, love, creativity, faith, companionship, hope, and so on are to be valued over anything that we can grasp in our hands.

Do you preach to a multigenerational gathering? Play with the concepts of hiding and seeking. A curious toddler will giggle with delight playing peekaboo. A preschooler will hide in the same place over and over, and still be surprised when you find them. Youth move on to the game of "Sardines," which is "Hide and Seek" in reverse. Instead of "it" seeking those who are hiding, "it" hides and the seekers quietly join "it" in the hiding place until everyone is reunited. How might this simple game provide an accessible introduction to the idea of being hidden in God with Jesus? There is something about the scattered players coming together at the end of the game that evokes an image of God's expansive realm.

Even when playing a game, hiding alone can be unsettling. There is the fear of never being found. With Christ as our hiding companion, we do not have to fear being alone. He is our companion on this life journey, and God is our hiding place. Expand upon this idea of God as our hiding place, a source of shelter. If we are hidden in God, then we may also say that God is never hidden from us. God is ever accessible to us.

The paradox here is this: though we are hidden in God, we do not hide from the world. Like the game of "Sardines," we want our

4. On the early church's sacramental practice, one excellent resource is James F. White, *Introduction to Christian Worship*, 3rd ed. (Nashville: Abingdon, 2001).

friends to discover this perfect hiding place. We are concealed in God's love and presence, even as we are immersed in and exposed to the world. After the resurrection, the disciples continued to conceal themselves, unable to understand the promise. The Holy Spirit would soon propel them outward, so that they might reenter the world and welcome others into the shelter of God's love.

As with the disciples, hiding is not always a game. Christians in nations throughout the world hide for fear of persecution. Still others are forced into a life of invisibility. Those lost to human trafficking may disappear forever. Might you invite someone to share their story of being freed? As Christ labored to seek out the lost (and stolen), so must we. Educating our churches about these injustices expands understanding and empowers people to advocate for change.

These verses offer multiple paths. What does your congregation need to hear this Easter? Following Jesus is neither easy nor uncomplicated; Easter is neither easy nor uncomplicated. Yet Easter is our hope: we sing, we baptize, we anoint, we seek. Christ is risen! He is risen indeed!

CATHY CALDWELL HOOP

John 20:1–18

1 Early on the first day of the week, while it was still dark, Mary Magdalene came
to the tomb and saw that the stone had been removed from the tomb. 2 So she
ran and went to Simon Peter and the other disciple, the one whom Jesus loved,
and said to them, "They have taken the Lord out of the tomb, and we do not know
where they have laid him." 3 Then Peter and the other disciple set out and went
toward the tomb. 4 The two were running together, but the other disciple outran
Peter and reached the tomb first. 5 He bent down to look in and saw the linen
wrappings lying there, but he did not go in. 6 Then Simon Peter came, following
him, and went into the tomb. He saw the linen wrappings lying there, 7 and the
cloth that had been on Jesus' head, not lying with the linen wrappings but rolled
up in a place by itself. 8 Then the other disciple, who reached the tomb first, also
went in, and he saw and believed; 9 for as yet they did not understand the scripture, that he must rise from the dead. 10 Then the disciples returned to their homes.

11 But Mary stood weeping outside the tomb. As she wept, she bent over to
look into the tomb; 12 and she saw two angels in white, sitting where the body of
Jesus had been lying, one at the head and the other at the feet. 13 They said to her,
"Woman, why are you weeping?" She said to them, "They have taken away my
Lord, and I do not know where they have laid him." 14 When she had said this, she
turned around and saw Jesus standing there, but she did not know that it was
Jesus. 15 Jesus said to her, "Woman, why are you weeping? Whom are you looking
for?" Supposing him to be the gardener, she said to him, "Sir, if you have carried
him away, tell me where you have laid him, and I will take him away." 16 Jesus said
to her, "Mary!" She turned and said to him in Hebrew, "Rabbouni!" (which means
Teacher). 17 Jesus said to her, "Do not hold on to me, because I have not yet
ascended to the Father. But go to my brothers and say to them, 'I am ascending
to my Father and your Father, to my God and your God.'" 18 Mary Magdalene went
and announced to the disciples, "I have seen the Lord"; and she told them that
he had said these things to her.

Commentary 1: Connecting the Reading with Scripture

The initial challenge for the preacher is that the Gospel reading for this day, Easter, includes only the first half of John 20, even though the whole chapter constitutes an integrated literary and theological unit. Taken in its entirety, John 20 portrays five different persons or groups who come to "believe" in the resurrection (that is, to put trust in the risen Christ and in the fullness of life available through him), and who come to that belief in five different ways: the "disciple whom Jesus loved" (John 20:1–10); Mary Magdalene (vv. 11–18); the disciples, minus Thomas (vv. 19–23); Thomas (vv. 24–28); and finally the readers/hearers of John's Gospel themselves (vv. 29–31). Since the second half of the chapter, John 20:19–31, is the Gospel reading for the Second Sunday of Easter, the preacher may want to "borrow" that passage in order to preach on the whole chapter or to preach a two-part series on ways to come to belief.

The chapter begins before dawn on Easter, "while it was still dark" (v. 1). The darkness is literal (it is after all before daylight), but it is also theologically symbolic, representing the world without the light of Christ. John's Gospel makes much of the imagery of light and darkness. Jesus is "the true light, which enlightens everyone" (1:9). Christ's light brings hope, but because the light exposes evil, Christ also brings judgment: "this is the judgment, that the light has come into the world, and people loved darkness rather than light because their deeds were evil" (3:19). People move from light to darkness, and vice versa. Jesus' own disciple Judas was called into the circle of light, but he joined with the forces of darkness, and when he leaves the Last Supper table to betray Jesus, John comments tersely and poignantly, "And it was night" (13:30). On the other hand, the Pharisee Nicodemus starts out in darkness—"He came to Jesus by night" (3:2)—but he ends up a caretaker of the light, tenderly caring for the body of Jesus (19:39–42).

In sum, in the Gospel of John the incarnation—the Word becoming flesh and dwelling among us (1:14)—precipitates a crisis and sets in motion an urgent and demanding choice between two paths: light and darkness. In John's theology, to trust that Christ is the way to fullness of life, and an abiding relationship with God is to walk in the light. To turn away from that way is to forfeit life and to choose death. "While you have the light, believe in the light," Jesus says, "so that you may become children of light" (12:36).

In 2017, a deranged man opened fire on the crowd at a music festival in Las Vegas, Nevada, killing fifty-eight people, and then took his own life. In an interview, one of the shooter's neighbors spoke of how little they knew of him. "It was like living next to nothing."[1] Like living next to darkness, perhaps?

So, it is "still dark" when Mary Magdalene goes to the tomb of Jesus. The rest of the scene is a mixture, misunderstanding intertwined with profound belief. Here Mary Magdalene represents the confusion and bewilderment the resurrection creates, and the beloved disciple embodies the deep faith called for by that event. Mary sees that the tomb is open and empty—that is to say, Jesus has already been raised, and the light is already shining in the darkness (see 1:5)—but Mary does not yet comprehend. She is much like the disciples who, during Jesus' triumphal entry into Jerusalem, "did not understand these things at first" (12:16) but later came to realize the truth. Mary's own awakening to faith will happen later (20:11–18). The preacher may wish to explore how faith often moves slowly from disorientation to deep conviction.

Notice how many people in this passage are running. Mary runs to tell Peter and the beloved disciple that Jesus' body is missing. This news sets the two disciples running toward the tomb. All of this haste communicates that the resurrection is an emergency. Something has happened that demands urgent action, even though the first responders do not fully know what has occurred.

At first, Peter and the beloved disciple run stride for stride, but then the beloved disciple pulls ahead and outruns Peter. Many commentators have speculated about the significance of this footrace. Gail O'Day has pointed out that in John, the beloved disciple has "only one role: to embody the love and intimacy with Jesus that is the goal of discipleship in John."[2] If so, it is "love and intimacy with Jesus" that gets to Easter first. Indeed, both disciples peer into the tomb, but the beloved disciple becomes the first believer, the first child of the light. Like Mary, he did not understand everything. Like Peter, he did not grasp the connection between the Scripture and this resurrection (20:9). Even so, out of love and trust "he saw and believed" (v. 8). The preacher may want to explore how it is that some come to believe almost intuitively. They are not Scripture scholars or theologians, but they respond almost intuitively to the event of God in their lives and believe.

Not everyone follows this path. The next story in our passage returns to Mary Magdalene. Suddenly she is back at the cemetery "weeping outside the tomb" (v. 11). What is striking is that she sees so much and realizes so little. She sees "two angels in white" (v. 12) in the tomb

1. Barbara Liston et al., "Las Vegas Gunman Stephen Paddock Was a High-Stakes Gambler Who 'Kept to Himself' before Massacre," *Washington Post*, October 2, 2017; https://www.washingtonpost.com/news/post-nation/wp/2017/10/02/las-vegas-gunman-liked-to-gamble-listened-to-country-music-lived-quiet-retired-life-before-massacre/?utm_term=.e424aa4a2dd5.

2. Gail R. O'Day, "The Gospel of John," in Leander E. Keck et al., eds., *The New Interpreter's Bible* (Nashville: Abingdon, 1995), 9:491–875 (840).

(Peter and the other disciples saw only cloths), and she even sees Jesus himself but thinks he is the gardener. The light is breaking in all around her, but her grief and despair allow her only to see darkness and to think in terms of death.

What is it that turns this story? For the reader (who already knows that the "gardener" is Christ), the story turns when Jesus asks, "Whom are you looking for?" (20:15). Something clicks for the reader. These are the very first words Jesus spoke in John's Gospel (1:38), and now they are spoken again at the last. The story has come to culmination, and the disciples who were seekers at the beginning of John are mirrored by Mary at the end. Human beings are seekers questing for fullness of life, and John presents Mary as our patron saint. John makes it clear that what humanity truly seeks is what Mary found in that cemetery: the risen Christ, the light that shines in darkness, the embodied glory of God.

For Mary, though, the story turns when Jesus speaks her name, when the radically new presence of the risen Christ connects to the memory and intimacy of her relationship with Jesus. The preacher may want to explore how some come to faith when the gospel connects in a personal way. Another preaching possibility here is to consider how intimacy with Christ can move in two directions. Some may wish to turn it into nostalgia, yearning for an idealized past, which spotlights the importance of Jesus' word to Mary, "Do not hold on to me" (20:17). Jesus is not rejecting his relationship with Mary, but indicating the direction in which it will move. Deep relationships with Christ do not regress into the past, but move toward ascension, toward the glory of God, toward eternal life—toward the future promised in God.

THOMAS G. LONG

Commentary 2: Connecting the Reading with the World

The resurrection is laden with theological meaning and inspirational import. Easter is our annual reminder that the sting of death has no purchase over the gift of life. Resurrection Sunday is the perennial promise of God's provision that blooms through the concrete cracks of grief and despair. Without the resurrection, tragedy triumphs and our problems prevail. With the resurrection, however, beautiful hymns of hope spring from the human heart. William P. Mackay in 1863 had believers singing:

> Hallelujah! Thine the glory!
> Hallelujah! Amen!
> Hallelujah! Thine the glory!
> Revive us again.

The Gospel of John provides two related resurrection accounts. The first narrative, John 20:1–10, portrays Mary Magdalene finding the stone removed and Jesus' body missing. She runs to retrieve Simon Peter and another disciple. Mary Magdalene believes that human hands removed Jesus. Her response is plausible, since in John, unlike Mark's resurrection account (Mark 16:6–7), there is no angel present to declare Jesus' resurrection. A burial shroud is the sole remaining sign of Jesus' presence.

When the other disciple looked in the tomb, "he saw and believed" that Jesus rose from the dead. The Gospel writer's description is indeed a profession of faith on the part of the disciple. The absence of Jesus' body does not negate the hopes and spiritual strivings that the disciples carried to the tomb. To the contrary, Jesus' apparent disappearance underscores the disciples' conviction born of confidence in his promises.

One can imagine that these two disciples recalled Jesus' teachings. "In my Father's house there are many dwelling places. If it were not so, would I have told you that I go to prepare a place for you?" (John 14:2). The writer of John also records Jesus comforting his disciples with positive and prescient affirmations: "For the Father himself loves you, because you have loved me and have believed that I came from God. I came from the Father and have come into the world; again, I am leaving the world and am going to the Father" (16:27–28). Now they can reaffirm their convictions and faith in Jesus' promises.

Resurrection Sunday affords an opportunity to reaffirm our faith in God's promises. Even when personal circumstances are far from ideal, and it is difficult to discern God's presence, Jesus told his followers that he would not leave them as orphans; though "the world will no longer see me," Jesus says, "you will see me; because I live, you also will live" (14:18–19).

Holding fast to hope is more easily said than done. Many Christians want to believe that we will profess steadfast faith in the face of adversity. Peering into the empty areas of our lives and seeing evidence of God's care, however, is difficult. The disciples "saw and believed," but they quickly returned home. Maybe they went home to bear witness to Jesus' resurrection, though it is possible that they went home to mourn privately in their sadness and disbelief. Most believers realize that putting on a "face of faith" in public often belies the melancholy moments we experience behind closed doors. For it is when we are alone that feelings of fear and dread take residence in our hearts.

The second resurrection account, verses 11–18, speaks to this reality. Mary Magdalene remains at the tomb. She neither conceals her doubts nor masks her pain. An angel appears to engage Mary, which allows her to express her deepest fear: "They have taken my Lord, and I do not know where they laid him." This narrative provides us the chance to consider the many occasions on which we want to cry out like Mary, "They have taken my Lord."

Communities terrorized by mass shootings inevitably feel a sense of God's absence. Domestic terrorists attempt to steal any spirit of grace or goodness from our neighborhoods. Families directly affected by state-sanctioned violence indeed wonder where their Lord is hidden. Police officers have taken the lives of unarmed boys and men of color like Trayvon Martin, Eric Garner, Tamir Rice, Michael Brown, Philando Castile, Alex Nieto, and Stephon Clark. Their murders, coupled with the frequent refusal to hold anyone accountable, have undoubtedly caused many justice-loving people of faith to cry out, "They have taken my Lord, and I do not know where they laid him."

This is why Mary Magdalene's example is instructive. She remains at the tomb. She gives voice to her grief to whoever will listen. In the process, Jesus shows up. Just as God raised Jesus from the dead, Jesus lifts Mary's broken spirit. Resurrection Sunday represents renewal and revival. Those things that appear inconceivable can become plausible, and the unimaginable becomes tenable. The preacher has the opportunity to share examples all around us of where the improbable became possible, and those things that we thought were dead were brought back to life.

Consider the story of Jessie Little Doe Baird. She is a member of the Wampanoag community in Mashpee, Massachusetts. Years ago, Baird began to have dreams about people who looked like her but were speaking a different language. A street name in Mashpee caused her to wonder if she had been dreaming about the original Wôpanâak language, a language considered dead in the late nineteenth century. After years of studying with linguists at the Massachusetts Institute of Technology, scouring through old documents, and working within her local Cape Cod community, Jessie Little Doe Baird helped to revive the Wôpanâak language. Her daughter Mae became the first native Wôpanâak speaker in over a century, and in 2016 Massachusetts partnered with tribal families to open "The Children's House," a Wôpanâak language immersion school. Thanks to Baird's efforts, the Wampanoag community could say to the rest of us, "We are not dead! We still live here."[3]

There is also the story of middle-school student Vidal Chastanet and his principal Nydia Lopez at Mott Hall Bridges Academy in Brooklyn, New York. This school is located in one of the least resourced communities in Brooklyn, and many considered it among the worst places to send a child. When Humans of New York blogger Brandon Stanton stopped Chastanet on the street and asked him about his most significant influence, the young man named his principal, Ms. Lopez. Chastanet recounted how Ms. Lopez tells them every day that they matter. She refers to all students as scholars and changed the school colors to purple to signify royalty. Ms.

3. Anne Makepeace, dir., *We Still Live Here—Âs Nutayuneân,* PBS Indies, Independent Lens, documentary, 2011. DVD.

Lopez hoped to raise funds to take students on a campus visit to Harvard University. When Stanton publicized their story, not only did Ms. Lopez raise enough money to have students visit Harvard, with over $1 million in donations; Mott Hall Bridges Academy now offers a scholarship to support students' college pursuits.[4]

Resurrection Sunday should enliven, enrich, and encourage our souls, helping us to envision the impossible. We can take comfort even in the graveyards of our despair. In the words of twentieth-century poet and theology professor Amos Wilder:

> The immovable stone tossed aside,
> The collapsed linens,
> The blinding angel and the chalky guards:
> . . . .
> Retell, renew the event
> In these planetary years,
> For we were there and He is here:
> It is always the third day.[5]

JONATHAN L. WALTON

4. Caroline Kitchener, "What It Takes to Mentor Poor Kids," *The Atlantic*, July 25, 2017.
5. Amos N. Wilder, "The Third Day," in *Grace Confounding: Poems by Amos Niven Wilder* (Philadelphia: Fortress, 1972), 3.

Acts 10:34–43

34 Then Peter began to speak to them: "I truly understand that God shows no partiality, 35 but in every nation anyone who fears him and does what is right is acceptable to him. 36 You know the message he sent to the people of Israel, preaching
peace by Jesus Christ—he is Lord of all. 37 That message spread throughout
Judea, beginning in Galilee after the baptism that John announced: 38 how God
anointed Jesus of Nazareth with the Holy Spirit and with power; how he went
about doing good and healing all who were oppressed by the devil, for God was
with him. 39 We are witnesses to all that he did both in Judea and in Jerusalem.
They put him to death by hanging him on a tree; 40 but God raised him on the
third day and allowed him to appear, 41 not to all the people but to us who were
chosen by God as witnesses, and who ate and drank with him after he rose from
the dead. 42 He commanded us to preach to the people and to testify that he is
the one ordained by God as judge of the living and the dead. 43 All the prophets
testify about him that everyone who believes in him receives forgiveness of sins
through his name."

Commentary 1: Connecting the Reading with Scripture

Acts 10:34–43 is part of Peter's sermon within a dramatic story. The apostle, spurred on by his vision of the unclean animals, now (shockingly) stands in the house of the Gentile Cornelius, who himself has received a vision from God, assuring him that Peter will bring him godly teaching. We hear not only Peter's proclamation to Cornelius, but also the implications of that gospel for the church: "God shows no partiality, but in every nation anyone who fears him and does what is right is acceptable to him" (Acts 10:34–35).

Peter has been with Jesus in Galilee and Judea, in the Garden of Gethsemane, and in his arrest and trial. Though absent for the crucifixion, he has been restored by the risen Christ, and he knows about forgiveness. However, Peter and the church have yet to learn about the revolutionary power of Christ's work: the door has been opened for receptive Gentiles as well. Both the immediate and the larger literary context are important for interpreting this text; all these complexities cannot be shared in every homily, but they should inform the thinking of the preacher. For some sermons, such as one that dwells upon the wideness of God's mercy, preachers may decide to show explicitly how the overall narrative (alongside Peter's words) proclaims that particular truth.

Peter was learning even as he was preaching. Not only will he be stretched by entering the house of one previously unclean, but so too will all the apostles grow in the Jerusalem meeting that occurs immediately after this event. Here is the first major lesson that the church as a whole will learn. Jesus' actions have caused the veil of the temple to be torn, so that Gentiles also can live within the truth of the gospel. As Jesus had said, they would be his witnesses in Jerusalem, and Judea, and Samaria, and "to the ends of the earth" (Acts 1:8).

Peter's sermon presents several helpful and mysterious themes. First, the apostle reminds us that the good news is seen not only in its climax as Jesus dies, rises, and ascends, but in Jesus' entire life. There is no division between the "historical Jesus" and the Christ of faith. The very same one who "went about Judea and Galilee" and died also rose from the dead, eating and drinking anew with the apostles. Even more, it is he who will come, finally, at the last judgment. Peter's sermon fills out the meaning of Hebrews

13:8, that Jesus is the same yesterday, today, and forever. Some today divide the "Jesus of history" from the "Christ of faith." The preacher can correct this by showing how Peter's words depict Jesus as one who took on everything it is to be human, and yet who truly embodied (and embodies) our merciful and just God.

Next, we see that Peter describes Jesus' resurrection in two ways. First, "God raised him" (Acts 10:40). Jews in antiquity considered that the resurrection to life (see Dan. 12) was God's confirmation of the godly. Though it was a shock that Jesus had been resurrected *alone* and that the Gentile rule continued, God's affirmation of Jesus' ministry was nonetheless clear. Interestingly, in verse 41, Peter supplements this language with a contrasting phrase: "he rose from the dead." Jesus is not simply the recipient of God's breath of life, but is a principal in the drama. The Son "[has] life in himself" (John 5:26) and can lay down his life and "take it up again" (10:18). It may be difficult to see how both are true, but Peter joins these two perspectives, establishing both the Father's approval and Jesus as the One who conquered death. The preacher here may draw us into a paradox that illumines today's crisis of authority in the churches. We tend to play off order (or hierarchy) against autonomy, but if in Jesus we see that obedience and agency come together, we may learn more fruitfully to navigate the complexities of working with others, no matter what our position.

Third, Peter gives evidence for the resurrection and suggests its nature. He claims to be a witness to the risen Christ, one of the witnesses that God chose. Moreover, he mentions that the risen Jesus is no phantom, for he was able to eat and drink (Acts 10:41), though his life is infinitely more real than ours. Rather than thinking of the resurrection life as something vague and "only spiritual," we are reminded by the vividness of these stories that, alongside the resurrected One and those who will be raised to life eternal, our own present lives are not very "solid." In 2 Corinthians 5:1, Paul speaks about our present body as a "tent" that will be replaced by a permanent dwelling.

Fourth, he mentions the prophets who looked forward to this great event. Here, he is repeating the teaching of Jesus on the road to Emmaus and in the upper room that the books of the Old Testament all witnessed to him (Luke 24:27, 44). So we are taught how to read the Old Testament in continuity with the New.

Finally, Peter preaches the gospel in a nutshell: Jesus "is Lord of all" (Acts 10:36). We are so used to hearing the word "Lord" that we often gloss over it. Indeed, sometimes in our English versions, the word is translated as the honorific title "sir." On Peter's lips, it means a good deal more. For *kyrios* ("Lord") was the Greek term used to translate the Hebrew mysterious name for God revealed to Moses: YHWH ("I AM"). The preacher holds before us the secret of the ages: that the sovereign Lord of all has come among us, *as* one of us, to raise us to share intimacy with him.

The other lectionary readings for the day underscore Easter's joy. Psalm 118 calls us to "give thanks" for the Lord's steadfast love, and reminds us that God always surprises. Only the Lord could do such a thing, bringing life out of death, showing "steadfast love" (Ps. 118:2). Easter, the eighth day, becomes the passage way to new life: "This is the day that the LORD has made; let us rejoice and be glad in it" (Ps. 118:24). Our very gathering on Sunday (rather than the Sabbath) is a reminder that things have changed forever: we are part of a new creation brought into being by the One who conquered death.

When we consider today's Gospel reading (John 20:14), we are struck by how the grieving Mary Magdalene is (by the Holy Spirit? by the luminous presence of the risen Jesus?) "turned around," so that she recognizes the Lord: the Greek *estraphē* ("was turned") is passive, not active as our translations render it. Seeing things from this new perspective, she is to tell the disciples that God is now not only the Father of Jesus, but the Father of all believers. Accordingly, Jesus will breathe new life into his disciples, speaking peace and enlivening a whole new creation. Not only are we creatures who have received God's gift of life, but we are beloved members of the household of God, those upon whom he bestows the Holy Spirit.

Preachers can help us know that the reading leads us to consider Jesus' life as the pinnacle of salvation history, the mystery of the resurrection to which we look forward, the surprising activity of God that calls forth our thankfulness, the role of the apostles as witnesses, and the important place that each of us has in God's household.

EDITH M. HUMPHREY

Commentary 2: Connecting the Reading with the World

Here is an opportunity to preach the familiar Easter story from a different, possibly unsettling, viewpoint. Instead of remembering the testimony of women (which fell on deaf ears) or the foot race by Peter and John, or even Mary weeping in the garden, we have Luke's story of an expanding faith community. Peter, speaking to a Gentile household, shares a Twitter summary of Jesus' life. He begins with Jesus' baptism by John, recounts his healing ministry, remembers his death, celebrates his resurrection, and repeats his instructions to his followers to preach in his name. Peter, instructed by God, offers this good news to outsiders.

If we are truthful, we must admit that there are those in every congregation who do not find joy in the story of the empty tomb. For some, the accounts of the resurrection miracle cause more stress than happiness. The leap of faith expected at Christmas and Easter can simply be too much, though they may never admit it. As a result, some come to church on Easter prepared to tune out when the preacher steps up. Peter's account, with its emphasis on inclusion rather than exclusion, may offer a "back door" into the good news.

Peter's message takes the worshiper beyond the garden tomb, beyond the upper room, and beyond the road to Emmaus. Peter's message, with its minimalist description of Easter, boils this holy day's message down to its essence: God desires to redeem all of creation. God loves all of creation, in all its amazing diversity. "I truly understand that God shows no partiality," Peter preaches. God does not, but humans do. Could this be the Easter message of challenge and affirmation that your congregation needs to hear? Remind them that they are loved and welcomed by God, and called to love with the forgiving, compassionate wide love of God. Challenge the listeners to dig down and ask themselves to be honest about their own individual partialities. How might these biases color someone's experience of church, of God?

It would be worthwhile to spend a few moments of the sermon setting the context for Peter's speech, since this is as much Peter's conversion story as it is anyone else's. Read all of Acts 10 to prepare yourself for preaching. The words of truth that Peter shares with Cornelius and his family, words that lead to the baptism of the entire household, are words that Peter would have previously withheld from this family. Here we witness the good news crossing boundaries. The Acts text presents Easter through the multicolored lens of diversity, and this diversity will bring both blessing and complexity.

So who is in need of conversion? Peter would not have considered himself in that category. He was a witness to the resurrection; he preached resurrection. Many in your congregation may see themselves in the same light. As you consider the faces that will gather on Easter Sunday, whom do you see? Do you see a community in need of the same kind of conversion rehabilitation that Peter experienced? Christians sometimes ask one another, "When were you saved?" Some respond with an exact date, others a memory, others several moments. Some people point to that first Good Friday as the moment when salvation was extended to all.

This story invites believers to consider that salvation's mercies are ever unfolding within us. Peter knew and walked with Jesus, but he also denied Jesus and abandoned Jesus. He was familiar with the intentionally expansive way that Jesus engaged people, yet he could not comprehend that God wanted to take down all barriers, remove all walls. God spoke repeatedly to Peter through a dream, softening Peter's heart and opening Peter's mind to the expansiveness of God's realm.

Here is the question this text may pose for your congregation: Whom are we excluding? Whom do we deem as other, not worthy of receiving the gospel? Our lips and signs may have the "right" answer: "We welcome all!" Do the church's actions, the church's ministries, the church's worship correspond with those words?

Peter's acceptance of Cornelius's household got him into some hot water with the followers in Jerusalem (see Acts 11). The same risks exist today. Whenever the church seeks to expand its welcome, there will be resistance and concern. Within your own congregation's history there may be a defining moment when someone took a countercultural stand in defense of God's radical welcome. How did that play out within the community, and how did the experience influence future decisions? Another question also emerges: is the church not only willing to welcome those for whom the door has been shut, but also willing to go the extra step of patiently explaining that welcome to those who may not understand?

Chocolat, a romantic drama released in 2000, explores the damage the church does to itself and to others when it excludes instead of welcomes. A foreign woman arrives in a small town in France during the season of Lent, and opens a chocolate shop. From the color of the shoes she wears to her rejection of the Catholic Church, she does not fit in with the community. Gradually, many come to recognize that she embodies Christian values of compassion, peace, and justice. The young priest of the small town, Père Henri (Hugh O'Conor), is torn between pleasing the mayor with his legalistic interpretation of Christianity and his own more expansive beliefs. He finally finds the courage to preach this Easter sermon: "Do I want to speak of the miracle of our Lord's divine transformation? Not really, no. I don't want to talk about his divinity. I'd rather talk about his humanity, his kindness, his tolerance. I think that we can't go around measuring our goodness by what we don't do. By what we deny ourselves, what we resist, and whom we exclude. I think we've got to measure goodness by what we embrace, what we create and [whom] we include."[1]

A similar thread to pull from this text is found in the phrase "preaching peace by Jesus Christ." Although we know that Jesus' teaching and healing caused disruption and confusion for some, we are witnesses to his examples and teachings of how to live in peace. You may want to touch on some examples of Jesus' peacemaking: freeing the woman caught in adultery from shame and death (preventing an act of violence), restoring the isolated Zacchaeus to the community (addressing a corrupt system), overturning the tables of injustice at the temple (exposing a discriminatory and abusive practice). Jesus, the peacemaker, was continually taking action on behalf of the vulnerable. Carry this idea into the contemporary setting, and invite the Easter people gathered before you to imagine how they might live out Jesus' vision of peace.

As you celebrate the Easter message with your congregation, take the opportunity to make your listeners truly uncomfortable by reminding them that like Jesus' first disciples, they are also called to preach! One family at a time, one friend at a time, the early Christian community grew through the sharing of the good news of Jesus' forgiveness. Empower your congregants to claim their role as preachers. Encourage them to preach with their whole lives, embracing Jesus' vision of peace, his radical inclusion, and his delight in the world's diversity.

We can be thankful for Peter, for we all have our own "Peter" moments. Hot and cold. Clear-minded and confused. Peter was open to having his mind changed. Was there ever a better time to open our hearts and minds to renewal than Easter morning?

CATHY CALDWELL HOOP

1. *Chocolat*, directed by Lasse Hallström, based on the novel by Joanne Harris (Los Angeles: Miramax, 2000), DVD.

Matthew 28:1–10

1After the sabbath, as the first day of the week was dawning, Mary Magdalene
and the other Mary went to see the tomb. 2And suddenly there was a great earthquake; for an angel of the Lord, descending from heaven, came and rolled back
the stone and sat on it. 3His appearance was like lightning, and his clothing white
as snow. 4For fear of him the guards shook and became like dead men. 5But the
angel said to the women, "Do not be afraid; I know that you are looking for Jesus
who was crucified. 6He is not here; for he has been raised, as he said. Come,
see the place where he lay. 7Then go quickly and tell his disciples, 'He has been
raised from the dead, and indeed he is going ahead of you to Galilee; there you
will see him.' This is my message for you." 8So they left the tomb quickly with fear
and great joy, and ran to tell his disciples. 9Suddenly Jesus met them and said,
"Greetings!" And they came to him, took hold of his feet, and worshiped him.
10Then Jesus said to them, "Do not be afraid; go and tell my brothers to go to
Galilee; there they will see me."

Commentary 1: Connecting the Reading with Scripture

This familiar passage is a challenge. How might telling "the old, old story" engage contemporary congregations? There is the deeper challenge: a text that makes such a profound revelation—Jesus is risen—also creates mystery and surprises. Pursuing some of the surprises in this text offers a way forward for preachers.

The first surprise concerns why the women come to the tomb. Matthew scrubs out Mark's reference to spices, grief, and sadness. Rather, the two Marys come "to see the tomb" (Matt. 28:1). While the language of "seeing" has figured previously in scenes of literal healings, language of sight and blindness also functions as a metaphor for insight and understanding (13:14–16).

This metaphorical use explains why the women journey "to see the tomb." These women are Jesus' disciples who have "followed" him from Galilee (27:55). They have accompanied Jesus throughout his ministry in Galilee. They have witnessed his displays of God's reign/empire. They have heard his teaching that he must die and be raised (16:21; 17:22–23; 20:17–19). They have seen his prediction of crucifixion and death accomplished.

Knowing the tomb's location (27:61), in 28:1 they come expecting and looking for Jesus' resurrection. Verbs of "seeing" recur in verses 6–7, 10, and 17 to designate encounter with the risen Jesus. Matthew's account begins with expectation, insight, and encounter, not despair. The sermon could invite hearers to identify circumstances in their lives in which they might look for this new life that God creates.

What do the women "see"? The angel interprets the empty tomb to signify that Jesus has been raised, thereby confirming Jesus' teaching. Then they "see" or encounter the risen Jesus (28:9–10). Somehow, they recognize Jesus.

This is the second surprise: there is no description of Jesus' resurrection body. Jesus can be held and heard (vv. 9–10), and there is a subsequent encounter (vv. 16–20), but there is no description, just the affirmation of a resurrected body. Interpreters often affirm the continuity of the predeath and postdeath Jesus, but there is a more important connection.

Jesus' body has been abused, paraded, and voted on (27:20–23), tortured by whipping (v. 26), stripped (vv. 28, 31), costumed and mocked (vv. 29, 31), spat on and struck (v. 30), crucified and buried (vv. 32–60). His body has experienced the worst that imperial tyranny can inflict. Torture and crucifixion demeaned, rejected, and destroyed Jesus' bodily existence. Roman imperial agents killed him.

They cannot keep him dead. They cannot prevail against God's determined commitment to life and justice for all the bodies of the world. Raising Jesus' body enacts life in the midst of death, justice in the midst of injustice, wholeness in the midst of brokenness. It signifies God's life for all bodies.

Preachers might elaborate the significance of the risen Jesus having a body. It displays how much the just treatment of bodies and their interactions with other bodies matter in God's workings in the world. Injustice, tyranny, and disparities of power do terrible damage to bodies. Jesus' appearance as a body means that tyrannies do not have the final word—even though so often they seem to prevail. This resurrection story declares an alternative truth of God's workings. The sermon could emphasize the mission of the congregation as an Easter people who are empowered to acts of justice and change for homeless, hungry, violated, abused, sick, despairing, addicted bodies in our world.

One of the clearest expressions of resurrection in the biblical tradition occurs in 2 Maccabees 6–7. Seven brothers defy the tyrant Antiochus IV Epiphanes after he orders them to cease observing Torah and to renounce their identity in unfaithfulness to God. Their refusal results in terrible torture, one by one, while their mother is compelled to watch. They taunt the tyrant with assertions that God will raise them. The mother encourages her sons, "The Creator of the world . . . will in his mercy give life and breath back to you again" (2 Macc. 7:23). Faithfulness to Torah will secure the restoration of their tortured bodies and end the oppression of the Jewish people. Resurrection is somatic and societal; it repairs bodies and anticipates societal wholeness.

As with Jesus' resurrection, 2 Maccabees affirms resurrection as defiance of imperial tyranny. The expectation of resurrection relativizes destruction. Again, there is the affirmation that injustices against bodies matter and are corrected in the new reality of God's reign/empire in which resurrection participates. Preachers can help listeners hear and imitate the wider canon of Scripture's witness to acts of justice that defy destructive power.

There's a further surprise. Matthew 28:4 employs a powerful irony. It describes the soldiers that the alliance of political retainers, chief priests, and Roman governor Pilate had dispatched to keep Jesus in the tomb (27:62–66). As the angel proclaims resurrection and marks the tomb as a place of life, the soldiers "shook and became like dead men." These representatives of Roman power, apparently triumphant in inflicting death on Jesus, now become what they had inflicted. The demonstration of divine presence accompanying the angel's appearance (earthquake; rolling back the stone; his dramatic appearance) renders Rome's military lifeless.

The surprise is not that God has so acted. There's a long tradition of divine interventions that destroy or nullify imperial military power. Recall the Egyptian army drowned in the Red Sea (Exod. 14:21–31), Gideon's confounding of the Midianites (Judg. 7:4–23), the boy David felling the mighty Goliath and routing the Philistines (1 Sam. 17:40–54), God shutting the lions' mouths to protect Daniel from King Darius (Dan. 6); Judith beheading Holofernes, the general of the Assyrian king Nebuchadnezzar, to save the people (Jdt. 13). God can outpower any imperializing army, often, according to the tradition, by imitating violent imperial ways.

No actual soldiers are destroyed in this scene; life is asserted in a different key.

Here is the surprise: though God makes a habit of such interventions, the male disciples are oblivious to it. They run away (Matt. 26:56), though Peter remains a little longer (vv. 69–75). They do not run back. The male disciples do not wait expectantly for resurrection.

The focus remains with the two women. Not only do they look for resurrection, not only do they hear the angel's proclamation that "he has been raised, as he said." They are commissioned twice—once by the angel (28:7) and once by the risen Jesus (28:10)—to proclaim the resurrection gospel. It is not the elite and powerful, the successful and victorious, the males, who are entrusted with this proclamation. It is two women, marginal in a male-dominated society, who receive the identity as preachers and become central to the next chapter of this gospel story.

In a sense, this should not be a surprise. It is consistent with the rest of this Gospel, in which Jesus' attention has been especially focused on the marginal, on nonelites, the powerless, vulnerable, and broken. Yet we are so used to seeing the successful, the wealthy, the powerful, the dominant at the center that it is surprising to see the marginal on center stage. The preacher could develop examples of this centering of the margins in relation to the congregation's location and mission.

There is a final surprise. The women respond "with fear and great joy" (28:8). Resurrection is not unmitigated joy. The sermon could call hearers to the resurrection journey that comprises suffering and death, that opens up new worlds, that decenters and invades the present, that conflicts with the status quo and destabilizes our cultural normalcies. This journey embodies God's passionate, determined, relentless, unshakable commitment to life and justice for all bodies.

Fearful indeed—and joyful.

WARREN CARTER

Commentary 2: Connecting the Reading with the World

Matthew 28:1–10 boils over with supernatural events. Mary Magdalene and the other Mary, on the way to see Jesus' tomb, *felt* the earth move. They *saw* the angel, who caused the earthquake to roll back the stone, promptly sit upon it (Matt. 28:2). The angel, lightning-bright with clothes snow white, caused the guards to collapse as if dead (vv. 3–4). The women *heard* the angel say Jesus was raised from the dead and had left instructions for them to tell his disciples Jesus would see them in Galilee (vv. 5–7). Running to do the angel's bidding, the women suddenly *saw* Jesus, who greeted them. They grasped his feet. As they *touched* him, they *heard* him repeat the angel's directive (vv. 8–10). Matthew 28:1–10, a mere 208 words long, spends most of its words on things beyond nature. Interpretation of this passage calls for attention to supernatural things, historically and culturally.

On Easter Sunday, illuminating the historical context of the resurrection and of the one proclaiming it are both essential. The work of N. T. Wright demonstrates well the significance of historical investigation for resurrection preaching.[1] Wright argues that in a context of exile and oppression, some first-century Jews pinned their messianic hopes on the resurrection of martyred freedom fighters. From their ranks, the messiah would return to rule the kingdom of God on earth. Resurrection in this context always meant embodiment, Wright asserts. Only acceptance of Jesus' resurrection as a transformed physicality, he argues, makes sense of the formation of early Christian kingdom communities. The empty tomb mattered in that first-century context.

In verse 9, the two women "took hold of [Jesus'] feet." Dale C. Allison Jr. has drawn on the cultural history of feet and the supernatural to interpret this phrase as a claim to the embodiment of the risen Christ.[2] While affirming other interpretations of the foot holding—affection, submission, worship—Allison notes that interpreters throughout patristic and medieval times saw in this gesture confirmation of the risen Jesus' physicality. He buttresses this interpretation with a survey of ghost lore internationally. The bottom line: ghosts do not have feet, but Jesus did. The narrative affirms embodiment. Neither Wright nor Allison sees his work as proof of resurrection, but each draws on the history of the supernatural to clarify the gospel's meaning. In doing so, each leaves open the possibility of authentic spiritual (supernatural) encounters in human experience.

1. N. T. Wright, *The Resurrection of the Son of God* (Minneapolis: Fortress, 2003).
2. Dale C. Allison, "Touching Jesus' Feet (Matthew 28:9)," in *Studies in Matthew: Interpretation Past and Present* (Grand Rapids: Baker Academic, 2005), 105–16.

The historical and cultural contexts of the contemporary proclaimer of Matthew 28:1–10 are also significant for Easter proclamation in cultures that generally exclude genuine spiritual experience. The modern era, particularly in the Western world, defines reality in terms of rational, scientific evidence. The professions—business, medicine, law, and so on—and higher education's disciplines easily carry on without reference to reality beyond nature, or they struggle to find a way to integrate it. Folklore phenomenologist David J. Hufford says cultures have official belief systems promoted by authoritative social structures.[3] Modern official belief systems exclude the supernatural from existence in the real world. They consider spiritual experiences psychological or natural anomalies mislabeled with religious language. This increasing secularization supports a culture that suppresses, ignores, and explains away supernatural experience.

The church and professional ministry in this culture usually follow suit, which poses a problem for an institution rooted in supernatural realities. Many professional ministers reading commentaries like this one, and most people whom they hope to benefit by doing so, consider themselves to exist by virtue of education and daily practice in a mostly supernatural-free zone, for all practical purposes.

Commentary, interpretation, and proclamation in this historical circumstance tend to tiptoe around the possibility of the existence of angels or the transformed embodiment of a crucified man, preferring to address purely interior, psychological, subjective matters of faith, such as fear and joy (vv. 4, 8). At worst, religious authorities explain away claims to external sources for those interior reactions as hallucinations or delusions. At best, they suppose them fictive constructions by the early church, fabricated to create desired interior psychological states among their hearers. For example, the tomb might not be empty, but saying it was will create the same genuine interior faith as if it were true. They rewrite Paul, "If there is no [belief in] resurrection of the dead" (1 Cor. 15:13). The empty tomb does not matter; only belief in it does.

This critique is no proof for the historicity of the resurrection. It is a caution against complete surrender to a culture that rejects out of hand human experiences of transcendent reality. Modern culture has not eliminated such experiences. Hufford cites research that shows, rather, that people in secular cultures report spiritual experiences at about the same rate as in any other culture, including officially religious ones. The frequency is even higher among those with higher levels of education. Perhaps the preacher can cite a personal example.

A secular culture that excludes the possibility of supernatural events but has a population that regularly reports them informally is in denial. It is like the reality-resistant subjects in a classic card experiment. Subjects rapidly shown altered cards, such as a nine of spades painted red, without knowing that alternate forms were present, failed to see the altered cards at a much higher rate than subjects who knew beforehand that some cards in the deck might have been changed. People tend to see what they think is possible and resist seeing what they assume is not. Supernatural events change nature's normal "deck," but modern culture's official belief system gives no credence to those who see the changes. Is it always an illusion?

One task during Easter liturgy is to create a space where the *possibility* of supernatural realities is acceptable. This is not to be confused with proving the resurrection or dogmatic declarations of orthodox interpretations. It is to offer the hearer an intellectual, emotional, spiritual space to imagine that Mary Magdalene and the other Mary's Easter morning experiences might stand on their own, rather than require relabeling as hallucinations, delusions, or later fictive constructions.

Imagination is an essential tool for creating space for spiritual perception. In George Bernard Shaw's 1923 play *Saint Joan*, Robert de Baudricourt tells Joan that the voices she hears come from her own imagination. She answers, "Of course. That is how the messages of God come

3. David J. Hufford, "Beings without Bodies: An Experience-Centered Theory of the Belief in Spirits," in *Out Of the Ordinary: Folklore and the Supernatural*, ed. Barbara Walker (Logan, UT: Utah State University Press, 1995), 11–45.

to us." Easter calls us to imagine reality reborn. Imagine beings who exist only in two dimensions, like a living square drawn on a flat sheet of paper. If a three-dimensional sphere floated into the square's reality, it would appear to the square as an inexplicable ever-widening circle. Humans are three-dimensional beings whose spiritual experiences introduce another dimension. The idea is to point beyond the current horizon. Matthew 28:1–10 calls contemporary proclaimers to present possibility, not proofs.

Deliver the supernatural-saturated text of Matthew 28:1–10 to persons freed to believe the supernatural is possible, and they just might meet the living risen Christ on Easter morning. That would be good news worth telling the world.

WM. LOYD ALLEN

Second Sunday of Easter

Acts 2:14a, 22–32
Psalm 16
1 Peter 1:3–9
John 20:19–31

Acts 2:14a, 22–32

14But Peter, standing with the eleven, raised his voice and addressed them, . . .
22"You that are Israelites, listen to what I have to say: Jesus of Nazareth, a
man attested to you by God with deeds of power, wonders, and signs that God
did through him among you, as you yourselves know— 23this man, handed over
to you according to the definite plan and foreknowledge of God, you crucified
and killed by the hands of those outside the law. 24But God raised him up, having
freed him from death, because it was impossible for him to be held in its power.
25For David says concerning him,

'I saw the Lord always before me,
    for he is at my right hand so that I will not be shaken;
26therefore my heart was glad, and my tongue rejoiced;
    moreover my flesh will live in hope.
27For you will not abandon my soul to Hades,
    or let your Holy One experience corruption.
28You have made known to me the ways of life;
    you will make me full of gladness with your presence.'

29"Fellow Israelites, I may say to you confidently of our ancestor David that he
both died and was buried, and his tomb is with us to this day. 30Since he was a
prophet, he knew that God had sworn with an oath to him that he would put one
of his descendants on his throne. 31Foreseeing this, David spoke of the resurrection of the Messiah, saying,

'He was not abandoned to Hades,
  nor did his flesh experience corruption.'

32This Jesus God raised up, and of that all of us are witnesses."

Commentary 1: Connecting the Reading with Scripture

During the Easter season, the first lectionary reading is taken from Acts rather than from the Old Testament. Aside from providing a way of fitting Acts into the lectionary cycle, this practice makes thematic sense: what better way to celebrate the resurrection than to remember how it was first proclaimed? So it makes sense that in the first year in the cycle, and on the very first week after Easter day, the first lesson is the very first public proclamation of the resurrection, delivered by Peter on the day of Pentecost itself. According to Luke, it could not have come any earlier, because Jesus himself had commanded the disciples not to proclaim his resurrection until the Spirit had been poured out upon them (Acts 1:4; cf. Luke 24:49).

There no little irony here. On the one hand, the Easter message is that Jesus is alive; on the other, this news is made public by his followers only after he has been taken up to heaven and is thus no longer available to present "himself alive . . . by many convincing proofs" (Acts 1:3). None of this is spelled out in today's lesson, which simply quotes from Peter's sermon without reference to Jesus' commands or the descent of the Spirit; but the paradox, that the news of Easter goes out only after the risen Jesus himself is no longer available for inspection, is in many respects central to this reading. When he discusses Jesus' life and death, Peter appeals to his audience's own experience: Jesus was "a man attested to you by God with deeds of power, wonders, and signs that God did through him among you" (2:22) but whom these same auditors then "crucified and killed by the hands of those outside the law" (v. 23). By contrast, Peter's audience does not have any experience of the resurrection. *That* claim can be believed only on the basis of the testimony of Peter and his friends, who claim to be witnesses of this fact (v. 32).

This privileged access to knowledge of Jesus' fate would seem to put Peter and his companions in a superior position with respect to other Christians, since the faith of every other Christian down through the centuries depends on their eyewitness testimony. It seems consistent with ascribing these eyewitnesses such special status that when the eleven apostles gather to decide on a replacement for Judas, the decisive criterion for selection is that the person should be "one of the men who have accompanied us during all the time that the Lord Jesus went in and out among us, beginning from the baptism of John until the day when he was taken up from us" (1:21). On one level this seems only right: clearly only someone who actually saw the risen Jesus is qualified to "become a witness with us to his resurrection" (v. 22). Admittedly, after the apostles' demise, others who were not themselves eyewitnesses to the resurrection will carry on the preaching of the gospel, but in the first instance, in order to have a "share in *this* ministry" (v. 17), the primordial apostolic ministry upon which all later ministry depends, a person must have actually seen the risen Lord.

Yet if this reference to personal witness to Jesus' resurrection in Peter's sermon seems to give the apostles a privileged place in the church, the two other NT lectionary readings for the week paint a rather different picture. In the Gospel reading from John, for example, Jesus does not teach that eyewitnesses to his resurrection are worthy of any sort of special regard. Quite the contrary, he suggests that those who believe *without* having seen are superior those whose faith is based on sight (John 20:29). Similarly, when the same Peter who preached on Pentecost writes his letter to Christians in Asia Minor some years later, he praises them for believing in spite of the fact that they have never seen Jesus at all, whether before or after his crucifixion (1 Pet. 1:8).

In light of these observations, it is worth considering that Peter's Pentecost speech may not place quite the weight on the importance of the eyewitnesses that its immediate context in the narrative of Luke–Acts might initially suggest. Although Peter certainly does affirm his role as a witness to the resurrection, the bulk of the reading is not concerned with either explaining or defending this status. Indeed, when Peter first proclaims the resurrection in Acts 2:24 ("God raised him up"), he makes no reference at all to the role of the apostolic witnesses like himself or to their testimony. Instead, he undertakes an exegesis of Psalm 16 (which, not surprisingly, is also the psalm appointed in the lectionary for this Sunday). This psalm depicts David rejoicing that God's faithful presence not only secures life in the present ("he is at my right hand so that I will not be shaken," Acts 2:25; cf. Ps. 16:8), but also is such that, even in death, God "will not abandon my soul to Hades, or let your Holy One experience corruption" (Acts 2:27; cf. Ps. 16:10). The burden of Peter's exegesis is that, notwithstanding the psalmist's use of the first person singular, David could not have been speaking of himself, since the fact that "he both died and was buried, and his tomb is with us to this day" (Acts 2:29) proves that he most certainly did experience corruption. It follows that he must have been speaking prophetically "of the resurrection of the Messiah" (v. 31).

While Peter's line of reasoning makes sense as far as it goes, its relevance for belief in the resurrection of Jesus is not particularly clear, since the presence of biblical testimony that the Messiah would be raised, however convincing, does not in itself lend any support to the claim that Jesus has in fact risen. The latter claim would seem to remain completely dependent on the trustworthiness of the testimony of Peter and the other apostles. Yet the effect of citing this psalm seems precisely to draw attention away from Peter and his companions as a focus of theological interest in their own right. Instead of focusing on the role of Peter and his companions as witnesses to the news that Jesus has risen from the dead, the upshot of Peter's exegesis of Psalm 16 is to suggest that from one perspective the resurrection should not really be considered "news" at all, since it was predicted in Israel's Scriptures ("For David says concerning him," Acts 2:25; cf. Luke 24:25–27).

This is not to say that Peter was using the psalm text to claim that it was evident beforehand that Jesus would be raised from the dead. All the evangelists make it clear that the disciples had no expectation that Jesus would be raised from the dead. One way to understand the import of Peter's use of Psalm 16 in this reading is to remind us that even though the gospel comes to us through the witness of other human beings, the object of our faith is never other people, even the apostles themselves, but the God who certainly raised Jesus from the dead. However important Peter's witness may be here, at the beginning of the church, Peter points not to himself and the other disciples, but to God, as the one whose word secures the truth of the resurrection.

IAN A. MCFARLAND

Commentary 2: Connecting the Reading with the World

The first three Sundays of Easter this lectionary year walk us through the aftereffects of Pentecost according to Luke. The lection designated for the Second Sunday of Easter continues Peter's sermon, a sermon that begins with Peter's interpretation of Joel so as to make sense of the Spirit's arrival. While Acts 2:33–35 is omitted from the lectionary, extending Peter's sermon through verse 36 is a must. After all, in 2:33 Peter makes the direct connection between the exaltation of Jesus, both his resurrection and his ascension, and the promise of the Holy Spirit that then is poured out, as foretold, on the assembly. Acts 2 sets the liturgical tone for the meaning of the resurrection, and this portion of Peter's sermon centers on the why of the resurrection. To put it another way, Peter is preaching the *so what* of the resurrection. That is, we will be hard-pressed to make sense of the resurrection for and in our lives without the help and presence of the Holy Spirit. Preaching Acts 2 during Easter needs to tend to this theological assumption. Otherwise, we might too easily favor a resurrection theology that tries to disengage the empty tomb from the daily life of the church.

Set in the context of Easter, Peter's sermon suggests that the mission of the church is indeed to give witness to the meaning of the resurrection, over and over again, in our ever-changing times and places. This is a primary call of the church: not just to assume the resurrection or even to apologize for it, but to testify that Jesus' resurrection is the upending act that has set the Spirit loose. The very preaching of this sermon at this moment insists that the resurrection can never be an event located in the past of the church but is preached again and again when the Spirit's presence is sensed and professed. Moreover, the Spirit itself preaches the ongoing promise of the resurrection. The Spirit gives voice to this truth and gives us voice to utter this truth.

Preaching the resurrection in and for our time and place demands we believe that no power on earth other than God will have the final word, even when such power is perceived to have usurped God's own. Peter connects Jesus' power and authority to God's power and authority, thereby insisting that both Jesus' mission and his ministry were an overthrowing of earthly kingdoms, yet without the obvious indications to prove their defeat. This truth should change the course of how we choose to engage in the world. It means we look for and expect, albeit with anticipated difficulty, the ways in which God is actively fulfilling God's promises, just as David testified.

As central as Peter might appear in depictions of this scene, with the audience riveted by his proclamation, hanging on his every word, this is not likely to be the case for contemporary preachers attempting the same sermon. The absolute assertion that Jesus sits at the right hand of God, wields all authority and power, and is thus over every and any rule or reign that has come before or that will come after is unlikely to be an announcement received without question. How can we possibly make this case? What evidence can we provide to make such a statement believable?

Pentecost is proof, if you will, that the claim of Jesus' power is ours to make as preachers imbued with God's Spirit. In a sense, Pentecost is proof that Jesus' crucifixion, resurrection, and ascension are integral to God's mission because they reveal Jesus' victory over every power. Perhaps such proof, however, is not the kind of proof we typically assume we need. This is not proof by human standards, proof that demands evidence and argument. God is above such proof, but that is the very point of Peter's proclamation. Pentecost is God's claim of Jesus' authority. We preachers simply restate what the coming of the Spirit insists already: that God has upended the world's powers with the power of victory over death. We are witnesses of what God has done by raising Jesus from the dead (v. 32), and we are called to be witnesses in Jerusalem, in all Judea and Samaria, and to the ends of the earth (1:8).

Listening in on Peter's sermon, before we read ahead and hear the response of those to whom it is preached, provides an important opportunity for us who live day to day with the resurrection and Pentecost seemingly so far in our past. Peter's interpretation of Pentecost reminds us that as soon as we assume the resurrection is a long-ago event, we may very well miss the impact of God's life-giving Spirit in our present. Continuity is everything when it comes to interpreting God's activity in the world, which is why including verses 33–35 in the reading is so important. David himself, according to Peter, speaks about Jesus as the Messiah. Critical to interpreting the meaning of the resurrection is a constant hermeneutic of hindsight; the resurrection reveals the very character of God in retrospect.

If Pentecost cannot be connected to Jesus' resurrection, to say we have missed the point might very well be the biggest understatement of the last two millennia. This is an important corrective when preaching the meaning of Pentecost. All too often Pentecost preaching is mostly a forward-looking endeavor, and Acts seems to provide solid evidence for this homiletical move. Pentecost is often called, incorrectly, "the birth of the church," and so it becomes easy to leave the past behind in favor of God's new mission through Jesus to the Gentiles. Here is where Peter's sermon is an ecclesial necessity and most vital. Peter here reminds us that the pouring out of the Spirit was never and could never be a onetime event. It is this constancy of the Spirit as God's presence and power at work to which we give witness. We give witness to this truth whenever and wherever we see the world's powers being toppled by God's power.

As a result, including verse 36 as the proper end to Peter's sermon is critical, because it reminds us of how desperately we need the Holy Spirit to be able to recognize God's reign in the world. Peter's conclusion ("Therefore let the entire house of Israel know with certainty that God has made him both Lord and Messiah, this Jesus whom you crucified") is an accusation of our human brokenness. This is indeed what we do: kill off and crucify anyone or anything that can offer such an abundance of life. We find such promise to be too good to be true, just too hard to believe, especially if the promise is for the wretched masses Luke imagines. Can such abundant life really be God at work? Of course, time and time again, we are quick to cast the blame for Jesus' death on others.

Before interpreting Acts, the preacher must remember Luke, reread Luke, be reminded of Luke's focus and trajectory, a trajectory that assumes that the good news of the empty tomb will be rejected (Luke 24:11), a temptation to which none are immune. Without the Holy Spirit, we are incapable of the kind of witness to which we are called, a kind of witness committed to seeing the continuity of God in a world where leaders and systems fall far short of fulfilling the sure promises of God.

KAROLINE M. LEWIS

Psalm 16

[1]Protect me, O God, for in you I take refuge.
[2]I say to the LORD, "You are my Lord;
I have no good apart from you."

[3]As for the holy ones in the land, they are the noble,
in whom is all my delight.

[4]Those who choose another god multiply their sorrows;
their drink offerings of blood I will not pour out
or take their names upon my lips.

[5]The LORD is my chosen portion and my cup;
you hold my lot.
[6]The boundary lines have fallen for me in pleasant places;
I have a goodly heritage.

[7]I bless the LORD who gives me counsel;
in the night also my heart instructs me.
[8]I keep the LORD always before me;
because he is at my right hand, I shall not be moved.

[9]Therefore my heart is glad, and my soul rejoices;
my body also rests secure.
[10]For you do not give me up to Sheol,
or let your faithful one see the Pit.

[11]You show me the path of life.
In your presence there is fullness of joy;
in your right hand are pleasures forevermore.

Connecting the Psalm with Scripture and Worship

Psalm 16 is one of the most striking of the psalms of trust or confidence. Following on the sequence of Psalms 13–15, which trace the movement from fear to confidence, Psalm 16 proclaims the confident state of the righteous ones who dwell with God.[1] Described as a psalm of conversion,[2] in it the psalmist welcomes instruction and rejoices in "a goodly heritage" (Ps. 16:6) with hopes for the future. The themes of conversion and hope are appropriate for the Second Sunday of Easter, in which the more somber echoes of Good Friday are still in recent memory, even as the resurrection continues to be celebrated.

The transition between the end of the first reading from the Acts of the Apostles and the

1. J. Clinton McCann, "Psalms," in *The New Interpreter's Bible* (Nashville: Abingdon, 1996), 6:732.
2. Mitchell Dahood, *Psalms I*, Anchor Bible 16 (Garden City, NY: Doubleday, 1966), 87.

beginning of the psalm is a sharp one. Given the proclamation of the ancient *kerygma*—the claim that Jesus, who was crucified, has been raised—the hearer might expect a more exuberant beginning to the responsorial psalm. Instead, we find "Protect me, O God, for in you I take refuge" (v. 1). This plea for refuge and protection, with which the psalm begins, can be seen as a response to Peter's accusation in Acts 2:23 that "this man [Jesus], you crucified and killed by the hands of those outside the law." The Good Friday memories of violence are here used to evoke repentance and a new beginning. Peter invites the crowd to join him in his own movement from the denials of Good Friday to hope in the resurrection. God will protect those who cry out to God even, and especially, when they cry out in repentance for the evil that they have done. The roots of Christianity are thus found in repentance and forgiveness.

In the midst of this tension, Psalm 16 grounds the emotional Easter experience, both for the disciples and for the contemporary assembly, by connecting the church with the faith that has gone before and highlighting the resurrection hope that defines this season. Hearers will likely notice the way that the responsorial psalm echoes the first reading: "I saw the Lord always before me, for he is at my right hand so that I will not be shaken. . . . my flesh will live in hope. For you will not abandon my soul to Hades. . . . you have made known to me the ways of life" (Acts 2:25–28). This lengthy quotation is significant in two ways. First, Peter's easy quotation of the psalm is indicative of the prominent role that the Psalms played in the literature and life of the New Testament era. Second, the psalm, while providing a bridge from fear and shame to the confidence of conversion and forgiveness, also highlights the eschatological hope of resurrection.

Peter's quotation of Psalm 16 exemplifies the use of the Psalms as a lens for interpreting the paschal mystery. Contemporary assemblies might carry the more familiar memory of Jesus' quotation of Psalm 22 as a lens for understanding his death. In Acts, Peter makes use of a different psalm to interpret the resurrection. He builds on the idea that the reference to "refuge" in the first verse can be associated with the temple in which he is speaking. The temple itself represents the idea of sanctuary or hope of what one scholar calls "social restoration."[3] Here the preacher might ponder contemporary symbols of refuge in the context of the community's hopes and needs for restoration in the Easter season.

While it would be inaccurate to suggest that the psalmist knew of a doctrine of resurrection, the psalmist (and others) can express confident hope in a future spent in God's presence. This hope, which is grounded in relationship rather than doctrine, can help Christians today to focus on the "who" of God rather than the "how" of the doctrine of resurrection. Peter's quotation invites his hearers into a confident, if theologically vague, trust in God who will not "let your faithful one see the Pit" (Ps. 16:10). This understanding is the cause of gladness, rejoicing, and a sense of security in which a person can sleep well at night.

Here it can be worth noting that while the lectionary situates Psalm 16 as a response to Peter's early morning preaching at Pentecost, the psalm has also traditionally been associated with compline. This latter connection is likely due to the reference to "rest[ing] secure" (v. 9) and to being instructed "in the night" (v. 7). This context connotes the security of having completed the work of a long day and finding oneself safely at home. At this point one turns to God, open to the kind of instruction that wells up from one's own heart. While not all members of the congregation will hear the echo of night prayer, the alternative context invites reflection on resting confidently in God with gratitude for what has been and hope for what will come.

The confident tone of Psalm 16, in dialogue with the hard teaching of Peter in the temple, invites listeners to dwell in tensions, even amid the overarching theme of assurance in the hope of resurrection. Today's Gospel account of "doubting" Thomas also conveys something of

3. McCann, "Psalms," 732.

the erratic emotional experience of the disciples in the days and weeks after the resurrection; fear, confidence, shame, joy, grief, doubt, gladness, and hope swirl around the disciples in a time that must have been experienced as a blur of early mornings and late nights. While the disciples might have experienced these emotions particularly strongly during the days after the resurrection, it is also the case that contemporary families experience the turmoil of fear and hope due to sickness, loss, new opportunities and expectations, throughout the calendar year and even during the Easter season.

RHODORA E. BEATON

1 Peter 1:3–9

[3]Blessed be the God and Father of our Lord Jesus Christ! By his great mercy he has given us a new birth into a living hope through the resurrection of Jesus Christ from the dead, [4]and into an inheritance that is imperishable, undefiled, and unfading, kept in heaven for you, [5]who are being protected by the power of God through faith for a salvation ready to be revealed in the last time. [6]In this you rejoice, even if now for a little while you have had to suffer various trials, [7]so that the genuineness of your faith—being more precious than gold that, though perishable, is tested by fire—may be found to result in praise and glory and honor when Jesus Christ is revealed. [8]Although you have not seen him, you love him; and even though you do not see him now, you believe in him and rejoice with an indescribable and glorious joy, [9]for you are receiving the outcome of your faith, the salvation of your souls.

Commentary 1: Connecting the Reading with Scripture

The Christians to whom the author of 1 Peter writes this opening blessing and exhortation are caught in a tension commonly experienced by followers of Jesus: they are reveling in the glory of their "new birth" (1 Pet. 1:3), while at the same time suffering affliction as a consequence of their identification with the resurrected Christ. The author (probably not Peter) acknowledges this tension and encourages his readers to stay the course by naming another, related tension that defines their existence. That is, they are waiting for their salvation to come, even as they are working their salvation out in this world and life. Their faith in the resurrected Christ leads to suffering, he reminds them; but their hope is that salvation in the life to come will be free of suffering. Their hope for an inheritance that is "imperishable, undefiled, and unfading" (v. 4) allows them to survive, and even see the benefit of, their suffering in the here and now.

Holiness, suffering, and salvation are themes of the letter and are treated as mainstays of all Christian life. The believers who are being encouraged in their faith as those who are "exiles" (1:1) and "aliens" (2:11) in this world are likely Gentile converts who are being mocked and persecuted by their neighbors for trying to live holy lives. Lewis Donelson and other New Testament scholars explain that the recipients of this letter live amid Roman citizens in a "culturally, religiously, and politically diverse environment."[1] Preachers might note that, as is true for Christian believers in our day, the believers to whom 1 Peter was written were not appreciated for speaking evangelically about their faith, as though everyone should follow suit. One reading the text might imagine that the neighbors were particularly aggravated when believers associated conviction about Jesus Christ's resurrection with living lives of holiness that contrasted to their own.

Evidence that the audience of 1 Peter passed judgment that was directed at those around them, and that this provoked persecution, can be seen in 4:3. Here, in contrast to the lives of the believers, the neighbors' lives are said to be characterized by "licentiousness, passions, drunkenness, revels, carousing, and lawless idolatry." More poignant than the neighbors' presumed rage at such characterizations might have been their "surprise" at losing friends to conversion (4:4). First Peter is relentlessly clear that holiness precludes these behaviors and requires

1. Lewis R. Donelson, *I & II Peter and Jude*, New Testament Library (Louisville, KY: Westminster John Knox, 2010), 10.

others, including action (1:13), obedience to the truth (1:22), exercising mutual love (1:22), and blessing others (3:8).

The argument that suffering is a hallmark of a holy lifestyle, highlighted in the opening blessing, is a controversial one today, and preachers should name it as such as they consider the teachings of the text. To think of suffering as a "test" (4:12) that somehow proves the "genuineness" of faith (1:7) and is therefore beneficial, is one step removed from arguing that we should, therefore, pursue it as a good. The exhortation included with the opening blessing does not take the argument that far. Indeed, the Gentile Christians are instructed to rejoice, not because they suffer, but because their "various trials" will certainly one day come to an end (1:6–7). Suffering will be no more when salvation is "revealed in the last time" (v. 5).

This beatific vision of the fullness of salvation bookends the letter. In the opening blessing, it is described in inviting and even triumphant terms. The genuine faith of believers will give way to "praise, glory, and honor" (v. 7); Christians will "love," "rejoice," and be filled with an "indescribable and glorious joy" (v. 8). At the close of the letter, the vision is a bit less enthusiastic, taking on, instead, a more reassuring tone. In the end, after this "little while" of suffering that connects them to all Christians in the world (5:9), believers will be "restored," "supported," "strengthened," and "established" in God's "eternal glory in Christ" (v. 10). The closing promises are more tempered than the opening ones, perhaps because they follow the sobering content of the letter, where believers are charged not only to endure suffering, but to submit to the hierarchical structures of this world for the purpose of modeling exemplary behavior and thereby bearing witness to the faith: civilians to government officials (2:13), slaves to masters (2:18), wives to husbands (3:1).

Today's preachers might note that, though these instructions will likely cause great consternation for Christians who believe they are called to stand against unjust social structures, they do raise important questions for believers in all places and times:

How do disciples of Jesus Christ discern when to defy the expectations of culture and when to conform to them? How do Christians live with the "indescribable joy" highlighted in the opening blessing while at the same time either defying or conforming to cultural mores antithetical to their hope? Two further questions might be helpful for preachers grappling with what joy and salvation look like in light of the instructions in chapters 2 and 3: (1) What difference might it have made to their decision to conform to institutional structures that the readers of 1 Peter were likely lower-class laborers?[2] (2) What difference might it have made that they believed Jesus would soon return (4:7)?

The opening blessing in 1 Peter resonates deeply with other texts for this Lord's Day. Psalm 16 reassures readers that they are protected by God, even though they are surrounded by those who worship idols and live unholy lives. Acts 2:14a, 22–32 tells the story of "the resurrection of Jesus Christ from the dead" referenced in 1 Peter 1:3, testifying that the salvation associated with this event precipitates rejoicing and fills believers with hope. John 20:19–31 tells another story that helps elucidate the text from 1 Peter 1, which in verses 8–9 insists that readers "love, believe, and rejoice" in a Christ they have not seen.

The story of Thomas might be used by the preacher both to acknowledge parishioners' reticence to accept that which they cannot see and to assure them that they, like Thomas and the readers of 1 Peter, can nonetheless be converted to the living hope that will save them. In Thomas's case, conversion is provoked by the appearance of Jesus, so Thomas actually can see, and then believe. In the case of the believers to whom 1 Peter is written, their holy lives are joined with the life of the resurrected Christ and used by God to help others see, glorify God, and be saved (2:12; 3:1).

The rejoicing that suffuses this opening blessing is found in other biblical stories where God promises mortal beings they are participants in something imperishable. Abraham believes God's promise that he will have a multitude of descendants (Gen. 15:6); Mary responds with

2. Donelson, *I & II Peter and Jude*, 10.

"let it be with me according to your word" when told she will bear the Savior (Luke 1:38). With the recipients of 1 Peter, these two are filled with hope, but then comes Mount Moriah (Gen. 22) and the infanticides ordered by King Herod (Matt. 2). Abraham trudges up that mountain, and Mary ponders. With the author of 1 Peter, they, and believers everywhere, struggle to make sense of this world and its sufferings, in light of the salvation God has promised. It is a task of the preacher to honor sufferings while bearing witness to this promise; it is the task of Christians to live out the salvation of the future in the here and now, even if doing so alienates them from the world.

CYNTHIA L. RIGBY

Commentary 2: Connecting the Reading with the World

On this Second Sunday of Easter, the excitement and joy of the resurrection begin to give way to the realities of living out our Easter faith. This day is traditionally called Low Sunday, either from the misunderstood Latin word *laudate* for "praise" or from the feeling of letdown that follows the celebration of Easter. In any case, this day brings to mind the malaise we experience after many of life's celebrations, be they graduations, weddings, or other pinnacles of personal achievement. The graduate must face the often-challenging next phase of life by getting a job or pursuing further education. The newlyweds move on from the reception or honeymoon to the hard work of building a life together. Whatever the celebration, there comes a time when the party is over, the confetti must be cleaned up, and the revelers must return to life as usual with all its joys and challenges.

Peter (or, more accurately, the author writing under the name of Peter) addresses a group of Christian communities scattered throughout Asia Minor who are experiencing a similar kind of disappointment in the closing decades of the first century. Enough time had passed since Jesus' resurrection that they realized his promised return would not be as imminent as they had hoped. Instead, they were forced to figure out how to live out their Christian faith day to day, letting go of neither their hope nor their expectation of Christ's reappearance, while realizing that they were in this race of faith for the long haul. Peter's words encouraged them in their formation of true Christian community and in their pursuit of faithful witness to the surrounding cultures.

Those surrounding cultures, however, proved to be resistant to their witness. They became the source of the "various trials" (1 Pet. 1:6) suffered by the communities to which Peter wrote. Their Christian faith had alienated them from their neighbors, giving rise to a sense of cultural ostracism at best and more severe persecution at worst. That predicament bears striking similarity to the situation in which many Christian communities find themselves today, yielding a clear connection between this text and the contemporary church. Like them we ask, What does it mean to live as Easter people? What does it mean to profess Christian faith decades, even centuries removed from the resurrection? What does it mean to continue to "believe in [Christ] and rejoice with an indescribable and glorious joy" (v. 8) when we might be mocked or ignored for our efforts?

Preachers can easily connect to the challenge of articulating the value of Christian faith for twenty-first-century life, pointing to the work of modern apologists such as C. S. Lewis who have made what has been called "the case for Christianity." Indeed, this text provides the perfect opportunity for addressing the questions of how Christian faith remains relevant for our postmodern, skeptical age and why the church remains the best vehicle for the continued work and witness of Christ in the world.

That continued work and witness, however, come at a price today, even as they did for the churches across Asia Minor in the late first century. Peter's words remind us of the "various trials" (v. 6) we might face before "Jesus Christ is revealed" (v. 7). Despite how much we would prefer it to be otherwise, signing on for the way of the cross and following Jesus means accepting the possibility of suffering as he did. While we may never be called to endure the kinds of trials endured by some Christians in previous ages or in places around the world today, Peter's words challenge us to deepen our faith as we experience the pain and injustices of daily life. Preachers will have no trouble helping listeners understand Peter's reference to faith that is "tested by fire" (v. 7). No matter our life circumstances, trials will come along that will challenge our faith. Those trials may come *because of* our witness—the kinds of trials Peter is addressing—or they may become *an occasion for* our witness. No matter what those trials may be or how they come to us, however, Peter assures us that we are "protected by the power of God through faith" (v. 5).

That assurance of protection leads to another clear preaching connection that arises from this text: the juxtaposition of *suffering* and *hope* that defines Christian faith. This text names what modern psychological studies continue to reveal: the power of *hope* and *faith* in enabling us to cope with the challenges of life. Physicians and psychologists who have worked with and studied critically ill patients note the healing and sustaining benefits of having a belief in something beyond the present reality. Books such as *Love, Medicine and Miracles* by Bernie Siegel; *Head First: The Biology of Hope and the Healing Power of the Human Spirit* by Norman Cousins; and, more recently, *Being Mortal* by Atul Gawande testify to the ways in which hope enables the sufferer to endure and sometimes even overcome physical and emotional suffering.[3] As followers of the resurrected Christ, we have been given "a living hope" (v. 3) that will enable us to endure whatever we experience.

Nowhere is the healing and sustaining power of hope more clearly expressed than in the tradition of spirituals from the African American community. Enslaved people who were suffering severe physical, mental, and emotional abuse transcended their misery by means of hope in a God who, they believed, had not abandoned them. Their visions of a sweet chariot that would swing low to carry them home, a balm in Gilead that would make the wounded whole, and a Savior who knew the trouble they had seen gave them strength to endure the unendurable. The spirituals can provide a "teachable moment" for white communities of faith as they learn from and are inspired by the experiences of those whose faith was tested in unimaginable ways. Invoked with cultural sensitivity and a sincere desire for Christian community, the words and melodies of the spirituals echo through the years and across racial boundaries, demonstrating an expression of profound faith in the midst of profound suffering.[4]

In addition, our text is framed in doxological language, beginning with an ascription of praise ("Blessed be the God and Father of our Lord Jesus Christ!," v. 3) similar to those found in the opening salutations of many of Paul's letters and ending with an appeal to believers to "rejoice with an indescribable and glorious joy" even though we "have not seen" (v. 8) Christ. Peter's words echo Jesus' blessing in today's Gospel text about doubting Thomas, a blessing on those, like us, who have not seen him yet believe.

The preacher can find countless examples of faithful individuals throughout Christian history who did not see but believed, individuals whose witness inspires us to hold fast to faith today. History tells us that some of those Christian witnesses, from saints of the early centuries of the church to the Namugongo martyrs of Uganda in the late nineteenth century, sang songs of praise as they were marched to their deaths. Peter's words remind us that, even on this Low Sunday, we, like those brave Christian martyrs of old, can lift our heads and raise our voices in praise, knowing that we have received "the salvation of [our] souls" (v. 9) in the resurrection of Jesus Christ.

BEVERLY ZINK-SAWYER

3. Bernie Siegel, *Love, Medicine, and Miracles: Lessons Learned about Self-Healing from a Surgeon's Experience with Exceptional Patients* (San Francisco: Harper & Row, 1986); Norman Cousins, *Head First: The Biology of Hope and the Healing Power of the Human Spirit* (New York: Penguin, 1990); Atul Gawande, *Being Mortal: Illness, Medicine, and What Matters in the End* (London: Profile Books, 2014).

4. For more on the origin and power of the spirituals, see James H. Cone, *The Spirituals and the Blues: An Interpretation* (Maryknoll, NY: Orbis, 1992), and Velma Maia Thomas, *No Man Can Hinder Me: The Journey from Slavery to Emancipation through Song* (New York: Crown, 2001).

John 20:19–31

19When it was evening on that day, the first day of the week, and the doors of
the house where the disciples had met were locked for fear of the Jews, Jesus
came and stood among them and said, "Peace be with you." 20After he said this,
he showed them his hands and his side. Then the disciples rejoiced when they
saw the Lord. 21Jesus said to them again, "Peace be with you. As the Father has
sent me, so I send you." 22When he had said this, he breathed on them and said
to them, "Receive the Holy Spirit. 23If you forgive the sins of any, they are forgiven
them; if you retain the sins of any, they are retained."

24But Thomas (who was called the Twin), one of the twelve, was not with them
when Jesus came. 25So the other disciples told him, "We have seen the Lord." But
he said to them, "Unless I see the mark of the nails in his hands, and put my finger
in the mark of the nails and my hand in his side, I will not believe."

26A week later his disciples were again in the house, and Thomas was with
them. Although the doors were shut, Jesus came and stood among them and
said, "Peace be with you." 27Then he said to Thomas, "Put your finger here and
see my hands. Reach out your hand and put it in my side. Do not doubt but
believe." 28Thomas answered him, "My Lord and my God!" 29Jesus said to him,
"Have you believed because you have seen me? Blessed are those who have
not seen and yet have come to believe."

30Now Jesus did many other signs in the presence of his disciples, which are
not written in this book. 31But these are written so that you may come to believe
that Jesus is the Messiah, the Son of God, and that through believing you may
have life in his name.

Commentary 1: Connecting the Reading with Scripture

John's (Three) Resurrection Testimonies. Many associate John 20:19–31 primarily with "doubting Thomas," but our passage is part of three resurrection narratives found in chapter 20. These three stories interweave concerns about seeing, touching, and believing in the resurrection. The first involves Peter and the disciple whom Jesus loved when they see the empty tomb (John 20:2–10). Second is Mary Magdalene's testimony, "I have seen the Lord" (v. 18). Third, the gathered believers echo Mary's testimony when they testify to Thomas (v. 25). In these three narratives, seeing involves repeated attention to Jesus' hands and side (vv. 20, 25, 27). There is also a concern with touching Jesus, though Jesus' command to Mary—"Do not hold on to me" (v. 17)—becomes a command that Thomas touch him (v. 27).

Moreover, there are actually two stories in our passage occurring eight days apart (v. 26). Both times, Jesus presents himself to the gathered community by passing through locked doors and bids those gathered a traditional Jewish greeting, *Shalom,* "peace" (vv. 19, 26). Each time, he presents his wounds (vv. 20, 27). Each time, he teaches or commissions the believers. In the first commissioning, Jesus gives the Holy Spirit to the believers by breathing on them, grants them the right to forgive and retain sins, and sends them into the world as he himself has been sent (vv. 21–23). That is, the first story relates the birth of the church. The second story then focuses less on Thomas's disbelief than on the miracle of believers who have never seen, believers for whom John writes his Gospel (vv. 29–31).

Connecting to the Passion. Several themes from John's Passion Narratives in chapters 13–19 recur in our passage. In this, the first gathering of believers since John 13, Jesus' greeting, "Peace," recalls Jesus' gift of peace in 14:27 and again in 16:33. There, Jesus gives them a gift that counters the very fear the disciples are experiencing in 20:19. Jesus then shows the disciples his wounds, not "the father" as Philip had requested (14:8–9). Is it perhaps possible to see God only by looking upon Jesus' wounds? Jesus' scarred side hearkens back to his wounding in 19:34. So also, the joyful response of the disciples in 20:20 enacts the promises in 16:20–22 that their pain would turn to joy when Jesus sees them again.

The One Who Rose for Us

May nothing seen or unseen begrudge me making my way to Jesus Christ. Come fire, cross, battling with wild beasts, wrenching of bones, mangling of limbs, crushing of my whole body, cruel tortures of the devil—only let me get to Jesus Christ!

Not the wide bounds of earth nor the kingdoms of this world will avail me anything. I would rather die and get to Jesus Christ, than reign over the ends of the earth. That is whom I am looking for—the One who died for us. That is whom I want—the One who rose for us. I am going through the pangs of being born. Sympathize with me, my brothers! Do not stand in the way of any coming to life—do not wish death on me. Do not give back to the world one who wants to be God's; do not trick him with material things. Let me get into the clear light and manhood will be mine. Let me imitate the Passion of my God. If anyone has Him in him, let him appreciate what I am longing for, and sympathize with me, realizing what I am going through.

Ignatius of Antioch, "The Letter to the Romans," from *Early Christian Fathers*, ed. Cyril D. Richardson, Library of Christian Classics (Philadelphia: Westminster, 1953), 105.

Jesus then sends the believers, a theme reminiscent of his teaching in chapter 17, especially 17:18. Next, he breathes on the believers, saying, "Receive the Holy Spirit." This Holy Spirit is the Advocate and "the Spirit of truth that the world cannot receive," a Spirit who will testify on Jesus' behalf and "guide [the believers] into all the truth" (14:16–17, 26; 15:26; 16:13). Jesus' gift of the Spirit presupposes that he has returned to "him who sent me" (16:5). Has Jesus ascended between seeing Mary Magdalene (20:17) and his appearance to the believers (20:19)? The protagonist of the second narrative in our passage, Thomas, is the disciple who asked about where Jesus was going and the way (14:4–5). Finally, note that the life promised in 20:31 echoes the discussions of life in 14:6 and 17:2–3. A sermon might consider how these stories reflect and perhaps even amplify the promises Jesus makes before his crucifixion.

Connecting to John's Gospel. This passage also connects to passages throughout the Gospel of John. For instance, his miraculous appearance in the evening recalls Jesus' walking on water at the same time of day (6:16). Jesus stands among them, just as he did when John the Baptist testified (1:26). The believers' rejoicing mimics that of the friend of the bridegroom (3:29) and of Abraham (8:56). Jesus' breathing the Holy Spirit onto the disciples underscores that he himself gives the Holy Spirit (1:32–33; 3:34; 7:39). As for Thomas, his willingness to die with Jesus in 11:16 belies his supposed faithlessness. The "many other signs" Jesus did points us back to the signs that Jesus performs in John's Gospel (2:11; 4:54; 6:14; 9:16; 12:17–18).

Thematically, throughout John, Jesus refers to himself as one "sent by God" (see esp. 3:16–17). Jesus' commission leads in turn to the sending of the believers (20:21). As a theme, believing resounds throughout John's Gospel (e.g., 1:12–16; 3:15–18), culminating in "blessed are those who have not seen and yet have believed" (20:29). Moreover, the question of what Jesus "has seen" (3:11, 32; 6:36, 46; 8:38) parallels the testimony of what the disciples have seen (20:25, 29) and have believed. A sermon might note that Jesus' ministry continues beyond the cross, to the generations to come, generations who have not seen, but have believed.

One uncomfortable recurrence in 20:19 is John's deep animosity toward the Jews (*Ioudaioi*) (see 2:18; 5:16, and many other passages). Modern interpreters should remember this conflict primarily as an internal struggle among believers, never one intended to be extrapolated to geopolitical or interfaith relationships.

Lectionary Themes. Luke's narrative in Acts 2:14a and 22–32 joins John in underscoring that the first proclaimers of the resurrection bore witnesses to the *risen* Christ (see Acts 2:32; John 20:25, 29). Further, in both Acts and John, Jesus' ministry gains legitimacy because of the signs he performed among the people, signs that Peter claims were evidence of divine attestation (Acts 2:22; cf. John 20:30). However, an interesting tension emerges also. Through a quotation of the Septuagint translation of Psalm 16, the author of Luke–Acts claims that Jesus' flesh does not see decay (Acts 2:27, 31; Ps. 16:10).[1] Yet Jesus' flesh clearly suffers at least an injury; otherwise John 20:20, 25, and 27 do not make much sense. This tension suggests that the resurrected Christ comes to us with wounded flesh, both with eternal power and human frailty.

In addition to its quotation in Acts 2:22–32, Psalm 16 resonates with the Gospel's assertion that God makes known the ways of life (Ps. 16:11; John 20:30–31). Further, the psalmist's confession, "You are my Lord," harmonizes with Thomas's confession, "My Lord and my God" (Ps. 16:2; John 20:28).

Themes of restoring or giving life also resonate with 1 Peter 1:3–9. The writer praises God for giving the community new birth into a living hope (1 Pet. 1:3; cf. John 20:31). John's commendation of those who have not seen echoes the acclamation of the epistle writer to the audience of 1 Peter (1 Pet. 1:8; John 20:29).

Canonical Connections. As in all the Gospels, Jesus rises on the first day of the week (John 20:19), later an important gathering day for the early church (Acts 20:7). Jesus' appearance through locked doors on resurrection day in John parallels Luke's account (Luke 24:36–49). However, there are several key differences. Unlike John's Jesus, Luke's Jesus eats before the gathered (Luke 24:42–43). Further in Luke, Jesus teaches about the suffering of the Messiah, the proclamation of repentance, and the forgiveness of sins (Luke 24:46–47). Forgiveness in Luke does not rest with the disciples, as it does in John. Moreover, Luke's Jesus does not give the Holy Spirit by breathing on the believers on Easter evening, as John's Jesus does (John 20:22); Luke saves that for Pentecost. It can be tempting to reconcile these different Easter stories. What emerges when we let John tell a different story, one aimed at those who believe when they have not seen?

MARGARET P. AYMER

Commentary 2: Connecting the Reading with the World

Doubt Is Part of Faith. For the Protestant Reformers, the doctrine of justification is key, a concern summed up by the Latin phrase *sola fide* ("by faith alone"). Underlying the Protestant emphasis on the doctrine of justification is the question, What must I do to be saved? Martin Luther argued that the Roman Catholicism of his day taught justification by works, whereas the apostle Paul taught a doctrine of justification by faith. In other words, the sinner is *not* justified *because* he or she believes, but faith is our recognition that God provides all we need for justification. Because humanity is fallen, wounded and damaged by sin, we are in need of salvation—a state we cannot achieve on our own. Yet in the twenty-first century the words "justification by faith" have become unintelligible in an increasingly secular culture—and maybe even in many of our churches.

As the Pew Research Center has documented, as of 2014 religiously unaffiliated people represented 23 percent of the adult population of the

1. The Hebrew of Ps. 16 refers to "the Pit" (*sachat*) not "decay" (*diaphthora*) as it does in the Septuagint.

United States.[2] Young adults in particular are more likely to identify as "nones," with millennials (those born 1981–1996) constituting 35 percent of the religiously unaffiliated. Perhaps Thomas, the apostle who refused to believe Jesus had risen from the dead unless he could first put his fingers in the mark of the nails or place his hand in the wound at Jesus' side, is the patron saint of the nones. To the religious none, faith is primarily a matter of intellectual assent to a series of (somewhat incredible) theological claims, such as the virgin birth, the incarnation, and the resurrection of the dead. Two thousand years of human history and scientific progress stand between the events of the resurrection and our generation of believers who have been educated to approach religious claims with skepticism and conditioned to grant final authority on questions of truth to "science." So the image of today's millennial generation looking for nail holes in the Savior's hands seems somehow appropriate. Yet this is no reason to disparage an entire generation. After all, Thomas—one of the Twelve—doubted too. What's his excuse?

Paul Tillich once wrote, "Doubt is not the opposite of faith; it is one element of faith."[3] The implication for making the Christian faith intelligible to a skeptical audience is that we need to reeducate ourselves about *how* to communicate faith to others. Granted, one aspect of religious faith involves granting intellectual assent to a series of propositional statements: God exists, God is love, God is best known through reading Scripture, Jesus is the Son of God. Yet faith is more adequately conceived as a relationship based on trust, established over a long period of time and grounded in an interpersonal encounter in what the Jewish philosopher Martin Buber has described as an I-Thou relationship.

In other words, until we have nurtured the idea that faith is not a series of beliefs but a process of getting to know another person, we stand little chance of breaking down the intellectual obstacles skeptics use to justify unbelief. There is a place for apologetics in Christian theology, but persuasion—not coercion—is a better tool for evangelization, as evidenced by the philosopher Søren Kierkegaard, who suggests that the most apt analogy for those desiring to know God is to read Scripture as "a lover who has received a letter from his beloved—I assume that God's Word is just as precious to you as this letter is to the lover. I assume that you read and think you ought to read God's Word in the same way the lover reads this letter."[4]

In this context, doubt is not a personal or moral failing but merely a natural step in the development of an intimate personal relationship—the most important personal relationship anyone can have. Like all personal relationships, faith needs to be nurtured and encouraged if it is to grow. Therefore, there is no room for judgment or condemnation when addressing doubt.

Making Room for Doubt. I am always moved by the painting *The Incredulity of Saint Thomas* by the Italian baroque painter Michelangelo Merisi da Caravaggio (1571–1610). Caravaggio is known for incredibly realistic and detailed paintings that use dramatic lighting and shadow to portray the human condition in all its grandeur *and* in all its grittiness. This particular painting illustrates the episode in John's Gospel that gave rise to the expression "doubting Thomas." John recounts that a week after the cross and resurrection, Jesus appears among his disciples again; this time he confronts Thomas, saying, "Put your finger here and see my hands. Reach out your hand and put it in my side. Do not doubt but believe" (John 20:27). It is this very moment—when Jesus takes Thomas by the hand and guides the doubting apostle's finger—that Caravaggio captures in all its grotesque anatomical detail. Jesus grabs Thomas by the wrist and actually guides his hand to the spear wound in his side, and Thomas morbidly satisfies his curiosity by sticking a finger right in the wound and probing around.

Inspired by the starkness of this painting, two points grab me about our passage. First, Jesus

2. Michael Lipka, "A Closer Look at America's Rapidly Growing Religious 'Nones,'" Pew Research Center (May 13, 2015). http://www.pewresearch.org/fact-tank/2015/05/13/a-closer-look-at-americas-rapidly-growing-religious-nones/.

3. Paul Tillich, *Systematic Theology* (Chicago: University of Chicago Press, 1975), 2:116.

4. Søren Kierkegaard, *For Self-Examination/Judge for Yourself!*, ed. and trans. Howard V. Hong and Edna H. Hong (Princeton, NJ: Princeton University Press, 1990), 26.

is not offended by Thomas's doubts and seeks to overcome them with these reassuring words: "Do not doubt but believe" (v. 27). Second, once confronted by incontrovertible evidence, Thomas admits the error of his ways and makes a confession of faith: "My Lord and my God!" (v. 28). I take great comfort from this story, precisely because Jesus welcomes our doubts while reaching out to overcome those doubts. In fact, over the years, many have come to consider Thomas the first Christian theologian, insofar as the vocation of theologian involves a lifetime of dancing with doubt; yet in the end—after many struggles and objections—the theologian joins "doubting Thomas" in confessing faith in Jesus Christ as our Lord and God.

Unfortunately, many Christian believers have been reared to think that doubt stands against faith. Some self-righteous Christians even use this very Gospel story as a condemnation of doubt because of what Jesus said to Thomas: "Have you believed because you have seen me? Blessed are those who have not seen and yet have come to believe" (v. 29). This is proof-texting at its worse. After all, the story is not about judgment and condemnation. It is about *reassuring* Thomas in the midst of his doubt *so that* he can come to faith. Recall Jesus' reassuring words to Thomas, "Do not doubt but believe" (v. 27).

Unless I am mistaken, the Protestant Reformation was founded on the belief that all we need is grace, *sola gratia*. What if many Protestants have turned faith into a "work"? What if too many Protestants are all too quick to condemn those who find some aspect of our Christian faith hard to believe? Doubt is not a sin. Yes, Jesus praises those who are able to believe without benefit of incontrovertible evidence, but he does not reject Thomas because of his doubt. Instead he embraces Thomas, takes him by the hand, and provides Thomas with all the evidence he needs to come to faith. *This* is grace in action.

RUBÉN ROSARIO RODRÍGUEZ

Third Sunday of Easter

Acts 2:14a, 36–41
Psalm 116:1–4, 12–19
1 Peter 1:17–23
Luke 24:13–35

Acts 2:14a, 36–41

14But Peter, standing with the eleven, raised his voice and addressed them, . . .
36"Therefore let the entire house of Israel know with certainty that God has
made him both Lord and Messiah, this Jesus whom you crucified."
37Now when they heard this, they were cut to the heart and said to Peter and to
the other apostles, "Brothers, what should we do?" 38Peter said to them, "Repent,
and be baptized every one of you in the name of Jesus Christ so that your sins
may be forgiven; and you will receive the gift of the Holy Spirit. 39For the promise
is for you, for your children, and for all who are far away, everyone whom the Lord
our God calls to him." 40And he testified with many other arguments and exhorted
them, saying, "Save yourselves from this corrupt generation." 41So those who
welcomed his message were baptized, and that day about three thousand persons were added.

Commentary 1: Connecting the Reading with Scripture

The body of today's first reading follows almost directly on the heels of last week's (as we are reminded by the repetition of Acts 2:14a at the outset). Still, there are differences: last week's lesson was a verbatim transcript of Peter's Pentecost sermon. Today's reading focuses more on its immediate effect on the crowd of "devout Jews from every nation under heaven living in Jerusalem" (Acts 2:5) who had gathered to listen to it. As part of the story of Pentecost, the reading continues and sets a pattern for Luke's account of the growth of the church in the later chapters of Acts: first, the public proclamation of Jesus' resurrection from the dead (in the first instance by his immediate disciples, who alone were witnesses to his risen life) and then the reception of that message as gospel—good news—by people not heretofore associated with Jesus' story.

This pattern of the movement of the gospel, from the disciples outward, is a defining feature of the book of Acts. In this it differs from the Gospel of Luke, to which it serves as a sequel (see Acts 1:1–2). Whereas the Third Gospel both begins and ends in Jerusalem (the focal point of God's earthly presence in first-century Jewish understanding), the narrative of Acts begins in Jerusalem but moves ever farther afield—to Samaria, Antioch, Asia Minor, Greece—culminating with Paul's arrival in Rome, the capital of the empire. Moreover, this movement outward includes not merely the gospel's audience but also its ministers. As the book progresses, Luke's focus shifts from the work of Jesus' earthly associates (especially Peter) to that of Paul, who, although a witness to the resurrection (see Acts 9:3–6; 1 Cor. 15:8), did not know Jesus prior to his death.

At the point in the story where today's lesson falls, however, things have just begun to move from the center as we hear of the very first postapostolic converts to what would soon come to be called "the Way" (Acts 9:2). In many respects, the pattern of response recorded here provides a template for subsequent narratives of evangelization in Acts, in which preaching leads to conversion and baptism (8:12; 10:48; 13:48; 14:1; 16:13–15, 31–33; 18:8), sometimes, as here, with a mention of the numbers involved (see 4:4; 19:5–7).

At the same time, there is one striking difference between the account here and later episodes in Acts. That difference relates to the immediate effects of apostolic preaching on its audience. In today's lesson, it seems, *all* who heard "were cut to the heart" (2:37). Although it is not clear that everyone went on to believe and be baptized,[1] there is no indication that either Peter's sermon or the "many other arguments" (v. 40) that followed provoked any hostile response—a point that is all the more remarkable, given that twice in the sermon Peter had accused his listeners of being the agents of Jesus' crucifixion (vv. 23, 36).

By contrast, Luke's account of the subsequent spread of the gospel pointedly supplements accounts of believing reception with emphasis on the hostility produced by Christian preaching, among both Gentiles (19:23–29) and (in a way that can only make the present-day reader profoundly uncomfortable, given the long history of Christian anti-Semitism) Jews (13:42–45; 14:1–2; 17:1–5). This pattern reaches a crescendo in the final scene of the book, where—notwithstanding Luke's explicitly noting that there was division among Paul's Jewish audience, with some believing and others not (28:24)—Paul seems to declare God's wholesale rejection of Israel (28:25–28). Such a judgment stands in striking contrast to Peter's insistence in today's lesson—made to people he names as Jesus' executioners!—that "the promise is for you" (2:39).

This declaration sits almost exactly at the center of today's lesson and demands further attention, for it is the one genuinely theological statement in the reading. Peter's sermon had been largely descriptive: a report of what had happened to Jesus. Today's lesson offers a follow-up that is primarily cast in the imperative: first, "Repent and be baptized" (2:38), and then, "Save yourselves from this corrupt generation" (v. 40). In between these two exhortations stands the reason for it all: "For the promise is for you, for your children, and for all who are far away, everyone whom the Lord our God calls to him" (v. 39).

This statement makes it clear that Peter's injunctions to his audience are not the orders of a dictator, but rather appeals made in the name of a loving God to receive a new life that is offered freely. They should thus be taken in the same vein as those other imperatives, "Take, eat," and "Drink from it, all of you" (Matt. 26:26–27 and pars.). In particular, Peter's statement speaks directly to the problem of the hostility or indifference the preaching of the gospel elicits elsewhere in Acts.

What becomes of those who ignore or actively reject the good news? As already noted, even in this passage, there is at least the suggestion that for all Peter's efforts, not everyone who was present went on to be baptized that day. However, the statement that "the promise is for you, for your children, and for all who are far away," undercuts any notion of their eternal reprobation. Even if some that day ignored the message, the promise remains for them and their children, as well as "for all who are far away." If Peter is to be taken at his word here, "everyone whom the Lord our God calls to him" includes simply *everyone*: the promise is for all, without exception.

One might view the perspective on Christian preaching presented in this lesson as representing the ideal case: a sermon that had included both indictment and promise ("you crucified and killed. . . . But God raised him up," 2:23–24) is shown to elicit from its hearers both repentance (the proper response to indictment) and faith (the proper response to promise). In this respect, it ties in with the Gospel lesson for today, which tells the story of the disciples on the Emmaus road. If Peter's sermon on Pentecost is the first properly "church" sermon (following the convention that Pentecost is the birthday of the church), Jesus' words to Cleopas and his unnamed companion arguably is its prototype, in that Jesus, like Peter, speaks words of judgment (Luke 24:25 and Acts 2:23), followed by interpretation of the OT (Luke 24:27 and Acts 2:25–31). In both cases the listeners are deeply moved (Luke 24:32 and Acts 2:37).

If today's Gospel may be read as providing the background or prototype for the kind of speech that should characterize Christian evangelization, the epistle lesson from 1 Peter speaks

1. It is certainly possible that "those who welcomed his message [and] were baptized" (v. 41) included everyone present, but that does not seem the most natural reading of the text.

to the aftermath of the process of conversion described in Acts 2. The writer presumes that the gospel has been already heard ("You know that you have been ransomed. . . . You have come to trust God," 1 Pet. 1:18, 21), and baptism received ("You have purified your souls. . . . You have been born anew," 1 Pet. 1:22–23). In light of these two facts, believers are instructed to "love one another deeply from the heart" (1 Pet. 1:22). In this way, Peter's letter supplements the message of his Pentecost sermon by reminding us that the point of the gospel is not simply personal assurance of God's favor (though it is most certainly that, too) but also devotion to one another.

IAN A. MCFARLAND

Commentary 2: Connecting the Reading with the World

Set in the liturgical context of Easter, the reaction to Peter's sermon, a sermon that boldly connects Pentecost to Jesus' death and resurrection, should cause us to take a second look at our own reactions. A few weeks out from the empty tomb, it is easy to relegate the resurrection to a onetime event that happened too long ago to make the same kind of difference now that it did back then. Acts 2, smack dab in the middle of Easter, suggests that the Spirit will not and cannot let that happen. The Spirit's arrival confirms that the resurrection was never a correction of a mistake or validation of a plan gone wrong. That the resurrection—and the crucifixion for that matter—was integral, essential, and inherent to God's "ends-of-the-earth" mission of love is perhaps a harder pill to swallow than if we had simply to look over or make excuses for a botched mission.

The truth is that the church needs regular reminders of its identity. We should be a people constantly responding to the meaning of the resurrection, a resurrection to which the Spirit testifies on a daily basis. As soon as the church loses sight of this vision, it has indeed let go of the expansive scope of God's vision, at least according to Luke–Acts. So verse 36 is the ultimate postresurrection confession. Jesus is indeed Lord. Jesus sits at the right hand of God. Jesus is the Messiah, God's anointed one who brings about salvation. This is the heart of the church's confession and witness. This is the only proper response to the resurrection.

Responding to Pentecost and thereby the meaning of Jesus' resurrection, however, is not for the faint of heart. In fact, hearing the truth of the empty tomb "cuts to the heart" (Acts 2:37). It just plain hurts when we realize our own complicity in the sidelining of the resurrection and our own compliance in making the resurrection only something to which we look forward, instead of something in which we delight daily. Responding to the resurrection is immediate, and it is now. "What should we do?" (v. 37) is exactly the question we should ask, not once or twice over the course of our Christian life, but every single day.

This daily response to the resurrection is exactly what "repentance" means in the context of Acts 2. Peter is not requiring a kind of moral confession, acknowledging sin, saying sorry, or forcing an admission of guilt, so much as he is demanding a change in perspective. After all, that is exactly what the resurrection does, with the help and power of the Holy Spirit. This change in how we see things is essential to moving forward. Nothing can remain the same. Fundamentally, Pentecost confirms that the resurrection was and will always be the new perception of the world to which the church gives witness. The resurrection has caused a massive reorientation of the world as we have known it. So we must ask, How will we live in this world now transformed by the resurrection? What should we do? Perhaps put on a new set of glasses so as to see the world in all its resurrected splendor.

It is in this new perspective of life over death, of gain in the midst of loss, of breath when loss seems to have the most power, that baptism is best understood. Baptism signals this change of perception; it signals a commitment to viewing the world and being in the world in a way that anticipates victory over death. Baptism

The Work of God within You

I thought it might be good at this point to give some instruction in the way to come to a true understanding of the Word of God and to a personal experience of the fact that you are taught of God. For if we are not versed in Scripture, how are we to tell whether the priest who teaches us is expounding the pure truth unadulterated by his own sinful desires?

First, we must pray inwardly to God, that he will kill off the old man who sets such great store by his own wisdom and ability.

Second, when the old man is killed off and removed, that God will graciously infill us, and in such measure that we believe and trust only in him.

Third, when that is done we shall certainly be greatly refreshed and comforted, and we must constantly repeat the words of the prophet: Lord, God, strengthen that which thou has wrought in us. For 'let him that thinketh he standeth take heed lest he fall," as Paul says.

Fourth, the Word of God does not overlook anyone, and least of all the greatest. For when God called Paul, he said to Ananias: "He is a chosen vessel unto me, to bear my name before the princes and kings of the earth." Again, he says to the disciples (Matt. 10): "And ye shall be brought before governors and kings, that ye may testify unto them concerning me."

Fifth, it is the nature and property of the Word to humble the high and mighty and to exalt the lowly. That was the song of the Virgin Mary: "He hath put down the mighty from their seats, and exalted them of low degree." And again, John proclaimed concerning Christ (Luke 3): "By him shall all the hills be brought low, and the valleys filled, etc."

Sixth, the Word of God always attracts and helps the poor, comforting the comfortless and despairing, but opposing those who trust in themselves, as Christ testifies.

Seventh, it does not seek its own advantage: for that reason Christ commanded his disciples to take neither scrip nor purse.

Eighth, it seeks only that God may be revealed to men, that the obstinate may fear him and the lowly find comfort in God. Those who preach in that manner are undoubtedly right. Those who cautiously beat about the bush for their own advantage, defending the teaching of man instead of holding and expounding the doctrine of God, are false prophets. Know them by their words. They make a fine outcry: The holy Fathers! Is it nothing that man can do? and the like. But for all their complaining they do not complain that the Gospel of Christ is slackly proclaimed.

Ninth, when you find that the Word of God renews you, and begins to be more precious to you than formerly when you heard the doctrines of men, then you may be sure that this is the work of God within you.

Tenth, when you find that it gives you assurance of the grace of God and eternal salvation, it is of God.

Eleventh, when you find that it crushes and destroys you, but magnifies God himself within you, it is a work of God.

Twelfth, when you find that the fear of God begins to give you joy rather than sorrow, it is a sure working of the Word and Spirit of God.

May God grant us that Spirit. Amen.

Ulrich Zwingli, "Of the Clarity and Certainty of the Word of God," in *Zwingli and Bullinger*, trans. G. W. Bromiley, Library of Christian Classics 24 (Philadelphia: Westminster, 1953). 93–95.

represents this alternate way of seeing things. As a result, baptism should also function as a claim on our purpose. Baptism cannot be reduced to a onetime event, any more than the resurrection can be left behind in the history books of the church. Baptism propels us forward into the larger mission of witnessing to the ends of the earth. Baptism becomes an outward sign, an observable act, that acknowledges our change of sight. We know our full purpose when we insist that God's reign, as demonstrated in Jesus' resurrection and the giving of the Spirit, alters our interpretation of the world. With this new understanding of what God did in the resurrection of Jesus and what God is now up to in the world, it is like being gifted with a new set of eyes, new lenses through which to see God at work. Imagine, for example, viewing a painting of a Bible story you have never seen before. All of a sudden, there are details in the story that come to life.

This baptism also means the forgiveness of sins. The verb here for forgiveness (*aphesin*, v. 38) can also be translated "release of sins," which better fits the ethos of Acts. Forgiveness is release from that which might silence witness or muffle testimony, from that which might lead to a denial of God's power. Released and forgiven, we are freed to imagine our own participation in God's all-encompassing reign. We are freed to embrace a turning of the world upside down, rather than finding ways to pretend that the world can stay the same. We are freed to see the potential of Pentecost, that the Spirit's arrival is "for all who are far away, everyone whom the Lord our God calls to him" (v. 39).

Peter's sermon then comes full circle: they, *all of them*, will receive the gift of the Holy Spirit. Any attempt to limit or circumvent the vastness of God's vision is certain to be overcome by God's expansive grace. The power of the Spirit, witnessed in Acts 2:1–13, is but viewed only at this point in a mirror dimly. Twenty-six chapters are still left to watch the Spirit at work in Acts. We cannot leave the Spirit's work in the past. In fact, it is the Spirit's presence that enables us to perceive the Spirit at work now and in the days to come.

That we should protect ourselves from "this corrupt generation" (v. 40) makes more sense if we have in mind the final section of Acts 2 and its focus on the communal results of Jesus' resurrection and the Spirit's presence. The hallmarks of the community outlined in verses 42–47 function as the very obverse of a corrupt generation. That is, the activities of this now Spirit-filled community named in the final verses of chapter 2 are directly opposite the behaviors of the corrupt communities of this generation. While Peter's imperative is most often translated as "save yourselves" (*sōthēte*, v. 40), it is a passive imperative, "be saved." So Peter insists that we are not the agents of our own salvation; such agency belongs only to God.

Once again, Peter reminds us of who ultimately has the power, who is really in charge. It is another way for Peter to insist that all along, God has been the primary actor in the events that Peter has witnessed. Peter probably said more in his sermon, words and sentences not directly quoted by Luke; this testifies both to the importance of Peter's interpretation of Pentecost and to the limitless nature of what we can say about God. God's activity cannot be contained, by either the number or the content of our words. The ultimate affirmation of the extent of the reach of the resurrection, the ascension, and the pouring out of the Holy Spirit is provided in the final numbers of those added to the assembly. Three thousand persons is not a number to overlook, and it is what we ourselves should anticipate when the gospel is preached.

KAROLINE M. LEWIS

Psalm 116:1–4, 12–19

[1]I love the LORD, because he has heard
  my voice and my supplications.
[2]Because he inclined his ear to me,
  therefore I will call on him as long as I live.
[3]The snares of death encompassed me;
  the pangs of Sheol laid hold on me;
  I suffered distress and anguish.
[4]Then I called on the name of the LORD:
  "O LORD, I pray, save my life!"
. . . .
[12]What shall I return to the LORD
  for all his bounty to me?
[13]I will lift up the cup of salvation
  and call on the name of the LORD,
[14]I will pay my vows to the LORD
  in the presence of all his people.
[15]Precious in the sight of the LORD
  is the death of his faithful ones.
[16]O LORD, I am your servant;
  I am your servant, the child of your serving girl.
  You have loosed my bonds.
[17]I will offer to you a thanksgiving sacrifice
  and call on the name of the LORD.
[18]I will pay my vows to the LORD
  in the presence of all his people,
[19]in the courts of the house of the LORD,
  in your midst, O Jerusalem.
Praise the LORD!

Connecting the Psalm with Scripture and Worship

Psalm 116, a psalm of thanksgiving, is also one of the Hallel Psalms (Pss. 113–118) which are sung during Passover.[1] The historical and contemporary liturgical contexts are important, as is the current setting as a dialogical response to this week's first reading from the Acts of the Apostles. The liturgical season invites deeper reflection on the Easter sacraments of baptism and Eucharist.

Psalm 116's unusual opening sets the stage for the themes of loving dialogue that develop in the pairing of psalm and first reading. As J. Clinton McCann points out, the Psalms in general rarely mention humans who explicitly express love for God.[2] Psalm 116 is the exception, beginning with a proclamation of love. The speaker explains this love with reference to the claim that God "has heard my voice and my supplications" (Ps. 116:1). The psalmist loves because he or she has been heard. This is the invitation to a lifelong, loving relationship: "I will call on [God] as long as I live" (v. 2). Contemporary people might ask, What might this example of listening and loving

1. J. Clinton McCann, "Psalms," in *The New Interpreter's Bible* (Nashville: Abingdon, 1996), 6:1147–49.
2. McCann, "Psalms," 1148.

mean for us in our relationships with God and with one another?

A geographical link between the psalm and the reading from Acts grounds the dialogical reality of the worship that humanity offers to God across generations. In the first reading, Peter's preaching occurs against the backdrop of the temple, the place where the psalms were most frequently sung by Levite choirs. Here Peter preaches of God's promise to forgive sins "for you, and for your children, and for all who are far away" (Acts 2:39). In liturgical reply, the psalmist also speaks of a promise—a human one this time. The speaker refers to "vows [made] to the LORD in the presence of all his people, in the courts of the house of the LORD, in your midst, O Jerusalem" (Ps. 116:18–19). The psalms have accompanied and facilitated the worship of God for generations. The vow of which the psalmist speaks, which is also referenced as a kind of refrain in verse 13, has been made in the temple ("the courts of the house of the LORD," v. 19). In temple worship, an act of gratitude might have been accompanied by a sacrificial offering ("I will lift up the cup," v. 13) and possibly also by the singing of the psalm itself.

In the case of the psalm and the first reading, the promises and vows that are offered between God and humanity take on liturgical, and even sacramental, qualities. In Peter's preaching, it is not the human, but "the Lord our God" who calls (Acts 2:40) and promises, inviting sinners to seek baptism and salvation. The human beings listen to God's voice and "about three thousand persons" (v. 41) welcome Peter's message and begin a new way of life with God that day. They, and we, can now express the words of the psalmist with increasing confidence: "I love the LORD, because he has heard my voice and my supplications" (Ps. 116:1).

Given the seasonal focus on Christian initiation explicitly evoked by the baptismal description in Acts, it is also appropriate to consider these readings in light of the new birth of Christian life and contemporary sacramental celebration. Emphasizing the breadth of the experience of life with God, the psalmist contrasts "the snares of death" (v. 3) with the experience of relationship with the God who saves lives (v. 4). McCann notes that the word "precious" in verse 15, which might in the Christian context be regarded as referring to the spiritual value of the death of Jesus, is better translated "costly." The death is not exclusively positive, but is regarded as a kind of costly expense, since "the whole point of the psalm is that God wills life and works to make life a reality."[3] Paired with the vivid baptismal imagery of Acts 2, Psalm 116 celebrates the new life and freedom of the paschal mystery that are the gifts of the resurrection and life in the church.

In the contemporary liturgical context, the account of the Pentecost baptisms can certainly be invoked as a reminder of baptism, or even a liturgical framework for the celebration of baptism if any in the assembly have requested it during this season. Building on this theme, Psalm 116 can be understood to evoke an invitation to the Table in continuity with the invitation to the font. In Year A, Psalm 116 has most recently been proclaimed on Holy Thursday. This commemoration of the Last Supper that Jesus shared with his disciples evokes the liberating themes of the Passover and the cups of wine that are consumed during the singing of Hallel Psalms, of which Psalm 116 is one.

On Holy Thursday the cup imagery is also evoked explicitly in the second reading, in which Jesus "took the cup also, after supper, saying, 'This cup is the new covenant in my blood'" (1 Cor. 11:25). If the psalm were to be sung using the same musical setting as used on Holy Thursday, the connection to the Lord's Supper could be highlighted with reference to the idea of lifting up "the cup of salvation and call[ing] on the name of the LORD" (Ps. 116:13). If community members are being or have been baptized during the Easter season, the combined readings offer an opportunity for mystagogical preaching regarding these sacraments and their relationship.

RHODORA E. BEATON

3. McCann, "Psalms," 1149.

1 Peter 1:17–23

17If you invoke as Father the one who judges all people impartially according to
their deeds, live in reverent fear during the time of your exile. 18You know that you
were ransomed from the futile ways inherited from your ancestors, not with perishable things like silver or gold, 19but with the precious blood of Christ, like that
of a lamb without defect or blemish. 20He was destined before the foundation of
the world, but was revealed at the end of the ages for your sake. 21Through him
you have come to trust in God, who raised him from the dead and gave him glory,
so that your faith and hope are set on God.
22Now that you have purified your souls by your obedience to the truth so that
you have genuine mutual love, love one another deeply from the heart. 23You
have been born anew, not of perishable but of imperishable seed, through the
living and enduring word of God.

Commentary 1: Connecting the Reading with Scripture

There is a bit of a twist built into the opening clause of our passage. Verse 1:17 is pointedly addressed to those who call God "Father"; readers falling into this category would likely have in mind that the Father God they call upon is merciful and protective, as described just a few verses earlier (1 Pet. 1:3–5). Here, however, God's fatherhood is associated with judgment, not care.[1]

Even more unnerving, perhaps, is the idea that Christians will be judged "impartially according to their deeds" (v. 17), right alongside those who do not have faith in Jesus Christ (see also 4:17). The assertion that believers will be judged by their deeds might seem jarring, especially to contemporary Protestant Christians who subscribe to the Reformation emphasis that salvation comes, as Ephesians 2:8–9 says, not by works, but by faith alone. Preachers might raise the question of how the author of 1 Peter understands the dynamics of salvation, and what can be learned from his approach. What is the benefit of salvation in Christ, if Christians are judged alongside everyone else?

The theological logic of the passage is further complicated, for contemporary readers, by the language of "ransom" used in verse 18. We might assume that it is the lives of believers that are ransomed by "the precious blood of Christ" (v. 19). What the text actually says is that Christians are "ransomed from the futile ways inherited from [their] ancestors." First Peter is here reminding the community that Christ's blood has set them free from the hedonistic lifestyle of their nonbelieving Gentile neighbors (see 4:3). How, exactly, does Jesus' death accomplish this?

Preachers and teachers reflecting on the model of the atonement operative in this passage should take note of the author's commitment to reinforcing the connection of the community of Gentile believers with the history of Israel. Throughout the letter, believers are identified as those who are "alien" and in "exile," drawing a link between their suffering (as those who are being afflicted by their nonbelieving neighbors) and the suffering of the Israelites. Directly preceding our passage, the author makes reference to the prophets of Israel who sought to identify the timing of the "sufferings" and "glory" of Christ (1:10–11).

Here the author goes on to suggest not only that the believers are joined to the traditions of Israel, but that the prophets were serving on

1. This "reversal" is noted by Lewis B. Donelson in *I & II Peter and Jude*, New Testament Library (Louisville, KY: Westminster John Knox, 2010), 45.

their behalf (1:12). This audacious claim, however, does not serve as justification for believers becoming self-congratulatory. On the contrary, it is precisely because they participate in this legacy that believers should strive to behave "obediently" (1:14), even as a form of rejoicing in their inheritance. As the blood of carefully selected animals sealed Israel's covenantal relationship with God, so the blood of Christ, "like that of a lamb without defect or blemish" (v. 19), makes trust in the God "who raised him from the dead and gave him glory" possible for the Gentile believers (v. 21).

The preacher might point out that the author seems to leap to a new subject, mutual love, in verse 22. However, 1 Peter understands love as the obvious topic next to be discussed, treating it as a natural corollary to "obedience to the truth" (v. 22). His logic for the connection is evident in verse 23. It runs something like this: (1) The believers live obedient lives oriented in relation to the truth of their eternal hope in Jesus Christ; (2) the believers are changed by way of these obedient behaviors; they are "born anew . . . by the living and enduring word of God" and begin to manifest "imperishability" in their character and interactions (1:23); and (3) transformation occurs in the lives of the believers, made evident in the cardinal sign that they "love one another deeply from the heart" (1:22). While it is not included in our passage, the argument is capped off by the citing of Isaiah 40:7a and 8 in verse 24, reminding readers of their connection to the legacy of Israel, even while exhorting them to focus not on the flesh that passes away (see also 1 Pet. 2:11), but on the "word of the Lord" that endures.

Chapter 2 continues to describe what mutual love looks like in the life of the community: it eschews "all malice, and all guile, insincerity, envy, and all slander" (2:1). Chapter 3 adds that to love means to have "unity of spirit, sympathy . . . a tender heart, and a humble mind" (3:8). A Sunday school teacher might ask, Can you imagine what our churches today would be like if we loved in the manner described in 1 Peter? In order to do so, the letter reminds us, we need to focus our attention in a place that is likely, for us, counterintuitive: not on ourselves and our own loving, but on the truth of God's word.

Connecting with the other lections, we may spotlight key themes, including conversion, sacrifice, and the character of Christian life. Both Acts 2:14a, 36–41 and Luke 24:13–35 describe changes to the "heart" that come with recognizing one's relationship to the death and resurrection of Jesus Christ. Those listening to Peter are "cut to the heart" when they realize they have crucified the Messiah (Acts 2:37); the disciples feel their "hearts burning within [them]" when supping with the risen Lord (Luke 24:32). Like our passage in 1 Peter, these texts communicate that a change takes place at the core of those who are "born anew" (1 Pet. 1:23) as they recognize their relationship to Jesus Christ.

Importantly, these lections presume a corresponding recognition that one is related to the cloud of witnesses who have also been changed. As 1 Peter celebrates the connection of the Gentile believers to the Israelites, for example, so Jesus in the Luke text draws connections between his history and the words of the prophets, commenting that the disciples have been "slow of heart" to believe (Luke 24:25). The preacher connecting these texts might ruminate that, while conversion always affects the heart, it might look different in distinct parts of the biblical witness. In Acts and 1 Peter, conversion arrives as an immediate event. In the Gospels, the disciples experience it as a slow process.

Sacrifice is connected to obedience, in these texts, as part of the character of Christian life. Psalm 116 mentions "thanksgiving sacrifice" (Ps. 116:17) in the context of alluding to the death of the faithful (v. 15), servanthood (v. 16), and "paying vows" (vv. 14–18). Repentance, as a component of conversion, involves sacrificing old behaviors and "futile ways" for new (Acts 2:37; 1 Pet. 1:18). Connections might be made to additional texts that associate the sacrifice made in Christian life, not with the death of believers, but with their commitment to living in submission to the word of God. One striking connection occurs between 1 Peter 2:5 and Romans 12:1–2; 1 Peter talks about believers making "spiritual sacrifices" and Romans about "living sacrifices." In both of these texts, Christian life is marked not only by turning from the world and being transformed, but by participating, as priests, in the very will and ministry of God.

Noting this might help the preacher imagine what life characterized by "mutual love" looked like for the community of 1 Peter. Perhaps it was not as focused as we might fear on submitting to hierarchical structures (see 1 Pet. 2 and 3), as it was on not allowing the perishable expectations of a broken world to distract believers from living into their imperishable hope.

CYNTHIA L. RIGBY

Commentary 2: Connecting the Reading with the World

As our journey into the Easter season deepens, so does the reality of both the joys and the obligations of being followers of Jesus Christ. In last week's text, Peter pronounced a blessing upon those in churches across Asia Minor who believed in Christ without seeing him and held fast to their faith despite persecution and rejection. Now Peter moves from what scholars have identified as an *indicative* mood that describes the benefits of faith to an *imperative* mood that commands believers to live in a way that reflects the salvation they have been given through Christ's resurrection. In what is essentially a call to a holy way of life, Peter offers the church a vision of what it looks like to be the people of God and challenges the communities to which he wrote and the community of the church today to live into that vision.

This portion of 1 Peter 1 echoes the sense of alienation that was acknowledged earlier in the chapter and characterized the first-century churches who received Peter's letters. While the suffering that accompanied that alienation is not explicitly noted in this text, Peter uses the word "exile" (1 Pet. 1:17) to describe the state of the Christians in Asia Minor. While we are aware of Syrian, Sudanese, Rohingyan, and others experiencing literal exile from their homelands because of their ethnic or religious backgrounds, most of us in twenty-first-century North America will preach and hear this text from places of comfort. Nevertheless, we cannot ignore the feeling of exile that pervades many churches today and gives rise to an important contemporary connection to this text.

Scholars and observers of the present-day church such as Walter Brueggemann and William Willimon have invoked the idea of exile to describe our current condition.[2] Ongoing conversations about the increasing number of Americans who identify as "nones" (those with no religious affiliation) and about the marginalization of the church connect directly to Peter's words as we explore ways to live out our faith in the face of cultural alienation.

The exilic nature of the Christian experience in a world that seems disinterested in traditional religious faith points to a sacramental dimension of this text, as we are reminded of our baptismal commitments. While Peter makes no explicit mention of baptism in this or last week's text, there are clear baptismal references both early in the chapter, where we are assured that God "has given us a new birth" by means of Christ's resurrection (v. 3), and later, when Peter declares that we "have been born anew . . . through the living and enduring word of God" (v. 23).

That new birth comes with great benefits that are named early in the opening verses, including a "living hope," an "inheritance" kept for us in heaven, the protection of "the power of God," and nothing less than "the salvation of [our] souls." It also comes with costs, including possible suffering and social ostracism such as the Christians in Asia Minor were experiencing and as Christians in places such as North Korea, Afghanistan, and Somalia are experiencing today. Our baptisms mark us as the beloved children of God, but they also mark us as odd in a world that is resistant to the gospel.

2. See Walter Brueggemann, *Cadences of Home: Preaching among Exiles* (Louisville, KY: Westminster John Knox, 1997), and Erskine Clarke, ed., *Exilic Preaching: Testimony for Christian Exiles in an Increasingly Hostile Culture* (Harrisburg: Trinity Press Int., 1998).

That oddness, however, is the beginning of what sets us apart as "holy" (v. 16) as we live lives that reflect the qualities of God. The text clearly describes some of those qualities, suggesting ethical imperatives for the contemporary church. The opening verse of today's text speaks to important national conversations swirling around us. God is described as "the one who judges all people impartially according to their deeds" (v. 17). We live in a culture that is torn apart by judgments made on the basis of race, class, creed, and other qualities that serve to divide us from one another. We regard those who do not look, think, act, or speak like us as "others" to be feared and even despised.

The preacher will not have to look far to find examples—perhaps from his or her own community—of the kinds of judgments we invoke upon each other and how those judgments cause pain and alienation. One of the dimensions of holy living described in this text is emulation of the kind of impartial judgment that God bestows upon us. We can be thankful that examples of those who embody such holy living are also abundant, as faithful people manage to move beyond their judgments and come to regard each other in a new way, reaching out to one other in generosity and love.

Such love—"genuine mutual love," love that comes "deeply from the heart" (v. 22)—is another mark of the holy life. Peter's words echo those of Jesus in the commandment he gave to his disciples the night before his death to "love one another" as he loves us (John 13:34). Such love should be the defining quality of the church, but too often we regard that commandment lightly and fail to love "deeply." The preacher can explore what loving "deeply" might mean for the lives of individual believers and for the witness of the church. There are countless stories and depictions in literature, art, and music of the transformative power of love when shared with others.

In addition, genuine love enables us to overcome "the futile ways inherited from [our] ancestors" (1 Pet. 1:18), raising an important psychological connection to this text. Human experience from the OT to the present day has demonstrated the destructive power of "the sins of the fathers" that are visited upon future generations. Much psychotherapy is devoted to uncovering and addressing the baggage we all carry with us from our families of origin and from past life experiences. Psychotherapists such as Edwin Friedman and Ronald Richardson have identified how "the futile ways inherited from [our] ancestors" (v. 18) can distort the people we might otherwise become.[3]

Those same psychotherapists, however, also affirm that we can, with help, overcome brutal childhoods and past indignities. One of the ways in which people have been able to move beyond the paralyzing and distorting power of those inherited "futile ways" is by means of faith in a loving, forgiving, redeeming God. As with stories demonstrating the transformative power of love, preachers can find countless stories of individuals who have found, in God's grace in Jesus Christ, personal redemption and the power to move beyond past injustices.

The text concludes with an affirmation of our baptismal identity as those who have been "born anew . . . of imperishable seed" (v. 23). The metaphor of "seed" serves as a reminder that, as those who have been made holy "through the living and enduring word of God" (v. 23), what we *are* and *do* has lasting consequences. The "genuine mutual love" (v. 22) we show for one another and for all of God's creation, along with other dimensions of our holy living, enable the church to plant "seed" that will take root and spread across the world and down through the ages, bearing witness to God's grace in Jesus Christ.

BEVERLY ZINK-SAWYER

3. See Edwin H. Friedman, *Generation to Generation: Family Process in Church and Synagogue* (New York: Guilford Press, 1994), and Ronald W. Richardson, *Family Ties: A Self-Help Guide to Change through Family of Origin Therapy* (Bellingham, WA: Self Counsel Press, 2011).

Luke 24:13–35

[13]Now on that same day two of them were going to a village called Emmaus, about seven miles from Jerusalem, [14]and talking with each other about all these things that had happened. [15]While they were talking and discussing, Jesus himself came near and went with them, [16]but their eyes were kept from recognizing him. [17]And he said to them, "What are you discussing with each other while you walk along?" They stood still, looking sad. [18]Then one of them, whose name was Cleopas, answered him, "Are you the only stranger in Jerusalem who does not know the things that have taken place there in these days?" [19]He asked them, "What things?" They replied, "The things about Jesus of Nazareth, who was a prophet mighty in deed and word before God and all the people, [20]and how our chief priests and leaders handed him over to be condemned to death and crucified him. [21]But we had hoped that he was the one to redeem Israel. Yes, and besides all this, it is now the third day since these things took place. [22]Moreover, some women of our group astounded us. They were at the tomb early this morning, [23]and when they did not find his body there, they came back and told us that they had indeed seen a vision of angels who said that he was alive. [24]Some of those who were with us went to the tomb and found it just as the women had said; but they did not see him." [25]Then he said to them, "Oh, how foolish you are, and how slow of heart to believe all that the prophets have declared! [26]Was it not necessary that the Messiah should suffer these things and then enter into his glory?" [27]Then beginning with Moses and all the prophets, he interpreted to them the things about himself in all the scriptures.

[28]As they came near the village to which they were going, he walked ahead as if he were going on. [29]But they urged him strongly, saying, "Stay with us, because it is almost evening and the day is now nearly over." So he went in to stay with them. [30]When he was at the table with them, he took bread, blessed and broke it, and gave it to them. [31]Then their eyes were opened, and they recognized him; and he vanished from their sight. [32]They said to each other, "Were not our hearts burning within us while he was talking to us on the road, while he was opening the scriptures to us?" [33]That same hour they got up and returned to Jerusalem; and they found the eleven and their companions gathered together. [34]They were saying, "The Lord has risen indeed, and he has appeared to Simon!" [35]Then they told what had happened on the road, and how he had been made known to them in the breaking of the bread.

Commentary 1: Connecting the Reading with Scripture

On the Way to Emmaus. The first appearance of the resurrected Christ in Luke's Gospel takes place on the Emmaus road on the afternoon and evening of the day of resurrection (Luke 24:29, 33). The risen Christ appears to a disciple named Cleopas (v. 18) and the person who shares his house (v. 29), possibly his wife. Jesus inserts himself into their heated conversation, explaining the scriptural support for the suffering of the Messiah (vv. 25–27). Yet their eyes are kept from recognizing him until he blesses and breaks bread in their home (vv. 16, 31).

Luke's telling of this interaction centers around themes of gradual recognition and understanding, marked by the repetition of themes around seeing (vv. 16, 31, 35); of the word "heart," the seat of knowledge and deliberation (vv. 25, 32); and of words about knowledge, understanding, and recognition (vv. 16, 18, 31, 35). The disciples testify that their "hearts burned" (v. 32), that is, their understanding deepened, "on the road," that is, in the process of walking with and listening to the Christ over a journey of seven miles, likely several hours of walking and listening (v. 13).

Luke also records here the resurrection-day trauma and befuddlement of the faith community. Verses 19–24 beautifully capture a perception of Jesus as a prophet "strong in deed and word before God and the people," a hoped-for redeemer or liberator of Israel (v. 21). The words of these two disciples (v. 19) also record a sense of being betrayed by one's leaders (v. 20) and reiterate their incredulity of the women's testimony about the tomb (vv. 22–24).

Luke's Passion and Resurrection. In the Emmaus story, Luke retells the passion and resurrection of Jesus, highlighting their critical moments. Jesus' breaking bread in Emmaus recalls his bread breaking, three days earlier, at Passover in Jerusalem (22:17–19). Jesus' assertion that the Christ must suffer (24:26) echoes Jesus' desire to eat Passover with the disciples "before I suffer" (22:15). The fervent discussion of the Emmaus disciples (24:15) recalls the fervent questioning regarding who might betray Jesus (22:23). The Emmaus disciples seem to echo those who mocked the notion that Jesus might be a prophet (22:64; 24:19). Additionally, the appearance to Simon at the end of the Emmaus story recalls Jesus' warning that Simon would be tested but that he would return (22:31–32; 24:34). In their conversation with Jesus, the two disciples also recall the crucifixion (23:21–33) and burial of Jesus' body (23:52, 55). Further, they discuss with bafflement the events of that morning, the women's testimony of the empty tomb, the vision of divine messengers, and the confirmation of the empty tomb by Peter (24:1–12).

However, a curious turn in the narrative occurs when the two disciples discuss their leaders' treatment of Jesus. Here they use the Greek word *paradidōmi* (24:20), a word more commonly used in Luke for Judas's betrayal of Jesus (22:4, 6, 21–22, 48). Indeed, the only official connected with the word *paradidōmi* in the passion is Pilate, who hands Jesus over to crucifixion. This reflects a tendency in Lukan theology to place more blame for Jesus' death on the temple elites than on Roman occupiers.

Connecting to Luke–Acts. At the beginning of the Gospel, Luke writes, "I too decided . . . to write an orderly account for you . . . so that you may know the truth concerning the things about which you have been instructed" (1:4). Thus, Luke's concern with understanding and the parallel themes of sight, recognition, and appearance extend throughout the Gospel and Acts. Jesus joins the two disciples unrecognized on the road, just as Jesus had earlier entered the boat of Simon Peter unrecognized (5:1–11). Luke says that the Emmaus disciples' eyes were "seized" (NRSV "kept from recognizing," Gk. *krateō*), suggesting perhaps a divine action that is reversed when their eyes are later opened during the breaking of the bread (24:16, 31). This recalls others for whom eyes and understanding are linked. Consider Simeon as he sings the Nunc Dimittis (2:29–32) or the blinding and restoration of Saul of Tarsus (Acts 9:1–19). By contrast, Jesus weeps because the things that make for peace are hidden from the eyes of Jerusalem (Luke 19:42). Further, Jesus' reported appearance to Simon (24:34) echoes other miraculous appearances in Luke's Gospel, including Gabriel to Zechariah (1:11), Moses and Elijah on the mountain (9:31), the tongues of fire (Acts 2:3), and Paul's vision of a man from Macedonia (16:9).

Additionally, the possibility that one of the Emmaus disciples was Cleopas's wife recalls to mind the role of women in Luke and Acts. Women support Jesus' ministry (Luke 8:1–3), are part of Jesus' teaching (15:8–10), and are present at Jesus' death and resurrection (23:55–56; 24:1–10). This continues into Acts with women such as Tabitha (Acts 9:36–42), Rhoda (12:13), and Lydia (16:13–15).

Lectionary Themes. In Acts 2:14a, 36–41, Peter places blame for Jesus' crucifixion on his Jerusalem audience, as did the Emmaus disciples (cf. Luke 24:20). Then Peter reveals that God has appointed this crucified Jesus as Lord and Christ (Acts 2:36; Luke 24:26, 35). Just as in Emmaus, the hearts of Peter's listeners bear the impact of his teaching (Acts 2:37; Luke 24:32).

Psalm 116 echoes two themes of the Emmaus story. The psalmist prays, "Save my life," and proclaims that the deaths of God's holy people are precious to God (Ps. 116:4, 15), which recalls the testimony of the Emmaus disciples of Jesus' suffering, death, and resurrection (Luke 24:20, 23, 35). Further, the psalmist vows to take the cup of salvation and call upon the name of the Lord, which is reminiscent not only of the Emmaus meal but Jesus' final Passover and the cup of the new covenant (Luke 24:30; cf. 22:19–20).

In 1 Peter 1:17–23, the author asserts that his congregation has been ransomed by Christ. Hear this in parallel to the Emmaus disciples' hope for the redemption of Israel; "redeem" and "ransom" both translate the same Greek verb, *lytroomai*. Further, the author's testimony about the blood of Christ recalls the suffering of the Christ in the Emmaus story (1 Pet. 1:19; Luke 24:20). To the Emmaus disciples, Jesus teaches that suffering precedes the Christ's entering his glory. The Petrine author testifies that God did indeed raise Jesus from the dead and has given him that promised glory (1 Pet. 1:22; Luke 24:26, 34).

Canonical Connections. The Emmaus story testifies to the presence of Christ in the breaking of bread. In Jesus' ministry, bread is often blessed and broken (Matt. 14:19; 15:36; 26:26; Mark 6:41; 8:6; 14:22; John 6; 1 Cor. 11:23). Further, bread breaking marked the early church even at its very beginning (Acts 2:46; 20:7, 11; 27:35). How is the church still marked by the breaking of the bread today?

Emmaus also reminds us to attend to the sojourners. Cleopas identifies Jesus as someone sojourning (*paroikeō*) in Jerusalem (Luke 24:18). In the past, God's people had been sojourners, migrants wandering through lands that they did not own (Acts 7:6. 29; Heb. 11:9). As Christians, we are citizens in heaven, but we remain sojourners here on earth (Eph. 2:19; 1 Pet. 1:17; 2:11). How might today's church continue to attend to the sojourners?

Finally, in the open eyes of the Emmaus disciples, we remember those whose eyes first opened to knowledge, Adam and Eve (Gen. 3:5–7). In the hospitality of the Emmaus disciples we recall Lot (Gen. 19). In these stories, understanding comes from God, the source of all knowledge. To what new understandings is God calling the church today? What will be revealed to us in the breaking of the bread?

MARGARET P. AYMER

Commentary 2: Connecting the Reading with the World

Their Eyes Were Opened. Søren Kierkegaard condensed the Christian gospel to its bare essence:

> Even if the contemporary generation had not left anything behind except these words, "We have believed that in such and such a year the god appeared in the humble form of a servant, lived and taught among us, and then died"—this is more than enough. The contemporary generation would have done what is needful, for this little announcement, this world-historical *nota bene*, is enough to become an occasion for someone who comes later, and the most prolix report can never in all eternity become more for a person who comes later.[1]

Kierkegaard's point is that contemporaneity to the events of the Bible is no guarantee of faith, so whether one is an eyewitness to the miracles of Jesus or two thousand years removed from those events, empirical evidence does not necessarily lead to faith. In other words, the work of God's Spirit in transforming the believer is the foundation of faith, and the very means by which God's revelation is accepted as reliable by

1. Søren Kierkegaard, *Philosophical Fragments: Johannes Climacus*, ed. and trans. Howard V. Hong and Edna H. Hong (Princeton, NJ: Princeton University Press, 1987), 104.

believers. Without the divine act of revelation and the accompanying gift of grace that enables us to recognize this divine disclosure as coming from God, the details concerning the life, ministry, death, and resurrection of Jesus of Nazareth remain abstract historical facts.

The Christian doctrine of revelation teaches that knowledge of God is possible *only* by an act of God. While it is possible to see traces of God in the beauty and order of creation, *we need grace* to recognize the truth in front of us. Therefore, even witnessing something miraculous is undermined by the human capacity for doubt and mistrust. When Jesus walked alongside the two travelers on the road to Emmaus, they were kept from recognizing him. Sadly, despite everything Jesus had said and done to prepare the disciples for his death and resurrection, their doubts undermined their trust in him as God's promised Messiah: "But we had hoped that he was the one to redeem Israel" (Luke 24:21). As readers of the Gospel of Luke, we are in on the secret; we know who the stranger is and what he has accomplished. Still, the story serves as a primer for understanding how God overcomes disbelief and how believers experience that moment of personal enlightenment and awakening.

The passage also confirms that the act of divine self-disclosure is intrinsically connected to the written Word, as Jesus overcomes the travelers' blindness by providing an *authoritative* interpretation of Scripture: "beginning with Moses and all the prophets, he interpreted to them the things about himself in all the scriptures" (v. 27). Scripture mediates God's revelation. At the heart of *Christian* theology is the assertion that the death and resurrection of Jesus are the culmination of God's covenant with Israel. Paradoxically, it takes the risen Jesus to explain this hidden message contained in the sacred Scriptures of Israel. Furthermore, it is the risen Jesus who then teaches the church how to read and understand the whole of Scripture through the lens of his earthly life and ministry.

In the Breaking of the Bread. The Emmaus Walk, a Protestant adaptation of the Roman Catholic *Cursillos de Cristianidad* ("short courses in Christianity") designed to teach lay people how to become effective Christian leaders over the course of a three-day retreat, is a popular worldwide phenomenon. The movement's name comes from our passage in Luke. The group's mission statement is simple: "Empowering leaders to be the hands and feet of Christ." One of its stated goals for the weekend retreat is "to participate in the daily celebration of Holy Communion and to understand more fully the body of Christ."[2]

A growing number of Protestants do not celebrate Communion regularly, or if they do, it is without understanding that, according to Scripture, the breaking of bread in solemn remembrance was the chief act of early Christian worship. In sixteenth-century Geneva, the consistory required the celebration of the Lord's Supper a minimum of four times a year, though John Calvin urged a greater frequency, celebrating the sacrament *every* Sunday, once at the dawn service and again at the main midmorning service, so as to accommodate as many schedules as possible. In fact, Calvin describes the communion as "a spiritual mystery, which cannot be seen by the eye, nor comprehended by the human understanding," yet in the bread and the wine "we may say that Jesus Christ is there offered to us that we may possess Him." Thus he appeals to believers that they not abstain from the Supper too often, since God wants us to approach the sacrament in repentance, not perfection: "For if we allege as pretext for not coming to the supper that we are still weak in faith or in integrity of life, it is as if a person excuse himself from taking medicine because he is sick."[3]

The language in our passage recalls Jesus feeding the five thousand as well as the Last Supper with his disciples, so the comparison to the Lord's Supper is easily and naturally made. In fact, the pacing of the scene, in which there is act of table fellowship (v. 30) that leads to an act

2. See http://emmaus.upperroom.org/about.

3. John Calvin, "A Short Treatise on the Lord's Supper," in *John Calvin: Writings on Pastoral Piety*, ed. and with trans. by Elsie Anne McKee (New York: Paulist, 2001), 106–8.

of revelation (v. 31) echoes the earliest liturgical form of the communion recorded in 1 Corinthians 11:23–26. Furthermore, Luke links the reading and interpretation of Scripture with the breaking of bread, which leads to confessing that Jesus is Lord (24:34).

The Rule of Faith. Before the NT canon was finalized, the early church fathers were guided by an oral tradition that originated in the preaching of Jesus and the apostles known as the *regula fidei* or "rule of faith," which resembled an earlier and shorter version of the Apostles' Creed. In essence, this rule served as a summary statement of core Christian beliefs, such as faith in the one God who created heaven and earth and who became human for our salvation. Our passage contains vital fragments of this early creed to remind us that while faith is grounded in a transformative encounter with God, this encounter also has a concrete content: (1) continuity between the Old and New Testaments (vv. 25–27), (2) the necessity of Jesus' death on the cross (v. 26), (3) an affirmation that Jesus is the Messiah (v. 26), and (4) confirmation of God's promised resurrection (v. 34).

Accordingly, though faith involves an element of personal trust precipitated by a transformative encounter with God, this trust involves a number of *specific beliefs* that communicate who God is, what God is like, and how best to relate to God as God. Belief is not the mechanical end product of a series of intellectual affirmations. It is a gift of God, an act of divine self-revelation in which the believer is joined in covenant with God, which brings with it reliable knowledge of God. Just as Cleopas and his companion were moved to share what they witnessed (v. 35), we are called to share the faith we have been given.

RUBÉN ROSARIO RODRÍGUEZ

Fourth Sunday of Easter

Acts 2:42–47
Psalm 23
1 Peter 2:19–25
John 10:1–10

Acts 2:42–47

42They devoted themselves to the apostles' teaching and fellowship, to the
breaking of bread and the prayers.
43Awe came upon everyone, because many wonders and signs were being
done by the apostles. 44All who believed were together and had all things in
common; 45they would sell their possessions and goods and distribute the proceeds to all, as any had need. 46Day by day, as they spent much time together in
the temple, they broke bread at home and ate their food with glad and generous
hearts, 47praising God and having the goodwill of all the people. And day by day
the Lord added to their number those who were being saved.

Commentary 1: Connecting the Reading with Scripture

Today's first reading continues directly from last week's, bringing to a conclusion the story of the first Pentecost. Last week, the lesson described the immediate effects of the first Christian sermon as delivered by Peter to a cosmopolitan crowd of Jews who had gathered in astonishment at the commotion that ensued when the Spirit descended on the assembled disciples. In response to this sermon, we were told how the members of that audience were "cut to the heart" (Acts 2:37) and urged to repent, and how they responded by welcoming the gospel message and being baptized. The reading for today completes the story by describing the life led by those who came to believe on that first Pentecost Sunday.

The description is brief, but evocative. Perhaps it is to be a model for the ongoing life of the church, but it does stand at the beginning of the church's history as an anticipation of the end, when all the saints in heaven gather as equals around the throne of the Lamb. Most strikingly, it suggests an erosion of any distinction between sacred and secular, since the newly baptized committed themselves both to common worship ("the apostles' teaching and fellowship, to the breaking of bread and the prayers," Acts 2:42) *and* to common life in the world (for they "were together and had all things in common," v. 44). Moreover, this new form of life seems to have left a positive impression even on outsiders, for we are told that the fledgling community secured "the goodwill of all the people," so that "day by day the Lord added to their number those who were being saved" (v. 47).

It is often remarked that Luke provides a highly idealized picture of the church's early days, and even a fairly superficial reading of Acts supports that judgment. At the same time, this blanket characterization masks important features of the book's narrative trajectory in which the church's situation becomes progressively more fraught, even as the gospel message moves beyond the confines of Jerusalem to Judea, Samaria, Asia Minor, Greece, and, ultimately, Rome itself. Seen in this broader perspective, the situation described in Acts 2 represents an initial state of harmony in Christian life that almost immediately passes away.

Thus, in the very next episode in Luke's narrative, Peter (after preaching a sermon very similar to the one he gave on Pentecost) is promptly arrested by the temple authorities (4:1–3), inaugurating a relationship of conflict with the Jewish leadership that continues right through the end of the book with the arrest and trial of Paul (chaps. 21–26). Nor are the threats to the church merely external. Tensions also arise within the community itself. For example, the practice of sharing possessions leads to the terrifying story of Ananias and Sapphira, two converts who are both struck dead for failing to share their wealth fully with the community and lying about their resources (5:1–11). There is further trouble in this same sphere, as disputes over the distribution of food among widows from different ethnic groups requires apostolic intervention (6:1–4). More controversy arises over the implications of the gospel message—specifically, whether Gentile converts (a category of believer not yet even on the horizon in Acts 2) need to observe the whole of the Mosaic law. While an apostolic council manages to hammer out a compromise solution (Acts 15), the question continues to fester and emerges again at the end of the book in connection with the events surrounding Paul's arrest (see 21:17–29).

When viewed in relation to all that will follow in Luke's narrative, the situation described at the end of Acts 2 is paradoxical. In one respect, the three thousand or so persons (2:41) who form the first community are not a patch on the numbers that will join later. The very next episode in Acts yields five thousand believers (4:4), Peter's arrest notwithstanding. Subsequent chapters report unnumbered converts from all around Palestine and the eastern Mediterranean. At the same time, the harmony and consensus that Luke ascribes to the church's first days are not sustained and never regained. In short, at the same time that the church grows more "catholic" by virtue of its geographic and demographic spread, it also becomes, seemingly, more fractured, both internally and with respect to its relationship with the wider world.

In this context, it is helpful to place this lesson in relation to the day's other readings. It has the distinction of being the only lesson that does not invoke the pastoral imagery of sheep and shepherds, the traditional focus of the Fourth Sunday of Easter (sometimes called Good Shepherd Sunday for that reason). Among the other three lessons, the psalm arguably offers the most thematically obvious connections with the text from Acts, inasmuch as Luke's description of the serene existence of the first community, dwelling at peace with one another and those about them, parallels the psalmist's calm assurance that God will provide what we need for sustenance, protect us from all evil, and secure a life of abundance, goodness, and mercy.

By contrast, the other two lessons are more suggestive of the tensions that will accompany the growth of the church in the period after those halcyon days immediately following Pentecost. The author of 1 Peter has external threats to the community in view, leading him to exhort the congregations of Asia Minor to which he writes to follow Jesus' example of grace under pressure when facing persecution, just as sheep follow their shepherd. The Gospel reading is more suggestive of internal dangers, the threat of false leaders who try but fail to lead the sheep to destruction: "the sheep . . . will run from him because they do not know the voice of strangers" (John 10:4–5).

Interestingly, however, Jesus' own role in this Gospel text is unclear. In the first part of the reading, he speaks of the shepherd as the one who enters the sheepfold by the gate, in contrast to the one who "climbs in by another way" (v. 1). These verses thus seem to suggest that Jesus is the shepherd, but things are not that simple. For when Jesus realizes that his audience has failed to understand his pastoral metaphor and attempts to explain what he means, he identifies himself not with the shepherd ("I am the good shepherd" comes only later on in the chapter and is reserved for this same Sunday in Year B of the lectionary) but with the gate to the sheepfold. Moreover, as Jesus works with this image, the figure of the shepherd, the leader whom the sheep need to follow in order to find good pasture, simply drops out: "Whoever enters by me will be saved, and will come in and go out and find pasture" (v. 9), apparently without any need of a shepherd to lead them.

The theme of the church as a leaderless flock is not central to John or Acts; in fact, after John 10 the next concentration of pastoral imagery comes in chapter 21, when the risen Jesus commissions Peter as the community's shepherd. Nevertheless, the disappearance—however temporary—of the shepherd figure in John 10:7–10 has an echo in the account of the church in Acts 2:42–47, where—again only temporarily—the life of the community can be described without reference to any one member having authority over another. It is not a situation that will last, nor is there any indication Luke intends it to be a model for the ongoing life of the church, but it does point to the church's eschatological expectation and hope.

IAN A. MCFARLAND

Commentary 2: Connecting the Reading with the World

At this point, we have arrived at the final reading of three weeks in the lectionary that take us through Acts 2 in the Easter season. So interpretation of this last lection should reflect backwards, to the beginning of Acts 2 and the event of Pentecost, but should also be attentive to the foreshadowing of what is to come. That is, this vision of community should be carried forward to the lections from Acts remaining as well as into the Pentecost season. The meaning of Pentecost for the community of the faithful, particularly in the midst of the season of Easter, is not something to let go of too quickly. We do so at our own peril, leaving behind a liturgical and ecclesial connection that will be harder to make as the weeks progress. As we move into the season of Pentecost, we inevitably need Pentecost's connection to resurrection to avoid our "ordinary" Pentecostal preaching.

It is worth the preacher's time to contemplate, only a few Sundays away from Easter, the meaning and function of a community defined and determined by the resurrection. The ways in which the Easter truth, the Easter proclamation, makes a distinct claim on the church's communal identity should be at the center of post-Easter preaching. Otherwise, both the resurrection and Pentecost become individual moments in the lives of believers, personal professions that allow us to negotiate and navigate the meaning of the resurrection and Pentecost without attention to the other, without acknowledging how our role in the community of the faithful might have to change going forward.

Resurrection is not simply a personal claim that secures your after-death reality. Resurrection brings you into a community that follows Jesus in order to live as Easter people. We need the community so as not to forget who we truly are. It is too easy these days to individualize our faith confessions, as if they did not make a difference for how we move about in the world and how we view the other. Resurrection, fundamentally, is a communal affair, a promise that directs a way of living now and determines a community in our future.

It would be easy to dismiss this passage as having any sort of significant demands for our contemporary congregations and communities of faith. After all, the entire description seems rather idyllic, a utopian Christian community living an ideal beyond our practical grasps. Perhaps that is true in some ways. Perhaps we have allowed it to be. The ethical and moral implications of the community described in these last verses of Acts 2 seem far beyond possibility, given our contextual circumstances and expectations of acceptable living and social norms. Again, perhaps this is an excuse, a way to wiggle out of the demands that the resurrection and the giving of the Holy Spirit make. If we are honest, we might admit that too often we are satisfied with the lowest common denominator when it comes to ethics and morality. It is as if we expect to fail and so we set the bar low, justifying our inability to achieve such high standards of Christian community. Why we are willing to settle? Why we are so quick to consider this description of community as beyond our natural reach?

Maybe that is the point. On our own, left to our own devices, achieving such ideals is impossible. However, with the power of the Holy Spirit, we are at the very least called to lean into this kind of community. Moreover, the Spirit might just teach us how to expect it.

How we attempt to navigate the structures of community, particularly when community constructs are in peril, is a noteworthy question these days. This is likely most obvious in the ways in which dystopian literature and films have captured the cultural imagination. Consider, for example, the AMC television series

The Walking Dead. Left without certain and dependable paradigms, how does community get constructed? What are the standards for communal living, and who gets to define those standards? What are those marks that make community possible in the first place?

With the Spirit's help, we might just be able to get behind some of these criteria of a post-Pentecost, resurrection-centered Christian community. We might suppose that we can spend more time together (v. 46). After all, for many church members, church still remains a time-devoted aspect of life. Breaking bread at home and eating food with glad and generous hearts is likely an activity that is possible and might even be fun to pursue (Acts 2:46). Praising God is still within the realm of possibility, though temporary or halfhearted praise of God does not work for Luke when a primary characteristic of believers in Acts is constancy of worship (v. 47).

Things get a little more difficult when it comes to other identifiers of Christian community, especially when it is a community that believes in the resurrection and expects the Holy Spirit actually to show up. Having the goodwill of all the people is not a trait that too many would associate with Christian communities these days (v. 47). In fact, the opposite might be true.

Of course, how "goodwill" is defined would be a critical task of the preacher, especially in the context of the theology of Luke–Acts. At the same time, we must acknowledge the lack of goodwill toward the other expressed by certain Christians and Christian communities. We do not have to look far to name the ways in which groups that identify as Christian actively discriminate against minoritized persons in the purported name of biblical principles. Where, how, and why the opposite of goodwill is executed in our contexts becomes a critical component to preaching this passage. Goodwill that marks a community as distinguishably Christian is a characteristic most in peril in our days.

Still we have yet to come to terms with verses 44–45. Of course, these verses are contextually defined, but how and why we allow that to be an easy excuse toward dismissal of their demands is worth a sermon all on its own. The practicalities are apparent, and the challenges are most certainly evident. However, as soon as we let the practicalities and challenges excuse actual wrestling with the vision of Christian community exemplified in this passage, we should pause and ask ourselves, Why? Why do we so quickly dismiss these demands? Why do we so immediately eschew this community's response as something beyond our reach? Have we relegated the sharing of possessions to first-century ideals? Might we imagine that something different might be observable in how we are community?

A resurrection community should be perceptible. At the very least, this passage provides an opportunity for us to ask our own communities if this is true for them. If the belief in the resurrection and its power to transform lives here and now is not perceivable in all that we do and say with each other and with others, the very center of a Christian community is at stake. When we start to think that fellowship, the sharing of meals, whether the Lord's Supper or a church picnic, prayer and praise, mutuality and support, and having glad and generous hearts are all things beyond our abilities, then Pentecost has indeed become a relic of the past.

KAROLINE M. LEWIS

Psalm 23

[1]The LORD is my shepherd, I shall not want.
   [2]He makes me lie down in green pastures;
he leads me beside still waters;
   [3]he restores my soul.
He leads me in right paths
   for his name's sake.

[4]Even though I walk through the darkest valley,
   I fear no evil;
for you are with me;
   your rod and your staff—
   they comfort me.

[5]You prepare a table before me
   in the presence of my enemies;
you anoint my head with oil;
   my cup overflows.
[6]Surely goodness and mercy shall follow me
   all the days of my life,
and I shall dwell in the house of the LORD
   my whole life long.

Connecting the Psalm with Scripture and Worship

On this Good Shepherd Sunday, in which Psalm 23 is proclaimed with a Gospel reading in which Jesus compares himself to the gate of a sheepfold, it can be especially helpful to consider one of the most well-known and best-loved psalms in a fresh context. Considering Psalm 23 as a response to another well-known passage from Acts regarding the ideals of the earliest Christians can open new, yet related, opportunities for reflection.

As with previous weeks, the temple setting of Acts reminds us of the temple setting of the psalms. McCann notes that despite the agrarian imagery that is usually emphasized—the "green pastures," "still waters" (Ps. 23:2), and even "dark valley[s]" (v. 4)—the reference to the "house of the LORD" in verse 6 could be seen as a reference to the temple. In this light, the imagery of table, oil, and cup (v. 5) could evoke items associated with temple worship and the feasts that might follow.[1] While these are also items of everyday usage, here that everyday usage is placed in the specific context of a life lived with God. Such imagery could be used to build on the connections to the Lord's Supper that emerged in the previous week's readings.

In the midst of this everyday imagery, both readings also indicate an eschatological ideal in which any individual can say with confidence, "I shall not want" (v. 1). In contrast to the experiences of loss or fear, the psalmist speaks confidently of a life of "goodness and mercy" (v. 6) spent in the company of the Lord. As one scholar points out, the verb "to follow," which is here applied to "goodness and mercy," in fact has the sense of "pursue," a word that in the Psalms is often used to describe the actions of

1. J. Clinton McCann, "Psalms," in *The New Interpreter's Bible* (Nashville: Abingdon, 1996), 6:769.

Serve God and Have God in Your Heart

Take care, as one living in a foreign land, do not prepare for yourself one thing more than is necessary to be self-sufficient, and be prepared so that whenever the master of the city [of this world] wants to expel you because of your opposition to his law, you can leave his city and come to your own city and joyfully conform to your law, free from insult. Take care, therefore, that you serve God and have him in your heart; work God's works, remembering his commandments and the promises that he made, and trust him to keep them, if his commandments are kept. So, instead of fields buy souls that are in distress, as anyone is able, and visit widows and orphans, and do not neglect them; and spend your wealth and all your possessions, which you received from God, on fields and houses of this kind. For this is why the Master made you rich, so that you might perform these ministries for him.

Shepherd of Hermas, in *The Apostolic Fathers*, ed. Michael W. Holmes (Grand Rapids: Baker, 2004), 419, 421.

enemies.[2] Here we find that good rather than evil actively pursues the one who walks with God. In the case of the psalm, this confidence is placed directly in God, who is depicted as a competent and loving shepherd. The shepherd protects, comforts, nourishes, and restores. While these phrases are familiar, one might dig deeper, asking, What does it mean for God to "restore my soul"? Are there things in our lives that lead to a sense of erosion of the soul? What might the experience of restoration be like?

The reading from the Acts of the Apostles can help to answer this question. The description in Acts is also that of an eschatological ideal of the church. Here, members of the community, like the psalmist, can confidently say, "I shall not want" (v. 1). No one will want for anything, because it is clear that the people "had all things in common" and distributed "to all, as any had need" (Acts 2:44–45). Those in the Acts community are depicted as being as happy as the metaphorical sheep in Psalm 23. Rather than having "a table [set] before" them (Ps. 23:5), "they broke bread at home" (Acts 22:46). Instead of an overflowing cup (Ps. 23:5), they eat "with glad and generous hearts" (Acts 22:46). Their companionship (bread sharing) protects, comforts, nourishes, and restores them. Since each is acting in response to her or his belief, and most likely also to the baptism that was described in the previous story (Acts 2:36–41), community members place their confidence in God's "goodness and mercy" (Ps. 23:6), which have called together a community of generous people who care about one another.

The final verse of the passage from Acts invites listeners to consider what it means to be saved. In the Gospel reading, Jesus, referring to himself as the gate to the sheepfold, says, "Whoever enters by me will be saved, and will come in and go out and find pasture" (John 10:9). Psalm 23 could also be seen as a succinct answer to questions about the experience of salvation: here it is a life spent wandering the right path through pastures and valleys with God. The model community in Acts provides a concrete example of the lived reality of salvation in the church community. They have entered through the gate of baptism in Christ and are now about the business of coming in, going out (see John 10:9), and helping others to find restoration for their souls.

As the church continues to celebrate the Easter feast, images of overflowing tables and cups can be brought together with the image of a thriving community in Acts. Contemporary listeners might be invited to reflect on the relief that a poor individual or family in first-century Jerusalem might have felt on joining the community of believers; suddenly the kingdom of God has been realized for this person or family. The hungry are given good things not due to charity, but out of the justice established by the community's practice. All have become needy, yet all can be confident that their needs will be met. Both the need and the bread are shared.

RHODORA E. BEATON

2. McCann, "Psalms," 768.

1 Peter 2:19–25

[19]For it is a credit to you if, being aware of God, you endure pain while suffering unjustly. [20]If you endure when you are beaten for doing wrong, what credit is that? But if you endure when you do right and suffer for it, you have God's approval. [21]For to this you have been called, because Christ also suffered for you, leaving you an example, so that you should follow in his steps.

> [22]"He committed no sin,
> and no deceit was found in his mouth."

[23]When he was abused, he did not return abuse; when he suffered, he did not threaten; but he entrusted himself to the one who judges justly. [24]He himself bore our sins in his body on the cross, so that, free from sins, we might live for righteousness; by his wounds you have been healed. [25]For you were going astray like sheep, but now you have returned to the shepherd and guardian of your souls.

Commentary 1: Connecting the Reading with Scripture

Any preacher or teacher who studies this lection in its scriptural context will immediately notice it does not include verse 18, the verse that addresses the teachings that follow to "slaves." The verse is one of the most controversial in the New Testament, because it seems to (and has historically been used to) endorse slavery. "Accept the authority of your masters with all deference," it reads, emphasizing that this is to include masters who are "harsh" as well as those who are "gentle" (1 Pet. 2:18). This instruction sets up the argument of our passage, which is that any suffering slaves experience as a consequence of bad behavior or disobedience to the master receives no "credit." "God's approval" is the reward for those slaves who "do right" and "suffer for it" (v. 19). Given that verse 18 clarifies the verses that follow, why is it omitted from our passage?

New Testament scholar Joel Green suggests that although verse 18 mentions household "slaves" (*oiketai*), the author is, first and foremost, addressing all members of the community. Two verses prior, 1 Peter referenced them together as God's "servants" (*douloi*, v. 16). In moving to discuss how household slaves should interact with their "non-Christian masters," the author is speaking to a "microcosm" of the broader dynamic in which the Gentile Christians are "a marginal group within the wider world."[1] Slavery is treated as but one instance of how all Christians in the community are expected to "accept the authority of every human institution" (2:13).

This line of argument might help to make sense of why verse 18 is not included in our lection. Perhaps it was thought that the risk of misunderstanding verses 19–21 to apply only to household slaves would be greater if the verse, with its pointed reference to "slaves," was included. Yet the preacher or teacher will also want to reflect on some problems that may have factored into the logic for omitting verse 18, however unintended. For example, if it is true that all members of the community are in some way "slaves" in relation to their nonbelieving neighbors who are afflicting them, what do we then make of the parallel paradigm, in the following chapter, that wives "accept the authority of [their] husbands" (3:1)? Are all members of

1. Joel Green, "1 Peter 2:19–25," in *Feasting on the Word: Preaching the Revised Common Lectionary, Year A, Volume 2,* ed. David L Bartlett and Barbara Brown Taylor (Louisville, KY: Westminster John Knox, 2010), 437.

the believing community somehow called to be submissive wives to their non-Christian "husbands" (non-Christian neighbors) in hopes they will be "won over" (3:1)? Perhaps; but sermons should not neglect the more straightforward reading of the texts: that 1 Peter really is emphasizing that literal slaves should submit even to abusive masters, and that wives should think of their husbands as their "lord" (3:6).

How do we hear these texts as the Word of God, even when we disagree? As Phyllis Trible has suggested, perhaps we can learn something about what God is saying to us about slavery, submission, and oppressive power dynamics from our resistance to texts like these and their history of interpretation.[2] At the very least, the suggestion might be made that the people of God read this text *descriptively* (taking the context of 1 Peter into account) instead of *prescriptively* (treating the instructions in the letter as though they should be followed in every place and time).

Our passage goes on to make two important sets of distinctions, one concerned with types of suffering and the other with possible responses to it. First: there is suffering that is a consequence of wrongdoing, and there is suffering that is a consequence of "doing right" (v. 20). Second: one can respond to suffering caused by abuse by "returning abuse," or one can respond by refusing to "threaten" and instead entrusting oneself "to the one who judges justly" (2:23). The author exhorts the believing community to follow Christ's example in suffering so closely that any suffering will be interpreted as a consequence of their holiness. Similarly, the believers are not to retaliate, but to set the "eye for an eye" of Exodus 21:24 paradigm aside in favor of Jesus' teaching (see Matt. 5:38–39) and example (1 Pet. 2:21–25; also note Suffering Servant images in Isaiah, especially Isa. 53:3).

First Peter insists this approach to suffering is his readers' calling (1 Pet. 2:21); throughout the letter he emphasizes that their identity is different than it was before, different than the nonbelieving neighbors around them. They are to be "holy" (1:16), "obedient to the truth" (1:22), and living in light of their new birth in relation to that which is "imperishable" (1:23). They are to set themselves apart, as those who are "precious in God's sight" (2:4), as "spiritual houses" (2:5) who live differently and suffer accordingly as "God's own people," "a chosen race, a royal priesthood, a holy nation" (2:9). Clearly, these descriptions connect the audience of 1 Peter to Israel as well as to Christ.

Those who study this text in preparation for teaching or preaching may productively ponder how the writer understands the relationship between Jesus' suffering, the sufferings of the world, and salvation. This is a controversial subject in our day, and we want to be careful not to glorify suffering in ways that serve to justify or perpetuate it. First Peter is not necessarily showcasing suffering, but rather trying to make sense of the community's lived experience of suffering in light of their faith (see also 4:12). There are at least three pastoral points of reassurance embedded in the author's exhortation to help the believers live in relation to their "imperishable hope" (1:1–5) even in their difficult day-to-day lives: (1) God is aware of what is happening and is on the side of the holy sufferer (2:20); (2) suffering is a mark both of one's identification with Christ and of one's identity as chosen (2:21); and (3) the sufferer is ultimately in the hands of the one who "judges justly" (2:23). This last reassurance picks up on the theme of judgment that appears elsewhere in the letter, turning it from a trial that should invoke holy fear (see 1:17; 4:17–18) to a blessing that should inspire utter trust (2:23; 4:19).

The theme of sheep and shepherds appears at the end of the passage and reappears in the final chapter in the context of identifying the leadership of the believing community with Jesus, the "chief shepherd" (5:4). In relation to our passage, the reader is not yet any kind of assistant shepherd, but a sheep who has "gone astray" (1 Pet. 2:25; also Isa. 53:6) and been found by Jesus, the "guardian" (1 Pet. 2:25). Other lections for the day use similar imagery to assure believers that they are being cared for, even as they suffer. "The Lord is my shepherd . . . even though I walk through the darkest valley," testifies the psalmist (Ps. 23:1, 4). Jesus in John 10:1–10 calls himself both shepherd of

2. See Phyllis Trible, *Texts of Terror: Literary-Feminist Readings of Biblical Narratives* (Minneapolis: Fortress, 1984).

the sheep and gate by which they enter the fold "and find pasture" (John 10:9).

John 10:10 resonates with the themes of joy, hope, and new life in 1 Peter, all of which characterize the lives of the believers even as they suffer. "I came that they may have life, and have it abundantly," Jesus says. To which the community of 1 Peter might say, "Amen," and then add, "therefore we 'live for righteousness' for 'by his wounds we have been healed'" (1 Pet. 2:24).

CYNTHIA L. RIGBY

Commentary 2: Connecting the Reading with the World

Peter here addresses head-on what he hinted at in the first chapter: the reality of suffering for those who claim Christian faith. Peter makes clear not only *why* we must accept the reality of suffering as part of our Christian identity ("because Christ also suffered" for us, 1 Pet. 2:21), but also *how* we must suffer (without returning abuse or threat, entrusting ourselves instead "to the one who judges justly," v. 23). Christian suffering in light of Christ's suffering on our behalf then becomes both a necessary part of the holy living to which we are called in the previous chapter and a witness to those who would persecute us.

This portion of 1 Peter 2 also includes what was a typical "household code" of the Greco-Roman era: a set of cultural norms that regulated how various members of a household would behave. Such codes were prevalent in ancient texts and set roles for family members (husbands, wives, and children), servants, and slaves. The elephant in the room is what the Revised Common Lectionary parameters for this lection *exclude*: that is, verse 18, which states the obligation of slaves to their masters. Preaching this lection, therefore, loses some of the painful power it might otherwise have as a reminder of times in antiquity, the recent past, and still today when the enslavement of other human beings has been all too normal and persistent.

Peter implores all of us who seek to live into our Christian identity, no matter our human identities, to acknowledge suffering as a necessary component of our faith. He places that reality in a clear christological context, stating that we have been "called" to suffer "because Christ also suffered for [us]" (v. 21), leaving an example for us to emulate. The specific kind of suffering addressed by Peter is the pain "you endure when you do right and suffer for it" (v. 20). From NT times to the present day, believers have chosen to put themselves in harm's way in order to be faithful to their understanding of God's claim on their lives and to counter evil on behalf of others.

The preacher can point to any number of examples from just the past century of those who suffered for doing what they believed was right. One example is that of Eric Liddell, a Scottish Olympian, whose story was popularized in the movie *Chariots of Fire*. Liddell, a Scottish track star and committed Christian, refused to run in the qualifying heat for the 100-meter race in the 1924 Paris Olympics, his best event, because it was held on a Sunday. That chapter of his story ended well when he unexpectedly won the gold medal in the 400-meter race. However, Liddell faced many challenges during his years as a missionary in China. During the Japanese occupation of that country in World War II, Liddell was detained with other Westerners and died in 1945 in an internment camp.[3]

There are many stories of other Christians who suffered for doing what they believed was right, as we see from examples of those who were inspired by their faith commitments to risk their lives for the sake of others during World War II. One story is that of Corrie ten Boom and her family, who hid Jews from the Nazis in the Netherlands during the early 1940s. When their efforts were discovered, ten Boom and her family were imprisoned, and some of them

3. To learn about hardships in the camp where Liddell was held, see Langdon Gilkey, *Shantung Compound: The Story of Men and Women under Pressure* (San Francisco: HarperOne, 1975).

died. She survived to tell her story of standing up for what was right in the face of evil and how her faith gave her courage not only to survive the horrors of the Holocaust but also to reach a place of peace and forgiveness for those who had wronged her.[4]

German theologian Dietrich Bonhoeffer is another example of someone who suffered for doing what was right in the era of World War II. Bonhoeffer and several clergy colleagues were imprisoned and eventually executed for their participation in the Confessing Church, which opposed the Nazi regime. Along with his martyrdom, Bonhoeffer's *Letters and Papers from Prison* and other writings on Christian discipleship have inspired Christians across the world in many ways: from opposing oppressive governments to working for justice in their communities, all in an effort to do what is right after the example of Christ.[5]

More recent examples of those who suffered for doing what is right include leaders of the civil rights and liberation theology movements. The 1950s and 1960s in America exposed bitter cultural divides but gave rise to equally powerful witnesses over issues of race. A leader of that movement, Martin Luther King Jr. was inspired by Peter's words, "When he was abused, he did not return abuse" (v. 23), and by Christ's example in advocating the nonviolent resistance that came to shape the civil rights movement. Other leaders of that movement, most notably Georgia Congressman John Lewis, continue to share their experiences and to work toward more equitable and just laws for all people. Building on such examples of nonviolent Christian witness, church leaders in other parts of the world, such as Archbishop Óscar Romero of San Salvador, have lost their lives in an effort to seek justice and freedom for others.

Beyond the challenging exhortation to endure suffering for what is right that is addressed to individual Christians and to the community of faith, there are some comforting words in the closing verses of this text. "[Christ] himself bore our sins in his body on the cross," Peter assures us, "so that, free from sins, we might live for righteousness" (v. 24). There is a sense of confidence and freedom that comes from that knowledge. We are confident that we "have God's approval" (v. 20), as stated earlier in the text. Therefore, we can take risks on behalf of ourselves and others as we pursue what is right and "live for righteousness" (v. 24). Not only that, but "by [Christ's] wounds [we] have been healed" (v. 24), pointing to a helpful psychological connection that emerges from this text.

We all have personal and corporate wounds that need to be healed, places where brokenness threatens our existence as individuals and as communities. The social fabric of our nation continues to be shredded by polarized opinions on many divisive issues. Add to that the despair that plagues so many individuals as evidenced by current epidemics of substance abuse and broken relationships. Our hope for healing what ails us is that "balm in Gilead that makes the wounded whole," as suffering slaves of nineteenth-century America sang. Peter reminds us, as he did first-century Christians, that our only hope for healing lies in our once-wounded and now-resurrected Lord, who heals us and leads us into a new way of life according to his example.

That resurrected Lord, Peter concludes, is "the shepherd and guardian of [our] souls" (v. 25). The liturgical context for this text is Good Shepherd Sunday. The Gospel lesson tells us that Jesus called himself the shepherd whose voice was recognized by his sheep. It is interesting that this text from 1 Peter begins with the acknowledgment of painful suffering but ends with the pastoral depiction of a guardian shepherd. For us, that juxtaposition is a powerful reminder that no matter what we experience as we hold fast to our faith in Jesus Christ and risk our lives for what is right, we are always brought back into the fold and guarded by the grace of the Good Shepherd.

BEVERLY ZINK-SAWYER

4. See Corrie ten Boom, *The Hiding Place* (Washington Depot, CT: Chosen Books, 1971).
5. See Dietrich Bonhoeffer, *Letters and Papers from Prison* (New York: Touchstone, 1997) and *The Cost of Discipleship* (New York: Touchstone, 1995).

John 10:1–10

1 “Very truly, I tell you, anyone who does not enter the sheepfold by the gate but
climbs in by another way is a thief and a bandit. 2 The one who enters by the
gate is the shepherd of the sheep. 3 The gatekeeper opens the gate for him, and
the sheep hear his voice. He calls his own sheep by name and leads them out.
4 When he has brought out all his own, he goes ahead of them, and the sheep
follow him because they know his voice. 5 They will not follow a stranger, but they
will run from him because they do not know the voice of strangers.” 6 Jesus used
this figure of speech with them, but they did not understand what he was saying
to them.

7 So again Jesus said to them, “Very truly, I tell you, I am the gate for the sheep.
8 All who came before me are thieves and bandits; but the sheep did not listen
to them. 9 I am the gate. Whoever enters by me will be saved, and will come in
and go out and find pasture. 10 The thief comes only to steal and kill and destroy.
I came that they may have life, and have it abundantly.”

Commentary 1: Connecting the Reading with Scripture

Jesus' Shepherd Sayings. John 10:1–5 begins with a *paroimia* or proverb, a saying that describes an ethical way of being (see John 10:6). The proverb Jesus tells first describes the difference between a thief and a shepherd, beginning with how each enters the sheepfold (vv. 1–2). The distinction continues beyond the point of entry. Verses 3–5 describe the familiarity between the shepherd and sheep: they know his voice, and the shepherd knows their names. A second distinction then emerges between the shepherd and a stranger whose voice the sheep do not know and whom they will not follow (v. 5). The stranger may not be a bandit, but neither is the stranger the shepherd. Thus, this proverb explains how to be a good shepherd: enter correctly, know the doorkeeper, and get to know each sheep by name. However, the audience does not seem to follow (v. 6).

In verses 7–10, Jesus begins to explain the proverb with an “I am” (Gk. *egō eimi*) statement meant to point to Jesus' divine character. In verses 7 and 9, Jesus identifies himself with the door or gate of the sheepfold. Sheep who enter through Jesus receive salvation and find pasture (v. 9), that is, life in abundance (v. 10). Disturbingly, the statement also polemicizes “all who came before” Jesus as thieves and bandits (v. 8). The identity of these persons is unclear, and interpreters should take care that they not use this passage to defame all Jewish prophets and teachers who preceded Jesus. A sermon writer should be cautious not to superimpose unknown first-century-CE tensions onto twenty-first-century situations.

On Shepherds and Sheep: Connecting to John 10. Chapter 10 marks one of the final chapters of John's Gospel before Jesus' passion. At the end of the chapter, tensions threaten to become violent during the Hanukkah festival when Jesus asserts his oneness with God (10:22, 30). These tensions serve to explain why Jesus does not immediately go to Lazarus when he becomes ill in chapter 11.

Wandering all over chapter 10 are metaphors of sheep and shepherds, metaphors that connect this chapter to the earlier *paroimia* in verses 1–10. The latter metaphor Jesus claims for himself, changing from “I am the gate” (10:7–10) to “I am the good shepherd” (10:11, 14). Jesus thus claims the characteristics of the shepherd in 10:1–5. He is not only the door or gate through which the shepherd enters. Now he is the shepherd, the one whose voice the sheep know (10:14, 27–29; cf. vv. 2–4). However, the contrast in this section shifts from bandit to hired hand. While hired hands will not steal, neither will they give their lives on behalf of sheep that they do not own, a veiled rebuke of the Jerusalem leadership. By contrast, the good shepherd not only owns but cares for the sheep, even at the cost of life itself (vv. 12–15).

Moreover, Jesus here declares the existence of "sheep that do not belong to this fold" (v. 16), perhaps a nod toward a Gentile mission. These also will be included, protected by Jesus the gate (vv. 7–10) and defended by Jesus the good shepherd (vv. 11, 14).

Connecting to John's Gospel. During Jesus' passion in John, various characters enact the roles described in the *paroimia*: Judas, the thief (12:6); Barabbas, the bandit (18:40); and an unnamed enslaved girl, the doorkeeper (18:16–17). "Sheep" recurs in 21:16–17 when Simon Peter receives instruction to feed Jesus' sheep. Although not explicit, Simon Peter thus enacts the role of the hired hand (18:15–27), making his restoration in chapter 21 that much more poignant.

John's Gospel also includes ongoing themes of listening to Jesus' voice (3:29; 5:25, 28; 11:43; 18:37) and of the positive results of following Jesus (1:37–43; 8:12; 12:26: 21:19–21). Further, just as the shepherd goes ahead of the sheep, Jesus goes ahead of his disciples to prepare a place for them (14:2–3, 12, 28; 16:28). These followers Jesus calls "his own," echoing 1:11, and foreshadowing 13:1. Just as the sheep enter and exit through the gate, so also those who wish salvation and to approach God must enter through Jesus (3:17; 14:16). Those who enter, who listen, who follow have life (10:10), a recurring refrain throughout John's Gospel (3:15–16, 36; 5:24, 26, 39–40; 6:40, 47, 53–54, 68; 8:12; 20:31).

The gate and shepherd metaphors in chapter 10 join several other "I am" statements in John's Gospel, including Jesus as bread of life (6:35); light of the world (8:12); the resurrection (11:25); the way, the truth, and the life (14:6); and the true vine (15:1). With each of these, John highlights characteristics of Jesus for the community of faith. A sermon might explore how the images of sheep, shepherd, and gate illustrate Jesus' character and ministry among us today.

Connecting to the Lectionary. Psalm 23 describes God as a shepherd. Like the shepherd in John 10:1–5, God leads the sheep out into good pasture (Ps. 23:3a). Those who follow receive food and water, protection and care, "goodness and mercy," even in the valley of the shadow of death. Thus God, the good shepherd, goes ahead of the sheep, and the sheep follow and find good pasture (cf. John 10:4, 9). Perhaps Jesus alludes to this psalm when he promises that those who enter through him will have abundant life (John 10:10).

The author of 1 Peter also invokes this metaphor when reminding his audience that they have returned "to the shepherd and guardian of your souls" (1 Pet. 2:25). This shepherd also goes ahead of the sheep, suffering on their behalf, leading them by example (1 Pet. 2:21) and ultimately granting them life (John 10:10; 1 Pet. 2:24). Once more, there are consonances between this passage and John 10:1–10, especially the *paroimia*. A sermon might consider the relationship between Jesus the gate and God the shepherd and how these metaphors point to God's love for us.

Canonical Connections. Metaphors of sheep and shepherds abound throughout the canon of Scripture, particularly among the Psalms and prophets. Whether in lament (Ps. 44:11, 22) or in simple self-description, many writings use the metaphor of "sheep" to describe God's people. Perhaps the most familiar of these comparisons describes the relationship between God and God's people as that between a shepherd and sheep (Pss. 95:7a; 100:3). The obverse also applies. Throughout Scripture, when God's people appear to be wandering aimlessly without leadership, the writers describe them as sheep without a shepherd (Num. 27:17; 1 Kgs. 22:17; 2 Chr. 18:16; Matt. 9:36; Mark 6:34).

Just as the call of the shepherd leads to the following of the sheep, so also similar call stories echo Jesus' command to his earliest disciples, "Follow me" (e.g., Matt. 4:20, 22). Those who follow become like Barsabbas and Matthias of Acts 1:23, disciples who go in and out with their fellows through the gate (John 10:9; Acts 1:21–23). The "going before" of the shepherd in John 10:4 evokes God's going ahead of God's people as a pillar of fire and of cloud (Exod. 13:21), leading them out into a land flowing with milk and honey. In addition, one may hear echoes of the return from exile as God promises to go before God's people to level the mountains (Isa. 45:2).

However, the Gospel writer also reminds us of Jesus going ahead of his disciples to Jerusalem (Luke 19:28); going first can be perilous for the shepherd. A sermon on these themes might consider the connections between discipleship and being God's sheep. What can we trust God to do? What response does God expect from us?

MARGARET P. AYMER

Commentary 2: Connecting the Reading with the World

In the Fold. There is perhaps no more pervasive image in the Bible than that of a shepherd tending his flock. From Abel who was a "keeper of sheep" (Gen. 4:2, 3) to Jacob who tended his own sheep (Gen. 30:40), from Moses who cared for his father-in-law's flock (Exod. 3:1) to David who was given charge of his father's flocks despite being the youngest son (1 Sam. 16:11), there are multiple instances in Scripture where sheep and shepherds convey important theological insights. Reflecting the prominence of flocks and herds in the cultures of the ancient Near East, the Bible uses the occupation of shepherd many times over to depict God as caring over God's people, from the ubiquitous Psalm 23 ("The Lord is my shepherd, I shall not want") to Jesus proclaiming himself "the good shepherd" (John 10:11).

Given the economic dependence the early nomadic culture of Israel had on its flocks, it is not surprising to see the image of God as a shepherd leading his people to safe pastures (Exod. 15:13, 17). If God is Israel's shepherd, and God's anointed leaders are shepherds appointed to care for God's people, then two distinct themes (perhaps providing material for two different sermons) emerge from this passage in John's Gospel. First, John 10:1–6 establishes the need for the community ("the sheep") to have a strong leader ("the shepherd of the sheep"), because there are enemies intent on leading God's sheep astray. In the early church, leaders were instructed to "tend the flock of God" (1 Pet. 5:2), and the titles used for them—elder (*presbyteros*) and bishop (*episkopos*)—had direct links to the work of shepherding. Furthermore, to have the kind of shepherd the flock trusts—whom the sheep will follow because they know his voice—the early church was in agreement that such leaders "must be above reproach" (1 Tim. 3:2).

Second, the text also makes clear that while the church must employ capable women and men to shepherd God's "flock," ultimately, there is only one shepherd: Jesus Christ, our Lord and Savior. This is why at this point in his sermon Jesus shifts from the image of the shepherd guarding his sheep to the (equally pastoral) image of the gate: "I am the gate. Whoever enters by me will be saved, and will come in and go out and find pasture" (John 10:9). In the end there is only one shepherd, and the task of God's appointed shepherds here on earth is to lead the flock to its one true Lord, in whom we find abundant life (v. 10).

They Will Not Follow a Stranger. A friend of mine once served a Spanish-language, rural congregation whose members included undocumented migrant farm workers. During his years as pastor of this poor and marginalized community, the church grew in membership and had become "home" to a subset of the US population that often lives in hiding and shuns public involvement. Eventually, several of these undocumented men and women answered the call to leadership and became ordained elders in the congregation *despite* their undocumented status. Sadly, my friend eventually took a call elsewhere, in order to pursue further studies, and had to say goodbye to this congregation. Needless to say, his decision to leave caused much grief among the members, especially among those undocumented elders who accepted the mantle of leadership based on their belief that as their shepherd this pastor would protect them. The pastor called a public forum to alleviate the fear and growing mistrust, at which one of the elders accused him by saying, "You are not a good shepherd; you are a stranger, and we no longer know your voice." Transitions in pastoral leadership are always difficult, compounded in this instance by the undocumented status of many church members, but my friend took advantage of the situation to remind the church that there is only one shepherd—the Good Shepherd—and so long as we trust in him, the Lord will always provide trustworthy leaders. In fact, God had already done so by calling elders who, despite their undocumented status, accepted the responsibility to tend this threatened but growing community.

Careful What You Pretend to Be. Humorist Kurt Vonnegut in his novel *Mother Night* (1962) wrote that this is the only story he has written whose moral he knows. It is the story of Howard W. Campbell Jr., an American who moved to Germany in 1923 at the age of eleven. He became a famous playwright but then a propagandist for the Nazi war machine. Unbeknownst to anyone but himself and a now-dead agent of the US War Department, Campbell was not a Nazi but an American double agent pretending to be a Nazi, in order to help the Allied cause. Unfortunately, Campbell played too convincing a Nazi, and found himself in a prison cell in Jerusalem awaiting trial as a war criminal. The moral of the story is this: "We are what we pretend to be, so we must be careful about what we pretend to be."[1]

In our passage, we are told that the church is God's flock, and the elders and pastors are God's shepherds. We are also told that the sheep know and trust the shepherd. A close relationship between the shepherd and the sheep is assumed, and the possibility that the shepherd might be a wolf in sheep's clothing is never considered. However, numerous clergy abuse scandals have led us to be mistrustful of people in positions of leadership. Thus, instead of reading this text as a call for sheep passively to accept the shepherd's authority, I choose to read it as a caution to anyone considering the call to church leadership. In other words, regardless of your office—be it deacon, elder, or pastor—people will look to you for guidance. They will trust you simply by virtue of your office. With such power comes great responsibility (Voltaire, 1793; Spider-Man, 1962). As always, Jesus serves as the model for authentic leadership, and it is his voice that ought to be trusted.

No one is born a leader. Like all things in life, it takes work and dedication to nurture the virtues that make one a good shepherd, and character—while at first taken on trust—is quickly exposed by our actions. The text makes it clear that a shepherd speaks truth, is reliable, and works for the good of the flock. Accordingly, when the shepherd calls, the sheep not only recognize the voice; they trust it and follow it, because they have come to know that voice as reliable and constant. I was ordained solo pastor of a rural congregation in a town of eight hundred people at the ripe old age of twenty-five. You can imagine the anxiety caused by the words of one elder (a man many years my senior) when he said to me, "Many people see you as the spiritual leader of this community."

Vonnegut was right. You are what you pretend to be. Thank God I had the wisdom to imitate those mentors and peers in ministry who lived lives of *imitatio Christi* ("imitation of Christ") and modeled for me a humble example of servant leadership. Even when I felt the sheep did not listen to me (v. 8)—which was often—I always prayed that they would listen to him.

RUBÉN ROSARIO RODRÍGUEZ

1. Kurt Vonnegut, *Mother Night* (New York: Dell Publishing, 1966), v.

Fifth Sunday of Easter

Acts 7:55–60
Psalm 31:1–5, 15–16
1 Peter 2:2–10
John 14:1–14

Acts 7:55–60

> [55]But filled with the Holy Spirit, he gazed into heaven and saw the glory of God and Jesus standing at the right hand of God. [56]"Look," he said, "I see the heavens opened and the Son of Man standing at the right hand of God!" [57]But they covered their ears, and with a loud shout all rushed together against him. [58]Then they dragged him out of the city and began to stone him; and the witnesses laid their coats at the feet of a young man named Saul. [59]While they were stoning Stephen, he prayed, "Lord Jesus, receive my spirit." [60]Then he knelt down and cried out in a loud voice, "Lord, do not hold this sin against them." When he had said this, he died.

Commentary 1: Connecting the Reading with Scripture

Today we hear of a violent *death* precipitated by bold proclamation of the *resurrection*—this during the church's seven-week celebration of victory *over* death won *by* that resurrection. Today's first reading is a terse, dramatic account of a mob execution, a lynching by stoning. The stark juxtaposition of death and life is arresting, especially on this liturgically upbeat day. To give this text wide berth in sermon preparation would be understandable, but following that impulse would be unfortunate. Acts shows up in the lectionary infrequently as it is, and there are evocative preaching possibilities in the apparent incongruity of an execution precipitated by proclamation of the resurrection.

First, preachers will need to put this text in the context of the early chapters of Acts, beginning with the whole of chapter 7. Indeed, the six appointed verses make little narrative sense apart from the fifty-three before them. Those verses comprise an extended speech by soon-to-be-martyr Stephen, delivered before religious leaders. Stephen serves as his own defense attorney against two charges: blasphemy and sedition against the temple and the law. (Defendants in court proceedings are advised not to serve as their own counsel. The oral-argument strategy Stephen employs seems good evidence for the admonition.) He does not address the charges directly, let alone offer evidence to rebut them. Although he is the one on trial, he assumes the role not of a defense attorney, but of a prosecution lawyer, the prosecutor of his prosecutors. It is hardly surprising that he ends up getting himself killed!

Stephen's accusatory challenge consists in reading the history of God's redemptive investment in the life of Israel from the underside. He recounts how throughout that history, God's people have consistently resisted and sabotaged God's purposes, both by rejecting the efforts of God's designated salvation agents (Joseph and Moses most particularly) and by persecuting one prophet after another. The pattern has culminated in the treatment of Jesus by those now accusing Stephen. It is not he but they who are guilty of the charges they have falsely brought against him: "You are the ones that received the law as ordained by angels, and yet you have not kept it" (Acts 7:53).

The charge is leveled here against fellow Torah followers, but the gospel will provoke analogous rejections from many other quarters. The resurrection of Jesus is no "happily ever after" resolution of a standard story line. His "overcoming" of death entails continual confrontation by his followers against death-dealing actions, dispositions, behavior patterns, and systemic structures from traditions, religious and secular alike, that repudiate the prospect and reject the challenge of resurrection life.

The author of Acts seems intent on driving this point home; it is the fourth such resurrection proclamation and confrontation story deployed in the first few chapters of the narrative overall. Each one escalates in conflict over the one before. While recounting these might be unnecessary or inadvisable in this day's sermon, preachers will be helped to recall these earlier accounts in which resurrection proclamation and strong pushback are dramatically interplayed:

1. Peter and John's healing of a disabled beggar in the temple (3:1–4:4)
2. Peter and John's interrogation by "the rulers, elders, and scribes assembled in Jerusalem" (4:5–31)
3. The jailing, interrogation, and flogging of the apostles by the Sanhedrin (5:12–42)

Strikingly, these conflict scenes are framed by the temple healing act of Peter and John and the "great wonders and signs among the people" done by Stephen (6:8). Simple acts of healing, it seems, can foment systemic social and religious disruption!

It also may be worth attending to the apparent disconnect between what Stephen does (and dies for) and the job description for which he is ordained in Acts 6:1–7. Along with Philip and five others, he is appointed to ensure that the credibility of the gospel—food for the soul—is not compromised by an issue regarding food for the body. Hebrew widows are perceived as receiving inequitable preference in food distribution over Hellenist widows. Stephen and his colleagues are charged with overseeing fairness in food supply, thereby ensuring that resurrection *practice* is in full accord with resurrection *preaching*.

This task might appear to be more logistical than theological—except, of course, that theology apart from moral and sociological logistics would hardly be incarnational. Rather than presuming to transgress his designated vocational boundaries (for Stephen as for Philip, see Acts 8), resurrection practice and preaching are all in a day's work. Might the "signs and wonders" Stephen does include his strategic and hands-on social actions that gesture toward the full meaning of resurrection? That would be congruent with the proclamations and practices of the Lord, whom Stephen sees in a validating vision just before he dies. Might those actions of Stephen be just as threatening in his social setting as were those of the one he serves? Racial and ethnic tensions—especially regarding distinctive sacred beliefs, sacred practices, and sacred spaces—are prevalent throughout the book of Acts. Religious turf wars abound. The preaching and practice of resurrection tend to evoke earthquakes on spiritual landscapes.

Two other connections are worth noting. Stephen is described not once but several times as "full": full of the Spirit (6:3, 5; 7:55), full of faith (6:5), and full of grace and power (6:8). This "fullness" is given narrative resonance by the way Luke describes how Stephen responds to his stoning. He commends himself to God and asks God to forgive his executioners (7:59–60), which resonates profoundly with the response of Jesus at his crucifixion (Luke 23:34, in some manuscripts, and 23:46). Clearly, whatever the content of Stephen's "fullness," it has to do with an integrated way of being, not simply a rush of strong feeling. Both Jesus and Stephen practice resurrection in the way they confront and undertake their physical deaths. In so doing, both defy spiritual death and invalidate its power.

The church may still be in the season of Easter, but by now the lilies in the sanctuary have wilted, the festive "Welcome, Easter Morning" hymns have run their course, and the trumpets have been packed away till Christmas. Resurrection-appearance Gospel lessons ended two weeks ago. Everyone may still be saying "Alleluia" on cue, but the energy level has fallen. The hard edge of Easter toward which the Stephen story points, however, is seconded by the "living stone," "cornerstone," "rejected stone," "stumbling stone" interplay that we hear in

1 Peter 2, where the metaphors are not unartfully "mixed" but deliberately juxtaposed. What is "death" and what is "life," what is "darkness" and what is "light" depend on where and with whom we stand.

The readings from John that will take us from here to the end of the season are more resonant still: words of Jesus depicted as spoken to his disciples *before* his death and voiced to John's own preaching community and to us as Easter affirmations. There we will find words at once compassionate and steely, addressed in reassurance to troubled hearts. These are presence-promising, Way-showing words of Truth and Life. Life in the resurrection is not just life as resuscitation. It means loving one another (John 13:34) and practicing the presence of the risen Christ.

Witnesses to that deep truth can be found throughout the Scriptures. Moses and Miriam, Puah and Shiphrah, Elijah and Elisha, Isaiah and Jeremiah, Amos and Hosea, Barnabas and Paul all stand up for the God of life by standing up to the powers of death. Preachers are sometimes counseled to preach a lot of Easter on Good Friday and a lot of Good Friday on Easter. They can do that when they preach on the death of Stephen.

DAVID J. SCHLAFER

Commentary 2: Connecting the Reading with the World

On this Fifth Sunday of Easter, the lectionary reading bears witness to the resurrection of Jesus and the promises the resurrection encapsulates. Due to the prominence of Stephen's vision into heaven of "Jesus standing at the right hand of God" (Acts 7:55–56), this story is befitting of the liturgical season. It confirms that the risen Lord is indeed in place by God's side to advocate on behalf of all believers and humanity. Furthermore, it confirms Jesus' promise of the Holy Spirit to equip disciples to proclaim the gospel before synagogues and councils (Luke 21:12–16), even to the ends of the earth (Acts 1:8), as well as to empower them to stand firm in the face of persecution even unto death.

This story of Stephen and his martyrdom is unfamiliar to many, and its peculiarity as a lectionary story is magnified by this being the only time in the three-year cycle a Christian community may even hear of it. Stephen is a faithful Jew who becomes a fierce and devout disciple of Jesus. Accused of blasphemy (6:11), he is brought before the Jerusalem council. During his testimony, he chastises the council—not as a Christian but as a fellow Jew—for their shortsightedness as theological and religious leaders in their persecutions of Jesus' disciples. Stephen knows from the Scriptures the covenant community's pattern of rejecting God's chosen prophets and leaders (7:38–40, 51–52); he recognizes that the council is following in their ancestors' footsteps. As the high priests, scribes, Pharisees, and other leaders become enraged by his testimony, Stephen, being "filled with the Holy Spirit" (v. 55), has a vision. This is where our lectionary text begins.

Stephen's vision is evidence of Jesus' resurrection and God's reign. For second-generation disciples experiencing the aftermath of the second temple's destruction and seeking signs of kingdom promises, his testimony provides solace and comfort in knowing that God sees the plights, pains, and persecutions of the faithful. The tomb, Rome, and the council could not abolish the power of Jesus or the proclamation of the gospel throughout the world. Jesus has ascended upon his heavenly throne, sits in his rightful place, and assumes his authority.

As Jesus' body was never imprisoned in the tomb, God's Spirit was never confined to the temple. In context, Stephen's message must have sounded blasphemous; however, this truth was revealed under the temple's rubble. God is in every time and place, active and present in our midst. The work of God is not sequestered within the four walls of any human edifice; instead, it engages the world and invites believers to realize the work of the kingdom in the present day.

While Stephen's vision affirms hope in Jesus' postresurrection existence, it also confirms God's call for the church to speak hard truths even to and about itself. Jesus stands as one in agreement with Stephen and the audacity with which he speaks. In that moment, Jesus empowers and supports a disciple who has followed him and taken up the cross (Luke 9:23). Stephen stands at the edge of life because he has confronted the local leaders about their opposition to God's will and purpose. His bravery is a model for the church to do likewise. God calls the church to exhort leaders and the public to protect vulnerable citizens from abuse, to provide housing for the homeless, and to legislate so that the humanity of all is lifted up. Within the church, leaders have to repent for its hostility toward women's ordination, its participation in racial injustice, and its treatment of LBGTQIA+ community.

Stephen's execution was not a consequence of his care for widows (Acts 6:1–6) or even his miraculous works (6:8). He died because he told a hard truth to the council about their disregard of God's prophetic word through the ages. In the wait for the eschaton, the Christian church is called to be like Stephen and tell hard truths to society's leaders, especially other Christian leaders, who profess to care for the welfare of others and to follow God, while their rhetoric and actions remain antithetical to God's prophetic word and the examples of Jesus. The lectionary invites the reader to examine her moral obligation to speak boldly and to remember Jesus' promise to empower her and imbue her message with the wisdom of the Holy Spirit, even in difficult arenas.

The narrative's focus on the crowd as much as Stephen is no coincidence. Rhetorically, it functions as a mirror for faith communities to examine themselves, not as a tool of condemnation against the Jewish council or Jews in general. The crowd reflects an unsavory reality of faith leaders whose ears were closed, sometimes intentionally, to the truth about how they—and we—have fallen short of our most cherished commitments. Oftentimes, the church acts like the crowd. It has covered its ears, facilitating the death of many honorable people and causes. It has covered its ears to sexual abuses and domestic violence behind its doors and the doors of its parishioners. It has covered its ears to the protests of those being victimized by xenophobia. It has closed its ears to poverty and the theft of resources of one nation by nations that were already rich. Too often, the Christian church has not only ignored calls to stop injustice but also colluded in the subordination of women, the attempted erasure of indigenous people, enslavement, and abuses of children.

The story warns the audience not to be like the population of faithful who did not believe the prophets, truth tellers, and gospel preachers of the day because their message did not conform to their beliefs, perceptions, and engagement in world. Today too many of us avoid the truth. Politicians have called reliable news sources fake media, even as the journalists report what they see and hear. Algorithms on social-media sites and browsing patterns isolate people into curated news sources that only agree with our worst impulses, insulating communities into echo chambers. The story cautions the faith community to listen widely and with discernment for God's instructions, especially when it may contradict what we already believe.

Lastly, we cannot ignore the introduction to and presence of young Saul, later to be known as Paul. His presence is ambiguous. A young leader in training, he may have volunteered or been coerced to witness Stephen's execution. It is possible that Saul was caught up in the spectacle, much a like a person watching a train wreck and unable to look away. Alternatively, he could have volunteered to watch the council's coats in order to do his part in mediating justice. Although the author's intent for introducing Saul this way is unattainable, it foreshadows Saul's later life as Paul. As Saul, he becomes known for his relentless persecution of Jesus' disciples. As Paul, he experiences brutality, rejection, and even execution from those who refuse to believe the gospel of Jesus Christ and his resurrection promises. In this moment, Saul gets a peek into his own life and the consequences of speaking truth to power.

While celebrating the risen Lord and the powerful witness of Stephen who becomes known as the first Christian martyr, the lectionary pushes readers. It calls disciples to listen intently, even to material that may be enraging, for difficult truths that have the potential to be as transformative as the gospel itself. Listening to the truth, even when inconvenient, contributes to growth, to maturation, and to the ability for individuals and communities to live into their greatest potential as they realize God's kingdom on earth as in heaven.

BRIDGETT A. GREEN

Psalm 31:1–5, 15–16

[1]In you, O LORD, I seek refuge;
 do not let me ever be put to shame;
 in your righteousness deliver me.
[2]Incline your ear to me;
 rescue me speedily.
Be a rock of refuge for me,
 a strong fortress to save me.

[3]You are indeed my rock and my fortress;
 for your name's sake lead me and guide me,
[4]take me out of the net that is hidden for me,
 for you are my refuge.
[5]Into your hand I commit my spirit;
 you have redeemed me, O LORD, faithful God.
. . . .
[15]My times are in your hand;
 deliver me from the hand of my enemies and persecutors.
[16]Let your face shine upon your servant;
 save me in your steadfast love.

Connecting the Psalm with Scripture and Worship

Psalm 31 is considered a lament or psalm of complaint. Its structure can be described as "chaotic" or "irregular," and is perhaps indicative of the tumult that has overtaken the life of the psalmist.[1] This sense of chaos makes the psalm especially suitable on the lips of Stephen, who is the first of the Acts community to be put to death for his faith. While others have been arrested and released (Acts 4:21–23) or rescued, seemingly by divine intervention (5:19), Stephen's experience shifts rapidly from a discussion of biblical exegesis (7:2–53) to expulsion from the city and death by stoning. Recalling the threats in response to Jesus' prophetic preaching at the synagogue in Nazareth (Luke 4:16–30), the pairing of Psalm 31 with this passage from Acts highlights, first, the development of a comparison between Stephen and Jesus and, second, a message of consolation to all who trust in God during times of persecution.

The pairing of Psalm 31 with the martyrdom of Stephen serves to illustrate the close connection that Luke develops between Jesus and Stephen. This connection has two effects. It emphasizes the holiness of Stephen by connecting him to Jesus. It also suggests that the death of Jesus was an act of martyrdom like that of Stephen and other Christians who would follow him.

The first element of the comparison is developed in repeated use of the imagery of God's "hand" in both the psalm and Acts. The psalmist makes two references to the hand of God: "into your hand I commit my spirit; you have redeemed me, O LORD, faithful God" (Ps. 31:5), and "my times are in your hand; deliver me from the hand of my enemies and persecutors" (v. 15). The first instance is referenced by both Jesus and Stephen at the moments of their deaths. Jesus quotes the psalm, specifically entrusting his spirit into his Father's hands

1. J. Clinton McCann, "Psalms," in *The New Interpreter's Bible* (Nashville: Abingdon, 1996), 6:800.

during the crucifixion described in Luke 23:46. Stephen does not mention God's hand explicitly, but entrusts his spirit directly to "Lord Jesus" (Acts 7:59), whom he has seen at the right hand of God (vv. 55–56). Although not a direct reference to this psalm, listeners might also note Stephen's "Do not hold this sin against them" as an echo of Jesus' "Father, forgive them, for they do not know what they are doing" (Luke 23:34). It is this week's psalm that is the liturgical lynchpin between Jesus' death and Stephen's death.

Stephen's death is clearly modeled on the death of Jesus, thus setting an example for all Christians and also highlighting the reality of Jesus' death as a form of martyrdom. While this emphasis can easily be lost in broader soteriological discussions of the paschal mystery, the emphasis on martyrdom may have been important to Christians of earlier generations. Luke Timothy Johnson notes that the emphasis in Acts on Stephen's experience of being "filled with the Holy Spirit" and thus able to see Jesus in heaven "standing at the right hand of God" (Acts 7:55) is reminiscent of the events of Jesus' baptism (Luke 3:21). Stephen becomes "a spokesperson for the people."[2] His impending witness of martyrdom is thus set up in comparison to the baptism that began Jesus' public ministry.

As a response to Stephen's suffering and death, Psalm 31 includes the standard elements of the lament: complaint followed by trust in God. While Stephen certainly has cause for complaint, the overwhelming emphasis in Acts is on trust in God and generosity of spirit. Like the psalmist, Stephen can say, "My times are in your hand" (Ps. 31:15), even as he realizes that his deliverance from "the hand of my enemies and persecutors" (v. 15) will be an eschatological one.

The contrast between the hand of God and the hand of enemies (a common theme in the Psalms) is especially striking here. The hands that throw stones cannot compare to the heavenly vision of "Jesus standing at the right hand of God" (Acts 7:55). The "stones" that are cast are paltry in comparison to the image of God as "a rock of refuge . . . a strong fortress to save me" (Ps. 31:2b). Stephen does not seem to expect an earthly salvation, but has confidence in God who inclines an ear (v. 2a), in contrast to those who cover their ears to avoid the words of the prophets. Here it can be noted that the verses immediately preceding the reading from Acts include the following accusation from Stephen: "You are just like your ancestors. Which of the prophets did your ancestors not persecute?" (Acts 7:51–52). This persecution is perhaps at the root of the sin and violence for which Stephen prays that they might be forgiven (v. 60).

In the midst of the Easter season, Psalm 31 and the martyrdom of Stephen serve as reminders that the paschal mystery continues. Violence and death persist in the world. Like Stephen, some members of the assembly may have wondered how a situation could go from "just talking" to a violent argument. Like the psalmist, some may fear "the net that is hidden for me" (Ps. 31:4) or the shame that lingers in a long-kept secret. While it is not at all easy, the Easter difference is that like Stephen, members of the assembly are "filled with the Holy Spirit" and thus can see with the eyes of faith. In this state, they can witness to "the glory of God" as Stephen does, or like the psalmist pray with hope: "Let your face shine upon your servant" (v. 16). The good news is that the hand of God is indeed a refuge, even though chaos remains present.

RHODORA E. BEATON

2. Luke Timothy Johnson, *The Acts of the Apostles,* in Sacra Pagina, vol. 5 (Collegeville, MN: Liturgical Press, 1992). 139.

1 Peter 2:2–10

[2]Like newborn infants, long for the pure, spiritual milk, so that by it you may grow
into salvation— [3]if indeed you have tasted that the Lord is good.
[4]Come to him, a living stone, though rejected by mortals yet chosen and precious in God's sight, and [5]like living stones, let yourselves be built into a spiritual
house, to be a holy priesthood, to offer spiritual sacrifices acceptable to God
through Jesus Christ. [6]For it stands in scripture:

"See, I am laying in Zion a stone,
  a cornerstone chosen and precious;
and whoever believes in him will not be put to shame."

[7]To you then who believe, he is precious; but for those who do not believe,

"The stone that the builders rejected
  has become the very head of the corner,"

[8]and

"A stone that makes them stumble,
  and a rock that makes them fall."

They stumble because they disobey the word, as they were destined to do.
[9]But you are a chosen race, a royal priesthood, a holy nation, God's own people, in order that you may proclaim the mighty acts of him who called you out of
darkness into his marvelous light.

[10]Once you were not a people,
    but now you are God's people;
  once you had not received mercy,
    but now you have received mercy.

Commentary 1: Connecting the Reading with Scripture

Today's reading takes us to the theological center of 1 Peter; it gives the church an identity designed to sustain it in the midst of suffering. The theology of 1 Peter is shaped by its recipients' experience of persecution. Like many other NT texts, this one must help its recipients understand persecution. It must convince them that it is not an indication that they have displeased God and not an indication that they have chosen the wrong god. Throughout the whole of 1 Peter, the author assures those suffering persecution that God loves them and that they have made the right choice. He acknowledges that they are now "aliens and exiles" in their own cities (1 Pet. 2:11; also 1:1) because of their faith but assures them of blessings from God that outweigh and outlast the suffering. Since that is the case, they must remain faithful despite persecution.

In the Greek, this lection begins in the middle of a sentence. The first verse of chapter 2 calls the baptized to rid themselves of various vices; then verse 2 gives the obverse: grow into the salvation they have received. The author urges them to desire the transformation salvation offers as newborn infants crave milk. The image of milk does not carry the implication that the readers are immature, as it does in 1 Corinthians 3:2. Rather, the milk's purity is a contrast to the vices of 1 Peter 2:1. This passage sees growing to embody salvation as a lifelong process. Alluding to Psalm 34:8, this metaphor envisions God as a nursing mother who nurtures her infant. Here that life is faithfulness to the demands of the Christian life.

Verses 4–10 summarize much of what 1 Peter has said to this point and provide the basis for the exhortations to right living and faithfulness in persecution that follow in the rest of the letter. The crucial function of these verses is to give the church an identity that encourages its readers to remain faithful, even though they face persecution. Verse 4 introduces an identity of Christ that is given scriptural support in verses 6–8. Verse 5 provides an identity for believers that receives scriptural support in verses 9–10.

The author identifies Christ as the "living stone" that has been rejected by humans but is chosen and valuable to God. Identifying Christ in this way is an important strategy for 1 Peter. The author makes the suffering and subsequent vindication and resurrection of Christ the pattern for believers' lives. Following this pattern, verse 5 identifies believers as "living stones." They can expect, then, that their lives will follow the pattern seen in Christ, the paradigmatic living stone.

Calling the recipients living stones leads to other metaphors. These stones are being built into a house, and they as a community are forming a holy priesthood. In this capacity, they offer "spiritual sacrifices," which verse 9 suggests are the proclamation of God's salvation. The identities of living stones (in parallel with Christ), of God's house, and of a priesthood all offer the readers status that persecution denies them. Still, the author must interpret these images if they are to assure his readers of this meaning.

Verses 6–8 use texts from Isaiah and the Psalms to explain what it means to call Christ a living stone. Isaiah used the metaphor of a cornerstone to proclaim that the strength of God's presence would remain within Jerusalem despite the unfaithfulness of its leaders (Isa. 28:16). Our author sees Christ as the unshakable presence of God in whom one can trust. First Peter uses Isaiah's promise that those who trust this stone will be vindicated to reassure his persecuted readers. The sure strength of the cornerstone is emphasized with the citation from Psalm 118:22, where the person who was disregarded by those around him is exalted by God's power. Christ is the exemplar of this kind of God's saving activity and the one who brings salvation to others. Like those in Isaiah's day who rejected the word of God (Isa. 8:14), those who refuse to believe in Christ and who persecute God's people are tripped up, rejected by that unmovable stone. The living stone image presents a pattern of rejection by outsiders and vindication by God. This aspect of the image is what 1 Peter wants its readers to recognize in their identity as living stones.

In verses 9–10, the author returns directly to assigning identities to believers. In contrast to those who reject Christ and fall, they are "a chosen race, a royal priesthood, a holy nation, God's own people." The author takes for his church the descriptions of Israel in Isaiah 43:20–21 and Exodus 19:6. His point is not to supplant Israel. He has no interest in a critique of the Israel of his day. Rather, he is identifying his church with the pattern of God's acts seen in the exodus and the return of Israel from exile. Again, that pattern is that those rejected or oppressed by others are the objects of God's salvation.

That is what his church needs to hear. Just as God saved Israel out of slavery, so God will save them beyond the persecution they now endure. Verse 10 reiterates this pattern with its citation of Hosea. After God has Hosea name his children so that they point to alienation from God and destruction, God promises restoration and salvation by renaming them. The author identifies this church with those who were once alienated but now have been made God's people and those who receive God's mercy.

Naming the church in these ways ties it to the paradoxical experience of being rejected by the world while being vindicated and exalted by God. The pattern is seen in the exodus, the return of Israel from exile, and most especially in Christ, the living stone that provides the exemplar for their lives as living stones. Seeing this pattern can help them serve God, even in the face of opposition and rejection. It assures them that God's gracious acts are more powerful than the forces that work against God's will.

This imitation of Christ in the midst of persecution is exemplified in Stephen's martyrdom (Acts 7). Stephen's trust that God would vindicate him imitates Jesus' trust in God to vindicate him (Luke 23:42–46). Moreover, we might notice another layer of imitation when Stephen forgives his tormenters just as Christ forgave those who crucified him.[1] The other lectionary texts also point to trusting God in difficult situations. The psalmist thanks God for rescue from a difficult situation (Ps. 31:1–5, 15–16). John 14:1–14 has Jesus assure his disciples that God's care for them extends beyond this world but is also a help within the world. Christ shows us who God is and that God will be present with us through him.

This text from 1 Peter is an Easter text because it points us to the power of God seen in the resurrection of Christ. It asserts that God's resurrection power promises that God will vindicate the faithful. No opposition, oppression, or rejection—not even death—is as powerful as God's determination to be with and to raise those who are faithful. This text invites sermons about the assurance that God's faithfulness affords the oppressed and suffering. It also suggests sermons about our identity as living stones who imitate Christ, *the* living stone, by trusting in God as we work for the good of those around us. Our identity as a royal priesthood further calls the church to mediate the presence and will of God to the world.

JERRY L. SUMNEY

Commentary 2: Connecting the Reading with the World

In 1 Peter, we hear a vivid exhortation that draws upon the memory and narrative of God's action and promise to encourage new groups of believers. So how can this letter speak to Christian communities today, almost two thousand years after the life, death, and resurrection of Jesus?

It is important to understand how this message would have been heard in its original context, those churches in the Roman provinces of Asia Minor. The Christian communities in these provinces would have likely been small groups in relatively rural areas. From the text, we can tell that their social status was marginal. They would have likely endured scorn from the local populace on account of their religious identification as followers of Jesus. Locals—particularly in their rural communities—would have treated these neighbors with hostility and would likely have often scapegoated them for drawing the ire of the Roman gods whenever famine, flood, or some other natural scourge afflicted these communities.

Given their "outsider" identity, the author's message here is certainly an assurance of belonging and purpose. Composed of both Israelites and Gentiles, these churches would have understood the imagery of the "cornerstone" and the embodiment of the now-destroyed Jerusalem temple. As the author employs scriptural understandings of "rejection" (1 Pet. 2:7), darkness (v. 9), and nonidentity (v. 10), many would likely hear undertones of their own experience with the culture around them. As 1 Peter reminds them that they are called by God to be a new "spiritual house" (v. 5) composed of "living stones" (v. 4), they are to live out their calling together, not as individuals but together, by offering "spiritual sacrifices" (v. 5), that is, a communal life that is pleasing to God. As they do so, the author assures them with the language of the covenant in the Hebrew Scriptures that they are called to be "a chosen race," that they are "precious" (v. 4), and indeed "God's own people" (v. 9), a part of the larger, universal church.

So how do we connect with this marginalized Christian community today? Before proceeding, we must be attentive to a particular temptation. We must resist the temptation to correlate the situation of a group of believers facing social rejection with the situation of the church in the United States or the West today. Despite the inclination of Western Christians to view themselves as rejected or ostracized, we rarely face situations today in which our own congregation is our exclusive source of community and positive participation in the world.

Certainly, some Christian communities, especially in other parts of the world, find themselves

1. There are text-critical questions about the authenticity of Luke 23:34.

in situations like those addressed by 1 Peter: scorned and in precarious social and political positions. However, many of us live with a vastly different experience, in which our status in our political environments is secure and our identification with Jesus and Christianity more broadly empowers rather than endangers our status within the larger communities in which we live.

Acknowledging this, we can find in the passage at least four preaching connections. First, there is a moment that lends itself to liturgical reflection. Falling on the Fifth Sunday of Easter, the passage offers us a chance to reaffirm with these early Christian communities in Asia Minor that "indeed, we have tasted that the Lord is good." The wording of verse 3 implies and invites an affirmation: "Indeed, we have!" After the excitement of the Easter proclamation threatens to yield to the more quotidian realities of Ordinary Time, perhaps this is a time to pause and renew our communal identity. As 1 Peter will remind us, that identity is defined by a connection with the Jesus who was rejected and who is yet precious in God's sight. This moment is a perfect time to celebrate communion or perhaps even a larger common meal together that offers a chance to liturgically engage the sense of taste, remembering as the bread and wine touch our tongues that indeed the Lord is good, and in this we celebrate our connection to the rejected and risen one.

Second, the idea that we are to offer "spiritual sacrifices" within the spiritual house built from the "living stones" of the church is one that values community, a valuing that tends to chafe against our mores today. God's people in 1 Peter are spoken of as a group ("a chosen race, a holy nation"), not as individual members. This communal temple in which we worship God *together* stands amid a society that is increasingly isolated. We experience the world today, more than ever before, as atomized individuals, with marketing algorithms on social media and internet sites pumping information to us that has been designed to appeal to our particular desires. This passage, however, reminds us that the Christian life cannot be so reduced to individual efforts and achievements. Against this wave of isolating information, the passage urges the church to take seriously its calling to be a place of vibrant conversation, relationship, and community.

Third, the full pain of rejection is something that many of us experience in a deeply personal as well as horrifically communal way. Bullying and societal scorn have profound consequences on the psyche. Teen suicide rates in the United States have risen significantly since 1999.[2] At

The Christ in Each Other

Once, when I was the only guest one Sunday night at a women's monastery, the sisters invited me to join them in . . . the community's procession into church. . . .

I didn't realize it at the time, but the sisters' invitation was an uncommon act of hospitality, and not being able to amble into church on my own to find a choir stall pushed me into recognizing what the sisters already sensed, that Christ is actively present in their worshipping community. Not as a static idea or principle, but a Word made flesh, a listening, active Christ who in the gospels tells us that he prays for us, and who promises to be with us always.

Walking slowly into church in that long line of women taught me much about liturgical time and space. I found to my surprise that the entire vespers service had more resonance for me because of the solemn way I had entered into it. Our procession was also a reminder of the procession of life itself; the older sisters with their walkers and canes had set a pace that the younger women had to follow. The prioress was my partner; we brought up the rear. "We bow first to the Christ who is at the altar," she whispered to me, as the procession lurched along, "and then we turn to face our partner, and bow to the Christ in each other." "I see," I said, and I did.

Kathleen Norris, *Amazing Grace: A Vocabulary of Faith* (New York: Riverhead Books, 1998), 162-63.

2. See Holly Hedegaard, Sally C. Curtin, and Margaret Warner, "Suicide Rates in the United States Continue to Increase," in *National Center for Health Statistics Data Brief*, no. 309 (2018).

the same time, school shootings are becoming increasingly common, almost as though the rage of rejection in each one is physically directed outward at those who are perceived to have caused it. There is certainly no simple, spiritual solution to this pain. Yet, perhaps in this passage, we learn that even as this particular community experiences rejection, they are "chosen" and "precious." In this promise, we glimpse the importance of having a place to belong, an identity that teaches us who and whose we are. Belonging and identity help us find ways to witness to the good news of Christ. This good news involves extending that identity to others and living daily into the idea of acceptance of others in bearing pain and struggle together.

Finally, if a major aspect of our identity as a church is that we have "received mercy" (v. 10), then this has cultural and political implications. Western life today is often marked by judgmental reactions when private errors are made public. More often than not, social-media sites have provided a platform on which these harsh, judgmental, and unnuanced tribal views can thrive. A church defined by mercy has a calling to exhibit that same mercy in its public behaviors and the online presence of its people. In voicing mercy online and offline alike, we demonstrate the "marvelous light" (v. 9) of God.

Politically, this identification as a people granted mercy illuminates our criminal justice system. The American prison system is not predicated on the idea of mercy or even leniency. Political platforms, in fact, often present the idea that what our nation needs is tougher laws, longer mandatory sentences, and reduced parole. Perhaps a community defined by having been shown mercy might be moved to carry that understanding of calling "out of darkness into his marvelous light" (v. 9) to those that previously had not been shown mercy (v. 10). Certainly, there is ample opportunity in the United States today for the church to lift its voice in both political and social witness to the power of grace for the incarcerated in our midst.

BRIAN S. POWERS

John 14:1–14

[1]"Do not let your hearts be troubled. Believe in God, believe also in me. [2]In my Father's house there are many dwelling places. If it were not so, would I have told you that I go to prepare a place for you? [3]And if I go and prepare a place for you, I will come again and will take you to myself, so that where I am, there you may be also. [4]And you know the way to the place where I am going." [5]Thomas said to him, "Lord, we do not know where you are going. How can we know the way?" [6]Jesus said to him, "I am the way, and the truth, and the life. No one comes to the Father except through me. [7]If you know me, you will know my Father also. From now on you do know him and have seen him."

[8]Philip said to him, "Lord, show us the Father, and we will be satisfied." [9]Jesus said to him, "Have I been with you all this time, Philip, and you still do not know me? Whoever has seen me has seen the Father. How can you say, 'Show us the Father'? [10]Do you not believe that I am in the Father and the Father is in me? The words that I say to you I do not speak on my own; but the Father who dwells in me does his works. [11]Believe me that I am in the Father and the Father is in me; but if you do not, then believe me because of the works themselves. [12]Very truly, I tell you, the one who believes in me will also do the works that I do and, in fact, will do greater works than these, because I am going to the Father. [13]I will do whatever you ask in my name, so that the Father may be glorified in the Son. [14]If in my name you ask me for anything, I will do it."

Commentary 1: Connecting the Reading with Scripture

At the end of John 13, Jesus warned his disciples that he would lay down his life for them, and so chapter 14 begins with Jesus' words: "Do not let your hearts be troubled." These are reassuring words of hope in God through Jesus. As a good leader, Jesus does not forsake his followers and is not asking anything of them that he is not willing to endure himself. Certainly, this was good news for disciples who had left everything to follow Jesus.

This invites us into a possible sermon consoling those who are anxious about the future, whether it be an illness, a family matter, a job-related concern, or larger political uncertainties. Jesus invites us to trust in him in spite of troubling times. It is also an invitation to a deeper level of discipleship, one that may involve risk. We might discern the shape of such trust in Jesus' response to Thomas's poignant question, "Lord, we do not know where you are going. How can we know the way?" (John 14:5). Not only does Jesus reassure the disciples, he directly responds to Thomas's question with a road map of sorts. In the midst of uncertainty, he asks the disciples to follow him. Even as Jesus is announcing his death, he insists that he is the way, the truth, and the life, and they can continue to trust in him. Jesus assures the disciples that they will go with him to the same place where he is going. Clearer than the precise eschatological location of such a place is the certainty of Jesus' promise.

Of course, the reference to a dwelling place in "my Father's house" in verse 2 has found its way into more than one homily and memorial service, ensuring the grieving that their loved one is embraced and cared for in the afterlife. This phrase can also be interpreted more broadly into an eschatological message about the end times. Verse 3 promises that Jesus is going to "prepare a place for you." This shows the very personal side of a God who knows us personally and cares about our salvation.

Coupled with verse 2's reference to "many dwelling places," there is space for a sermon about particularity and universality or unity within diversity. The Gospel writer offers an image of Jesus who is both preparing a room for you (personal), and yet his Father's house has many rooms (universal). This can help shape a wider imagination about our tolerance for difference, which is especially helpful in a world in which our personal opinions are constantly challenged by the diversity of God's creation. John depicts a Jesus who can relate to us while offering enough rooms for others.

Another possible sermon direction is an evangelistic sermon emphasizing Jesus' declaration to be "the way, and the truth, and the life" (v. 6). This is a very direct statement that preaches well for seekers and new believers. It can be an invitation for those needing direction and clarity in their lives to follow Jesus. This phrase is succinct as it points us to a three-point sermon that develops each topic in greater detail. A preacher can use her imagination to interpret the way as a path or journey toward a deeper relationship with Jesus. One example is a mountain-climbing guide who leads us out of the base camp to higher altitudes. Secondly, we are seeking the truth in Jesus and his moral and spiritual teachings. Lastly, the reference to life represents abundance, new opportunities, and all that is plentiful.

There are other phrases in our passage that can be infused with new life in our preaching. "No one comes to the Father except through me" can be a perhaps surprisingly helpful connection to interreligious dialogue and living with our Jewish and Muslim neighbors in a post-Holocaust, post-9/11 world. Generally speaking, there are three ways to understand how Christianity relates to other faith traditions: exclusivism, inclusivism, and pluralism. The traditional stance has been that the only way to salvation is through faith in Christ Jesus and that all others are condemned. This stance, though, has led to beliefs such as supersessionism, the belief that Christians replaced Jews as God's chosen people and that the Jews were responsible and thus held liable for Jesus' crucifixion. The inclusivist position states that there are non-Christians who act like Christ, such as Gandhi, who will be saved by God. The pluralist position argues that there are many faith traditions that lead to salvation, like bicycle spokes that lead to the hub.

A traditional interpretation of this passage is the exclusivist position that Jesus is the only way to salvation in the Father. However, the realities of anti-Semitism and religious pluralism in our communities have brought into question the usefulness and accuracy of such an interpretation, especially in light of the need for greater interreligious dialogue and understanding. Having a personal relationship with Christ and believing that he is the way to salvation does not preclude an attitude of respect, interreligious dialogue, and religious freedom. After all, we serve a God who is much bigger than our capacity to understand. We, Christians, claim to know God only *through* Jesus Christ. We can see this in Jesus' response to Philip's request to "show us the Father," when Jesus replies, "Whoever has seen me has seen the Father" (v. 9). Jesus is God's love incarnate in human form. Jesus is Immanuel, God with us. We can experience an intimate relationship of love, trust, and assurance in Jesus, and at the same time not be threatened by other religious traditions. It is possible to be a faithful Christian and believe that Jesus is the way in one's personal experience without invalidating the experience of the other.

Changing gears from the theological to the practical, the verses describing the father-son relationship can also be interpreted as a model family and invite a sermon on family relationships. Jesus' intimate relationship to the Father is an example for those who struggle with family conflicts, brokenness, and disconnection. There are members of our congregations who long for intimacy and reconciliation in family relationships that have been damaged by hurt, abuse, or neglect. This passage can offer a message of hope and reconciliation. If a father figure or parent is not physically or emotionally present in one's life, Jesus offers an image of a heavenly Father who is trustworthy and available for us in the absence of a healthy relationship with our biological family.

Lastly, this passage concludes with an emphasis on the works that result from our relationship with the Father. When we believe in Jesus, he says that we will "do the works that I do" (v. 12). Jesus does not stop there; he states that when we believe in him, we are capable of doing even "greater works than these." This is an invitation to be a disciple of Jesus who is not only a believer but also a follower and a doer. This is a helpful counterbalance to an understanding of the Gospel of John that is spiritualized and overemphasizes a personal relationship with Jesus without the resulting social responsibility and fruits of the Spirit that come with discipleship. The passage invites us to continue the works of love, compassion, and service to others that Jesus embodies throughout his ministry on earth. The Christian life is not a truncated gospel about belief in Jesus for the sake of my own personal salvation; rather it is about living out the gospel message in all areas of our life "so that the Father may be glorified" (v. 13).

PHILIP WINGEIER-RAYO

Commentary 2: Connecting the Reading with the World

We do not understand what Jesus means when he says, "In my Father's house there are many dwelling places" (John 14:2), until we make room for placeless people: international students, internally displaced persons, refugees, unhoused people, Dreamers, addicts, differently abled people, foster children, domestic-abuse victims, ignored or abused elderly folks, among too many others. When Jesus evokes the Jewish wedding custom of a groom going to prepare a place for his bride and then formally coming again to take her to live as part of his larger family, Jesus is making space and describing his relationship with disciples as a marriage.

Among the disciples, we may imagine some surprised looks and wry smiles at the marriage imagery, but the point is clear enough: they are family. They are part of an extremely large family, coming together and building a distinctive household, thanks to the person and work of Jesus. On the heels of Jesus washing his disciples' feet and instructing them to do likewise, forgiving a traitor, giving a new commandment to love, and then noting that even a close friend will deny him, the invitation is sweet. Do not let your hearts be troubled. Trust that God has space for you, no matter how unreliable, proud, or unfinished you may be. Live as a member of God's own household, acting in the distinctive way this household acts.

What is that way? Jesus shows us. His life is the witness and way. Jesus walks among and sees even the overlooked. He befriends a range of people. He heals. On this night, he eats with his disciples. He washes their feet. He forgives and reconciles in advance with those about to betray or deny him. When facing what is ahead, Jesus embodies peace and courage. What does it mean to follow "the way, and the truth, and the life" (v. 6) of Jesus? It means living the way he lived; embodying the values, postures, and truths he embodied; and spending our lives sharing the freeing, reorienting, abundant life of God. It means incarnational, relational, and missional living. It means living our story as Christ's story, as part of the same family, set up and sent out to show the needed love of God, who welcomes, creates space, and empowers us to "do the works that I do, . . . in fact, . . . greater works" (v. 12).

John 14:6, however, has a dreadful history. Plucked out of context and weaponized, it has been wielded as a triumphant statement of Christian superiority, a public challenge to other religions and individuals who disagree. It has been treated as if Jesus offered a mic-drop ultimatum. It has been made to sound as if Jesus suddenly stopped his private conversation with friends and issued a worldwide proclamation to all people, demanding explicit, universal, unequivocal belief in him.

Yet on the night Jesus prepares for death, forgives those who will betray him, witnesses to many rooms in God's house, and lines out how his family should live after he is gone, Jesus is not threatening or condemning outsiders. The night Jesus washes feet and prepares to do something so self-giving, humiliating, and terrifying as dying on a cross, Jesus does not issue a proud ultimatum. Instead, Jesus speaks to insiders, exhorting his family to witness to the God we know and see in him, urging them to keep living this way, this truth, this life, even after he is gone and especially when it is tough.

If Jesus had aimed for his disciples to embody a narrow exclusivity, he might have said, "My Father's house has just a few reserved rooms, so get your act together and command the world to do the same." Instead, in his last hours, Jesus teaches his disciples to live as he lived, revealing the stunning abundance and welcome of God. He exhorts them to live as the way, truth, and life that reshapes a pain-filled, broken world.

Liturgically, it may seem strange to return to precrucifixion stories during Eastertide. Yet this is the season's purpose: to rejoice in the power of the resurrection and retune ourselves to what it means that Christ is risen. Jesus' Farewell Discourse does not consist only of parting words of comfort. Rather, Jesus poses an ethical challenge and asks us to focus on what is next. A sermon might do the same, pointing beyond Jesus' death and resurrection. It might direct disciples to the future and what it means to be embraced with Jesus' life as the way, truth, and life for us, all thanks to the resurrection power Jesus lets loose in this world, shattering the power of death in its many forms.

Alternatively, a close reading of this text might prove liberating to congregants who struggle with this text's imperialistic use or even with the Bible's validity as a whole, given the ways John 14:6 has been punitively interpreted. Sometimes, preaching must include naming that which should be disavowed, and Christian proclamation of this text has too often focused on a single verse proclaimed without regard to larger context. Thus, another option is to preach the full content of these verses.

The world yearns to see the John 14 way of life Jesus lifts up embodied in the lives of real neighbors, coworkers, leaders, and friends. We yearn to see it in our own lives. Regardless of personal convictions about Christianity's exclusive claims, Christians largely agree that Jesus represents a decisive and authentic revelation of God. Preaching God's call to the way of life embodied in Jesus and preaching Christ's resurrection power loose in the world, enabling us to live this way, and to do so even more faithfully (v. 12) could be timely and profound. Forgiven, we forgive. Reconciled, we pursue ministries of reconciliation. Given reason to hope, we live boldly.

In short, the passage is about inclusivity. God's house has many rooms. Jesus has prepared a place for us where unexpected people become family. Consequently, disciples can live as compelling a life as Jesus did, embodying the joy, openness, and justice we know in Jesus Christ. This text asks the church about its focus. Is our life as a church a powerful manifestation of the life of Jesus? What does our table fellowship look like? Whom do we heal? Whose feet are we washing? How do we help others find family and place in the household of God? Who is around us? Whom is God inviting us to see? For whom do we create home?

The church is clearly being called to reshape its rhythms, postures, and priorities to make room for placeless people. We are being urged to recognize that church is not an end in and of itself but is an instrument of God's mission. The question is whether we need to adjust our concentration, easing our laser focus on programs, budgets, members, and internal church life and, instead, building the engagement of all members with people outside the church walls whom God may be intentionally bringing into our life for God's own kingdom purposes.

Courageous conversations and intentional boundary crossing are not optional. Jesus removed barriers, drew alongside the stranger, and prepared "many dwelling places" within his Father's house. The moment is now to join in this life-changing, life-giving work of making place. The moment is now to take seriously the witness of our lives. Let us act in the distinctive way God's household acts, living our story as Christ's story, as part of the family sent to show the deeply needed love of the One who welcomes, creates space and family for all, and empowers us to "do the works that I do and, in fact, . . . greater works than these" (v. 12).

LINDSAY P. ARMSTRONG

Sixth Sunday of Easter

Acts 17:22–31
Psalm 66:8–20
1 Peter 3:13–22
John 14:15–21

Acts 17:22–31

22Then Paul stood in front of the Areopagus and said, "Athenians, I see how extremely religious you are in every way. 23For as I went through the city and looked carefully at the objects of your worship, I found among them an altar with the inscription, 'To an unknown god.' What therefore you worship as unknown, this I proclaim to you. 24The God who made the world and everything in it, he who is Lord of heaven and earth, does not live in shrines made by human hands, 25nor is he served by human hands, as though he needed anything, since he himself gives to all mortals life and breath and all things. 26From one ancestor he made all nations to inhabit the whole earth, and he allotted the times of their existence and the boundaries of the places where they would live, 27so that they would search for God and perhaps grope for him and find him—though indeed he is not far from each one of us. 28For 'In him we live and move and have our being'; as even some of your own poets have said,

'For we too are his offspring.'

29Since we are God's offspring, we ought not to think that the deity is like gold, or silver, or stone, an image formed by the art and imagination of mortals. 30While God has overlooked the times of human ignorance, now he commands all people everywhere to repent, 31because he has fixed a day on which he will have the world judged in righteousness by a man whom he has appointed, and of this he has given assurance to all by raising him from the dead."

Commentary 1: Connecting the Reading with Scripture

"Always be ready to make to make your defense to anyone who demands from you an accounting for the hope that is in you." Thus counsels 1 Peter 3:15 in today's epistle lesson. The author appends a qualification: "yet do it with gentleness and reverence." This principle of evangelism is both moral and rhetorical, facilitates congruence between medium and message, and is fully in play as Paul addresses Stoics, Epicureans, and other Athenian intellectuals at the Areopagus. Paul has been summarily dismissed by some as a "babbler," but is given an opportunity for a hearing by others who, even if they are only vaguely curious, see no better way to pass the time than by listening to "something new" (Acts 17:16–21).

How different a resurrection proclamation this is from the one that we heard last Sunday in Acts 7:55–60! At its outset, Paul's message is seemingly more respectful of the tradition he addresses than was that of Stephen to his accusers. Yet both Paul's presentation and that of Stephen are particularly pitched to the religious and cultural roots of their respective audiences (Israel's salvation history narrative in Stephen's case, the Athenian tradition of philosophers and poets in Paul's). Both speeches directly challenge the manifestations of idolatry entrenched within each setting. Neither address can be deemed a clear success in terms of how many hearts and minds it changes. Yet Paul's resurrection proclamation does win a few converts, and more importantly perhaps, it portends the promise of a further hearing on the part of some (vv. 32–34). Stephen's proclamation moves no one—except, of course, to stone him.

Is this sufficient evidence on which to judge Stephen's speech a proclamation failure and Paul's of value limited at best? Perhaps, if the standard against which preaching success should be measured is Pentecost. On that occasion, sneering dismissals notwithstanding (2:13, 15, "They're just drunk!"), Peter's sermon produces results the likes of which have seldom been achieved by preachers since. Yet, maybe a "souls saved," results-based criterion for assessing the sermons of Paul and Stephen is not the indicator most appropriate. After all, Stephen is described at his speech's end as "filled" with the same Holy Spirit (7:55) as the one that "fills" the disciples (2:4) and sends them into the marketplace on the feast of Pentecost.

These three sermons from the book of Acts (about which we hear in three of four succeeding Sundays at the end of the season of Easter) comprise a spectrum regarding the results they generate: wide embrace at Pentecost, limited reception in Athens, total rejection at the trial in Jerusalem. Yet all three occupy a prominent place in Acts, which can perhaps be characterized as an anthology of contextual gospel preaching, for each proclamation is called forth by specific preceding events, and each is followed by the further unfolding of actions precipitated by that sermon.

The sermons in their respective settings are not just words sandwiched between stories; rather, the sermons themselves are the very "acts" of the apostles. Their sermon words are Holy Spirit–charged "speech acts"; they are *words* that *work*. The emphasis of this homiletical anthology is not which sermons "worked" and which ones did not. All have their place in an unfolding trajectory that both bears witness to and further embodies the work of the Word made flesh.

As the season of Easter comes to a close, the focus of our preaching shifts from proclaiming "Christ is risen!" to examining what it means for us to live in light of the resurrection. It may be worth a preacher's preparation time to review other resurrection proclamations that Acts recounts. The briefest survey reveals a remarkable variety. Some sermons are longer (22:1–21) while some are shorter (14:15–17). Some are addressed to crowds (2:14–36), others to individuals (8:31–37); some to Jews (11:5–17), others to Romans (10:34–43). Sermons are delivered before audiences ranging from eager to interested, skeptical to hostile. Some are addressed to persons of political prominence (24:10–21), others to ordinary folks (28:26–28). Some (like Stephen's in Jerusalem) are rigorous defenses against false charges. Some (like Paul's in Athens) are apologias before agnostics. Some (like Paul's valedictory to Christians in Ephesus) are words of comfort and encouragement to members of the Christian community (20:17–35). At least one, do not forget, puts a listener to sleep (20:7–12).

Whether or not any of these sermons find their way into the sermon under preparation for this coming Sunday, it is a worthwhile exercise in homiletical spirituality. It is humbling, reassuring, encouraging, empowering for those heading toward the pulpit to refresh their imaginations and spirits with a rapid review of how many different voices comprise the great chorus of witnesses to the resurrection, as well as how many different styles are required to address different listeners in different situations. Preachers like Peter, Paul, Stephen, Aquila, Priscilla, and Apollos all have their place, and each voice is essential in bearing witness to the fullness of God's life-transforming power

There is an underlying thread tying together Peter's sermon addressed to "devout Jews from every nation under heaven" (2:5), Stephen's defense before accusers in a kangaroo court, and Paul's interfaith dialogue attempt before the Athenian intelligentsia: an effort to honor and to engage seriously religious/philosophical/theological traditions. Yet all these preachers are also in a situation analogous to that which the Johannine Jesus alerts his followers to expect regarding "the Spirit of truth, whom the world cannot receive, because it neither sees him nor knows him" (John 14:17, in today's Gospel lection). Establishing connections, cultural or

Our Debt of Love Unceasing

Are not these inestimable benefits bestowed upon thee by thy Creator enough for thee, to make thee render to Him continual thanksgiving and pay to Him thy debt of love unceasing, when thou considerest how at the beginning of thy creation He called thee by His goodness out of nothing, or rather out of the dust of the earth to so great a height of dignity? Apply to thine own life the words of the Saints. Hear what is said concerning a Saint. This then is the praise given to a Saint: *With all his heart he praised the Lord*. Behold that end whereunto thou wast created; behold the task which thy Master hath set thee to do. For to what end should God have raised thee up by so glorious a privilege in thy creation but that He desired thee to give thyself to His praises without ceasing? Thou wast then created to praise thy Creator, so that, being occupied in nothing else than His praises, thou mightest here by the service of thy righteousness draw nearer unto Him and hereafter attain to the life of blessedness. For His praise makes thy righteousness in this world, and thy happiness in the world to come. But if thou praisest, praise Him from thy whole heart, praise Him by loving Him. For this is the rule of praising that is given to the Saints: *With all his heart he praised the Lord and loved God that made him.*

Praise therefore, and praise with thy whole heart, and love Him whom thou praisest. For he praiseth, but not with his whole heart, whom prosperity persuadeth to bless God, but adversity restraineth from the office of blessing. Again he praiseth but loveth not, who in the praises of God, seeketh to have anything by his praising beside God Himself.

Praise therefore, and praise worthily, so that to the utmost of thy power there be in thee no charge, no thought, no contemplation, no carefulness of mind, that is void of the praise of God. Let no worldly prosperity divert thee, nor any worldly adversity restrain thee from His praise. For thus thou wilt praise the Lord with thy whole heart and with love also; thou wilt seek from Him nothing else than Himself, that He may Himself be the goal of thy desire and the reward of thy labours, thy consolation in this life of shadows and thy possession in the blessed life to come. Hereunto wast thou created, that thou shouldst bear a part in His praises for ever and ever, and this thou shalt more fully understand, when thou, being lifted up by the blessed vision of Him, shalt see that by His mere free bounty thou, when thou wast not, wert out of nothing created to such happiness, and created, called, justified, glorified unto such unspeakable bliss. For the contemplation of such things will give to thee a love that shall not weary of praising Him forever, of whom and by whom and in whom thou shalt rejoice that thou art blessed with good things so great and so unchangeable.

Anselm of Canterbury, "That the End for Which We Were Created Was to Glorify God for Ever," from *The Devotions of Saint Anselm of Canterbury*, ed. Clement C. J. Webb (London: Methuen & Co., 1903), II.59-60.

historical, religious or philosophical, can take a resurrection-proclaiming preacher only so far, precisely because resurrection *is* a bridge too far.

What can be despaired over as an impossible task because of the unbridgeable gap, however, can be understood by the Christ-is-risen preacher as a place for the shaping of an empty and open space for the work of the Spirit. Again and again in Acts, while the Spirit makes use of preaching preparation and proclamation, it is the Spirit and only the Spirit that makes the converting connection. Preachers were then, and are now, dependent upon and promised the gift of an "Advocate" (John 14:16) that, abiding in us, releases us from preaching-productivity anxiety.

The same Advocate frees us as well to frame an Easter preaching space with as much sensitivity to situation and listener as we can, knowing that our preaching can produce various responses, as Stephen, Paul, and Peter would confirm. Of course, this important message *to* preachers is an important message *for* preachers to share in sermons addressed to the faithful. Members of our congregations preach resurrection one way or another, by their words that are acts and acts that are words, in a world that God inhabits and continues to call into resurrection life.

Going into his preaching encounter with the Athenians, Paul is "deeply distressed" to see that the city is full of idols. Yet, rather than retreating from the scene or undertaking a frontal attack, he engages what he finds, respectfully and dialogically. Drawing attention to those idols and initially critiquing them by means of ideas ready to hand and widely acknowledged in Greek culture, Paul tries to assist his listeners to see both *through* and *beyond* those idols. His preaching style is characterized by gentleness and reverence. What contemporary idols do preachers and parishioners encounter in contemporary cultural settings? How can Easter preaching acts be analogously framed? The prospects are as provocative and wide as the preacher's perception and imagination.

DAVID J. SCHLAFER

Commentary 2: Connecting the Reading with the World

That Jesus' resurrection is the most critical event in human history is a great understatement, especially for Christians. However, even Christian believers need reassurance that our Savior lives. As the church moves into its sixth week after the majesty and splendor of Resurrection Sunday, the lectionary provides a striking testimony of God's plan for humanity and the Messiah.[1]

In his speech to the Athenian council, Paul points to the depths of God's plans, plans that reach as far back as the beginning of creation. Sometime after attending Stephen's stoning (see last week's lectionary text, Acts 7:55–60), Paul finds himself surrounded by stones and altars dedicated to idols (Acts 17:16). Among them he observes one inscribed to an "unknown god" (v. 23). Despite being unknown to the residents of Athens, God, as the creator of earth and all in it, knows them all. People's ignorance of God's character does not preclude them from God's grace and the power of the resurrection.

While quoting a local poet, Paul explains that the Greeks—actually all humans—have always had a deep awareness of God. The Athenians may not be able to articulate their search and encounter with the Divine, but art allows deep expression for what is not easily apparent or known. Moreover, art is multilingual, speaking about and to the matters of the soul in a way that is accessible to both creator and audience.

Art, of course, is a major expression of humanity's search for and encounter with the Divine. For instance, "Hallelujah" from Handel's *Messiah* aurally brings the hearer into the awe and a majesty that surrounds the birth of Jesus, God incarnate. John Coltrane's *A Love Supreme* expresses the saxophonist's spiritual devotion and quest for God that grew from his personal struggles and addictions. With the creative groans and sighs of his melodies, we experience both intensity and release when God encounters the soul. In the vivid illustrations of the biblical narratives by Chinese artist He Qi and depictions of biblical characters with brown skin in the works of Laura James, we can imagine ourselves in the testaments of God's love and power. God's plan is expansive and does not rely on our ability to articulate it fully. Our constant searching and groping for divine revelation is evidence of God's commitment to draw near to us (v. 27).

For the first disciples, who lost Jesus' physical presence; for the first audience, who lost the second temple; and for modern listeners, who had neither, Paul's speech reassures believers that God's power transcends human power and human-made edifices. Confined by neither persons nor buildings, God's salvation is accessible to all. Similarly, while enfleshed within a first-century, devoutly Jewish man who is Mary's son, the body of Christ has become the billions

1. Beverly Roberts Gaventa, *The Acts of the Apostles* (Nashville: Abingdon, 2003), 253.

of believers throughout time and space who proclaim the gospel in word and deed. After all, the church is not a building where we worship; church is actually the activity of worship in the world in service and glory to God. Such a vision of church emboldens Christians to share with the world the love, hope, and generosity we find in the freedom of grace and gospel.

Therefore, the text teaches us that with grace comes responsibility. Every person in every place is to repent. Verses 30–31 reveal God's plan for the Messiah as judge and redeemer. As Paul's christological teaching comforts those seeking the resurrected Lord, it illustrates the limitless nature of God's love and its accounting for our human response through a life of righteousness and justice.

With his proclamation that God created all people from one ancestor (v. 26), Paul asserts the unity of humanity. Humanity is to be in community with God and one another, sharing in the gifts of dignity, justice, freedom, equality, and resources, as already espoused in the Jewish Scriptures. Such sharing is more than something we understand or believe or confess; it is an ethical mandate and the foundation for human relationships in accordance to God's kingdom.

Throughout US history, African American luminaries have turned to Paul's speech, particularly Acts 17:26, as the biblical foundation for their political rhetoric advocating for human rights, equality, and unity. Benjamin Banneker (1731–1806), an African American freeperson and a third of the team who surveyed and planned Washington, DC, used the text to attest to the intellect and character of other African Americans against the dangerous rhetoric of black inferiority as asserted by then–secretary of state Thomas Jefferson.[2] Frederick Douglass (1818–95) appealed to the conscience of white Christians using this verse in his abolitionist papers and speeches. Demetrius K. Williams observes, "For Banneker and other blacks, it was not enough to hold a particular idea to be true, but especially for Christians, those who hold the Bible as authoritative, that conviction should compel or motivate one to action."[3] In addition to affirming the humanity of other African Americans and equality for all before God, these leaders challenged white Christians who claimed or leaned into a culture of racial superiority.

In Paul's proclamation in Athens, God calls all people to repent and to live righteously. Although Paul is speaking specifically to Gentile nonbelievers, his is a message for believers as well. As a lectionary text, it becomes an exhortation for Christian self-examination and dedication to live, much like the admonition of African Americans to the whole Christian body. Jesus' impending judgment should evoke individual, ecclesial, and societal introspection and action to realize God's kingdom through just treatment and fairness to all. The church's work includes the eradication of subordination, indignities, and suffering throughout the human family.

Paul's approach in proclaiming the gospel to the Athenians is a testament to God's expansive plan. With an ethnographer's curiosity, he strives to connect with the community he visits, even in spaces of discomfort. Without condescension or berating, he uses a rhetorical strategy that resonates with the audience and respects their culture. While Paul's mission is to introduce the gospel of Jesus and to transform lives, his goal is to persuade. Despite disagreeing with what he observes, he is neither dismissive nor patronizing.

As congregations enter new communities or welcome diverse worshipers, they would do well to learn from Paul's example and avoid colonizing tendencies in our welcome of others. In his observation of what was foreign to him, Paul discovers a purpose in the altar to the unknown god that enriches his anthropology and theology. He understands the Athenians' belief system, which allows him to deepen his own belief and give expression to it. He is open to the transforming

2. Demetrius K. Williams, "The Acts of the Apostles," in *True to Our Native Land: An African American New Testament Commentary* (Minneapolis: Fortress, 2007), 236.
3. Williams, "Acts," 236.

power of God to work in and through him while he labors in planting a Word. Paul knows that the gospel of Jesus both incarnates and transcends culture and never discriminates. It is available to anyone who will listen.

Paul's encounter with the Athenians demonstrates God's generosity in the gifts of the gospel and the Holy Spirit. These gifts are accessible to all who seek God and the teachings of Jesus. Additionally, they are for those who encounter the good news through the testimony and lived examples of believers.

In the end, God's overall plan for humanity surpasses earthly imagination and limits. As Christians, we look to the resurrection to renew our faith as recipients of and participants in God's plan. As creator of all things in heaven and earth (v. 24), God unifies humans to Godself and to one another.

BRIDGETT A. GREEN

Psalm 66:8–20

8Bless our God, O peoples,
let the sound of his praise be heard,
9who has kept us among the living,
and has not let our feet slip.
10For you, O God, have tested us;
you have tried us as silver is tried.
11You brought us into the net;
you laid burdens on our backs;
12you let people ride over our heads;
we went through fire and through water;
yet you have brought us out to a spacious place.

13I will come into your house with burnt offerings;
I will pay you my vows,
14those that my lips uttered
and my mouth promised when I was in trouble.
15I will offer to you burnt offerings of fatlings,
with the smoke of the sacrifice of rams;
I will make an offering of bulls and goats.

16Come and hear, all you who fear God,
and I will tell what he has done for me.
17I cried aloud to him,
and he was extolled with my tongue.
18If I had cherished iniquity in my heart,
the Lord would not have listened.
19But truly God has listened;
he has given heed to the words of my prayer.

20Blessed be God,
because he has not rejected my prayer
or removed his steadfast love from me.

Connecting the Psalm with Scripture and Worship

In his two-volume work, the evangelist Luke traces the power of the Holy Spirit throughout time and place. At the outset, Luke 1 tells of the angels' annunciations to Zechariah and to Mary, and throughout the book of Acts, the evangelist traces the apostolic travels by which the Spirit's power is manifest to the whole of the Roman Empire. Among the narratives and twenty-eight sermons and speeches in Acts is today's first reading, Paul's proclamation of the gospel at the Areopagus in Athens, a site renowned in antiquity as a Greek religious and cultural center. The song of the angels to shepherds in the town of Bethlehem in Luke 2 is now in Acts 17 heard in Paul's preaching of the risen Christ at one of the empire's most stunning centers of public life.

The lectionary invites the assembly to respond to Paul's sermon by joining in the second half of

Psalm 66. Some verses of this psalm are cast in the plural, as if all the members of Israel are at praise, and some verses are cast in the singular, as if the author is offering a personal song of gratitude. This alternation between plural and singular is common in the Psalms, and indeed is a mark of Christian worship, in which the individual and the assembly weave in and out of one another. So it is that if this is a Sunday on which it is difficult for me to praise God, I trust to the rest of the baptized community to carry me along with their song.

The psalmist hopes that the "peoples," that is, those who are outside of the community, will hear and join in the praise. As we sing the psalm, we are joining with Paul, who is preaching to the polytheists and intellectuals of Athens. "Come and hear," we call out, appealing as did Paul especially to "God-fearers," persons outside of the faith community who are nevertheless seeking God. Paul's sermon addresses these outsiders by speaking of creation and the earth's diversity of religious devotion, while the psalm testifies to the memory of Israel, which was tested and oppressed but then led safely through their wanderings, "through fire and water." (At this phrase, Christians, although not the psalmist, might recall the fire of the Holy Spirit and the water of baptism.) Thus the first reading has recalled creation, and the psalm has echoed the history of salvation. So also Christians in their testimony speak to one another and anyone who will listen of the magnificence of the creation, the wonder of the human being, and the history of divine merciful protection for all the people.

Gratitude for God's saving of the people leads to the psalmist's glad-hearted participation in the prescribed religious ritual of offering sacrifices at the temple. Perhaps the verse about "vows" reminds us of our promises at baptism. The psalmist joins in the temple sacrifice, and we recall Paul's discussion of the world's practices of religious devotion. Luke has set this striking sermon ascribed to Paul within sight of the temples of the Acropolis, all those altars of sacrifice a backdrop to his testimony to Christ (Luke is indeed a master of narrative).

The truth is that there is no life without death. Most of what we must eat to live comes from the death of some other life, and even the birthing mother willingly offers her life so that the child will survive. Thus in many religious traditions worshipers gave to the deity some living thing as a sign of their personal devotion. Christians have likened the execution of Jesus to such a sacrifice of another's life for my own; so, as Christians singing this psalm, we might think of Christ's crucifixion, our "offering" in "the temple."

The first reading concludes with Luke's characteristic call to repentance and a life marked by righteousness, and also in the psalm we claim to have removed from ourselves iniquity: some liturgical Psalters translate verse 18 as "evil in my heart." The final verse of the psalm begins with the phrase "Blessed be God." The word "bless" has circular meaning in the Bible: we bless—that is, we praise—God, and God blesses—that is, God favors—us. "Bless" is a word describing the relationship between God and the covenant people, the God whom Paul testifies is "not far from each one of us." Since it is "in God" that we humans live, such a mutual relationship is readily offered to us all.

Paul's comment about gods who are formed "by the art and imagination of mortals" is an example of the biblical proscriptions against believers portraying images of the Divine. Some in the Reformed tradition in Christianity maintain the historic Calvinist rejection of any and all crafted images of God. Yet in praying the psalms we do indeed engage in verbal imaginative imagery. Here in Psalm 66, God is a being who was active in history, a leader of the people, whose glory resides in a house, who gladly receives the fire and smoke of sacrifices, a divinity who loves humankind. Our minds endeavor to form a composite picture of such a God, and as Christians, we are assisted in this religious exercise by seeing on the mountaintop the cross of Jesus Christ and in a cave an empty tomb.

GAIL RAMSHAW

1 Peter 3:13–22

[13]Now who will harm you if you are eager to do what is good? [14]But even if you
do suffer for doing what is right, you are blessed. Do not fear what they fear,
and do not be intimidated, [15]but in your hearts sanctify Christ as Lord. Always be
ready to make your defense to anyone who demands from you an accounting
for the hope that is in you; [16]yet do it with gentleness and reverence. Keep your
conscience clear, so that, when you are maligned, those who abuse you for your
good conduct in Christ may be put to shame. [17]For it is better to suffer for doing
good, if suffering should be God's will, than to suffer for doing evil. [18]For Christ
also suffered for sins once for all, the righteous for the unrighteous, in order to
bring you to God. He was put to death in the flesh, but made alive in the spirit,
[19]in which also he went and made a proclamation to the spirits in prison, [20]who in
former times did not obey, when God waited patiently in the days of Noah, during
the building of the ark, in which a few, that is, eight persons, were saved through
water. [21]And baptism, which this prefigured, now saves you—not as a removal of
dirt from the body, but as an appeal to God for a good conscience, through the
resurrection of Jesus Christ, [22]who has gone into heaven and is at the right hand
of God, with angels, authorities, and powers made subject to him.

Commentary 1: Connecting the Reading with Scripture

This reading contains some of the most difficult christological passages and troublesome exhortations in the NT. Our passage follows a section that calls believers to live honorably in their social station, ending with a quotation of Psalm 34 that emphasizes doing good. Verses 13–17 describe a part of that doing of good, and verses 18–22 provide that conduct a christological foundation. This christological material also undergirds the exhortations that follow.

First Peter addresses churches that are experiencing persecution. This persecution probably consists mostly of economic and social harassment, but cases could easily lead them to unfriendly courts. It also seems likely that claiming to be a "Christian" (1 Pet. 4:16) could already lead to arrest. So it is unexpected when 3:13 continues the sentiment of Psalm 34 by asking, "Who will hurt you if you are trying to do right?" They know that many will hurt them for right behavior, and verse 14 acknowledges that some do suffer for righteousness. Declaring those who suffer unjustly "blessed" echoes the Beatitudes (Matt. 5:10) and the call not to fear others draws on Isaiah 8:12–13. Here, "blessed" does not mean "happy." Instead, "blessed" is an eschatological promise that the suffering believers now experience cannot do them ultimate harm. Further, the author says their good lives would make their accusers ashamed of their slanders. It is not clear whether this being ashamed happens now or at the day of judgment.

Verse 17 cites a common saying of the era, that it is better to suffer for doing good than for doing evil (see, e.g., Plato, *Polit.* 285E), but 1 Peter adds that such suffering is better if God wills it. The emphasis is not on God choosing some people to suffer but on God's will that believers do good—even if it leads to suffering.

Verses 18–22 interpret the readers' suffering through the life of Christ. These verses assert that Christ sets the example of accepting suffering for doing God's will. He is the example because his suffering was not the end of the story. After his suffering, God vindicated his life through the resurrection. Christ is more than an example here; he is also the Savior through whom you can be sure that you will receive God's blessings if you remain faithful in suffering.

The NT often talks about the death of Jesus as a means of salvation (e.g., Mark 10:45; John 11:50–53; Rom. 5:8; 1 Cor. 15:3–5; 2 Cor. 5:14). First Peter 3:18 is one of the very few NT passages in which the suffering of Jesus is represented as being itself salvific. The author has changed a traditional statement to support his larger argument, which contends that when the readers suffer for doing good, they are following the example of Jesus. The author of 1 Peter does not have in mind an atonement theory that says Christ's sufferings needed to match what sinners deserve in order to be efficacious. His point is that Christ endured unjust suffering for the benefit of others and that God vindicated that way of living through the resurrection and through giving salvation through Christ. Recalling Christ's willingness to suffer for our good can remind us of God's love for us and of the expectation that the saved imitate Christ by living in a way that privileges the benefit of others.

The description of the salvific work of Christ and God in verses 18–22 is difficult to follow. It seems to cite a number of traditions and preformed liturgies that have been altered to fit the argument. First, he says that Christ was killed "in the flesh" but made alive "in the spirit" (v. 18). Flesh and spirit refer to different realms. The flesh represents existence in the earthly realm, while spirit designates a realm of a different sort of existence, a resurrection existence. This coheres well with Paul's description of the resurrection body of Christ in 1 Corinthians 15.

Next, he says that Christ "made a proclamation to the spirits in prison" (3:19). Some see here a basis for the idea that Christ descended to preach to people in hell between his death and resurrection. However, this is not a reference to humans who had died. Rather, these imprisoned spirits are the powers responsible for causing the evil that led to the flood (v. 20). Jesus' proclamation to them does not offer salvation. Instead, it announces the sealing of their doom by God's exaltation of Christ. Christ does not descend into hell to tell them this but rather announces it in his progression of upward movement to the right hand of God. In the ancient world, people envisioned a series of levels or realms between earth and God's realm. The higher one went, the more powerful the being. Here, God has imprisoned the spirits of Genesis 6 in one of these levels. So the prison is not in a region *below* but in a region appropriate to the kinds of beings they are. Christ's resurrection and ascension are the sign that their defeat is permanent, and he proclaims that defeat to them as he ascends.

Reference to the flood leads the author to draw a parallel between Noah and members of his churches. As a few were saved from the evil around them in the ark, so now the few in Peter's church, on whom evil is inflicting suffering, are saved by the waters of baptism. It is not the act of baptism that saves them, but through it they have access to the blessing of Christ's resurrection. Our passage ends with a reference to the exaltation of Jesus to a position above all other powers of the cosmos. This makes it certain that those who suffer for their faith will ultimately experience salvation in the Christ who has power over all forces that oppose him and his people.

This passage seeks to strengthen believers who are experiencing unjust suffering by assuring them of God's vindication, mediated to them through the exalted Christ. They are encouraged to see their suffering as an imitation of Christ's willingness to suffer for others. While this can be great comfort to those trapped in unjust suffering, it is also very dangerous. Such passages have been used to encourage wives to remain with abusive husbands and to tell the oppressed or enslaved to accept their suffering as an imitation of Christ. This is certainly an illegitimate use of what this text says.

The recipients of 1 Peter had no means to escape their suffering other than denying their faith. When those in power call on those below them to suffer to imitate Christ, it is always a violation of the gospel. Those who call on the less powerful to suffer place themselves among those who will experience the eschatological shame of having harmed God's people. Those who are caught in unjust suffering can, however, look to 1 Peter for the assurance that such suffering does not have the last word. They can interpret their suffering through the death and resurrection of Christ which gives them assurance that they will receive God's salvation.

This text offers us assurance that difficulties, even tragedies, cannot separate the faithful from the salvation God gives us in the exalted Christ. It is also a call for the church to be a community that models putting the good of others ahead of one's own good. This is a call particularly to those among us who hold significant status: we must be sure to privilege the needs of those of lesser status, just as Christ gave up status by coming to earth and dying on the cross for us.

JERRY L. SUMNEY

Commentary 2: Connecting the Reading with the World

"Who would want to harm you if you do good?" Weary of the world and as students of history, we might answer with an indignant, "Are you serious?" First Peter recognizes this reality as well. The groups in Asia Minor to whom it was written likely lived in a vulnerable social position as "aliens and exiles" (1 Pet. 2:11) and would have been subject to a great deal of suspicion from the local populace. When natural disasters occurred, the people with strange gods were convenient scapegoats. While Christians here were less likely to be caught up in events like the fire in Rome in the mid-60s CE that was set by Nero, but for which he subsequently blamed and executed Christians, they still faced a good deal of contempt and ostracism from their neighbors.

First Peter recognizes that these believers are in a difficult position, and its guidelines for their behavior are guided by an idea that whatever they do, their words and actions must give testimony to Christ and to all that is therefore "good."

In this passage, we hear the exhortation to live in order to "sanctify Christ" (3:15) both in our hearts and outward behavior. This call to holy living can certainly relate to the difficulties of disciplining our behavior (particularly in the face of the ridicule of others) in order to have a "good conscience" (v. 21) before God.

This passage, like the passage from 1 Peter last week, includes several exegetical pitfalls that we must avoid. The first revolves around the notion of being persecuted for moral behavior. It is easy to read ourselves into the position of the church seeking to do good and equating the ideological opponents we might encounter in our society with those who would seek to harm us for our proper stances. This position has a tendency to close off dialogue and harden carefully constructed boundaries between groups who might disagree over sociopolitical issues. The passage exhorts believers in the opposite direction. The church here is called not to turn inward upon its own "goodness" but to present the gospel outward. So perhaps it is helpful to suspend the idea that our behavior is inherently proper at the outset of our interpretation, in order that we might pay closer attention to how the passage calls us to live into our baptisms as an appeal for "a good conscience" (v. 21).

In addition, the interpreter must also be wary of the idea of "redemptive suffering" and its shameful history within Christian theology. Passages like this one have been used to dismiss the complaints of those in situations of systemic oppression.[1] For example, the suffering of women in abusive relationships has been historically neglected with the understanding that their suffering might actually be a "spiritual" benefit. Certainly, we may accept that our own behavior may come with consequences that we are prepared to bear, but we should be wary of how much we undermine the gospel in attempting to make meaning of *someone else's* suffering.

With these two cautions in mind, I offer three ways in which we might find resonances with this passage. First, in terms of an ecclesial and social context, the passage sets the standards for Christian behavior in a way that is defined independently of the surrounding culture. Our society appears to be increasingly polarized

1. John Calvin argues that this verse indicates that "persecutions ought to be borne with resignation." Yet, as James Cone discusses in *A Black Theology of Liberation* (Maryknoll, NY: Orbis, 1970), 28, the problem arises when those in power attempt to ascribe this meaning to the suffering of the oppressed.

and agitated. We can find ourselves drawn into responding to vitriol and hyperbole in kind. The author here reminds us that our calling is different. We are to respond to our neighbors with "gentleness and reverence," both in order to validate the authenticity of our witness and to keep a "good conscience" (v. 21) ourselves. The church embodies this when it cultivates spaces where believers and members of the community can engage without insult and attack but with deliberately exercised care and concern.

Today we are called to maintain faithfulness in these principles amid means of dialogue that would continually seek to force us to join the fray and respond with anger and insult as a first instinct. Our public discourses on so many issues reflect this fury and outrage at those who disagree with us. The passage roots itself in the idea that we should "not fear what they fear" (v. 14), that our calling is set in a different realm of motivations. This suggests that faithfulness and fear of the Lord motivate Christians, rather than the fear of looking foolish, of not accumulating wealth, of being scorned. The passage suggests that our behavior as committed Christians must be different, full of the grace and patience reflected in God's actions in Christ. If we do otherwise, we undermine the "good news" and pollute it with hypocrisy and hostility.

Second, since this letter is written to those who hold a precarious position with the urging that they should continue to do what is right, even if it entails suffering, there is a connection with those who occupy this same position in our society today. A significant percentage of American political rhetoric in the past few years has become increasingly hostile to undocumented (and even to legal) immigrants. Protection of those in this status is a consistent theme of Scripture,[2] and in our current environment, Christians should note that protecting immigrants and demonstrating grace in this way may come at a cost.

Finally, this passage speaks to the difficulty of discerning a "good" moral path today and points to grace in this struggle for a "good conscience." As a German pastor in the 1930s, Dietrich Bonhoeffer was initially an ardent pacifist. As the war dragged on, Bonhoeffer concluded that there were no "good" moral choices, that any action was a decision between "wrong and wrong."[3] He argued that the only responsible thing to do was to accept that we occasionally have to take on guilt for the sake of others in imitation of Christ. We cannot justify our own actions, but we throw ourselves on the mercy of God. One might paraphrase Bonhoeffer's insight in terms of an "appeal to God for a good conscience" (v. 21) in a morally confounding world.

Few of us find ourselves in the same moral crucible Bonhoeffer endured, yet our public discourse certainly makes it extremely difficult to discern what is true, what is morally good, what is even real. Politicians no longer argue over the best ways to solve a problem but over the reality that defines the problem. What is a value to one church, political organization, or even an individual friend is the evil, root cause of suffering to another.

The end of this passage, however, contains a moment of grace: the reminder that baptism saves us, not by taking away our sin but as "an appeal to God for a good conscience" (v. 21). Baptism is not an act that instantly makes all things right; rather, it joins us in hope to Christ. That is, baptism embraces the promises of forgiveness and of a cleansing from the moral and spiritual pollution that seems unavoidable today. How can we embody such "grace" for those who experience this moral pain?

BRIAN S. POWERS

2. See Exod. 22:21; Lev. 19:33–34; Deut. 10:17–19; Isa. 56:1–8; Jer. 7:5–7; and Luke 10:25–37, among other passages.
3. Dietrich Bonhoeffer, *Ethics*, trans. Reinhard Krauss, Charles C. West, and Douglas W. Stott (Minneapolis: Fortress, 2009), 284.

John 14:15–21

[15]"If you love me, you will keep my commandments. [16]And I will ask the Father,
and he will give you another Advocate, to be with you forever. [17]This is the Spirit
of truth, whom the world cannot receive, because it neither sees him nor knows
him. You know him, because he abides with you, and he will be in you.
[18]"I will not leave you orphaned; I am coming to you. [19]In a little while the world
will no longer see me, but you will see me; because I live, you also will live. [20]On
that day you will know that I am in my Father, and you in me, and I in you. [21]They
who have my commandments and keep them are those who love me; and those
who love me will be loved by my Father, and I will love them and reveal myself
to them."

Commentary 1: Connecting the Reading with Scripture

This passage opens with a bold challenge: "If you love me, you will keep my commandments" (John 14:15). Discipleship stares us in the face. We also see the connection between a personal relationship with Christ and a testimony of love and service to others. This challenges the stereotypes of both evangelical Christians, who tend to prioritize conversion but are sometimes short on outreach and social justice, and so-called liberal Christians, who are advocates of social justice but tend to neglect evangelism. Jesus emphasizes both/and, a holistic Christian faith that maintains that both evangelism and justice are necessary aspects of the Christian life. This message of a holistic gospel is reiterated in verse 21 when Jesus states, "They who have my commandments and keep them are those who love me."

This reminds me of the passage in which the Pharisees attempted to trick Jesus by asking him which was the most important commandment (Matt. 22:37–39). Jesus wisely replied that we ought to love the Lord with all our heart, mind, and strength and to love our neighbors as ourselves. Jesus did not separate love of God from love of neighbor. Just as a healthy spiritual life involves a personal relationship with Jesus Christ, it also produces an outward expression of the fruits of the Spirit (Gal. 5:22–23).

While the first half of John 14 focuses on the relationship between Jesus and the Father, verse 16 offers insight into the role of the third person of the Trinity when Jesus points to the sure arrival of "another Advocate." This could serve as an invitation to a Trinitarian sermon about the three persons of the Godhead. The NRSV chooses "Advocate" as its translation of *paraklēton*, while the footnote offers the alternative rendering of "Helper." As Jesus foretells his death, he asks the Father to send the Holy Spirit to abide with his followers.

The preacher might focus on the inner workings and roles of the three persons of the Godhead with a particular emphasis on the Holy Spirit. One manifestation of that relationship is found in the Greek term *perichōrēsis*, which illustrates the divine dance in the intimate and harmonious relationship between the Father, Son, and Holy Spirit. The three persons interrelate with distinct characteristics yet with the fluidity of being one God.

It might also be helpful to connect John's invitation into Trinitarian thinking with a more recent attempt to imagine the complexity of divine identity. William Young's book *The Shack*[1] sold more than twenty million copies and climbed the bestseller list before being

1. William P. Young, *The Shack* (Thousand Oaks, CA: Windblown Media, 2007).

made into a movie. Sometimes controversial, the book depicts the main character, Mack, recovering from an abusive relationship with his father, finding a note to meet with "Papa" in an abandoned shack. The plot takes several twists and turns until Mack is reconciled with the Father through the Son with the assistance of the Holy Spirit. The book depicts the Father as an African American woman and the Holy Spirit as an Asian woman. Nevertheless, evangelical Christians bought the book in droves and participated in book studies to deepen their understanding of the Holy Trinity through Young's fictional account. The popularity of this book speaks to the curiosity and difficulty we have in understanding the mystery of the Holy Trinity.

Metaphors often fall short in explaining the fullness of the Holy Trinity. Recent efforts have described the Trinity as the liquid, ice, and vapor forms of water; as the yolk, white, and shell of an egg; and even as a boom box that can play the radio, a CD, or a cassette. Yet none of these metaphors can grasp the mystery of the Holy Trinity; they are simply inadequate to the task. As Paul states elsewhere, "For now we see in a mirror, dimly" (1 Cor. 13:12).

Of the three persons of the Trinity, the Holy Spirit is by far the least discussed and understood by the mainline Protestant traditions. John's reference to the Holy Spirit is an invitation to preach and teach on this overlooked and often misunderstood person of the Trinity. Some churches wait every year until the day of Pentecost to discuss the Holy Spirit; however, pneumatology is at the center of John's theology. Peruvian Pentecostal theologian Bernardo Campos calls on all Christians to embrace the Holy Spirit as God's gift to the whole church.[2] He believes that many Christians abdicate their access to the power of the Holy Spirit and assume that only Pentecostals can speak of Pentecost. Campos reasserts that Pentecost was an event for all of Christianity and we all have access to the Holy Spirit as an advocate. Clearly in this passage, Jesus is offering the Holy Spirit to all Christians, just as he prepares for death, resurrection, and ascension.

As we interpret how the three persons of the Trinity relate to one another, it is revealing that Jesus says, "And I will ask the Father, and he will give you another Advocate" (John 14:16). This places God the Father as the source of the Holy Spirit. The Eastern and Western Christian traditions split in large part over their interpretation of this passage in what became known as the *filioque* controversy. The Western or Latin church meeting at the Council of Toledo in 589 added the phrase "and the Son" (*filioque*) to the Nicene Creed, while the Eastern church continued to believe that the Holy Spirit proceeds only from the Father. This eventually led to the great schism in 1054 between Eastern and Western Christianity. This leads to an opportunity to speak of unity in diversity, just as the Trinity is three in one.

Without entering more deeply into the ecumenical councils and this theological controversy, it might suffice to say that the Holy Spirit is advocate or helper. This is a consoling message for Christians, to know that we are not alone. In an insular Western capitalist culture, societal ills such as alcoholism, drug addiction, gambling, pornography, and consumerism are often the result of attempts to fill a void left by loneliness. Perhaps this explains the ill-conceived attempts to find intimacy as expressed in the country music lyric, "Looking for love in all the wrong places."

An understanding of the Holy Spirit as the consoler can be especially profound for those who have suffered a loss or face anxiety about an uncertain future. Just as Jesus warns the disciples that he will leave them soon and offers the Holy Spirit as a consoler to be "in"—or as the NRSV footnote states, "among"—you. Invariably, there are persons in our congregations suffering from loss, separation, and broken human relationships. Verse 18 especially highlights this message by using the term "orphaned" to refer to the followers who might feel forsaken by Jesus' death.

Another possible sermon trajectory is a word of encouragement for the beleaguered. Sometimes people feel tired and struggle to continue on. Ministry, just like life, can throw challenges

2. Bernardo Campos, *El Principio Pentecostalidad: La Unidad del Espiritu, Fundamento de la Paz* (Salem, OR: Publicaciones Kerigma, 2016).

at us, and people lose sight of their first love of Jesus. The Gospel of John offers food for Christians on the journey stating that "the world will no longer see me, but you will see me" (John 14:19). In other words, although it may seem that Jesus has abandoned us or is not in sight, he is with us, accompanying us, and will reward us.

PHILIP WINGEIER-RAYO

Commentary 2: Connecting the Reading with the World

"In the beginning was the Word," the opening of John affirms. An entirely new world came from the miracle of words and the Word of God. Now, at the end of Jesus' life as in its beginning, Jesus is summoning a new world into being. Within the next twenty-four hours, Jesus will have been tried, unjustly convicted, tortured, and executed as an enemy of the state, and Jesus' followers will face real decisions. Who will they be, once Jesus is gone? Will they be a part of an understandable world of vengeance, victims, and victors? Will they, rather, live in the world Jesus is creating where those who love him do something about it, not just paying lip service but actually carrying out his commandments? Will the disciples live in fear or root themselves in God's love, which casts out fear (1 John 4:18)? Recognizing that they may feel abandoned, vulnerable, and even orphaned by God, Jesus promises an Advocate who will be with them even after he is gone.

In Eastertide, this text is sobering. We too live between worlds and, caught between them, we worry. We worry about melting ice caps, jobs, health care, and politics. We worry about having enough and being enough, about measuring up or about contributing too much or too little. We worry about the poor and disenfranchised, about being safe and valued, about the world future generations will inherit. We worry about people with different worldviews and priorities, about the church and its future, about the fidelity and presence of God. We can wear ourselves out with worry.

Jesus invites us into a different world, one in which he reigns, love is widespread, and we are not orphaned but have an ever-present Advocate. Poised between reality and hope, vacillating between thinking of this moment as a crushing moment of difficulty or a wondrous moment of possibility, when sharing the love of God is our call and the world's deepest need, we are invited into a world where we who love Jesus resist temptations to forget or doubt him, instead trusting and following his commandments (John 13:34).

Rather than living as if Jesus is dead and gone, we celebrate him alive and active. Invited into a reciprocal relationship of loving and being loved, we love as a bodily act of testimony and resistance to the seductive world of anxiety. We live as citizens of the new world Jesus is summoning. We remain voices of hope that resist despairing over what has not yet happened but draw attention to God among us (14:17, 19, 21). We revel in resurrection, not as the culmination of God's work, but as the inauguration of a new world filled with the presence and power of Jesus extending past the empty tomb into our lives and beyond. We move our lives into coherence with the new reign and rule of Jesus.

Like disciples before us, we are neither helpless, powerless, nor abandoned. As Easter people, we declare and live into God's new world, resisting the temptation to reduce our faith to a privatized narcotic and instead embracing the world-generating, world-changing commandments of Jesus.

Beyond this personal connection to resist the lure of anxiety, there is also an ecclesiastical connection to draw. Throughout the Farewell Discourse, Jesus speaks to a community. After all, imagining and living beyond our present circumstances requires community, for no one can robustly and sustainably hope alone. In speaking to a group, he returns time and again to a central theme: love. Love has been embodied in the washing of the disciples' feet and prioritized in the issuance of a new commandment that they love one another (13:34–35). It has been expressed in the foretelling of denial, followed immediately by the comforting call, "Do not let your hearts be troubled" (13:36–14:1).

Now, love bookends this lectionary excerpt as if Jesus was using the brain science dictum: repeat to remember. Repeat to remember. Repeat to remember. This message was so important that Jesus used his final hours to reinforce it: you are people who are loved, and so love. It is your defining characteristic (13:34; 14:15, 21). Relationship with God is not contingent on physical presence but builds from a shared willingness to live the love exemplified by Jesus' life.

People yearn for meaning in their lives. We want to live distinctively and make positive impacts together. Consequently, we might explore questions like these in a sermon: How do we as a community love in the way Jesus commands, models, and empowers? Such love is more than emotion or sentiment. As Jesus was sent by the Father, so we are sent. What might it look like to love deeply and seriously the few blocks or few miles around our church building? What does it mean that we are located where we are? Furthermore, what does it mean that the love of God is reciprocal (14:15, 21)? How do we allow ourselves to be loved and open ourselves to the gifts, kindness, beauty, and goodness of others? We need to be loved as much as we need to share love. What it means to be people of God is to be people who, thanks to the love of God we know in Jesus, actively share and receive love.

A third preaching connection could focus on engaging the Holy Spirit and the difference she makes in our lives. Verse 16 includes John's first reference to the Holy Spirit. The Greek word for Holy Spirit (*paraklētos*) can be translated many ways: "Comforter," "Counselor," "Helper," "Intercessor," "Advocate." As Jesus goes to the Father, it is not only that he will advocate for and be with disciples from far away. Alongside this, "another Advocate . . . [will] be with you forever" (v. 16). Jesus was the first Advocate, and now God sends another. Consequently, we understand the Holy Spirit when likening her presence with us to Jesus' presence and way of being with his first followers.

A constant companion like Jesus, the Holy Spirit is not remote but is "Comforter," alongside and present. As "Counselor" and "Spirit of Truth," the Holy Spirit teaches and reminds us of all that Jesus did and said (v. 26). As "Helper," the Holy Spirit assists disciples everywhere with obeying Jesus' commands and recognizing God in our midst (vv. 17, 19). As "Intercessor," the Holy Spirit prays for us and intervenes with God on our behalf. As "Advocate," the Holy Spirit stands alongside us, walking with us, assisting us, and working with and for us when our faith leads us crosswise with the powers that be. How freeing it is to know that we are neither alone nor solely dependent on our own strength! The Spirit of truth abides with and in us (v. 17). We are not orphaned (v. 18), nor do we orphan others by walking with them only from a distance.

Knowing this, the disciples overcame the fear that had so characterized the beginning of the night, and they went out into a difficult world with love, intentionality, and peace (v. 27), as we now can do. We can do this because the Holy Spirit is present and the power of death already defeated. Even when we are tired and have had enough, we can be loving and peace-filled because we are called, not just to be alongside others as Jesus was intimately alongside. Instead, we are given the Holy Spirit who actively works in our lives. When we doubt it, the Holy Spirit even helps us see and believe again.

LINDSAY P. ARMSTRONG

Ascension of the Lord

Acts 1:1–11
Psalm 93
Ephesians 1:15–23
Luke 24:44–53

Acts 1:1–11

[1]In the first book, Theophilus, I wrote about all that Jesus did and taught from the
beginning [2]until the day when he was taken up to heaven, after giving instructions through the Holy Spirit to the apostles whom he had chosen. [3]After his
suffering he presented himself alive to them by many convincing proofs, appearing to them during forty days and speaking about the kingdom of God. [4]While
staying with them, he ordered them not to leave Jerusalem, but to wait there for
the promise of the Father. "This," he said, "is what you have heard from me; [5]for
John baptized with water, but you will be baptized with the Holy Spirit not many
days from now."

[6]So when they had come together, they asked him, "Lord, is this the time when
you will restore the kingdom to Israel?" [7]He replied, "It is not for you to know the
times or periods that the Father has set by his own authority. [8]But you will receive
power when the Holy Spirit has come upon you; and you will be my witnesses
in Jerusalem, in all Judea and Samaria, and to the ends of the earth." [9]When he
had said this, as they were watching, he was lifted up, and a cloud took him out
of their sight. [10]While he was going and they were gazing up toward heaven,
suddenly two men in white robes stood by them. [11]They said, "Men of Galilee,
why do you stand looking up toward heaven? This Jesus, who has been taken up
from you into heaven, will come in the same way as you saw him go into heaven."

Commentary 1: Connecting the Reading with Scripture

While he was *going* up, they were *gazing* up, Luke says of the disciples. Followers of Luke's story line probably follow their gaze or fix on the watchers. What do *they* see that *we* do not? Artists fill this question space with visual representations. Sceptics raise eyebrows, dismissing ascension assertions as empirically indefensible. Cynics sneer at presumed media manipulation—reason swamped by sense-clogged feeling. All these visions, however, divert attention from elements in Luke's wider story world that, while seemingly peripheral to the central focus, are curious and seemingly incongruous. After all, there are conflicting elements in Luke 24 and Acts 1, the author's two accounts of Jesus' ascension. On this Sunday, the Liturgy of the Word starkly juxtaposes these differing story features.

First, *when* did the ascension occur? Luke 24:50–51 seems to indicate it happens at the end of an eventful Easter day. Acts 1 places it after forty days of postresurrection "convincing proofs" from the risen Lord. Second, *from where* did Jesus go up? The Mount of Olivet (Acts 1:12) or close to Bethany (Luke 24:50). Third, the stories concur that the disciples return to Jerusalem after the ascension. They are found in public, in the temple, blessing God, as Jesus just blessed them—if we follow the narrative sequence in Luke's Gospel. On the other hand, however, if the story from Acts 1 is extended beyond verse 11—where the disciples' heavenward gazing is summarily checked by "two men in white robes"—the disciples are found in a smaller, indoor, and private space, "in the room upstairs," where they are "constantly devoted to prayer" and selecting a successor to the recently self-executed Judas. Each of these narrative discrepancies alone is eye-catching, assuming one is not looking up to heaven. Taken together, they deserve preaching attention, especially since Luke is a consummate storyteller, a master of detail.

Attention demanding as these divergent details in parallel renderings of a single narrative might be, focusing on them too closely could distract us from what might be a further, even more significant disparity, one generated (ironically) by a point of *agreement* in the two accounts. This postascension/pre-Pentecost consonance appears to be in some tension—not just narrative but theological—with two places early on in Luke's Gospel. Immediately after the ascension and following Jesus' explicit instructions (Luke 24:49), the disciples spend several days waiting around until they are "clothed with power from on high." Acts 1:8 corroborates this directive: Jesus promises that the disciples will receive power when the Holy Spirit comes upon them. Yet twice during his ministry, Jesus has *previously* conferred power and authority on disciples, the Twelve in Luke 9:1–6 and "seventy others" in Luke 10:1–12, 17–24. *Then*, he grants them immediate power to undertake a mission of proclamation, exorcism, and healing, while after the ascension they must wait until the rushing, violent wind-like sound and divided tongues "as of fire" descend from heaven on Pentecost.

Before setting a homiletical direction, however, preachers would do well to recall John's account of the ascension, especially the admonition of the risen Lord to Mary forbidding her to touch him since he has "not yet ascended to the Father" (John 20:17). Jesus goes on to instruct her to inform the disciples that he will be ascending to God the Father, his Father and theirs too.[1] As we have already encountered in the Acts reading for Easter 5, Stephen, just before his stoning, is given a vision of Jesus at God's right hand (Acts 7:55–56). Various ascension references in the epistles tend to conflate or conjoin Jesus' resurrection and ascension in terms of how they signify his exaltation and glorification. For example, there is Paul's reference to Jesus sitting "at the right hand of God" (Rom. 8:34), his more extensive detail in the Christ hymn (Phil. 2:5–11, esp. v. 9), and a more indirect allusion in Romans 10:6. Hebrews describes Christ as having "passed through the heavens" (Heb. 4:14), being "exalted above the heavens" (7:26), and having entered the heavenly sanctuary (9:24). Note also 1 Peter 3:21–22 for yet another "gone into heaven at the right hand of God" reference.

Christ's resurrection and ascension as his *exaltation* are given a full rhetorical orchestration of doxological expression in today's epistle text of Ephesians 1:15–23. His "right hand in the heavenly places" position is elaborated in over-the-top superlatives: "far above" any other form of "rule," "authority," "power," "dominion," as well as above "every name that is named, not only in this age but also in the age to come." Just in case we missed the point, God has "put all things under his feet and has made him the head over all things." *That* is exaltation for you, stratospherically beyond the upward-straining gaze of anyone whose feet are rooted on the earth—or so it would surely seem.

The two men in white robes[2] who stand right beside the upward-looking, neck-straining, eye-squinting disciples say something surprising: the One taken up to heaven will come to them in the same way they have seen him go. Maybe that is "the Second Coming." Maybe it means Pentecost (if we allow "in the same way" a little interpretive breathing room). Maybe both, but also something more. It may be that storyteller Luke may, through his many disorienting perspectival shifts, be shaping a space for theological imagination in the church and in its preachers.

Biblical accounts of theophanies (think Abraham, Jacob, Moses, Gideon, Isaiah, Zechariah, Mary, Jesus' transfiguration) seem to come, in

1. Cf. John 7:33 as well as the consolation, assurance, and continuing connection Jesus proclaims in the Farewell Discourse (14:12, 28; 16:5, 10, 28).

2. For an understanding of the two "men" (both here and in Luke 24:1–7) as Moses and Elijah, who are also depicted by text and tradition as being taken up to heaven, see A. Katherine Grieb, following Luke T. Johnson, in *Feasting on the Word: Year B, Volume 1* (Louisville, KY: Westminster John Knox, 2008), 479–83.

their narrative presentations, "from the top down." The ascension, however, seems to be going "from the ground up." Of course, as often, and not inappropriately, understood, this leave taking gives the disciples space (and requires that they take it) to move without their supervisor in ready, tangible reach, as was the case in the Gospel of Luke when the Twelve and the seventy are sent out on what we might call "evangelism internship trips." Now the range of their mission has been radically extended: to the ends of the earth.

What to make of all this? If the author of Ephesians has it right, the exaltation of Jesus is not intended primarily to put us in our place. Rather, the ascension helps us perceive and appropriate the power of the risen Lord as the "fullness of him who fills all in all" (Eph. 1:23). Hence this interpretive hypothesis: Luke's back-and-forth—between descriptions of when and where the ascension happened and of what subsequent spaces prior to Pentecost the disciples were in and out of—may suggest or at least permit preachers to envision the ascent of the Lord and the descent of the Spirit as continually complementary moves. The presence and power of the triune God is a continual dynamic of ascending and descending (cf. Gen. 28:10–22 and John 1:43–51). This "up and down" movement both facilitates and animates the "in and out" and "back and forth" movements to which Luke bears witness in the Gospel and in Acts.

DAVID J. SCHLAFER

Commentary 2: Connecting the Reading with the World

Ascension of the Lord can be a time when we experience Jesus' presence differently. Like our apostolic ancestors, we are in between the majesty of Resurrection Sunday and the wonder of Pentecost. Although Jesus is lifted out of the earthly scene, he becomes omnipresent in the mission and ministry of the church. Our text from Acts prepares us to encounter Jesus and experience the expansion of the gospel through the power of the Holy Spirit and with the faithful work of his apostles.

Our passage begins a new volume of a long narrative history. It shifts focus from Jesus' active ministry on earth to the "acts of the apostles," pivoting from Jesus' physical presence to his absence. For the writer of Luke–Acts, Jesus' resurrection is a decisive moment in, though not the climax of, the Christian story.[3] Forty days after his resurrection, Jesus commissions his apostles to continue spreading the good news and then takes his leave when he ascends into heaven to his throne of glory.

During this transition, Jesus is quite present in the text. Notice that Acts 1:1–11 contains the final scene of Jesus teaching his apostles. Luke grounds the apostles' mission and frames the book of Acts by reminding the reader about "all that Jesus did and taught" (Acts 1:1). Along with a prologue with elements similar to the Lukan Gospel, this text signals the continuation of Jesus' mission. Rhetorically, the story reminds us that the kerygma of God's kingdom does not end with Jesus' exit; rather, the good news spreads and ministry expands because of the perpetual power of his words and actions to give life. After his ascension, his omnipresence is realized through the baptism and empowerment of the Holy Spirit as well as in the miraculous power of his name in the life and ministry of the church. Female and male disciples alike (vv. 2, 14)—along with Stephen, Cornelius, Lydia, Apollos, Priscilla, Aquila, and others throughout the millennia—become emissaries of God's love and grace.

The resurrected Jesus' final teachings center on the kingdom. No other theme or topic of discussion is mentioned during the risen Lord's forty days (see v. 3). Although the story omits the

3. Jesus' crucifixion and resurrection are the climax of his life story. However, the climax to the Christian story has yet to occur. It will come at the Parousia, the second coming of Christ, at the coup de grâce of sin and evil when all believers will join the heavenly chorus.

details of his message, the conversation seemingly generates the apostles' hopes for transformation and reforms on earth. They are looking forward to experiencing God's work in the restoration of Israel's kingdom (v. 6). Their concern speaks to their desire for freedom from Roman rule. Some might scoff at the apparent narrowness of the disciples' earthly focus. Some will say that their inquiry suggests a self-determination to regain their political sovereignty, a concern rooted in nationalism.[4] However, the apostles' question demonstrates their sociopolitical and material concern for the well-being of their community. Poverty, hunger, dehumanization, and amoral treatment suffocate their daily existence under a colonizing regime. They see God's power changing their immediate circumstance while forging an eschatological future. Through the voices of the apostles, Luke acknowledges that God's reign has political *and* theological implications and that they are intertwined.

Jesus does not rebuke the disciples' question. Instead, Jesus legitimizes the need to be attentive to earthly matters while doing kingdom work. His response eradicates any assumption that the disciples could imagine how God's plan will be manifested (e.g., their ministry among Gentiles). At first glance, it appears that Jesus is saying that the disciples ought not to be concerned with such issues (see v. 7). It is true that the apostles do not know God's plans, especially those regarding geopolitical, material import. However, knowing God's timing is less significant than God's mission for them to be empowered by the Holy Spirit as witnesses and conveyors of the good news (v. 8). This, however, is no passive mandate. They are to be actors within God's salvific plan, following and expanding the mission Jesus started.

This is both an ethical charge and an ecclesial charter. Ethically, believers are commissioned to go throughout the world to tend to earthly matters by creating societies reflective of God's liberation from the ravages of hunger, the indignities of social hierarchies, the injustices of tyranny. Ecclesially, the church is responsible for expanding God's kingdom with the words and actions of Jesus. Consequently, they are laying a counterclaim to any imperial force that subordinates people for material gain and restricts access to resources that provide for human flourishing.

Jesus prepares the apostles for the unexpected nature of God's plan. Human vision cannot comprehend the scale and scope of the divine project. God's salvation extends to all people from Jerusalem to the ends of the earth, disrupting and penetrating boundaries, whether political, cultural, or ethnic. God's sovereignty supersedes any earthly claims, imperial power, or political ambitions, even those of the apostles (cf. Luke 1:52). As the narrative unfolds, the apostles must expand their vision and their reach to realize God's kingdom. Strangers become family. Enemies become colleagues. Unknown regions become home. God's global mission is uncomfortable, even disconcerting, as it compels the apostles to redefine their understanding of God's chosen. Even as we may think we know the Spirit's movement, God continues to surprise us and expect us to reach deeply and broadly to spread the good news.

In this story, we must confront the inevitable: Jesus' absence. As Jesus ascends, the apostles gaze up, likely lost in the magnitude of the moment and overwhelmed with future anticipation. Life without Jesus must begin. However, the two men in white robes refocus their attention away from heaven and back to earth. Here they stand in the gap, awaiting the Holy Spirit's power and preparing to start their mission. The prophecy that Jesus will return as he left is not a foretelling of the Parousia, but more than likely a looking forward to Pentecost. Through the Holy Spirit and the evocation of his name, Jesus becomes (omni)present throughout the mission and ministry of the church. Though absent in his fleshed form, Jesus lives through and among us as the body of Christ.

In 1979, Roman Catholic Bishop Ken Untener of Saginaw, Michigan, composed the prayer "A Future Not Our Own" in celebration

4. Cf. Carl R. Holladay, *Acts: A Commentary* (Louisville, KY: Westminster John Knox, 2016), 74; Willie James Jennings, *Acts* (Louisville, KY: Westminster John Knox, 2017), 17.

of departed priests.[5] Often misattributed to Bishop Óscar Romero, the prayer is a reminder that the work of the kingdom is ours to bear but not always ours to see in its fullness: "We are workers, not master builders; ministers, not messiahs. We are prophets of a future not our own." In today's lectionary, we celebrate the presence and prepare for the absence of Jesus, knowing that the mission to which he calls us is ours to bear; but during our earthly journey we will never fully see and know the great depths and heights of God's overall plan. Yet each member of the church can identify with the apostles, gazing up at the ascending resurrected Lord. In his absence, we are made ready every day to spread the gospel and to do the work of the kingdom, baptized in his power.

BRIDGETT A. GREEN

5. Bishop Ken Untener, "Prayer Reflection Archbishop Oscar Romero: A Future Not Our Own." Archdiocese of Southwark. http://www.rcsouthwark.co.uk/romero_prayer.html.

Psalm 93

[1]The LORD is king, he is robed in majesty;
the LORD is robed, he is girded with strength.
He has established the world; it shall never be moved;
[2]your throne is established from of old;
you are from everlasting.

[3]The floods have lifted up, O LORD,
the floods have lifted up their voice;
the floods lift up their roaring.
[4]More majestic than the thunders of mighty waters,
more majestic than the waves of the sea,
majestic on high is the LORD!

[5]Your decrees are very sure;
holiness befits your house,
O LORD, forevermore.

Connecting the Psalm with Scripture and Worship

Although the two biblical accounts of the ascension (Luke 24:50–53 and Acts 1:1–14) were written by the same evangelist, the second telling of this story, appointed as the first reading on Ascension Day, includes more details than the first. Only the account in Acts states that the ascension took place forty days after the resurrection, and only Acts records the appearance of two men robed in white, whom, however, we recall from the Lukan account of the empty tomb. Thus, in different ways both accounts tie the ascension to the resurrection, and both place the event at a ritually significant time, whether on the Sunday of the resurrection or at the conclusion of a forty-day period of religious intensity. We recognize in Christian memory over the ages the value of Luke's detailed narratives, for the ascension story became a beloved way to conclude the life of Jesus, who has now returned to God's realm above the sky. Jesus, although beyond our sight, is now reigning in our hearts and throughout the cosmos.

The details in many Bible stories rely on this ancient cosmology of a three-tier universe, which some scholars assert would no longer have been literally believed by a first-century educated author such as Luke. Yet even in our time we speak as if the sky were "up" and as if things divine, such as the sainted dead or heaven or God, were up above the sky. We have, however, deleted from our worldview the idea that rain clouds are above the sky. Those rain clouds that release their water onto the earth through windows opened in the sky (see, e.g., Gen. 7:11) are for the Israelites the evidence of God's having tamed the wild waters of the sea. At creation, when God puts the waters of the earth in their place, and at the flood, when God destroys the earth by water and recreates a new earth, and at the exodus, when God drowns the oppressors in the waters of the sea, God shapes chaotic waters into the wellspring of life.

In our time, when many Christians find it difficult not only to attend worship on a Thursday but even to hear the narrative of the ascension as good news, a strong connection between ascension and baptism is welcome. During those times and places when Christianity was dominant, sometimes even exclusive, baptism became a birth ritual of little religious significance and only for the infant's immediate family.

However, we Christians in the twenty-first century are in some ways back to the third century: small numbers of Christians, with no support from government, with a recurrence of martyrdom, surrounded by many competing religions and a thriving religious syncretism—and an increasing number of adult baptisms. With Christianity once again a minority religion, baptism once again has high value as a distinctive sign of membership in the religious community and a treasured marker of lifelong commitment to God. The Revised Common Lectionary proclaims the importance of baptism, especially in its baptismal focus during Lent. In Psalm 93, appointed for Ascension Day, Christians read the ancient water imagery as reminiscent of our own water ritual.

We Must Never Be Ashamed

We all live under the threat of being put to shame, and rightly so. This would not only imply that we have blundered here and there, but that our whole life, with all our thoughts, desires, and accomplishments, might be in truth, in God's judgment and verdict, a failure, an infamy, a total loss. This is the great threat. This is why the ground shakes under our feet, the sky is covered with clouds, and the earth, so beautifully created, darkens. Indeed we should be put to shame.

But now we hear the very opposite. "You shall never be ashamed." What I would like to do, dear brothers and sisters, is to ask you, each and all, to get up together and like a choir repeat: "We must never be ashamed!" Each one would have to repeat it for himself and lastly I would repeat it for myself: "I must never be ashamed!" This is what counts. We shall not be, I shall not be ashamed, not when looking up to him. Our radiance will be and must be a sign that we will not be put to shame. It is an evidence of the relationship established between God and ourselves. And this is the power of the relationship: what is true and valid in heaven, what Jesus Christ has done for us, what has been accomplished by him, man's redemption, justification and preservation, is true and valid on earth also.

Karl Barth, "A Sermon on Ascension Day," in Karl Barth, *Prayer and Preaching*, trans. B. E. Hooke (London: SCM, 1964), 124–25.

As our response to the narrative of the ascension, we join in Psalm 93 to laud God as king, not only of Israel, but of the whole earth. The fact that the ancient poem makes of God a male monarch, usually translated as "king," may be less bothersome for Christians when we are able to see that divine sovereignty primarily in the ministry of Jesus Christ.

Although a number of what are termed enthronement psalms praise the kingship of God over creation and the community, the fact that Psalm 93 is appointed for Ascension Day can highlight baptism for us. Verses 2–4 of Psalm 93 celebrate the imagery of God's victory over raging waters at creation. Those waters, so alien and terrifying to an ancient landed people, were tamed by God, although we still hear their roar of wild might. When Christians hear of God's water, we think of baptism, in which the terrifying otherness of raging seas has been contained by God, as if God said to the seas, "Thus far shall you come, and no farther" (Job 38:11). Likewise, in baptism, the power of water to drown is turned by the mercy of God into a sweet washing, the horror of the sinking of the *Titanic* into our regularly marking our foreheads with water from the font.

The final verse of Psalm 93, "holiness befits your house," situates us with the assembly in the nave (think: navy) of our church. It is God's holiness that fills this house; Christ's presence is no longer merely in Jerusalem but throughout the cosmos; that divine indwelling makes of us all a holy people.

Not bad for a Thursday.

GAIL RAMSHAW

Ephesians 1:15–23

[15]I have heard of your faith in the Lord Jesus and your love toward all the saints,
and for this reason [16]I do not cease to give thanks for you as I remember you in
my prayers. [17]I pray that the God of our Lord Jesus Christ, the Father of glory, may
give you a spirit of wisdom and revelation as you come to know him, [18]so that,
with the eyes of your heart enlightened, you may know what is the hope to which
he has called you, what are the riches of his glorious inheritance among the
saints, [19]and what is the immeasurable greatness of his power for us who believe,
according to the working of his great power. [20]God put this power to work in
Christ when he raised him from the dead and seated him at his right hand in the
heavenly places, [21]far above all rule and authority and power and dominion, and
above every name that is named, not only in this age but also in the age to come.
[22]And he has put all things under his feet and has made him the head over all
things for the church, [23]which is his body, the fullness of him who fills all in all.

Commentary 1: Connecting the Reading with Scripture

Ephesians is the only Pauline letter that has both a blessing of God and a thanksgiving at its opening. Among the undisputed letters, all have a thanksgiving except Galatians, while 2 Corinthians 1:3–7 substitutes a blessing of God for a thanksgiving. Ephesians includes both, as it emphasizes the greatness of the salvation that God gives through Christ. Ephesians renews its giving of thanks in 3:1 and 14 and then has a doxology in 3:20–21. So the opening section of the letter (chaps. 1–3) is marked by repeated prayer and thanksgiving.

As is usually the case with Pauline opening thanksgivings, 1:15–23 telegraphs themes that will be important throughout the letter. These themes are picked up in other thanksgivings in chapters 1–3. Pauline thanksgivings usually emphasize things about the recipients for which Paul is grateful, but in Ephesians, the recipients' praiseworthy characteristics are mentioned only in verse 15, where the writer mentions their reception of the gospel and love for other believers. This thanksgiving has less to do with the recipients than with the wondrous nature of the gospel. It asks God to help the readers recognize just how magnificent it is. Similarly, the prayer begun in 3:1 describes at length the greatness of the gospel. Then, the central request of the prayer of 3:14–19 is that the recipients be able to understand the amazing riches they are given in Christ.

The astonishing, really incomprehensible, nature of the gospel is central to Ephesians. A principal purpose of this letter is to demand and celebrate the unity of Jews and Gentiles in Christ. The author of Ephesians is a Jew who in places distinguishes himself and his people from Gentiles (e.g., Eph. 2:1–2, 11–13, 17, 19; 3:1). The antipathy of Jews toward Gentiles is palpable as Ephesians names them "dead in trespasses" (2:1) and "aliens" (2:19). When the church began, all its members were Torah-observant Jews and remained such. The church struggled for decades as it tried to discern how Gentiles could be part of the people of God without Torah observance of the sort practiced by Jews. Some had argued that Gentiles must fully become proselytes to be church members (Acts 15:1–5; Gal. 2:1–10). Paul was among those who argued that Gentiles fulfill the "righteous demands" of the law without full proselyte conversion (Rom. 3:28; 8:4; Gal. 6:6–16).

On the other side, anti-Semitism was well known in the ancient world. Given the questions about the legitimacy of their presence in the church, Gentile believers seem to have harbored some offense. It seems that the predominantly Gentile church to which Ephesians is addressed was wondering whether it needed to maintain ties with predominantly Jewish congregations and with the heritage of Israel. Ephesians insists that the church must remain connected to the promises God made to Israel and to the heritage of this same people.

This letter argues that the unity of Jews and Gentiles in Christ is one of the nearly unbelievable gifts that the gospel bestows. It is a shocking act of God; it is the "mystery of Christ" (Eph. 3:4) that God could bring together Jews and Gentiles into a single community. This uniting of the two is an eschatological mystery that was hidden from previous generations (3:4–6). It is still astonishing to the author of Ephesians that God could accomplish such a feat. This unity demonstrates the power and richness of God's love.

While the theme of unity runs throughout Ephesians, it is not an easy sell, either to the Gentiles who are addressed or to Jewish believers. So Ephesians bases this miraculous achievement on the resurrection and exaltation of Jesus. In 1:15–23, the author prays that God will help the readers understand how rich the gifts are that they receive and to know that the possession of those gifts is secured for both Jews and Gentiles through the power of God that raised Jesus from the dead and exalted him to the highest place in the cosmos. The ascension and exaltation of Christ are essential for Ephesians and its message of the unity of all in Christ. That exaltation of Christ sets him above all powers that might try to separate people from God's love and from relationship with one another in Christ.

It is from that place of power that Christ defeats divisive forces that appear in the present or will appear in any future. The Ephesian believers must all submit to the one who is the head of a church composed of a mixed group of Jews and Gentiles (1:22–23). It is through the exalted Christ that God brings to life all who were dead in their sins (2:4–7). It is the risen Christ who has made peace for both sides (2:14–16) and is the one body in which they all exist (4:6). It takes the kind of power that God displays in the raising and exaltation of Jesus to heal the rifts between these opposing groups and make them a single community of the saved. In this one body, they are to live up to their calling as God's newly created family (4:1–3; 5:1–2). All of this is made possible by the astonishing power of God that was exercised in the resurrection and exaltation of Jesus, with the purpose of saving Jews and Gentiles in a single community. All can be united because believers are in Christ, and Christ is above all things, including the obstacles to unity that now structure the world.

The lectionary psalms for today both celebrate the power of God. God's power is evident in God's sovereignty over earthly rulers (Ps. 47) and in God's sustaining the world (Ps. 93). These praise psalms laud God's power as it was known in Israel. Ephesians draws on these and similar thanksgivings for God's power as it describes how God has acted in the ascension and exaltation of Jesus. Ephesians sees the power that the psalmist praised now exercised in even more astounding ways.

The readings from both Acts and Luke contain assertions that none of those present understood in their fullness. Of course, Luke intends for "repentence and forgiveness of sins" to be proclaimed "to all nations" (Luke 24:47), this to include, and perhaps specifically target, Gentiles. When his other telling of the ascension has the angel say that the disciples will be witnesses to "the ends of the earth" (Acts 1:8), he must include Gentiles among the hearers. So the oneness of Jews and Gentiles for which Ephesians argues is already narrated as part of the original intention of God in raising and exalting Jesus.

The ascension of Jesus is a demonstration of God's power that intends to draw all people into the blessings God offers in Christ. Those blessings exceed our imaginations and are so abundant that they spill over into the whole world. That eschatological act of taking Christ into heaven is an irreplaceable part of God's plan to be recognized as the God of the whole world, whose intentions to save will not be thwarted by our divisions.

This passage suggests a number of important sermon themes. The ascension and exaltation of Christ that this text celebrates not only create the church's unity; they also empower the church to embody this unity in the face of ethnic and social divisions. In addition, this text gives a basis for us to proclaim that God's resurrection power enables the church to reject evaluations of others that are based on race and social status. Finally, this text assures us that the unity God gives in the exalted Christ is stronger than any divisions our churches may face.

JERRY L. SUMNEY

Commentary 2: Connecting the Reading with the World

Some of the most compelling theological ideas in the Christian faith are those rooted deeply in the mysteries of the Christian faith and connected insightfully to a particular context. This Ephesians 1 passage, in many ways, provides a metaphorical example of such a theology and contextual mystery. For modern scholars seeking to interpret this passage faithfully for our world and to understand the initial context of the letter, Ephesians itself has proved to be something of a cypher. While its author and original audience are named by the text, scholars have reason to doubt that either is as advertised. Many believe that the author of Ephesians was inspired by Paul's writings and translated traditionally Pauline concepts for a community situated in a slightly later historical context. There is even evidence that the first few theologians to reference the letter understood it to be addressed to different cities; Irenaeus of Lyon held that it was indeed addressed to the community at Ephesus, while Marcion quoted it as being addressed to the church at Laodicea.[1] In other words, the original context and reception of this passage are cloaked in mystery. So how do we proceed in interpreting it? I suggest that we do so boldly! We might acknowledge the mysterious origin before turning to the eloquent speech for God and the profound and yet particular hope it expresses for Christians in the power of Christ.

So what can we discern? Well, by all accounts the letter offers us a glimpse into communications between early churches. If not written by Paul, it appears to apply his thought to the situation of the larger church in the world. The author of Ephesians here gives a forward-looking statement as a profound assurance that the readers belong to the body of Christ. Starting with a thankful opening, the author's recognition of the major Christian virtues of faith and love (Eph. 1:15) moves him to a future vision of hope in Christ that is occasioned by a spirit of "wisdom and revelation" (v. 17). That hope is grounded in their own connection to Christ, who is extolled in cosmic ways as one given ultimate authority over "all rule and authority and power and dominion" (v. 21). The assurance to the believers is that they belong to the community intimately as the very body of Christ in the world.

So how do we hear these lofty and vague blessings, exhortations, and proclamations in a meaningful way in our concrete context today? First, the letter reminds us that one of the building blocks of a community rooted in faith, love, and eschatological hope is a true and abiding sense of thanksgiving, of gratitude for others.[2] Rearing children in an age of school shootings, cyber bullying, and smartphones is an enterprise fraught with anxiety. Yet recent studies indicate that one of the best protections against the depression, envy, and materialism that can work out in children and adolescents in such destructive ways is the regular practice of gratitude. Some psychologists argue that even late in life, the practice of acknowledging the contributions of others, of offering thanks to them and regularly thinking about the ways one is fortunate in the world, leads to greater community engagement, confidence, and even physical health.[3] The letter's greeting perhaps illustrates that gratitude is something not simply known or a quality possessed but something that must be practiced, said, and written over and over again.

1. See Shirley Jackson Case, "To Whom Was 'Ephesians' Written?," *The Biblical World* 38:5 (1911): 315–20.
2. See Diana Butler Bass, *Grateful: The Transformative Power of Giving Thanks* (San Francisco: HarperCollins, 2018) for a discussion of how our personal sense of gratitude often gets lost in our routines, practices, and public discourses.
3. See Jeffrey J. Froh and Giacomo Bono, *Making Grateful Kids: The Science of Building Character* (West Conshohocken, PA: Templeton, 2014).

Liturgically, as we celebrate the ascension of the Lord, the passage grounds the church's identity in this sense of gratitude, faith, and love while looking toward the future hope we find in Christ. The coming weeks in the liturgical calendar will focus on Pentecost and the birth of the church in the power of the Spirit. Christians will rightly celebrate the first proclamations of Christ's resurrection and the offer of forgiveness that create new believers and rapidly expand the church and its scope.

In this liminal moment, however, there is perhaps the opportunity to recall the element of gratitude as formative in connecting the early Christian communities. It can perhaps feel like an intimate, emotional moment in the life of the early, still relatively small church, akin to a shared moment of love or grace between parents over coffee before the kids wake up or between friends before the larger party arrives. In the liturgical calendar, this time can be imagined as a moment when the church's members have experienced the goodness of faith and love, even while they await the universal proclamation of Pentecost that extends that grace to others.

From an ecclesial standpoint, the church today, while making some strides toward unity, remains fractured by schism. The breaks between different traditions are often driven by long and deep histories of struggle, disdain, oppression, and violence. Perhaps, in this regard, some of these separations even serve a positive and protective, if temporal, end. Many groups of Christians nonetheless remain locked in bitter dispute and have deemed "apostate" other groups that profess to follow Christ, convinced of the other groups' grave errors about particular theologies.

This passage takes a markedly different approach, which serves perhaps to interrupt our concerns for doctrinal purity; it celebrates, rather than scrutinizes and judges, the Christian faith of others. Moreover, it celebrates a group that the author has seemingly never met (see v. 15). He does not mention names or include specific greetings, as Paul's authentic letters always do as they close. Yet the prayer he offers in our passage is for their continued blessing and their inclusion in the coming reign of God. This may serve as a powerful example that we can follow today: without losing sight of our real, tangible differences, we might celebrate thankfully the faith of others.

Finally, it is hard to overstate the political implications of the claim here that God has placed Christ "above all rule and authority and power and dominion" (v. 21). For the church, of which Christ is the head, all other claimants to ultimate authority, power, and responsibility are hereby rendered to be false. This does not necessarily connote that we may live without any need for political allegiances, wise leaders, or sound governance. Rather, it sets the standard for what *is* wise, sound, and good.

Ephesians holds in no small way that Christ is the absolute authority for the church. Any allegiance to political party or particular leader must be subordinate and accountable to the example of Christ. It also negates all claims to rule that are based on the promise of "absolute security" or which demand loyalty to a particular group or leader. Perhaps even harder for Western culture today is the idea that Christ is set over all "power and dominion," that is, the spiritual forces that pull us in different directions and influence our desires. The "bad guys" among these are easy to name: racism, misogyny, xenophobia, violence, envy, greed. Yet there are others that just as insidiously ensnare us. Comfort, complacency, satisfaction, egoism: these work more subtly on our conscious nature, yet as this passage reminds us, these too are subordinate to Christ, as he forms the body of the church.

BRIAN S. POWERS

Luke 24:44–53

[44]Then he said to them, "These are my words that I spoke to you while I was still
with you—that everything written about me in the law of Moses, the prophets, and
the psalms must be fulfilled." [45]Then he opened their minds to understand the
scriptures, [46]and he said to them, "Thus it is written, that the Messiah is to suffer
and to rise from the dead on the third day, [47]and that repentance and forgiveness
of sins is to be proclaimed in his name to all nations, beginning from Jerusalem.
[48]You are witnesses of these things. [49]And see, I am sending upon you what my
Father promised; so stay here in the city until you have been clothed with power
from on high."

[50]Then he led them out as far as Bethany, and, lifting up his hands, he blessed
them. [51]While he was blessing them, he withdrew from them and was carried up
into heaven. [52]And they worshiped him, and returned to Jerusalem with great joy;
[53]and they were continually in the temple blessing God.

Commentary 1: Connecting the Reading with Scripture

This passage comes at the end of the Gospel of Luke, right after the walk to Emmaus and Jesus appearing to the disciples in the upper room. Jesus calms the frightened disciples with these ten verses prior to his ascension. He places his crucifixion and resurrection on the third day in the context of the larger narrative as written in the law of Moses, the prophets, and the Psalms. In verse 45 Jesus teaches the apostles to read the Scriptures, and the subsequent verse informs the reader that he sees himself as living into a larger biblical narrative. Verse 48 involves the apostles as witnesses and then informs them that they will be sent out from Jerusalem.

For readers today, this is a reminder of the continuity between the Old and New Testaments. Jesus offers us an assurance that God can be trusted because God follows through on promises. This is an invitation for a possible sermon topic on connections between Judaism and Christianity. Jesus clearly views himself as a continuation of the biblical narrative, rather than the start of something entirely different. A sermon can emphasize Christianity's Jewish roots rather than the differences that led to such beliefs as supersessionism. Such beliefs argued that Christians replaced Jews as God's chosen people and led to years of persecution, culminating in the Holocaust. This passage clearly places Jesus within the biblical narrative of the whole of the Bible.

Another way to enter into the text would be to help the congregation see themselves as part of the narrative and identify with the disciples. Much has happened in a short period of time in this text, and the disciples' fears are certainly understandable. Just one short week ago and five chapters back (Luke 19:28–53), Jesus had entered the city of Jerusalem triumphantly, and the people had welcomed him with chants of

"Blessed is the king
  who comes in the name of the Lord!
Peace in heaven,
  and glory in the highest heaven!"

"Hosanna," they had shouted, and the disciples thought that the movement was alive and well. Now Jesus has been arrested, tortured, and crucified, and they are hiding in the upper room, scared for their lives. How would we feel if this were us? Three times, Peter denied knowing Christ. Cleopas and an unnamed disciple walked to Emmaus just to get out of town. Certainly, they were afraid that they could be arrested and accused of being followers of Jesus. They were scared that they would also be crucified.

It is astonishing to think of how surprising Jesus' appearance must have been to the disciples. Luke states that they were "startled" and "terrified" and thought that they were seeing a ghost (24:37). Jesus offers a message of peace and reassurance; do not worry, he teaches them, because everything is going according to plan. Jesus reminds the disciples that he had told them what was to come and that all that had happened to him was written in the law of Moses, the prophets, and the Psalms (v. 44). Here may be a good place for a funny sermon illustration about listening—or the lack thereof. The telephone game is one example: a simple message is whispered in a person's ear, and as the message is transmitted around the circle it is altered, intentionally or unintentionally, before it reaches the final person in the circle. Jesus has been telling the disciples about the prophecies and yet they are still caught off guard by his sudden appearance.

Today it seems that we live in a world that is moving too fast. A twenty-four-hour news cycle with political upheaval, juicy controversy, major weather events, and threats of nuclear war keeps us glued to our screens. How can we have peace in the midst of such turmoil? It is precisely when the disciples are most fearful and uncertain about the future that Jesus appears to the disciples and says, "Peace be with you" (v. 36).

Not only does Jesus offer calm; he is living proof of victory over death. Jesus has been raised and thus has overcome evil with good. This is the victory of light over darkness, love over hate, and life over death. Jesus appears to the disciples to assure them that everything he has preached and prophesied is indeed true, and they will be victorious. Jesus moves the disciples from fear to action. They are moved from paralysis and become protagonists. This is the good news of the gospel.

Jesus not only appears. He explains his appearance in the context of the larger biblical narrative and invites the disciples to participate in the resurrected life. So another possible preaching trajectory is that we are not just passive observers of this story; we are active agents, participants, protagonists in the ongoing proclamation of the good news. Jesus declares, "You are witnesses of these things" (v. 48). Here is an opportunity to invite your congregation to avoid the dangers of the "bystander effect," which keeps us from further action. Instead, Luke's Jesus invites us to be participants in the story of resurrection and bear witness to others. This can be a place to conclude the sermon with an invitation to discipleship, an invitation for the congregation to be not just hearers of the Word, but doers of the Word who witness to the living Christ.

Last, this passage concludes with the story of the ascension. Verse 52 states that Jesus was lifting his hands and blessing the disciples when he was "carried up into heaven." The footnote in the NRSV states that some ancient versions do not include this verse; however, other Bible passages, such as Mark 16:9, state that Jesus "was taken up into heaven and sat at the right hand of God." Here emerges a possible sermon topic about the three offices of Christ: prophet, priest, and king. In this passage we see Jesus play the role of prophet visioning the future (v. 44). We also see Jesus as priest to the disciples as he "opens their minds to understand the scriptures" (v. 45). Then Jesus consoles their fears before sending them out as witnesses (vv. 48–49). Lastly Jesus ascends to his throne in heaven as king. In these few verses you can illustrate how Jesus fulfills the three offices of the lordship of Christ. As followers of Christ today, we can take great solace in his roles as prophet who speaks truth to power, a priest who shepherds his flock, and a king who is our Lord.

Another sermon topic can be about the challenge of waiting for something. In verse 49, Jesus commands the disciples to "stay here in the city until you have been clothed with power from on high." Today's society is about efficiency. We do not like to wait. We are used to having everything at our fingertips. We can order a package from Amazon and receive it within twenty-four hours. We have thirty-minute fast food delivery. We have become spoiled with the belief that we can have what we want when we want it. This is a good teaching moment on the value of waiting. Jesus leaves the disciples in limbo, and the Gospel writer leaves the readers waiting for what the Father promised. Fortunately, the Gospel of Luke is continued in the Acts of the Apostles, so we know that the day of Pentecost is coming.

PHILIP WINGEIER-RAYO

Commentary 2: Connecting the Reading with the World

The liturgical time in the weeks between Easter and Pentecost is a wonderful time for a sermon on living *in between*. Between turning in a final exam and receiving the grade. Between planting a garden and enjoying its bounty. Between spring cleaning and summer vacation. In-betweenness is not only seasonal. I am enduring a significant health challenge but have no diagnosis or effective treatment yet. My daughter is capable, independent, and entering adulthood, but she is still my little girl. The churches with which I work are start-ups, fully church yet still becoming. So much of life is lived in between.

This season, not to mention Ascension Day in the Christian tradition, reminds us that we need awareness and skills to live faithfully while in-between. Easter has come and gone. Christ is risen. A new world with Jesus as ruler is here, and we seek to align our lives with his regime. Yet we wait for the fullness of resurrection power to be manifest. We wait for the promised Holy Spirit to show up and make a difference. Sometimes, we wait well, knowing that good things come to those patiently focused less on themselves and more on God. Other times, we feel lost, betrayed, or let down, as if waiting for anything in our instant-gratification culture proves God does not love us.

In Jesus' final, preascension words in Luke 24:44–53, we hear that the centuries of waiting, testifying, and prophesying are finally fulfilled. After looking back, Jesus looks forward. We hear that disciples, both then and now, will witness what God is doing and be clothed with power from on high. Then Jesus blesses them, withdraws, and in-between time sets in. However, rather than grieving a lack of closure or God's seeming unwillingness to meet a list of needs and wants, the followers of Jesus receive his blessing, observe his departure, and live with intentionality and great joy, reveling in what they have. They learn to watch, listen, be together, wait, bless, and worship. They do not have all the answers, but they have more important things: clear directive from God (Luke 24:47–49), each other (vv. 44–53), blessing (vv. 50–53), and—one of the riches that can be mined from the in-between time—joy (vv. 52–53).

Interim times teach, change, and prepare us. They help us learn to appreciate and mine all moments, both the expected and unexpected seasons, the welcome and the difficult stretches of life. In-between times can forge in us a skill that the faithful of all ages have to learn: the art of waiting. When those rare moments of closure and new beginnings actually occur and then wear off, God is in the in-between time, teaching and reforming us once again, helping us rejoice in the reality that we are neither stagnant nor completed.

An alternative sermon connection could concentrate on Ascension. Grounded in the poetic imagination of ancient Near Eastern cultures, in which kings ascended to reign[1] much as David went up to Jerusalem, Jesus' ascension lifts him up, sharing God's power and reigning in majesty, "seated at the right hand of God the Father Almighty." With free rein to roam the heavens and earth and a view from on high that sees all, Jesus Christ can do on a cosmic scale what Jesus of Nazareth did locally: defend the persecuted, feed the hungry, bring justice. Because Jesus now reigns, we are empowered to act differently and pursue our lifelong vocation: bringing our lives in line with Jesus' reign.

A third sermon direction could explore what it means to be witnesses. We know what we do not like about Christian witness, and it can be healing to name expressions of Christendom evangelism we need to disavow. Inaccessible

1. See also Pss. 24:3; 68:18; 139:8.

language needs to be left behind, as do invitations to "personal salvation" that encourage private spirituality and equate faith more with inward journey than with visibly transformed life. In some Christian witness, people hear not what the witnesses love about their faith but what is wrong with their own faith. Still other regrettable witness involves pushing conformity to particular ideas, practices, and beliefs. Witness starts to feel like an effort to make another person change. Such witness misses the mark when we do not share what is life-giving or hopeful about what we have found in Jesus, but instead simply warn others about continuing down their current paths.

Welcome witness involves sharing something good. After all, "gospel" literally means "good news"! The disciples experienced the risen Christ, knew the world to be changed, and found themselves changing with it. Being witnesses of these things involved sharing their own experiences, in their own ways. Similarly, so many of us are deeply enriched by hearing how Jesus is present in another's life, how we sense God calling and empowering us to change, or how we have met God during a difficult season. People are hungry for meaning and yearning to know they are valued. Furthermore, God is already at work in people's lives, bringing out the divine image in them. It is not up to us to "convert" anyone. We are free simply to join God in God's work, sharing our own experiences and asking others about theirs, treating all people as fellow image-bearers, and remaining open to authentic conversation that shapes conversation for all.

Post-Christendom witness is about responsive conversation rather than a fixed message. Such witness seeks conversation and connections between life experience and the gospel. Today's winsome witness values honesty, humility, vulnerability, courage, and respect. Ask your community how you could encourage reciprocal, relational witness.

One last sermon connection could focus on a prominent theme at the close of the text: blessing. While Jesus blesses the disciples, he is carried away as if still hallowing them with blessing that does not end. There are many ways Jesus could have said goodbye, particularly given the brutality and betrayals of his last days. Yet he chose blessing. He looked at his disciples and told them what they had meant to him and what he was hoping for them. He said something real, something remarkable, given how difficult it can be to say things that reflect what matters most to us.

We do not know the details of what Jesus said, but it may not matter. We know a blessing when we hear it. It knows us. It speaks deeply to our needs, fears, and hopes. It sees someone for who she is or something for what it is, looks with compassion past what some might see, and pronounces good. To give blessing is to see with divine perspective. In a world that invites critique and celebrates perfection, blessing does not wait for perfection to arrive. It recognizes and names dignity and holiness, however imperfect the vessel, and one thing this world deeply needs from all of us is more pronunciation of blessing.

Far from the purview of Jesus and clergy alone, this is the call of all Christians. Perhaps our blessings are not to be limited to one another but can and should extend to God and to all creation—noticing God, trees, birds, and fresh baked bread, blessing them and calling them good. To bless requires attentiveness, time, humility, and nerve. How else should we who are created in the image of God behave?

At the end of Luke, those gathered receive blessing that continues as Jesus disappears into the clouds. What happens next is breathtaking. Jesus is gone, and his followers are filled not with sadness but deep joy, even as they themselves repay the favor and continuously bless God.

LINDSAY P. ARMSTRONG

Seventh Sunday of Easter

Acts 1:6–14
Psalm 68:1–10, 32–35
1 Peter 4:12–14; 5:6–11
John 17:1–11

Acts 1:6–14

[6]So when they had come together, they asked him, "Lord, is this the time when you will restore the kingdom to Israel?" [7]He replied, "It is not for you to know the times or periods that the Father has set by his own authority. [8]But you will receive power when the Holy Spirit has come upon you; and you will be my witnesses in Jerusalem, in all Judea and Samaria, and to the ends of the earth." [9]When he had said this, as they were watching, he was lifted up, and a cloud took him out of their sight. [10]While he was going and they were gazing up toward heaven, suddenly two men in white robes stood by them. [11]They said, "Men of Galilee, why do you stand looking up toward heaven? This Jesus, who has been taken up from you into heaven, will come in the same way as you saw him go into heaven."

[12]Then they returned to Jerusalem from the mount called Olivet, which is near Jerusalem, a sabbath day's journey away. [13]When they had entered the city, they went to the room upstairs where they were staying, Peter, and John, and James, and Andrew, Philip and Thomas, Bartholomew and Matthew, James son of Alphaeus, and Simon the Zealot, and Judas son of James. [14]All these were constantly devoting themselves to prayer, together with certain women, including Mary the mother of Jesus, as well as his brothers.

Commentary 1: Connecting the Reading with Scripture

This text is part of the hinge between Luke's account of the ministry of Jesus and his account of the time of the church in Acts. Just at the end of his Gospel, after Luke briefly summarizes the period after the resurrection, this story and Acts 1:15–26 (which tells about the restoration of the Twelve by the addition of Matthias) move the reader inexorably forward into the experience of Pentecost. There the reign of God takes on new form and power. While the first few verses of Acts point us backward to the historical time of Jesus, this text has the effect of moving us forward. Luke tells the story of the ascension twice, once as a conclusion to his Gospel, and now as part of the initiation of a new age, a new story that he is eager to tell in Acts. This text thus plays a role both as ending and beginning, both literarily and theologically. It sews together these two great ages that Luke has chosen to narrate.

The Gospel text appointed for this Sunday (John 17:1–11), the beginning of the high-priestly prayer, has a similar function. Even as Jesus is preparing to leave his disciples by entering into his glory on the cross, laying down his life for the sake of his friends, he points forward by praying, "The words that you gave to me I have given to them" (v. 8). He announces that he is no longer in the world, but that the disciples are. The mission of love, embodied in his life, is already moving forward in the disciples. Even in the Gospel of John, it is hard to determine whether this text is truly a farewell discourse or a prelude into the time of the Holy Spirit. It too sews together the ages.

Luke reshapes the ascension story in his second recitation. There are few examples in Scripture where one author tells the same story twice. We can see Luke's editorial hand at work, reframing the story in Acts to accomplish his homiletical and theological intent. In the first telling of the story (Luke 24:50–53), Jesus' last gesture is to lift up his hands in benediction, a fitting end to his ministry that calls forth the response that has often been elicited by the presence of Jesus—from shepherds in Bethlehem to the centurion at the cross. They respond by giving praise to God. After Jesus' ascension, the disciples return to Jerusalem filled with great joy and a desire to worship.

In Acts, there is no benediction. After a cloud takes Jesus out of sight, two men in white robes appear to the disciples, asking, "Why do you stand looking up toward heaven?" The men tell them that Jesus will come again just as he left. They point the disciples ahead into history. This departure is not an ending, but another step in the forward movement of God's reign. Perhaps this is why Luke invites the two men in white garments into the story. We find two men at other significant turns in the scriptural narrative. At the transfiguration (Luke 9:28–36), Moses and Elijah appear to give us clues about Jesus' identity, even as the story moves from Galilee toward Jerusalem. At the empty tomb, the women encounter the two men who ask the life-changing question, "Why do you seek the living among the dead?" (Luke 24:5).

This ascension story in Acts glows with the light of transfiguration and resurrection. By connecting these stories with the two men, Luke hints that resurrection is not a onetime experience but a promise and an expectation for the future. It also connects us to the entire salvation history, from Moses to Elijah to Jesus—and now to this band of disciples.

You can feel this movement in Luke's two volumes. The entire narrative of Luke–Acts puts us on a geographical timeline, as summarized by Jesus in Acts 1:8: "You will be my witnesses in Jerusalem, in all Judea and Samaria, and to the ends of the earth." Luke leads us toward Jerusalem in his Gospel. Acts will now move us from Jerusalem outward to Judea and Samaria. At the end of Acts, we find Paul summarizing the fulfilment of the promise, "Let it be known to you then that this salvation of God has been sent to the Gentiles; they will listen" (Acts 28:28). The gospel now resides in Rome, the center of the Mediterranean world, where it is poised to go out to the ends of the earth.

This geographical movement highlights another of the primary messages of Luke–Acts: the inclusiveness of the gospel. We have been hearing all along about how the Holy Spirit carried those first disciples across boundaries of language, culture, and religious tradition, an ever-widening circle of good news that does not reach a conclusion, but rather suggests that, by arriving in Rome, it is set for another grand expansion. Could this be another reason that the two men caution the disciples about staring up into heaven? The movement of the Holy Spirit is not in the clouds with the historical Jesus but is being revealed on earth in a new way. Luke invites his readers to keep their eyes open for the next movement of the good news.

"You will be my witnesses" becomes the true hinge in the story. All along, Luke has been hinting that the followers of Jesus are more than observers. At the beginning of Luke, the witnesses are considered to be eyewitnesses (Luke 1:2). Here, at the beginning of Acts, the term shifts to witnesses. With this, Luke is moving us into a next generation, from those who were with Jesus to those who have an encounter with the resurrected Jesus through the Holy Spirit. The ascension narrative sets up the disciples—and us—to be ready for an outpouring of power from on high.

The reign of God, announced in the life, death, and resurrection of Jesus, is now left to this unlikely band of disciples standing on Olivet staring, slack-jawed, into the heavens. This text points us toward them as the key for how the gospel will go to the ends of the earth. Of course, they do not see it yet. Pentecost is yet to come, but Luke lets us in on the story. The link between the time of Jesus and the ongoing presence of the resurrection is, indeed, the community that trusts he is coming, the community that is waiting to be given the words and the courage to leave behind everything to follow.

This truly is the perfect text for the Seventh Sunday of Easter. It is appointed between the liturgical celebration of Ascension Day last Thursday and the celebration of Pentecost next Sunday. For many of us, by now, the celebration of Easter has wound down, and the church already strains to move forward into a new mode under the power of the Holy Spirit in the extraordinary time of the church. We cannot keep the trumpets sounding and the organ on full blast for the full fifty days. We are ready for something that moves us into ordinary life. Luke's second account of the ascension does exactly that. Maybe Luke's last question is for us on this Last Sunday of Easter, standing on the threshold of a new age, wondering how the story in this age can possibly move forward: "Why are you just standing there? *You* are my witness."

BRADLEY E. SCHMELING

Commentary 2: Connecting the Reading with the World

The preacher will immediately notice that today's reading from the Acts of the Apostles, the first lesson of the set of lectionary texts, is the account of the ascension: Jesus is lifted up into heaven (Acts 1:9). So begins the narrative arc of this book. The apostles are trustworthy witnesses of all that Jesus said and did and straightaway, without his earthly presence, they are to bear this witness to the ends of the earth. The time of their mission is now. Indeed the last thing Jesus says to them is that the Holy Spirit will empower them and they will witness to his life, ministry, death, resurrection, and ascension to all peoples of the earth.

Congregations that follow the church's calendar know that this Sunday falls during the fifty days of Easter, that stretch of paschal days between the First Sunday of Easter and Pentecost Sunday. This reading is appointed for the Seventh Sunday of Easter, which is the Sunday closest to the fortieth day after Easter, the day of the ascension. The introductory remarks of the Acts of the Apostles (Acts 1:1–5), coming just before today's appointed passage, provide a summary account of all that has transpired in the life and ministry of Jesus Christ. Readers learn that Jesus has appeared and spoken about the kingdom of God "during forty days" (1:3). Though Jesus' ascension to heaven is mentioned in Matthew, Mark, Luke, and John (as well as in other New Testament books), the verse in our passage lets us know that the ascension occurred on the fortieth day after the resurrection. Some contemporary ecclesial bodies keep the feast of the Ascension on the actual fortieth day, while others commemorate it on this Seventh Sunday of Easter.

Whether Ascension is celebrated on the fortieth day or on this Sunday, the preacher encounters it in this text. It is described here in Acts more fully than in any other account. Narratively and theologically the ascension is both an end and a beginning. In the narrative of Luke–Acts, it concludes, as the first chapter of Acts describes, the earthy events in the life of Jesus Christ. It is his last earthly event after his birth, baptism, temptation in the wilderness, ministry, passion, death, and resurrection. It marks the turn to the apostles' ministry.

Theologically it turns our focus toward the outpouring of the Holy Spirit, commemorated on Pentecost Sunday, and to the mission of the church that will be apparent in all of the appointed readings for the Sundays after Pentecost. The apostles now lose the earthly presence of Jesus, yet gain his continuous presence by the power of the Holy Spirit. The Spirit of the risen and ascended Christ is no longer bound by space or time and is always present.

The preacher may explore how this dynamic is present in the life of the congregation. Do we corporately relate to Christ as a historic past-tense person rather than as the One whose abiding presence is everywhere and always? We can see this distinction when our worship focuses too much on the past historical events of Christ, at the expense of worship that understands these past events have a present and true claim on us now. Some Christians seem to relate to Jesus as if he lived only long ago and now is distant from us.

Instead, the Acts passage and the account of the ascension speak to Christ's ongoing presence and power in the lives of believers, and throughout the earth. Those who believe Christ's present-tense presence shape worship language, songs, and rites that proclaim Christ's presence and work in our midst. We trust his promises to be with us. Some sermons play with the language of ascension: Jesus neither is absent nor has he absconded, but he has ascended to the place of glorification and authority (John 17). He ascends to a different place and way of being present.

In our passage the apostles ask Jesus if he will restore the kingdom; they seem to mean the power of Israel as it was at the time of David. He responds in a way that undercuts their hopes for a time frame or for insiders' knowledge: it is not for them to know. Yet Jesus promises the apostles that the power of the Holy Spirit will come upon them and that they will witness in the city of Jerusalem, the region of Judea and even Samaria, and beyond those places to the ends of the earth. Then he is taken up into heaven, and while the apostles stand gazing as he ascends, two men or beings instruct them not to stand and stare.

The text tells us that the apostles return from Olivet to where they are staying in Jerusalem. It names the eleven (minus Judas Iscariot) and concludes with a description of the apostles at communal and prayerful devotion along with "certain women" (1:14). In many ways this account parallels the story of the transfiguration, even down to the detail of the two men or angelic beings who appear as part of the story. Here too followers of Jesus are told to go about their ministries. They are not to remain on the mountain of the transfiguration, nor are they to stand about gazing up toward the sky. They, we, are to get on with the work of witnessing to him.

This text, coming as it does as the first reading on this Seventh Sunday of Easter, turns us to the horizon of the church and our continued mission. Congregations living and worshiping according to the witness of the church's year have been reading from the Acts of the Apostles throughout these fifty days of Easter. We are immersed in stories of the early church's ministry, how Jesus' apostles were telling the good news of his death that overcame the powers of sin and death, and how they were performing miracles and healings in his name. These accounts from Acts take the place of Old Testament readings just for these fifty days, and today's reading is the capstone of these Acts readings. Individually and as church we encounter the ascension again.

The preacher might preach a fresh commissioning to the gathered church. Is the congregation standing about gazing up to the sky, or is it expectantly on the road, back to the city with all its needs, trusting in the arrival of the Holy Spirit? Those apostles witnessed to persons who had not heard the story of Jesus Christ. They performed miracles, teachings, and healings. They not only spoke about him but they acted on his promises of new life. The preacher can explore where the church is boldly witnessing, in word and deed, to Christ's life-giving presence in today's world. More than that, the preacher can explore how such witness comes from confidence that God is present, active, and committed to sustaining God's followers by the power of the Holy Spirit. This Spirit empowers us for leadership even as we wait on Christ's return.

The last verses of this passage tell us that the eleven apostles, all observant Jews, gathered with Jesus' family and "certain women" and "devoted themselves to prayer" (v. 14). This is a witness for the church today: we wait upon God together. The preacher can help a congregation reflect on how it understands itself as a missionary community rather than a collection of individuals, and that none of our congregations stand on their own. We are part of the global company of Spirit-infused witnesses to the reestablishment of the reign of God.

JENNIFER L. LORD

Psalm 68:1–10, 32–35

1Let God rise up, let his enemies be scattered;
let those who hate him flee before him.
2As smoke is driven away, so drive them away;
as wax melts before the fire,
let the wicked perish before God.
3But let the righteous be joyful;
let them exult before God;
let them be jubilant with joy.

4Sing to God, sing praises to his name;
lift up a song to him who rides upon the clouds—
his name is the LORD—
be exultant before him.

5Father of orphans and protector of widows
is God in his holy habitation.
6God gives the desolate a home to live in;
he leads out the prisoners to prosperity,
but the rebellious live in a parched land.

7O God, when you went out before your people,
when you marched through the wilderness,
8the earth quaked, the heavens poured down rain
at the presence of God, the God of Sinai,
at the presence of God, the God of Israel.
9Rain in abundance, O God, you showered abroad;
you restored your heritage when it languished;
10your flock found a dwelling in it;
in your goodness, O God, you provided for the needy.

. . . .

32Sing to God, O kingdoms of the earth;
sing praises to the Lord,
33O rider in the heavens, the ancient heavens;
listen, he sends out his voice, his mighty voice.
34Ascribe power to God,
whose majesty is over Israel;
and whose power is in the skies.
35Awesome is God in his sanctuary,
the God of Israel;
he gives power and strength to his people.

Blessed be God!

Connecting the Psalm with Scripture and Worship

Scholars have described Psalm 68 as being among the most difficult psalms to translate, and with the least apparent internal logic. Famously, it has even been proposed that the psalm is actually only the opening lines of several psalms, almost a table of contents of some psalms not included in our Bible. However, verses 1–10 and 32–35, the beginning and ending of the psalm, can indeed serve the assembly on the Seventh Sunday of Easter in surprisingly appropriate ways.

In the first place, the psalm rehearses the history of Israel, as it were the backstory of the history of the church. Before the origins of Israel and the worship of Yahweh, it was Baal who as Canaan's sky-god "rides upon the clouds" (Ps. 68:4), and in the course of history, the people of Israel now name this sky-god Yahweh, the LORD (v. 4). This God cares for orphans and widows, that is, all the needy, who are cited as representatives of the whole people (vv. 5, 10). This God had freed Israel from their forced labor as prisoners in Egypt (v. 6), led the people through the wilderness (v. 7), appeared to them on Sinai (v. 8), and settled them in a land watered by abundant rains (v. 9). Thus God has brought the people from death into life, and to this God the people sing their praises (v. 34). Indeed, the psalm states that not only Israel, but all the kingdoms of the earth (v. 32) will come to praise the Lord.

This condensed history of the people of Israel complements Luke's emphasis in both the Gospel and in Acts, since Luke maintains that it is within human history that God saves the people. We recall the passage in Luke 3:1–2, in which the evangelist carefully proposes the precise historical timing of the birth of Jesus. The first reading for this Sunday situates us in the church's historical narrative, after the ascension of Jesus and in the original center of Christianity, the city Jerusalem, from which the church will expand throughout the known world. True to what we might expect from Luke, present to receive the power of the Holy Spirit are Mary (see Luke 1–2), the women (see Luke 8:1–3), eleven of the disciples (see Luke 6:12–16), and Jesus' brothers (see Luke 8:19–21).

Secondly, Psalm 68 includes several references to God's abode above the sky. "Let God rise up," begins the psalm. As "rider in the heavens," God speaks with a mighty voice. Christians singing this ancient song rightly think of Luke's narratives of the ascension, through which the third evangelist describes the culmination of the ministry of Jesus. At the ascension, Christ enters the divine realm to reign with God, no longer solely over Israel, but now over the entire cosmos. Thus the archaic poetic imagery that describes God as residing above the earth makes this psalm appropriate for Christian praise at and around the festival of the Ascension.

The emotion that fills the psalm is exuberant joy. One might imagine that when the Savior leaves the scene, the community is sorrowful. The Psalms, though, the first hymnbook of Christians, call us to exult, to be jubilant, to praise the majesty of an awesome protector. At the ascension, it is not that Jesus leaves us, but that—using the poetic phrase of the Scriptures—Christ is now at the right hand of divine authority, dispensing power and strength to all the people.

The concluding verses of the psalm applaud the very voice of God. Although there are many issues about which groups of Christians disagree, Christians do concur on this, that the Bible is the Word of God. That is, in the Scriptures read in assembly and in faithful proclamation of that Word, the baptized hear the voice of God. (In some churches, the assembly stands for the upcoming Gospel reading, for it is as if Jesus himself has entered our room, and we acknowledge his voice by rising in respectful attention.) So it is that within several minutes, our assembly has traversed several thousand years: beginning in testimony to ancient theophanies; moving through legendary history and tribal memories into the kingdom of Israel; then encountering Jesus and acclaiming him as the Son of God, who ascended from Jerusalem into the majesty of God; assembling with other believers to spread the word from Jerusalem "to the ends of the earth"; arriving here together on a Sunday morning a week before Pentecost, to receive power from the Holy Spirit, just as Luke said we would. We are not afraid of the might of enemies, of a parched land, or indeed of the martyrdoms that are once again threatening the church—Peter, cited in today's reading from Acts 1, was among the first believers martyred, says Christian history—for "awesome is God in his sanctuary."

What indeed is our worship space, our holy place, but the very sanctuary of God?

GAIL RAMSHAW

1 Peter 4:12–14; 5:6–11

4:12Beloved, do not be surprised at the fiery ordeal that is taking place among you
to test you, as though something strange were happening to you. 13But rejoice
insofar as you are sharing Christ's sufferings, so that you may also be glad and
shout for joy when his glory is revealed. 14If you are reviled for the name of Christ,
you are blessed, because the spirit of glory, which is the Spirit of God, is resting
on you. . . .

5:6Humble yourselves therefore under the mighty hand of God, so that he may
exalt you in due time. 7Cast all your anxiety on him, because he cares for you.
8Discipline yourselves, keep alert. Like a roaring lion your adversary the devil
prowls around, looking for someone to devour. 9Resist him, steadfast in your
faith, for you know that your brothers and sisters in all the world are undergoing
the same kinds of suffering. 10And after you have suffered for a little while, the
God of all grace, who has called you to his eternal glory in Christ, will himself
restore, support, strengthen, and establish you. 11To him be the power forever
and ever. Amen.

Commentary 1: Connecting the Reading with Scripture

On this Seventh Sunday of Easter, 1 Peter underlines a sobering reality: the triumph of Christ's resurrection does not prevent Christians from suffering. In fact, the first-century church faced suffering and even persecution for their faith. This dual experience of triumph and persecution, which seems like a contradiction, makes sense only in light of both Christ's suffering *and* God's ultimate victory through Christ's resurrection.

God's triumph over evil is celebrated throughout the Hebrew Bible and in the psalm for today: "Let God rise up, let his enemies be scattered; let those who hate him flee before him" (Ps. 68:1). The power of Christ's resurrection permeates the New Testament, but so too does the reality of suffering. Because the ancient church celebrated the victory of God over the powers of evil, death, and the devil at Eastertide, the question of suffering becomes even more poignant and agonizing than in Lent. The audience of 1 Peter certainly asked, as believers do today, If God has won the victory through Christ's resurrection, then why is there so much evil, persecution, and suffering in the world? How do we respond?

First-century Christians wrestled with these painful questions. In the early years of the Christian movement, the situation had certainly gone from bad to worse. In the last decade of the first century, official persecution under the emperor Domitian had become more intense and intentional. The fourth-century Christian historian Eusebius recounted a story that Domitian interrogated Jesus' relatives as a way to extinguish the Christian movement. As emperor, he liked to be addressed as *dominus et deus* ("lord and god"). As a result, he found Christians' resistance to proclaim him as such—because they reserved that title for their God and Savior alone—to be, frankly, treasonous. This makes sense of why most scholars date 1 Peter around 90 CE.

There are some other clues in this letter. The title "Babylon" for Rome (1 Pet. 5:13) was not used until after the temple in Jerusalem was destroyed in 70 CE. Similarly, the word "elder" that the writer uses for himself in 5:1 does not fit Peter as adequately as "apostle." Finally, the sophisticated level of Greek does not seem appropriate to Peter, a Galilean fisherman. Thus the writer is probably not the apostle (Peter was likely martyred in the mid-60s), but a disciple writing in Peter's name and honoring his legacy. In this historical context, the Christian community of the first few decades after Christ's death and resurrection found themselves to be a tiny minority, often intensely disliked by the surrounding pagan and imperial world.

This passage has an easily discernible three-movement structure: First of all, there is the reality of persecution by the pagan world. Second, the passage exhorts Christians to respond with resolute trust in God. Third, the result will be that God in Christ "restores, supports, strengthens, and establishes" believers (5:10). The simplicity of this structure, of course, should not obscure the difficulty of living it out in the first century—or the twenty-first, for that matter—since religious persecution is prevalent in various parts of the globe.

The first part of this passage (4:12–14) demonstrates that, although suffering is painful when it happens to the Christian church, it mirrors the life of Jesus, who (though he was the Messiah or king) also suffered (v. 13). Even more, the "burning" (one word in the original Greek becomes "fiery ordeal" as a necessity of translation) has as its outcome to test and thus refine Christians (v. 12). This echoes a phrase earlier in the letter, where 1 Peter describes that "your faith . . . is tested by fire" (1:7). With a striking similarity to Jesus' words in the Beatitudes—followers were blessed when "persecuted for righteousness' sake" (Matt. 5:10)—1 Peter adds that God promises the Spirit to abide with believers in times of trial. First Peter 4:13 points to "sharing Christ's sufferings," using a word that connotes communion and fellowship in Christ's "suffering," which is repeated twice in this lectionary passage (5:9, 10). This recalls that Christ was not only resurrected. He suffered first. In all this, the promise is that the "Spirit of God is resting on you" (4:14). The early Christians experienced the Spirit's presence in all circumstances—and that is why they were blessed.

The second section of today's passage (5:6–11) exhorts the listeners ("listeners" because this letter would generally have been read aloud) to submit to God and to humble themselves with the confidence that God cares. In 5:7, as Jesus also teaches in Matthew 6:25–34 and Luke 12:22–33, Christian believers move away from anxiety about their sufferings as they rely on God. All three verses lead back to Psalm 55:22, "Cast your burden on the LORD, and he will sustain you." Verses 6–8 present a series of commands: "humble yourselves," "cast all your anxieties" on God, and "discipline yourselves," with the promise that God "will exalt you" and will demonstrate divine support.

The final command moves to the devil and the Christians' need to stay alert. Why? The "slanderer" or "backbiter" (the literal meaning of the Greek word for "devil") is a "lion" (5:8). To first-century ears, this would not be a zoo animal behind the bars of a cage, but a frightening predator in the wild. So Christians were to "keep alert" (5:8). Verse 9 is not actually a command ("resist the devil"), but an epithet of the devil as "whom you resist," as if this is simply a fact. Ultimately, the passage leads to a stirring promise in 5:10, which gave the Christian churches hope: God will "restore, support, strengthen, and establish you." Is this promise only in the future, in the age to come, in the new heaven and the new earth (Rev. 21), or can believers claim this in the here and now as well? What does 1 Peter mean by "in due time" (5:6) and after "a little while" (5:10)?

Already the assurance has been given that "the end of all things is near" (or alternatively, "at hand" in 4:7). "Lord, is this the time when you will restore the kingdom to Israel?" the disciples ask in the lectionary passage from Acts 1:6. The answer: "It is not for you to know the times or periods that the Father has set by his own authority" (Acts 1:7). Instead, and in the meantime between the Now of Christ's resurrection and the Not Yet of the new heaven and the new earth, believers live out their witness to the gospel (Acts 1:8). So the answer to "when" remains a bit unclear and dependent solely on God's divine decision.

However, the New Testament abounds with the eschatological hope of the new heavens and the new earth, and even of their imminent arrival. This is where the accent lies in this passage from 1 Peter. It establishes the original Christians' ultimate hope. Nevertheless, there may be moments when the God who raised the crucified Messiah will also do this work of restoring his people here, in this age. All in all, believers can be convinced that God will act at

Beyond the Cross, the Kingdom

His mind was similarly liberated from spiritual subjection to the existing civil powers. He called Herod, his own liege sovereign, "that fox" (Luke 13:32). When the mother of James and John tried to steal a march on the others and secure for her sons a pledge of the highest places in the Messianic kingdom (Matthew 20:20-28), Jesus felt that this was a backsliding into the scrambling methods of the present social order, in which each tries to make the others serve him, and he is greatest who can compel service from most. In the new social order, which was expressed in his own life, each must seek to give the maximum of service, and he would be greatest who would serve utterly. . . .

Christ's ideal of society involved the abolition of rank and the extinction of those badges of rank in which former inequality was incrusted. The only title to greatness was to be distinguished service at cost to self (Matthew 20:26-28). All this shows the keenest insight into the masked selfishness of those who hold power, and involves a revolutionary consciousness, emancipated from reverence for things as they are. . . .

Jesus was not a child of this world. He did not revere the men it called great; he did not accept its customs and social usages as final; his moral conceptions did not run along the grooves marked out by it. He nourished within his soul the idea of a common life so radically different from the present that it involved a reversal of values, a revolutionary displacement of existing relations. This idea was not merely a beautiful dream to solace his soul. He lived it out in his own daily life. He urged others to live that way. He held that it was the only true life, and that the ordinary way was misery and folly. He dared to believe that it would triumph. When he saw that the people were turning from him . . . unutterable sadness filled his soul, but he never abandoned his faith in the final triumph of that kingdom of God for which he had lived. For the present, the cross; but beyond the cross, the kingdom of God.[1]

1. Walter Rauschenbusch, *Christianity and the Social Crisis*, Library of Theological Ethics (Louisville, KY: Westminster/John Knox, 1991), 86, 87, 89–90.

some point because the Lord has the power to bring all this about (5:11).

Even in this seventh week after the Easter celebration, believers realize they will face affliction, but do so with the assurance of God's ultimate triumph. In some ways, this should not surprise us. It is the reality that comes with following a crucified and risen Messiah. In fact, Christians must realize that suffering is inevitable, but equally so is the promise of victory.

GREG COOTSONA

Commentary 2: Connecting the Reading with the World

Jesus has disappeared into heaven in glory, leaving his friends and disciples behind. What now? Whether or not your congregation or tradition makes much of the feast of the Ascension, these verses from 1 Peter offer insights and instructions for any Christian community or person feeling left in a lurch, abandoned by God, or enduring any kind of suffering.

As you prepare for this sermon, reflect on particular ways your congregation or community may be feeling alone or in the midst of "fiery ordeals" right now. Read the text and imagine God is speaking through this letter directly to you and to them. Invite your listeners near the start of your sermon to take a moment and consider something they might be going through personally right now, and to hold this in their hearts and minds as they listen.

First Peter reminds us not to be surprised by adversity or tough times. Too often, we believe that to be "normal" is to be happy, carefree, healthy, and successful. All of Scripture can witness this is not the case. To be normal is to struggle. In 1 Peter, fledgling Christian communities were minorities, not fitting in either among non-Christian Gentiles or among the Christians who were also Jews. Yet they were not alone, as the writer declares: "your brothers and sisters in all the world are undergoing the same kinds of suffering" (1 Pet. 5:9). Part of being Christian, if we are doing it right, is enduring some kind of alienation from the wider culture. God cannot promise to protect Christians from suffering. More often in the New Testament, Christians in particular—Paul, Peter, Stephen, Mary—are asked to endure suffering, usually in order to witness to the gospel or to act from love or nonviolence.

Dietrich Bonhoeffer, pastor and theologian, spent 1930 at Union Theological Seminary in New York, and he fled Nazi Germany briefly in 1939 for safety in the United States. However, before long he felt an irresistible longing to return to be with his people despite the danger. He wrote to theologian Reinhold Niebuhr: "I have made a mistake in coming to America. I must live through this difficult period in our national history with the Christian people of Germany. I will have no right to participate in the reconstruction of Christian life in Germany after the war if I do not share the trials of this time with my people."[1]

Our temptation in the face of threat or suffering may be to escape, or to build up fortifications of protection around us, not realizing that we are intensifying our suffering through isolation or abandoning our neighbor, who may also be alienated and struggling. Standing apart or running away from our communities, friends, family, or even danger, is not, in the end, the way toward redemption and healing, at least not in Christ.

However, these are not uncommon responses. Even the disciples, after watching Jesus disappear from their sight into heaven, locked themselves in the upper room. It was not until the Holy Spirit descended at Pentecost and drove them back out into public life that they saw their destiny was tied up with other people—people all over the world. Early Christians also tended to band together in small groups and to worship in secret locations for safety. It was only because of brave believers like Paul, Peter, Barnabas, and Lydia, who reached out despite their fears or reservations to preach, teach, welcome, and organize, that the Christian faith spread and changed the lives of so many people. We must not hide inside our own heads, congregations, or neighborhoods so that our view of reality gets distorted, thinking we are alone in our pain or safer inside ourselves than connected in community. We are not "the only ones." We are not alone. We have one another and God, who has promised always to be with us (Isa. 41:10; Matt. 28:20).

First Peter invites us to see suffering and alienation not as something merely to endure but as a means of blessing. He insists we should "rejoice insofar as [we] are sharing Christ's sufferings" and teaches that "if [we] are reviled for the name of Christ, [we] are blessed" (1 Pet. 4:13–14). *Rejoice?* Feel *blessed* in suffering? How can this be? Suffering is something we want first to fix or eliminate, but suffering and rejection are where we can learn compassion and vulnerability; both are needed to create true relationship, with people and with God.

Jean Vanier, founder of the L'Arche movement for people with developmental disabilities, reflected in an interview, "Weakness is not an evil. But it can be and should become the place where [I] can meet people . . . [and] realize that I need a savior. I need Jesus."[2] Our suffering, alienation, and fiery ordeals are the places where we can see we are not God and that we need love, community, and Jesus.

We are members of Christ's body. When we suffer, we share in Jesus' sufferings and rejection, just as Jesus shares in ours. Just as Jesus was condemned and suffered for and with the whole human race on the cross, so there is an intimacy with him in our own suffering and estrangement that we can feel in prayer, in meditation, or in our thoughts and awareness. This

1. Letter quoted in Renate Bethge, *Dietrich Bonhoeffer: A Brief Life* (Minneapolis: Augsburg Fortress, 1991), 54.
2. Jean Vanier, interview with "The Work of the People," http://www.theworkofthepeople.com/become-weaker. Undated.

is especially if we are suffering or alienated for the sake of the gospel; for instance, for the sake of someone in need, for the poor and oppressed, to resist oppression, to do the right thing, or for the purpose, simply, of being true to ourselves. However we may be suffering, we can know that Jesus is suffering with us and loving us through it. As 1 Peter writes, we are blessed, "because the spirit of glory, which is the Spirit of God, is resting on [us]" (4:14).

Still, 1 Peter instructs us not to focus as much on suffering or alienation as on the power and love of God. We cannot let ourselves be so weighed down by struggle that there is room for nothing else within us, including our relationships with God and one another. To make room, the writer offers four directions in verses 6–9: (1) humble yourselves, (2) cast your anxiety on God, (3) discipline yourselves and remain alert, and (4) resist the devil. These may sound harsh; they certainly encourage us to depend less on ourselves and more on God, to lean on Christ, to wait on the Spirit. The poet Jan Richardson, in her poem "Stay,"[3] puts it this way:

For now,
hear me when I say
all you need to do
is to still yourself,
is to turn toward one another,
is to stay.

Wait
and see what comes
to fill
the gaping hole
in your chest.

In this pause between Ascension and Pentecost, after Christ has ascended but before the appearance of the Holy Spirit, not unlike the pause of all creation, waiting for the return of Christ to redeem the earth, encourage your people to remember that God never leaves us, no matter how things may seem. Even when we feel forsaken in our struggles, God invites us to turn to one another to find community and solidarity. God invites us to lean on Jesus, who bears our burdens with us, who can bring blessing out of suffering, and who offers us a love and power greater than we could ever muster alone.

HEIDI HAVERKAMP

3. Jan Richardson, "Stay," in *Circle of Grace: A Book of Blessings for the Seasons* (Orlando, FL: Wanton Gospeller Press, 2015), 161–62.

John 17:1–11

[1]After Jesus had spoken these words, he looked up to heaven and said, "Father, the hour has come; glorify your Son so that the Son may glorify you, [2]since you have given him authority over all people, to give eternal life to all whom you have given him. [3]And this is eternal life, that they may know you, the only true God, and Jesus Christ whom you have sent. [4]I glorified you on earth by finishing the work that you gave me to do. [5]So now, Father, glorify me in your own presence with the glory that I had in your presence before the world existed.

[6]"I have made your name known to those whom you gave me from the world. They were yours, and you gave them to me, and they have kept your word. [7]Now they know that everything you have given me is from you; [8]for the words that you gave to me I have given to them, and they have received them and know in truth that I came from you; and they have believed that you sent me. [9]I am asking on their behalf; I am not asking on behalf of the world, but on behalf of those whom you gave me, because they are yours. [10]All mine are yours, and yours are mine; and I have been glorified in them. [11]And now I am no longer in the world, but they are in the world, and I am coming to you. Holy Father, protect them in your name that you have given me, so that they may be one, as we are one."

Commentary 1: Connecting the Reading with Scripture

As Eastertide draws to a close, the Gospel reading for the Seventh Sunday of Easter focuses on the end of Jesus' time on earth. In prayer, he looks back on his life and ministry. This retrospective also provides a glimpse of what lies ahead as Jesus anticipates the new reality of resurrection and what it will mean for his relationship with his followers. Notions of glory shine through the Gospel and the accompanying texts, a glory both fully realized in God and God's Son, and a promised glory yet to be fulfilled. This tension is evident in the lack of understanding about Jesus and his ministry from those he encounters, his disciples, and others, elsewhere in the Gospel (John 5:39–44; 8:27; 10:1–6; 12:16; 14:5, 8–9; 16:18, 30–31; 20:9), in the Synoptic Gospels (Matt. 16:23; Mark 6:52; 9:32; Luke 2:50; 9:45), and in the lection from Acts (Acts 1:6).

The second half of the Gospel of John (chaps. 13–21) has been called the Book of Glory.[1] Jesus' public ministry, described in the first twelve chapters of John, called the Book of Signs, has come to a close, and he is preparing his disciples for what lies ahead. The Book of Glory begins around the table where Jesus kneels to wash their feet (13:1–11). This action points to the strange nature of the glory of God made manifest in Jesus. It is a servant glory, lacking in the kind of powerful signs of glory some of his followers were hoping for.

John 17:1–11, the first part of what is known as Jesus' high-priestly prayer, concludes his Farewell Discourse (chaps. 14–17), which is similar in form and timing to Moses' last words and prayer in Deuteronomy (chaps. 32 and 33).[2] Speaking with his followers, Moses looks back

1. Raymond E. Brown, *An Introduction to the New Testament* (New York: Doubleday, 1997), 334–35.

2. For a discussion of the parallels between Moses' farewell and Jesus' Farewell Discourse, see Raymond E. Brown, *The Gospel according to John XIII–XXI*, Anchor Bible 29A (New Haven, CT: Yale University Press, 1970), 744–45.

on their life together before blessing them in prayer, just as Jesus does.

Jesus' prayer takes place at the table where he has eaten a pre-Passover meal with his disciples, washed their feet, and commanded them to do the same for each other (John 13:12–17). Jesus prays for himself, that he may be glorified in God's presence, and he prays with tenderness for his disciples, voicing his love for them, here as elsewhere (13:1a, 34; 14:21; 15:9).

Concluding the Farewell Discourse, the prayer serves as a turning point, moving toward the passion. "The hour has come" (17:1), as Jesus has known it would (13:1). Even as he looks back on his ministry (17:4), he knows there is no going back. The prayer is Jesus' final blessing, his almost-last words, for his closest followers. In the first part of the prayer, Jesus prays only for the disciples (v. 9), not the world. He then expands the circle of discipleship to "those who will believe in me through their [the disciples'] word" (v. 20). In so doing, Jesus reaches across the boundaries of time to unite us with him in his glory, a glory that comes through suffering (vv. 20–23). With the disciples, we too listen in on the prayer; we too are its beneficiaries.

As Jesus prays, he repeats his declaration that the hour has come for God to glorify him (13.1; 17:1). In other words, the culmination of Jesus' ministry is now. This "now" has both past and future aspects. Jesus glorified God on earth in the past by finishing the work he was given to do (17:4); he now asks also to be glorified with God in the life to come. That future glory is a restoration of the glory that he knew with God before time began (vv. 5, 24). As announced in John 1:14, the glory of God that is beyond time entered the world in a particular time in the person of Jesus. Now at the end, he prays to return to the presence of that eternal glory. There are echoes, here, of Philippians 2:5–11, of a preexistent Christ dwelling in glory with God before creation and then taking on human form, "the form of a slave" (Phil. 2:7b). Having humbled himself, Christ kneels to wash feet before being restored to glory with God for all eternity.

The theme of glory—past, present, and future—is also woven through the other readings for this Sunday. Psalm 68 paints a picture of God's transforming glory: protecting the vulnerable (Ps. 68:5); giving the lonely a home (v. 6); freeing the captives and punishing those who rebel (v. 6); causing rain to fall and restoring the wilderness (vv. 8, 9); providing for the needy (v. 10); evoking praise from the people (v. 32). The psalmist describes the realization of God's intention for the world, the love that God has for the world (John 3:16) that is affirmed throughout Scripture. This is akin to the work Jesus was given to do that glorified God (17:4): healing, restoring, feeding, tending the flock. Just as Jesus has made God's name known (John 17:6, 11), so the psalmist calls on the people to do the same, in song and praise and exultation (Ps. 68:4).

In the passage from 1 Peter, the promise of sharing in Christ's glory, which God will reveal in some future time, becomes the hope that sustains those who are persecuted: as they are united with Christ in suffering, so they will be united with him in glory. Past faithfulness and present endurance will yield to glory (1 Pet. 4:14). In the tension of the "already and not yet," the glory is not only a future reward but a present reality. A suffering, servant glory, "the spirit of glory, which is the Spirit of God" (1 Pet. 4:14), is already with the believers.

As the Easter season ends, the reading from Acts anticipates the Day of Pentecost and points to a new season in the liturgy and in the church. Acts 1 describes the glory of the ascension, as Jesus is lifted to heaven in a cloud and holy messengers appear. The disciples are still hoping for earthly glory through the restoration of the kingdom to Israel. They are grounded in the present, anxiously asking the risen Christ if this is the time (*chronos*, as contrasted to Jesus' sense of *kairos*; see Acts 1:6). Instead of participating in Israel's restoration to power, they are to receive Christ's power and become Christ's witnesses (Acts 1:8). Their vocation is to continue glorifying God on earth by fulfilling the work they have been given to do in the here and now, just as Jesus did. That glory will lead to their suffering and servanthood.

Glory is an attribute of God that is mentioned again and again in the OT, usually rendered in Hebrew as *kavod*, a word that connotes weightiness. The Psalms, for example, are filled with references to God's glory, often displayed in power, might, and majesty. Although it was not possible to look on God's face and live, Moses nonetheless asked to see God's glory (Exod. 33:18). In the person of Jesus, according to John, we have all been granted a glimpse of God's glory (John 1:14, 18)—not a distant transcendent glory, but a glory made manifest in suffering, service, and love.

MARTHA C. HIGHSMITH

Commentary 2: Connecting the Reading with the World

Preaching the Gospel of John throughout the Easter season in Year A is a tough and demanding task for even the most seasoned preacher. John's particular theological worldview and vocabulary make it a challenge for the preacher to draw immediate and relevant connections between the text and the context in which he or she is preaching. The Seventh and last Sunday of Easter marks the final installation of three Sundays of Jesus' Farewell Discourse, bringing the Easter season to a close with Jesus' own prayer for the disciples and, by continuation, for the current community of believers.

While we know that Jesus has a close relationship with God and an intentional prayer life, we do not often get a window into the exact words of those prayers. In Matthew and Luke, we have the Lord's Prayer as a result of the disciples asking Jesus how they should pray, but Jesus' own prayers are somewhat mysterious. When Jesus does pray out loud, his prayers are relatively brief, especially when compared with this farewell prayer in John 17. In this particular prayer, Jesus is acting as an intercessor, primarily praying on behalf of his disciples.

In his hymn "Alleluia! Sing to Jesus," W. Chatterton Dix refers to Jesus as "Intercessor, friend of sinners," and asks, "Earth's redeemer, plead for me." There are times when we feel unworthy to approach God ourselves and we ask someone else to intercede on our behalf. Just as Jesus intercedes for us as the one who is both human and divine, so members of the communion of saints also serve as intercessors. According to the Council of Trent, "the saints who reign together with Christ offer up their own prayers to God for [humanity]."[3] Though sometimes disparaged during the Reformation era, when there was concern about praying to saints rather than directly to God, the concept of requesting intercession has a long history.

In most Christian traditions, we dedicate a substantial part of worship to intercessory prayer. Though we also pray for our own needs, intercessory prayer is prayer explicitly on behalf of others. During this time of worship, we often pray by name for individuals connected to the community, particularly those who may be sick or suffering. We also intercede with prayer for victims of particular natural disasters or terrorist attacks.

In our national dialogue, intercessory prayer has gotten a bad reputation, due to the prevalence of the phrase "thoughts and prayers" on social media in the wake of tragedies like school shootings. The tendency of politicians and public figures to offer thoughts and prayers without taking meaningful action has led to the mockery of the phrase. Jesus' own intercessory prayer connects prayer and action, praying for the disciples as he prepares for his passion and resurrection.

Jesus' prayer gives the preacher an opportunity to discuss the Christian calling to pray for others. Many people in the pews have had a situation in which a specific prayer for someone was not answered—that a cancer would go into remission or that a soldier would come back from war. However, we do not pray for some deus ex machina to fix everything so that we can forget about it. Praying for others puts us in solidarity with those with whom Jesus was in solidarity: the poor, the hungry, the sick, and the forgotten. We pray to remember. We offer intercession to be in communion with them, and we pray for the grace of God to inspire us and strengthen us to be the body of Christ, to make our thoughts and prayers into concrete actions.

3. *The Canons and Decrees of the Sacred and Oecumenical Council of Trent*, ed. and trans. J. Waterworth (London: Dolman, 1848), 234.

The last verse of the designated Scripture portion provides another avenue for connecting this text to the mission and goal of the unity of the church (although the preacher is always free to expand the text and read more of Jesus' farewell prayer!): "And now I am no longer in the world, but they are in the world, and I am coming to you. Holy Father, protect them in your name that you have given me, so that they may be one, as we are one" (17:11). The final phrase of that verse is echoed later in verses 21, 22, and 23. The oneness of those given to Jesus, his disciples, is to mirror the unity of the Father and the Son.

Given what we know about the state of the Christian church, we might argue that Jesus' own prayer for the unity of the church has been ineffective. From the beginning, Jesus' followers found themselves at odds over theology and gradually split into factions. With the Protestant Reformation, those splits rapidly multiplied. At times, these divides were particularly ugly, resulting in the deaths of those deemed heretics. Theological disagreements over ecclesiology were complicated by issues of money and power between heads of state and the church. In contemporary contexts, Christians more often make the news for suing one another over property than for cooperating in mission.

Aimed at counteracting the trend of division, the modern ecumenical movement can be traced to the first couple of decades of the twentieth century. Much of the world was consumed with war, and the hope was for the church to be an agent of reconciliation. Eventually, the World Council of Churches met for the first time in 1948, with the goal of the whole church overcoming differences in order to be an example of hope, peace, and unity.

The struggle of ecumenism is to balance the desire to conform to Jesus' prayer that we all may be one with the particularities of our own theological commitments. While Christ and his unity with the Father and the Holy Spirit is our primary point of unity, our diverse geography, language, liturgy, and theology affect how that is expressed. Is it even possible for us, after all of this time and with our human tendency toward sin and division, to "be one" as Jesus and the Father are one?

With the secularization of the Western world and the loss of cultural capital that Christianity used to enjoy, our current moment is ripe for the opportunity to live into Jesus' prayer for his disciples through more ecumenical cooperation. Some Protestant denominations have entered into agreements intended to foster ecumenical relationships through sharing of clergy and by recognizing the particular gifts and strengths of one another. Today, the way people select a faith community is also based less on denominational loyalty or specific theological premises, leading unintentionally to more ecumenically oriented lives and general goodwill toward Christians of other types.

Our usual understanding of unity involves minimizing differences or distinctiveness. Despite Jesus' prayer for unity, we might hesitate to give up what makes our particular tradition or denomination unique. Ultimately, if our model for unity is the relationship between Jesus and the Father or, more broadly, the Trinity, we have a model of unity in diversity. The Father, the Son, and the Holy Spirit are one, and they are also three persons. They are individual and also consubstantial. To be one as Jesus and the Father are one is to be unified but also distinct.

Frankly, as the church, we have little problem with distinction and more struggles with unity. Jesus' prayer for us, his disciples and his church, is that we may be one in him. That very unity is a gift and a grace from God that we strive to live into as our Christian vocation.

KIRA SCHLESINGER

Day of Pentecost

Numbers 11:24–30
Psalm 104:24–34, 35b
1 Corinthians 12:3b–13
John 20:19–23
Acts 2:1–21
John 7:37–39

Numbers 11:24–30

[24]So Moses went out and told the people the words of the LORD; and he gathered seventy elders of the people, and placed them all around the tent. [25]Then
the LORD came down in the cloud and spoke to him, and took some of the spirit that was on him and put it on the seventy elders; and when the spirit rested upon them, they prophesied. But they did not do so again.
[26]Two men remained in the camp, one named Eldad, and the other named Medad, and the spirit rested on them; they were among those registered, but they had not gone out to the tent, and so they prophesied in the camp. [27]And a
young man ran and told Moses, "Eldad and Medad are prophesying in the camp."
[28]And Joshua son of Nun, the assistant of Moses, one of his chosen men, said,
"My lord Moses, stop them!" [29]But Moses said to him, "Are you jealous for my
sake? Would that all the LORD's people were prophets, and that the LORD would
put his spirit on them!" [30]And Moses and the elders of Israel returned to the camp.

Commentary 1: Connecting the Reading with Scripture

Texts from the book of Numbers are infrequent in the Revised Common Lectionary, so this text provides an opportunity to explore a period of Israelite history that is often overlooked. This fourth book of the Torah tells the story of the wilderness sojourn as it transitions from the first generation that escaped from slavery in Egypt to the second generation, who will enter the promised land. The book gets its English title from the census information that is recorded in the first chapter. The Hebrew title, however, is "In the Wilderness." This is a more accurate summary of the contents of the book and the setting of the historical narrative.

The book can roughly be divided into three major sections. The first (chaps. 1–10) revolves around preparations for life in the wilderness. There are instructions on how the camp is to be arranged, and the ministry of the Levites is prescribed. The second section (chaps. 11–25), in which our text is located, describes the chaotic life of being a community in the wilderness. In this section the sojourners make their way to the edge of the Jordan but are afraid of the nations that inhabit the promised land. They refuse to enter Canaan and so are punished, extending the wilderness wandering to forty years. The third section of the book (chaps. 26–36) provides instructions on how life was to operate after the wilderness. The entire book moves us from Mount Sinai to Moses' last sermon in Deuteronomy.

Numbers 11:24–30 is part of the complaint narrative. After only three days of travel from Mount Sinai, the people "complained in the hearing of the LORD" (Num. 11:1). God's anger burns at the edges of the camp. Then a rabble, a group among the sojourners who have a strong craving, stir up the people to weep and complain over their lack of meat. They are tired of the manna, the miraculous bread provided for them daily. It is not good enough for them, they say. When Moses hears of the complaint, he despairs about his leadership. He cries out that he is not able to carry the people alone; the burden is too heavy. He is even ready to die rather than continue in leadership. So the Lord instructs Moses to gather seventy leaders and take them to the tent of meeting, where the Lord will take some of Moses' spirit and share it with the leaders.

This is not the first time that Moses has struggled to carry the weight of leadership. In Exodus 17, Moses struggles to hold his arms up during a battle with the Amalekites, so Aaron and Hur hold them up for him (Exod. 17:8–13). In Exodus 18:13–26, Moses' father-in-law, Jethro, notices how difficult it is for Moses to judge so many cases; it is taking a heavy toll on him. He suggests that Moses train a group of judges to handle the ordinary cases so that the load is shared among a community of judges. Moses' decision in Numbers 11:24 to choose the seventy leaders to share in the charismatic and prophetic dimensions of leadership is another step in the sharing and structuring of leadership.

A sermon might well explore this familiar dynamic between charismatic leadership and the need to institutionalize that spirit; or the need for church leaders to create structures of support, lest they suffer burnout. God's people have always needed to build structures that can carry and distribute the power that comes from God's presence. In fact, it seems to be necessary for prophetic leadership to be shared if it is to be effective. Jesus himself sends out the seventy because the "harvest is plentiful but the laborers are few" (Luke 10:1–12).

Yet even this need to institutionalize is never as ordered or clear as might be hoped. Eldad and Medad, names that have a wonderful poetic ring, have not gathered with the seventy in the traditional place where God speaks to Moses and the people. They are not at the center of the camp at the tent of meeting, but are outside the sphere of holiness. They are among the people. This is noteworthy, particularly in a book where spheres of holiness are ordered and defined. Clearly, God's Spirit does not abide by the rules that the priestly writer has articulated. Eldad and Medad speak with the same prophetic power as those chosen.

Perhaps the listener needs a reminder that God regularly speaks outside the boundaries of even the most sacrosanct and approved "camp." The young Joshua is bothered by this breach of order, but Moses, who has been more regularly in contact with the sometimes capricious and regularly unpredictable God, sees the bigger picture, wishing that all of God's people would be captured by the Spirit's prophetic power.

Moses' prayer links these texts to Pentecost (Acts 2:1–21) and the outpouring of the Holy Spirit, where the entire gathered assembly is either speaking prophetically or understanding the prophetic utterance in their own languages. We can trace a line from the Hebrew prophetic tradition to this moment in Jerusalem, when the church becomes the community where all, indeed, do share in the Spirit's charismatic power.

In fact, a movement has been set into motion that will require building and institutionalizing the Spirit, but will, at the same time, be regularly challenged to expand its circle to include more who come under the Spirit's power. Peter's vision to eat both clean and unclean animals (Acts 10) will expand the Spirit's reach beyond the Jewish community. The church will struggle with this widening. Mark's Gospel offers a glimpse into an experience almost identical to the story of Eldad and Medad in the wilderness. The disciples hear of someone casting out demons in Jesus' name. Their first reaction is to ask Jesus to make them stop. Jesus, appearing next to Moses in the transfiguration a few verses before, says, "Whoever is not against us is for us" (Mark 9:38–41).

Eldad and Medad become signs that God's Spirit can blow in directions not predicted or even acceptable according to tradition or sacred text. The Spirit, breathing between the Lord and Moses, breathing between Moses and the seventy, eventually breathing between Jesus and the disciples on Pentecost, always breathes across boundaries to include other prophets who are among the people. These texts teach us to look beyond the regular people and places to find prophetic utterance. God is always at work both in the center and at the edge, among people we have not expected.

Finally, this text occurs in liminal space, in a threshold place where one way of being has dissolved and another is forming. The experience of Mount Sinai is fresh, yet the journey toward the promised land is only now taking concrete shape. The people are on the move, but it turns out that moving forward into the promise is more complicated, difficult, and filled with anxiety than anticipated. Leadership is harder because the reality of a people on the way is also taking concrete form. Blessings, once a source of delight and hope, turn out to be ambiguous and fleeting. There is a developed sense of being a chosen group, a people of covenant, but the community contains "rabble" whose craving and whining affect the whole community. It is significant to note that the freshness of expanded authority and spirit comes when the full and realized implications of being a covenant people are also fully realized.

BRADLEY E. SCHMELING

Commentary 2: Connecting the Reading with the World

The preacher serving in an ecclesial tradition that follows the church's calendar knows that this passage from the book of Numbers is assigned for Pentecost Sunday and therefore has something to say about the gift and work of the Holy Spirit. The preacher will be well served to read and think about the connections between the other lectionary texts from John, Acts, and Psalm 104. If the preacher does not use this text from the book of Numbers and uses the Acts reading in its place, then the text from 1 Corinthians is the epistle reading for the day. The point here is that the Day of Pentecost, and the other appointed readings for this day, serve as interpretive lenses for reading this text. If the preacher is in a church tradition that does not interact with the church's year, then the preacher encounters a story in Numbers 11:24–30 that says things about charismatic leadership and the gift of God's Spirit in human beings.

We have a curious story on our hands, and preachers have questions to answer. Where is Moses at this point in Numbers? Why is he gathering seventy elders and placing them around the tent? What is this tent? Has the Lord come down in a cloud before? What spirit does the Lord take from Moses and put on these seventy elders? Why does the text retain this detail about the spirit-infused elders who prophesy: "But they did not do so again" (Num. 11:25)? These questions arise from only the first scene.

The second scene has two men, elders presumably, remaining in the camp and prophesying. We read that they were registered (serving as representatives of the community) but had not gone out to the tent (v. 26). Overhearing their prophesying, someone else runs to report this prophetic action to Moses and Joshua. Joshua implores Moses to stop the two men from prophesying. Moses' reply to Joshua suggests that he is of a different mind about this prophetic activity: "Would that all the LORD's people were prophets, and that the LORD would put his spirit on them!" (v. 29). Moses and the elders return to the camp.

At first glance verse 29 seems to make clear this text's connection to the day of Pentecost and all the ways that the church hopes for the activity of the Holy Spirit. The verse tells us that Moses was supportive, not antagonistic, regarding the prophesying of Eldad and Medad. Joshua may have thought they were upstarts and outliers, but Moses, Joshua's superior, commends what the two men have done (v. 29). Moses wishes that everyone would carry out this prophetic action, that God's spirit would be upon everyone.

With those words the reader is left to trust the agency of this spirit and the origin and purpose of this prophetic speech. If Moses wishes for this, so should we. This chapter and the one following are a collection of stories regarding Moses' leadership and his charisma, or gifts of prophetic leadership. His is not an inherited leadership but a charismatic one. These stories, and our passage in particular, deal with how the charisma of spirit is transferred to others.

All of these connections are pertinent to the ways Christians think about the gift of the Holy Spirit. Would that all have a share of this spirit and go about prophesying like Eldad and Medad! Our spirited leadership is not sanctioned by inheriting an office but by God's gift of the Spirit in our lives. Also, our spirit-filled pronouncements may not be anticipated or welcomed by others, perhaps even (especially?) by those already in leadership positions, like Joshua. These connections arise from this story, and the preacher could explore ways that members in a congregation react to other members' spirited proclamations. How do we play out our own hierarchies of leadership within congregations? Whose spirited leadership is sanctioned? Who is silenced? Whose spirited proclamation is questioned?

The preacher can, additionally, help us reflect on our spirited leadership in the world. Some persons are gifted with spirited speech and can raise their voice in public and private forums, influencing others' return to God. Others may prophesy by actions, God's spirit working in them as they write or parent or even shop in ways that beg for attention to God's intentions.

Yet the preacher should move with care when identifying the work of the Spirit. Many of us think ourselves to be persons who bring the vibrant, new, disruptive Spirit to situations. Perhaps we are. Perhaps, however, we are instead the Joshua of our situation, a sanctioned Spirit-filled leader in our own right, but one who could be surprised by how God's appointed Spirit moves in others, even at times disrupting our preconceived notions.

Our text is part of the Israelites' wilderness journey account with Moses as their leader. They follow the Lord whose daytime presence is a cloud and whose nighttime presence is a pillar of fire. When the Lord pauses (as cloud or fire), they set up the ark of the covenant, and each tribe sets up its own encampment. When the Lord moves again, by fire or cloud, they follow. Chapter 11 begins with the Israelites' complaints about life in the wilderness.

The Israelites' ongoing and detailed complaints about the manna (vv. 1–10) have brought about the Lord's ire and fiery vengeance. They are tired of manna and they want meat. Moses complains to God about the complaining people (vv. 11–15) and says that "they are too heavy for me" (v. 14). The Lord responds, "Gather for me seventy of the elders of Israel. . . . I will take some of the spirit that is on you and put it on them" (vv. 16–17a). The Lord does this so that "they shall bear the burden of the people along with you so that you will not bear it all by yourself" (v. 17b).

Our text today is the account of the Lord's promise coming true. The Lord takes some of the spirit that was in Moses and gives it to those seventy elders. It is significant to Numbers that this spirit-sharing occurs in the context of a complaining people and is, in fact, an indirect response to the people's complaints. The people complain to Moses, Moses complains to God, and God acts to alleviate Moses' burden. The Lord's promises do not end with the transfer of spirit. The verses immediately following our passage detail God's sending meat (in the form of quails) to the complaining people. It is a curious story of the Israelites gathering quails, eating, and dying by the Lord's plague (vv. 31–35). Complaint (and punishment) and spirited leadership are present in our text.

Perhaps the preacher could help us think about God's promised and present Spirit in the midst of times full of complaints. According to the scenes surrounding our story, the Lord's ire and wrath are stirred up. Yet God does not withhold God's gift of the spirit. Seventy elders (an auspicious number) receive the spirit. God has heard Moses' complaint and transfers a share of God's spirit to these elders so that Moses does not bear the entire leadership burden. It is an account of God's sustenance in wilderness times, even alongside God's punishment of such complaints. The transfer of the spirit comes for communal sustenance; the spirit comes through the community and for the community. According to the text, the spirited action of the seventy ceases too soon (v. 25). Is that true for us as well?

JENNIFER L. LORD

Psalm 104:24–34, 35b

24O LORD, how manifold are your works!
In wisdom you have made them all;
the earth is full of your creatures.
25Yonder is the sea, great and wide,
creeping things innumerable are there,
living things both small and great.
26There go the ships,
and Leviathan that you formed to sport in it.

27These all look to you
to give them their food in due season;
28when you give to them, they gather it up;
when you open your hand, they are filled with good things.
29When you hide your face, they are dismayed;
when you take away their breath, they die
and return to their dust.
30When you send forth your spirit, they are created;
and you renew the face of the ground.

31May the glory of the LORD endure forever;
may the LORD rejoice in his works—
32who looks on the earth and it trembles,
who touches the mountains and they smoke.
33I will sing to the LORD as long as I live;
I will sing praise to my God while I have being.
34May my meditation be pleasing to him,
for I rejoice in the LORD. . . .
35b Bless the LORD, O my soul.
Praise the LORD!

Connecting the Psalm with Scripture and Worship

On Pentecost, the fiftieth day of Easter, the church completes its annual celebration of Christ's resurrection by praising God for the gift of the divine Spirit given to the church and the world. However, for Christians, every Sunday all year long is a celebration of Jesus' resurrection, and so Pentecost does not so much conclude Easter as manifest it for the remainder of the year. Assemblies are advised to avoid any silliness that might accompany some Happy Birthday of the Church party, for Luke's two volumes tell us that the Spirit of God, the very breath of life in the creation of all things, bestowed life into believers throughout history, was encountered in the ministry of Jesus and in the lives of his associates, and is now recognized as enlivening the whole assembly and indeed the cosmos itself.

The first reading may be the Pentecost narrative from Acts 2, in which the fire and wind of Mount Sinai are replicated in the fire and wind in the Jerusalem house. God comes not only to Moses, but to each of the gathered believers, the divine flame shining on each person's forehead. Alternatively, the first reading may be the story of Moses' God-given authority now shared with seventy elders, and—in a delightfully comic conclusion to the story—even with those who for some reason had not made it out to the tent. Both choices proclaim the reception of God's Spirit, no longer to only a few designated leaders, but now to great numbers of the people, even to those who were absent. On Pentecost, one way to say, "Christ is risen!" is to say to one another, "Receive the Holy Spirit," as if we are Moses or Peter, pouring God's blessings out for everyone.

The psalm chosen for Pentecost is the last twelve verses of Psalm 104, a hymn to God the Creator. In verses 24–25, we affirm that, far from being birthed on this fiftieth day, the divine Spirit was active already in creating the world. For a landed people like the ancient Canaanites, the sea represented unbounded chaos, the terror of existence outside of human civilization, and in verses 25–26 the psalmist dismisses any fear of the sea by praising God for its wonder. It would be helpful if the service folder for this Sunday included a picture of the Leviathan of verse 26, so that the assembly catches the meaning of this fascinating Israelite claim, that the ancient Near Eastern sea monster, who churns up the waters and swallows drowned sailors, is in reality only a grand sea creature that God created for sheer enjoyment. Verses 27–28 acknowledge God as not only the original Creator, but also as the preserver of the life on earth, by providing food for all creatures.

It is mainly verses 29–30 that have led to Psalm 104 being selected for the festival of Pentecost. The complex Hebrew noun *ruach* can be translated as "wind," "breath," or "Spirit," and our differing biblical translations have chosen one of these three possible options as most appropriate for each context. So in Genesis 1:2, what is it that comes from God to sweep over the waters? In Genesis 2:7, what does God give to the creature of dust that it may become a human? Much of Christian tradition has heard Psalm 104:29–30 as if it were referring to the Spirit of God granting life to the whole creation. Thus on Pentecost Sunday, God's Spirit is praised for enlivening not only the church but the whole cosmos, even the sea monsters. According to Trinitarian theology, the Spirit of God is the Spirit of the risen Christ. In recent decades, churches are attending to the transformative power of the divine Spirit not merely in the self, and not only in the church, but throughout the whole of creation. Psalm 104 is a banner proclamation for this ecological understanding.

The last verses of Psalm 104 return our memory to the smoking crest of Mount Sinai. We might think of the church as yet another volcano, burning with a divine mystery and summoning all the baptized to praise. It is usual for Christians to omit the curse in verse 35; yet despite contemporary sensibilities, such a petition is rather like the characteristic Christian hope for heaven, where evil will be over and gone. In verse 35, the psalm's final reference to "my soul" calls each of us to praise, the individual joining in the communal response to the first reading, the single human within the amazing diversity of creatures enjoying life from the Spirit. On this earth it is we humans who received from the Creator the gift of speech and who can sing out our Hallelujah, our "praise the Lord."

GAIL RAMSHAW

1 Corinthians 12:3b–13

[3b]No one can say "Jesus is Lord" except by the Holy Spirit.

[4]Now there are varieties of gifts, but the same Spirit; [5]and there are varieties of services, but the same Lord; [6]and there are varieties of activities, but it is the same God who activates all of them in everyone. [7]To each is given the manifestation of the Spirit for the common good. [8]To one is given through the Spirit the utterance of wisdom, and to another the utterance of knowledge according to the same Spirit, [9]to another faith by the same Spirit, to another gifts of healing by the one Spirit, [10]to another the working of miracles, to another prophecy, to another the discernment of spirits, to another various kinds of tongues, to another the interpretation of tongues. [11]All these are activated by one and the same Spirit, who allots to each one individually just as the Spirit chooses.

[12]For just as the body is one and has many members, and all the members of the body, though many, are one body, so it is with Christ. [13]For in the one Spirit we were all baptized into one body—Jews or Greeks, slaves or free—and we were all made to drink of one Spirit.

Commentary 1: Connecting the Reading with Scripture

The passage for this Sunday of Pentecost—that is, the birthday of the Christian church—emphasizes the power of the Spirit of God. In 1 Corinthians 12, Paul takes up the topic of God's power and reminds his hearers that the principal outworking of the Spirit is the unity of God's people. As he has written at the beginning of this letter (1 Cor. 1:10–17), his desire is that "there be no divisions," but instead that the church be "united." Paul dislikes intensely any divisions among Christ's people.

In fact, Paul believes that the giving of the Spirit on the day of Pentecost, and the gifts of the Holy Spirit, have a very specific effect: they bring about the unity of the body of Christ—yet the churches in Corinth are a mess. They are divided and unruly. Only two decades after Jesus' death and resurrection, the Christian communities in this Greek cosmopolitan center are a confused mayhem of competition. They also do not like Paul very much (which can be discerned by even a cursory reading of 2 Corinthians). Nonetheless, assured of his apostleship, Paul takes up this authority (with varying degrees of success) to try to bring this motley assortment together under the one Lord, Jesus the Christ.

Churches in this day were assemblies of Christians in private houses, since cathedrals or sanctuaries did yet not exist. This may have made physical unity difficult, since Christians met in homes, as Paul indicates later when he greets Aquila and Prisca, "together with the church in their house" (16:19). Each would thus be a different assembly (or church). This situation might have led them to declare "I belong to Paul," "I belong to Apollos," or "I belong to Cephas"—which in fact they did proclaim (1:12). Paul despised this approach because all Christians belong to the one Lord Jesus (1:13). By separating themselves into factions, they denied this in practice.

In the passage for today, Paul is addressing "spiritual persons" (see 12:1), that is, persons endowed with spiritual gifts. The Corinthian Christians were competitive and dismissive of other Christians. They particularly prized their "tongues," their glossolalia, that is, heavenly language given directly by the Spirit and thus not a known human language. In chapter 14, Paul describes tongues as indistinct, like the sound of a flute or harp (14:7), as a prayer without the mind but in the Spirit (vv. 14–15), and even as apparent lunacy (v. 23). Still, Paul never doubted the existence of tongues and even boasted later in this letter, "I thank God that I speak in tongues more than all of you" (v. 18). Nonetheless, despite whatever dazzling display tongues presented, "the primary token of the indwelling Spirit, the indispensable evidence that one is truly 'spiritual,' is not glossolalia, but love," as F. F. Bruce has summarized the passage at hand.[1]

To illustrate his point, Paul drew on a common analogy of the time for the "body politic"—that all the citizens who make up the *polis*, or the city, have diversity of abilities in their unity as one city, like a human body. It is something all human beings know. Feet are not eyes, an ear not a nose, our beating heart not an elbow; yet each of those members, and more, is needed to make a fully functioning body. Most of all, the body cannot consist solely of a mouth that speaks heavenly, and therefore unknown, languages.

What brings unity? The brief two-word statement "Jesus Lord" (the original Greek implies the "is") represents the essential confession of early Christians (see 1 Cor. 8:6; Rom. 10:9; 2 Cor. 4:5; Phil. 2:11). Before baptism, they were asked, "What do you believe?" Their response was, "Jesus (is) Lord." Then they were baptized. These two words in Greek reveal that the work of the Spirit is not discerned by way of dramatic manifestations as much as in the simple confession of believers that Jesus is Lord. While this confession was not flashy, it was dangerous, since it set up a strong contrast to the popular assertion that "Caesar is Lord."

Paul's call to Christian unity is a central theme throughout his letters (for example, Rom. 12:4–8). What does unity look like? In verse 4 of 1 Corinthians 12, Paul balances "varieties of gifts" with "the same Spirit." In verses 8–9, "the same/one Spirit" is repeated for emphasis. In other words, there is diversity in unity and unity in diversity, with neither of these more important than the other. Interesting to note is that Paul probably coined the word for "gifts" in verse 4 (not the same word as in Rom. 12:1). His word, *charismata*, emphasizes God's grace and demonstrates that anything activated by the Spirit (see v. 11) is given by God as a gift to the church.

The focus throughout is best expressed in verse 6: "the same God who activates them all." Paul focuses on *God's* work in all this: the source, not the manifestation. In fact, the psalm for this Sunday describes that this is the Creator Spirit that animates all life (Ps. 104:30). In 1 Corinthians, God and the Spirit are interchangeable, and "one" recurs throughout the passage and appears three times in this short closing verse (1 Cor. 12:13) in this passage.

"Tongues" appears to be a favored gift of the Corinthians. Because it was a language not known to any human speaker, it required interpretation (v. 10). Interestingly, this seems to contrast with the experience at Pentecost in today's reading, Acts 2:1–21 (esp. vv. 8–11), where tongues are known human languages, though given spontaneously to nonnative speakers.

One has to remember Paul's concern for unity in the body of Christ. After this passage, and before he returns to *charismata* in chapter 14, he emphasizes in chapter 13 the gift that characterizes the Christian community. It is *agapē*, a love that is "patient" and "kind" (1 Cor. 13:4), a love that does not "insist on its own way" (v. 5).

Two further questions often arise in the discussion of "spiritual gifts" or *charismata*: Is this list exhaustive? No, because Paul enumerates various additional gifts in other places (e.g., Rom. 12:6–8; Eph. 4:11), which suggests he emphasized the gifts pertinent to each particular Christian community. Second, are these gifts different from natural abilities? Some seem to be, such as speaking in tongues, but others, like "administration" (in the Rom. 12 passage) would look very much like a natural ability. However one answers that question, for Paul, the particular listing of spiritual gifts did not nearly equal the significance of Christians using them to serve together in the unity of the Spirit.

In closing, it is worth nothing that the Jewish festival of Pentecost celebrated the giving of the Law and that the Christian holiday of the same name celebrates the giving of the Spirit who fulfills the Law by bringing the unity of

1. F. F. Bruce, *I & II Corinthians*, The New Century Bible Commentary (New York: HarperCollins, 1981), 117.

love. This matches Jesus' summary of the Law in which he cites Deuteronomy 6:5 and Leviticus 19:18: "You shall love the Lord your God with all your heart, and with all your soul, and with all your mind" and "You shall love your neighbor as yourself" (Matt. 22:34–40).

Thus, during the season of Pentecost, Christians realize that the Spirit's central work is not to activate spectacular displays of *charismata*, but to create unity through the diverse gifts of the body of Christ.

GREG COOTSONA

Commentary 2: Connecting the Reading with the World

Every Pentecost, we recognize the coming of the Spirit on that wondrous day two thousand years ago in Jerusalem, and the ongoing gift of the Spirit in our lives and churches. Paul, writing to the Christians in Corinth only about twenty years after the day of Pentecost, was already reflecting on the ongoing life of the Spirit. The churches of his letters were communities of ordinary people seeking to live out the gospel in their ordinary lives. Like us, they were not present for Pentecost in Jerusalem, to feel the wind or see the tongues of fire, but they could experience the Spirit through love, joy, vocation, spiritual gifts, and transformative community.

How is the Holy Spirit working in your congregation today? How is the Holy Spirit calling forth gifts and vocations? How is the Holy Spirit calling people into community? The Holy Spirit is like God's border collie—trying with boundless energy to herd us together into groups, to testify in word and action to all the world that "Jesus is Lord" and God is love.

Scripture is clear, especially in the book of Acts and the letters of Paul, that the Holy Spirit bestows on us wisdom and gifts for doing this work, for building one another up and spreading the good news of Jesus. Paul has two similar, though not identical, lists of these gifts. one in today's reading and one in Romans 12:6–8. These lists can seem vague or a bit fantastic, with gifts like "utterance of knowledge," prophecy, and working of miracles, which can be a bit hard to define or sound superhuman. Paul's lists were not meant to be definitive or grandiose but to name gifts he saw already at work in individuals in those particular communities. As you prepare this sermon, you might take some time to consider the gifts of the Spirit already alive and active in your congregation. What are the particular ways your members and neighbors love to serve one another? What activities or ministries do they find irresistible? In what ways are they longing and yearning to grow? By not focusing on their flaws or ways they do not want to grow, these sorts of questions can offer clues to the gifts and the movement of the Spirit already afoot.

What is a "gift of the Spirit" anyway? Paul's list of examples is long, as if to remind the Corinthians that the Spirit is not exclusive or limited, but diverse and generous. While we can look in our modern churches for the gifts he mentions, like faith, wisdom, discernment, healing, prophecy, or even speaking in tongues, we can also expand Paul's list to include other activities, ministries, or talents that our folks may be using to build up one another and the larger community.

One online inventory of spiritual gifts includes playing a musical instrument, convening a group, and giving spiritual advice, as well as activities we may consider more mundane, like working behind the scenes, giving money, or fixing things when they break. All are essential to faith and ministry together. A gift of the Spirit can be anything we do easily and well and choose to share for the "common good" (v. 7). Our gifts are marked by both our individual joy and community need.

Frederick Buechner's insight, along these lines, is memorable and helpful: "The place God calls you to is the place where your deep gladness and the world's deep hunger meet."[2] Paul might add that the gifts of the Spirit also

2. Frederick Buechner, *Wishful Thinking: A Seeker's ABC* (San Francisco: HarperOne, 1993), 118.

somehow proclaim or demonstrate that "Jesus is Lord" or, as he writes earlier in the letter, show "Jesus Christ, and him crucified" (1 Cor. 2:2).

Gifts are not a hierarchy of achievements or a proof of faith. A gift of the Spirit is not something earned. Paul tells the Corinthians that their spiritual lives and actions are not about personal worthiness or effort, but pure *gift*: the result of the grace, desire, and activation of the Spirit. They are simply part of who we are! We tend to believe that faith and ministry are the result of personal decision, agency, and preference, whether we think of ourselves as spiritually worthy or spiritually lacking. You might invite the congregation to consider their spiritual lives, even their church attendance, as "gifts of the Spirit" that are given by God by grace rather than rewards they must work to deserve, or exercises they must practice the "right way." Our gifts are not talents to develop to be good enough for God, but gifts God has given to us for our own enjoyment as well as for the common good.

What a strange message this is to us in the modern world, where our primary role in society is as consumers: choosing when and how to use, take, purchase, and accumulate the products offered to us. We easily can "wear" spirituality rather than practice it, with "spiritual" clothes, jewelry, tattoos, knickknacks, and trips, rather than investing in the vulnerable and risky transformation of our hearts and minds. We may measure Christian worthiness in exterior signs like Sunday attendance, "good" behavior, Bible study, or volunteer work. We may even judge our own worthiness more harshly than others', discounting our right to belong, participate, or even pray, because we believe our spiritual merits do not measure up. Christian community and faith are gifts of the Spirit, not something to be earned. They are gifts not only to us as individuals, but to our entire communities, both inside and outside the church. Paul emphasizes that our gifts work together, each particular and unique, but none better or less worthy than another.

Finally, the gifts of the Spirit are not just fun or fanciful, but gifts with revolutionary potential. Stanley Hauerwas and William Willimon put it this way: "To be made holy by the work of the Holy Spirit is to be made part of a community of truth that makes friendship possible in a world of violence and lies."[3] There is more at stake when we proclaim that "Jesus is Lord" than our own behavior or salvation. The life of our church can be transformative, for both the congregation within and the world without, as a "community of truth" and a place where friendship is possible. You might ask your congregation to reflect and consider this quotation in the context of their own life together, with opportunity to talk more in your adult education time or to write thoughts on index cards or Post-it notes to display and share in your fellowship hall.

We do not need to see flames of fire or hear each other speaking in tongues to know the Holy Spirit is among us. Paul teaches us that the Spirit works among us through our gifts and relationships. We are one body in Christ, each with gifts from the Spirit to use together in proclaiming the gospel. The gifts of the Spirit are *gifts*, not a checklist, not a spiritual Olympics requiring training and bestowing medals on the best of the best. They are to be used for the common good, not for ourselves alone. They can bring diverse and differing people together in friendship, "Jews or Greeks, slaves or free." Pentecost can continue in our lives as individuals and communities as we allow the Holy Spirit to work in and through us, declaring that "Jesus is Lord" and making his love known to all, even in the face of violence and lies.

HEIDI HAVERKAMP

3. Stanley Hauerwas and William Willimon, *The Holy Spirit* (Nashville: Abingdon, 2015), 76.

John 20:19–23

[19]When it was evening on that day, the first day of the week, and the doors of the house where the disciples had met were locked for fear of the Jews, Jesus came and stood among them and said, "Peace be with you." [20]After he said this, he showed them his hands and his side. Then the disciples rejoiced when they saw the Lord. [21]Jesus said to them again, "Peace be with you. As the Father has sent me, so I send you." [22]When he had said this, he breathed on them and said to them, "Receive the Holy Spirit. [23]If you forgive the sins of any, they are forgiven them; if you retain the sins of any, they are retained."

Commentary 1: Connecting the Reading with Scripture

Does the Holy Spirit come as wind and fire, or as a breath of peace? The Gospel for the Day of Pentecost offers a different perspective from the Acts lection that is frequently the focus of preaching and worship. Both lections illuminate, in various ways, the unifying and transforming power of the Holy Spirit, as do the accompanying texts for the day. The reading from John's Gospel describes a turning point for the disciples: it is the moment they (except for Thomas) come to believe that the Lord is still with them (John 20:20–25), the moment their fear is transformed to joy.

John 20:19–23 is a brief account of Jesus' second postresurrection appearance and the first to the disciples. The lection follows John's accounts of the Last Supper, the passion, and the discovery of the empty tomb. "On that day" (v. 19), the day of resurrection, some of the disciples were huddled together in a locked room. Peter and the disciple Jesus loved had gone to the tomb after Mary Magdalene told them it was empty. They had seen for themselves and believed her account (20:8–9) but did not understand that Jesus had risen from the dead. Their confusion apparently continued even later, after Mary announced to them that she had seen the Lord. Instead of rejoicing, the disciples were afraid—afraid of the religious leaders, afraid perhaps that they too would be persecuted and killed. It was in this fear-filled room that Jesus appeared and, as he had promised (14:25–27), gave the gifts of peace and the Spirit.

Some scholars see Jesus' greeting of peace not as a wish or a prayer but rather as a statement of fact. It may be more appropriately translated "Peace to you" rather than as the future hope implied in the construction "Peace be with you," with its added verb.[1] The disciples were far from peaceful, however. The text implies that they still did not understand who Jesus was, that they still could not see him even right in front of them, until he held out the proof in his wounded hands and side. When they finally saw Jesus (20:20b), he repeated his greeting. Perhaps this time they believed he was a reality.

The peace Christ extended empowered the sending of his disciples. No longer need they remain frozen in fear. Instead they were sent as Jesus had been sent (17:18). The Spirit was to be their Advocate, one who would be with them and fill them forever (14:16–17), teaching and reminding them (14:26) of all Jesus had said. In these ways the Spirit would show them that now they were to do as he had done when he was in the world. With the breath of Jesus, they were given the power to forgive sins and the power to retain sins (the preacher might

1. Raymond E. Brown, *The Gospel according to John XIII–XXI*, Anchor Bible 29A (New Haven, CT: Yale University Press, 1970), 1021.

note that this is in some contrast to Matt. 6:14–15, where lack of forgiveness toward others results in lack of forgiveness from God). Some interpreters take this to mean that the disciples were given power to "hold" the unforgiven sins of others until the final judgment.[2]

A Full Baptism of the Spirit

Dear sisters in Christ, are any of you also without understanding and slow of heart to believe, as were the disciples? Although they had seen their Master do many mighty works, yet, with change of place or circumstances, they would go back upon the old ground of carnal reasoning and unbelieving fears. The darkness and ignorance of our natures are such, that, even after we have embraced the Saviour and received his teaching, we are ready to stumble at the plainest truths! Blind unbelief is always sure to err; it can neither trace God nor trust him. Unbelief is ever alive to distrust and fear. So long as this evil root has a place in us, our fears cannot be removed nor our hopes confirmed.

Not till the day of Pentecost did Christ's chosen ones see clearly, or have their understandings opened; and nothing short of a full baptism of the Spirit will dispel our unbelief. Without this, we are but babes—all our lives are often carried away by our carnal natures and kept in bondage; whereas, if we are wholly saved and live under the full sanctifying influence of the Holy Ghost, we cannot be tossed about with every wind, but, like an iron pillar or a house built upon a rock, prove immovable. Our minds will then be fully illuminated, our hearts purified, and our souls filled with the pure love of God bringing forth fruit to his glory.

Julia A. J. Foote, "A Word to My Christian Sisters," in Julia A. J. Foote, *A Brand Plucked from the Fire* (New York: G. Hughes, 1879), 115–16.

The gift of the Spirit is both present and promised throughout the Gospel of John. Jesus is the one on whom the Spirit rests, the one who will baptize others with the Holy Spirit (1:33). The Spirit is as unpredictable as the wind (3:8), without limits (3:34), life giving (6:63), and truth telling (14:17; 15:26; 16:13). The peace that accompanies the gift of the Spirit, Jesus' peace, is also unpredictable. It is not the world's peace (14:27) but a peace that will endure even in the face of persecution (16:33).

From the beginning, the Spirit, the *ruach* of God, is a creative force (Gen. 1:2; 2:7) moving over chaos and bringing life. Just as God breathed into the human, the *adam*, so God breathes into all creatures, as the psalm lection declares: "When you send forth your spirit, they are created; and you renew the face of the ground" (Ps. 104:30).

In Ezekiel's vision of the valley of dry bones (Ezek. 37:5, 6, 9, 10), the Spirit, also *ruach*, restores life and is the agent of resurrection and restoration (37:12–14). Just as in Genesis, without the breath of the Spirit there is no life. It was the mystical encounter with the risen Jesus and the gift of that same Spirit that breathed new life into the disciples.

In the alternate lection for the day, Numbers 11:24–30, the Spirit of God brings the gift of prophecy, a gift ideally not limited to a few but offered to "all the Lord's people" (Num. 11:29). Whether breathing creation into existence or being poured out on ancient prophets, the Spirit is transformational. In this broad context, the gift of the Spirit in the locked room in Jerusalem must also be seen as transformational, changing the disciples from a fearful, defensive group into those who are Christlike, sent into the world like Jesus (John 17:18) to do the work of God. This unity with Christ is also a unity with God (17:11, 21–23; 1 John 3:24). It is the love of God in Christ, a perfect love abiding with them forever, that has cast out their fear (1 John 4:18).

In John, Jesus himself gives the Holy Spirit to the disciples on the evening of the day of resurrection, and it comes as a breath of peace. Luke–Acts, however, places the coming of the Holy Spirit almost fifty days after the resurrection

2. Brown, *Gospel according to John XIII–XXI*, 1024.

and following the ascension. The risen Jesus has promised the gift of the Spirit (Acts 1:5, 8) but is not present when it comes in a violent wind and tongues like fire (Acts 2:2–3). The Spirit gives the disciples the power to speak so all in the known world can understand. The disciples who had been confused about Jesus' mission (Acts 1:6) are now transformed into his witnesses.

Although the Spirit is manifest in different ways in the two passages, the effect is similar: disciples once confused or fearful are filled with the Spirit and given Christlike power. In either case, the Spirit is disruptive: lives are changed, people are transformed. The disciples are sent out to continue the work of Jesus in the power of the Spirit. They, and those who come after them, do this through the diversity of the transformational gifts the Spirit bestows, as described in 1 Corinthians 12, another lectionary text, where "each is given the manifestation of the Spirit for the common good" (1 Cor. 12:7). The work of the Spirit has a unifying effect, resulting in the many members of the body being one with each other (1 Cor. 12:12), as they are one with Christ (cf. John 17:21–23), baptized into one body in the one Spirit (1 Cor. 12:13).

The gift of the Holy Spirit, whether with its wind and flame or peace and life-giving breath, changes everything. With the first disciples, we find ourselves rejoicing and no longer fearful (John 20:20b), sent into the world (John 20:21b), blessed with a diversity of spiritual gifts (1 Cor. 12), and knowing the fullness of life through God's life-giving breath (Ps. 104:30). The Spirit breaks through barriers: locked doors; language; individualism; fear; racial, ethnic, and social divisions. The Spirit transforms, renews, unites, and sends us into the world to carry on the work both begun and fulfilled in the life of Jesus.

MARTHA C. HIGHSMITH

Commentary 2: Connecting the Reading with the World

These five verses from the Gospel of John are not what we normally associate with Pentecost, even though many of the traditional themes are present. The giving of the Holy Spirit, the beginning of the church, and even the focus on breath and wind all show up with a distinctly Johannine twist. Bringing out the differences between this passage and the Pentecost event in Acts can create an opportunity for new insights about the Holy Spirit and her role, a topic often neglected from the pulpit except on the feast of Pentecost. The congregation has previously encountered these verses just a few weeks ago on the Second Sunday of Easter as part of the story of Thomas the Twin. This feast day marks the end of our Easter celebration in the liturgical year, with our text recounting three major events that occur on the same day: the discovery of the empty tomb, the first appearance of the risen Christ, and Christ's giving of the Holy Spirit. For Pentecost, this text can function as a hinge between liturgical seasons, looking at how we continue to live out Easter and Pentecost even as we transition into Ordinary Time.

Twice in the span of three verses, Jesus greets the disciples with "Peace be with you." While a typical greeting, neither the context nor the person offering the greeting is conventional. Jesus mysteriously enters the room despite the doors being locked, a testament to his resurrected body. The disciples have locked themselves inside out of fear. In contrast to their fear, Jesus offers peace, not merely a greeting but an offering of the peace promised in the Farewell Discourse (John 16:33). This peace is, as the hymn "O Master, Let Me Walk with Thee" puts it, "the peace that only thou canst give," a peace that surpasses our earthly fears and anxieties.

There are many things in our contexts and in the broader world that incite fear within us, fear that is frequently stoked by television news or social media. We fear the unknown in times of upheaval and transition. We fear for our economic security and that of our children. We fear the loss of the institutions that have shaped us. We even fear for our physical security in places we formerly thought were safe, like schools, churches, hospitals, and movie theaters.

In the wake of mass shootings around the United States, some of which have taken place at churches, many places of worship have reevaluated their security plans. Out of the fear of being sitting ducks during a worship service for an armed intruder bent on causing harm, some have opted to lock doors as a means of controlling who can enter and when. Of course we want to protect ourselves, our children, and other vulnerable people in our midst, but we must balance this with our belief in the risen Christ, who enters in spite of our locked doors and greets us with his peace. The gifts of the Holy Spirit and of Christ's peace do not remove or negate our fear, but grant us the knowledge and grace not to let that fear dictate our terms of engagement with the world.

When we greet each other with the peace of the Lord in our worship service, it can frequently devolve into a social hour rather than serving its proper function. Greeting one another with the peace of Christ is an action and event that is full of hope and gravitas when we can encourage one another to proclaim the gospel without fear or anxiety. Jesus' second greeting of "peace be with you" in 20:21 is directly linked to his sending of the disciples into the world. Instead of catching up on the latest gossip or trading compliments on apparel, exchanging the peace of Christ with one another could be a reminder that, whatever our fears and anxieties, the risen Christ is present among us and sends us out in the world to bear witness.

The presence and importance of breath as the means by which Christ gives the Holy Spirit to the disciples is another avenue ripe for exploration and meditation. Breath or wind is one of the traditional manifestations of the Holy Spirit, and here it is directly breathed from the resurrected Christ. Not the rushing wind or the tongues of fire from Acts, this giving of the Holy Spirit mirrors the breath of life with which God animates the first human. Even without the scientific knowledge that we now have, people have long understood the biological and spiritual power of the breath. Our lives begin and end with breath, from that first cry of a newborn outside the womb to the deathbed vigil, watching for the last independent breath.

The breath is a powerful life force, and its quality is also crucial to our well-being. We are reminded in yoga or meditation practices to breathe deeply, from our diaphragms, not shallowly from the upper part of our lungs. It is the breath that helps everything else in our body function, bringing in oxygen and expelling waste products. Spiritually, we can use the breath as a focus for centering ourselves and calming our minds. In a moment of crisis or anxiety, we are advised to take two or three deep breaths to calm our racing hearts. The parallels between our breath and the Holy Spirit lie in how crucial each of them is. Though their presence is more often felt rather than seen, they are still absolutely required for our physical and spiritual life and health.

Having received the Holy Spirit directly from the mouth of Jesus, part of the mission and calling for the disciples, and subsequently the church, is to be sent out into the world to embody reconciliation and the forgiveness of sins. While we might normally think of sin as a moral failing, John's Gospel posits sin as a theological failing, an inability to recognize Jesus as a revelation of God. Thus, Jesus' sending of the disciples as he was sent by God is intertwined with the mission of proclaiming Jesus' identity.

Too often, rather than witnessing to Jesus' identity as God, the church desires to function as the gatekeeper and judge over what is and is not "sinful" in our society and culture. Rather than the church being "for" something with a positive mission of preaching Jesus as the Son of God, the church is seen as being against any number of things, particularly those viewed as progressive by secular society. Many of those who have fallen away from the church would cite the church's historical stances of being anti-women, anti-LGBTQ+, and anti-sex as things that they came to find unacceptable. Instead of being identified as witnesses to the power of the risen Christ and the breaking of barriers by the Holy Spirit, Christians and the church are too often seen as those who are not as ready and willing to forgive as they are to retain sins.

To be the people of God in the world is to be empowered by the Christ-breathed Holy Spirit and sent into the world to witness to who Jesus is as the revelation of God. This is the task not only of the leaders but of the entire faith community. On Pentecost, as the church celebrates its beginning as a community of faith, we have a chance to recommit to this mission of being "for" Christ and not just "against" what we might see as being wrong with the world.

KIRA SCHLESINGER

Acts 2:1–21

1When the day of Pentecost had come, they were all together in one place. 2And suddenly from heaven there came a sound like the rush of a violent wind, and it filled the entire house where they were sitting. 3Divided tongues, as of fire, appeared among them, and a tongue rested on each of them. 4All of them were filled with the Holy Spirit and began to speak in other languages, as the Spirit gave them ability.

5Now there were devout Jews from every nation under heaven living in Jerusalem. 6And at this sound the crowd gathered and was bewildered, because each one heard them speaking in the native language of each. 7Amazed and astonished, they asked, "Are not all these who are speaking Galileans? 8And how is it that we hear, each of us, in our own native language? 9Parthians, Medes, Elamites, and residents of Mesopotamia, Judea and Cappadocia, Pontus and Asia, 10Phrygia and Pamphylia, Egypt and the parts of Libya belonging to Cyrene, and visitors from Rome, both Jews and proselytes, 11Cretans and Arabs—in our own languages we hear them speaking about God's deeds of power." 12All were amazed and perplexed, saying to one another, "What does this mean?" 13But others sneered and said, "They are filled with new wine."

14But Peter, standing with the eleven, raised his voice and addressed them, "Men of Judea and all who live in Jerusalem, let this be known to you, and listen to what I say. 15Indeed, these are not drunk, as you suppose, for it is only nine o'clock in the morning. 16No, this is what was spoken through the prophet Joel:

17'In the last days it will be, God declares,
that I will pour out my Spirit upon all flesh,
and your sons and your daughters shall prophesy,
and your young men shall see visions,
and your old men shall dream dreams.
18Even upon my slaves, both men and women,
in those days I will pour out my Spirit;
and they shall prophesy.
19And I will show portents in the heaven above
and signs on the earth below,
blood, and fire, and smoky mist.
20The sun shall be turned to darkness
and the moon to blood,
before the coming of the Lord's great and glorious day.

21Then everyone who calls on the name of the Lord shall be saved.'"

Commentary 1: Connecting the Reading with Scripture

This passage is one of the few readings assigned for every year of the lectionary cycle, which underscores its significance in the life of the church. As such, it is extremely rich in its connection with the entire canon, especially in relation to the whole document of Luke–Acts and also to the other lectionary readings, especially John 7:37–39. The text is so thick with meaning and wider connections that we will be hard pressed to do it justice; its testimony seems nothing short of miraculous. Anxiously awaiting the arrival of the promised Spirit, the apostles and other "believers" (120 in all, according to Acts 1:15) were together in Jerusalem celebrating the feast of Pentecost. Pentecost, seven weeks after Passover on the liturgical calendar, is a significant event because it is traditionally linked to the giving of the Law. The disciples had been instructed to wait "for the promise of the Father," when they would be "baptized with the Holy Spirit" and "receive power when the Spirit came upon them" (Acts 1:4, 5, 8). At that point they were instructed to be Christ's "witnesses in Jerusalem, in all Judea and Samaria, and to the ends of the earth" (1:8).

The Pentecost story, it is agreed by most exegetes, belongs to the wider biblical story of the Gospel of Luke, called by many interpreters simply Luke–Acts. Pentecost stands in the middle of Luke–Acts, near the beginning of the book of Acts. David Bartlett, biblical interpreter and homiletician, asks that we "notice that at the beginning of both ministries, that of Jesus [Luke] and that of the church [Acts], Luke shows us how deeply grounded the new covenant is in the old."[1] In fact, many understand the day of Pentecost to be the birthday of the wider community, the church, which is joined to Jesus the Jewish prophet. There is a revision of the older covenant associated with the Law (and thus linked to Pentecost) into the new covenant exemplified and sealed in Jesus the Christ.

The reading fits into the longer story of Luke–Acts. Just as Jesus could not explain his ministry without turning to Isaiah, so Peter explains Pentecost in reference to Joel. Joel 2:28–32 announces the last days, when the Spirit will be poured out on all flesh, and all who call on the name of the Lord will be saved.

The passage in Acts 2 makes it quite clear that the powerful gift of the Spirit in tongues of fire upon those gathered in Jerusalem on the day of Pentecost came "not for the sake of the church but for the sake of the world," as Bartlett puts it. The profusion of languages denotes this worldwide significance. This event is universal and unlimited, not provincial or limited; thus many, perhaps even all, nations are addressed. Surely generations of readers have stumbled over the pronunciation of "Phrygia and Pamphylia" among others in the table of nations in 2:8–11. It is hard not to be astonished at the range of peoples who each heard the apostles in their own language. The catalog, which goes on for four verses, leads us to ask, What does this mean?

Some have seen the Pentecost event as a sort of reversal of the confusion of languages that took place at the tower of Babel in Genesis 11:1–9. Perhaps better read, however, Pentecost does not so much reunite all languages and cultures as enable that diversity to be witnessed, as persons understood what was being said. The author of Acts prefigures the movement of the story of Jesus into all the world through references to multiple peoples and cultures. If the Gospel of Luke represents the life and teachings of Jesus of Nazareth, Acts recounts the way the gospel was carried to Corinth, Antioch, Philippi, and even to the Gentiles. Pentecost is thus the beginning of universal evangelism.

We should not miss the emphasis on the power of the Spirit. Clearly this is the Spirit that Jesus promised the apostles he would send, who would enable them to do "signs and wonders" beyond those of Jesus himself. Christians cannot simply ignore the power and the capabilities that were given to the apostles and other believers. Jacob Myers asks, "What if Luke's intention . . . is to break apart a theology that is wrapped up in ethnic identity" and expand or even rebuild the foundations so that "God's bigger vision" of power "might burst forth"?[2]

There are also hints that Luke is "linking the Pentecost event with the renewal of the Sinai covenant," in the words of Mikeal Parsons.[3] This new covenant may be broadening the work of the Spirit to extend to all peoples, including even future generations. The citation of Joel is "remarkably inclusive," as Parsons notes: sons, daughters, young and old men, male and female

1. David Bartlett, "Commentary on Acts 2:1–21," www.workingpreacher.org/preaching.asp?xcommentary_id=71.
2. Jacob Myers, "Commentary on Acts 2:1–21," https://www.workingpreacher.org/preaching.aspx?commentary_id=1296.
3. Mikeal C. Parsons, "Commentary on Acts 2:1–21," https://www.workingpreacher.org/preaching.aspx?commentary_id=2066.

slaves. All receive the Spirit. Joel 2:28–32 is replete with images of theophany that join the rush of the violent wind, the tongues of fire, the smoke, and the sun turned to darkness; these images are reminiscent of the pandemonium that happened at Pentecost predicted by Peter in his sermon. Something colossal is afoot. This citation from Joel is a bridge both to what precedes Pentecost and what follows it. In effect, the Joel prophecy is fulfilled in the Pentecost event. Just in case we missed it, Peter is announcing that this event has powerfully inclusive significance for all genders, ages, and nationalities.

The other lectionary readings for the day (Num. 11:24–30; 1 Cor. 12:3b–13; John 20:19–23) reinforce the themes of the promise of the Spirit and of power. There are two preaching images in the 1 Corinthians reading: one of the distribution of gifts and the other of the interdependent working of the various parts of the body joined and knit together in one Spirit. Particularly relevant to our commentary here is John 7:37–39, which may be understood to hearken back to the passage from Joel announcing that the messianic age has begun. The preacher might use Joel 2:28–32 as a forceful way of tying the promise-fulfillment theme together.

After the resurrection, Jesus promises to send power from on high ("the promise of the Father") upon his followers. In this Pentecost passage he fulfills that promise, surely calling on power that belongs only to God. As Richard Hays puts it, "the outpouring of God's Spirit demonstrates that the risen [and ascended] Jesus is seated at God's right hand where he possesses the divine authority. . . . Simply put, Jesus has the authority to send the Spirit because . . . he is 'Lord.'"[4]

Acts 2:1–21 is the nexus point of the messianic age. Scripture up to the time of this event has moved toward the life and teachings of the Messiah. The Gospels recount that life and those teachings. In Acts 1 Jesus commissions his disciples to go out into all the world. This is where the proclamation hits the road. In short, the lectionary readings fill out and reinforce the Pentecost themes. Not only are they cohesive; they all point toward different implications for the preacher and for the life of the church. In each of our readings the Spirit comes upon believers, empowering them to be the living water, which Jesus has promised. Indeed, the promised gift made to the disciples by the risen Lord in John 20:22, when he exhorts them to "receive the Holy Spirit," is extended at Pentecost and continues to be manifest now.

L. SHANNON JUNG

Commentary 2: Connecting the Reading with the World

In Acts 2:1–4, God confirms the coming of the Spirit with three signs. The most significant, though, is the worship in tongues, that is, in languages that the worshipers have never learned. Luke repeats this on two other occasions when God pours out the Spirit, although on those occasions, Luke is silent about whether those present can understand those who are speaking in tongues (Acts 10:46; 19:6). Because many present at Pentecost recognize the languages on this occasion, they ask what is happening (2:12), and Peter responds that this indicates that Joel's prophecy about God empowering his people prophetically is being fulfilled (2:16–18).

Scholars today differ as to whether this phenomenon of worshiping God in unlearned tongues must always involve real languages or if it can be speech, inspired by the Spirit and uttered by someone with a specific gift for speaking, that only God understands. Paul uses the same wording as Luke to refer to prayer understood only by God (1 Cor. 12:10; 14:2, 13).

For Paul, what matters more than the specific linguistic features of the communication is the heart's affective communication with God (13:1; 14:2, 14–15). Paul emphasizes the benefit of praying in tongues for personal spiritual renewal. Although Luke presumably would

4. Richard B. Hays, *Reading Backward: Figural Christology and the Fourfold Gospel Witness* (Waco, TX: Baylor University Press, 2014), 71.

have agreed, his emphasis in this passage is elsewhere. He describes the occasion in Acts 2 by noting that God inspires the believers to worship in human languages they cannot speak. In addition, there are people present who can understand and participate (Acts 2:11).

On this occasion, tongues serve as a sign explaining what this outpouring on Pentecost is all about: God's Spirit is empowering God's servants to speak God's message across all human barriers, as promised in Luke 24:47–49 and Acts 1:8. Although this promise was first and foremost for Jesus' first disciples, it is quite clear that it extends to all of Jesus' followers for all generations (2:38–39).

Like witness (1:8) and prophecy (2:17–18), worship in tongues is a form of speech for God that God's Spirit empowers. If some believers are empowered to worship God in other people's languages, how much more can God empower us to cross all cultural barriers with the gospel?

Many parts of the church have learned from Acts 2 and offer lessons to the rest of us, for example, the monastic movements and Anabaptists who have taken seriously the model of Acts 2:44–45. Pentecostal and subsequent charismatic renewals challenge the rest of the church by how seriously they have taken Acts 2:4–18. Starting with the Azusa Street revival in 1906, these renewals have grown from a handful of people to an estimated half a billion or more—perhaps the largest movement in Christianity today next to the Roman Catholic Church, with which it overlaps.

Although outsiders often defined the Christian Pentecostal movement by one of its most distinctive traits, speaking in tongues, many recent observers trace more of the movement's long-range success to another characteristic feature.[5] From its beginning at Azusa Street, led by African American holiness preacher William Seymour, interracial, cross-cultural empowerment was at the heart of the movement. Around the world, it often appealed to the poor and those who felt excluded culturally, socially, or academically from much of the mainstream church. Of course, charismatic renewal has diversified across classes and denominations, and some of its forms would be barely recognizable to the first Pentecostals. On the whole, however, its growth illustrates a key feature of this passage: the empowerment of the Spirit thrusts us across all human barriers.

This feature of the narrative becomes even clearer in the verses that follow. In 2:5–13, Jewish people from around the world are present for the festival. In this passage, Luke provides a list of peoples, probably evoking for much of his audience the Bible's first such list in Genesis 10. The passage that follows Genesis 10 is Genesis 11:1–9, the account of the tower of Babel, but whereas in Genesis 11 God comes down to scatter the languages and divide peoples, here the Spirit comes down to scatter languages to establish a new, multicultural unity in Christ.

Although an early witness to the Azusa Street revival celebrated that "the color line is washed away in the blood," human depravity soon enough reared its head. Accustomed to a range of worship styles, including that of his own African American community, Seymour welcomed loud and joyful worship (often evident in the Psalms), as well as quiet. Seymour's key mentor on the matter of tongues, however, was accustomed only to a quiet experience of the Spirit. Thus he rejected this worship; further, he reportedly derided the revival in racist terms. Like too many people even today, Seymour's white mentor failed to transcend the racial prejudices of his day.

After this confrontation, Seymour emphasized this other dimension in Acts 2, to which the tongues-speaking pointed. As far as Seymour was concerned, persons ought not to claim to be full of the Spirit, no matter how much they spoke in tongues, if they could not love their brothers and sisters in Christ across racial lines. Some of our churches today are culturally monolithic for geographic reasons; one cannot expect the same racial diversity in rural Iowa as in Flushing, Queens, New York, for example. Some of our churches, however, are monocultural because of residential segregation or cultural insensitivity.

5. See esp. Allan Heaton Anderson, *To the Ends of the Earth: Pentecostalism and the Transformation of World Christianity* (New York: Oxford University Press, 2013).

We may need to learn from William Seymour and from Luke's picture in Acts.

In Acts 2, God pours out the Spirit on "all flesh" (2:17), though Peter himself does not recognize that this promise transcends even ethnic boundaries until he meets Cornelius (10:28, 47). Although the ethnic and cultural barrier is the primary one on which Acts focuses, Acts reveals that the principle does not stop there.

God's promise in Joel crossed barriers of age, gender, and free or slave status. Luke elsewhere illustrates also God speaking through both genders and all ages (Luke 2:36; Acts 21:9–10). Jarena Lee, Julia A. J. Foote, Catherine Booth, and other earlier women preachers rightly understood the liberating message of the Spirit's empowerment in this passage. Many of the women in ministry worldwide also belong to the renewal movements of the Spirit mentioned earlier. Although some passages in the NT do accommodate the cultural limitations of the day, others point beyond these to God's ideal (Gal. 3:28). Paul valued his fellow ministers who were women (Rom. 16:1–7; Phil. 4:2–3), and Luke recognizes that God's gifts, including empowerment to speak for God, are not limited by gender (Acts 2:17–18).

Peter changes Joel's wording with respect to slaves: now the Spirit is for all who are *God's* servants (2:18). This might remind us that *all* of us come to God as servants, on the same level—though Luke probably understands this more clearly than does Peter! Although Joel's wording already crossed class barriers, the new wording virtually eliminates such classes. The world still evaluates us in socioeconomic terms, but Jesus' followers must value and treat each other as brothers and sisters of equal dignity.

The Spirit in Acts thrusts us across human barriers to honor our Lord among all peoples. The Spirit also empowers believers together, regardless of ethnicity, class, or gender, as partners in this mission, equally dependent on God's enablement. Perhaps it is time for us, like the first disciples, to pray for the enablement of God's transforming Spirit.[6]

CRAIG S. KEENER

6. For fuller detail on Acts 2:1–21, see Craig S. Keener, *Acts: An Exegetical Commentary* (Grand Rapids: Baker Academic, 2012–2015), 1:780–920.

John 7:37–39

[37]On the last day of the festival, the great day, while Jesus was standing there, he cried out, "Let anyone who is thirsty come to me, [38]and let the one who believes in me drink. As the scripture has said, 'Out of the believer's heart shall flow rivers of living water.'" [39]Now he said this about the Spirit, which believers in him were to receive; for as yet there was no Spirit, because Jesus was not yet glorified.

Commentary 1: Connecting the Reading with Scripture

This passage is one of the Gospel readings for Pentecost Sunday. In it, Jesus refers to the gift of the Spirit. That gift is realized on the day of Pentecost. This gift is a mark of the incoming messianic age and Jesus' proclamation of himself as living water.

Commentators view chapters 5–12 in John's Gospel as consisting of two primary types of material. One is the seven signs and wonders that Jesus performs in his public ministry; the other is the building conflict with unbelievers, the chief priests (Sadducees), and the Pharisees. These materials are intertwined. As Jesus went about healing, feeding, and teaching, the religious authorities and unbelievers became more and more threatened by his ministry. Some commentators believe John may be seeking to bolster the confidence of the community of Jewish Christians who had been expelled from the synagogue. Others believe the Fourth Gospel was addressed especially to Gentile Christians. In either case, we have here a world-changing claim: Jesus is in effect proclaiming that he is the river of living waters that flows both from himself and from the Spirit, and that believers will receive this Spirit.

The passage takes place in Jerusalem at the Feast of Tabernacles. One of the three major annual festivals in the Jewish year, the Feast of Tabernacles was a time of much joy in Jerusalem; Jewish men were obliged to attend. During Jesus' day it had "taken on the significance of remembering God's provision for the people of Israel during their wilderness wanderings," according to Elisabeth Johnson.[1] For seven days water was carried in a golden pitcher from the Pool of Siloam to the temple as a reminder of the water from the rock in the desert (Num. 20:2–13) and as a symbol of hope for the coming messianic deliverance (Isa. 12:3). Water is a powerful image of life, celebration, and provision in Scripture.

Jesus identifies himself as the source of living water on the "last day of the festival" (John 7:37–38). This causes division in the crowd. Some say Jesus is in fact the prophet and Messiah (v. 40); others that the Messiah could not come from Galilee. (v. 41) This repeats the same dispute that had taken place earlier in the week when Jesus implied that his teachings are from God (7:28–29). After this claim, the chief priests and Pharisees are doubly eager to get the temple police to arrest Jesus on the spot.

John may have intended to mirror a contemporary dispute for his readers and to bolster the confidence of the community by demonstrating that Jesus Christ is living water. Nevertheless, on the last day of the festival, the great day, Jesus has a second teaching, our lectionary text for this Sunday. Water ceremonies were a significant part of the Festival of Tabernacles. Some of the rabbis saw in the festival's water ritual an invocation of the Holy Spirit. Thus it is highly symbolic. In this powerfully symbolic context, Jesus says: "Let anyone who is thirsty come to me, and let the one who believes in me drink. . . . 'Out of the believer's heart shall flow rivers of living water'" (7:37b–38).

1. Elisabeth Johnson, "Commentary on John 7:37–39," www.workingpreacher.org/preaching.aspx?commentary_id=2046.

"Here, at this festival that celebrates God's provision in the wilderness, Jesus offers the living water that quenches all thirst and is a source of life eternal."[2] He is now the living water of life that comes from God, the one who will offer the Spirit of living water to others. John explains: "Now he said this about the Spirit, which believers in him were yet to receive, for as yet there was no Spirit, because Jesus was not yet glorified" (v. 39). Pentecost was still to happen; only then would the full outpouring of the Spirit be experienced.

Our lectionary text has a twofold character. First, it is the announcement that Jesus is the true water of life, who turns the symbol into reality. Second, it is a promise that believers will become channels of life to others, through Christ's Spirit given at Pentecost.

Often in John's Gospel, water and Spirit are joined together. Jesus tells Nicodemus he must be born again, by water and the Spirit (3:5). He explains to the Samaritan woman at the well that he is the living water and that God is Spirit (4:7–26). Living water, joined with the Spirit, is used by John as a "symbol of the revelation of God in Christ which satisfies all spiritual thirst[3] (4:10–15). This is the reason John sets the event at the Feast of Tabernacles rather than Pentecost, showing the linkage between the living water and the Spirit that clearly prefigures Pentecost as described in Acts 2:1–21.

It might be easy for Christian believers to miss the promise and opportunity extended by Christ, whether they were present at the Feast of Tabernacles or Pentecost, or whether they are living in our present day. Jesus claims to be living water; moreover, he claims that out of believers will flow rivers of living water. When the Spirit came to believers at Pentecost, they—and now we—became the rivers of living water. We are those upon whom the Spirit came.

The other Gospel reading for Pentecost is John 20:19–23. In John's Gospel the promised Spirit comes at Passover, or Easter, rather than at Pentecost, as it does in Luke–Acts. The promise made at the Feast of Tabernacles in the John 7:37–39 text is fulfilled at Passover. John reinterprets all three Jewish festivals in light of God's incarnation in Christ. The festivals that celebrate the deliverance from Egypt (Passover), the presence of God the Spirit (Pentecost), and the provision of God (Tabernacles) find new significance in light of God's sending his only Son to tabernacle among us, and the Son's sending the Spirit to abide with us.

Both Gospel readings emphasize the giving of the Spirit, as does the Pentecost text. Both also have a connection to the prophet Joel. In chapter 2 of Joel there is the promise that God will make provision for his people. The sending of grain, wine, and oil; the pouring down of abundant rain; and plentiful food (Joel 2:18–27) are themes that resonate with the traditions of the Feast of Tabernacles. They precede the promise of Yahweh to pour out his Spirit on all flesh: sons, daughters, old men, and slaves. This passage from Joel (2:28–32) is recited as part of Peter's Pentecost speech. The miracles at Pentecost resolve once again the conflict between those who held that Jesus was Messiah and those who denied it.

John quite clearly in both lectionary passages, as throughout his Gospel, is calling people to believe and to stand firm. He is claiming the Spirit for all the thirsty who come to Jesus. Jesus invites all to come and drink from the living water, the Spirit who guides disciples into faith and truth. Belief is a gift of the Spirit. All those who are hungry and thirsty are to be welcomed as children of God, an all-inclusive God, as Pentecost so clearly models.

These passages, together with the Pentecost text, the images of 1 Corinthians 12:3b–13, and Numbers 11:24–30, all point to the promise of the Spirit of Jesus Christ. They are the basis of evangelism and the source of strength for every believer. They are the gift of faith.

L. SHANNON JUNG

2. Johnson, "Commentary on John 7:37–39."
3. Johnson, "Commentary on John 7:37–39."

Commentary 2: Connecting the Reading with the World

For each of the eight days of the Festival of Booths (John 7:2), priests would draw water from the Pool of Siloam, lead a procession to the temple, and pour out the water in the temple. They foreshadowed what was announced in the Scripture readings on the last day of the festival. These passages, Ezekiel 47 and Zechariah 14, promised that a river would flow from Jerusalem or, more specifically in Ezekiel, from the temple. Revelation 22:1–2 depicts the consummation of this vision in the new Jerusalem, but John 7 speaks of its foretaste already beginning at Jesus' death and exaltation.[4]

On the last day of the festival, Jesus cites the Scripture read on that day and invites those who are thirsty and believe in him to come to him and drink from him (7:37–38). John explains that the living water that Jesus refers to is the Spirit (7:39). The Spirit is also the water of eternal life he offered to the Samaritan woman in John 4:10–14. It fits a motif that runs through this Gospel: Jesus' water of the Spirit is better than the water of John's baptism (1:26, 33), better than the water of ritual purification (2:6, 9), better than the water of Jacob's well (4:12–14), and better than the water of a pool associated with healing (5:1–9). Jesus is even better than the water used for this festival, from the Pool of Siloam (9:1–7). In other words, there is no greater "water" than the water that Jesus offers here.

Jesus' promise lies at the very heart of our faith. Whereas the OT associates empowerment by God's Spirit especially with prophets and leaders, throughout the NT the activity of God's Spirit marks all of Jesus' followers. If we entrust our lives to Christ, then God's own Spirit, the third person of the Trinity, lives inside us. No gift could be greater than that.

Since the European Enlightenment, some Christians have stressed the human, rational character of Christianity. In many respects, this emphasis has greatly benefited the church; we have a faith that makes sense on Christian premises, and in many respects makes sense even apart from them. Sometimes, however, we have acted as if we could accomplish God's work or understand God's ways by merely human effort. Nothing could be further from the NT message. In Enlightenment terms, Christianity from the start has been inescapably supernatural, which may be one reason that some of its claims disturb many modern people. Nevertheless, many Christians continue to testify of supernatural transformation and other experiences, not least an experience of the supernatural God. In language more characteristic of the early apostolic church, Jesus' followers comprise a movement dependent on God's Spirit.

What does this activity of the Spirit look like? John speaks elsewhere of being born from above from the water of the Spirit (3:3–5). To use John's language elsewhere, God's Spirit changes us from having a devilish nature (8:44) to being God's children (1:12–13). This new life does not mean that we are perfect or that we can boast of our virtue; it does mean that there is a new agent of transformation at work inside us.

John also speaks of the Spirit joining us in our witness for Christ (15:26–27; cf. 16:7–11). When we speak about Christ, we can depend on God to work far beyond what our own merely human efforts could do by themselves. Those of us preachers who are shy may take special encouragement from this promise.

In this Gospel, the Spirit also enables us to have personal relationship with Jesus (16:13–15). In John 15:15, whatever Jesus heard from the Father, he made known to his disciples, his friends. In 16:13, whatever the Spirit hears, the Spirit will likewise reveal, honoring Jesus (16:14–15). We can experience an intimate, trusting relationship with Jesus like the relationship that his first disciples had.

"Living water" was an ancient expression for fresh, flowing water, the kind of water that one gets from "rivers" (7:38), not from typical wells (4:14). Jesus' words here suggest an inexhaustible, unending supply. We may feel at the limit of our God-given strength and ability, but

4. For fuller discussion of this background, see Craig S. Keener, *The Gospel of John: A Commentary* (Grand Rapids: Baker Academic, 2003), 1:721–30.

we look to a Lord whose supply remains fresh. Some church traditions emphasize a single, special experience of the Spirit; some other church traditions emphasize a second experience of the Spirit. The Spirit's work in us is not limited to a first or second experience. God's Spirit is always available.

What does that mean in day-to-day practice? Certainly it does not mean that we will always feel God's Spirit or feel spiritual. It *does* mean that we have the right to expect God's Spirit to work in us regularly. Sometimes God works in our lives in the deepest ways when we sense or recognize God's presence the least; it is often only after hardships that we realize how much they made our faith grow. In good times or bad, God's Spirit is with us to help us better understand God's heart toward us, and therefore better live our lives in the recognition of God's presence.

Recognizing God's love for us is harder for some of us than it is for others. If we have experienced abuse or broken trust, trust does not come as easily, even toward God. However, the Bible repeatedly reminds us that God is far from the proud and near the broken (e.g., Ps. 138:6). God knows where each of us begins and shows special patience for those who need the most help in recognizing and believing Christ's love.

The ultimate expression of that love is in the cross. John 7:37–39 shows that depending on God's Spirit also requires dependence on Jesus, who died for us. John's pneumatology is christocentric (cf. 14:26; 15:26; 16:14–15). John does not speak of "spirit" as merely some mystical feeling with no content. He speaks of the Spirit that specializes in helping us know the real Jesus (cf. 1 John 4:1–3). The Spirit was not yet available when Jesus spoke, because Jesus had not yet been glorified.

What does it mean for Jesus to be glorified? Jesus sometimes reveals his glory in this Gospel through signs (e.g., 2:11; 11:4, 40). This passage refers to Jesus' ultimate glorification in this Gospel, which begins with his crucifixion (12:16, 23–24). When Jesus is enthroned on a cross, crowned with thorns (19:2–5, 19), Jesus reveals the Father's glory—God's heart for the world laid bare. As his side is pierced, not only blood but water flows out (19:34). Physically, this may reflect the puncturing of the pericardial sac, releasing fluid around the heart, but why does John take space to record and emphasize this point (19:34–35)? Presumably to remind us that the promised "water" of the Spirit has now become available.

This Gospel, known for its wordplays in Greek, includes one at the cross. When Jesus died, he "gave up his spirit," a natural description of death (19:30). The Greek phrase can also be translated this way: "he gave the Spirit." It cost Jesus everything to make the Spirit available to us, so it is gross disrespect to him to neglect his gift. John explains that Jesus refers here to believers *receiving* the Spirit (7:39). The water of the Spirit flows from Jesus to believers. Essentially, Jesus is saying, "I am the foundation stone of God's new temple. Let the one who wills, come and drink freely from the water of the river of life!"

CRAIG S. KEENER

Contributors

O. WESLEY ALLEN JR., Lois Craddock Perkins Professor of Homiletics, Perkins School of Theology, Southern Methodist University, Dallas, TX

RONALD J. ALLEN, Professor of Preaching and New Testament, Christian Theological Seminary, Indianapolis, IN

WM. LOYD ALLEN, Professor of Church History and Spiritual Formation, McAfee School of Theology, Mercer University, Atlanta, GA

LINDSAY P. ARMSTRONG, Executive Director, New Church Development, Presbytery of Greater Atlanta, Atlanta, GA

MARGARET P. AYMER, The First Presbyterian Church, Shreveport, Louisiana, D. Thomasen Professor of New Testament Studies, Austin Presbyterian Theological Seminary, Austin, TX

ERIC D. BARRETO, Weyerhaeuser Associate Professor of New Testament, Princeton Theological Seminary, Princeton, NJ

RHODORA E. BEATON, Associate Professor of Sacramental and Liturgical Theology, Aquinas Institute of Theology, St. Louis, MO

LEIGH CAMPBELL-TAYLOR, Interim Pastor, Morningside Presbyterian Church, Atlanta, GA

WARREN CARTER, Professor of New Testament, Brite Divinity School at Texas Christian University, Fort Worth, TX

DIANE G. CHEN, Professor of New Testament, Palmer Theological Seminary of Eastern University, St. Davids, PA

GREG COOTSONA, Professor of Comparative Religion and Humanities, California State University, Chico, Chico, CA

JEROME F. D. CREACH, Robert C. Holland Professor of Old Testament, Pittsburgh Theological Seminary, Pittsburgh, PA

SARAH BIRMINGHAM DRUMMOND, Dean and Professor of Ministerial Leadership, Andover Newton Seminary at Yale Divinity School, New Haven, CT

JANE ANNE FERGUSON, Associate Minister, Plymouth Congregational Church, Fort Collins, CO

DAVID GAMBRELL, Associate for Worship, Office of Theology and Worship, Presbyterian Church (U.S.A.), Louisville, KY

DAVID G. GARBER JR., Associate Professor of Old Testament and Hebrew, McAfee School of Theology, Mercer University, Atlanta, GA

BRIDGETT A. GREEN, Assistant Professor of New Testament, Austin Presbyterian Theological Seminary, Austin, TX

W. SCOTT HALDEMAN, Associate Professor of Worship, Chicago Theological Seminary, Chicago, IL

HEIDI HAVERKAMP, Author, Episcopal priest, DeKalb, IL

MARTHA C. HIGHSMITH, Pastor, McClure Memorial Presbyterian Church, Castle Hayne, NC

JOHN C. HOLBERT, Lois Craddock Perkins Professor Emeritus of Homiletics, Perkins School of Theology, Southern Methodist University, Dallas, TX

CATHY CALDWELL HOOP, Pastor, Grace Presbyterian Church, Tuscaloosa, AL

CAMERON B. R. HOWARD, Associate Professor of Old Testament, Luther Seminary, St. Paul, MN

JAMES C. HOWELL, Senior Pastor, Myers Park United Methodist Church, Charlotte, NC

EDITH M. HUMPHREY, William F. Orr Professor of New Testament, Pittsburgh Theological Seminary, Pittsburgh, PA

L. SHANNON JUNG, Cole Professor Emeritus of Town and Country Ministry, Saint Paul's School of Theology, Overland Park, KS

CRAIG S. KEENER, F. M. and Ada Thompson Professor of Biblical Studies, Asbury Theological Seminary, Wilmore, KY

KAROLINE M. LEWIS, Associate Professor of Biblical Preaching and The Marbury E. Anderson Chair in Biblical Preaching, Luther Seminary, St. Paul, MN

MICHAEL L. LINDVALL, Pastor Emeritus, Brick Presbyterian Church in the City of New York, New York, NY

THOMAS G. LONG, Bandy Professor Emeritus of Preaching, Candler School of Theology, Emory University, Atlanta, GA

JENNIFER L. LORD, The Dorothy B. Vickery Professor of Homiletics and Liturgical Studies, Austin Presbyterian Theological Seminary, Austin, TX

IAN A. MCFARLAND, Regius Professor of Divinity, University of Cambridge, Cambridge, UK

ANDREW NAGY-BENSON, Pastor, Congregational Church of Middlebury, Middlebury, VT

MIKEAL C. PARSONS, Professor and Macon Chair in Religion, Baylor University, Waco, TX

JULIE PEEPLES, Senior Minister, Congregational United Church of Christ, Greensboro, NC

BRIAN S. POWERS, Bernard William Vann Fellow in Christianity and the Military, The Michael Ramsey Centre for Anglican Studies, Durham University, Durham, UK

SALLY B. PURVIS, Retired Minister, Lakewood United Church of Christ, St. Petersburg, FL

GAIL RAMSHAW, Professor Emerita of Religion, La Salle University, Philadelphia, PA

CYNTHIA L. RIGBY, W. C. Brown Professor of Theology, Austin Presbyterian Theological Seminary, Austin, TX

RUBÉN ROSARIO RODRÍGUEZ, Associate Professor of Systematic Theology, Saint Louis University, St. Louis, MO

KATHRYN SCHIFFERDECKER, Professor and Elva B. Lovell Chair of Old Testament, Luther Seminary, St. Paul, MN

DAVID J. SCHLAFER, Independent Consultant in Preaching and Assisting Priest, The Episcopal Church of the Redeemer, Bethesda, MD

KIRA SCHLESINGER, Interim Rector, St. Ann's Episcopal Church, Nashville, TN

BRADLEY E. SCHMELING, Senior Pastor, Gloria Dei Lutheran Church, St. Paul, MN

CAROLYN J. SHARP, Professor of Homiletics, Yale Divinity School, New Haven, CT

BRENT A. STRAWN, Professor of Old Testament, Duke Divinity School, Durham, NC

JERRY L. SUMNEY, Professor of Biblical Studies, Lexington Theological Seminary, Lexington, KY

JONATHAN L. WALTON, Plummer Professor of Christian Morals and Pusey Minister in the Memorial Church, Harvard University, Cambridge, MA

PHILIP WINGEIER-RAYO, Dean and Professor of Missiology and Methodist Studies, Wesley Theological Seminary, Washington, DC

REBECCA ABTS WRIGHT, C. K. Benedict Professor of Old Testament and Biblical Hebrew, The School of Theology, the University of the South, Sewanee, TN

JOHN W. WURSTER, Pastor/Head of Staff, St. Philip Presbyterian Church, Houston, TX

BEVERLY ZINK-SAWYER, Professor Emerita of Preaching and Worship, Union Presbyterian Seminary, Richmond, VA

Author Index

Abbreviations

C1	Commentary 1	G	Gospel
C2	Commentary 2	OT	Old Testament
E	Epistle	PS	Psalm
FR	First Reading (when not from the Old Testament)	SR	Second Reading (when not from the Epistles)

Numerals indicate numbered Sundays of a season; for example, "Lent 1" represents the first Sunday of Lent, and "Easter 2" the Second Sunday of Easter.

Contributors and entries

Scripture Index

Scripture citations that appear in boldface represent the assigned readings from the Revised Common Lectionary.

OLD TESTAMENT

APOSTOLIC FATHERS